Programming with C++

B.L. Juneja
Department of Mechanical Engineering
I.I.T. Delhi, New Delhi – 110016

Anita Seth
Institute of Engineering and Technology (IET)
DAVV University, Khandwa Road
Indore

PUBLISHING FOR ONE WORLD

NEW AGE INTERNATIONAL (P) LIMITED, PUBLISHERS

New Delhi • Bangalore • Chennai • Cochin • Guwahati • Hyderabad
Jalandhar • Kolkata • Lucknow • Mumbai • Ranchi
Visit us at **www.newagepublishers.com**

Published by New Age International (P) Ltd., Publishers
First Edition: 2009
Reprint: 2009

Branches:

- 36, Malikarjuna Temple Street, Opp. ICWA, Basavanagudi, **Bangalore**. ✆ (080) 26677815
- 26, Damodaran Street, T. Nagar, **Chennai**. ✆ (044) 24353401
- CE-39/1016, Carrier Station Road, Near Paulson Park Hotel, Ernakulam South, **Cochin.** ✆ (0484) 4051303
- Hemsen Complex, Mohd. Shah Road, Paltan Bazar, Near Starline Hotel, **Guwahati**. ✆ (0361) 2543669
- No. 105, 1st Floor, Madhiray Kaveri Tower, 3-2-19, Azam Jahi Road, Nimboliadda, **Hyderabad**. ✆ (040) 24652456
- RDB Chambers (Formerly Lotus Cinema) 106A,1st Floor, S.N. Banerjee Road, **Kolkata**. ✆ (033) 22275247
- 16-A, Jopling Road, **Lucknow**. ✆ (0522) 2209578
- 142C, Victor House, Ground Floor, N.M. Joshi Marg, Lower Parel, **Mumbai**. ✆ (022) 24927869
- 22, Golden House, Daryaganj, **New Delhi**. ✆ (011) 23262370, 23262368

ISBN : 978-81-224-2613-7

Rs. 375.00

C-09-06-3747

Printed in India at Glorious Printers, Delhi.
Typeset at Inhouse.

PUBLISHING FOR ONE WORLD
NEW AGE INTERNATIONAL (P) LIMITED, PUBLISHERS
4835/24, Ansari Road, Daryaganj, New Delhi-110002
Visit us at **www.newagepublishers.com**

Preface

C++ is an excellent programming language both for procedural as well as object oriented programming and lends support to more diverse applications compared to any other computer programming language. This one reason that C++ now is used in more than 80% of all the softwares that is being produced these days. Naturally, those with sound knowledge of C++ have access to many job-opportunities. However, many students feel that programming with C++ is a difficult task. In this book, the presentation of the subject has been designed keeping in view the difficulties of the students. Almost every topic is followed by illustrative examples, so that the readers may easily grasp the content.

In programming, one learns much more quickly through actual live programs than by simply reading volumes about how to program. Every chapter of the book contains illustrative examples in the form of well designed live programs which the reader may use for learning as well as for his/her applications. The programs are designed to bring out the salient features of the underlying principle or coding technique. The book contains more than 450 live programmes. This feature of the book is highly useful for those doing self study of C++ language.

The book also contains an extensive coverage of STL and other recent additions to C++ Standard Library. STL contains function templates and class templates which are meant to be reused by professionals in their application programmes. In fact, the reuse of well established software is at the heart of object oriented programming. The book contains a large number of live programs for illustrating the applications of the STL functions and algorithms. Thus the book is highly useful to professionals as a ready reference.

The first few chapters of the book deal extensively with the procedural programming. This style of programming is still used extensively for small length programs. Also, a good grounding in procedural programming prepares the students for more difficult topics pertaining to classes, operator overloading, inheritance, object oriented programming (OOP), template functions and template classes as well as container classes such as vector, list, deque, sets, multisets, maps, multimaps, stacks, queues, etc. All these topics are dealt in sufficient detail as well as a large number of illustrative live programs are included. This part is highly useful to students as well as software professionals. These templates are meant to be reused in professional application software.

Almost all the topics generally used in C++ programming are covered in the book. The contents of the book have already been class tested. From the responses of students, the authors feel confident that the book should be useful for students pursuing science and engineering, BCA, MCA and those appearing for examinations of Department of Electronics Society. Authors are also confident that the book will prove its worth to software professionals as well as to those pursuing self-study.

B.L. Juneja
Anita Seth

Acknowledgements

The authors would like to record their gratitude to the Director of IIT Delhi and Director of Institute of Engineering and Technology, Indore, for providing general facilities for carrying out the writing of this book. Authors are grateful to the Head of Department of Electronics and Telecommunication, IET Indore, and Prof. J.P. Subrahmanyam, Head of Department of M.E., IIT Delhi for encouragement and inspiration.

The authors are particularly grateful to Professor Arun Kanda and Professor S.G. Deshmukh – the previous Head and Associate Head of Mechanical Engineering Department, IIT Delhi, for providing facilities to Dr. B.L. Juneja to teach the subject to the graduate students of Mechanical Engineering Department. This has given him the opportunity to test the material in class environment. We are highly grateful to Prof. P.V.M. Rao of Mechanical Department, IIT Delhi for allowing use of computer laboratory and helping with necessary software.

Authors are also grateful to Professor G. Singh of Maryland University, USA for his valuable advice, encouragement and for providing the syllabi of the courses on C++ being taught at American Universities.

Authors are grateful to Dr. Nitin Seth of Mechanical Department, IET Indore, presently working as Professor, Indian Institute of Foreign Trade, New Delhi for his valuable suggestions and general help in presentation of material.

For accomplishing a work like writing of this book, it requires, besides the efforts of the authors, the advice and help of the persons closely associated with the authors. The authors are indeed grateful to Mr. Rajiv Kapoor, Mr. Bharat Kalra and all the colleagues for their valuable suggestions and encouragement.

The last but not the least, authors are indeed grateful to Mrs. Asha Seth and Mrs. Pushpa Juneja for providing the moral support and help so that the work could be completed.

B.L. Juneja
Anita Seth

Contents

CHAPTER

1 Introduction to C++

1.1 COMPUTER AND COMPUTER LANGUAGES

Computer has become an essential element of our modern society. Work in offices, factories, selling outlets, research and development laboratories, teaching, telecommunication, sports, and even home entertainment are all being controlled by computers. Not only that, most of our future developments are closely linked with the developments in computer systems which involve development in hardware as well as software. This is reflected in the rapid developments in computer hardware that we see today. Super computers that are capable of doing trillions of instructions per second is the talk of the day. The personal computers whether desktops or laptops have capabilities and speeds much better and prices much less than the mainframe computers of just a decade ago. Only machines are not enough. Robust and efficient software is needed to make these machines to perform to the fullest extent. Computer languages are the bases of efficient software.

A typical computer hardware (Fig. 1.1) consists of one or more **microprocessor** chips connected to the supporting chips and other electronic circuits. These chips include cache and primary memory chips usually called **RAM** (Random Access Memory). Besides, the microprocessor is also connected to bulk storage memory devices such as **floppy disc**, **CD ROM** (Compact Disc Read only Memory), **hard disc** and **magnetic tapes** etc. The microprocessor chip which is the main chip is also called **CPU** (Central Processing Unit). Its internal structure consists of circuits which form a number of **registers** (typical number is 16), an **arithmetic unit**, a **logic unit** and a **control unit.** It has large number of terminals for connection to external devices (for instance a typical CPU has as many as 478 terminals). Out of these a group of terminals is for data input and data output, another group is for memory addresses and still another group for control purposes. Besides, several terminals are for **interrupt** service. An interrupt is like gate crashing. Suppose some program is being processed in the computer and you interrupt that program and start your own program. The computer first saves the ongoing program status, takes up your item, and after finishing work on it, it resumes the ongoing program. Every CPU supports a set of instructions designed by its manufacturer. We need not go into details of the complex circuitry, however, some of the names mentioned above are often used in software and a programming student should be familiar with them. A beginner in programming will most probably be using a desktop personal computer (PC). A typical PC cabinet is illustrated in Fig. 1.2. The input/output devices that a reader would in general come across are shown in Fig. 1.3.

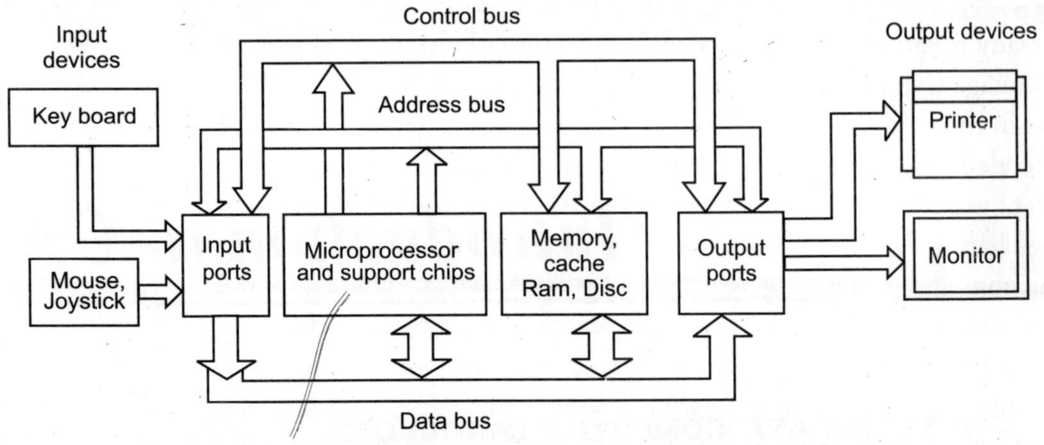

Fig. 1.1: Components of a computer system. Bus lines carry electrical pulses from one device to another. Arrows show the data flow

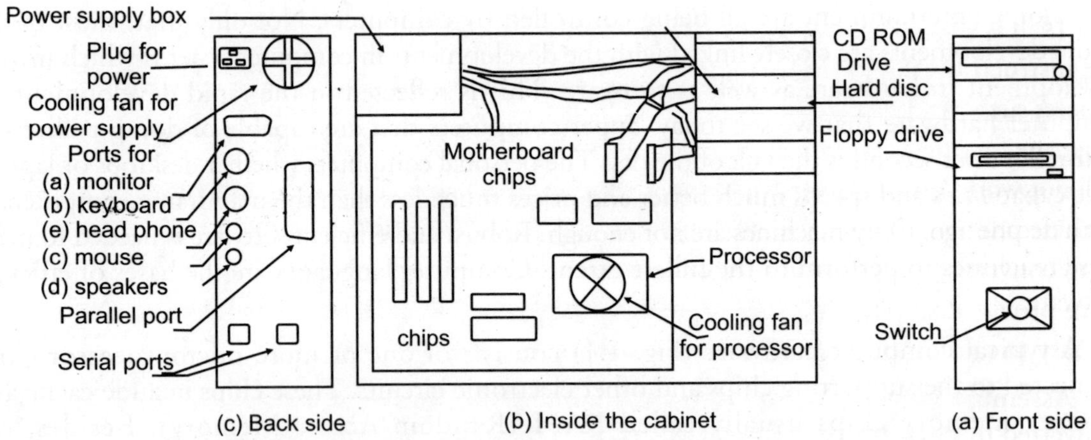

Fig. 1.2: A typical desktop computer cabinet. The various ports may be placed differently on different models

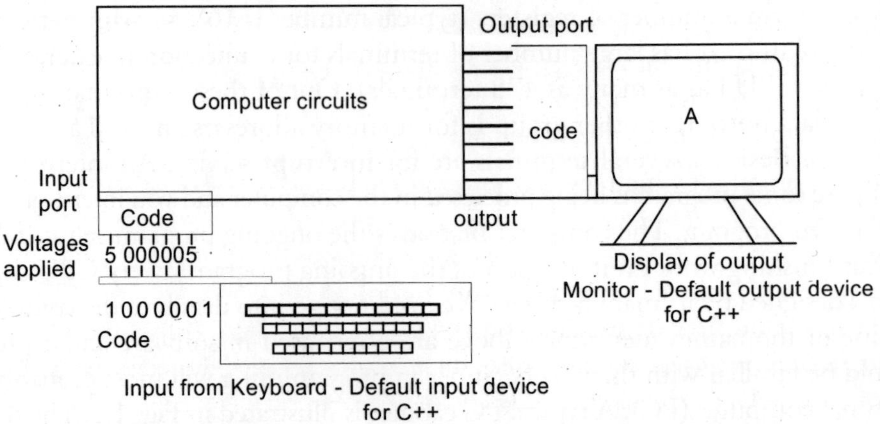

Fig. 1.3: A PC (personal computer) and standard input/output devices

MACHINE LANGUAGE

As already mentioned, a computer is a collection of electronic circuits driven by application of high voltage (typical value is 5 volts) at some points and low voltage (typical value is 0) at other points in the circuit. We may designate (code) high voltage as 1 and low voltage as 0. Thus the basic code for computer instructions consists of sequences of 1s and 0s such as 00111110. The values of variables, which are numbers, can also be represented in binary numbers (discussed later in the chapter) which are also sequences of zeros and ones. Thus a program which comprises instructions and data may be written as a series of sequences of zeros and ones. There are different instruction formats (combinations of opcodes, codes and data) so that the processor can make out which sequence of 0s and 1s is instruction and which is data. The first number in an instruction is opcode followed by data. Some instructions may not have any data to act upon. The complete set of these instructions for a CPU is called **machine language code** or simply **machine language.** This is the language which machine understands.

A program written in machine language will consist of a large number of sequences of 0s and 1s. It is very difficult to write such programs and debug them in case there is an error. Besides, the instruction codes for processors made by different manufacturers are different for the same process such as addition or storage of a value etc., therefore, the program written in one machine language for one microprocessor will only work on computers having similar microprocessor but will not work on computers based on other microprocessors. That is to say, there is no **portability** of these programs. Moreover, it is very cumbersome to write and debug programs in binary codes or to convert a program made for one make of CPU to another make of CPU. These two factors have provided impetus for development of **high level programming languages** which should be easy to understand, debug and be portable.

Assembly language is the next development. In this the instructional codes have been converted to more readable forms, for example, for one processor instruction such as MOV AX 116 means move the immediate data that is 116 to destination register AX. The word MOV is short form of MOVE. Assembly language instructions such as MOV, ADD which stands for addition, SUB which stands for subtraction etc. are called **mnemonics**. A program written in assembly language needs a software called **assembler** which converts the program consisting of mnemonics and data into machine language. In this case also the programs are not portable. Nevertheless, the programs written in assembly language are easier to read as well as easier to debug than those written in machine language.

In the development of a high level language there has always been an endeavour to make the language as near to the language that we speak as possible. It is worthwhile to note that the programs written in machine language are the most efficient in execution, because there is nothing between the code and the machine as is the case with high level languages. All high level computer languages need a **compiler** or **interpreter** to convert the program instructions and data into machine language for its execution, because, the machine understands only its own language, i.e. sequences of 0s and 1s.

C Language

BCPL was one of the earliest high level computer language developed in 1967 by Martin Richards for writing **operating system** which is a software needed to control various processes in computer applications. Later the language B was developed by Ken Thompson who added many new features in the language.

C was developed mainly from B by Dennis Ritche. Soon C became popular with programmers and it remained so for several decades. It is still used in several applications. It is a structured high level language. Programs written in C are easy to write and debug as well as the programs are portable. The code is nearest to the assembly language and thus is quite efficient. However, the code written in C language needs a compiler to convert the different instructions and data into machine language.

Because of popularity of C many companies produced compilers for C. A **compiler** is a software which converts the program into machine language. Because of the widespread use of C, it became necessary to standardize the syntax and functions of the language so that the programs could run with compilers developed by different organizations and on different platforms. The American National Standard Institute (ANSI) prepared a standard document for C as a national standard which later with some modifications was also adopted by ISO (International Organization for Standardization) as an international standard. The first standard C document was published in 1990. It is known as **ISO/IEC 9899-1990, Programming Language – C.** The C language according to this document is also called **C-90.**

With further development of C, it became necessary to revise the earlier standard. The revised standard was ratified by ISO in 1999. The document is known as **ISO/IEC 9899-1999, Programming language – C.** The language according to this standard is known as **C - 99** and it is in vogue at present.

In order to meet the variety of demands from the real world problems, several computer languages have been developed over the same period. These languages are more tuned to the typical applications that these languages are put to. The number of these languages is quite large and it is difficult to give even brief discussions of all these languages. Many of these could not gain any popularity and are dead. However, some of these became popular and have been in use for a number of years. The popular ones are Basic and Visual Basic, Cobol, Fortran, Logo, Prolog, Pascal, Lisp, Ada, Simula, Smalltalk, etc. After the development of C++, another language Java has been developed. Java is more user friendly. However, C++ is a very versatile language and finds applications in many diverse fields and hence is very popular.

1.2 A BRIEF HISTORY OF C++

In eighties an average large C program was of the order of a few thousands of lines of code. With really large programs the difficulties with C language became more apparent and researchers were busy finding better options. C++ is a redevelopment of C carried out by Bjarne Stroustrup when he was working with AT&T during 1983-1985. Inspired by the language Smalltalk and Simula which are object oriented programming (OOP) languages, he added the concept of classes, in order to impart similar capabilities in the then widely popular C language. Classes are the basis of OOP. Initially the new language was called **C with classes.** The name C++ was coined later by Rick Mascitti in 1983. The symbol (++) is an operator in C which increases the value of an integer variable by 1. The name C++ aptly shows that C++ is oneup on C. The C++ is also often called as **better C**.

The C++ programming language became popular soon after it was officially launched. As a result, scores of programmers got involved, who have not only tested the codes and recognised the pitfalls, but have also added reusable program modules to C++ Standard Library which is a large collection of well tested and reusable programs which facilitate the writing and execution of diverse applications. It became necessary to standardise C++ as well. So an ISO committee was formed in 1995 and C++ standard was ratified by ISO in 1998. The document is officially known as **ISO/IES 14882-1998, Programming Language – C++.** The language according to this standard is briefly referred to as **C++ 98.** Later a revise version of the standard with minor corrections and clarifications was published in 2003. This document is known as **ISO/IEC 14882::2003.** This is the standard being followed at present. This is also available in the book form with name "The C++ Standard" and published by John Wiley Ltd.

In fact, there has been continuous development in the language. Addition of inheritance of classes, operator overloading and polymorphism has enhanced the application of the language. The addition of template functions and template classes has given rise to generic programming. A remarkable enhancement to the language is the addition of Standard Template Library as a part of C++ Standard Library. These programs can be used straightway by the programmers to create new applications as well as new programs. Addition of *namespace* has added additional flexibility in combining programs written by different programmers without running the risk of ambiguity of same names being used for different variables in different sections of the program. These developments in C++ have enhanced the capabilities of C++ enormously. A very large program may be broken into small modules and classes, which may be developed by different programmers and tested for their performance before combining them into one large program. These developments have given extensive capability to C++ to have reusable program modules and classes which comprise the C++ Standard Library.

1.3 MAJOR ADDITIONS FROM C TO C++

There has been continuous effort for upgrading C++ by way of adding new algorithms, applications and other additions such as namespace, etc. It is really difficult to make a detailed list of all these items, however, below only major developments are listed which are responsible for major advantages of using C++ over C.

(1) Classes which provide a mechanism for data abstraction, encapsulation of data and functions, information hiding and object oriented programming.

(2) Operator overloading.

(3) Inheritance.

(4) Polymorphism.

(5) Addition of namespaces.

(6) Template functions and template classes which lead to generic programming.

(7) Addition of STL (Standard Template Library).

(8) Many new keywords.

1.4 SOME ADVANTAGES OF C++ OVER C

C++ allows procedural programming as well as object oriented programming and generic programming. In seventies and eighties generally procedural programming were used for short as well for long programs which comprised a few thousands to hundred thousands lines of code. The present day big programs comprise millions of lines of code. In procedural programming, there are many problems in production of really large programs. Debugging is one major problem. Even after successful implementation the maintenance of the software is not easy. It is difficult for a new programmer to comprehend the different sections of the program.

The inclusion of classes has added the advantage of object oriented programming to C++, though, it is also an efficient language in procedural programming. The inheritance of classes in C++ has also made easy to reuse the existing class programs. If you have made a class program, verified and tested and later you wish to add new things into it, you can do it without modifying the tested and verified program. You simply make another class program which inherits the existing class and adds the new features into it. The original program remains intact and is used in the new program without any modification. Later on you can make still another class which inherits any one or both of the already developed classes and adds new features to the whole program. This allows a continuous addition of new features in an already running program without disturbing the existing classes.

Operator overloading gives the facility for applying the same operators that we use for fundamental types to the class objects as well. Thus the operations on vectors, complex numbers, strings and other class objects are made easier. The operator overloading gives a large extension to C++.

The addition of inheritance and polymorphism in C++ has extended the scope of use of existing software. A big program may be designed to comprise convenient reusable components or modules comprising different classes. It is possible to extend or modify the components as explained above in case of classes. The various sub-programs may be re-assembled in different ways to make new programs. Debugging of a big program becomes easy because each class and module can be tested and verified independently of the whole program. Another major advantage is that a number of programmers or teams of programmers may be involved in developing different modules of a big program which is difficult in procedural programming. In C++ there is another advantage that these modules may be seamlessly combined without a clash of names of variables and functions by *using namespaces*. Also the syntax in C++ is easier than that in C. It is because of all these advantages that C++ is used in more than 80% of all the software that is being created these days.

Though C++ is often called as superset of C, however, there are differences as well. Many students ask this question. Is it necessary to learn C for learning C++? The answer is no.

For learning C++ it is not necessary to first learn C. If you already know C it will certainly help, because, the concepts in procedural programming are similar. If you do not know C there is nothing to worry because C++ is best learned on its own and you would be avoiding confusion because of some differences in syntax in the two languages.

1.5 RANGE OF APPLICATIONS OF C++

C++ has now emerged as one of the most advanced and most popular computer language developed so far and has highest diversity in its applications. A comprehensive list of applications has been compiled by Bjarne Stroustrup, the originator of C++ himself and is available on internet at the following address.

http://www.research.att.com/~bs/applications.html

The list includes the names of companies who have developed many different softwares for diverse applications and in which C++ has been used. Here we list some of the application fields in which C++ has been used for producing software. These are listed below. The list is largely based on the above mentioned reference.

A Partial List of Fields of Applications of C++

(i) Operating Systems and component in windows XP and other OS components.
(ii) Software for e-commerce.
(iii) Customer service software such as electronic ticketing, car and flight reservations, etc.
(iv) Telecommunication services.
(v) Real time control applications.
(vi) 2-D and 3-D animations and games.
(vii) Multiprocessor multimedia software.
(viii) Portable set up box and digital TV software.
(ix) CAD software.
(x) Software for medical instruments and systems.
(xi) Java virtual machine (JVM).
(xii) Telephones services.
(xiii) Mobile phones billing systems and other infrastructural facilities.
(xiv) Irrigation control systems.
(xv) Speech recognition and dictation systems.

The interested reader should consult the above mentioned internet site of Bjarne Stroustrup for more information.

1.6 COMPILERS FOR PROGRAMMING WITH C++

For execution of programs written in C++ you need to load a compiler software on your computer. The function of compiler is to compile the program that you have written and present the code to computer in machine language for execution. Besides this, the compilers in integrated development environment also assist the programmers by pointing out the mistakes in the program listing. This aspect is very useful for learning C++, because, not only beginners even experienced programmers would make mistakes in writing the code and if the compiler does not point it out, the programmers will have to struggle hard to find it out. This an excellent facility and a beginner should get acquainted with the error pointed out by compiler and the remedial action. This can best be done by first have a correct program, then introduce different types of errors one by one and find the response of compiler. A few trials will acquaint a beginner with the common errors and the remedial actions needed for them.

There are many compilers available in market. Some are free and may be downloaded from internet. Some are paid but available on trial basis for a specified period while others are on payment systems. The reader is advised to see following internet sites for obtaining more information.

(i) An incomplete list of C++ Compilers - by Bjarne Stroustrup at following address.
http://www.research.att.com?~bs?compilers.html

(ii) Google Directory of C++ compilers – at the following address.
http://www.rafb.net/efnet_cpp/compilers

Some of the free compilers for windows are given below.

(i) Borland C++ 5.5
(ii) Dev-C++
(iii) LCC-Win32
(iv) Microsoft Visual C++ Toolkit 2003

For Multi-platform a free compiler is

(i) GCC

For imbedded C++ applications a free compiler is

(i) djgpp for intel 80386 (and higher)

It is better to start with an integrated development environment (IDE) like MS Visual C++ 6.

1.7 The C++ STANDARD LIBRARY

It is a rich collection of programs on classes, functions and template classes and template functions which are helpful in program writing and in its execution. Every program requires applications of several functions of C++ Standard Library. These functions are included in the program by including the header files which contain these functions (see Chapter 2 for header files). Standard Template Library (STL) has also been made part of C++ Standard Library. STL mainly comprises container classes such as vectors, lists, deque, associative containers such as sets, multisets, maps, multimaps, etc. and near-containers such as C++ strings, etc. Also it has iterator classes which help in traversing through the containers. These programs can be directly used by a programmer to create different applications. Besides, there are more than 70 algorithms in STL which may be used by programmers for creating new applications and programs. All these are, in general, supported by C++ compilers of good companies.

1.8 PROGRAM DEVELOPMENT IN C++

The start is made by installing one of the compilers described above on the computer. However, for a beginner it is better to work with an IDE like MS Visual C++ 6, which does text editing, compiling, linking and makes a binary file of the source code (the program typed by the programmer) which is loaded on to RAM for execution. A C++ program consists of a sequence of statements typed by the programmer from top to bottom with the help of text editor. It is presumed that a beginner will go through the documents provided with the compiler regarding the instructions for its loading and running. The programmer after typing the program, can direct for compiling. The programmer may get a list of syntax errors in the typed version of the program. Some compilers also indicate the location of the error (the line in which error is there) in the program. The programmer should correct these errors and again direct for compiling. When the text of the program is error free, the programmer can direct for run or build the program. The different elements in the process of making, compiling and running a program are also illustrated in the Fig. 1.4. See Appendix E for starting with Microsoft Visual C++ 6.0.

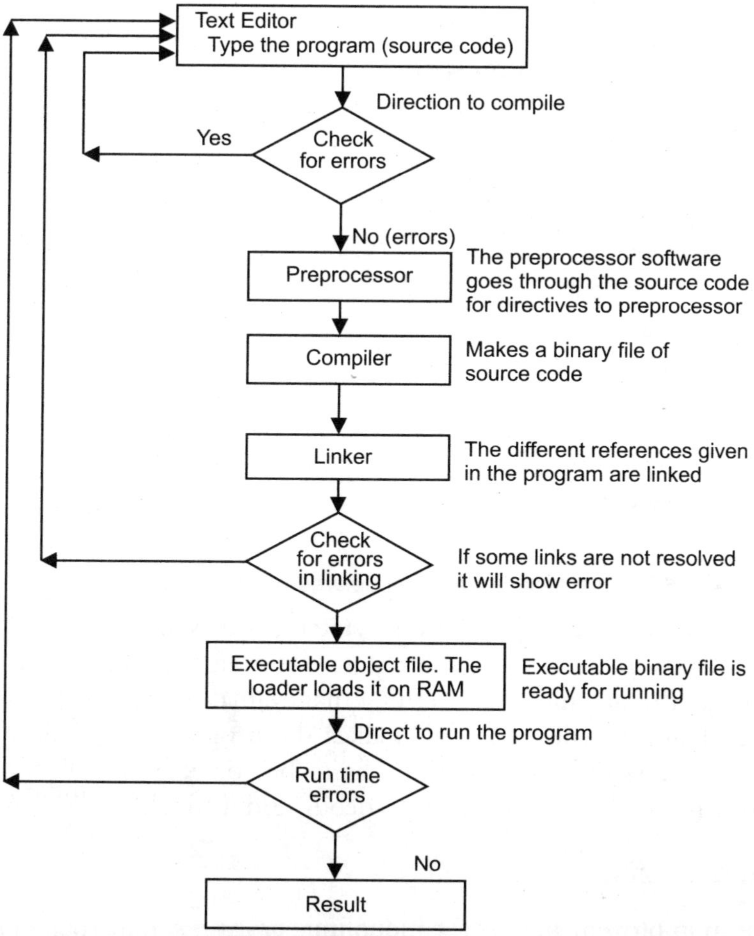

Fig. 1.4: Sequence of processes in development of a program in C/C++ language. (Also See Appendix E for more details on starting programs in C++)

All these processes are integrated, a programmer has only to type the program, give direction to compile, correct any error if indicated and then give direction to run the program. The various processes illustrated in the figure are internal to the compiler.

1.9 PROGRAMMING TECHNIQUES

With the development of programming languages the different programming techniques also evolved. The distinguishable techniques are listed below.

1. Unstructured or monolithic programming.
2. Procedural Programming
3. Modular Programming
4. Object oriented Programming

For C++ we are mainly concerned with procedural programming and object oriented programming. However for sake of being able to appreciate the differences, all the techniques are described briefly below.

UNSTRUCTURED / MONOLITHIC PROGRAMMING

The general structure of a monolithic program consists of global data and statements which modify the data and finally it contains the output statements. A sample is shown in Fig.1.5.

```
// Main program
Data
Statement1
Statement2
Statement
____________
Statement1
Statement2
end
```

Fig. 1.5: Programming in an unstructured programming language

The program is executed from top to bottom, statement by statement. If similar evaluations are to be carried out at several places in the program, for example, statement1 and statement2 in above illustration, all the statements concerning that evaluation have to be repeated at all the places where the evaluation is desired. This makes the program very lengthy. Besides, any modification in the process of the evaluation has to be corrected at so many places in the program. Such programs are lengthy, difficult to debug and difficult to maintain.

PROCEDURAL PROGRAMMING

These programs are an improvement over the monolithic programs. If a group of statements carry out similar action at several places in the program, such a group is taken out of the main program and is placed in a subprogram called subroutine or procedure or function. In the main program the subroutines or functions are called. When a subroutine is called, the main program is paused and control shifts to the subroutine till it is finished. Its return value if any is fed to the main program which is resumed from where it was left. It is illustrated in Fig.1.6.

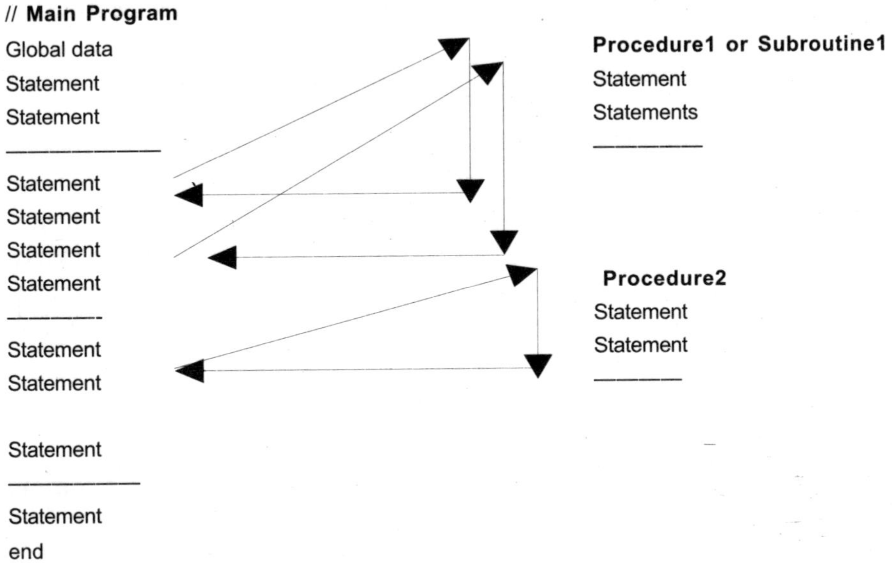

Fig. 1.6: Procedural programming

A procedural program is more structured. The different procedures or subroutines can be checked independently of the main program, thus debugging becomes easier. It is also easier to maintain the program. The drawback is that if the subroutine is small and is called many times in the program, the overload of calling makes the program inefficient.

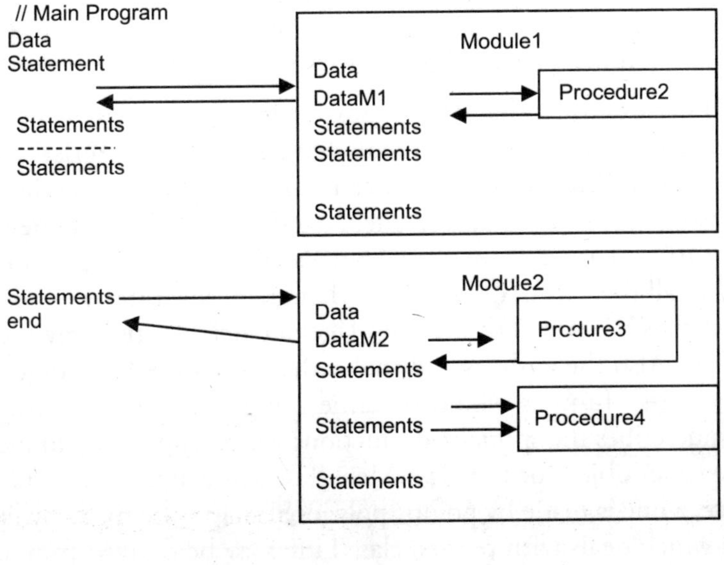

Fig. 1.7: Modular programming

Modular Programming

In this type of programming the similar procedures are grouped together into modules. Thus the whole program may consist of modules and connecting statements. The main program supplies data and co-ordinates the different modules. It is illustrated in Fig.(1.7).

1.10 OBJECT ORIENTED PROGRAMMING

In this technique an important factor is the data abstraction. The different procedures or functions are built around the abstract data. Thus the data and functions are encapsulated in a single structure called 'class'. The classes are the bases of object oriented programming (OOP). The classes create new data types besides the fundamental types which are already defined in C++. In a class, the different functions/procedures are defined according to the data that an object of the class must have. In the following the concept of classes and objects are explained with analogies from the physical world.

Classes and Objects

Every object in the real world is unique in itself. However, there are some common characteristics that it shares with other objects and which give a feeling that there is a group of objects which are different from others and form a class. For instance, a common characteristic of all fishes is that they live in water. So fishes form a class of objects that is different from the class of those who live on ground. Among the fishes there must be many classes or groups such as star fish, whales, jelly fish, etc., which can be differentiated because of their size, shape, colour, behaviour, etc. These characteristics give them a separate identity and they can be taken in separate groups or classes though all of them live in water, which is a common characteristic. Therefore, the different classes of fish may be derived from a common class, say class Fish. This is called **inheritance**. Thus we may make a program to describe the common characteristics of all fishes while the programs that describe the characteristics of only whales or only star fish form the classes which are **inherited** from or are **derived** from the class Fish.

Let us take another example, that of humans, which form a class which is different from those of tigers, cats and dogs. But all animals have some characteristics common among themselves. All belong to a class which we may call class Animals. Among the humans also there are two distinct classes, that of men and women. So the class Men may be derived from class Humans which in turn is derived from class Animals. The data and functions which form the class Animal apply to all the classes downstream that are derived from it, i.e. that of class Men and class Tigers and class Women. For the class Tiger a particular tiger say the one in the zoo is an **object** of this class. Also the authors and the reader of this book are **objects** or **instances** of class Humans. The class Humans would describe the general characteristics of all humans. Similarly class Men describes the specialised functions which apply only to men. Any particular man is an instance or an object of the class Men. The same argument applies to many other objects. For instance, a line is made by points, polygonal shapes are made by lines. Thus we may make a class Point which deals with points, class Line may be derived from class point and so on.

DATA ABSTRACTION

Every object of real world has a large amount of data associated with it. The data describes various characteristics, some of which may be common with other objects. But for a program which is limited by its purpose and scope some of the data associated with objects of a class may not be useful for the purpose of the program and hence may not be needed. We have to select the data most appropriate for the purpose of the program as well as it should be uniformly applicable to all the objects of the class, for which the program is being prepared. In fact, if we make a model of the behaviour of the objects of the class, the desired data in the model is the abstract data.

CLASSES V/S PROCEDURAL PROGRAM

In C++ a class is a sort of blueprint or design in programming that describes the characteristics of a group of objects which share some common characters. A class comprises data members and function members. Some of the function members are defined with data members as parameters while others may serve as an interface for other functions declared private in the class, still others may be friend functions, etc. When the class is implemented, the functions members operate on the actual data of an object to bring out characteristics of the object. The actual object data is substituted for the data members in the functions contained in the class.

One may ask the question, what is the difference between a class and a procedural program because both involve data and functions? The class program differs in many ways. In case of procedural program if it comprises the same functions and data as in the class, can certainly bring out characteristics of one object. For second object, the program is again run with changed data. However, in case of class, several objects can co-exist each having its own data, while the functions in class are shared by all the objects. Some function may involve interaction of objects of different classes.

The class has also the advantage of information hiding. The user need not know how the program is being implemented. Also the user can not have direct access to object data if the same is declared private in the class. Thus it enhances the data security. The classes can also be inherited by another class. The process of inheritance is not limited, it is endless. Thus inheritance makes it possible to reuse the program in a large number of other programs without any modification. Still another question remains. Why should we call classes as object oriented programming?

This question deals with the actual implementation of classes. In a procedural program a user may call any function and may operate it with data already in the program or with user input data as planned in the program. In fact, the whole program is before the user who can easily temper with data members and functions. In case of class, the function call is linked with an object of the class. The functions of a class can not be called without linking it with the object. Thus a class program gets implemented only if at least one object is validly defined with its data on which the functions of the class may operate. A class program is only for its objects. The kind of data that the objects must possess so that they can become objects of the class is also defined by the **constructor function** or another public function in the class declaration. Below is an example of simple class with name Rectangle. Statements that follow double slash (//) are comments and are not part of the program. The first 9 lines comprise the class declaration.

The main program starts after this. At this stage many readers are not acquainted with some of the statements and key words written below, nevertheless, one can make out the difference between this and the procedural programming.

PROGRAM 1.1 – Illustrates a class program.

```
class Rectangle                  // declaration of class with name Rectangle
{                                // class body starts with {.
private :                        // access label
int Length ,Width;               // private data
public :   // access label
void Setsides ( int a, int b){Length= a , Width = b;}
 //void Setsides() is public function for accessing private data
int Area (){return Length * Width;}
};                               // class declaration ends here.


#include <iostream> //main program starts from here
using namespace std;

int main()                       // Main function
{
Rectangle Rect1, Rect2;          // Rect1 and Rect2 are two objects of
                                 // class Rectangle
Rect1.Setsides(50,40);           // Rect1 calls function Setsides().See
// the dot operator (.) between Rect1 and Setsides().
Rect2.Setsides(30,20);           // Rect2 calls function Setsides()
cout<<"Area of Rect1 = "<< Rect1.Area() << endl;
//Rect1 calls function Area(). See the dot operator between the
    //Rect1 and Area.
cout<<"Area of Rect2 = " <<Rect2.Area()<<endl;
                // Rect2 calls function Area()
return 0 ;
}                                // end of program
```

The statements after // are the comments. They are not part of program. Following is the output of the two cout statements in the main program.

```
Area of Rect1 = 2000
Area of Rect2 = 600
```

The above program is an example of object oriented program. It consists of class declaration for objects which are rectangles. The name of class is Rectangle. Rect1 and Rect2 are two objects (rectangles) of this class. See that function calls are linked with the objects on whose data they operate, i.e., Rect1.Setsides(50, 40) and Rect1.Area(). The dot operator (.) provides the link. If you simply call the function like Area() it will not work. So class is implemented only for its objects. The various class functions are linked to the object for their execution.

INFORMATION HIDING

Classes also allow the hiding of the data members as well as some function members by declaring them as **private** in the class declaration. This is illustrated in the above program in which int length and int width are declared as private. Private members are accessible only through other functions declared **public** in class declaration. Private data and functions are not directly accessible even by the objects of the class. The objects of class may access its public data and function members.

The class itself may be hidden from the user who only includes it (includes the name of class) in the program and deals with the interface provided by public functions in the class like Setsides () and Area () in the above example. In case of class program, a user of the program is like a driver of a car who only knows about pedals (accelerator, clutch and brake) and steering wheel and light switches which are the **public interfaces** or we may call them as public functions. The driver does not know the complex mechanism behind the pedals and steering wheel. In fact, a driver need not know all that just for driving the car. Similarly in a class program, the data and some member functions may be totally hidden from the user of the program. Because after a class code has been tested, debugged and verified we may store in a separate file. The class code may not be available to user who only includes the relevant filename in his/her program. Besides a class may be derived from another class which also may be having private members. The intention is to hide as much as possible from the user of the program and classes provide the mechanism for this. This is called **information hiding.**

1.11 OPERATOR OVERLOADING

In most of the programs, we often use operators such as +, –, /, etc. These are used for operations like addition, subtraction, division, etc. Let us take operator +. This operator is defined to add two integers or two decimal point numbers. Now if you want to add two vectors this operator will not work because a vector has a magnitude and a direction. To overcome the problem of direction, in vector mathematics, we add components of vectors. For example in case of two dimensional vectors, x-component of vector **A** is added to x- component of vector **B** and y-component of vector **A** is added to y-component of vector **B**. Here the vectors are shown by bold letters. Let A_x and A_y be components of **A** and B_x and B_y be components of **B**. Let **C** be the resultant vector with components C_x and C_y. So the addition of **A** and **B** is expressed as below.

$$C_x = A_x + B_x$$
$$C_y = A_y + B_y$$

We can, however, overload the operator + to carry out above additions, that is, we redefine the functionality of + operator so that it will do the above two additions and will find C_x and C_y.

With this facility we can write the following code in our program.

```
C = A + B ;
```

This statement will do $A_x + B_x$ and assign it to C_x and do $A_y + B_y$ and assign it to C_y. Thus we can do vector addition with the same operator +. This is called **operator overloading.**

Similarly other operators may also be overloaded if so needed. You will yourself appreciate that such a provision gives a tremendous extension to C++. There are many applications of operator overloading such as in manipulation of vectors, complex numbers, matrices, any object that is represented by more than one value can be dealt with the help of operator overloading.

1.12 INHERITANCE

We have already discussed that classes may be formed for the objects which have some common characteristics. These characteristics are passed on to the classes that are derived from the base class. The derived class inherits the base class without any modification while it may add more specialized characteristics to the objects. The process is called **inheritance.** There is no end to the process of inheritance. One may derive another class which inherits any one or more of the already derived classes. Inheritance makes it possible to reuse an already tested and working class program. Thus a big program may be divided into such classes which may be useful in the present program as well as other programs. The Fig.1.9 illustrates the application of inheritance.

For sake of illustration let us consider two dimensional space. We all know that a line is made of points, other shapes say polygons are made out of lines. The shapes like square, rectangle and hexagon are polygonal shapes. Therefore, the functions of class Point are also useful in class Line. Similarly the functions of class Line are useful in class Polygons and that of polygons are useful in classes Square, Rectangle and Hexagon. Therefore, the upstream classes may simply be inherited instead of repeating their code again and again in downstream classes.

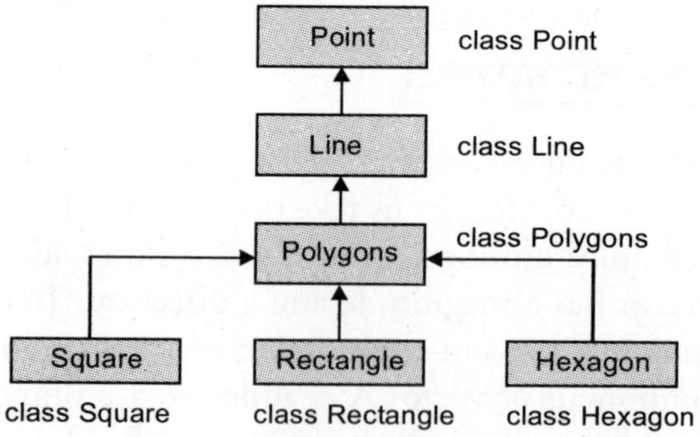

Fig. 1.8: Inheritance

Thus inheritance helps in the reuse of the already established software. In the chain of inheritances shown in Fig.1.8, the class Point is base class for class Line. Similarly the class Line is base class for class Polygon which is also base class for class Square, class Rectangle, etc. A class may have more than one class as base classes. An object of class Square is also an object of class polygon but an object of class Polygon is not an object of class Square. This is because class Polygon does not know about the classes downstream like class Square.

1.13 POLYMORPHISM

Polymorphism is a Greek word which means the ability to take different forms. In the previous section we have seen how the operator + may be overloaded to carry out different operations.

This is an example of polymorphism. However, in such cases the choice of function is known at the compile time itself. Therefore, this is called **static binding** or **early binding.** The **run time binding** or **late binding** or **dynamic binding** is one in which the choice of appropriate function is carried out during execution of the program (Fig.1.9). This is realised through declaration of **virtual functions** in the base class and by use of base class **pointer.** A pointer is a variable whose value is the address of another object to which it points.

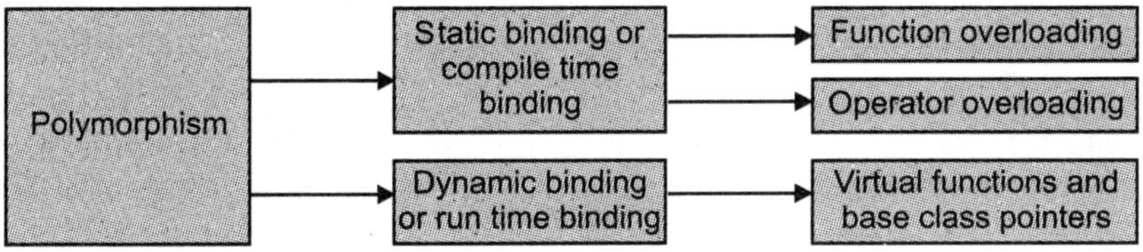

Fig. 1.9: Polymorphism

1.14 NUMBER SYSTEMS

Since computer operations are ultimately connected to manipulation of numbers in the binary form, it is worthwhile to know about different number systems which will be often used in the programs. Below we deal with the number systems such as decimal, binary, octal and hexadecimal systems. We normally use decimal system in our daily life calculations. This is a system with base 10 and digits are 0, 1, 2, 3, 4, 5, 6, 7, 8 and 9. Perhaps mankind started counted on fingers and there are ten fingers so is the base of our number system. Suppose we have a number 456, it can be written as below.

$$4 \times 10^2 + 5 \times 10^1 + 6 \times 10^0 = 400 + 50 + 6 = 456$$

Here you see that apart from the value of digit, its position in the number also matters. In 456, the first digit 6 is at unit place and has value 6 while the digit 5 is at a place next to unit and which has place value 10. Therefore, this 5 has value $5 \times 10^1 = 50$. Similarly the digit 4 is at hundredth place has value $4 \times 10^2 = 400$

However, computer systems work on binary system. Binary system has a base 2. In a binary number such as 1110111, the digit at unit place (right most) has place value $2^0 = 1$. For the next digit, the place value is $2^1 = 2$. So if the digit is 0 its value is 0 but if the digit is 1 its value is 2. Similarly the digit at hundredth place has place value = 1×2^2 , i.e. 4. In other words, digit 1 in the hundredth place is equivalent to 4. Below we have tabulated the conversion of decimal numbers from 0 to 10 to binary numbers.

Decimal number	Binary number	Conversion of binary into decimal
0	0	$0 \times 2^0 = 0$
1	1	$1 \times 2^0 = 1 \times 1 = 1$
2	10	$1 \times 2^1 + 0 \times 2^0 = 2 + 0 = 2$
3	11	$1 \times 2^1 + 1 \times 2^0 = 3$
4	100	$1 \times 2^2 + 0 \times 2^1 + 0 \times 2^0 = 4$

5	101	$1 \times 2^2 + 0 \times 2^1 + 1 \times 2^0 = 5$
6	110	$1 \times 2^2 + 1 \times 2^1 + 0 \times 2^0 = 4 + 2 = 6$
7	111	$1 \times 2^2 + 1 \times 2^1 + 1 \times 2^0 = 4 + 2 + 1 = 7$
8	1000	$1 \times 2^3 + 0 \times 2^2 + 0 \times 2^1 + 0 \times 2^0 = 8$
9	1001	$1 \times 2^3 + 0 \times 2^2 + 0 \times 2^1 + 1 \times 2^0 = 9$
10	1010	$1 \times 2^3 + 0 \times 2^2 + 1 \times 2^1 + 0 \times 2^0 = 8 + 2 = 10$

Numbers with base 8 and base 16 are also used. The numbers of digits in the different systems are given in Table 1.1.

Table – 1.1

Number system	Base	Digits
Binary	2	0, 1
Octal	8	0, 1, 2, 3, 4, 5, 6, 7
Decimal	10	0, 1, 2, 3, 4, 5, 6, 7, 8, 9
Hexadecimal	16	0, 1, 2, 3, 4, 5, 6, 7, 8, 9, A, B, C, D, E, F

The digits A, B, C, D, E and F in hexadecimal system are equivalent to 10, 11, 12, 13, 14 and 15 respectively in the decimal system. A number such as 0000000111001000 may be converted back to decimal number as given below.

$1 \times 2^8 + 1 \times 2^7 + 1 \times 2^6 + 0 \times 2^5 + 0 \times 2^4 + 1 \times 2^3 + 0 \times 2^2 + 0 \times 2^1 +$

$0 \times 2^0 = 256 + 128 + 64 + 8 = 456$

In the above exercise it is shown that each place in the binary number has a power of the base 2. Thus for the digit on the extreme right the power is zero, so for value it is multiplied by 2^0 or 1. For the next digit the power is 1, so its value is obtained by multiplying it by 2^1, and so on.

Figure 1.10 illustrates the conversion of a decimal number into a binary number.

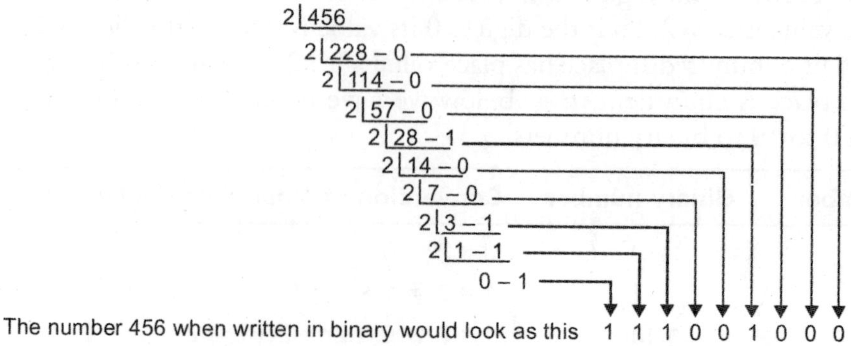

Fig. 1.10: Converting a decimal number into binary

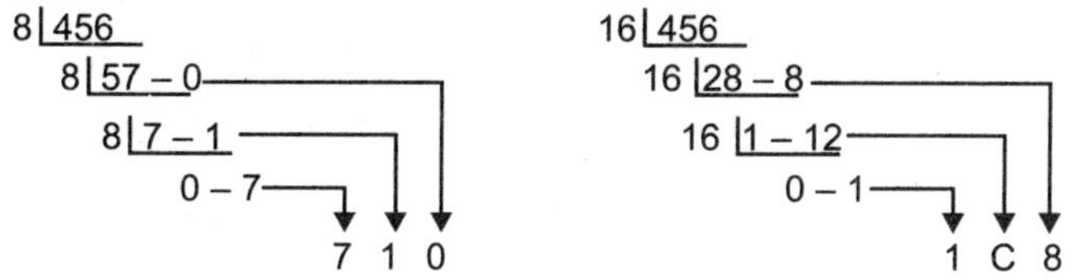

(a) Octal (a) Hexadecimal

Fig. 1.11

The same number 456 may also be written in octal or hexadecimal system as well. We repeat the exercise of Fig.1.10 for octal and hexadecimal systems as shown in Fig.(1.11a) and Fig. (1.11 b) respectively. The following table shows the number 456 in different number systems.

Table – 1.2

Number system	Base	Representations of decimal number 456
Binary	2	111001000
Octal	8	710
Decimal	10	456
Hexadecimal	16	1C8

In a computer program the octal numbers are preceded by 0 (zero) and hexadecimal numbers are preceded by 0x or 0X. Thus 456, in octal is 0710 and in hexadecimal it is written as 0X1C8. For conversion from binary to octal or hexadecimal see the following grouping of digits.

Binary equivalent of 456	111	001	000
Octal	7	1	0
Binary equivalent of 456	1	1100	1000
Hexadecimal	1	C	8

For converting binary into octal, make groups of binary digits with three digits in each group starting from extreme right. The decimal digit represented by each group is the digit in octal representation. In the above example, starting from right, the first group of three binary digits are all zero. So the octal digit is also zero. The second group 001 is equivalent to octal 1. The third group 111 is equivalent to 7. So the number in octal representation is 0710.

Similarly for the hexadecimal representation from binary, make groups of four binary digits as illustrated above. Make a hexadecimal digit out of the four binary digits. The right most group (1000) evaluates to 8. The next group 1100 evaluates to 12 in decimal which is C in hexadecimal. The last group is only 1. So the number 456 in hexadecimal representation is 0X1C8 or 0x1c8. **In a program, decimal numbers should not be preceded by zero (0).**

FRACTIONAL NUMBERS

In a decimal system a fractional or a decimal point number say 456.25 may be written as

$$456.25 = 4 \times 10^2 + 5 \times 10^1 + 6 \times 10^0 + 2 \times 10^{-1} + 5 \times 10^{-2}$$

Same method applies to binary fractional numbers. Say we have a number

$x = 111001000.01$

in binary. It may be converted to decimal system as below.

$$x = 1 \times 2^8 + 1 \times 2^7 + 1 \times 2^6 + 0 \times 2^5 + 0 \times 2^4 + 1 \times 2^3 + 0 \times 2^2$$
$$+ 0 \times 2^1 + 0 \times 2^0 + 0 \times 2^{-1} + 1 \times 2^{-2}$$
$$= 256 + 128 + 64 + 8 + 0 + 0.25 = 456.25$$

For converting 0.25 from decimal system to binary, we have to successively multiply it by 2 till it is 1 or non-fractional as below.

$$0.25 \times 2 \times 2 = 1$$

Therefore, the number 0.25 in decimal system is equal to 0.01 in binary.

Exercise – Convert the fraction 0.1, 0.2 and 0.5 from decimal system to binary.

Solution

Conversion of 0.1—Multiply 0.1 successively by 2, till it is 1 or just more than 1.

		Binary fractional number
$.1 \times 2 = .2$	less than 1	.0
$.1 \times 2 \times 2 = .4$	less than 1	.00
$.1 \times 2 \times 2 \times 2 = .8$	still less than 1	.000
$.1 \times 2 \times 2 \times 2 \times 2 = 1.6$	now multiply fraction .6 as below	.0001
$.6 \times 2 = 1.2$	now multiply fraction .2 as below	.00011
$.2 \times 2 \times 2 \times 2 = 1.2$	now multiply fraction .2 by	.00011001

Therefore .1 of decimal = .00011001 of binary. As shown above the fraction could still continue.

Conversion of 0.2 of decimal into binary

$0.2 \times 2 \times 2 \times 2 = 1.6$	fraction part now left is .6	.001
$.6 \times 2 = 1.2$	fraction part now left is .2	.0011
$.2 \times 2 \times 2 \times 2 = 1.6$	fraction part now left is .6	.0011001

Therefore .2 of decimal = .0011001 of binary.

Similarly it can be shown that .5 of decimal = .1 of binary.

1.15 BITS AND BYTES

The smallest unit of computer memory is a **bit,** which may have values either 0 or 1. In computer we often deal with groups of bits. A group of 8 bits is called a **byte**. The characteristics of a memory is that if a bit has been set to one it will continue to remain in that state until it is reset to zero. And if it is reset to 0 it would remain so unless it is set to 1. A simple example is that of a switch. When you press the switch, it switches on a light, and it continues to remain on untill you put it off or reset it. When a switch is put on it connects a high voltage to the light circuit. We may call it as state 1. When it is put off the circuit voltage becomes zero. We may call it a state 0. In electronics there are circuits which are called *flip-flops.* A flip-flop is just like a switch. When it has high voltage (≈ 5 V) on its output point we say it is set and when the voltage at its output terminal is 0 we say it is at zero or reset.

The output state can be manipulated by input signal to the flip-flop. Thus we can make its output 0 or 1 as we wish just like a switch which can be put on or put off, the difference being that in case of flip-flop it is done by electronic circuit while in case of manual switch it is done manually. We have qualified the switch as manual because switching can also be done electronically. **Each flip-flop is one bit of memory.** A bit can have value 0 or 1. Now you understand why binary numbers are used in computers. Binary numbers also have only two digits, one is 0 and second is 1. Computer memory also has two states 0 or low and 1 or high. If we have an array of such flip-flops, some set high or at 1 and some set to low or at 0 at their outputs, we can represent a binary number. For instance, Fig.1.12 shows four bits. They have the place values from unit for the bit on extreme right to 8 for bit on the extreme left. If all the bits are set (have value 1) the total number stored is equal to 8 + 4 + 2 + 1 = 15 in decimal system.

Bit number	3	2	1	0
Binary number (when set)	1	1	1	1
Place value	$2^3 = 8$	$2^2 = 4$	$2^1 = 2$	$2^0 = 1$
Number stored when all the bits are set = 1 × 8 + 1 × 4 + 1 × 2 + 1 × 1 = 15				

Fig. 1.12

Below in Fig. 1.13 we show 4 flip-flops by four squares numbering from 0 to 3. *In computer terminology the counting starts from 0.* Here we take right most bit (Fig.1.13) as the 0th bit at the unit place. In programming also as you will see in the chapter on arrays that the first member of an array is the 0th element. So it is better that you make a habit to count from 0. The next flip-flop (shown by square at 1) is at place where place value is 2. The flip-flop next to it (3rd from right and numbered as 2) has a place value $2^2 = 4$ and the last has place value $2^3 = 8$.

Now if the bit 0, 1 and 3 are set (each equal to 1) and bit 2 is 0. The number stored is 11. It is explained below.

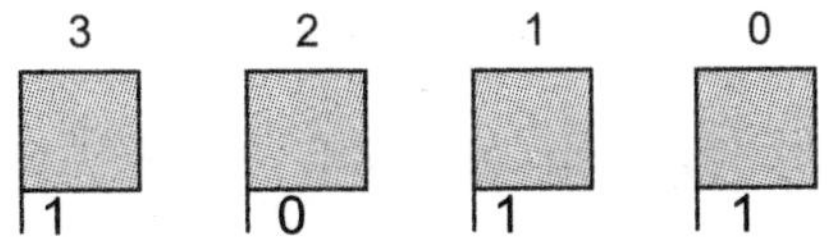

Output state

Number held $1 \times 2^3 + 0 \times 2^2 + 1 \times 2^1 + 1 \times 2^0 = 8 + 0 + 2 + 1 = 11$

Fig. 1.13

Starting from right of Fig.1.13, the 0th bit is high representing 1, the next one is also high but it is one digit to the left of 0th bit. So here 0 is zero, but 1 is equal to $1 \times 2^1 = 2$. Similarly at the third place it is zero so it is equal to $0 \times 2^2 = 0$. At the fourth place the bit is high so it represents $1 \times 2^3 = 8$. So the total of all these is 11. Similarly, if all of them were high they would represent a number 15, and when all of them are low they represent 0. So a set of 4 memory bits can hold any number from 0 to 15 or from 0 to $(2^4 - 1)$. Similarly, if we have 8 bits of memory arranged as shown in Fig.1.14, we can store any number from 0 to $(2^8 - 1) = 0$ to 255.

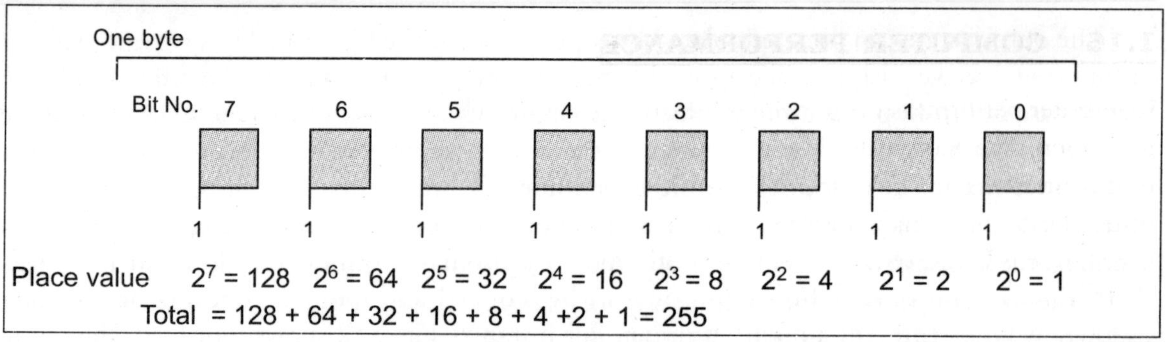

Fig. 1.14: One byte can store any positive number from 0 to 255

So one byte can hold any positive number (unsigned number) from 0 to 255. Similarly if the number is unsigned (positive) 2, 3 and 4 bytes can hold numbers as given below.

2 bytes (16 bits) can hold an unsigned number from 0 to $(2^{16} - 1) = 0$ to 65535

3 bytes (24 bits) can hold any unsigned number from 0 to $(2^{24} - 1) = 0$ to 16,777,215

4 bytes (32 bits) can hold any unsigned number from 0 to $(2^{32} - 1) = 0$ to 4,294,967,295

Often we have to deal with positive as well as negative numbers (**signed** numbers). In such cases, the left most bit of the memory block allocated to the number is reserved for sign. If this bit is 0 the number is positive and if the bit is set to 1 the number is negative. So for storage of signed number we now have one bit less. Therefore, for signed numbers the maximum value of number that can be stored on a n-bit memory becomes $(2^{n-1} - 1)$. Thus the ranges of signed numbers that can be stored on 1, 2, 3 and 4 bytes are as follows.

Range of signed number that 1 byte can hold

$$= -2^{8-1} \text{ to } (2^{8-1} - 1) \text{, i.e. } -128 \text{ to } 127$$

Range of signed number that 2 byte can hold

$$= -2^{16-1} \text{ to } (2^{16-1} - 1) = -32768 \text{ to } 32767$$

Range of signed number that 3 byte can hold

$$= -2^{24-1} \text{ to } (2^{24-1} - 1) = -8388608 \text{ to } 8388607$$

Range of signed number that 4 byte can hold

$$= -2^{32-1} \text{ to } (2^{32-1} - 1) = -2147483648 \text{ to } 2147483647$$

In general, characters such a 'A', 'b', etc., are stored in one byte, short integers (whole numbers) are stored in two bytes, integers are stored in 4 bytes. The floating decimal numbers are stored in 4 bytes for single precision (float) and in 8 bytes for decimal point numbers with double precision.

1.16 COMPUTER PERFORMANCE

Computer performance is generally measured by how quickly it performs a task. If it takes more time then its performance is low. The speed of CPU (frequency of its oscillator) is one factor that contributes to the efficiency. But processor does not work alone. It works with support of other electronic chips whose speed is equally important. Besides, the type of program that it is handling, the language of program, etc., all affect its performance. Among the devices that support CPU, the most important ones are the memory devices in which the processor stores the data and extracts data from. Generally the speed of memory devices is much lower than the speed of the processor and this low speed becomes a drag on the processor because it has to wait till the process of storing data or process of extracting data is completed. Fig.1.15 shows the different memory devices which are used by the processor to carry out a program. Different memory devices have different speeds and hence the cost (Fig.1.16). The performance of a memory device is measured by the access time. This is the time taken by memory for extraction of a data. The fastest memory which is closest to the processor is L1 cache memory which in some processors is on the processor chip itself. It has the minimum access time of the order of 1 to 2 nano-seconds (1 nano-second $=10^{-9}$ sec.). Then comes the L2 cache memory that may be on a separate chip. Its access time is nearly twice that of L1. Then comes the RAM the main memory which is extensively used by processor. The cache memories are also part of RAM. Speeds and prices of memory devices vary over a good range. The slowest are the bulk storage memories such as hard disc, magnetic tape etc., and their access time varies from seconds to minutes. Fig.1.16 gives an idea of the access times of different memory devices.

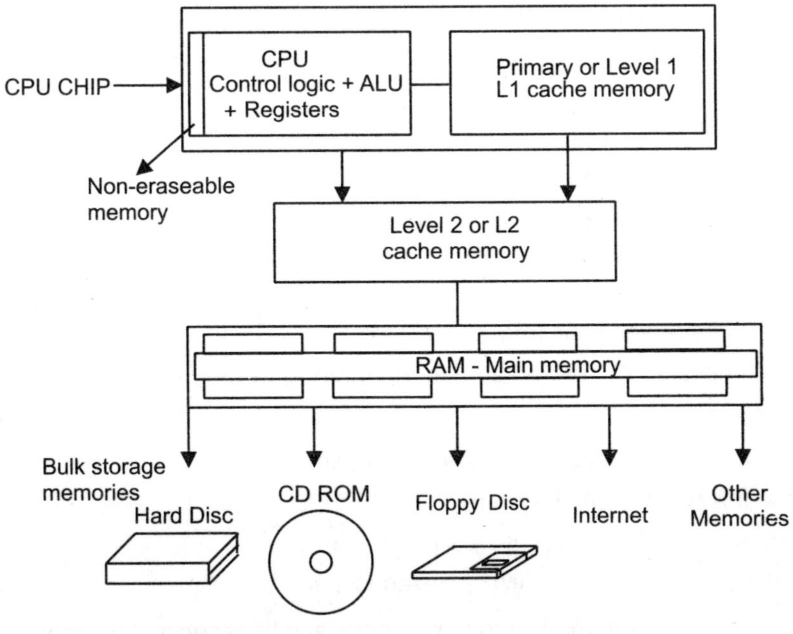

Fig. 1.15: Types of memories in a computer

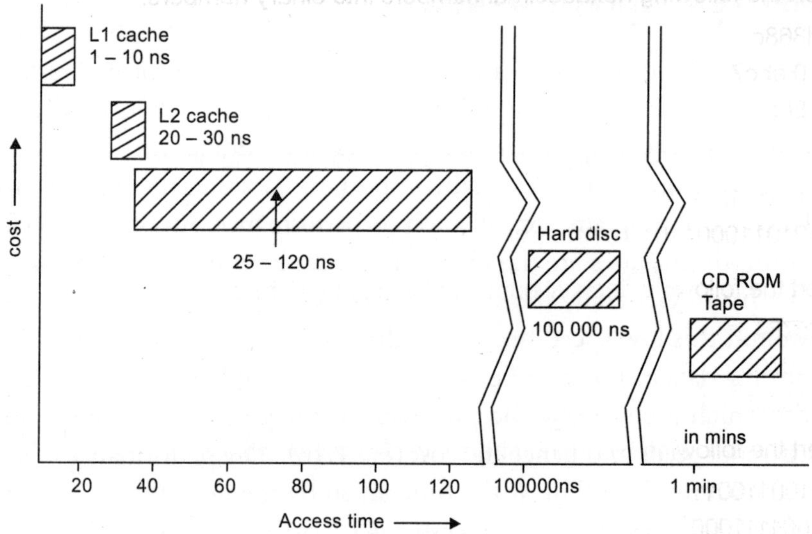

Fig. 1.16

It is logical to infer that a computer with large L1 and L2 would perform better. Besides L1 and L2, the computer performance also depends on RAM and the quality of program. A program is more efficient if it generates less machine code. In this respect the programs written in machine language are the fastest because there is nothing between the program and the processor. The programs written in assembly language come next , i.e. take more time as these have to go through the assembler. The programs written in a high level language have to be converted into machine language by a compiler or interpreter. Naturally these programs take more time than those written in assembly language. Programs in C++, when compared with other high level languages on efficiency scale, come midway, nearly as good as java.

EXERCISES

1. What do you understand by following terms?
   (i) Machine language
   (ii) Assembly language
   (iii) High level languages
2. What are the major additions from C to C++?
3. What is a compiler? Why is it needed to run a program written in C++?
4. What is a class?
5. What are the different types of computer memories?
6. Explain the following number systems.
   (i) Decimal (ii) Binary
   (iii) Octal (iv) Hexadecimal
7. Convert decimal number 46535 into binary, octal and hexadecimal numbers.

8. Convert the following hexadecimal numbers into binary numbers.
   (i) d368c
   (ii) f 0 abc7
   (iii) 368c
9. Convert the following binary numbers into hexadecimal numbers.
   (i) 1110101011001
   (ii) 1010110001101.10101
10. Convert the following decimal numbers into binary numbers.
   (i) 65784
   (ii) 100765
   (iii) 133.25
11. Convert the following binary numbers into decimal numbers.
   (i) 11001100110
   (ii) 10011110001.111
   (iii) 11110111111
12. How are the hexadecimal numbers differentiated from octal numbers in output from a computer?
13. What do you understand by the following terms?
   (i) Microprocessor (ii) Compiler
   (iii) Assembler (iv) Interpreter
14. What do you understand by the following?
   (i) RAM (ii) ROM
   (iii) L1 cache memory (iv) L2 cache memory
15. What do you understand by the following terms?
   (i) Flip flop
   (ii) Bit
   (iii) Byte
16. Explain the following terms.
   (i) Inheritance
   (ii) Operator overloading
   (iii) Polymorphism
17. What do you understand by object oriented programming?
18. How are binary numbers stored in a computer?
19. What are classes and objects?
20. How big a number may be stored in 3 bytes if it is one of the following?
   (i) signed number (ii) unsigned number
21. A class program is to be made for determining area of any polygon. What data is required for the purpose?

22. Distinguish between the following styles of programming.
    (i) Procedural programming.
    (ii) Modular programming.
    (iii) Object oriented programming.
23. Distinguish between the following terms.
    (i) Class and object
    (ii) Base class and derived class
    (iii) Data abstraction.
24. What data should be printed on a driving licence of a person? (Hint: use data abstraction)
25. What data should be printed on the identity cards of students of a technical institute?
26. The city police decides that all domestic servants should carry an identity card. What data do you think should be printed on it?
27. The employees of a bank are required to wear an identity card during working hours in the bank. What data do you think should be printed on it?

❍❍❍

CHAPTER

2 Structure of a C++ Program

2.1 INTRODUCTION

A typical program in C++ may comprise a list of statements involving variables (objects whose values may change during the execution of program), constants (whose values do not change), operators like +, –, etc. and functions, etc. Computer recognises them by their names just like you are recognised by your name. Obviously, no two variables or constants should have same name. However, functions may have same name if their parameters are different. It must be emphasised here that **C++ is a case sensitive language**, which, means that it will take 'A' and 'a' as two different objects. Similarly Area, area and AREA are three different objects. Therefore, while writing a program the name of a variable, constant or a function should be written consistently in the same fashion throughout the program.

Like any other high level programming language, C++ also has certain rules, special syntax and keywords to help the programmers to write a program and execute it. Keywords have special meanings for the compiler and are used to control and execute the program. Naturally, these words should be used in a program only for the purpose they are meant for. Their use as names of variables, constants, functions or objects will create errors in the program. The keywords used in C++ are listed in Table 3.2 in Chapter 3. Besides these, there are a number of files called **header files** and functions in **C++ Standard Library** which help in the execution of the programs. Therefore, every program has to include the header files which are required by the program.

The keywords as well as names of files and functions in C++ Standard Library are in general defined in lower case. As already mentioned the keywords should not be used as names, however, if the case of any letter in a keyword is changed it is no longer a keyword. Thus a safe bet is that the starting letter in a name may be made capital.

Also C++ is highly typed language which means that the data is categorized into different **types**. For example, whole numbers form a category called integers. So when a variable whose value can only be in whole numbers, is declared we write **int** (short form of integer) before its name. The int is its **type**. Variables which have values in floating decimal point numbers such as 2.4 or 3.14159, etc. form another category. For declaration of such variables we write **float** or **double** before their names. For variables which have values in form of characters are of type **char.**

An **interactive program** requires the user of the program to put in some data during the execution of the program. The data may comprise numerical values, or a string of characters which may be a statement or simply yes or no. In the following we first learn the essential tokens of a C++ program which are a must in every program.

2.2 COMPONENTS OF A SIMPLE C++ PROGRAM

Program 2.1 given below, illustrates the essential components or tokens of a C++ program. In this program it is desired to put two sentences or messages on the output device. If the output device is not specified in the program, the monitor of the computer is the default output device. In such a case, the output will be displayed on the monitor. Monitor is connected to one of the output ports of the computer. Similarly keyboard is the default input device.

PROGRAM 2.1 – A sample program which displays two messages on monitor.

```
#include <iostream.h>
int main()
{ std::cout<<"Hello, Welcome to programming with C++!\n" ;
std::cout <<"Are you interested to join?"<< std::endl;
return 0 ;
}
```

HEADER FILES

The first line of the Program 2.1 is #include <iostream.h> in which the symbol # is a pre-processor directive. It is a signal for pre-processor which runs before the compiler. The statement directs the compiler to include the **header file** <iostream.h> (input/output stream) from **C++ Standard Library** in this program. The file **<iostream.h>** has the procedural software in the form of functions which are used with its two objects **cin** and **cout** for performing input and output respectively. The cin is used along with **extraction operator** (>>) for input and cout is used along with **insertion operator** (<<) for output. The name of a header file when included in a program is enclosed between a pair of angular brackets < >. The header file name may as well be enclosed between double quotes " ". When the header file name is enclosed between angular brackets the pre-processor searches for it only in C++ Standard Library. The angular brackets indicate to pre-processor that it is part of C++ Standard Library. When it is enclosed between double quotes (" "), the pre-processor first searches the directory in which the file containing the directive #include appears. If this search is not successful, the search goes to C++ Standard Library. Therefore, generally for a user defined header files the name is written in double quotes and for the C++ Standard Library header file, the name is written in angular brackets.

Any program requiring standard input, i.e. from keyboard, and standard output, i.e. to monitor, must include the header file **<iostream.h>**. You may include other header files as well from C++ Standard Library if your program requires them. For example, if you want to carry out evaluation of mathematical functions like square-root, sin(θ), cos (θ) or log (6), etc., you must include the header file **<cmath>**. The header file cmath has the software for evaluation of many such functions. For including more than one header file in a program, these should be written in successive lines as illustrated below. Only one header file is written in one line.

```
#include <iostream>
#include <cmath>
#include <cstdlib>
```

Also note that there is no comma or semicolon or full stop anywhere in any of the above three lines or at the end of lines. The earlier convention of writing the header file with extension (.h) such as <iostream.h> is now not recommended and is written simply **<iostream>**. Similarly the other header files such as <math.h> and <stdlib.h> are now written as <cmath> and <cstdlib>. Both versions are supported by compilers. The difference between the two is that header file having names like <xxxx. h> have their names in global namespace while those without (.h) have their names in **namespace std** which is being increasingly used now. The term *namespace std* and its use is explained latter in this chapter.

INT MAIN( ) OR VOID MAIN( )

The second line of the above program (int main()) indicates the beginning of the program. In C++ the parentheses ( ) are used to indicate that the identifier or name on its left is a function. Here main () is also a function. **Every program in C++ must have only one main() function.** The word *int* stands for integer. Here int main() means that function *main()* is a return type function which returns an integer value. In case of a return type function the last statement is return *value;* . In the present case the last line of the program reads **return 0;**. If the above program runs successfully, it will return 0 to the system. For some compilers the statement return 0; is optional but if you are working with Microsoft C++ Visual 6 compiler, this statement is required, otherwise, the compiler will show error. The code lines after int main() and enclosed between the left brace '{' and right brace '}' form the body of the program which may have several lines of code. The left brace '{' is placed at the beginning and the right brace '}' is placed at the end of a program. In general, a program may have several pairs of these braces in its body as well. These are used for various purposes, however, the above two braces are essential.

A typical program in C++ is illustrated below in Fig. 2.1. It starts with names of header files to be included in the program. These are followed by function **int main** () or **void main** () and then the body of program enclosed in the curly braces{}. These braces generally contain expressions, statements and operators with a purpose to carry out some action on the data presented to the program. Expressions are the conditions if fulfilled the statement following the expression is carried out. In the program sample you will observe that all the **statements in a C++ program end with a semicolon** (;). Besides the statements, the program may contain conditional expressions like the one illustrated in Fig.2.1, i.e., if(expression). Such expressions do not end with semicolon (;).

```
# include <iostream>
int main ()
{Statement;
if(expression)
{Statement;
 ——;
 }
Statement;   // comment
return 0;
}
```

Fig. 2.1: A typical program statements

The body of Program 2.1 comprises two output statements and the line return 0;. The last line has already been discussed above. The output statements are discussed below.

OUTPUT STATEMENT – USE OF COUT

The first output statement of Program 2.1 is repeated below for ready reference.

```
std::cout<<" Hello, Welcome to programming with C++!\n" ;
```

The C++ standard library functions and classes are defined under namespace **std.** The operator (::) is the **scope resolution operator**. The line std :: cout means that we are calling an object **cout** which is defined under namespace std or which belongs to header file <iostream.h> of C++ Standard Library. The object cout is used with the **stream insertion operator** (<<). During the execution of the program the operator << inserts the argument on its right hand side into the output stream. In the present program the statement on the right of operator << is a string of characters enclosed between double quotes (" "). A string of characters as defined by ASCII (see Appendix A) and enclosed between double quotation marks is put to output stream as it is written. Even if it contains a keyword or digit or any other symbol, it would go to output stream as it is written without any change.

2.3 ESCAPE SEQUENCES

Some characters preceded by back slash character (\) like the one at the end of the above output statement, i.e. "\n", have a special meaning for the compiler. Back slash (\) is an escape character. The combination "\n" represents an **escape sequence** which directs the cursor to new line. Thus "\n" is new line character. It directs the cursor to next line, naturally any statement on the right hand side of "\n" will go to next line. But, \n has to be enclosed between double quotes like "\n". In some situations it may not be possible to put this symbol along with other statement as it has been done above, and, if it is desired that the output should now shift to next line, then it may be written in a separate line as illustrated below.

```
std::cout<<"\n";
```

Similarly, a back slash followed by character 't', i.e. , "\t" represents an escape sequence which moves the cursor to right by certain spaces in the same line. The number of spaces for the shift may be modified by adjusting the setting. The other such escape sequences and their actions are described in Table 2.1 below.

Table 2.1 – Escape sequences

Escape character	Description of action
\a	Bell or beep is generated by the computer on program execution.
\b	Back space. Moves cursor to previous position.
\f	Form feed. Advances cursor to next page.
\n	Shift to new line.
\r	Carriage return. Positions the cursor to the beginning of current line.

Contd...

\t	Horizontal tab. Moves the cursor by a number of spaces or to next tab stop in the same line.
\v	Vertical tab.
\\	Displays a back slash character (\).
\'	Displays a single quote character (').
\"	Displays a double quote character (").
\?	Displays a question mark (?).
\0	Null termination character. Signifies end of a character string.
\o	Code for octal numbers.
\x	Code for hexadecimal numbers respectively.

The next line in Program 2.1 is also an output statement, enclosed in double quotes. After the quotes is the end of line code (std::endl;). In this code we have used scope resolution operator (::) because we are calling *endl* which belongs to C++ Standard Library. The effect of *endl* is similar to that of "\n", i.e. it directs the cursor to new line. Thus what follows *endl* goes to the next line. Both the "\n" and std::endl may be used any number of times in the same code line. The output will correspondingly go to different lines.

The last line in the Program 2.1 is return 0; and it has already been explained above. The expected output of the Program 2.1 is the display of two messages on the monitor as given below.

```
Hello, Welcome to programming with C++!
Are you interested to join?
```

When a function does not return any numeric value as in the present case of main() we may as well write its *type* as `void`. Thus we could have written `void main()` in place of `int main()` in the above program. But in that case the statement `(return 0;)` is not required. This applies to any other void function as well. However, if we do not specify `int` or `void` before `main()` compiler would take it as `int` by default.

COMMENTS

The comments are not part of a program but are included so that the programmer can later remember what the program and its various variables stand for. It is a good practice to include comments, particularly for big programs which involve a large number of variables. A week after writing the program, the programmer may forget what the program does or what the different variables stand for. The comments help not only in recollecting the program written a few days ago, they also help even during writing a program particularly if it is a big program.

A comment may be introduced by first putting double slash (//) followed by the comment up to end of the line. It can be put anywhere in the program. The compiler simply neglects what follows the double slash (//) up to the end of line. Therefore, a comment may be put in the same line as the code or in a new line but after the double slash (//). If the comment is long and goes to next line, another double slash (//) is needed before the next line. Alternatively, a long comment may as well be enclosed between the C type comment symbols, i.e. /* before the start of comment and */ at the end of the comment. Both these methods are illustrated in Program 2.2.

PROGRAM 2.2 – It illustrates how to include **comments** and use of **void main () in place of int main().**

```
// A program with comments
#include <iostream>
void main()

//Anything written after double slash is neglected up to the
//end of line. The comment can be put anywhere in the program.

{ std::cout << "Hello, Welcome to programming in C++! \n";

/* Notice the blank spaces in the beginning of the first two lines, and also
the missing lines. All these blank spaces are neglected by compiler. Comments
may also be put in the c-style, i.e. between the symbols/ * and */ as done in
this comment.*/
std::cout <<"Are you interested?"<<std::endl;
/* When you use void main() do not include the statement 'return 0;', because
the void functions do not return any value*/
//and compiler will show it as an error if return statement is included.
}
```

In the above program there are too many comments and program code is submerged in them, so the code lines are made bold so that these are distinctly visible. The first line is a comment. The output is same as for Program 2.1. Notice that blank spaces are introduced in the first three lines. Also after void main () in program body a line is blank. All these are called **white spaces** and are neglected by the compiler. Therefore, you may write the program as you like so that it is easily readable. There is no requirement that every line must start from the beginning. In above program int main()is replaced by void main(). Since void functions are non-return type functions so the statement return 0; is not included in the program.

The Program 2.3 given below illustrates application of some of the escape sequences listed in Table 2.1. Remember that they have to be enclosed in double quotes (" ").

PROGRAM 2.3 – Illustrates application of some escape sequences.

```
#include <iostream>
int main()
{
 std::cout<<"Hello,\a\'Welcome to programming with C++!\'\n";
```

```
   /* Inclusion of character "\a" will cause the computer to generate a sound
(a beep) when program is executed */

  std::cout<<"Hello,\\ Welcome to programming with C++!\\\n";
     // This prints \ see 2nd line of output.

  std::cout<<"      Welcome to programming with C++!\rHello\n";

  // inclusion of \rHello brings Hello to the front of line.
  Std::cout<<"Hello\t Welcome to programming with \t\"C++!\"\n";

   // The character \" puts double quotes to the statement
  return 0;
  }
```

The expected output is given below.

```
Hello,'Welcome to programming with C++!'
Hello,\ Welcome to programming with C++!\
Hello Welcome to programming with C++!
Hello    Welcome to programming with      "C++!"
```

The program has been made self explanatory with the help of comments included in the program. You may verify them from the output. In implementing the first line of code after int main(), the computer makes a sound like a beep. In the second line of output slashes are put. In the third line of output the word *Hello* has been bought forward to the beginning of line. But you have to keep space for it otherwise it will replace some characters of welcome. In the 4th line of output the application of tab "\t" has shifted the cursor by a few spaces. So in the output we find space after *Hello* and after *with*. Also note that C++! has been enclosed in double quotes.

THE CIN

In many interactive programs the user is required to put in some data. In the following program we make use of function **cin** (the standard input stream) for this purpose. This is used along with the operator >> which is called **extraction operator.** This is followed by the name of variable in whose memory block the data has to be stored. The input data should be of same type as that of the variable declared. The operator >> directs the data to *cin*. **After typing the data for cin, do press the '*enter-key*', otherwise, the computer will not proceed further.** The following program illustrates the application of cin.

PROGRAM 2.4 – Application of cin in a user interactive program.

```
#include<iostream>
int main()
{
```

```
int length =0;  // length is the name of variable of type int
int width=0, area=0; //width and area are also names of variables.
 std::cout<<"Write the length and width of a rectangle: " ;
          // output statement
  std::cin>> length>>width;   // Input statement
 area = length*width;    // computation of area

std::cout <<"length = " <<length<<"\t width = "<<width<<"\t area = "
<<area<<endl;    // output statement

return 0 ;}
```

You should note that in the above program all the code lines except the first two end with semicolon. The first line comprises the header file and the second is *int main()*. A common mistake by a student involves use of semicolon at wrong places. You would also observe that all the code lines in the above program do not start from extreme left. As already mentioned above, in C++ the white spaces are neglected. So it does not matter where you start the line. The program may be written in a way so that it is easier to read. The operation of above program is explained below.

2.4 VARIABLE DECLARATION AND MEMORY ALLOCATION

In Program 2.4, the second code line after int main() declares an integer variable by name 'length'. The word *length* is identifier or name of the variable, just as you are identified by your name. When you declare a variable, a block of memory is allocated for it for putting its value. In this case 0 is assigned to it. The size of the memory block depends on the *type* of variable (see Chapter 3 for details). The declaration of a variable in a program is done by first writing its *type*, give space then write the name or identifier for the variable as illustrated below.

`type identifier ;`

This is illustrated below.

```
int n ;  // The statement declares an integer with name n.
```

The details of fundamental *types* in C++ are discussed in detail in Chapter 3. Here we may mention that the five *types* of data described in Table 2.2 below are the most common in C++. Examples of their use are also given in the table.

Table 2.2* – Most commonly used data types

Type	Description	Examples of declaration
void	no data type (used with functions & pointers)	void main() void F();
int	whole number or integer	int length; int k = 6;
float	decimal point number. (single precision)	float y; float PI =3.141;

Contd...

double	decimal point number (double precision)	double A; double PI = 3.141592653;
char	all alphabets like A, b, C along with symbols as defined in ASCII code (see Appendix A)	char ch; char x = 'A'; Here ch and x are names of variables. 'A' is the value assigned to variable x.

* See Chapter 3 for more details.

In the 5th line of Program 2.4 two more variables are declared with names 'width' and 'area'. You may declare any number of variables of same type in a single line. The type should be mentioned at the start of line and the variable names should be separated by comma (,).

Before a variable is used in the program it should be initialized which means that a value should be assigned to it, otherwise the complier will show error or warning. To start with we have assigned 0. As already mentioned above when a variable is declared a block of memory is allocated for storing its value. The value may be either assigned by the programmer or calculated during the execution of program. With the declaration of three variables, i.e. length, width and area the compiler allocates three blocks of memory. A graphical illustration of this is given in the Fig.2.2.

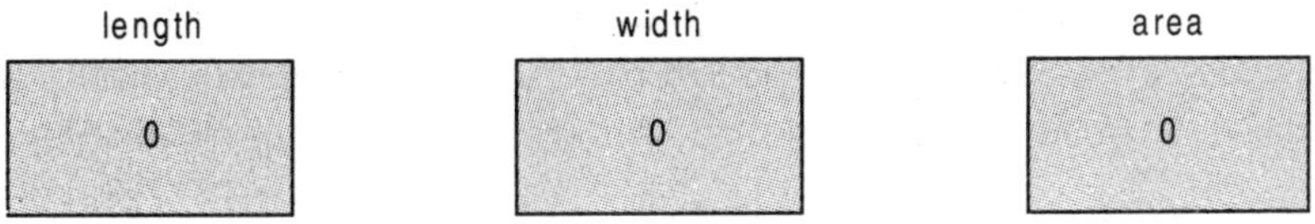

Fig. 2.2: Allocation of memory blocks on declaration of variables

At the time of declaration of variables in Program 2.4 we assigned 0 values to length, width and area, so the allocated memory blocks show 0. The actual values are entered by the user when the program runs (user interactive program). On clicking to run the program it displays following sentence on the monitor.

```
Write the length and width of a rectangle:
```

At the end of line you will find a blinking cursor. Here you have to enter two numbers. You may type one say 15, then *give a space* and type second number. In this case, 4 has been typed. After typing, the line would look like as given below.

```
Write the length and width of a rectangle: 15 4.
```

After typing 15 and 4 **press the *'enter-key'***, with this the extraction operator (>>) will direct the two values to std::cin which will place them in the memory blocks allocated for them when they were first defined. The number 15 will be placed in the memory block allocated for length and number 4 will be placed in the memory block allocated for width. The Fig. 2.2 now changes to the following.

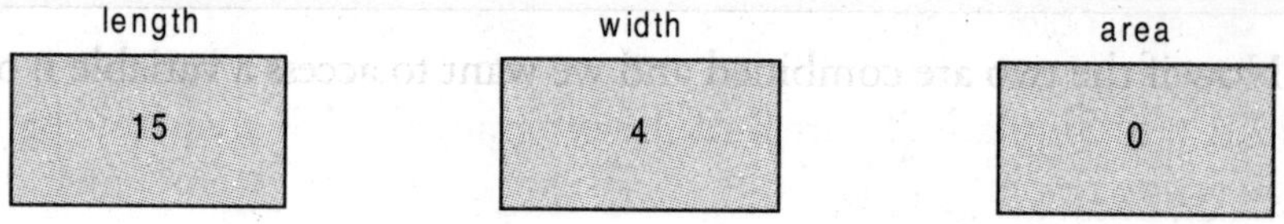

Fig. 2.3: Condition of allocated memory blocks after completion of cin function

In the next code line of the program the two numbers are multiplied and the product is assigned to area. Assignment is carried out with operator (=). On the left side of the operator we write name of variable and on its right side the value to be assigned. This line of program is processed by three operations, i.e. (i) the numbers 15 and 4 are copied from their locations then (ii) these are multiplied and (iii) the product is placed at the memory location reserved for area. After the variable area is assigned the product (60), the 0 is replaced by 60. The Fig. 2.3 now changes to the following figure.

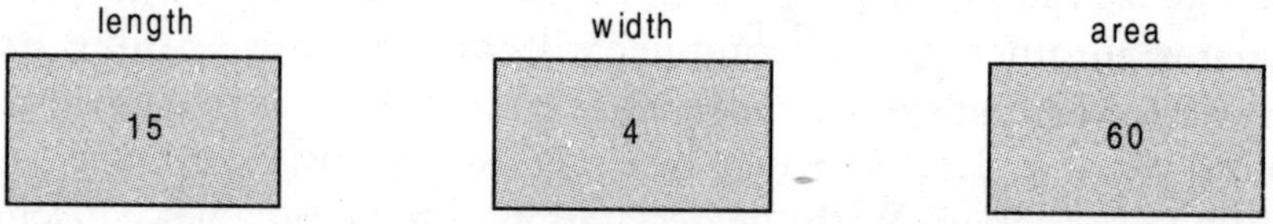

Fig. 2.4: Condition of allocated memory blocks after assignment of product to area

The next code line in the Program 2.4 is the output statement. For execution of this line the numbers from the three locations are copied and displayed on the monitor. The words in double quotes are displayed as they are typed in the program. Values of variables are put where their names appear in the cout expression of the program. So you get the display as given below.

```
Write the length and width of a rectangle: 15 4
length = 15      width = 4      area = 60
```

2.5 NAMESPACES

Namespaces is a powerful feature of C++ language. It enables the programmer to group a set of objects or functions under one name. All the classes, objects and functions of C++ Standard Library are defined under *namespace std*. We can simplify the writing of *std :: cout* to *cout* and *std :: cin* to *cin* by including the following directive in the program.

```
using namespace std;
```

Note that this line ends with a semicolon. The namespaces are useful when you are combining two or more parts of a program and you are afraid that some of names of different variables may be same in the two parts. To distinguish that a particular set of names belongs to a particular part of program we make use of namespace. Say we may put the declaration

```
namespace XA
```

in the beginning of part A and similarly put

```
namespace XB
```

for the part B. Now if the two are combined and we want to access a variable n of program part A we can write XA :: n. Similarly if part B of the program also has a variable by name n we can access it through scope resolution operator as XB::n . Even though the name is same (n) the values in two cases would be as assigned in XA and XB respectively.

More details of using namespace are discussed in Chapter 20. Here we contend with that by adding *using namespace std;* in the beginning of the program, the *std::* is no longer needed with cout and cin and other names belonging to C++ Standard Library such as endl, etc. The following program illustrates the application of namespaces and the directive 'using namespace std'. First, a group of names n, m, k and R are declared under namespace NS1. The same names are again declared under namespace NS2. The two sets of name are used in a program with application of scope resolution operator :: or by adding the statements such as,

using namespace NS2;

Under this statement the names belonging to NS2 can be used without the scope resolution operator but the names belonging to NS1 will have to use *NS1::* before their names.

PROGRAM 2.5 – Illustrates application of namespaces.

```
#include <iostream>
using namespace std;  // use of std namespace

 namespace NS1    //no semicolon at end of line
 { int n = 3;
 float m = 2.5;
  int k = 2;
  double R = n*m*k; }

 namespace NS2  //no semicolon at end of line
 {float n = 4.0;  //Names are same as in NS1 but values are
// different.
  int m = 2 ;
  double k = 3.0 ;
   double R = n*m*k; }
  int main()
{ int Square;
 int Product ;
  using namespace NS2;
  Square = n*n + m*m ; // values under NS2 are used
 Product = NS1::k * NS2::m; // k belongs to NS1 and m to NS2
 cout << "Square = " << Square << ",\t Product = " <<  Product<<endl;

cout<< " R = "<< NS1::R <<endl; // This R belongs to NS1
cout << " R = " <<NS2::R<< endl; // This R belongs to NS2
 return 0 ;
 }
```

The output is as under. The output is made self explanatory by using comments.

```
Square = 20,     Product = 4
R = 15
R = 24
```

2.6 USER INTERACTIVE PROGRAMS

In a user interactive program the user is required to feed the data asked by the program. Program 2.4 discussed above is an example of user interactive program. The Program 2.6 given below is yet another example of the same. The program makes use of the object **cin** of <iostream> header file. The difference between the two programs, i.e. 2.4 and 2.6 is that in Program 2.6 we have used the directive **using namespace std;** which simplifies the writing of names belonging to C++ Standard Library, for example, instead of writing std :: cout we simply write the code as cout.

PROGRAM 2.6 – This program illustrates the application of cin and use of namespace std.

```
#include <iostream>
using namespace std;
int main()

{ int D;
 float PI ;
   // Here D stands for diameter and PI stands for π.
 double A, C;
  // A stands for area and C stands for circumference.

cout<<"Write values of D and PI:";
cin>> D>>PI;  //statement for input of D and PI
cout<<"You have written the values as D = "<<D<<" and PI = " <<PI<<endl;
// endl may be used in place of "\n"

 A = PI*D*D/4;  // computation of area
 C = PI*D;    // computation of circumference
 cout <<"D = "<< D <<", A= "<< A <<" and C= " <<C <<endl;
 return 0;
}
```

On clicking to run the program, the following statement is displayed on the monitor.

```
Write values of D and PI:
```

You will see a blinking cursor at the end of line. There you type the value of diameter, in this case it is typed 10. Give a space and write value of PI and **press enter-key**. The program will not proceed further if you do not press enter-key. The output of the program as displayed on monitor is given below.

```
Write values of D and PI:10 3.14159
You have written the values as D = 10 and PI = 3.14159
D = 10, A= 78.5398 and C= 31.4159.
```

Also note that in the above program we have used *endl* ; (end line) instead of std::endl; because we have used the directive `using namespace std;` in the beginning of the program.

2.7 FORMATTING THE OUTPUT

Often we need to format the output. There are many functions for the same but at present we take only a few that are provided in <iostream>. However, more details are discussed in Chapter 19. Here we discuss only the following.

(i) Putting spaces between items of output, i.e. use of " " or tab "\t"
(ii) Controlling width of output.
(iii) Control of precision for float and double numbers.
(iv) To put the floating decimal point number in scientific notation.
(v) Use of fill() function to fill empty spaces.
(vi) Codes for right and left justification.

First we take the case of providing spaces. Even if you write the output statement in a fragmented manner as illustrated in Program 2.7, they would be put together by operator << unless spaces are specified. One method of providing space is by enclosing the blank spaces in double quotes like " ". Because any statement or blank spaces enclosed between double quotes is sent to output stream as it is written. Alternatively, space character "\t" called tab may be used to provide a preset space. It has to be enclosed in double quotes like "\t" and you may use single "\t" or multiple tabs as in "\t\t\t", etc. The number of spaces for each "\t" may also be set.

PROGRAM 2.7 – Multiple use of operator **<<** , the tab **"\t"** and " **\n** " in output statement.

```
#include <iostream>
using namespace std;
int main()
{
cout<<"Hello"<<" Nat";   // Natasha is broken into pieces
cout<<"as"<<"ha,"<<"\n\tGood"<<" Morning!\n"; // use of "\n" and "\t"
cout<<"When are you going to market?"<<endl;
return 0;
}
```

The output of the above program is given below. You will notice that even though the words have been fractured into pieces in *cout* statements, but in output these are placed together one after another in the same order.

```
Hello Natasha,
        Good Morning!
When are you going to market?
```

The above program also illustrates the use of tab "\t" to provide space. The second line of output is printed with a margin because "\t" has been put before Good and after new line character "\n" in the program,(see "\n\tGood" in the program).

The following program shows that assignment can also be done by putting the value to be assigned in parentheses following the variable identifier. Moreover, the values are assigned in scientific notation.

PROGRAM 2.8 – Illustrates scientific notation and assigning the values.

```
#include <iostream>
using namespace std;
void main()
{
 double C (4.56E9); // Number expressed in scientific notation
  // the value is assigned by putting it in brackets
 double D = 6.54e9;
 double E = 675.987654;
 char Kh('B'); // assignment by putting the value in brackets.

cout <<"C = " << C <<" "<<", D = " << D<<endl;
cout <<" C+D = "<< C+D<<endl;

char ch = 'A';
cout <<"Kh = "<<Kh <<"    "<<"ch = "<<ch <<endl;
cout <<scientific << E<<endl;
  // asking for output of E in scientific notation
}
```

The expected output is given below.

```
C = 4.56e+009 , D = 6.54e+009
 C+D = 1.11e+010
Kh = B    ch = A
6.759877e+002
```

The above program illustrates that we can also assign a value to variable by putting the value in parentheses immediately following the variable name. Another example is given below.

```
double C(4.56E9);
```

This is equivalent to the following.

```
double C = 4.56 E9;
```

Also the code `kh('B');` assigns the value `'B'` to `char kh`.

We may also ask for output in scientific notation. This is illustrated in the last output statement in the program in which the code <<scientific is added in the output statement, as a result of which the number 675.987654 has been displayed as 6.759877e +002 in the output.

FUNCTION WIDTH ()

The function width() is associated with the object cout and is coded as below.

```
cout.width(unsigned int n);
```

Here n, a positive number, specifies the spaces desired in output. The following program illustrates the use of function width()and left and right justification. The default setting is right justification. If the output characters are less than n spaces, the remaining will be blank spaces.

PROGRAM 2.9 – Illustration of function width() and right and left justification.

```
#include <iostream>
using namespace std;
int main()
{ int x ;
 double A ,y ;
 cout<<"Write one int and one double number: ";
 cin >> x >>y;
cout.width(20);
cout.setf(ios::right); // right justified
cout<<"x = "<<x<<endl;
  cout.setf(ios::left); // left justified
  cout<<"x = "<< x<<"\n";
  cout<<"y = "<<y<<"\n";
  A = x+y;
  cout<<"Value of A = " <<A<<"\n";
  return 0;
}
```

The expected output is given below.

```
Write one int and one double number: 4000000 5.2E8
              x = 4000000
x = 4000000
y = 5.2e+008
Value of A = 5.24e+008
```

As already mentioned the right justification is the default justification, if left justification is desired it has to be specified. The *ios* is the base input /output class. The detailed discussed of these is given in Chapter 19 in which *ios* class is discussed. Since we have not dealt with classes as yet, we take it as a code. The second observation of the output is that if input is in scientific notation output is also in the same notation.

FUNCTION PRECISION ()

In the next example we take up the use of `precision()` function along with `width()` function. Code for `precision()` is similar to that for `width()` function. It is illustrated below.

```
cout.precision(unsigned int m);
```

where m represents the number of digits desired in the output. The function `precision ()` is linked with object cout by dot (.) operator. Function `precision ()` is used only for floating decimal point numbers, i.e. for float and double.

PROGRAM 2.10 – Illustrates application of function precision().

```
#include <iostream>
using namespace std;
int main()
{
    int A ;
    double PI ,B ;
    A = 4567543;

 PI = 3.141592653589793238;
 B = 245.7654329832;
 //If precision is not specified, default precision is 6
cout <<"PI= "<< PI <<"\tA = "<<A<<"\tB = "<<B<<endl;
cout.precision(4);

    cout <<"PI= "<< PI <<"\tA = "<<A<<"\tB = "<<B<<endl;
    cout <<"PI= "<< PI <<"\tA = "<<A<<"\tB = "<<B<<endl;

 cout.precision(8);
 cout <<"PI= "<< PI <<"\tA = "<<A<<"\tB = "<<B<<endl;
 return 0;
}
```

The output is given below.

```
PI= 3.14159      A = 4567543     B = 245.765
PI= 3.142        A = 4567543     B = 245.8
PI= 3.142        A = 4567543     B = 245.8
PI= 3.1415927    A = 4567543     B = 245.76543
```

See the result carefully. The first line of output is the default output without any specification in the program. 6 digits are printed for decimal variable while integer is printed in full. For the second line of output we specified `precision(4)`. So only 4 digits have been printed for the floating decimal point numbers, while the integer A has been printed full. For the last line of output we increased the precision to 8. For the numbers with decimal points 8 digits are displayed while the integer number is written full. The precision setting continues till a new setting is encountered. In the next example we take the case of insufficient width setting. When the width setting is less than that required for output the width setting is neglected.

PROGRAM 2.11 – Illustrates the case of insufficient width setting.

```
#include <iostream>
using namespace std;
int main()
 { int A = 867564;
    double p = 4.532678;
    double m = p/5;

cout.width(12);
cout <<A <<"\n"<< p<<"\n"<< m << endl;

cout.precision(4);
cout.setf(ios::left);
cout <<"A = "<<A<<"\t"<< "p = "<<p<<"\t"<< "m = "<<m << endl;

cout.precision(20);cout.width(10);
// width setting is less than precision setting.
cout <<p<<"\t" << m << endl;
return 0;
}
```

The output is given below.

```
      867564
4.53268
0.906536
A = 867564      p = 4.533        m = 0.9065
4.5326779999999998        0.9065356
```

Compare the outputs with the specifications given in the cout statements. The effect of width() setting remains only up to the first line of output. In the first line of the output A is printed in 12 spaces on the right side. It has 6 digits and there are 6 blank spaces on the left of it. The second and third lines of output are not affected. Also for the second and third line of output the default precision setting is 6 so 6 digits are displayed in output. For the 4th line of output the precision setting is 4 so only 4 digits are displayed in case of p and for m. Integer numbers are not affected by precision setting. For the next line of output, precision is set at 20 while the width setting is 10. Therefore the width setting has been neglected. While the width setting affects only the next line of output, the precision setting remains till it encounters a new setting.

FUNCTION FILL()

If the width setting is more than the number of characters in the output, there would be some empty spaces which may be filled with a character such as dash(-) or some other character by using fill () function. The character desired to fill with is put in the argument. It has to be enclosed by single quotes. Thus for filling with character dash(-) we write the code

```
cout.fill('-');
```

See the following program for illustration.

PROGRAM 2.12 – Illustrates application of fill() function.

```
#include <iostream>
 using namespace std;
int main()
{
cout.width(15); //hello will be written in 15 spaces
cout.fill('-'); //fill the empty spaces with dash(-)

cout<<"Hello,"<<endl;
cout.width(40); //the output be written in 40 spaces,
cout.fill('*'); //fill the empty spaces with '*'

cout<<"Welcome to"<<"   "<<"programming in C++!"<<endl;
cout.width(36);
cout.fill('$');  // fill empty spaces by '$'

cout<<"Are you learning C++ ?"<<endl;

return 0;
}
```

The expected output is given below.

```
---------Hello,
******************************Welcome to programming in C++!
$$$$$$$$$$$$$$Are you learning C++ ?
```

The output shows that first line of output is in 15 spaces and 9 spaces have been filled with dash. In the next line of output, the 40 spaces are up to end of 'Welcome to'. Moreover no filling has taken place in the blank spaces in between the statement.

The `cout.fill()` function persists beyond the immediate next line of output statement till `next fill()` function is encountered. This is illustrated in the following program. For undoing the previous setting, include an empty fill setting as illustrated below. For more details see Chapter 19.

```
cout.fill(' ');
```

PROGRAM 2.13 – Illustrates fill() function along with width() and precision().

```
#include <iostream>
using namespace std;
int main()
 {
 int x =205;
double PI=3.141592653589793, y=4564.2318765;

 cout.fill('-');
  cout.width (6);
   cout<<x<<endl;

 cout.precision(8); cout.width(16);
 cout<<PI<<endl;
  cout.precision(6);
   cout.fill(' ');
    cout.width(10);
 cout<<y<<endl;

return 0;
 }
```

The expected output is as below.

```
---205
-------3.1415927
 4564.23
```

In the above program the empty spaces are desired to be filled with dash ('-') in the output for x. Therefore the function `cout.fill('-');` has been added before the output statement for x. In the next output statement for PI the function `cout.fill()` has been omitted but we find that filling by dash continues. Therefore, for removing the fill() function setting an empty fill function `cout.fill('');` has been added before the output statement for y, so no fill symbol appears in output of y. For more details see Chapter 19.

2.8 FUNCTION cin.getline() v/s cin

For entering a string of characters as we come across in names, messages etc., we can make use of `getline()`. It is coded as below.

```
char message [20]= "Good morning!"
cin.getline (message, int n, ch) ;
```

Here message is a string of characters. It can have 20 characters including the Null character ('\0') which marks the end of string (see Chapter on C-strings for more details on strings).

Of the arguments of `getline ()`, 'message' is the name of string, the int n (a positive number) is the number of characters to be read and ch is the name of character on encountering of which it would stop reading. This is illustrated in the following program. In the program the user is asked to enter a name. The maximum number of characters to be read is specified as 30. The limiting character ch is specified as below.

```
char ch = 'L';
```

Whenever a value is assigned in form of a character, it should be enclosed in single quotes as shown above.

PROGRAM 2.14 – Illustrates the application of function **getline().**

```
#include <iostream>
using namespace std;
int main()
 {
 char Name1 [30] ;
 char ch = 'L';
 cout<< "Enter a short name :";
 cin.getline(Name1, 30, ch);
 cout<<"\nName1 = " << Name1;
return 0;
}
```

The expected output is as given below.

```
Enter a short name :Tata Motors Ltd

Name1 = Tata Motors
```

The name entered was Tata Motors Ltd. The output shows that on encountering the letter 'L' the reading stopped. So output is only Tata Motors.

The following program illustrates the difference between cin and `cin.getline ()`. The function `getline()` reads the whole line including the blank spaces while cin does not read blank spaces. It takes a blank space as end of the value.

PROGRAM 2.15 – Illustrates difference between **cin.getline()** and **cin.**

```
#include <iostream>
using namespace std;
int main()
 {
     char word [30];
           cout<<"Write two small words : ";
                 cin.getline(word,30);
```

```
cout<<"You have written "<< word<<"\n";
 cout<<"Write two small words : ";
 cin>> word;

cout<<"You have written "<< word<<"\n";
 return 0;
 }
```

The expected output is given below.

```
Write two small words : TATA MOTORS
You have written TATA MOTORS
Write two small words : Tata Motors
You have written Tata
```

On running the program the following line appears on the monitor

```
Write two small words :
```

So two words TATA MOTORS were typed and entered. The function `cin.getline ()` reads the two words and the output is given in the next line of output. Again another line given below appears on screen.

```
Write two small words :
```

This time the words entered are Tata Motors. These are read by cin. From the output you see that only Tata is printed. This is because cin stops reading when a blank space is encountered. While in case of `getline()` it reads blank spaces as well as characters.

EXERCISES

1. What are the program tokens in a simple C++ program?
2. What do you understand by expression ' # include <iostream>' in a program ?
3. How do you declare an integer variable, a variable with value in floating decimal point number and a character variable in a C++ program?
4. What for fill() function is used ?
5. Is it mandatory to write *return 0 ;* as last line in all the C++ programs?
6. How would you include comments in the listing of a program?
7. What are header files?
8. What are *void* functions?
9. What is C++ Standard Library?
10. What do you understand by terms 'namespace' and 'namespace std' and the directive 'using namespace std ; '?
11. What do the following stand for? What are they called?

(i) "\t"
(ii) "\n"
(iii) /* */
(iv) //

12. Make a program to illustrate the effect of precision setting when the argument of the function precision is less than the number of digits before the decimal point.

Answer:

PROGRAM 2.16 – Illustrates **precision ()** and **width()** functions

```
#include <iostream>
using namespace std;
void main()
 {
 double PI = 3.14159265358;
 double B = 67543687.897;
      cout.precision(4);
 cout<< "B = " << B <<" PI = "<<PI<<endl;
 cout.setf(ios::fixed); //output in normal notation.
 cout.precision(5);
 cout<<"B = " <<B <<endl;
 }
```

The output shown below shows that in scientific notation the output consists of 4 digits. For output in fixed notation the precision setting has given 5 digits after decimal point.

```
B = 6.754e+007 PI = 3.142
B = 67543687.89700
```

13. Select the correct *type* of variable for the following quantities.
    (i) Temperature of hot water in degrees centigrade.
    (ii) Volume of a bucket.
    (iii) Number of machines in a workshop.
    (iv) For writing values like 'A', 'B' etc. in a program

14. How would you write input and output statements when the directive 'using namespace std;' is not used?

15. What do you understand by function **precision ()** ?

16. How would you unset the already set fill() function?

17. Find errors in following declarations and write the correct versions.
    (i) Int n ;
    (ii) int 8 = n;
    (iii) char ch = a ;
    (iv) Char alpha = A;

(v) Double M = 6.78;

18. What for we use the function **width()**?

19. Which of the following statements are true?
    (i) Every C++ program must have one main () function.
    (ii) Statements in a C++ program must end with a semi-colon (;).
    (iii) In C++ all the variables must be declared in the beginning of the program.
    (iv) A C++ program always ends with return 0 ; .

20. Find errors in the following program. Rewrite a correct version of it.

```
include <iostream>
 int main ()
 int n , m ;
 {n = m + 4;
  m = 5.5;
cout << m << " "n<< endl;
cout >> m*m <<endl;
}
```

21. Write a program to make character 'D' with character ('*') .
22. Make program for finding area of rectangle with sides in floating point numbers.
23. Make a program to make filled triangle with apex at the top by using ('*') for filling.

Answer: The following program is made to write different number of asterisk(*) in successive lines to make a solid triangle as illustrated in the output below.

PROGRAM 2.17 – Illustrates program for making a figure – solid triangle

```
#include  <iostream>
using namespace std;
int main()
{cout<<"      *\n     ***\n    *****\n   *******\ n
*********\n***********"<< endl;
return 0 ;
}
```

The output is given below

```
     *
    ***
   *****
  *******
 *********
***********
```

24. Make a program for making filled right angle triangle with base parallel to horizontal plane.

Answer:

PROGRAM 2.18 – Illustrates program for making a solid right angle triangle.

```
#include  <iostream>
using namespace std;
 int main()
{ cout<<"\t     *\n\t     **\n\t   ***\n\t   ****\n";
 cout<<"\t *****\n\t******"<< endl;
return 0 ;
}
```

The output of the program is given below.

```
          *
         **
        ***
       ****
      *****
     ******
```

25. Make a program to make a figure of letter H with the symbol (*) .

Answer to Q.25

PROGRAM 2.19 – Illustrates program for making a figure like the character H

```
#include  <iostream>
using namespace std;

void main()

{ cout<<"\t*      *\n\t*       *\n\t*       *\n\t********\n";
cout<<"\t*      *\n\t*       *\n\t*       *\n" ;
}
```

The output is given below.

```
*      *
*      *
*      *
********
*      *
*      *
*      *
```

26. Make a program to print the message “Hello, Welcome to Programming in C ++”. The print statement in the program be written in two lines with the message broken as “He” , “ll”, “o”, welcome” in first line and “ to programming in C++ “ in second line.

Answer:

PROGRAM 2.20 – An exercise in output statement

```
#include <iostream>
using namespace std;
int main()
{
 cout<<"He"<<"ll"<<"o,"<<"Welcome";

cout<<" to programming in C++!\n";
 return 0;
 }
```

The output is given below.

```
Hello, Welcome to programming in C++!
```

27. Make a program to print T and S with character '*' as done for H in Q.25.

28. Make a program to print the + sign with the help of * symbol.

29. Write the expected output of following program.

PROGRAM 2.21 – An exercise to illustrate use of "\n" and "\t"

```
#include <iostream>
//use of tab, namespace, new line character.
using namespace std;
int main()
{
cout<<"\tHello,\n\tWelcome to\n programming in C++!\n";
return 0;
}
```

Answer:

The expected output is as below.

```
    Hello,
    Welcome to
programming in C++!
```

30. Write the expected output of following program.

PROGRAM 2.22 – Exercise for finding output of a program

```
#include <iostream>
int main()
{
std::cout<<"Hello,\a\'Are you coming to C++ class? \'\n";
std::cout<<"Hello,\\Are you coming to C++ class?\\\n";
std::cout<<"      Are you coming to C++ class?\rMohan\n";
```

```
std::cout<<"Hello\tAre you coming to C++ class?\n";
return 0;
}
```

Answer:

The expected output is given below.

```
Hello,'Are you coming to C++ class? '
Hello,\Are you coming to C++ class?\
Mohan Are you coming to C++ class?
Hello      Are you comming to C++ class?
```

31. Identify errors in the following program. Correct them and run the program.

```
// Program for correction.
    #include <iostream>;
   using namespace STD;
int main();
 {
 int x =205;
  double PI=3.141592653589793, y=4564.2318765;

 cout.fill('-');
        cout.width (6)
           cout<<x<<endl;

 cout.precision(10); cout.width(8);
     cout<<PI<<endl
         cout.precision(6);
               cout.fill(' ');
                  coutwidth(10)
  cout<<y<<endl;

return 0;}
```

❍❍❍

CHAPTER 3

Fundamental Data Types in C++

3.1 FUNDAMENTAL DATA TYPES

In C++ data is differentiated into different categories or **types** such as integers or whole numbers (*type* is **int**), decimal point numbers (*type* is **float** or **double**), characters (*type* is **char**), etc. However, C++ also allows **user defined types** such as class objects or structures for which the name of the class or the structure is their *type* (see Chapter 11). The data *types* which are implicitly defined in C++ are the **fundamental data types** which form the subject matter of this chapter.

We all know that computers work on numbers expressed in binary. Anything that is entered into a computer whether these are numbers which we use in our daily calculations or these are instructions and operators such as +, –, / ,etc., or are alphabets such as A, b, C, etc., all are stored in the form of binary numbers which are sequences of 0 and 1. For instance, when we type text on keyboard connected to computer the letters are stored in computer memory in the form of binary numbers according to **ASCII code** which is followed universally (see Appendix A). **ASCII** (pronounced as 'as-key') stands for American Standard Code for Information Interchange. In this code, every letter or symbol has a value. For instance, character 'A' has value 65 and is stored as 1000001 in computer memory, similarly character 'B' is equivalent to 66 and computer stores it as 1000010 and so on. Also when we retrieve the same data on the computer monitor or printer it should display or print A for 'A' and B for 'B' and not 65 and 66. That implies that the **type** of data that is entered or retrieved from computer must be specified.

As per ASCII code the characters and symbols have values which range from 0 to 127 and thus can be stored in one byte of memory. A number like 6574594 or like 123452.9876754326 would require much more memory space. Also whole numbers and numbers with decimal point are stored differently and require different memory spaces. When a variable is declared by putting its *type* followed by its *name* (or identifier), the compiler allocates a block of memory space for storing the value of the variable. The size of the memory block depends on the *type* of the variable. For every *type* of variable a different but a limited space (in number of bytes) is allocated by the compiler, the size of which depends on the system hardware, operating system and the compiler.

By declaring the *type* of a variable, the type of data that the variable can have also gets known. For example, if the type of a variable is `int`, the variable is an integer or whole number. The values that may be assigned to it should also be integers or whole numbers. Moreover, with each *type* a particular set of operations are associated. Thus by specifying the *type* we, in fact, refer to a class of variables on which a particular set of operations may be performed. Besides integers, decimal point numbers and characters, there are other *types* in C++ such as Boolean type, enumeration type, etc. Table 3.1 below lists the different fundamental types in C++.

Table 3.1 – The **fundamental types** in C++ and the codes

Type	Code
(A) Integral type – These comprise the following types.	
(i) Boolean type	`bool`
(ii) Enumeration type	`enum`
(iii) Character type which includes	
(a) Characters	`char`
(b) Unsigned characters	`unsigned char`
(c) Wide character	`wchar_t`
(iv) **Integers** – These comprise	
(a) Short integers	`short`
(b) Integers	`int`
(c) Long integers	`long`
(d) Unsigned short integers	`unsigned short`
(e) Unsigned integers	`unsigned int`
(f) Unsigned long integers	`unsigned long`
(v) **Floating decimal point types** – These comprise	
(a) Normal precision or single precision	`float`
(b) High precision or double precision	`double`
(c) High precision or double precision	`long double`

INTEGERS

Integers are associated with every aspect of our life. A simple example is that of counting, such as number of members in a family, number of passengers in a bus, number of gun shots fired or number of events, etc. In all such cases whole numbers are used. Because, there cannot be a half passenger in bus or one quarter member in a family or one fourth shot fired. The whole numbers whether they are positive or negative are called *integers.* A whole number may be *short* such as number of members in a family or very *long* number such as number of seconds in a century. Naturally they require different sizes of computer memory for storage. The program must allocate sufficient memory to store the short as well as long number. If the number is bigger than the memory allocated then a part of number may get truncated or reduced in size which will lead to errors. Also if memory allocated is too big it would be wasteful use of memory space. Therefore, whole numbers are differentiated according to their size. Thus there are three types of whole numbers as distinguished by their size. They are called short, integer and long and the codes for the three are written as **short, int** and **long.**

On most of the 32 bit computer systems short is stored in 2 bytes. Two bytes comprise 16 bits. Out of the 16 bits the leftmost bit is reserved for sign (+ or –), hence only 15 bits are available for storing the number. Therefore, the range of numbers that may be stored as *short* is from -2^{15} to $+(2^{15}-1)$, that is from – 32768 to + 32767 (see Chapter 1 for details).

On a similar system, *int* is allocated 4 bytes (32 bits). In this case also the leftmost bit is reserved for sign (+ or –). Therefore, the range of numbers that can be stored varies from -2^{31} to $+(2^{31}-1)$ that is from – 2147483648 to + 2147483647. The long is also allocated 4 bytes, therefore, its range is also the same as for int.

Unsigned Integers

There are many applications where only positive integers are permitted. To illustrate this point we take the case of computer memory which consists of bits. These are grouped into bundles of 8 each called bytes. In RAM bytes are numbered in a sequence. A number in this sequence is the address of a byte. This number cannot be negative. It is just like that your house number cannot be negative. These are called unsigned numbers. The signed numbers can be positive or negative, but **unsigned numbers are always positive**. The unsigned numbers are also short unsigned numbers, integer unsigned numbers and long unsigned numbers. These types are respectively coded as **unsigned short**, **unsigned int** and **unsigned long**. On a 32-bit system unsigned short is allocated 2 bytes, but no bit is needed for sign, therefore, the range of unsigned short is from 0 to 65535. Similarly the range of **unsigned int** on most systems ranges from 0 to $(2^{32}-1)$, i.e. from 0 to 4294967295.

Floating Decimal Point Numbers

There are quantities which cannot be expressed as whole numbers. For example, if you take your weight, it is quite unlikely that it would be an exact number of kilograms. It may be to say 55.25 kilogram. The number 55.25 can also be written as 221/4, i.e. a fraction. Therefore, such numbers are also called fractions or floating point numbers. The term floating point has originated from the method the number is stored in computer. Say the number 75.25 is to be stored. In binary it is written as 1001011.01. The number is stored as $.100101101 \times 2^7$. On a 32 bit system the number 1001011 01, is stored on the 23 bit segment of the 32 bits while the power 7 or 111 in binary, is floated, i.e. it is stored separately on the remaining 8 bit segment.

The leftmost bit (32nd bit) is kept for sign (+ or –). In scientific notation also we often float the decimal point. The number 7685.43 may be written as 7.68543×10^3. Therefore, in scientific notation the number 7685.43 is expressed as 7.68543 e+3 or 7.68543 E+3 in C++. So such numbers are called floating point numbers. These numbers may also be +ve or negative. Both the integers and fractions when grouped together are called **rational numbers.**

Now consider a number like π which is the ratio of circumference of a circle to its diameter. This number cannot be expressed exactly as ratio of two whole numbers or a fraction. It can only be approximated to a ratio. For instance, we often use the approximate value of π as 22/7. In the same category are the numbers like $\sqrt{2}$, $\sqrt{3}$ or $\sqrt{5}$, etc. All such numbers are called **irrational numbers.** They are also stored just like floating point numbers.

As far as computer program is concerned we differentiate between whole numbers or integers and numbers with floating decimal point because they are stored differently in the computer memory. We also discussed that whole numbers are differentiated according to size as well.

Similarly, the floating point numbers are differentiated according to the **precision** required, i.e. the number of digits after the decimal point. They are respectively called and coded as **float**, **double** and **long double.** On most 32 bit systems a float has seven significant digits and is allocated 4 bytes of memory while a double has 15 significant digits, nearly double the precision of float. It may get 8, 10, 12 or 16 bytes for storage on different systems. The memory spaces generally allocated for a float, double and long double are given in Table 3.3.

CHARACTERS

The alphabets along with some other symbols are called characters. In C++ characters are stored according to ASCII code (See Appendix A). For example, a few of the values are listed below.

Character	Value as per ASCII	Character	Value as per ASCII
A	65	a	97
B	66	b	98
____	____	____	____
0 (digit)	48	1 (digit)	49
5 (digit)	53	9 (digit)	57

According to this code the numerical values of alphabets and other symbols range from 0 to 127 and in the extended IBM list up to 255, which can be written in 8 bits or one byte. Therefore, each character is allocated one byte for its storage.

THE ENUMERATION TYPE

As described in the introduction, fundamental types are defined in C++, besides a programmer may create his/her own data types through classes. The enumeration type may also be used to define user's own data type. The enumeration type is an integral data type. Its syntax is as follows.

enum typename { enumerator_list_of_objects};

The syntax is illustrated below with examples.

enum Day { Monday, Tuesday, Wednesday, Thursday, Friday, Saturday, Sunday};

In the above case, Monday would have a value 0, Tuesday would have value 1, Wednesday 2 and so on. In the above declaration if you put Monday = 1 as illustrate below then, Tuesday would have value 2, Wednesday 3 and so on.

enum Day { Monday =1, Tuesday, Wednesday, Thursday, Friday, Saturday, Sunday};

The enum may also be used to define a number of **integral constants** as given below.

enum Data { A = 100, B = 100, C = 400, D = 500 , E = 600};

or

enum Marks { correct =2, wrong = – 1, not_attempted = 0};

BOOLEAN TYPE

Yet another type is the Boolean type integer which is coded as bool. When we examine a logical statement it may be either **true** or **false**. We may associate a number say 1 for true and 0 for false. For example, let us have a conditional statement such as, *if* (*A* > *B*) in a program. Now if this condition is actually true, 1 will be sent to the system. If it is false, 0 will be sent to the system. In this way the system will know whether the condition is true or false.

3.2 DECLARATION OF A VARIABLE

Declaration of variables was briefly discussed in Chapter 2, more details are given below. A variable may be declared as below.

type identifier;

Here *type* is the data type such as int, float or double, char, etc., as listed in Table 3.3. A variable must have a name with which it is identified. It is just like that you are identified by your name. The *type* must be written in lower case. For example an integer with name Age is declared as below

```
int Age;
```

Note that the line ends with a semicolon (;). Any variable before it is used in the program should be initialized as well, i.e. a value should be assigned to it. In C++ it is not necessary to declare and initialize all the variables right in the beginning. It may be done anywhere in the program but before it is actually used in the program. Initialization is done by using assignment operator (=) as illustrated below.

```
int Age;
Age = 22;
```

The above two lines may be combined as given below.

type identifier = initial value;

```
int Age = 22;
double PI = 3.1415926535;
```

The computer output for both float and double will be according to the default precision set in the computer which is generally 6 digits. However, you can change it by specifying another precision value. Code for setting precision has already been discussed in Chapter 2.

A variable of type character is also declared as below.

char identifier ;

For example a variable with name ch and value 'A' is declared and assigned as below.

```
char ch = 'A' ;
```

With this definition of ch, the compiler would allocate one byte for storing the value of ch. It may also be declared as a string as given below.

```
char ch[] = "A";
```

In this case two bytes are allocated by compiler for ch[], i.e., one for 'A' and one for NULL character ('\0') which is appended by the system and marks the end of string (see the output of Program 3.16).

Below is another example of declaration of a variable which has value as a string of characters. In all such cases the value is enclosed in double quotes and number of characters in the string +1 are put in square brackets.

```
char River[6] = "Ganga";
```

Here *River* is the name of a char variable and in the above definition its value is "Ganga". In the above declaration the number of elements of the string "Ganga" are 5 plus the Null character, so total is 6. When the declaration and initialization are together we need not put the number of elements. The compiler can count the number of elements. Thus we could have also written as below.

```
char River [ ] = "Ganga" ;
```

Consider the declarations of following variables, i.e. Digits and Plus are declared and values '5' and '+' are assigned respectively.

```
char Digit = '5' ;

char Plus = '+' ;
```

Here Digit is the name of a variable of type char and character '5' is assigned to it as its value. According to ASCII code, character '5' has a value 53. Similarly '+' is assigned to variable Plus. The character '5' is not the usual 5 used in calculations. Similarly here '+' is not the usual operator +. Here it is a character. The characters as per ASCII code have values from 0 to 127 (IBM extended list is up to 255) and therefore, are allocated one byte for storing one character. The wchar_t, also called as wide character type, cannot be stored in one byte. Two bytes are allocated for its each character. It belongs to **Unicode character set** which is an international standard character set and is also supported by C++. This character set includes characters of different languages of world such as Latin, Greek, Bengali, Devnagari, Gurmukhi, geometric shapes, mathematical symbols, technical symbols, etc. The interested readers are advised to refer to reference "*The Unicode Standard, Version 2.0* by Unicode Consortium" - Addison- Wesley, 1996.

3.3 CHOOSING AN IDENTIFIER OR NAME FOR A VARIABLE

Computer identifies a variable by its name just as you are identified by your name. When a variable is declared the compiler allocates a block of memory for placing the value of the variable in it. In fact, for the computer that allocated block of memory is the variable and you can get to the value stored in this memory block by calling the name of the variable. The memory sizes allocated for different *types* may vary on different computers depending upon the hardware, the operating system and the compiler used. Table 3.3 gives the different *types* of variables and the sizes of memory blocks (number of bytes) generally allocated for different *data-types* on most computers. You may determine the same for your computer by running the Program 3.2, on your computer. The names of variables or identifiers should be carefully selected, because a valid identifier should comply with the following points.

1. **It can be a sequence of one or more characters including underscore symbol (_).** Example - *Barlength* or *Bar_length* are valid names.

2. **There should be no white (blank) spaces in an identifier. It should be a single word.** *Bar length* is invalid. *Box volume* is invalid while Boxvolume or Box_volume are valid.
3. **There should be no marked character in the identifier.**
4. **There is no limit on length of name in C++. However, in C it is limited to 32 characters.** Better have a check on the compiler you are using.
5. **Identifier should never start with a digit.** It should always start with an alphabet or underline symbol, however, digits can be part of identifier. 2A is invalid while A2 and _2A are valid.
6. **It should not have any other symbol except alphabets, digits and underscore symbol.** Example- Newdelhi_2 is valid but Newdelhi-2 or Newdelhi(2) are invalid identifiers.
7. **It must not be a keyword of C++.** A list of keywords is given in Table 3.2. Thus double or int are invalid identifiers while Double or Int or INT are valid identifiers.
8. **Besides the keywords the specific reserved words for the compiler should not be used as identifiers.**
9. **The alternative representations of some operators of C++ also should not be used as identifiers.** These 11 words are given below.

   and, and_eq, bitand, bitor, compl, not, not_eq, or, or_eq, xor, xor-eq

If one or more characters in the name is in upper case it is a safe bet against a keyword being used as name of a variable. A list of keywords is given in Table 3.2 below.

3.4 KEYWORDS

There are 63 keywords in C++. Out of these 32 are common with C. The keywords in C++ are listed in the table below. The common keywords are shown bold.

Table 3.2A – Keywords in C++

asm	auto	**bool**	break	case	**catch**
char	class	**const**	const_cast	**continue**	**default**
delete	**do**	**double**	dynamic_cast	**else**	**enum**
explicit	export	**extern**	false	**float**	**for**
friend	**go to**	**if**	inline	**int**	**long**
mutable	namespace	new	operator	private	protected
public	**register**	reinterpret_cast	**return**	**short**	**signed**
sizeof	**static**	static_cast	**struct**	**switch**	template
this	throw	true	try	**typedef**	typeid
typename	**union**	**unsigned**	using	virtual	**void**
volatile	wchar_t	**while**			

Table 3.2B – The 11 alternative representations of some C++ operators

and	and_eq	bitand	bitor	compl	not
not_eq	or	or_eq	xor	xor-eq	

PROGRAM 3.1 – Illustrates declaration of different types of variables.

```
#include <iostream>
using namespace std;
int main ()
{  int Dia   = 10 ;            //  variable Dia stand for diameter.
   double PI = 3.14159265358979323;
   float pi  = 3.14159265;
double Area_circle = PI* Dia*Dia / 4;
cout<<"PI =  "<<PI<<"\t pi =  "<<pi<<endl;
char ch = 'S';    // ch is the name of a variable with value 'S'
  cout << "ch = " << ch <<endl;
  cout<< "Area_circle = " << Area_circle<< endl;

    int m, n, p; // m, n, p are names of variables of type int
    m = 4;         // 4 is value of m
    n = 3;
    p =  m*m + n*n ;
cout <<"p = "<<p << endl;
 return 0;
 }
```

The expected output of the program is as below. The output for both float and double is according to the precision setting in the computer. In present case it is 6, so output is in 6 digits.

```
PI = 3.14159    pi = 3.14159
ch = S
Area_circle = 78.5398
p = 25
```

The following table lists most of the fundamental types and the memory allocated in general.

Table 3.3 – The different fundamental types and memory allocated for different types

S.No.	Variable type	Code for type	Examples of declaration	Memory(bytes) allocated in general
1.	character	char	char A, char ch;	1
2.	signed character	signed char	signed char ch;	1
3.	boolean	bool	bool M ;	1
4.	wide character	wchar_t	wchar_t ch;	2
5.	integer	int	int x;	4
6.	short integer	short	short n;	2
7.	long integer	long	long y;	4

Contd...

8.	unsigned short	unsigned short	unsigned short M;	2
9.	unsigned integer	unsigned int	unsigned int N;	4
10.	unsigned long	unsigned long	unsigned long X;	4
11.	float	float	float Weight ;	4
12.	double	double	double Area ;	8
13.	long double	long double	long double Area;	8

3.5 SIZE OF FUNDAMENTAL DATA TYPES

The function `sizeof()` returns the number of bytes allocated for its argument. The memory allocation for different types of data may be different in your computer because it depends upon the hardware and software being used. The following program makes use of the function `sizeof()` to determine the size of different types. It also includes wchar_t characters.

PROGRAM 3.2– Illustrates the application of function **sizeof().**

```
#include <iostream>
using namespace std;
//The program finds the memory allocated for different data types
int main()
{cout<<"Number of bytes reserved for following types."<<endl;
cout<<" For character  : \t" <<sizeof(char)<<"\n";
cout<<" For signed character : \t"<<sizeof(signed char)<<"\n";
cout<<" For wide character : \t"<<sizeof (wchar_t)<<"\n";
cout<<" For integer  : \t"<<sizeof(int)<<"\n";
cout<<" For short  : \t"<<sizeof(short)<<"\n";
cout<<" For long   : \t"<<sizeof(long)<<"\n";
cout<<" For float  : \t"<<sizeof(float)<<"\n";
cout<<" For double  : \t"<<sizeof(double)<<"\n";
cout<<" For long double  : \t"<<sizeof(long double)<<"\n";
cout<<" For unsigned short : \t"<<sizeof(short unsigned)<<"\n";
cout<<" For unsigned integer : \t"<<sizeof(int unsigned)<<"\n";
cout<<" For unsigned long : \t"<<sizeof(long unsigned)<<"\n";
wchar_t Wch = L'H';  // wide characters are preceded by L.
cout << " The size of Wch  : \t"<<sizeof (Wch)<< "\n";
return 0;
}
```

The expected output is given below,

```
Number of bytes reserved for following types.
```

```
For character                          : 1
For signed character                   : 1
For wide character                     : 2
For integer                            : 4
For short                              : 2
For long                               : 4
For float                              : 4
For double                             : 8
For long double                        : 8
For unsigned short                     : 2
For unsigned integer                   : 4
For unsigned long                      : 4
The size of Wch  :  2 //wide character takes 2 bytes
```

The following program illustrates the declaration of char variables and shows that some arithmetic operations may also be performed with them just as they are done on integral digits. You will also note that a digit such as 9 will have different value when it is used as a character ('9').

PROGRAM 3.3 – Illustrates use of variables of type char.

```
#include <iostream>
using namespace std;
int main()
{ char ch1,ch2,ch3, ch4, ch5 ,ch6,ch7,ch8;
 // ch1 to ch8 are simply names of variable. Their type is char

 ch1= 'A'; //The value of character A in ASCII code is 65.
 ch2 = 'z';  // Value of 'z' in ASCII code is 122.
 ch3 = ch2;
 ch4 = ch2 - '9'; // here '9' is character and not number 9.
// Value of character'9'in ASCII code is 57.Thus 122-57 = 65='A'.

ch5 = ')'*2;
//value of character')' in ASCII code is 41, so 41 × 2 =82=  character R
 ch6 = ch1 + 10;   //'A'=65,so 65 +10 = 85 ='K'
 ch7 = ch2 % ch1;   /* This operation gives remainder of
        122/65 which is 57= '9' */
ch8 = '9'*2;  // '9' = 57 on ASCII code so 57 × 2 = 114 = 'r'
cout<<" ch3 = "<<ch3 <<"\t ch4 = " <<ch4 <<"\tch5 = "<<ch5<<endl;
cout<<" ch6 = "<<ch6<< "\tch7 = "<<ch7<<"\tch8 = "<<ch8<<endl;
 return 0;
  }
```

The expected output is given below.

```
ch3 = z        ch4 = A        ch5 = R
ch6 = K        ch7 = 9        ch8 = r
```

The output results have already been explained by the comments given in the program. The characters are represented between single quotes like 'K'. The computer stores their numerical value according to the ASCII code.

CONSTANTS

C++ provides many different types of constants. For instance, in the above program we have seen a character such as 'A' is a constant value equal to 65. Similarly 'K' is another constant value. These are **character constants.** A sequence of characters enclosed between double quotes such as " Morning" is a **string constant.**

Similarly, "\n" or "\t' are constants which have special meaning for compiler and are known as escape sequences. These are discussed in Chapter 2.

Sequences of digits are integral constants. These may be decimal (base 10), octal (base 8) or hexadecimal (base 16). A decimal sequence of digits should not start with 0, because, in that case it would be taken as octal number by computer. Octal numbers are preceded by zero (0). The digits of the three systems have already been discussed in Chapter 1. If you see page 20 of Chapter 1, we have,

456 is a decimal number. Its equivalents in octal and hexadecimal are given below.

0710 is octal number. In this, 0 on extreme left indicates that it is octal number.

0x1c8 is hexadecimal number. 0x indicates that it is hexadecimal number.

Sequences of digits of base 10 are called decimal constants. Similarly, a digital sequence of base 8 is called octal constant and a sequence of hexadecimal digits is hexadecimal constant.

THE CONST AND VOLATILE

The const and volatile are attribute modifiers. A quantity, whether it is int, float, double, char or user defined type (a class object), if it is declared **const** its value cannot be changed in the program. One may declare a constant quantity as below.

const int Diameter = 10 ; // the statement fixes the Diameter to 10 units.

const float PI = 3.14159; // const float value which cannot be modified later.

const char kh [ ] = " Good Morning"; // a constant string of characters.

const wchar_t wch [ ] = **L** "Trip"; // a constant string of wide characters.

Note that the values in wide characters are preceded by L.

The **volatile** may be used in definition of a variable which may be modified from outside the program, It is decleared as **volatile int x;**

STORAGE CLASS SPECIFIERS

The following five storage class specifiers are supported by C++. These are **auto, register, extern, static** and **mutable**. These are disenssed below.

auto : The local variables belong to auto storage class. It is optional to use the specifier **auto.** Thus the declaration **int n;** is same as **auto int n** ;

The scope of these variables is the block of program (statements enclosed in a pair of curly brackets {}) in which they are created. During running of program, after the block is over the variables are removed from the memory and are not available.

static: A **static variable** may be a local or a global variable. Global variable may be accessed from any part of the program. Also see the section on scope of variables.

register : A CPU has a number of registers (16 is a typical number) for various purposes. A programmer may use the specifier **register** in the declaration of a variable if the same is desired to be loaded on a register so that it is readily (in less time) available to the processor. If the variable is frequently used in the program, the time of execution of program may decrease by this specification. However, it is the compiler which will decide if the recommendation can be honoured.

extern : The specifier **extern** gives the variable an external linkage and it may be accessed from another linked file.

mutable : An object of a class may be declared constant. However, if a data member of class is declared mutable, it may be modified in a constant object.

The following program illustrates extern, static, auto, register and bool data type.

PROGRAM 3.4 – Illustrates different storage class data.

```
#include <iostream>
using namespace std;
extern int n = 10;  // global variable
 int y = 5;   // global variable
int main()
 { static int D = 5;
 int x =7;
    auto int z = 25 ;
    cout <<"n*n = " <<n*n << ", y*y = "<< :: y *::y<<endl;
 register int m = 5;  // m to be loaded on a register
 cout << "Product m *D = "<< m*D <<endl;
 bool B = (x == y);  // B is a bool type variable
 bool C = (y*y == 25); // C is also bool type variable
 cout << "B = " << B<< ", C = " << C<<endl;
 return 0;
  }
```

The expected output is given below.

```
n*n = 100, y*y = 25
Product m *D = 25
B = 0, C = 1
```

The following program illustrates the static specifier.

PROGRAM 3.5 – Illustrates static storage class specifier.

```
#include <iostream>
using namespace std;
 static int n = 10;
 int main()
{{ int n = 20;
 int y = 8;
cout <<" y = "<<y << ", n = " << n <<" and ::n = "<< ::n<<endl;
 }
cout << "Outside the inner curly brackets n = " << n <<endl;
cout <<"And ::n = "<<::n<< endl;
return 0 ; }
```

The expected output is given below.

```
 y = 8, n = 20 and ::n = 10
Outside the inner curly brackets n = 10
And ::n = 10
```

The **enum** type may be used to define a number of integral constants as discussed on page 56. The following program gives an illustration.

PROGRAM 3.6 – Illustrates another example of enum data type.

```
#include <iostream>
using namespace std;
int main()
{ int n, m;
 double p, q;
  enum Day { Mon=1, Tues, Wednes, Thurs, Fri, Sat, Sun};
enum data { A = 10, B=5, C = 6};   // defining integral constants
  cout<< "Thurs = "<<Thurs<<endl;

n = Wednes + Mon;     // Addition
 p = Mon - Fri;     // Subtraction
  q = Sun/Wednes ;     //integer division
    m = A*B*C;    // using enum data

cout<<"n = " << n <<",\t p = " <<p <<endl;
 cout<< "q = "<<q <<endl;
 cout<<"Saturday=  " <<Sat<<"\n";
  cout<<  "m = " << m <<endl;

return 0;
 }
```

The expected output is given below, enum type has been used to define several integral values.

```
Thurs = 4
n = 4,      p = -4
q = 2
Saturday= 6
m = 300
```

3.6 SCOPE OF VARIABLES

The scope of a variable depends on the storage class to which it belongs, i.e. **automatic** storage class or **static** storage class. The local variables belong to **automatic** storage class. The keywords **auto** (generally not used) and **register** (if the variable is desired to be loaded on register) may be used before variable names. The scope of both these is limited to the nearest program block enclosed by braces { } in which they are defined. Figure 3.1 illustrates declarations of local variables which belong to automatic storage class and their scope along with the scope of **static** storage class variables.

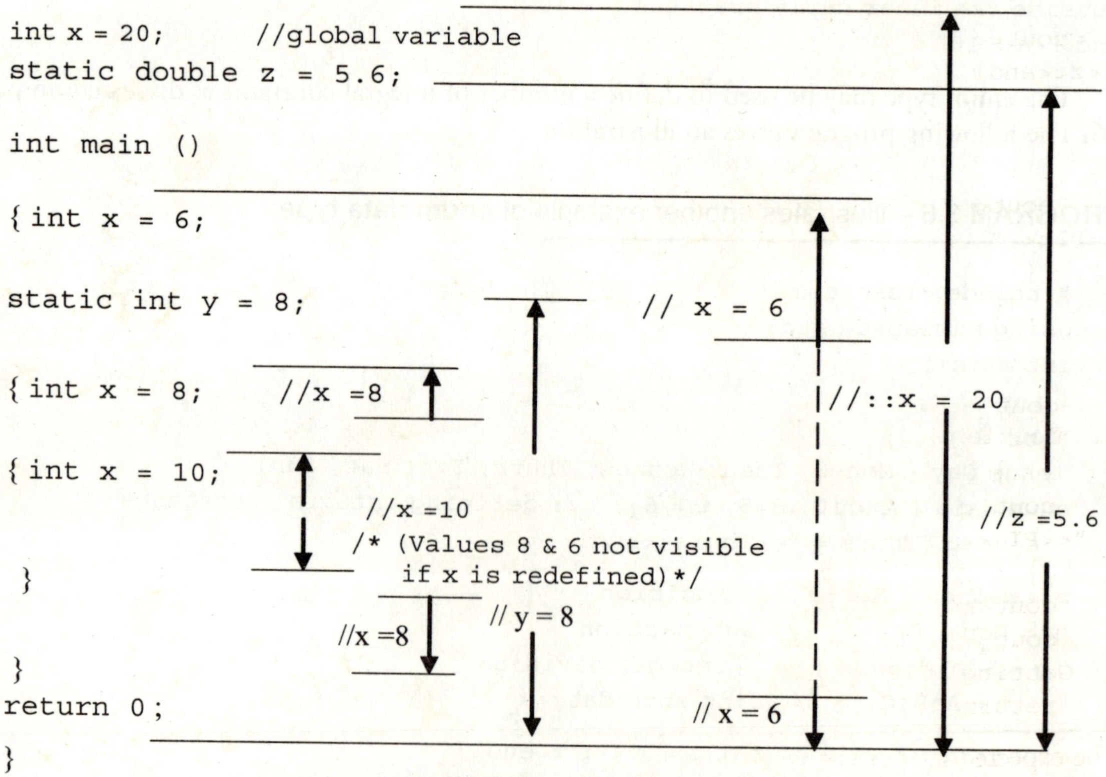

Fig. 3.1: Scope of variables

In the **static** storage class there are two categories, i.e. external or global variables and local **static** variables. The global variables are defined outside any class or a function declaration. Thus global variables are defined outside main (). Their scope is from the point of declaration to the end of program. Inside the main () they may be accessed with scope resolution operator (::). The static variables are declared with keyword **static** inside a function or out side a function. The scopes of local and global variables are illustrated in Fig. 3.1. The static data members for classes are discussed Chapter 12. The data declared **const** cannot be modified in the program. The declaration may be inside a function or outside a function. The following program illustrates the different categories.

PROGRAM 3.7 – The program illustrates the **scope of variables.**

```
#include <iostream>
int x = 8;                     // global variable
  double y = 2.2;                  // global variable
     using namespace std;
int main()
   { int x , y;
     const double PI = 3.14159;

const int z = 6;        // Value can not be changed in the program
          x = 11;                     //   variable in main()
          y = 9 ;                     //   variable in main()
cout<< "In main \t\tx = "<<x <<", y = "<<y<<"\t PI = "<<PI <<"\tz = "
<<z<<endl;
    {int x, y;
          x = 5;
          y = 4;
 cout<<"In outer braces         x = "<<x<<",    y = "<<y <<"\t PI = "
<<PI<< "\tz = "<< z << endl;
   {
    { int x, y;
         x = 20;
         y = 30;
 cout <<"In inner braces        x = "<<x<<", y = "<< y << "\t PI = "<<PI
<< "\tz = "<< z <<endl;
    }
 cout <<"In the outer braces     x = " <<x<< ",    y = " << y <<"\t PI
= "<<PI << "\tz = "<< z <<endl;
 }}
 cout<< "Outside the outer braces x = "<<x <<",      y = "<<y<<endl;
 cout << "In global scope          x = " << ::x << " y = "<<::y <<endl;
// Getting global value of x
 return 0;}
```

The expected output is given below.

```
In main                  x = 11,  y = 9   PI = 3.14159   z = 6
In outer braces          x = 5,   y = 4   PI = 3.14159   z = 6
In inner braces          x = 20,  y = 30  PI = 3.14159   z = 6
In the outer braces      x = 5,   y = 4   PI = 3.14159   z = 6
Outside the outer braces x = 11,      y = 9
In global scope          x = 8 y = 2.2
```

In the above output you see that values x=8 and y = 2.2 are global. In the mid portion of program and in the innermost braces '{ }', x and y have been declared again as x = 20 and y = 30. This is shown in the third line of output. In outer curly brackets the variables x and y have values 5 and 4 respectively (2nd and 4th line of output). But the scope of values x = 20 and y = 30 is only up to the closing of the innermost curly bracket. After the closure of inner and outer braces the values of x and y are again 11 and 9 respectively. That is illustrates by the last but one line of output in which the values of x and y are same as assigned in the beginning of program, i.e. x = 11 and y = 9, while in between the values are different. The variables PI and z do not change their values throughout the program because these are declared const. The global values are again same, i.e. 8 and 2.2. Note that global values have been declared above the main (). For accessing global variables the scope resolution operator (::) has to be used. The global values may be obtained any where in the program by using scope resolution operator (::) before the variable name. However, for local variables the scope are limited to nearest curly braces { } in which they are defined. The variables defined in a function have scope only up to the function.

3.7 TYPE CASTING

The change in *type* of a variable whether from one fundamental type to another fundamental type, or among user defined types, i.e. from an object of one class to object of another class or change of a pointer from one class to another class, etc., are called type casting. These may be carried out as below.

```
(type_now_desired) expression;          // C style of type casting
or
type_ now_desired (expression);         // C++ style of type casting
                // some take this also as c-type casting
```

Thus if `int A` is now desired to be changed to double it may be coded as,

```
(double) A;  // C style
or
double (A);   // C++ style
```

The code of following program gives a simple example as to why type casting is required.

PROGRAM 3.8 – Illustrates the need for type casting.

```
#include<iostream>
using namespace std;
int main()
 {int A = 3,B= 4, C =7;
 cout<< " A/B = " <<A/B <<endl;
  cout <<" C/B = "<< C/B <<endl;
  cout <<" A/(double)B = " << A/(double)B<<endl;
   cout <<" double (C)/B = " << double (C)/B<<endl;

   return 0;}
```

The expected output is below.

```
A/B = 0
C/B = 1
A/(double)B = 0.75
double (C)/B = 1.75
```

Division of int with another int results in int number and because A/B = 3/4 is a fraction, therefore, the output is 0. This is illustrated by the first line of output. Similarly the second division 7/4 results in 1 because the fractional part (.75) is neglected in integer division. But situation can be saved if we convert either numerator or denominator into a double number as done in the next two lines of output. In one case the denominator is changed to double and in second case numerator is changed to double. Now the output also contains the fractional part. More type conversions are illustrated in the program given below.

PROGRAM 3.9 – Program is another illustration of **type casting.**

```
#include <iostream>
using namespace std;
int main()
{
 int n ;
 double k = 3.675 , m1, m2 , p1,p2 ;
  char ch = 'B';
  n = int(ch);
 cout << "ch = "<<ch << "\t\t k = "<<k<<endl;
 k = int(k);

 cout << "n = " <<n << "\t \t k = "<<k<<endl;
 p1 = (int)7.5/3.0 ;
  p2 = (int) 7.5/3;
   m1 = int (4.5/2);
   m2 = int (4.5/2.2);

  cout<< " p1 = " <<p1 <<",\t p2 = "<<p2 <<endl;
  cout << " m1 = "<<m1<< ",\t m2 = "<<m2 <<endl;
  return 0;
 }
```

The expected output is given below.

```
ch = B                      k = 3.675
n = 66                      k = 3
 p1 = 2.33333,              p2 = 2
 m1 = 2,                    m2 = 2
```

The output shows that double k has been changed to an integer. The numerical value of character ch has been assigned to n. Numerical value of 'B' is 66. Note that value of p1 has not been changed to int while value of p2 has been changed. The difference is that value of p1 contains float type operand so it is taken float. Both m1 and m2 values have been changed to int because the type casting applies to the result of division because of brackets. Therefore, for conversion of *type* of the result of a calculation it is better to enclose the calculation part in brackets.

NEW TYPE CASTING OPERATORS IN C++

In C++ the following four new casting operators are defined.

```
static_cast < > ( )
dynamic_cast < > ( )
reinterpret_cast < > ( )
const_cast < > ( )
```

Some of these operators are meant to be used for specific applications. For instance dynamic_cast<>() is applied for runtime type information in inheritances with polymorphic base class. Since we have still not learnt about classes, pointers, inheritance and virtual functions, so the details of all of these cannot be discussed here. These are discussed in Chapter 15.

The application of static_cast <>() is however discussed below as it can be applied to fundamental types as well to user defined types. Unlike C-type casting in static_cast the constantness of the object is preserved. As applied to fundamental data types the static_cast <>() is coded as below.

```
static_cast <desired_type> (object);
```

Here we limit the application to the fundamental types like int, char and double. The following program illustrates its application.

PROGRAM 3.10 – This program illustrates conversion by static_cast <>()

```
#include <iostream>
using namespace std;

int main ()
{
 double n = 69.54, p =5.5, a ,m ;
 double s = 4.4563 , q = 2.45, b = 3.23 ;
s = static_cast<int>(s) + static_cast<int>(p);
   //s is assigned integral portions of s and p
cout<<"s = "<<s<<endl;

p = static_cast<int>(q);
m=65;
char ch = static_cast<char>(n) ;
    // double n is changed to a character
cout<< "ch = " << ch<< endl;
```

```
a = static_cast<int>(b)+ s;
  // s has already been changed to integer above
 cout<< "a = "<<a <<", \tp = " << p <<endl;
  cout <<"char m = "<<static_cast<char>(m)<<endl;
  cout<< "q = " << q << ", \t b = " <<b<<endl;
   cout<< "m = " << m<<endl;
 return 0;
}
```

The expected output is given below.

```
s = 9
ch = E
a = 12,       p = 2
char m = A
q = 2.45,        b = 3.23
m = 65
```

The first line of output, the s has been assigned the sum of integral parts of s and p. Hence, s = 9. The double n is cast into a character value. So n is first converted to int, i.e. 69 and then to character 'E' and the 'E' has been assigned to ch. Similarly, int m which has value 65 is converted into a character 'A'. The output for a , p and m can be similarly explained. The last two lines of output show that when cast converted values are assigned, the variable themselves do not change.

3.8 THE typedef

The typedef allows us to create alternative name for a *type* which may be a fundamental *type* or user defined *type*. For instance, with the following declaration we may simply write D in place of double.

```
typedef double D ;              // The typedef of double is D
```

The application is illustrated in the following program.

PROGRAM 3.11 – Illustrates application of typedef.

```
#include<iostream>
#include<cmath>
using namespace std;

 typedef double D ;
void main()
 {
 D x, y, Area ;  // Here D stands for double
  cout<< "Enter two point numbers : "; cin >> x>>y;
```

```
    Area = x*y;
    cout<< "Area = " << Area<<endl;
  }
```

The expected output is given below.

```
Enter two point numbers : 8.5 10
Area = 85
```

3.9 THE typeid () operator

The operator typeid () identifies the *type* of variable. Its real use is with dynamic objects created in inheritance with virtual functions and base class pointer wherein the information about *type* of object (to which class it belongs) is not available from the pointer (see Chapter 15). For fundamental *types* the operator is not of much use because these do not change *type*. Here we only show the use of the operator. It returns reference to *type* of its argument. It is coded as,

typeid(object);

For determining the name of *type* it is coded as below.

typeid (object).name();

The application is illustrated in the following program.

PROGRAM 3.12 – Illustrates application of operator typeid ()

```
#include <iostream>
using namespace std;
void main ()
{
 int x, y;
 double z;
if(typeid(x) == typeid(y))
 cout << "x and y are of same type."<<endl;
else
 cout<< "x and y are of different type. " <<endl;
 cout << "The type of z is "<< typeid(z).name()<<endl;
 cout<< "The type of y is "<< typeid(y).name() << endl;
}
```

The expected output of the program is given below.

```
x and y are of same type.
The type of z is double
The type of y is int
```

3.10 ARITHMETIC OPERATIONS ON VARIABLES

The operators including arithmetic operators are dealt in detail in the next chapter. However, here we introduce the arithmetic operators. The five arithmetic operators are listed in the Table 3.4 below.

Table 3.4 – Arithmetic operators

S. No.	Description of operation	Operator symbol
1.	Addition	+
2.	Subtraction	–
3.	Multiplication	*
4.	Division	/
5.	Modulus (returns remainder on division)	%

The following program illustrates some of the arithmetic operations.

PROGRAM 3.13 – Illustrates **arithmetic operations**

```
#include <iostream>
using namespace std;
int main()
 { int a = 4,b = 6, E;
double c,d,A,B,C,D;
 c = 2.6;
 d = 1.3;
 A = c + d;      // addition
  B = c - d;      // subtraction
   C = a/d;     // division
   D = d * d;       //multiplication
    E =b % a;       // modulus operator
cout<< "A ="<<A<<", B = "<<B<<", C= "<<C<<", D = "<<D<<", E = "<<E<<"\n";
return 0;
  }
```

The expected output is given below.

```
A =3.9, B = 1.3, C= 3.07692, D = 1.69, E = 2
```

3.11 FUNCTION swap()

Function `swap ( )` is a C++ Standard Library function. It exchanges the values of two variables. The variables should be of **same type**. See the following program for illustration.

PROGRAM 3.14 – Illustrates application of swap() function.

```
#include <iostream>
using namespace std;
int main()
{//swap function interchanges the values of same type variables
 int x ,y;
cout<<"Write two integers x = ";
cin>>x; cout<<" and y = "; cin>>y;
swap(x,y);
cout <<"After swapping: x = "<<x <<" and y = "<< y<<endl;
return 0;
}
```

In this program the user is asked to enter two integers for x and y. The program interchanges their values. The output of the program is given below.

```
Write two integers x = 35
and y = 45
After swapping: x = 45 and y = 35
```

It should be noted that variables used as arguments of function swap () must be of same type. The function swap() belongs to C++ Standard Library.

EXERCISES

1. What are the fundamental types? Why are these called fundamental types?
2. How do you declare a variable?
3. Which of the following identifiers are incorrect?

   (i) 5chairs (ii) Money
   (iii) template (iv) typeid
   (v) bitor
4. What are keywords in C++?
5. What do you understand by typeid () and typedef?
6. Is it necessary to declare all the variables right in the beginning in a C++ program?
7. What is the difference between the number 5 and the character '5'?
8. Can the keywords be used as variable name?
9. Which of the following statements are wrong? Also correct the wrong statements.

   (a) Int x = 7; (b) int y = 5.0;
   (c) double = 4.76548; (d) Float = 5.463;

10. Are the following initializations correct? If not, give the correct version.

    (a) int x = 6 ; (b) short int y = 8;

    (c) unsigned long = – 4500; (d) enum (Monday, Tuesday, Wednesday) ;

11. Differentiate between *double* and *long double* numbers.
12. What is wrong with following statements? Also give the correct version.

    (a) int x = 6.75; (b) int shot = 8;

    (c) char m = A; (d) double n = int (B);

13. What information do we get by using the function sizeof()?
14. Make a program to read three integer numbers and to calculate and display their squares and cubes.
15. Make a program to read, calculate and display the cubes of two small numbers which are entered by user.
16. Write a program that prints ASCII code for upper case alphabets A to C.
17. Write a program that reads length in inches and converts it into centimetres.
18. Write a program that converts Fahrenheit into centigrade.
19. What does swap() function do? Can it swap values of variables of different types?
20. Write a program to convert character variables into integers and integer variables into character variables.
21. What do you understand by scope of a variable?
22. Explain the difference between the following.

    (i) variable with global scope.

    (ii) variable with scope in main().

    (iii) variable with local scope.

23. Give examples of code of the above three types of variables.
24. Explain the scopes of global and static variables.
25. What is function scope?
26. What is the difference between a static variable and a constant.
27. Make a small program that asks the user to enter three numbers and displays their cubes.
28. Write the expected output of the following program.

PROGRAM 3.15 – Another example of **type-casting.**

```
#include <iostream>
using namespace std;
int main ()
{
int n = 80.54, p =5, a ,m ;
double s = 4.4563 , q = 2.45, b = 3.23 ;
s = int(s) + int(p);
cout<<" s = "<<s<<endl;
```

```
p = int(q);
m=65;
char ch = char(n) ;
cout<< " ch = " << ch<< endl;

a = int(b)+ s;

cout<< " a = "<<a <<", \tp = " << p <<endl;
cout <<" char m = "<<char (m)<<endl;
cout<< " q = " << q << ", \t b = " <<b<<endl;
cout<< " m = " << m<<endl;
return 0;
}
```

29. Make a program to illustrate the values of character '+' and size of "A".

PROGRAM 3.16 – Illustrates the values of characters '+' and size of "A".

```
#include <iostream>
using namespace std;

int main()
{ char River [6] = "Ganga";
char ch[] = "A";

char Plus = '+';
cout<< "Character + = " <<int(Plus)<<endl;
cout << sizeof (ch)<<endl;
cout<<River<<", " << ch <<endl;
return 0;
}
```

The expected output is given below.

```
Character + = 43
2
Ganga, A
```

○○○

CHAPTER

4

Operators

4.1 INTRODUCTION

Operators are instructions, represented by a single symbol or combination of symbols such as +, –, /, +=, &, etc., which are used in program statements to carry out some action on the data. The actions may be assignment, arithmetic operations, comparison of values of two variables, determination of address of a variable, pointing to memory location or linking an object to its class member, etc. C++ has a rich inventory of operators, however, in this chapter we shall be dealing with the following.

(i) Assignment operators
(ii) Arithmetic operators
(iii) Composite assignment operators
(iv) Increment & decrement operators
(v) Relational or comparison operators
(vi) Logical operators
(vii) Bitwise logical operators

Most of these operators are common with those of C. The symbols of these operators are shown in Table 4.1. Some of these we have already used in previous chapters, however, we have not examined their behaviour in detail.

C++ supports **unary**, **binary** and **ternary** operators. A unary operator takes one operand for its operation, a binary operator takes two operands and a ternary operator takes three operands. There is only one ternary operator in C++, i.e. selection operator (?:) which is discussed in the next Chapter. Examples of operators which are both unary and binary are + and –. These operators may be used to change the sign of a value in which case these are unary operators. These may also be used to add and subtract two quantities in which case they operate on two quantities and are binary. The **arity** of an operator is the number of operands it takes for its operation.

OPERATOR PRECEDENCE AND ASSOCIATIVITY

Consider the following simple calculation.

8 - 2*3

We know that its result is 2. But how is that result calculated? We first multiply 2 and 3 and then subtract the product (6) from 8. That means that multiplication has higher priority or precedence than the minus, otherwise if we first subtract 2 from 8 and then multiply the result would be 18. Each operator has a **precedence level** which decides its turn for operation when there are several operators in a statement. The operator with highest precedence is performed first followed by the one with the next lower precedence. The precedence levels of the operators are set in the complier and computer follows these rules during calculations.

Now if a number of operators having the same precedence level are there in a statement then how to decide as to which should be performed first. For example consider the following calculation.

20 % 3 * 5

The operators % and * have same level of precedence and both are binary operators. In the previous chapter we studied the modulus operator (%) which gives the remainder on division. Thus 20 % 3 = 2. In the above expression, if operation 20%3 is performed first the result is 10, otherwise if 3*5 is performed first the result is 5 because in that case 20 %15 = 5. In such cases the **associativity** of the operators comes to rescue. Since the operators are binary if the operations are performed left to right the result is 10 and if it is performed right to left the result is 5. The **associativity** of both % and * operators is left to right and thus the correct result is 10.

The operators in C++ are implicitly defined for variables of fundamental types. For user defined types such as class objects, C++ allows to redefine their functionality so that they can be used for class objects as well. The examples are (i) manipulations of vectors, (ii) manipulation of complex numbers, etc. For such cases the operators are overloaded (functionality is redefined) Even if the functionality of an operator is redefined (see Chapter 13) the arity, the precedence and the associativity of the operator do not change.

4.2 ASSIGNMENT OPERATOR

The basic assignment operator is (=) which is often called *equal to*. On the left of this operator we write the name of variable to which a value is to be assigned or l-value and on right side we write the value to be assigned to it or r-value. The l-value is the memory space in which the r-value is stored. Consider the following assignments.

```
int x = 5;          // Declaration and initialization
int y = 10;
y = x ;             // assignment
```

In the last statement, will the value of x be assigned to y or the value of y be assigned to x? The associativity of = operator is right to left, so value of x will be assigned to y. In this operation y becomes 5.

In the previous chapters we have already studied the two methods of declaration and initialization, which are illustrated below.

type identifier = value ;

type identifier (value) ;

The example are given below.

```
int x = 5, n = 3;
```

We may write such statements as given below.

```
int x , Age;          // declaration
float y ;             // declaration
y = 5.764;            // assignment
x = 5;                // assignment
Age = 22;             // assignment
```

The second method is illustrated below. .

```
int Age(22) ;     // Age is declared and initialized to 22.
```

Similarly a floating point variable may be declared and assigned as below.

```
float PI(3.14159);

double PI(3.1415926535);
```

Let Kh be name of a variable of type character. We want to assign the character 'B' to it. We may write the code as below.

```
char Kh;

Kh = 'B';
```

Or we may combine the above two statements as below.

```
char Kh = 'B';
```

or as,

```
char Kh('B');
```

Similarly a string of characters may be assigned. In the following the **<string>** header file is included in the program in order to declare variables of type *string*.

```
#include<string>

void main()

{string myname ;    // myname is a variable of type string

myname = "Monika";    /*"Monika" is the value assigned to  myname */

string Name ("Sujata"); // Name is assigned value "Sujata"
             string  name = "Mamta"; }
```

However, if the header file <string> is not included, a string variable may be declared as C-string. For such a case the assignment is illustrated below.

```
char myname [] = "Monika";
```

The constant 0 (zero) is of type int, however, it may be assigned to variables of all types. Thus we can write as below.

```
int x = 0;              //  It assigns 0 to int x.
float y = 0;            // It assigns 0.0 to float y
double d = 0;           //It assigns 0.0 to double d
char ch = 0;        //It assigns Null character '\0' to ch,
```

Table 4.1 – Operators common to C and C++

Operator symbol	Description of action	Operator symbol	Description of action
Arithmetic operators		,	Evaluate
+	Addition	**Increment/ decrement**	
–	Subtraction	++	Increment by 1
*	Multiplication	– –	Decrement by 1
/	Division	**Logical operators**	Also see chapter5
%	Modulus	&&	AND
Assignment operators		||	OR
=	Assignment	!	NOT
+=	Add and assign	**Bitwise operators**	
– =	Subtract and assign	&	AND
*=	Multiply and assign	|	OR
/=	Divide and assign	^	XOR
%=	Assign remainder	>>	Shift right
Relational operators	Also see chapter 5	<<	Shift left
==	Equal to	~	complement
>	Greater than	&=	Bitwise AND assign
<	Less than	|=	Bitwise OR assign
!=	Not equal	^=	Bitwise XOR assign
>=	Greater than or equal	<<=	Bitwise shift left and assign
<=	Less than or equal	>>=	Bitwise shift Right and assign
? :	Conditional operator		

Programs 4.1 and 4.2, given below, illustrate the assignment of different types of variables.

PROGRAM 4.1 – Illustrates different methods of **assignments.**

```
#include <iostream>
using namespace std;
```

```
void main()
{int P(20);            // This is equivalent to int P = 20;
     int M = 30;
     cout<<"P = "<<P<<",t M = "<<M<<endl;
double C (4.56), D ;   // double C(4.56) is equivalent to
                        // double C = 4.56
D = 6.54;
cout<< "C = "<< C<<",t D = " <<D<<endl;

char Kh('B');          // For assigning single char the single
                       // quotes '     ' are required
char ch = 'A';
cout << "Kh = "<< Kh << ",t ch = "<< ch <<endl;
}
```

The expected output is as below

```
P = 20,        M = 30
C = 4.56,      D = 6.54
Kh = B,        ch = A
```

The following program makes use of <string> header file which provides similar assignment operations as we do for int or char variables.

PROGRAM 4.2 – For a string of characters we may use class string (see Chapter 17).

```
#include <iostream>
using namespace std;
#include <string>
void main()
{   // In following Name1, Name2 and Name3 are names of strings.
string Name1("Mona Lisa");    // string of characters have to be
                              // put in double quotes "      "
string Name2 = "Gyatri";
string Name4 = "Malhotra";

string Name3;
Name3 = "Raman";              //Assignment = can be used for objects
                              //of class string.
cout << "Name1 = "<< Name1 <<endl;
cout << "Name2 = " << Name2 <<endl;
cout<<  "Name3 = "<< Name3 <<endl;
cout << "Name2 + Name4 = " << Name2 + Name4<<endl;
}
```

The expected output of the program is given below. Note that we have used header file <string> in the program. The objects of this class may be added as illustrated in last line.

```
Name1 = Mona Lisa
Name2 = Gyatri
Name3 = Raman
Name2 + Name4 = Gyatri Malhotra
```

4.3 ARITHMETIC OPERATORS

We have already discussed the arithmetic operators in Chapter 3. The different arithmetic operators are +, –, *, / and % which represent the addition, subtraction, multiplication, division and modulus. The application of these operators has also been illustrated in Program 3.13 in the previous chapter. The operator % is applicable only to integers and is generally used to test the divisibility of a larger integer by a smaller integer. If on division the remainder is zero then larger number is divisible by the smaller number. The following program illustrates the test of divisibility.

PROGRAM 4.3 – Illustrates the test of **divisibility of integers**.

```
#include<iostream>
using namespace std;

void main()
{ int A,B, m;

cout<< "Enter two integers :"; cin >> A >>B;
cout << "you have entered A = "<<A <<" and B = " << B<<endl;

if (A %B )            //the condition is if A%B is more than zero
cout<<"A is not divisible by B" <<endl;
else
cout <<"A is divisible by B "<<endl;
}
```

The expected output is as under. Two numbers 64 and 2 are entered. 64 is divisible by 2.

```
Enter two integers :64 2
you have entered A = 64 and B = 2
A is divisible by B
```

The following program calculates the roots of a quadratic equation $ax^2 + bx + c = 0$. Because this involves the evaluation of square root so the header file <cmath> is included in the program.

PROGRAM 4.4 – The program calculates roots of a quadratic equation.

```
#include <iostream>
#include <cmath>          //<cmath> header file is required for
           //calculating square root
using namespace std;
int main()
{                      // quadratic equation is: a x² + bx + c = 0
double  a,b,c, P, S;
 cout << "Enter the values of a,b and c :";
cin>>a>>b>>c;

 P =  b*b-4*a*c ;

 if( P < 0)         // If P is -ve, the roots are imaginary.
     { P = -P;
        S = sqrt(P)/(2*a);
cout<<"Root R1 = "<< -b/(2*a) <<"+" <<"i"<<S << " and Root R2 =
"<< -b/(2*a)<<"-" <<"i"<<S<<endl;
}
 else
  { S = sqrt(P) ;          // If P is +ve the roots are real.

cout  <<"Root R1= "<< (-b+ S)/(2*a)  <<",  and Root  R2 = "<< (-b -
S)/(2*a) <<endl;
}
  return 0;
}
```

The following two trials of the above program are carried out with different values of a, b and c. In the first case imaginary roots are obtained and in second case real roots are obtained.

```
Enter the values of a,b and c :4 10 10.25
Root R1 = -1.25+i1 and Root R2 = -1.25-i1
```

The following real roots are obtained when we enter $a = 4$, $b = 10$ and $c = 4$.

```
Enter the values of a,b and c :4 10 4
Root R1= -0.5,  and Root  R2 = -2
```

Precedence in Arithmetic Operators

All the arithmetic operators do not have the same precedence. Computer first evaluates those with highest precedence then it evaluates those with next precedence and so on. Table 4.2 gives precedence of arithmetic operators.

Table 4.2 – Arithmetic operators

Arithmetic operation	C++ operator	Order of evaluation
Parentheses	( )	First. If there are several nested pairs, the inner most pair is evaluated first. If in parallel, from left to right.
Multiplication, division, modulus	* / %	Equal. If there are several than left to right
Addition, Subtraction	+ –	Equal, If there are several from left to right

Below is an illustration of how an expression for A is evaluated by computer.

A = 5*((3 + 4) +6) – 2 *(3+4);

= 5*(7 + 6) – 2*(3+4)

= 5*13 – 2*(3+4)

= 5*13 – 2*7

= 65 – 2*7

= 65 – 14

= 51

In some cases when the expressions are not written carefully the precedence may give an unexpected result. This is demonstrated by following program.

PROGRAM 4.5 – Illustrates the effect of **precedence** on the value calculated.

```
   #include <iostream>
   using namespace std;

   int main()
   {
    int a = 15, n = 3,s = 8,  p = 6,r = 3,A ,B , P1,P2,P3 ;
    double C,D;
   A = n*a%p ;        // here first n and a are multiplied before
//the operation of %.
     B = n*(a%p);       // here () is evaluated first and the result
//is then multiplied to n.
       P1 = n% a*p ;
          P2 = (n%a)*p ;

              P3 = n%(a*p);

     C =(n +s +p +a)/r;           //bracket is evaluated first
```

```
D =  n + s+p+a/r;      //Here a/r is evaluated first. It is
                        // then added to n+s+p.
cout<< "A = " << A <<"\t B = " << B <<endl;
cout<< "P1 =" <<P1<<"\t P2 = " << P2 <<"\tP3 = "<< P3<<endl;
cout <<"C = "<< C <<"\t D = " << D << endl;
return 0;
}
```

The expected output is given below.

```
A = 3          B = 9
P1 =18         P2 = 18        P3 = 3
C = 10         D = 22
```

The above program emphasizes how the precedence can make a difference in the calculation. Let us take the line,

```
A = n * a % p ;
```

Though the precedence level of * and % is same but evaluation is from left to right so the above expression is equivalent to the following.

```
A = (n * a) % p ;
```

Therefore, the expressions A = (n * a) % p; and A = n *(a % p); would not give same result. Same is true for evaluation of P1, P2 and P3. The expression P1 = n%a*p ; is equivalent to the following.

```
P2 = (n%a)*p ;
```

But P3 = n%(a*p); is different because the priority has been changed. In this the expression (a*p) is evaluated first.

4.4 COMPOSITE ASSIGNMENT OPERATORS

C++ allows combining the arithmetic operators with assignment operator. The arithmetic operator is written first followed by assignment operator but not vice versa. Thus we write the code for add and assign as below,

```
B += 6;
```

which means that first add 6 to the present value of B and then assign the result to B. This is equivalent to the following statement.

```
B = B + 6;
```

Similarly the other operators may also be combined. All the composite operators are listed in Table 4.3. The applications of some of these are given in the Program 4.6.

Table 4.3 – Composite assignment operators

Operator	C++ expression	Equivalent expression	Explanation and use
`+=`	`B += 5;`	`B = B +5;`	`int B= 4;` `B +=5 ;` // makes B=9.
`-=`	`C -= 6;`	`C = C - 6;`	`int C = 10;` `C -= 6 ;` // makes C=4
`*=`	`D *= 2;`	`D = D*2;`	`int D = 10;` `D *=2;` // makes D=20
`/=`	`E /= 3;`	`E = E/3;`	`int E = 21;` `E /=3;` //makes E = 7
`%=`	`F %= 4;`	`F = F % 4 ;`	Divides F by 4 and remainder is assigned to F

In all the composite operators there should not be any space between the symbols. For instance, if we give space between + and = such as + = it may result in error.

PROGRAM 4.6 – The program illustrates the application of **composite operators**.

```
#include <iostream>
using namespace std;
int main ()
{
int m =3, n=4, p=5, s = 6, q = 11;
m += 2; // no space between + and =
n *= 4;
      p -= 3;
        s /=2;
            q %=4;
cout <<"m = "<<m <<", n = "<<n<<", p = "<<p<<", s = " <<s<<endl;
cout << "q = " << q << endl;
return 0;
}
```

The expected output is given below. The out put is self explanatory.

```
m = 5, n = 16, p = 2, s = 3
q = 3
```

4.5 INCREMENT AND DECREMENT OPERATORS

For increasing and decreasing the values of integral objects by unity, we may make use of increment operator ++ and decrement operator – – respectively. These operators may be placed before or after the variable name. When the operators ++ and – – are placed before the variable name, these are called pre-increment and pre-decrement operators respectively. When the operators are placed after the names then these are called post-increment and post-decrement operators. In case of pre-increment the present value of variable is first increased by unity and the incremental value is then used in the application. And in case of post-increment, the present value of variable is used in the application and then the value of variable is incremented. Same is the case of operator −−. The pre and post versions of ++ and −− are also elaborated in Table 4.4.

Also take care that there should not be any space between ++ or between −− because this may result in error.

Table 4.4 – Increment and decrement operators

Pre or post	Operator	Description
Pre-increment	++k	First increase the value of k by unity. Then evaluate current statement / function by taking incremented value.
Post-increment	k++	First use the current value of k to valuate current statements / function, and then increase k by unity
Pre-decrement	−−k	First decrease the value of k by unity and assign it to k. Then evaluate the statements / functions.
Post-decrement	k−−	First use the current value of k to valuate current statements / functions then decrease k by unity.

The following program illustrates the increment and decrement operators.

PROGRAM 4.7 – Illustrates increment and decrement operators.

```
#include <iostream>
using namespace std;
int main()

{int a = 6, p = 4,r=3,n =5,A,B,C,K ;

 A = 6*++n   ;
 cout << "A = "<<A <<"\t n = " <<n <<endl;
 K =  5*a-- ;
 cout<<"K = "<<K<<"\t a = " <<a << endl;

 B =r++*r++ ;
 cout<< "B = "<<B<<"\t r = "<< r << endl;
C = p--*p--;
cout<<"C= "<< C<<"\t p= " << p << endl;
return 0;
}
```

The expected output given below is self explanatory. However, it is also explained.

```
A = 36       n = 6
K = 30       a = 5
B = 9        r = 5
C= 16        p= 2
```

For the first line of output n = 5. The n is first incremented to 6 and then multiplied by 6 to give 36. The second line of output is obtained by multiplication of 5 with the initial value of a, which is 6. The variable a is then decremented to 5. The third line is obtained by multiplying r with r, taking the initial value. Then r is incremented twice. The last line of output is obtained similarly. The program below illustrates more such cases.

PROGRAM 4.8 – Illustrates application of **increment and decrement operators**.

```
#include <iostream>
using namespace std;
int main()
{int m=6,n=2,p=4,r=3,s=8,k = 4,a,b,c,d ;
a =++n+ ++m;
b = s++ * s++;
c =  p--*p-- ;
d = (--k* -- k)*++r ;
cout<<"a = "<<a<<",\tn = "<<n<<",\tm = "<<m<<endl;
cout<<"b = "<<b <<",\ts = " <<s<<"\n";
cout<<"c = "<<c<<",\tp = "<<p<<endl;
cout<<"d = "<<d <<",\tk = "<<k<<",\tr = "<<r<<endl;
return 0;
}
```

The expected output is given below.

```
a = 10,     n = 3,     m = 7
b = 64,     s = 10
c = 16,     p = 2
d = 16,     k = 2,     r = 4
```

In the first line of output a = (2 + 1) + (6 + 1) = 10. For the second line of output s is increased after the multiplication, so b = 8 × 8 = 64. But s has got increment twice, so its value becomes 10. Similarly in the third line of output the decrement in the value of p happens after the multiplication, therefore value of c = 16 and p has got decrement twice, so its value has decreased from 4 to 2. For the fourth line of output the value of k is pre-decreased twice because the decrement operator has higher precedence than the operator *. Similarly value of r is increased from 3 to 4 then multiplied with the first factor which is 4. So the result is 16.

As you have seen in the above program, in a complex expression wherein a variable appears several times, it would be better not to use increment or decrement operators because it becomes difficult for the programmer to keep track of changes in values. In the following program for the expression E = ++a*– –a*++a; you would expect for a = 6, the E = 7 × 6 × 7, but it is equal to 6 × 6 × 7. Because value of a is first increased to 7 and then decreased to 6 before the first multiplication. It is then increased to 7 and multiplied to 36.

Similar cases can arise in expressions like ++m*––m. If initial value of m is 4 you would expect the expression to evaluate to (4 + 1)(5 – 1) = 20 but program gives a value 16. Because the value of m is first increased then it is followed by decrement and then multiplication. So the expression evaluates as 4 × 4 = 16. Thus if we have an expression like

```
A = ++n * --n ;
```

The result is A = n*n ; with the initial value of n, because ++ and –– have higher precedence than *. But if you have an expression like

```
A = ++n *--p* --n;
```

It would evaluate as A = (n+1) *(p–1)*(n–1);

The following program involves product of three factors like the example given above, and it is interesting to note the results. Would you like to explain the results?

PROGRAM 4.9 – Illustrates use of operator ++ and –– in along with other operators.

```
#include <iostream>
using namespace std;
int main()
{
 int a = 6, n= 5,s =8,  p=4,r=3,A,B,C,K,M,D,E  ;
 A = ++n*--p * --n ;    // Equivalent to 6*3*5=90 and now p = 3
  cout << "n = "<<n <<", A = " <<A <<endl;
    B =  ++a*2*--a;  // This is equivalent to 7*2*6
      D = --a * ++a ;        // This is equivalent to 6*6
         E = ++a*--a*++a;  // Equivalent to 6*6*7 = 252
 cout<<"B = "<<B<<", a = " <<a << ", D = "<<D <<", E = " << E
<<endl;

   M = ++s*--s;      // equivalent to 8*8

 K =++r +4 --r ;   // Equivalent to 4+4-3=5
cout<< "K = "<<K<<", r = "<< r <<", M = "<<M<< endl;
     C =p++* 5*p--;    // Equivalent to p *5 *p and p =3
                        // See calculation for A above
cout<<"C= "<< C<<", p = " << p << endl;
return 0;
}
```

The expected output is given below.

```
n = 5, A = 90
B = 84, a = 7, D = 36, E = 252
K = 5, r = 3, M = 64
C= 45, p = 3
```

4.6 RELATIONAL OPERATORS

These operators are used to compare two variables and are generally used with conditional statements. For example, the code if(A==B) means if A and B are equal. Note that in this two 'equal to' signs (==) are used. Programmers often make a mistake by using single =. The other relational operators are explained in Table 4.1. These are explained as well as their applications are illustrated in Chapter 5.

4.7 BOOLEAN OPERATORS

Boolean operators are logical operators. They relate the logical statements. Let A and B be the two variable representing two logical statements. The logical variable have only two states that is either it is true or false. If it is true the variable has a value 1 or a positive value. If it is false it has value zero. The three Boolean operators are OR, AND and NOT. Table 4.5 gives details about these operators and their symbols.

Table 4.5 – Boolean Operators

Condition	Operator	Description
(i) A OR B	||	If either A or B or both are true then A|| B =1 It is false only when both A and B are false. In that case A||B = 0
(ii) A AND B	&&	If both A and B are true then A && B = 1 else A&&B =0 (It is false when any one is false)
(iii) NOT A	!	True if A evaluates to be false, i.e. If A is false then !A = 1 and false when A evaluates true, i.e. If A is true then !A = 0

The evaluation of various conditions in terms of true or false in different situations are given in Table 4.6(a,b,c) below.

Table 4.6 – (a), (b) and (c)

(a) A OR B

A	B	A||B
false	false	false
true	false	true
false	true	true
true	true	true

(b) A AND B

A	B	A&&B
false	false	false
true	false	false
false	true	false
true	true	true

(c) NOT A

A	!A
true	false
false	true

The program below illustrates the applications of Boolean operators.

PROGRAM 4.10 – Illustrates the application of **Boolean operators.**

```
#include <iostream>
using namespace std;
int main()
{ int p, q, r, s,t,x, y, z;
p =1;
```

```
q = 0;
r = 1;

s = p||q;
t = !q;
x = p&&q;
y = (p || q && r||s);
z = (!p || !q && !r || s);

cout << "s = "<<s << ", t = " << t <<", x = "<<x<< endl;
cout << "y = " <<y <<", z = "<<z<< endl;
return 0; }
```

The expected output given below should be verified by reader by calculations with help of Table 4.7(a,b,c).

```
s = 1, t = 1, x = 0
y = 1, z = 1
```

4.8 BITWISE OPERATORS

As already discussed in Chapter 1, a bit is the basic unit of memory. It can have only two states. If it is set its value is 1 otherwise it is zero. Bitwise operation means convert the number into binary and the carry out the operation on each bit individually. For example let us take the operation complement represented by symbol (~). Let us take a number

```
short A = 42;
```

A short number is stored in two byte or 16 bits. Therefore,

A when expressed in binary = 00000000 00101010

Complement of A is ~A = 11111111 11010101

The compliment operator changes the bit with value 0 to 1 and the one with value 1 is changed to 0. The different bitwise operators are listed in Table 4.7 below. It also illustrates codes.

Table 4 .7 – Bitwise operators

Operator	Description	Example of code
&	AND	`A&B ;`
|	OR	`A|B;`
^	XOR	`A^B ;`
>>	Shift right	`A >>2;//shift right by 2 places`
<<	Shift left	`A<<2;`
~	Complement	`~A;`
&=	Bitwise AND assign	`A &= B;`

Contd...

|=	Bitwise OR assign	`A |= B;`
^=	Bitwise XOR assign	`A ^= B;`
<<=	Bitwise shift left assign	`A <<= 2;` Shift left by 2 places and assign to A
>>=	Bitwise shift right assign	`A >>= 1;` Shift right by 1 place and assign to A

The operators AND, OR and XOR are explained in truth Table 4.8 below.

Table 4.8 – Bitwise operators AND, OR and XOR

Bit1= A	Bit2 = B	A&B	A|B	A^B
0	0	0	0	0
1	0	0	1	1
0	1	0	1	1
1	1	1	1	0

The programs given below explain the application of some of these operators.

PROGRAM 4.11 – Operator complement (~) is used to determine the maximum value of an integer that can be stored on my PC.

```
#include<iostream>
using namespace std;

void main()
{ unsigned A = 0;
A = ~ A;
cout << "A = "<<A  <<endl;
}
```

The expected output is given below.

```
A = 4294967295
```

The following program illustrates the application of bitwise AND operator (&).

PROGRAM 4.12 – Illustrates **bitwise AND operator.**

```
#include<iostream>
using namespace std;

void main()
{ short A =24;
```

```
short B = 8;
int C = A&B;
cout << "C = "<<C  <<endl;
}
```

The expected output is given below.

```
C = 8
```

The output is explained as below. A short number is stored in two bytes, therefore,

24 in binary is equal to	00000000 00011000
8 in binary is equal to	00000000 00001000
Bitwise AND is equal to	00000000 00001000

The result 0000000000001000 in binary is equal to 8.

The following program illustrates OR and left shift operators.

PROGRAM 4.13 – Illustrates the operators **OR** and **left shift (<<).**

```
#include<iostream>
using namespace std;
void main()
{ short A =42;
short B = 12;
int C = A|B;
int D = A<<1;

cout << "C = "<<C  <<endl;
 cout<< "D = "<<D <<endl;
}
```

The expected output is as under.

```
C = 46
D = 84
```

Explanation of output is given below. A short number is stored in two bytes or 16 bits. Therefore,

42 in binary is equal to	00000000 00101010
12 in binary is equal to	00000000 00001100
Bitwise OR operation results in	00000000 00101110

This is equal to 46 in decimal

For the variable D, the digits of A are shifted left by 1 place and assigned to D. So the original binary number 00000000 00101010 now becomes 00000000 01010100 which is equal to 84, i.e. the number gets multiplied by 2. Thus shifting a digit to left means multiplication by two.

PROGRAM 4.14 – Illustrates the operators **^** , **>>=** and **<<=** .

```
#include<iostream>
using namespace std;

void main()
{short A =42;

short B = 12;
 short C = 24;
   short D  = A^B;             // XOR operator
      C <<= 1;
          A <<=2;  // Shift to left by 2 places and assign
   B >>=2 ;       // shift right by 2 places and assign
 cout<< "A = "<<A<< " \tB = "<< B <<endl;
 cout << "C = "<<C  <<endl;
 cout << "D = "<< D <<endl;
}
```

The expected output is given below.

```
A = 168          B = 3
C = 48
D = 38
```

The binary equivalent of A = 42 has been shifted two places to left. So the number gets multiplied by 4. So A = 168. Similarly the right shift by two places in case of B divides it by 4.The binary equivalent of 24 has been shifted to left by one place and assigned to C. Therefore, C = 24×2 = 48. For A ^ B see the following explanation.

Binary equivalent of 42 is	00000000 00101010
Binary equivalent of 12	00000000 00001100
Bitwise XOR operation gives	00000000 00100110

This is equivalent to 38.

The following Program illustrates more of the compound assignment operators.

PROGRAM 4.15 – Illustrates the application of **operators ^=, &= and |=.**

```
#include<iostream>
using namespace std;
void main()
{ short A =20, D , E, F;
 short B = 18;
   short  C = 30;
       D = C^=B;
         E = A &=B ;
            F = C|=A ;
```

```
    cout <<"E = "<<E <<endl;
    cout  <<"F = "<< F <<endl;
    cout << "D = " <<D <<endl;
    }
```

The expected output is given below. Try to explain the output.

```
E = 16
F = 28
D = 12
```

Chapter 18 deals exclusively with operations on bit sets based on functions in <bitset> header file.

4.9 PRECEDENCE OF OPERATORS

Precedence is an important aspect of operators. A partial list of operators and their precedence is given in Table 4.9. The table does not include all the operators because we have not so far dealt with them. For a more detailed list see Appendix C.

Table 4.9 – A partial precedence table. Those higher in list have higher precedence

Operator	Type	Associativity
( )	Parentheses	Left to right
[]	Array subcript	Left to right
++ – –	Unary postfix	Left to right
++ – –	Unary prefix	Left to right
+ –	Unary plus, unary minus	Right to left
* / %	Multiplicative	Left to right
+ –	Additive	Left to right
<<	Bitwise left shift	Left to right
>>	Bitwise right shift	Left to right
<, <=, > , >=	Relational operators	Left to right
== , !=	Relational	Left to right
&	Bitwise AND	Left to right
^	Bitwise XOR	Left to right
|	Bitwise OR	Left to right
&&	Logical AND	Left to right
||	Logical OR	Left to right
= , *= , /= , %=, + =, – =	Assignment operators	Right to left
&=, ^=, |=, <<=, >>=		Right to left
Comma	Evaluate	Left to right

EXERCISES

1. State step by step the sequence of operations that a computer would follow to evaluate the following expressions. (Hint - use precedence of operators)
   (a) Z = 5 y + 3y(10y + 5/2) for y = 2.
   (b) Z = 7 y % 2 + 2(3 + (y % 3 + 2)) for y = 19
2. State the step by step order in which a computer would evaluate the following expressions? (Hint - use precedence of operators)
   (a) 5 * 5 *(4 + 6*8) +4;
   (b) 7 % 3 *(5 + 6*7) –5;
   (c) 8 * 3 % 5 *(3 * 5 % 2 – 6) –4;
3. What is wrong with the following codes in a program.
   (a) n*n(12 – n)(n + 3); (b) m % 3 (4 – m);
   (c) p *p(m + n);
4. Evaluate the following expressions for int n = 10;.
   (a) n * n % 3; (b) n*(n % 3);
   (c) (n*n) % 5; (d) n/3;
5. Explain the difference between pre and post increments, i.e. ++ n and n++.
6. Evaluate the following for int n = 8 ;
   (a) n += 3; (b) n += 2 % 3;
7. Evaluate the following for int n = 4;.
   (a) ++n*n++; (b) ++n*n– – ;
   (c) 2*++n + 3 * – –n; (d) ++n += 3;
8. Evaluate the following expressions for int n = 20 ;
   (a) n /= 5; (b) n += 8;
   (c) n %= 7;
9. Write a program to find roots of a quadratic equation.
10. Write a program to numerically prove that sin(A + B) = sinA .cosB + cos A. sinB.
11. Write a program to prove numerically that $(A + B)^2 = A^2 + B^2 + 2AB$.
12. Write a program which reads two integers numbers x and y and carries out the following bitwise operations on the numbers.
    (i) x & y; (ii) x |= y;
    (iii) x <<= 2;
13. Write a program to read 5 integers and to display their average value.
14. Write a program to display the average value and standard deviation of 10 integers.
15. Compare the precedence levels of following operators.
    + , – , / , *
16. What would be the value of following expression for int m = 10; in the following code?
    (i) m = ++m;
    (ii) m *= ++m;

17. Make a program to evaluate the following expressions for m = 6, n = 2 and (i) a = 0, b = 0, c = 0, d = 0, and e = 0. Repeat the same when (ii) a =1, b =1, c = 2, d = 2, and e = 2.

(i) a += 4 + ++m*n ;
(ii) b *= 3 + – – m*m ;
(iii) c += 2 +m *++m ;
(iv) d *= 2* + m*m– – ;
(v) e –= 2*++m / m– – ;

Answer –

PROGRAM 4.16 – An exercise in application of **increment/decrement operators.**

```
#include<iostream>
#include<cmath>
using namespace std;

int main ()
{
int m = 6,n = 2, a=0,b=0,c=0,d=0,e=0;
a +=4 + ++m*n ;
b *=3+ —m*m ;
c +=2 +m *++m ;
d *=2* + m*m-- ;
e -=2*++m / m-- ;

cout<<"a = "<<a<<", "<<"b = " << b<<", c = "<<c<<", d
= "<<d <<", e = "<<e <<endl;
return 0 ;
}
```

The expected output is as under.

a = 18, b = 0, c = 51, d = 0, e = –217

For the second case the values are
a = 19, b = 39, c = 53, d = 196, e = 0

18. Determine the output of following program.

PROGRAM 4.17

```
#include <iostream>
using namespace std;
int main ()
```

```
{
int m=3, n=4, p=5, s=6, q=31;
m += 2;
n *= 4;
p -= 3;
s /= 2;

cout <<"m = "<<m <<", n = "<<n<<", p = "<<p<<", s = "
<<s<<endl;
q %= 4 + (n /= 4);

cout << " q = " << q << endl;
return 0;
}
```

Verify your answer with the following output obtained by running the program.

```
m = 5, n = 16, p = 2, s = 3
 q = 7
```

❍❍❍

CHAPTER 5

Selection Statements

5.1 INTRODUCTION

Often we compare two or more items for characteristics such as size, number of items or quality, etc. For instance, if you have to select a bag out of two bags A and B, you may compare their sizes, say bag A is bigger than bag B. If you are looking for a bigger size, you may select A and discard B. In many real life situations our decision for further action depends on the result of such comparisons. In automatic control systems also the current conditions (values of parameters) for a process are compared with the set conditions and the differences decide the remedial actions. In programming for real life problems often the values are compared and the next step is decided by the outcome of comparison. In C++ like in other programming languages there is a set of operators which are used for the comparison of characteristics of two objects. These are listed in the Table 5.1 given below.

Table 5.1 – The operators for different relational (comparison) expressions

	Condition	Operator	Example	C++ code with *if*
(i)	equal to	= =	if m is equal to n	if (m == n)
(ii)	not equal to	! =	if m is not equal to n	if (m != n)
(iii)	greater than	>	if A is greater than B	if (A > B)
(iv)	less than	<	if C is less than D	if (C < D)
(v)	less than or equal to	< =	if M is less than or equal to N	if (M<= N)
(vi)	greater than or equal	> =	if m is greater than or equal to n	if (m >= n)

When we compare whether two numbers are equal or not we use (==) and not (=) because (=) is assignment operator. In the code m = n ; the value of n is assigned to m. Thus the operator (=) does not do any comparison. For comparison whether m is equal to n or not we must use ==. In the second line of the Table 5.1 we have a condition if m is not equal to n. The operator (!=) is opposite of the operator (==). Conditional comparisons may occur in a variety of problems. Generally comparison operators are used along with conditional expressions as illustrated in the last column of the table.

5.2 CONDITIONAL EXPRESSIONS

In C++ three conditional expressions are provided. These are (i) *if,* (ii) *if .... else* and (iii) *switch* .The *if* condition gives the option of single choice, i.e. if the conditional expression is true the statement following the condition is carried out. If the condition is false the following statement is discarded and program goes to next statement. In *if .... else* there are two choices. One choice is with *if* and the second choice is with *else.* If the conditional expression is true the statement following *if* is carried out otherwise the statement following *else* is carried out. In switch condition more than two choices are generally provided. There is no limit to the number of choices. Each switch condition may have its own choice condition. Similar results may also be obtained by using a chain of *if .... else* statements. All these are explained below.

5.3 THE *if* EXPRESSION

We often say like this "if you get marks equal to 50% or more than 50% you can get admission in the course". Another similar statement would be "If you know programming with C++ you are eligible for this job." A close examination of above expressions shows that the first part of the sentence is the condition prefixed with *if*, i.e. if this happens or if it is true then the second statement will follow. In case, the condition is not true the following statement is discarded and program proceeds to next statement. In a program it is written as given below.

if (conditional expression)

statement;

The first line of code is the condition. If the expression in the parentheses is true, the statement following the expression would be carried out, otherwise the statement would be ignored and the program would proceed further.

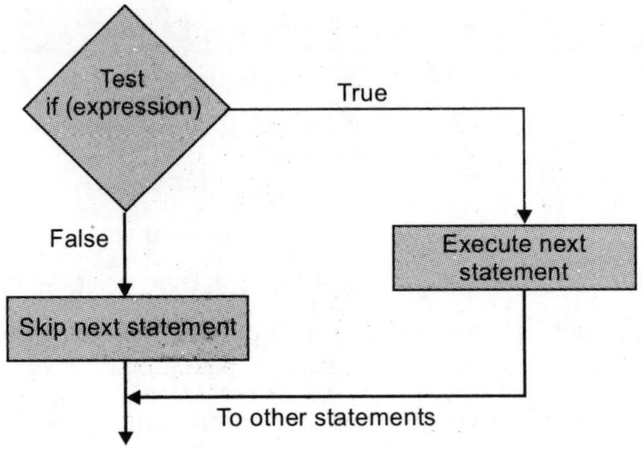

Fig. 5.1: Execution of *if* condition

Figure 5.1 illustrates the execution of *if* condition. You would also note that the *conditional expression is put in brackets and there is no semicolon at the end of line, while the following statement ends with semicolon.* The condition mentioned above has been used in the following program in which the user is asked to enter the marks obtained by him / her. If marks are more than or equal to 50%, the next line of the program will be executed, i.e. it will be displayed on the monitor. If the expression is not true nothing is displayed on monitor.

PROGRAM 5 .1 – Illustrates *if* condition

```
#include<iostream>
using namespace std;
int main()
{ int Marks;
  cout<<"Write your marks: ";
   cin>>Marks;
 if (Marks >= 50)   // conditional expression
 cout << "You are eligible for admission."<< endl;
return 0;
}
```

As you click for execution of the program, the sentence 'Write your marks: ' will appear on monitor with the cursor blinking at the end of the line. Here you type the marks obtained, say you type 60, and press the 'enter key', the second sentence '*You are eligible for admission.*' will appear on the monitor. The monitor will show the following two lines.

```
Write your marks: 60

You are eligible for admission.
```

In the following program applications of some more relational operators are illustrated.

PROGRAM 5.2 – Illustrates a multiple *if* (expressions)

```
#include <iostream>
using namespace std;
int main()
{ int n , m ,p;
  cout<<"Enter three integers."; cin>>m>>n>>p;
if(n == m)  // If n is equal to m Display the following.
  cout<<"n and m are equal"<<endl;
if(m !=n)  // If m is not equal to n, display the following
  cout << "n and m are not equal. "<<endl;
if (m >=p)  // If m is greater than or equal to p.
  cout <<"m is greater than p"<<endl;
if ( p>=m)
 cout<< "p is greater than m."<<endl;
 return 0;
}
```

The expected output is given below.

```
Enter three integers.30 30 40
n and m are equal
p is greater than m.
```

The values of m and n are equal, while p is greater than n or m. Therefore, the statements "n and m are not equal" and "m is greater than p" have been neglected because the *if* conditions preceding them are not true.

If more than one statements have to follow the *if (expression)*, the statements should be enclosed between curly braces { }. A sample is shown below.

if (expression)
{ Statement 1 ;
Statement n ; }

5.4 THE *if ... else* STATEMENT

In many of the real life situations two or more options are available. Single *if...else* condition may be used when there are two choices and a chain of *if...else* expressions may be used for more than two choices. The execution of an *if... else* expression is illustrated in Fig. 5.2 .

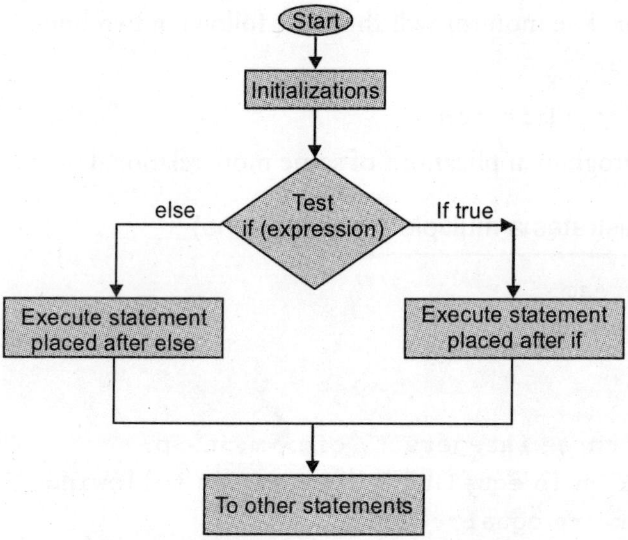

Fig. 5.2: Execution of *if ... else* statement

The code for two choices (*if...else*) may be written as below.

if (expression)
statement1 ;
else
statement2 ;

You may write the statements in a fashion that it is easier to read. Program 5.1 may be modified to Program 5.3 given below to get a response to any value of Marks that is entered.

PROGRAM 5.3 – Illustrates *if … else* condition

```
#include<iostream>
using namespace std;
int main()
{ int Marks;
 cout<<"Write your marks: ";
  cin>>Marks;
if (Marks>= 50)   // conditional statement
 cout << "You are eligible admission."<< endl;

else
 cout << "You are not eligible for admission." <<endl;
 return 0;
  }
```

On clicking for execution the user is asked to enter his /her marks. Say the marks entered are 46, the following will be displayed on the monitor.

```
Write your marks: 46
You are not eligible for admission.
```

Test for Divisibility

Suppose you want the program to test whether an integer number say *n* is divisible by another integer number say *m*. For this we use the modulus operator (%) which gives the remainder when one integer is divided by another integer. The code is illustrated below.

```
if( n % m)
    cout<< n <<" is not divisible by "<< m << endl;
else
    cout<< n <<" is divisible by "<< m << endl;
```

The above mentioned *if* (expression) is true if there is a remainder. Therefore, if it is true then n is not divisible by m. If there is no remainder, i.e. the condition is false then n is divisible by m. It is illustrated by the following program.

PROGRAM 5.4 – Illustrates the test for divisibility for integers.

```
#include<iostream>
using namespace std ;

int main()
 {
 int n, m ;
 cout << "Enter two integer numbers: " ;
 cin>>n >>m ;
```

```
if (n % m)
 cout<<"Number"<<n<< " is not divisible by"<<m<<endl ;
else
 cout<< "Number "<<n<<" is divisible by "<< m<<endl ;
 return 0 ;
 }
```

On running the program the following statement will appear on the monitor.

```
Enter two integer numbers:
```

The user is prompted to enter two numbers. At the end of line the user will find a blinking cursor. It is here that the user has to type two numbers. First type one number say 66, give space and type the second number say 3. *Then press the enter-key*. Unless you press the *enter-key* the program will not proceed further. As you press *enter- key* the following sentences will appear on monitor.

```
Enter two integer numbers: 66 3
Number 66 is divisible by 3
```

5.5 CONDITIONAL SELECTION OPERATOR (? :)

If there are two options to choose from, the conditional selection operator (? :) may be used in place of *if… else*. The code is quite compact and convenient. It is illustrated below.

condition ? statement1 : statement2

The above code means that if the *condition* evaluates true then *statement1* will be carried out, otherwise the *statement2* will be carried out. **Note that the two statements are separated by colon (:).** Suppose you give the name 'max' to the greater of the two numbers *m* and *n,* then for selecting the greater of the two the code may be written as below.

```
m>n ? max = m : max = n ;
```

That is if *(m>n)* is true then the greater of the two numbers is *m* or *max* = *m* and if it is not true then the greater of the two is *n* or max = *n.* Its use is illustrated in the following program.

PROGRAM 5.5 – Illustrates conditional selection operator

```
#include<iostream>
using namespace std;
 int main()
 { int A, B, C, D ,max, Max;

 cout<< "Write four whole numbers : " ; cin>>A>>B>>C>>D ;
cout<<"Maximum of first two numbers = " << (A > B ? A:B) << endl;
 max = ((A > B ? A : B) > C ? (A > B ? A : B) : C);
 cout <<"Maximum of first three numbers =" << max << endl;
```

```
Max = ((A> B ?A : B) > (C>D ? C:D) ? (A>B ? A:B) : (C>D ? C:D));
cout<< "Maximum of four numbers = " << Max << endl;
return 0;
}
```

The expected output is given below. The selection operator has been used to find maximum of two, three and four numbers. The numbers entered are 60, 45, 90 and 10. The output is self explanatory.

```
Write four whole numbers : 60 45 90 10
Maximum of first two numbers = 60
Maximum of first three numbers =90
Maximum of four numbers = 90
```

The following program gives a different application of the conditional selection operator.

PROGRAM 5.6 – Program illustrates a choice between two functions by ? : operator.

```
#include<iostream>
using namespace std ;
void MS1 (){cout<<"I will be the first.\n";}
void MS2 (){cout<<"You will be the first.\n";}
int main()
{
int mymarks,yourmarks;

cout<<"Write mymarks and yourmarks ";
cin>>mymarks >>yourmarks;

mymarks>yourmarks ? MS1() : MS2() ;
return 0 ;
}
```

The expected output is given below.

```
Write mymarks and youmarks 92 88
I will be the first.
```

5.6 THE *if ... else* CHAINS

More than one choices may be managed by a chain of *if . . . . else* expressions. The following program selects the name of the 4th day of the week out of 7 choices.

PROGRAM 5.7 – The program illustrates *if . . . . else* chain

```
#include<iostream>
using namespace std;

int main()
{ int m ;
 cout<< "Name the day which is day number ";
 cin>>m ;

 if (m == 1) cout<< "It is Monday" <<endl;
else
 if (m == 2) cout<< "It is Tuesday" <<endl;
else
 if (m == 3) cout<< "It is Wednesday" <<endl;
else
 if (m == 4) cout<< "It is Thursday" <<endl;

else
 if (m == 5) cout<< "It is Friday" <<endl;

else
 if (m == 6) cout<< "It is Saturday" <<endl;

else cout<< "It is Sunday" <<endl;
 return 0;
}
```

The expected output is given below.

```
Name the day which is day number 4
It is Thursday
```

Suppose you are preparing grade cards and you wish that on entering the marks the computer should also print an appropriate quotation depending upon the marks. The following program gives an illustration.

PROGRAM 5.8 – Another illustration of *if ... else* chain

```
#include<iostream>
using namespace std;
 int main()
{
 int Marks;
 cout << "Enter the marks: ";
 cin>>Marks ;

 if (Marks >= 90)
```

```
    cout<<"Excellent, keep it up";
   else
    if (Marks >= 80 )
    cout<<"Congratulations, you have got A grade."<<endl;
   else
    if (Marks >= 60 )
    cout<<"Very good, You have secured first class. "<<endl;

   else
    if (Marks >= 40 )
    cout<< "You have passed. You need to work hard."<<endl;
     /* The program will fail if the order in which the statements are written above is
altered.*/
   return 0;
   }
```

The expected output is given below.

```
Enter the marks: 75
Very good, You have secured first class.
```

The above program may fail to write correct quotation if the order in which the above statements are written is changed. However, if compound Boolean conditions are written, the program will deliver correct quotation irrespective of where the relevant statement is written.

5.7 SELECTION EXPRESSIONS WITH LOGIC OPERATORS

For compound comparative conditions such as '*if number n is greater or equal to 80 and less than or equal to 150*', etc. can be written with the help of Boolean logical operators which are given below. The output of Boolean operators are either true or false. When two statements are compared, either the condition is true which returns 1 to system or it is false which returns 0 to the system. With these return values the system gets to know whether the condition is fulfilled.

The three Boolean operators are as follows.

(i) AND (ii) OR (iii) NOT

Let A and B be the two logical statements. The following table discusses the characteristics of the three operators under different conditions.

Table 5.2 – Boolean operators

Condition		Description	Operator	Example of code
(i)	A OR B	True if either A or B or both are true. (It is false only when both are false.)	| |	A| |B ;
(ii)	A AND B	True if both A and B are true. (It is false when any one or both are false)	&&	A && B ;
(iii)	NOT A	True if A evaluates to be false, and false when A evaluates true.	!	!A ;

PROGRAM 5.9 – The program develops a truth table for the Boolean expression !A || B.

```
#include <iostream>
using namespace std;

int main()
{ // for details on for expression see Chapter 6 on Iteration.

for ( int A =0; A<2 ; A++)
 { bool S;
for(int B =0;B<2; B++)
 { S = !(A||B);
cout<< "A = "<<A << "  B = "<<B <<"  !( A||B)= " <<S<<endl;}}
return 0;
}
```

The expected output is as follows.

```
A = 0   B = 0   !( A||B)= 1
A = 0   B = 1   !( A||B)= 0
A = 1   B = 0   !( A||B)= 0
A = 1   B = 1   !( A||B)= 0
```

An application of compound expression using Boolean operators is given in Program 5.10 below. In this program we determine the maximum of the three numbers entered by the user.

PROGRAM 5.10 – Application of Boolean expressions for determining minimum of three numbers.

```
#include<iostream>
using namespace std;
main()
{
 int a,b,c;
 cout<<" Write three numbers: " ;
 cin>>a>>b>>c;
if (a>c && b>c)
 cout <<"The minimum of the three numbers is" <<c<<endl;
 else
if (c>b && a>b)

 cout <<"The minimum of the three numbers is " <<b<<endl;
 else
 cout <<"The minimum of the three numbers is " <<a<<endl;
 return 0;}
```

The program is run and three numbers 42, 25 and 75 are entered. The output of the program is given below.

```
Write three numbers: 42 25 78
The minimum of the three numbers is 25
```

In the following program the Program 5.8 is recoded with Boolean conditions so that the order of writing the statements does not affect the choice.

PROGRAM 5.11 – Illustrates Boolean conditions in *if … else* chain

```
#include<iostream>
using namespace std;
 int main()
{ int Marks;
  cout << "Enter the marks: ";
  cin>>Marks ;

 if(Marks >= 80 && Marks<90)
 cout<<"Congratulations, you have got A grade."<<endl;

else

 if (Marks >= 90)
  cout<<"Excellent, keep it up"<<endl;
else
 if (Marks >= 60 && Marks<80)
  cout<<"Very good , You have secured first class. "<<endl;

else

 if (Marks >= 40 && Marks<60)
 cout<< "You have passed. You need to work hard."<<endl;
 return 0;
}
```

The marks entered are 95 and the expected output is given below.

```
Enter the marks: 95
Excellent, keep it up
```

5.8 THE switch STATEMENT

When a multiple selection is desired we may use a *if – else* chain or *switch* statement. For large number of choices the *if – else* chain becomes unwieldy and confusing. A better method is the switch expression which is illustrated below.

```
switch (expression)
{ case value1 : statement1;
    break;
  case value2: statement2;
    break;
  case value3 : statement3;
    break;
  ..................
   case valuen : statementn;
   break;
    default : statement;  }
```

During execution of the program, the switch expression is evaluated. The expression should evaluate to an integer value. Its value is compared with the values mentioned in different cases mentioned under switch expression. If the value matches a value of a particular case, the statements in that case are carried out. If no case-value matches with the value of switch expression the program comes to the last statement which is a default statement. Provision of default statement is optional. It is useful in case of user interactive programs where the user may enter a wrong value by mistake. The statements contained in default case can remind the user that the data was wrong and prompt the user to enter correct data. After each case the statement **break;** is provided to get out of the switch at the end of a case which matched the key. If this is not provided, then all the statements following the match would also be carried out which is not desirable. The following points must be taken care of while using switch statement.

(i) The (expression) must evaluate to an integral value. Characters may also be used in the switch expression because characters also have integer value as per ASCII code.

(ii) The choices are enclosed between a pair of curly brackets.

(iii) Each case value is followed by colon (:).

(iv) All the statements following a match are carried out. After the colon there may be one or more than one statements. In case of multiple statements there is no need to put them between curly braces.

(v) The break statement should be given at end of every case, otherwise, all the cases following a match would be carried out.

The following figure illustrates the execution of switch statement.

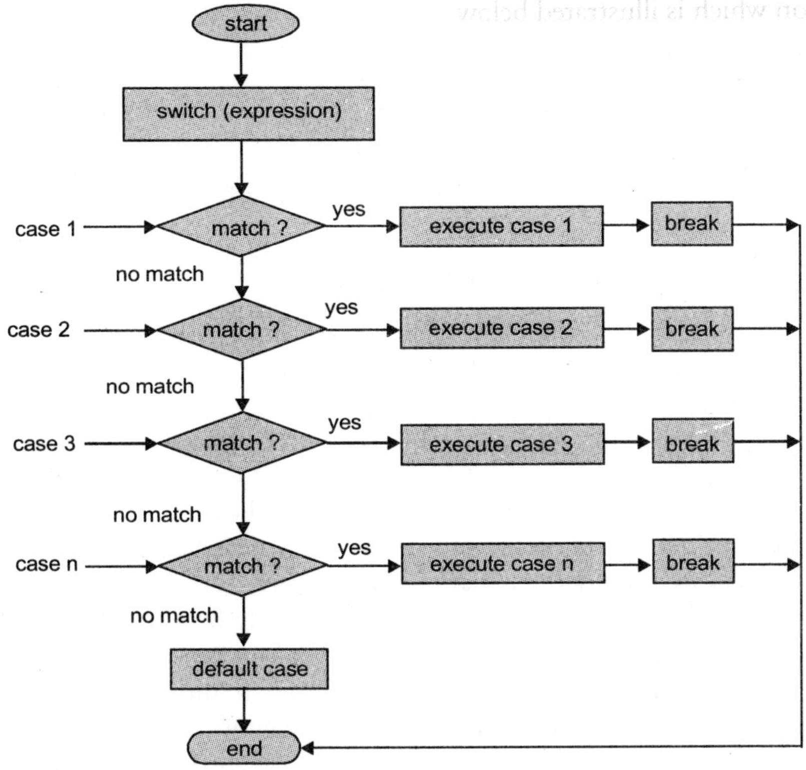

Fig. 5.3: Execution of switch statement

PROGRAM 5.12 – The program illustrates switch statement

```
#include<iostream>
using namespace std;
main()
{
 int m ;
 cout<<"Name the day which is day number ";
 cin>>m ;

 switch (m)
 {case 1:cout<<"It is Monday"<< endl; break ;
 case 2: cout<<"It is Tuesday"<< endl; break;
 case 3: cout<<"It is Wednesday" <<endl; break;
 case 4: cout<<"It is Thursday" <<endl; break;
 case 5: cout<<"It is Friday"<< endl; break;
 case 6: cout<<"It is Saturday"<<endl; break ;
```

```
case 7: cout<<"It is Sunday"<<endl; break ;
default: cout <<"The number entered is not in the range."<<endl;
}
return 0;
}
```

The following output is obtained when value 4 is entered form.

```
Name the day which is day number 4
It is Thursday
```

When the number 11 is entered for m we would get the following result.

```
Name the day which is day number 11
The number entered is not in the range.
```

Another example is that of online admissions. It may be desired to put the marks obtained by the student as the only criterion for admission. In the following program a student is asked to enter his/her percent marks and he/she gets the advice as to which course he/she is eligible for admission. Six choices are provided for marks, i.e. (i) below 45, (ii) 45 and above, (iii) 60 and above, (iv) 75 and above and (v) 90 and above. Since marks may be any number such as 46, 81, etc., we carry out integer division of the marks by 15 and it gives an integer value less than 7. Thus if marks are 78 the integer division by 15 will give 5 and if marks are 55 the integer division would give 3, and so on. Also note that several statements are inserted in each case without enclosing them in curly braces { }. Also note that each case ends with the statement break;. If break; statement is not provided then all statements following a match, including the cases after the match, would also be carried out which is obviously not desirable.

PROGRAM 5.13 – Another illustration of **switch statement**.

```
#include<iostream>
using namespace std;
int main()
{ int Marks;
 cout << "Enter your percent marks ";
 cin >> Marks ;
switch ( Marks/15)
{   // for 90 to 100 the division will give 6
case 6: cout<<"You can get admission in all branches"<<endl;
cout<< "Finish the admission formalities by week end"<<endl;
 break;
case 5 :   // for marks 75 to 89
cout<<"You can get admission in all branches except the science
courses."<<endl;
cout<< "Finish admission formalities before month end."<<endl;
 break ;
case 4:   // for marks 60 to 74
```

```
    cout <<"You are not eligible for Science and economics."<<endl;
    cout<< "Choose other courses by tomorrow."<<endl;
      break;
    case 3:     // for marks 45 to 59
    cout<<"You are eligible for English and Hindi courses only."<< endl;
    cout<<"Complete admission formalities soon."<<endl;
     break ;

    case 2:     // for marks 30 to 44
     cout<<"Sorry, Not eligible here."<<endl;
     cout<< "Better try correspondence courses."<<endl; break;

     default: cout << "Sorry, Marks entered are not correct" <<endl; }
// default case
     return 0; }
```

The expected output on entering marks 63 is given below.

```
Enter your percent marks 63
You are not eligible for Science and economics.
Choose other courses by tomorrow.
```

EXERCISES

1. What is wrong with the following code?

```
if(i> 4);
n = n + I;
```

2. What is wrong with the following code?

```
if (n % m)
cout<< "n is divisible by m";
```

3. Give an example of switch statement.
4. What are the Boolean logic operators?
5. Write a Boolean *if(expression)* for integer i to have values between 1 to 5 and between 20 to 25.
6. What is conditional selection operator? Make a small program to illustrate its application.
7. Show by constructing a truth table that the following Boolean conditions are equivalent.

   !(A||B) and !A&&!B

   Answer:

   The truth table is constructed below. For all values of A and B it is shown that !(A||B) and !A&&!B are equivalent.

Truth Table

A	B	!A	!B	!(A||B)	!A&&!B
0	0	1	1	1	1
0	1	1	0	0	0
1	0	0	1	0	0
1	1	0	0	0	0

8. Evaluate the two expressions !(A&&B) and (!A||!B) for all values of A and B (0 and 1) , and show that they are equivalent.

Answer: The following table shows that !(A&&B) and (!A||!B) are equivalent.

Truth Table

A	B	!A	!B	!A||!B	!(A&&B)
0	0	1	1	1	1
0	1	1	0	1	1
1	0	0	1	1	1
1	1	0	0	0	0

9. Use truth table to show that !A||B and A||!B are not equivalent.

Answer: From the truth table given below it is clear that the two expressions are not equivalent.

A	B	!A	!B	!A||B	A||!B
0	0	1	1	1	1
0	1	1	0	1	0
1	0	0	1	0	1
1	1	0	0	1	1

10. Write a compound Boolean *if(condition)* for the following situations.

    a. A varies from 0 to 10 but not between 4 to 6.

    b. B varies between 20 to 30 and between 40 to 50.

    Hint.

```
int A, B ;
if (A>=0 && A<4 || A > 6&& A <=10)
if (B>=20 && B<=30 || B>=40 && B<=50)
```

11. Make a program which asks the user to enter 4 numbers and program finds the maximum of the four by using conditional selection operator.
12. Make a program to select a number greater of the two numbers which are entered by user of the program using *if (expression)*.
13. Find mistakes in the following program which finds minimum of three numbers.

```
#include<iostream>
using namespace std;
int main()
{
int a,b,c;
 cout<<"Write three numbers: " ;
 cin>>a>>b>>c;
if(c<b && b<a )
 cout<< "The minimum of the three number is "<<c<<endl;
else
 if (b<c && c <a )
cout<< "The minimum of the three number is "<<b<<endl;
 else

cout<< "The minimum of the three numbers is"<<a<<endl;
return 0 ;
}
```

14. Make a program which asks the user to enter three numbers and finds the greatest of the three numbers using conditional selection operator.
15. Write a program to find the greatest of four numbers using the selection conditional operator.
16. Make changes to Program 5.11 in order to use switch statement in place of *if – else* chain.
17. Make a program for preparing the truth table for Q.7 above.
18. Make a program to prepare the truth table for Q. 8 above.
19. Find mistakes in the following program, correct it and run it.

```
#include <iostream> ;
using namespace std;
int main ()
```

```
{int x, y, max;
cout<<" Write two integers ";
cin >>x >>y;
 x > y : max = x ? max = y;
cout<<Max <<" is larger of the two numbers."<<endl;
 }
```

20. There are a number of mistakes in the following program. Locate the mistakes, correct and run the program.

```
 #include<iostream>
using namespace std;
 int main()
{ int Marks;
cout << " Enter your percent marks ";
cin>>Marks ;
switch ( Marks/15)
{
case 6; cout<<" You can get admission in all branches"<<endl;
break:
case 5 ;
cout<<" You can get admission in all branches except the science
courses."<<endl;
case 4;
cout <<" You are not eligible for Science and economics courses."<<endl;
break;
 case 3;
 cout<<"You are eligible in English and Hindi courses only."<<endl; break:
  case 2;   // for marks 30 to 44
cout<<"Sorry, Not eligible here, try correspondence courses."<<endl; break:
default; cout <<"Sorry, Marks are not correct"<<endl;    // default case
}
return 0;
}
```

❍❍❍

CHAPTER

6

Iteration

6.1 INTRODUCTION

In many programs it is required to repeatedly evaluate a statement or a whole block of statements with increment or decrement of some data in order to arrive at a result. Problems such as sum of numbers, calculations of numerical tables, numerical integration, automatic control, sorting of lists etc. are some examples. Repeated evaluation of statements is called iteration and recursion. The recursion is taken up in the chapter on functions while iteration which is also called looping is the subject matter of this chapter. In many programming languages *goto* statement is extensively used to go back and forth in a program. It is also used for making a loop. In C++ along with *goto* there are other better options such as *while, do..... while, for* etc. First let us start with the *while* statement.

6.2 THE *while* STATEMENT

In a program, the *while* statement or loop is incorporated as illustrated below.

while (conditional expression)
statement;

The above code means that as long as the conditional expression placed in parentheses evaluates true, i.e. it is more than zero, the statement following this will be carried out. In the while expression generally there is a variable whose limiting value is set to stop the loop. However, there are endless while loops as well, which will evaluate the following statement infinite number of times. Such loops have to be stopped with statements like **break;** after a variable attains a limiting value. The listing of Program 6.1 given below carries out addition of numbers, say from 1 to n. In the program the variables *n* , *i* and *Sum* are declared as integers. The number *n* is initialized as 10, *Sum* as 0 and *i* as 0. The *while* (*expression*) is used in the program as illustrated below.

```
while (i <= n)
Sum +=i++;
```

This above code means that as long as *i* is less than or equal to *n*, evaluate the following statement which is Sum +=i++;. As you know from previous chapter this statement means that add the value of *i* to value of *Sum* and assign this value to *Sum* and then increase i by 1 and again repeat the process. Thus the process is repeated again and again till $i = 10$. So Sum will become equal to 0 + 1 + 2 + 3 + 4 + 5 + 6 + 7 + 8 + 9 + 10 = 55. After the loop is over, the computer moves to the next statement which in this program is the output statement.

PROGRAM 6.1 – Illustrates ***while*** loop for determining sum of numbers from 1 to 10.

```
#include <iostream>
using namespace std ;
int main()
 {int n = 10, i= 0, Sum = 0;
while (i <= n)
 Sum += i++;
cout << "Sum of integers from 1 to 10 = " << Sum <<endl ;
return 0;
}
```

The expected output of the above program is given below.

```
Sum of integers from 1 to 10 = 55
```

The statement given in output is printed only at the end of loop, because the output statement is not included in the loop.

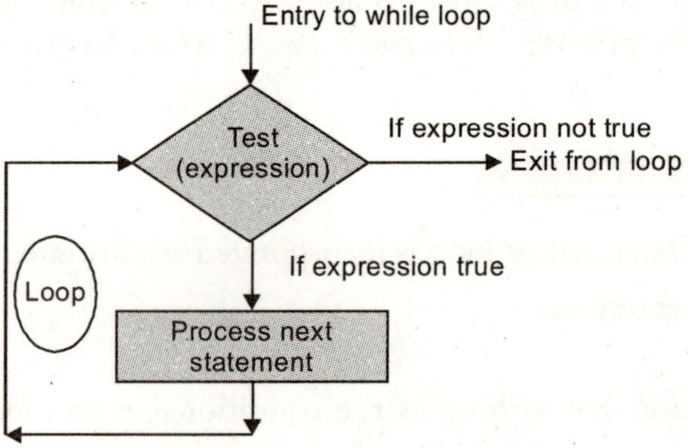

Fig. 6.1: The execution of a *while* loop

In Program 6.1 you must have noticed that the limit on the maximum value of i and its increment each time put a limit on the number of times the loop will run. If there is no limit on the maximum value of the variable i the loop will never end. One such condition may be *while*($i>=0$) followed by increment in i which starts from 0. Another example of endless loop is *while* (1), the condition most commonly used for having an endless loop is given below.

while (*true*)
statement;

The word true is a keyword of C++ and its value is 1. In such cases it is necessary to incorporate a break statement to get out of the loop. The different processes that take place in the implementation of a *while* loop are illustrated graphically in Fig.(6.1).

If more than one statements of code are desired to be included in the loop they should be enclosed between a pair of curly braces { } as given below.

while (expression)

{ statement1 ;

....

statementn ;}

In this way the whole block of statements from *statement1* to *statement n* becomes part of the loop. This is illustrated in the listing of Program 6.2 in which it is desired to determine the square roots of numbers 10, 20, 30 and 40, etc. and display them.

PROGRAM 6.2 – Illustrates ***while*** loop for determining square roots of numbers.

```
   #include <iostream>
   #include <cmath> /*Header file cmath required for square root.*/
using namespace std;
   int main()
   {int n = 10,N ,i=0;
   while( i<5 )  // Note that there is no semi-colon at the end.
   {N = i*n;
   cout <<"Number = " << N <<"\tSquare root = "<<sqrt(N)<<endl;
    i++;}
   return 0;
   }
```

The expected output from the program is given below.

```
Number = 0     Square root = 0
Number = 10     Square root = 3.16228
Number = 20     Square root = 4.47214
Number = 30     Square root = 5.47723
Number = 40     Square root = 6.32456
```

In the above program the header file <cmath> has been included because we wish to calculate square root of a number. The square root is evaluated by function sqrt() which belongs to <cmath> header file. By using curly brackets more than one lines of code following the *while(expression)* have been included in the loop. So we get output on every iteration. If the braces {} after *while (i<5)* are not used the output statement would be carried out after the loop is over, i.e. the following would be the output.

```
Number = 40  Square root = 6.32456
```

6.3 THE NESTED *while* STATEMENTS

When more than one parameters such as *i* and *j* are to be varied in a program and it is desired that for each value of *i*, the *j* be varied over its range of values, such conditions are called nested conditions. Program 6.3 given below illustrates the use of *while* condition for such a case. Such cases generally involve more than one statement of code. The *i* loop is the outer loop and *j* loop is the inner loop. The manner in which code may be written is illustrated below.

```
while (int i < n)
  { statements ;
    while (int j < m)
     { statements ;
         statement ; } }
```

PROGRAM 6.3 – The program illustrates **nested *while*** loops.

```
#include <iostream>
using namespace std;
   //The program illustrates nested while loop
void main()
{
int x =0,i=0 ;
cout<<"i\tj\tx\ty" <<endl;

while (i<=2)
 { int j = 0;    // outer while loop

 while (j<=2)
 { x+=(i+j);    // inner while loop
int y = x*x;

cout <<i<<"\t"<<j<<"\t"<<x <<"\t"<< y<<endl;
 j=j+1; }
 i =i+1;}
}
```

The output is given as under. For each value of i the j has been varied over its range of values (0 to 2).

```
i       j       x       y
0       0       0       0
0       1       1       1
0       2       3       9
1       0       4       16
1       1       6       36
1       2       9       81
```

```
2        0        11        121
2        1        14        196
2        2        18        324
```

6.4 COMPOUND CONDITIONS IN A *while (expression)*

For a condition such as *while (i>=2, j<= 4)* the *i* should have initial value of 2 or more so that the loop can start. If you put the initial value of *i* as 0 or 1 the loop will not start. In this *while* expression the termination of the loop is controlled by condition *j<=4*.

PROGRAM 6.4 – The program illustrates **compound condition** in ***while*** (expression).

```
#include <iostream>
using namespace std;
int main()
{
int x =0,i=2,y;
 cout<<"\ti \tx \ty" <<endl;
  while ( i>=2,i<=4 ) // compound while expression
 {
 x = 2*i;
  y = x*x;
  cout <<i<< "\t"<<x <<"\t"<< y<<endl;
   i =i+1; }
 return 0;
}
```

The expected output is given below.

```
i        x        y
2        4        16
3        6        36
4        8        64
```

More than one conditional expressions with different variables separated by comma (,) may be put in *while* expression as illustrated below.

```
while ( i>=2, j<=5, k <= 6)
```

In such cases the loop is terminated by the last condition in the expression. In the above mentioned case, the value of k controls the termination of loop. However, the output may as well depend on the compiler you are using. Program 6.5 provides an output.

PROGRAM 6.5 – Another example of **compound condition** in ***while*** expression.

```
#include <iostream>
using namespace std;
```

```
int main()

{
int x =0,i=2,j=0,k = 0,y;
cout<<"i\tj\tk\tx\ty" <<endl;

while (i>=2, i<=4,j<=5 ,k <=6 ) // compound while condition
{
x =(i+j+k);

y = x*x;
cout <<i<<"\t"<<j<<"\t" <<k <<"\t"<<x <<"\t"<< y<<endl;
j++;
i ++;
k ++;
}
return 0;
}
```

The expected output, given below, shows that the intermediate conditions, i.e. i <= 4 and j <= 5 are ineffective. The *while* expression is evaluated in every iteration. In case i <2 the loop will not start. Once started, the loop will stop when the last expression in the *while* (expression) evaluates false. For compliance of all the conditions it would be necessary to have the conditions connected by Boolean AND operator.

i	j	k	x	y
2	0	0	2	4
3	1	1	5	25
4	2	2	8	64
5	3	3	11	121
6	4	4	14	196
7	5	5	17	289
8	6	6	20	400

COMPOUND BOOLEAN CONDITION IN *WHILE* (EXPRESSION)

Generally in most of the programs only one condition in *while* expression is used, however, there is no bar to use compound conditions. This has been demonstrated in Program 6.5. If the expressions are simply separated by comma (,) the intermediate conditions may be overlooked, however, if they are connected by Boolean && operator the loop would end with any one variable reaching the limit. The Program 6.5 is modified and run again with Boolean condition as given below.

```
while (j<5&&i>=3&&i<=10)
```

With this expression the loop will end when any one condition is violated.

PROGRAM 6.6 – The program illustrates ***while*** *loop* with compound Boolean expression.

```
#include <iostream>
using namespace std;
int main()

{int x =0,i=3,j=0,y;
 cout<<"\ti\tj\tx\ty" <<endl;

while (j< 5 && i>=3 && i<= 10)
 { x+=(i+j);
 y = x*x;

cout <<"\t"<<i<<"\t"<<j<<"\t"<<x <<"\t"<< y<<endl;
 j++;
 i++;
}
return 0;
}
```

From output given below it is clear that i has been varied from 3 onward while due to the condition on j the loop is terminated at j = 4. If Boolean operators were not put and the variables were simply separated by (,) the loop would have gone to i = 10 and j would have gone to 7 beyond the condition j<5. The output of the program is given below.

```
i        j        x        y
3        0        3        9
4        1        8        64
5        2        15       225
6        3        24       576
7        4        35       1225
```

If, however, the above while expression is put as *while (j> = 0 || i> = 3 && i<= 10)*, and the initial value of i may be less than 3, the condition will evaluate to be true and the program would run from j = 0 to i = 10.

6.5 THE *do....while* LOOP

The use of *do...while* loop is similar to *while* loop except for the fact that the while condition is evaluated at the end of program, therefore, at least one computation would be carried out even if the while condition turns out false. The following figure illustrates the execution of *do ... while* loop.

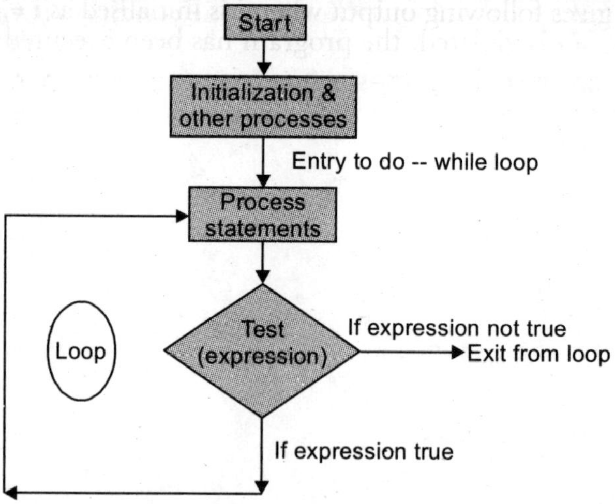

Fig. 6.2: Execution of *do — while* loop

The following program illustrates the application of *do … while* loop.

PROGRAM 6.7 – The program illustrates ***do --- while*** loop.

```
#include <iostream>
using namespace std;
void main()
{
int x =0,i =0 , y;
cout<<"i\tx\ty" <<endl;

do                          // start of do - - while loop
 {
x =2*i;
y = x*x;

cout <<""<<i<< "\t"<<x <<"\t"<< y<<endl;
 i++;}
while ( i<=3 );             //Test condition of do -- while loop
}
```

The expected output is given below.

```
i    x    y
0    0    0
1    2    4
2    4    16
3    6    36
```

The same program gives following output when i is initialised as i = 5 instead of i = 0. Even though the condition i <=3 is violated, the program has been executed for one time and gives the following output.

```
i          x          y
5          10         100
```

FACTORIAL OF A NUMBER

In the following program an application of *do...while* loop has been made to evaluate the factorial of positive numbers. The break command has been used when the factorial exceeds a certain value.

```
Factorial (n) = 1× 2 × 3 × 4 × 5 ... × ( n−1) × n
```

Or it may also be written as

```
Factorial (n) = n × Factorial (n-1)
```

which is a recursive form of function. This aspect is discussed in Chapter 7. In the following program the first form is programmed.

PROGRAM 6.8 – Illustrates calculation of **factorial numbers** with *do---while* loop.

```
#include <iostream>
using namespace std;

int main()
{
int x =0,i=0,factorial=1, limit = 500;
cout<<"i"<<"\tx"<<"\t" << "Factorial x" <<endl;

do
{ i =i+1;
x +=1;
factorial *= x;
cout <<i<<"\t"<<x <<"\t"<< factorial<<endl;
 }
while (factorial<limit );

return 0;
}
```

The output is given below. The output shows that maximum limit of 500 has been crossed. This is because the while expression is tested at the end of the loop, so when the condition is tested it is already beyond the specified limit.

```
i          x          Factorial x
1          1          1
2          2          2
3          3          6
4          4          24
5          5          120
6          6          720
```

6.6 ENDLESS *while* LOOPS

To get out of an endless loop such as *while*(true) we can make use of statement break; However, if you also want to get out of the program as well, you may use exit() function. With break statement one gets out of the loop while with exit() function one gets out of the program. The argument for *exit*() function is 0 or any integer. For some compilers 0 conveys successful termination. Thus it may be coded as

```
exit (0);
```

The function is placed after the statement where it is desired to get out of the program.

PROGRAM 6.9 – Illustrates use of **exit(0)** to terminate the endless loop and the program

```
#include <iostream>
using namespace std;

int main()
{cout<<"i\tx\ty" <<endl;
int x =0,i=0 ,y;
while (true)   // Endless while loop
{
 x = i*i ;
 y = x*x;
  if (y>300)
  exit(0);  // 0 or any integer value can be argument
 cout <<i<<"\t"<<x<<"\t"<< y<<endl;
 i++;
 }
 return 0;
}
```

The expected output is given below.

```
i       x       y
0       0       0
1       1       1
2       4       16
3       9       81
4       16      256
```

In the above program *while (true)* has been used, which is an endless loop. The loop is terminated by putting a limit on the value of one of the altering variable as the condition for exit. Such loops may also be terminated by using the statement *break ;* in the code. This is illustrated in the following program. You should note that the break statement ends with a semicolon.

PROGRAM 6.10 – The program illustrates **endless *while*** loop with **break** statement.

```
#include <iostream>
using namespace std;
int main(){
int x =0,i =1,y;
cout<<"i"<<"\tx"<<"\t" << "y" <<endl;

while (true)     //Endless loop
 { x +=i;
 y = x*x ;
  cout <<i<<"\t"<<x <<"\t"<< y<<endl ;
  i++;
if(i>= 6)
break;    // break statement
 }
return 0;
}
```

The expected output is as under.

```
i        x        y
1        1        1
2        3        9
3        6        36
4        10       100
5        15       225
```

6.7 THE *for* LOOP

The *for* loop is coded as given below.

for (initial value of variable ; conditional expression ; mode of increment /decrement) statement ;

There are three expressions inside the brackets separated by two semicolons. In the first expression the variable controlling the loop is initialised, i.e. its initial value is specified, in the second expression its final or limiting value is given, i.e. the value of the variable at which the loop should terminate, in the third expression the mode of increment/decrement is specified. The working of a *for loop* is illustrated in Fig. 6.3.

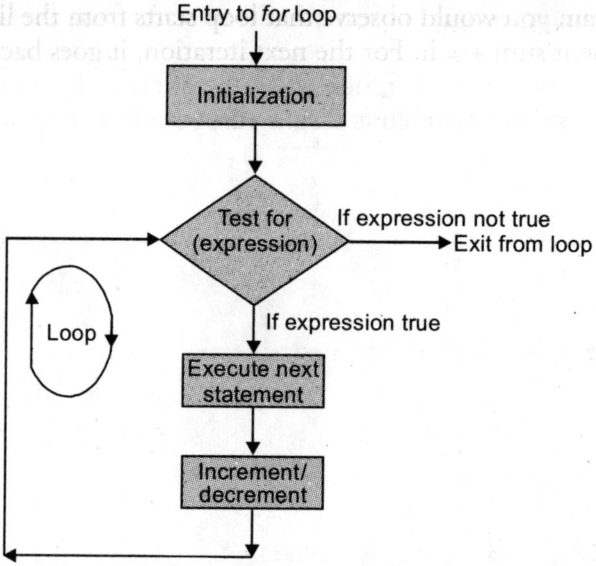

Fig. 6.3: Execution of a *for* loop

A *for* loop is illustrated below. In the following expression the variable i controls the loop.

for (int i = 0 ; i< = 10 ; i++)

statement ;

If more than one statements are to be included in the loop they should be enclosed between the curly braces {} as illustrated below.

for(int j = 20 ; j>=0 ; j–)

{ statement1;

____

statementn ; }

The program below carries out sum of numbers 1 to 10 with the help of *for* loop. The output is displayed at the end of loop.

PROGRAM 6.11 – Program illustrates ***for loop*** for sum of numbers from 1 to 10.

```
#include<iostream>
using namespace std;
main()
{int n = 10;
 sum=0 ;

for (int i=0;i<=n; i++) // beginning of loop statement
 sum += i;   // end of loop statements

cout<<"sum = "<<sum<<endl;
 return 0;
}
```

In the above program you would observe that loop starts from the line for (int i=0;i<=n;i++) and ends at the statement sum + = i;. For the next iteration, it goes back to the loop expression and repeats the process. So in every iteration the value of i is added to variable sum. At the end of looping process the sum is 55 which is displayed by output statement of the program. The expected output is given below.

```
sum = 55
```

ENDLESS *FOR* LOOP

You should note that *inclusion of the expressions in the brackets are optional but inclusion of the two semicolons is a must.* We may as well write the above *for* loop as

```
int i = 0;
for (; i<10; )
i++;                    // See program 6.26
```

We may write an endless *for* loop as below.

for (; ;)

In the above declaration there are no expressions except the two semicolons. This is an **endless *for* loop** and as already discussed above an endless loop may be stopped by using the break; statement. See the following program for an illustration.

PROGRAM 6.12 – Illustrates an **endless *for* loop**.

```
#include<iostream>
using namespace std;
int main()
{ int i =0,sum=0 ;

 for(;;) //endless for loop
{ sum += i;
if (sum >25) break; // break included to end the loop.
 cout<<"i= "<<i<<"    sum = " <<sum<<endl;
 i++;}
return 0;
}
```

The expected output is given below.

```
i= 0   sum = 0
i= 1   sum = 1
i= 2   sum = 3
i= 3   sum = 6
i= 4   sum = 10
i= 5   sum = 15
i= 6   sum = 21
```

6.8 COMPOUND CONDITIONS IN *for* (*expression*)

The *for* (*expressions*) may have conditions on more than one variables. In such compound conditions the variables are separated by comma as illustrated for *m* and *n* below.

for (int n =0, int m = 0; n <=3,m <=5; n++,m++)

In the above expression the initial values of variables are separated by comma (,), the limiting values are separated by comma and finally the modes of increments are also separated by comma. The different variables may have different modes of increment/decrement. In Program 6.13 given below two variables *n* and *m* are included in *for* loop with differing limiting values but similar modes of increment.

PROGRAM 6.13 – Illustrates **compound condition** in ***for*** (expression).

```
#include<iostream>
using namespace std;
int main()
{int n, m ;

for (n=2,m=0;n<=8,m<=3 ;n++,m++)
cout<<"n = "<<n<<", m = "<<m<<", product = " <<n*m<<endl;
return 0;
}
```

The expected output is as below.

```
n = 2, m = 0, product = 0
n = 3, m = 1, product = 3
n = 4, m = 2, product = 8
n = 5, m = 3, product = 15
```

In the above case the loop terminates at m<=3 and does not continue to n<=8. If the same program is run again with the condition *for(n=2,m=0;n<=3,m<=8 ;n++,m++)*, i.e. by interchanging the limits the loop will run up to m<=8. The control rests with the limiting factor which is last in the middle expression.

THE *FOR* LOOP WITH COMPOUND BOOLEAN EXPRESSION

If Boolean operators are used in *for* (*expression*) the above stated problem is not there, i.e. all the conditions are interconnected by Boolean operators. This is illustrated in the following program in which the *for* expression is

```
for (int i=0,j=0; i<= 4 &&j <= 16; i= i++, j= j+2)
```

In this expression the minimum limiting value is *i<=4* so loop will end at this value of *i*, because the limiting condition would evaluate true only up to *i <=4*. It is illustrated below.

PROGRAM 6.14 – Illustrates **compound Boolean condition** in ***for*** (expression).

```
#include <iostream>
using namespace std;
int main()
{ int Product;
for (int i=0,j=0; i<= 4 &&j <= 16; i++, j= j+2)
{ Product = i*j;
cout<<" i = "<<i<< "\tj = "<<j << "\tProduct = "<< Product<<endl; }
return 0;
}
```

The expected output is given below.

```
i = 0     j = 0     Product = 0
i = 1     j = 2     Product = 2
i = 2     j = 4     Product = 8
i = 3     j = 6     Product = 18
i = 4     j = 8     Product = 32
```

6.9 NESTED *for* LOOPS

If a function involves more than one variable and we want to evaluate it for different values of all the variables, we will have to use a nested *for* loop. For sake of illustration say we have a function with three integer variables *m*, *n* and *p*. If it is desired that function be evaluated for all values of *n*, *m* and *p* then a nested *for* loop, as illustrated below, may be used.

```
for ( int n=0; n<= A; n++)
 for ( int m=0; m<= B ; m++)
   { Statements;
    ----------
 for ( int p =0 ; p<= C ; p++)
    { Statements;
    --------- }
     }
```

Program 6.15 illustrates the code for a nested *for* loop for two variables *n* and *m*. In a similar way a program may be written with any number of nested loops.

PROGRAM 6.15 – Illustrates **nested *for* loops.**

```
#include<iostream>
#include<iomanip>
using namespace std;
int main()
{
```

```
    int n, m ;
    for (n=1;n<=3;n++)
     for(m=1; m<=2; m++)
     {cout<<setw(5);
   cout<<"n = "<< n<<"   m= "<<m <<"    product = "<<n*m <<endl;
    }
   return 0;
   }
```

The output of the above program is given below. You will observe that for every value of *n*, the variable *m* has been varied over its range of values, i.e. 1 and 2 .

```
n = 1   m= 1   product = 1
n = 1   m= 2   product = 2
n = 2   m= 1   product = 2
n = 2   m= 2   product = 4
n = 3   m= 1   product = 3
n = 3   m= 2   product = 6
```

6.10 GENERATION OF RANDOM NUMBERS

In many real life problems there is an element of uncertainty and require probabilistic or random sampling technique. Examples are in quality control, queues on service stations, computer games, etc. For treatment of such problems random numbers are required. A random number is one whose value cannot be predicted just as the time of occurrence of an earthquake cannot be predicted, at least, at present. It is nearly impossible to get truly random numbers, however, pseudorandom numbers may be generated. In C++ the following two functions are used which are provided in the header file **<cstdlib>**.

```
int rand();
void srand (unsigned seed);
```

The function `rand()` produces random numbers in the range from 0 to a maximum number called RAND_MAX provided in the header file. If only `rand()` is used it would produce same set of random numbers every time it is run. This is illustrated in Program 6.16 given below. However, if a seed number is provided to random number generator by the function `srand()` it would produce a different set of random numbers. Every time `rand()` is run a different seed number has to be provided to get a different set of random numbers. This is illustrated in Program 6.17 given on the next page.

PROGRAM 6.16 – Illustrates generation of **random numbers** with **rand()** function.

```
#include<iostream>
#include<cstdlib>
using namespace std;

int main()
```

```
{int n ;

for (n=1;n<=6;n++)
cout << rand()<<"\n";
return 0;
}
```

Output of the first trial: In the above program no seed number is fed and *rand*() function produces the set of 6 random numbers given in the output below. If the program is run again it will produce the same set of random numbers as illustrated in the second run of the program.

```
41
18467
6334
26500
19169
15724
```

The output of the second trial is given below. It is same as the output of first trial.

```
41
18467
6334
26500
19169
15724
```

From the above outputs it is clear that every time the random number function is called it will produce the same set of random numbers. Such a condition is not desirable because it smells some kind of setting. Many times, in situations such as in draw of lots it is required to assure the audience that the random number generated are not in any way biased. In such cases, a person from the audience may be asked to enter a seed number. This is a case where user of program provides the seed number. Program 6.17 given below solves this problem. In the first trial run, the seed number provided is 211and the random numbers generated are given in the output. In the second trial the seed number is 151 and we get a different set of random numbers in the output.

PROGRAM 6.17 – Illustrates **random number** generation with a **seed number**.

```
#include<iostream>
#include<cstdlib>
using namespace std;

int main()
{
int n , S ;
 cout<< "Write a positive seed number : ";
cin>> S;
```

```
  srand(S);

  for (n=1;n<=6;n++)
  cout << rand()<<"\n";
  return 0;
   }
```

With seed number 211, the following output is obtained.

```
Write a positive seed number : 211
727
14641
22258
756
22542
21137
```

With seed number 151 the output is as below.

```
Write a positive seed number : 151
531
25096
31752
31517
26260
14909
```

In programs such as computer games it is not possible for user to provide a seed number on every event in the game. In order to get around such problems we may make use of function time() defined in the header file **<ctime>**. The function `time(Null)` gives a number which is equal to the number of seconds elapsed up till now since 1st January 1970 Greenwich time 00:00:00. This number is always changing and can provide a different seed number every time `rand()` is run. The code is `srand (time(Null));`.

In the following program, time has been used for the seed number. The header file <ctime> of C++ standard library has been included. The code for using time () as seed number is as below.

```
long unsigned time(Null);
```

The program given below also displays the value of seed number.

PROGRAM 6.18 – Illustrates use of **time( )** as **seed number**.

```
#include<iostream>
#include<cstdlib>
#include <ctime>
using namespace std;
main()
```

```
{int n ;
long unsigned seed(time( NULL )) ;
 srand(seed);
 cout <<"seed = " << seed<<endl;
cout<< "The random numbers are as below."<<endl;
for (n=1;n<=6;n++)
cout << rand()<<"\n";
return 0;
}
```

The output is given below.

```
seed = 1183200663
The random numbers are as below.
29589
3656
1276
1828
24019
21122
```

Random Numbers in a Specified Range

For obtaining random numbers between zero and a limiting high value say High, we may take the modulus of random numbers generated by rand() with (High +1). However, if it is desired to obtain random number between two limits say High and Low we may use the following code.

```
Randnumber = rand() %(High - Low +1) + Low;
```

PROGRAM 6.19 – Illustrates generation of **random numbers** in **specified range**.

```
#include<iostream>
#include<cstdlib>
#include<ctime>
using namespace std;
int main()
{
 long Randnumber ;
long unsigned seed(time( NULL )) ;
  srand(seed);
  cout<< "seed = "<<seed<<endl;
cout<< "Random numbers in two digits (less than 100)"<<endl;
for (int n=1;n<=10;n++)
```

```
  { Randnumber = rand();
      cout << Randnumber %100<<"  ";
   }
cout << "\n";
cout<< "Random numbers for dice play (High = 6, Low = 1).\n";
for (int k=1;k<=10;k++)
 { Randnumber = rand();
  cout << Randnumber%6 + 1<<"  "; //for High = 6, Low = 1.
 }
return 0;
}
```

The expected output is given below.

```
seed = 1225696985
Random numbers in two digits (less than 100)
15 19 36 10 22 84 31 59 40 13
Random numbers for dice play (High = 6, Low = 1).
6 2 3 5 6 4 4 3 4 4
```

6.11 THE *goto* STATEMENT

The code *goto* is used in many programming languages for moving back and forth in the program. In C++ the code lines are not numbered as is the case in some other programming languages. Therefore, for using *goto* statement one needs to put in a label. At the starting point, i.e. point from where the jump is to be executed we simply code as *goto name_of_label* as illustrated below.

```
statements;
goto name_of_label ;            //code at point of jump
_______
statements;
name_of_label :          //code at destination of jump.
statements;
```

At the destination, the label name is put at the start of line and it has to be followed by colon (:) as illustrated above. Any other statement is put on right side of colon or in next line. In the following program we have put the label name as *Again.* So at the point of jump the statement is written as *goto Again;*. At the destination it is *Again:* . The following program illustrates the application of *goto* statement for iteration.

PROGRAM 6.20 – Illustrates use of ***goto*** statement for going back in program.

```
#include <iostream>
using namespace std;
int main()
 {
 int n , m ;
 cout <<"Write and enter two integers: " ; cin>> n>> m;
cout << "You have written the numbers as n= "<<n <<" and m = "<<m <<endl;

 Again :   //The label Again, see colon at end.
if(n<m)
 n++;
else
 m++;
if(n == m)
 cout<<"Now m = " << m<<" and n = " << n<<"\n";
else
 goto Again;   // Jump back to Again making a loop
 return 0;
 }
```

The expected output of the above program is given below.

```
Write and enter two integers: 40 60
You have written the numbers as n= 40 and m = 60
Now m = 60 and n = 60
```

In the following program *goto* command has been used for moving forward in the program.

PROGRAM 6.21 – The program illustrates ***goto*** command with a ***while*** loop.

```
#include <iostream>
using namespace std;
int main()
{
cout<<"i\tx\ty" <<endl;
 int x =0,i= 0 ,y;
while (true)
 { i =i+1;
 x = 2* i ;
  y = x*x;
if (y>100)
goto End;    // 'End' is the name of label.
cout <<i<<"\t"<<x <<"\t"<< y<<endl;
}
End:
return 0 ; }
```

The expected output is given below.

```
i      x      y
1      2      4
2      4      16
3      6      36
4      8      64
5      10     100
```

6.12 THE *continue* STATEMENT

The *continue* command may be used to bring the control back to the top of a loop before all the statements in the program are executed. The following program illustrates the application of *continue* and *goto* commands. In the program an integer 20 is decreased by 1 in each iteration till a number divisible by 7 is reached. On getting the number the *goto* statement takes the program to the end.

PROGRAM 6.22 – The program illustrates the use of ***continue*** and ***goto*** commands.

```
#include <iostream>
using namespace std;

int main()
 {
int n =7 , m=20 ;
 while(n<m)
 {m= m-1;
if (m% n ==0)
 goto end;
else
 continue; }
 end: cout<<"m = " << m<<" and n = " << n<<"\n";
  return 0; }
```

The expected output obtained on running the program is given below.

```
m = 14 and n = 7
```

6.13 INPUT WITH A SENTINEL

Sometimes it is not known as to how many entries will be there or the entries may be limited but you do not wish to count them. For such cases you may use an endless loop for input of data using *cin* function. You may also incorporate a conditional statement that if an entry value is equal to a specified value which is not likely to be there in the usual entries, the program should get out of loop and process the data already entered. This is called input with a **sentinel.**

The following program illustrates an application of input with a sentinel.

PROGRAM 6.23 – Illustrates input with a **sentinel**.

```
#include<iostream>
using namespace std;
main()
{
int Marks , Entry_no = 0 ;
double Av_Marks, total = 0.0;
while (1)
{ Entry_no++;
cout<< "Entry_no = " <<Entry_no <<endl;
cout<<"Enter the marks = "; cin >> Marks;

if (Marks >100) {cout<<"last entry not counted \n"; break;}
total = total + Marks;
Av_Marks = total/Entry_no;
}
cout << "Total Entries = " <<Entry_no <<endl;
cout << "Average Marks = " << Av_Marks << endl;
return 0 ;
}
```

In this program it is taken that the maximum marks are not going to be more than 100. So the condition for break has been put as if (Marks > 100) break; After getting out of the loop the program calculates the average marks obtained by students. The output of the above program is given below.

```
Entry_no = 1
Enter the marks = 50
Entry_no = 2
Enter the marks = 80
Entry_no = 3
Enter the marks = 90
Entry_no = 4
Enter the marks = 60
Entry_no = 5
Enter the marks = 44
Entry_no = 6
Enter the marks = 110
last entry not counted
Total Entries = 5
Average Marks = 64.8
```

EXERCISES

1. How do you write a *for* loop expression?
2. Give a sample code for endless *for* loop.
3. Make a program using endless *for* loop and use break; statement to get out of it.
4. Make a small program to illustrate an endless *while* loop and use *exit* () function to end the program.
5. Write a program using *while* loop to make a multiplication table of 1.25 from 1×1.25 to 10×1.25.
6. What is the difference between *while* loop and *do … while* loop?
7. Make a program using *for* loop to display square roots of numbers from 1 to 5.
8. Write a program to convert inches into millimetres and millimetres into inches.
9. The function 2y + 3xy –6zx + 4z is to be evaluated for x = 1 to 4, for y = 2 to 5 and z = 3 to 6. Write a program with nested *for loops* to achieve this.
10. Write an endless *for loop* to read a number of integers. It should exit when 000 is entered. The program should display total number of entries and average value of the entered data.
11. Make a C++ program to generate random numbers with seed number provided by user.
12. Make a program with *for loop* to generate 6 random numbers less than 1000 by using function *time()* for generating the seed number.

    Answer: Type and run the following program to get a set of random numbers less than 1000.

PROGRAM 6.24 – Illustrates generation of three digit random numbers.

```
#include<iostream>
#include<cstdlib>
#include<ctime>
using namespace std;
int main()
{
 long Randnumber ;
 cout<< "Random Numbers are"<<endl;
long unsigned seed= time( NULL ) ;
srand(seed);
for (int n=1;n<=6;n++)
{Randnumber = rand()%1000;
cout << Randnumber<<"\n";
}
return 0;
}
```

The following output is obtained by running the program.

```
Random Numbers are
411
809
767
51
671
123
```

13. Find mistakes in the following program. Correct it and run it.

```
#include <iostream>
using namespace std;
void main()
{
int x = 0;
do;
{
cout<< "\tcube of "<< x <<" = "<<x*x*x <<endl;
x +=1;
}
while(x<=4)
return 0;
}
```

14. Write an iteration program with endless *while* loop. Make use of `exit()` function to get out of it.
15. Make a program with *do—while* loop to calculate the square roots of numbers from 1 to 10.
16. Write a program with endless *while* statement and make use of break statement to terminate the loop.
17. Make a program to illustrate the use of *goto* statement.
18. Make program to illustrate the use of *continue* statement.
19. Make a program to evaluate the following function for x = 4 to 8, y = 2 to 3 and z = 5.

    $4x^3 z + 5 y z + 10 x y z$

20. Construct a program with *for loop* to evaluate a truth table for the Boolean expression. !(A||B)

Answer:

```
#include <iostream>
using namespace std;
int main()
```

```
{ int A , B ;
for ( A =0; A<2 ; A++)
{for(B =0;B<2; B++)
cout<< "A = "<<A << " B = "<<B << " !( A||B)= " << !(A||B)<<endl;}
return 0;
}
```

21. Make a program for integration of x in the limits specified by user.

Answer:

For integration of a function f(x) between the limits a and b, we follow the well known trapezoidal rule as illustrated below.

$$\int_a^b f(x)\,dx = h\left(\frac{1}{2}f_0 + f_1 + f_2 + f_3 + \cdots + f_{n-1} + \frac{1}{2}f_n\right) - \frac{nh^3}{12}f^{||}(\xi)$$

Where

$h = (b - a)/\,n$

$f_0 = f(a)$

$f_n = f(b)$

$f_k = f(a + k \times h)$

The last term goes to zero as *n* goes to ¥. The method is illustrated in the following program.

PROGRAM 6.25 – Illustrates calculation of integral of x between the limits specified by user.

```
#include <iostream>
#include <cmath>
using namespace std;
int main () {
double x , Lower_Limit , Upper_Limit , Integral , h, F;
int n = 100;
 cout<<"Enter the limits of integral :\n" ;
 cout<< "Upper_Limit = "; cin >> Upper_Limit ;
 cout<< "Lower_Limit = " ; cin>> Lower_Limit;
h = (Upper_Limit - Lower_Limit )/n;
 Integral = 0.5 * (Lower_Limit + Upper_Limit)*h;
 for ( int i =1; i<n; i++)
{F = (Lower_Limit + i*h)*h ;
 Integral += F; };
 cout << "Integral of x = " << Integral <<endl;
 return 0 ;
 }
```

The expected output is given below. The user has put in the limits as 8 and 2 so the result is 30.

```
Enter the limits of integral :
 Upper_Limit = 8.0
 Lower_Limit = 2.0
 Integral of x = 30
```

22. Make a program to integrate x^n in the range for x = a to x = b. Also develop a program to integrate any polynomial in the limits a to b.
23. Make a test program to illustrate endless *for* loop.
24. Make a program with *for* loop having only middle expression.

    Answer: The program is given below.

PROGRAM 6.26 – Illustrates *for* loop with only middle expression.

```
#include<iostream>
using namespace std;
main()
{int n = 10,sum=0, i=0 ;
for ( ;i<=10; )
{sum +=i;
i++;}
cout<<"sum = "<<sum<<endl;
return 0;
}
```

The program runs and output is as below.

```
sum = 55
```

❍❍❍

CHAPTER

7 Functions

7.1 INTRODUCTION

Generally we take a function as some formula type mathematical entity whose numerical value has to be found if parameters are given. However, in C++ along with the formula type, a function in the broader sense may be considered as a component of a big program. A large program may be divided into suitable small segments and each segment may be treated and defined as a function. These segments can be separately compiled, tested and verified. So division of a very large program into manageable smaller functions or modules not only makes the development process easier it also makes it possible to involve a large number of programmers in the development process. The different functions/program segments may be developed separately by different programmers and then combined into a single program. Such a scheme makes it easier to locate bugs. Moreover, the maintenance of a big program also becomes easier.

The purpose of a function is to receive data, process it and return a value to the function which has called it. The terms *calling function* and *called function* are derived from the telephone communication. The one who rings the number is the *calling* person and one who receives the call is the one *called*. The same terminology applies to functions. Thus the function which calls another function is the *calling function* and the function which is called is the *called function*. The different data variables that a function accepts for processing are called *parameters* of the function. The values that represent the parameters and are passed on to the function when it is called, are the arguments of the function. Some functions return a numeric value to the calling function. These are called **return type functions.** If a function does not return a numeric value we call it **void function**. A function may be void but it still may be processing integer type, floating type or other types of data. The function is still called void. Similarly a function may not be void but still may not have any argument to operate upon, in that case, its arguments are void.

A programmer should understand how to declare a function, define a function and call a function. In a program a function has to be declared and defined only once. Then it may be called as many times as required. The functions which are declared and defined by a programmer are called **user defined functions** or *programmer defined functions.* Besides, C++ Standard Library has a large collection of predefined functions which can also be used by a programmer. We have already dealt with some such functions such as swap (), sqrt (), etc. We shall discuss more of these in this chapter. Below, Fig.7.1 shows a general procedural program in which other functions are called.

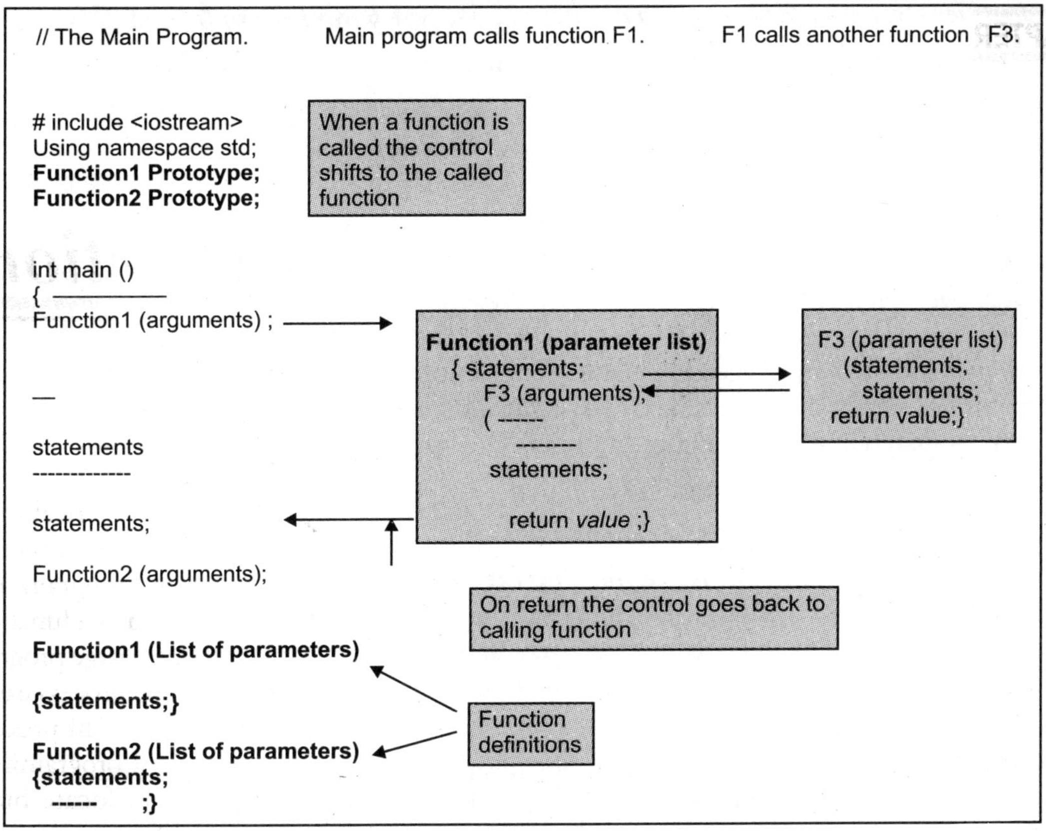

Fig. 7.1

Figure 7.1 shows that main program contains a number of statements and also function calls. When function F1 is called the action already taken by computer on main program is saved and control shifts to the called function F1. The function F1 during its execution calls another function F3 and the action already done in F1 is saved and control shifts to the function F3. On completion of F3 the control comes back to F1 and on completion of F1 the control comes back to the main program. The main program proceeds from where it was left when F1 was called.

7.2 USER DEFINED FUNCTIONS

A function has a head and a body. A complete definition of a function comprises both head and body. The head gives the information about *type* of function, name of function and a list of parameters enclosed in parentheses. The *type* of function is the type of data it returns. Thus if the data returned is integer the function *type* is *int*. If the function returns a floating point number, the *type* of function is *float* or *double*, etc. If the function does not return any numeric data its type is *void*. However, it is possible to separate the declaration of head or prototype of function and the definition of a function. A function body comprises statements and expressions enclosed between a pair of braces {} and which perform the task of function. The function definition which comprises both head and body, is illustrated below.

***type identifier* (*type parameter1, type parameter2, ---, type parameter n*)** // head of function

{statements ;} // body of function

In the above definition the first word is the *type* of function, it is the *type of data it returns.* The second item is identifier which is the name of function. The name may be decided in the same way as we decide the name of a variable. One has to follow the same rules as given in Chapter 3 for identifiers for variables.

The method of declaration of parameters (third item) is equally important. The parameters are written between a pair of parentheses ( ). The *type* of each parameter such as *int*, *float* , *double* , *char*, etc., has to be mentioned individually before the name of the parameter otherwise the compiler will take it as an integer by default. For example, suppose we want to define a function to represent the weight of a cubical body having length, width and height in whole numbers and density of its material in floating point number. The function definition is illustrated below.

```
double Weight (int Length, int Width, int Height, float Density)
 { return Length*Width*Height*Density ;}
```

Here the name of function is *Weight*. The first word *double* is its *type* because the *type* of return value is double. Length, Width, Height are names of three integer type parameters representing length, width and height respectively, and, Density is the name of a parameter which is a floating point number and represents density of material. You should note that each parameter is preceded by its *type* individually.

The body of function comprises the statements and expressions required to perform the task of function, and are enclosed between curly braces {}. In the above definition there is only one statement which returns the product of all the arguments. Arguments are the values of parameters, some authors call them as actual parameters. The following points should be noted when declaring a function head.

(i) All the parameters are enclosed in the parentheses and are separated by comma.

(ii) The *type* of each parameter is declared individually. If the type of a parameter is not mentioned the compiler may take it as an integer by default.

(iii) There is no semicolon at the end of head line if it is followed by body otherwise there is semicolon.(;) at the end of header.

Now we have to decide as to where the function definition be placed in a program. **A function cannot be defined inside another function.** Therefore, the definition cannot be placed inside the main () function. It has to be outside the main () function. In a program, function definition may be placed before *main()* function, above or preferably below the names of header files or it may be done after the end of *main ()* function. The declaration and definition may be separated as well, i.e. the declaration (function head followed by semicolon) or function prototype may be placed above the main () and definition (both head and body) may be placed below the end of the main () function. Some compilers require that function head or prototype be given before it is invoked in the main() function. The definition may be placed after the end of main () function. Fig. 7.2 illustrates the different placements of a function in a program. The function prototyping is discussed after this.

```
// Main program

# include <iostream>
using namespace std;
Function Prototype;
int main ()
{
statements ;
Function (arguments) ;   <-- // Function Call
________
 return 0; }

Function definition
```

Fig. 7.2 (a): Prototype above the main() and definition below the main()

```
// Main program

# include <iostream>
 using namespace std;
Function definition
int main ()
{ statements ;

 Function (arguments);   <-- // Function Call

return 0 ;
  }
```

Fig. 7.2 (b): With function definition above main, no prototype is needed.

```
//Main program
# include <iostream>
using namespace std;
Function head ;
int main ()
{ ________
 statements;
Function ( arguments );   <-- // Function Call
________
 return 0 ;
   }
Function definition
```

Fig. 7.2 (c): Function head declared above main () and function defined after main ()

Fig. 7.2 (a, b, c) – Where to place the definition of a function in a program?

7.3 FUNCTION PROTOTYPE AND RETURN STATEMENT

A function prototype comprises *type* and *name* of the function along with list of *types* of its parameters enclosed in brackets. It ends with a semicolon as illustrated below.

type identifier (*type-of- parameter1, type-of-parameter2*, … type-of- *parameter n*);

The prototype conveys the following information to the compiler.

(i) The type of function, i.e. the type of return value.

(ii) Number of parameters of the function.

(iii) Type of each parameter.

(iv) The order in which the arguments would be placed when the function is called.

The method of declaring the *function prototype* before the `main()` and the function definition (head and body) after main () function is more popular. It is illustrated in Fig.(7.2 a). In this arrangement you need not define all the functions right in the beginning of the program. Only function prototypes are given at the beginning.

It is very important that in function prototype the *type* of each parameter is mentioned individually and *types* are placed in the same order in which the corresponding arguments would be placed when the function is called. The names of parameters may or may not be given in the prototype, however the names are necessary in the head of function in the function definition. For example, the prototype of function Weight may be declared as below.

```
double Weight ( int, int, int, double) ;
```

Observe that names of parameters are not given. In fact names are not required to be given in the prototype of a function. Compiler does not take note of names in prototype. However, if you have mentioned names the complier will not give error either. Therefore, you may as well write the prototype of function Weight, discussed above, as

```
double Weight(int Length, int Width, int Height, float Density);
```

You should note that **a function prototype ends with a semicolon (;).**

For **calling the function** in the main() or in any other function you need to mention the name of function followed by arguments (values of parameters) in parentheses and end the line by a semicolon. The above function Weight may be called as below.

```
Weight (a, b, c, d);
```

Here a, b, c and d are the actual values of parameters or arguments (some authors call actual parameters). In this instance, Length takes value a, Width takes the value b , Height takes the value c and Density takes the value d. It is important that the values are put in the same order as declared in the prototype, because the compiler would take them in the same order. Also their *types* should be the same as declared in the prototype. For example if you put a = 4.5 while it stands for *int Length,* the compiler would chop off the fractional part and will take it as 4 which can lead to errors. Therefore, it is again reminded that **data arguments be given in the same order and type as given in the declaration of function prototype.** If this rule is not followed the program will give erroneous results.

Return Statement

When we call a function the program control goes to the first line of the called function and various statements of the function are evaluated. In case of void functions, the function ends at the occurrence of the last closing right brace (}). Thereafter, the control automatically comes back to calling function. It is optional to put the last statement in the function as

```
return;
```

In case of return type functions the return value is transferred to calling function through a return statement and then at close of last right brace (}) control passes on to calling function. Therefore, the last statement in the return type function is as below.

```
return value;
```

For instance, in the definition of Weight the last statement is as below (in fact body has only one statement).

```
{return Length*Width*Height*Density;}
```

On encountering the last closing brace '}' the control comes back to the main program at the point where it left at the time of function call.

A function returns only one value. However by using pointers one may get to parametric values and thus more than one values may be obtained (see Chapter 9 on pointers).

In Program 7.1 given below we illustrate a user defined function. It calculates the weight of a cubical body. In this program the function Weight has been defined before the *main* () function and hence, there is no need of function prototype.

PROGRAM 7.1 – Illustrates a **user defined function** which calculates the weight of a prismatic bar.

```
#include<iostream>
 using namespace std;
     // Function defined above main
double Weight ( int L, int W, int H, float Rho)
{return L*W*H*Rho ; } //Rho is density of material
int main()
 {
 int A =2,B = 3,C = 1 ;
 float D = 7.5;

cout<<" Length ="<<A<< ", Width = "<<B<< ", Height = " <<C <<", Density =
"<< D <<endl;
cout << " Weight of bar = "<<Weight(A,B,C,D)<< "\n ";
// A, B, C and D are taken in the order L,W,H,Rho declared in function head.
return 0 ;
}
```

The expected output of the program is given below.

```
Length =2, Width = 3, Height = 1, Density = 7.5
Weight of bar = 45
```

In the following program, the function has been defined at the end of main() function. In such cases it is required that function head followed by semicolon or prototype be declared before the main().

PROGRAM 7.2 – Illustrates **declaration of function** above main and **definition** below the main function.

```
#include<iostream>
 using namespace std;
 int Function (int x); //Function head or prototype in which
  // it is not necessary to put the names of variable.
```

```
int main()
 { int n;

 cout << "    Number   \t  Square" <<endl;
 for ( n = 0;n <=5;++n)
 cout<< "     "<< n <<"     \t" << Function(n) <<endl;
return 0;
}

 int Function(int x)    // Function head
 { int Square = x*x;  //Function body
  return Square; }
```

The expected output is given below.

```
Number      Square
0             0
1             1
2             4
3             9
4            16
5            25
```

In the following program function ptototype has been declared before main and function definition is given after the main (). In the function prototype only the *type* of each parameter separated by comma have been mentioned. The names of parameters need not be given in a function prototype. **A function prototype ends with a semicolon.** The following program calculates the sum of squares of two integers.

PROGRAM 7.3 – Illustrates placing **function prototype** before main() and **definition** at the end of main()

```
 #include<iostream>
 using namespace std;

int Funct(int , int ) ;                       // Function prototype
                                    // only types of parameters given.
int main()
 { int n , m;
 cout << "n       m     Sum of squares" <<endl;

for (int i = 0;i<=5;i++)
 { n = i;
  m = 2*i;
  cout<< n <<"\t"<<m <<"\t"<< Funct(n,m) <<endl;}
```

```
            // Function called as Funct(n,m)
    return 0;
    }
                                        // function definition
    int Funct(int x, int y)          // types and names both needed
     { int S = x*x + y*y; ;           // in head
      return S ; }
```

The expected output of the program is given below.

```
n         m      Sum of squares
0         0         0
1         2         5
2         4         20
3         6         45
4         8         80
5         10        125
```

In all the cases mentioned above you must have noticed that a function *is not defined in-side the main() function.* Inside `main()` it is only called by mentioning the function name with arguments in parentheses. For example, in the above program it is called as `Funct(n,m);`.

In the following program a function is defined to calculate the 4th power of an integer. Once defined the function may be called any number of times.

PROGRAM 7.4 – Illustrates **function definition** above the main ().

```
#include <iostream>
using namespace std;
 long power(int x)  // function definition before main ()
 {return x*x*x*x;}
int main()
{ int y = 2;
 double z;
 z = (power(y+2) -power(y))/ power(y);
cout <<"power(y) = "<< power(y)<<"\n";
cout<<"power(y+2) = "<<power(y+2)<< ", and z = " <<z<<endl;
return 0;
}
```

The program would give following result.

```
power(y) = 16
power(y+2) = 256, and z = 15
```

7.4 INTEGRATION OF A FUNCTION

For integration of a function $f(x)$ between the limits a and b, we follow the well known trapezoidal rule as illustrated below.

$$\int_a^b f(x)\,dx = h\left(\frac{1}{2} f_0 + f_1 + f_2 + f_3 + \cdots + f_{n-1} + \frac{1}{2} f_n\right) - \frac{nh^3}{12} f''(\xi)$$

Where

$h = (b - a)/n$

$f_0 = f(a)$

$f_n = f(b)$

$f_k = f(a + k \times h)$

The value ξ is a value between a and b. The last term goes to zero as n goes to ∞. The method is illustrated in the following program.

PROGRAM 7.5 – Illustrates integration of x^2

```
#include <iostream>
#include <cmath>

using namespace std;
double integral(double x ,double a, double b )
{
int n = 100;

double F, h, Sum ;

 h = (b-a)/n;
 Sum = h * ( b*b + a*a)/2;

for ( int k =1; k<n ; k++)
 {x = a + k*h;
  F = x*x;
  Sum = Sum+ h *F ;}

return Sum ;
}

int main()
{
double y ;
cout<<"Integral= "<< integral(y,2.0,4.0) <<endl;
return 0 ;
 }
```

The output is given below. It can be easily verified. $\int_2^4 x^2 = \frac{1}{3}(4^3 - 2^3) = 18.666\,6666$

```
Integral= 18.6668
```

7.5 FUNCTIONS WITH EMPTY PARAMETER LIST

Up till now we used the function as formula type, in which some numerical value is calculated and returned. But the function may, as mentioned in the introduction, just carry a message or it may be used to print or display, etc. Such functions are generally of type void and may not have any argument to act upon. Thus such functions may be defined as illustrated below.

```
void Display (void); // Display is the name of function
{cout << "You are learning C++."<< endl;}
```

Or simply

```
void Display ();
{cout << "You are learning C++."<< endl;}
```

In the following program a function is defined to display a message.

PROGRAM 7.6 – Illustrates a function with **empty parameter list**.

```
#include <iostream>
using namespace std;
void Display(void); //Function prototype, empty parameter list
void main()
{
Display();    // Program calls the function
}
void Display()    //Function definition
{cout<< "Come! Let us learn C++."<<endl;
cout<<"Have you any prior knowledge of C++?"<<endl;
cout<< "Or would you like to start from the beginning?" <<endl;
 }
```

The expected output is given below

```
Come! Let us learn C++.
Have you any prior knowledge of C++?
Or would you like to start from the beginning?
```

7.6 FUNCTION OVERLOADING

The term refers to more than one function having the same name in a program. The overloaded functions must have either different number of arguments or have arguments of different *type*. Even if one argument is of different *type* in the overloaded functions the compiler will not give an error signal.

This is illustrated in the following program in which three different functions having same name Product () are declared. The compiler can find the appropriate function by comparing the arguments. The prototype of one function is *int Product (int , int , int);* , of the second is *int Product (int, int);* which has different number of arguments though all are of type int and of the third function is *double Product (int, double);* . This function has same name but one parameter is int while other is double, besides its type is also different, so it is different from the other two.

PROGRAM 7.7 – Illustrates overloaded functions.

```
#include<iostream>
using namespace std;
int Product(int, int);              //Three functions with same name
int Product (int,int,int);
double Product( int, double);
int main()
{int a = 5,b = 6, c= 2;
double d = 5.5;

cout << "Product of a and b = " << Product(a,b) << endl;
cout<< "Product of a, b and c = " << Product(a,b,c) <<endl;
cout << "Product of b and d = " << Product(b,d)<< endl;
return 0;
}

int Product(int x, int y)   // definition of function
 {return x*y;}

double Product(int A, double B) // definition of function
 { return A*B;}

int Product(int n, int m, int k) // definition of function
 {return n*m*k;}
```

The expected output is given below.

```
Product of a and b = 30
Product of a, b and c = 60
Product of b and d = 33
```

7.7 THE inline FUNCTIONS

When a program consists of a large numbers of functions considerable time of computer is wasted in the function call routine that it has to follow. When a function is called, the processor saves the present status of the current program, evaluates the function and returns to resume the ongoing program. In case of frequently occurring small functions the overburden of function call may be considerable and can make the program inefficient. At the same time writing of the function code whereever it occurs in the program would make the program long and crude. It is not a welcome feature even for maintenance of the software. So the concept of **inline function** is evolved. We define the function only once in the program. It is preceded with key word **inline** as illustrated below. The compiler substitutes the code of the function whereever it is called in the program. An illustration of an inline function definition is given below.

```
inline int Cube(x)
{return x*x*x ;}
```

The following program provides an illustration. In the program a general power function has been defined for integers.

PROGRAM 7.8 – Illustrates **inline function.**

```
#include<iostream>
 using namespace std;
inline int Power(int x, int n)        // inline function
{ int P = 1;                          // definition
 for (int i =0; i<n ; i++)
  P *=x;
   return P; }
int main()
{ int A = 2, B = 3, C =5;
cout<< "A square = "<< Power(A,2);   // function call
cout << "\nB to the power 4 = "<< Power(B,4); // function call
cout<<"\nC to the power 3 = "<< Power(C,3)<<endl;//function call
 return 0;
  }
```

The expected output is given below.

```
A square = 4
B to the power 4 = 81
C to the power 3 = 125
```

7.8 USE OF #define FOR MACROS

The pre-processor directive #define is generally used to create symbolic constants. It may also be used to define very small functions or macros. Program 7.9 defines a macro for finding greater of the two numbers. Program 7.10 given on the next page finds the area of a rectangle by defining a macro. You will notice that no *type* is specified in the function.

PROGRAM 7.9 – A **macro** for finding maximum of two numbers.

```
#include <iostream>
using namespace std;
# define max(x,y) (x>y? x:y)
```

```
int main()
{ int A, B;
 cout<< "Write two integers :"; cin>>A>>B;
 cout << "Maximum of the two = " <<max (A,B)<< endl;
 return 0;
}
```

The expected output is given below.

```
Write two integers :60 75
Maximum of the two = 75
```

The following program is another example of macro.

PROGRAM 7.10 – A macro for finding area of rectangle.

```
#include <iostream>
using namespace std;

#define Area_Rect(x,y) ((x)*(y))
int main()
{
 double A, B;
 cout<< "Write sides of rectangle :"; cin>>A>>B;

 cout << "Area_Rect(A,B) = " <<Area_Rect(A,B) << endl;
return 0;
}
```

The expected output is given below.

```
Write sides of rectangle :30.5 4.5
Area_Rect(A,B) = 137.25
```

Factorial of a Number

Factorial of a number is also discussed in Section 7.11 of this chapter under the heading recursive functions. The factorial n is also written as n!. It is defined below.

```
n! = n(n-1)(n-2)(n-3) ...1
with 1! = 1 and 0! = 1
```

This can be achieved as below,

```
{int Factorial =1;
for ( int i =1; i<=n; i++)
Factorial *= i;
return Factorial; }
```

The factorial of a number may also be obtained as carried out in the following program.

PROGRAM 7.11 – Illustrates function to evaluate **factorial** of a number.

```
#include <iostream>
long fact(int i)

{ if (i < 0) return 0;
 int k = 1;
 while (i > 0)
 k *= i- -;
 return k;
 }
using namespace std;

int main()
{
    int n,m;
    long p;
    m = 5;
    n=3;
    p = fact(m)/fact(m-n);

cout <<"Factorial 6 = " <<fact(6)<<", Factorial 4 = "<<fact(4)<< ", p = "
<<p<<endl;

return 0;
}
```

The output obtained by running the program is given below.

```
Factorial 6 = 720, Factorial 4 = 24, p = 60
```

7.9 C++ STANDARD LIBRARY FUNCTIONS

The Standard C++ Library contains a large collection of predefined functions which may be called and used by programmers. Here we take the functions belonging to the header file <cmath>. However, there are many other functions in various header files in C++ standard library. We have already got the experience of using the functions `rand()`, `srand()`, `sqrt()` and `swap()` in the previous chapters.

For using a predefined C++ Standard Library function we have to include in our program the header file in which the function is defined. Some of the predefined functions in <cmath> header file are given in Table 7.1 below. In this table the arguments for the trigonometric functions such as sin(x) or cos(x), etc., are in radians, i.e. the values of x is in radians. Similarly the return value of function such as acos(y) = $\cos^{-1}$ (y) is also in radians.

There are a large number of other functions belonging to various header files such as <iostream>, <string> , <set> ,<map>, etc. These are dealt in the relevant chapters.

The following program illustrates, how to call C++ Standard Library functions and use them. If the result is expected in floating point number, better take it as *double.*

PROGRAM 7.12 – The program illustrates evaluation of some **functions of <cmath>.**

```
#include <iostream>
#include <cmath>
using namespace std;

int main()
 {

int a = 3600,b =10,c = -30 ,d = 3;
 double A,B1,B2,B1f,B1c,Cabs ,Dexp;
A = sqrt(a);                    // returns square root of a number
Dexp= exp(d);                   // returns e^d
B1 = log(b);                    // returns log of b to the base e
B2 =log10(b);                   // log(b) to the base 10
B1f=floor(B1);                  // returns lower integral value
B1c=ceil(B1);                   // returns just higher integral value.
Cabs =fabs(c);                  // returns absolute value

cout<< " Value of e to the power3= Dexp = " <<Dexp<<endl;
cout << " log of 10 to base e = B1 = " <<B1 <<endl;

cout << " log of 10 to the base 10 = " << B2 << endl;
cout << " Floor value of B1 = " << B1f << endl;

cout<< " Ceil value of B1 = "<<B1c<<endl;

cout<<" Absolute value of c = "<< Cabs <<" and A = "<<A<< endl;

return 0;
}
```

The output of the program is as below.

```
Value of e to the power 3 = Dexp = 20.0855
Log of 10 to base e = B1 = 2.30259
log of 10 to the base 10 = 1
Floor value of B1 = 2
Ceil value of B1 = 3
Absolute value of c = 30 and A = 60
```

The first line of output gives value of sqrt(a). The second line of output gives value of e^3. The third line of output gives log of 10 to the base e, the fourth line is the log of 10 to the base 10 so value is 1. The floor value of B1 which is 2.30259 is the next lower integer and so it is 2. Similarly the upper integer (ceil (B1)) value is 3. The value of c is – 30, so its absolute value is 30.

Table 7.1 – Some functions in **<cmath>** header file

Function	Description
Trigonometric Functions	
cos(x)	cosine of x, here x is in radians
sin(x)	sine of x, here x is in radians
tan(x)	tan of x, here x is in radians
acos(y)	inverse of cosine, output in radians
asin(y)	inverse of sine, output in radians,
atan (y)	inverse of tangent, output in radians
Other Functions	
round offs to higher integer value	
ceil (x)	Thus *ceil (2.76)* returns 3
exp(x)	returns value of e^x
fabs(x)	returns absolute value of x
floor(x)	rounds offs to lower integer value. *floor (2.76)* returns 2
log(x)	returns value of $\log_e$ (x)
$\log_{10}$(x)	returns value of $\log_{10}$(x)
sqrt(x)	returns value of square root of x
pow(n , m)	returns value of n^m

The calling of trigonometric functions of C++ Standard Library is illustrated in the Program 7.13 below. The value of angle in all these functions is in radians.

PROGRAM 7.13 – The program illustrates evaluation of **trigonometric functions**.

```
#include <iostream>
#include <cmath>
using namespace std;

int main()
{
 int a =60,b=45,c=30;
double alpha, beta, gama, C, S ,T ,theta, pi;
pi = 3.14159;
```

```
alpha = a*pi/180; //converting angle from degrees to radians.
 beta = b*pi/180;
 gama = c*pi/180;

C = cos (alpha); // calling trigonometric functions
 T = tan(beta);
  S = sin(gama);

 cout.precision(4); // number of digits desired in output
 cout << "cos 60 = " <<C <<endl;
 cout << "tan 45 = " << T << endl;
 cout << "sin 30 = " << S << endl;

theta = acos (0.5)*180/pi; // conversion of radians into degrees
cout << "cos inverse 0.5 = " << theta << " degrees" << endl;
return 0;
}
```

The expected output is given below.

```
cos 60 = 0.5
tan 45 = 1
sin 30 = 0.5
cos inverse 0.5 = 60 degrees
```

It may be reminded that for evaluations of trigonometric functions such as cosine, sine etc. the angles are expressed in radians. In case of inverse functions such as acos() or asin(), etc., the return values are also in radians. In the above program the angles are converted from degrees to radians for evaluations of sine, cosine etc. and from radians to degrees in case of inverse trigonometric functions.

7.10 PASSING ARGUMENTS BY VALUE AND BY REFERENCE

A reference to a variable is, in fact, an alias or another name for the same variable. Address of a reference is the same as that of the variable to which it is a reference. A reference to a variable is created by the declaration illustrated below.

```
int n = 10;
int& Number = n;
```

Here Number is reference to variable n. Similarly for other type of data we can create references as given below.

```
double Price = 5.6 ;
double & Money = Price;
    char ch = 'B'.
     char & kh = ch ;
```

Here Money is a reference to Price and kh is a reference to ch. Dealing with a reference is as good as dealing with the variable itself. If the value of reference is changed it also changes the value of variable. For more details on the topic see Chapter 9 on pointers and references.

When we pass the arguments to a function by value we pass on the copies of values of the variables to the function. The function may change the values of these copies but the values of variables are not changed because the function does not know where the variables are stored and hence cannot change values of variables. However, when we pass on a reference to a function, any change in the value of reference changes the value of variable. Also note that address of a variable, where its value is stored is same as that of its reference.

In the following program a function Swap() is declared and defined to interchange the values of two variables. The values of the two variables x and y are passed on to the function. From the output we see that though the function is alright but the values of x and y are not changed. The values of their copies m and n are changed but x and y remain unchanged. In Program 7.15 given on the next page, the values are passed on to the function by references and we find the values of x and y are now swapped.

PROGRAM 7.14 – Illustrates **passing arguments by value** to a function.

```
#include <iostream>
using namespace std;

inline void Swap ( int m, int n)
{
int Temp ;
Temp = m ;
m = n;
n = Temp;

cout<< "Address of m = " << &m <<endl;
cout << "Address of n = "<<&n <<endl;
cout<< "After swapping m = " <<m <<", n = " <<n <<endl; }
/*The program illustrates User defined Swap function.It interchanges the
values.*/
int main()

{
int x ,y;
cout<<"Write two integers "<<endl ;
cout << "x = ";cin>>x; cout<<" y = "; cin>>y;

Swap( x, y);

cout <<"\nx = "<<x <<", y = " << y << endl;
cout << "Address of x = " << &x <<", Address of y = "<< &y <<endl;
return 0;
}
```

From the output of the program, given below it is clear that values of m and n have been swapped but the value of the variables x and y have not been changed. Also the addresses of m and n are different from those of x and y.

```
Write two integers
x = 36
y = 66
Address of m = 0012FF24
Address of n = 0012FF28
After swapping m = 66, n = 36
x = 36, y = 66
Address of x = 0012FF7C, Address of y = 0012FF78
```

In the following program the values are passed of by references.

PROGRAM 7.15 – Illustrates **passing arguments by references** to a function.

```
#include <iostream>
using namespace std;

 inline void Swap ( int& m, int& n)
   //&m and &n are references to variables
 { int Temp ;
 Temp= m ;
 m = n;
 n = Temp;

 cout<< "Address of m = " << &m <<endl;
 cout << "Address of n = "<<&n <<endl;
 cout<< "After swapping m = " <<m <<", n = " <<n <<endl; }
int main()

{ /*The program illustrates user defined Swap function. It exchanges the
values of variables.*/

int x ,y;
cout<<"Write two integers "<<endl ;
cout << "x = ";cin>>x; cout<<" y = "; cin>>y;
Swap( x, y);

cout <<"\nx = "<<x <<", y = " << y << endl;
cout << "Address of x = " << &x <<", Address of y = "<< &y <<endl;
return 0;
}
```

The expected output of the program is given below.

```
Write two integers
x = 36
y = 66
Address of m = 0012FF7C
Address of n = 0012FF78
After swapping m = 66, n = 36

x = 66, y = 36
Address of x = 0012FF7C, Address of y = 0012FF78
```

From the output note the following points.

(i) The values of the variables are now interchanged. Here &m and &n in the function Swap (int & m, int & n) are references to x and y respectively.

(ii) The address of a reference is same as that of variable. For instance, the address of x is same as that of m, similarly the address of y is same as that of n.

7.11 RECURSIVE FUNCTIONS

Recursion is a programming technique in which the function calls itself again and again till the desired result is obtained. Naturally, in order to limit the number of times a function calls itself there has to be parameter which increases or decreases every time the function is called and a limit is put on its final value. The action is just like a loop. A **recursive function** is one that calls itself directly or indirectly in its definition. For instance, let us consider factorial of a number n.

n ! = n (n–1) (n–2) (n–3) ... 1

This can be put as

n! = n × !(n–1)

or Factorial n = n × Factorial (n–1)

In the above expression for the evaluation of factorial n, the function Factorial (n) calls itself in the form of Factorial (n–1). If programmed in this manner it would be called recursive function. In Program 7.11 we have already evaluated factorial n but in a non-recursive way.

PROGRAM 7.16 – Illustrates **recursive function** for determining a factorial.

```
#include<iostream>
 using namespace std;
 int F( int n )
{ if (n < 0) return 0;
if (n<=1) return 1;
else
return n* F(n-1);}
int main ()
```

```
{
cout << "Factorial(6) = " <<F(6)<<endl;
cout <<"Factorial (5) = "<<F(5)<<endl;
return 0; }
```

The expected output is given below.

```
Factorial(6) = 720
Factorial(5) = 120
```

FIBONACCI NUMBERS

Fibonacci numbers provide another example of recursive function. The numbers are in a series as 0 1 1 2 3 5 8 13 21…
which can be expressed in the following way.

fibonacci(0) = 0
fibonacci(1) = 1
fibonacci(2) = 1
fibonacci(3) = fibonacci(3–1) + fibonacci(3–2) = 2
fibonacci(4) = fibonacci(4–1) + fibonacci(4–2) = 3
fibonacci(5) = fibonacci(5–1) + fibonacci(5–2)= 5
fibonacci(n) = fibonacci(n–1) + fibonacci(n–2)

The above sequence of numbers may be programmed as a recursive function as illustrated in the following program.

PROGRAM 7.17 – Illustrates generation of **Fibonacci numbers.**

```
#include<iostream>
using namespace std;

int Fib(int n){ if (n ==0 || n <2) return n ;
else
return Fib(n-1) + Fib(n-2); }

main()
{
 for(int N=0; N<=11; N++)
 cout<< Fib(N)<<"   ";
 return 0;
}
```

The expected output is given below.

0 1 1 2 3 5 8 13 21 34 55 89

The following program does calculation of cubes of a series of numbers as a recursive function.

PROGRAM 7.18 – Illustrates a **recursive function** for finding cubes of integers.

```
#include <iostream>
using namespace std;
void Recf(int x)
{ int cube ;     //Definition of function
 cube= x*x*x;
 cout<< cube <<"  ";
 if (x> 5) exit(0);
 Recf (x+1);}

int main ()
{
int x =1;
Recf (x);
return 0;
}
```

The expected output is given below.

```
1  8  27  64  125  216
```

EXERCISES

1. How is a function declared and defined?
2. Where is the user defined function placed in a program?
3. What is prototype of a function?
4. Explain the terms 'passing arguments by reference' and 'passing arguments by value'.
5. Define a function to calculate the average value of a sample of values. Write a program to read a sample of ten numbers, and display the average value by using a function.
6. How do you call a function?
7. Can you define a function inside main()?
8. How can you modularise a program with the help of functions?
9. Define a function that returns the area of a regular polygon. Make a test program to evaluate the areas of an equilateral triangle and a square each having side equal to 10 units.
10. Define a function that accepts an integer as its argument and tests whether it is even or odd. Make a program to test the function.
11. Make a program to integrate x^n and test the program by evaluating integral of x^3 between the limits x = 5 and x =10.
12. The distance D between two points with co-ordinates (x_1, y_1) and (x_2, y_2) on a plane is given by

$$D = [(x_2 - x_1)^2 + (y_2 - y_1)^2]^{1/2}$$

Define a function that returns D. Make a test program which uses the above function to determine the distance between a point P(4, 8) and Q (7,12) and displays the same on the monitor.

13. The distance D between two points in a three dimensional space is given by

$$D = [(x_2 - x_1)^2 + (y_2 - y_1)^2 + (z_2 - z_1)^2]^{1/2}$$

Here x_1, y_1, z_1 and x_2, y_2, z_2 are the co-ordinates of the two points. Declare and define the function for D. Also make program which uses the function by calling it from main(). Determine and display the distance between points P(5, 6, 8) and Q (10, 12, 30).

14. Write a program which displays the message "Come! Let us learn C++ together.". Also write a program to test your function.
15. Define a function with name sqrof() which accepts an integer and returns square of the integer.
16. Define a function which chooses the greatest of three integers. Make a program which reads the three numbers from keyboard and displays the greatest number on the monitor.
17. Define a function with name powerof () which accepts two integers m and n as arguments and returns n^m.
18. Make a test program to test the function of Q.17 to determine the value of 4^4 and 2^{32}.
19. Make a program that generates Fibonacci numbers and displays the first ten numbers.
20. Define a function to integrate sin(x). Make a test program to evaluate the integral between the limits 0 to 180 degrees.
21. Make a program of a function which integrates a small polynomial between two specified limits.
22. What are macros? Give an illustrative example.
23. Find the mistakes in the following Swap function. Correct it and run it by making a test program.

```
inline void Swap ( int x, int y)
{ int temp ;
temp = x ;
x = y;
y = temp;}
```

❍❍❍

CHAPTER

8 Arrays

8.1 DECLARATION OF AN ARRAY

An array is a sequence of objects of the same *data type*. In computer, array elements are stored in a sequence of adjacent memory blocks. Each element of an array occupies one block of memory, the size of which is allocated according to the data *type* as discussed in Chapter 3. The declaration of **one dimensional array** is done as illustrated below.

type identifier [***number of elements in array***] ***;***

The above declaration of an array comprises from left to right the *data type* of elements of the array, such as `int, float, double, char,` etc., followed by the name or identifier of array, then the number of elements in the array put in square brackets. For example, an array of 4 bills having values in whole numbers may be declared as below.

```
int Bill [4];
```

Here Bill is the name of array. It has 4 elements as indicated by 4 in square brackets. The data type of its elements is int which is put in the beginning. But in this declaration we have not given the values of elements, i.e. still the array has not been initialized. One method of initializing the elements is by equating Bill [4] with values put in curly braces { } and separated by comma as given below. Fig. 8.1 shows how a one-dimensional array is stored in computer memory.

```
Bill [4] = {20, 30, 10, 15}; // initialization of an array
```

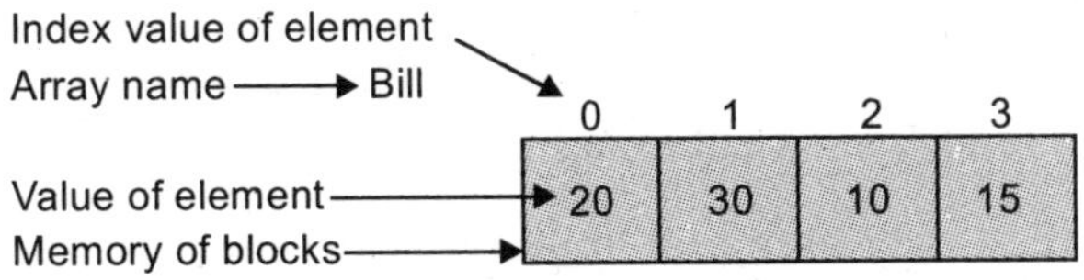

Fig. 8.1: One dimensional array in computer memory

The position of an element in array is called **array index** or **subscript** (Fig. 8.1). In case of the array `int Bill[4];` there are four elements. Their index or subscript values are 0, 1, 2 and 3. *Note that count for array elements or subscripts starts from 0.* Thus the first element of the array is Bill [0], second elements is Bill [1], the third is Bill [2] and fourth is Bill [3]. When the declaration and initialization of all the members are done together in same statement, we may or may not specify the number of elements in the square brackets. Thus the array Bill[4] may also be declared and initialized as below.

```
int Bill[] = {20,30,10,15};
```

With the declaration of an array having *n* elements, the compiler will allocate *n* memory blocks each of the size according to the data *type* for putting the values of elements of the array when these are initialized. Figure (8.1) illustrates the storage of the members of Bill [4] in the memory.

Arrays for other data types may similarly be declared and initialized. The array elements may be of type int , float, double, char or it may be an array of pointers, objects of a class or classes. For example an array with name Price consisting of 5 elements of type float, an array with name Weight with 7 elements of type double and an array with name Address having 100 characters may be declared as below.

```
float Price [5];   //The array can have 5 elements of type float
double Weight [7];  // The array can have 7 elements of type double
char Address[100];   // array can have 100 elements of type character
```

MULTI-DIMENSIONAL ARRAYS

If the elements of an array are arrays, the array is a multi-dimensional array. Let the 5 elements of an array Names be arrays of 30 characters each. It makes 'Names' a two dimensional array which may be declared as below.

```
char Names [5][30];
```

This array may be used to store 5 names each having up to 30 characters. Another instance of a two dimensional array having elements of type int is illustrated below in Fig. 8.2. It is declared and initialized as,

```
int M[2][5]= {5,2,3,2,4,6,7,8,9,8};
```

In computer memory a two dimensional array is also stored in the same way as shown in Fig.8.1, however, for a physical picture Fig. 8.2 shows how a two dimensional array may be visualised, i.e. two rows and 5 columns like a matrix.

M[2] [5]

5	2	3	2	4
6	7	8	9	8

Fig. 8.2: A two dimensional array

Similarly a three dimensional array may be declared and initialized as below.

```
int S[2][3][4]={2,1,3,4,5,8,9,7,6,5,4,8,1,2,3,4,6,7,8,9,2,4,6,3}
```

S[0][3][4]

2	1	3	4
5	8	9	7
6	5	4	8

S[1][3][4]

1	2	3	4
6	7	8	9
2	4	6	3

Fig. 8.3: A 3-dimensional array

For a physical picture we may visualise the array int `S[2][3][4]` as consisting of an array of two elements each of which is a two dimensional array. This is illustrated in Fig. 8.3.

8.2 ACCESSING ELEMENTS OF AN ARRAY

An array can have elements of one *type* only. All the elements of an array may be either integers, or floating point numbers or characters or class objects, etc., but they cannot be a mixture of different types. An element of an array is a variable of the *type* declared in the array declaration. It may be accessed by writing the name of array followed by index or subscript of the element in square brackets. Thus we may call the first element of array Bill[4] as Bill[0], the second element as Bill[1], the third element as Bill[2] and fourth element as Bill[3]. The ith element of array Bill is written as Bill[i–1]; because i starts from 0. Similarly in case of two dimensional array say M[2][5], we may call the an element belonging to ith row and jth column as M[i–1][j–1], this is because both i and j start from 0.

PROGRAM 8.1 – Illustrates declaration and initialization of an array.

```
#include <iostream>
using namespace std;
 main()
 { int Bill[4] = {20,30,10,15}; // Declaration and initialization
 double Price[5] = { 5.6, 8.3, 7.0, 6.3,7.8 };
 cout<<"Bill[0] = "<< Bill[0]<<", Bill[1] = "<<Bill[1]<<endl;
 cout<<"Bill[2] = "<< Bill[2]<<", Bill[3] = "<<Bill[3]<<"\n\n";

 for ( int i =0; i<5;i++ )    // for loop for Price output

 cout << Price [i] <<"  ";
return 0;
}
```

The output of the program gives the values of individual elements of the array as follows.

```
Bill[0] = 20, Bill[1] = 30
Bill[2] = 10, Bill[3] = 15

5.6 8.3 7 6.3 7.8
```

If the number of values assigned are less than the total number of elements declared in the array, zero is assigned to remaining elements. This is illustrated in the following program. If the array Bill[4] is initialized as below,

```
Bill[4] = {20,30};
```

the first two elements will have values 20 and 30 respectively. The remaining two elements will be assigned zero value.

PROGRAM 8.2 – Illustrates the consequence of assigning less number of values than the number of elements of array.

```
#include <iostream>
using namespace std;

int main()
 {
int Bill[4] = {20,30};
     // Two values are assigned while elements are four.

cout<<"Bill[0] = "<< Bill[0]<<", Bill[1] = "<<Bill[1]<<endl;
cout<<"Bill[2] = "<< Bill[2]<<", Bill[3] = "<<Bill[3]<<endl;
return 0;
  }
```

The expected output of the above program is given below.

```
Bill[0] = 20, Bill[1] = 30
Bill[2] = 0, Bill[3] = 0
```

In the output you see that Bill[2] and Bill[3], i.e. third and fourth elements have been assigned zero because in the initialization only two values are given. So the first two members are assigned these values.

If in the initialization, the number of values are more than the number of elements of the array, the compiler will show an error. See the following program.

PROGRAM 8.3 – Consequence of putting in more values than the array elements.

```
#include <iostream>
using namespace std;

int main()
 {
 int bill[4] = {20,30,12,21,4,32};
    // six values written while elements are only four.
 cout<<" bill[0] = "<< bill[0]<<", bill[1] = "<<bill[1]<<endl;
 cout<<" bill[2] = "<< bill[2]<<", bill[3] = "<<bill[3]<<endl;
return 0; }
```

The expected output is the following error message.

```
too many initializers
```

8.3 INPUT/OUTPUT OF AN ARRAY

As described above, the input/output of an array is carried out element by element. Therefore, either a *for* loop or *while* loop may be used for traversing the array. For example, if elements of an array *Bill[n]* having *n* elements are to be displayed on the monitor, we may write the code as below.

```
for (int i = 0; i<n; i++)
cout<< Bill[i]<<" " ;
```

The above statement will result in output of array elements in a single line, each element separated by spaces as given in double quotes " ". If it is required to mention identifier for each element along with its value, such as Bill[2] = 10 , we have to write the code as below.

```
for (int i =0; i<n; i++)
cout<< "Bill["<<i<<" ] = " <<Bill[i]<< ", ";
```

An illustration of output of the above code for array Bill[4] of Program 8.1 is given below.

```
Bill[0] = 20, Bill[1] = 30, Bill[2] = 10, Bill[3] = 15,
```

USE OF CIN FOR AN ARRAY

For interactive input by user of the program we can use *cin.* Since each member of an array has to be put in element by element so we may use a loop for the purpose. The following program carries out input of 5 members of array bill [5].

PROGRAM 8.4 – Illustrates user interactive input of array elements.

```
#include <iostream>
using namespace std;
int main()

{
 int bill[5];
  cout<<"Enter five integers :";
    for (int i=0;i<5;i++)
       cin>>bill[i];
  cout<<"\n";
   for (int j=0;j<5;j++)
      cout<<" bill["<<j<<"] = "<< bill[j]<<endl;
 return 0;
}
```

On clicking for running the program the following line will appear on the monitor with a blinking cursor at the end.

```
Enter five integers :
```

At the place of blinking cursor type 5 integers each separated by a space and then press the enter-key The following output will be displayed on monitor.

```
Enter five integers :10 30 40 20 50

bill[0] = 10
bill[1] = 30
bill[2] = 40
bill[3] = 20
bill[4] = 50
```

In C++ there is no check to see that you do not overstep the number of elements in the array while typing output statement. For example, if there are only 4 elements in the array you may ask for fifth or sixth element, the compiler will not show an error but the output for 5th and 6th member would be some garbage value. It is illustrated below.

PROGRAM 8.5 – Illustrates output when the number of subscript values are more than the number of array elements.

```
#include <iostream>
using namespace std;
main()
{
int bill[4] = {20,30,10,15};
 cout<<"The bill amounts are as under."<<endl;
  for (int i =0; i <6; i++)
    cout<<"bill["<<i<<"] = " << bill[i]<<"\n";
return 0;
}
```

The output is given below.

```
The bill amounts are as under.
bill[0] = 20
bill[1] = 30
bill[2] = 10
bill[3] = 15
bill[4] = 1245120 // garbage value, because bill[] has only 4
bill[5] = 4333209 // elements. These values do not belong to array.
```

In order to make sure that only exact number of elements are entered in any function accessing the array, the array size (number of elements) may be determined and used as illustrated below for `int bill[4]`.The code uses the function **sizeof()** which gives the number of byte allocated. Let us take size = number of elements in array and it is determined as below.

size = number of bytes allocated for array/number of byte allocated to one element.

The code for determining size of an array with integer elements and using it in output statement is illustrated below.

```
    int size;
  size = sizeof (bill) / sizeof(int);
  for ( int i =0; i< size; i++)
  cout << bill[i];
```

The application of this is illustrated in the following program.

PROGRAM 8.6 – Illustrates arithmetic operations on array elements.

```
#include <iostream>
using namespace std;
int main()
 {double sum=0 , average =0;
 double Price[5] ;
 cout<< "Write the Quotations."<<endl;
 for ( int i =0; i<5;i++)
 cin>> Price[i];
 int size = sizeof(Price)/sizeof(double);
        // size is the number of elements in array
 cout<<"size = "<<size<<endl;
 for (int j =0; j<size ; j++)  // use of size
 sum += Price[j];
 cout<<"Quotations are :";
 for(int k =0;k<size;k++)    // use of size
 cout<<Price[k]<<"  ";

cout<<"\nThe number in the sample = "<< size<<endl;
cout<<"sum = " <<sum <<endl;

cout<< "Average price = "<< sum/size <<endl;
return 0;
}
```

The expected output is given below.

```
Write the Quotations.
6.5 7.5 6.0 7.0 8.5
size = 5
Quotations are :6.5  7.5  6  7  8.5
The number in the sample = 5
sum = 35.5
Average price = 7.1
```

DIFFERENCE BETWEEN AN ARRAY AND A C-STRING

The C-strings which are also arrays of characters are discussed in the next chapter, however, it is worthwhile to bring out the differences between the two here. The following program brings out the difference in their storage in computer. A string of characters declared and initialized as

```
char Name[] = { "Delhi"};
```

is an array of characters, however, the system appends a Null ('\0') character at the end of string to mark the end of string. Therefore, the number of elements in the string increases by one, i.e. in the memory for "Delhi" there are 6 elements – 5 of Delhi and one '\0'.

PROGRAM 8.7 – Illustrates difference between an array and C-string.

```
#include <iostream>
using namespace std;
main()
{
double Weight [] = {5.4, 6.35,12.6};     // An array
char Name[] = { 'R','A','D','H','A'};    // An array
char ch[] = {"Radha"};          // A string. It can also be coded as
                                // char ch [] = "Radha";

cout<<"Size of Name = " << sizeof(Name)<<endl;;
 cout << "Size of ch = " << sizeof (ch)<<endl;

for (int i=0;i<5;i++)
cout <<Name[i] ;

cout<<"\n";
for (int j=0;j<3;j++)
cout<<Weight[j]<<"  ";
cout<<"\n";
cout <<ch ;
return 0;
}
```

The expected output is as below.

```
Size of Name = 5
Size of ch = 6
RADHA
5.4 6.35 12.6
Radha
```

The above program shows that a char array may be initialized by individual characters as well. In that case it is an array of characters without the Null character at the end. However, if a string of characters is assigned in any one of the following two methods the compiler appends the Null character at the end of string of characters to mark the end of string.

```
char ch[] = {"Radha"}; // or as below
char ch[]  = "Radha";
```

That explains that the difference between the array char Name[] and char ch [] is the Null character that is appended by the system at the end of string. Thus number of elements of string in the case of char ch[] = "Radha"; is one more than that in Name[]. This is because when we put it as a string in double quotes as in "Radha" the compiler attaches the Null (' \0') character at the end of the string, to mark the end of string. Moreover a string is treated as a single unit.

Swapping Elements of Two Arrays

As already mentioned the array as a whole cannot be assigned. Therefore, arrays cannot be swapped as a whole with another array. However, the swap operation may be carried out by swapping element by element. This is illustrated below.

PROGRAM 8.8 – Illustrates swapping of elements of two arrays.

```
#include <iostream>
using namespace std;
int main()
 {
 int bill[4] = {20,30,10,15};
 int Bill[5] = { 5, 6 ,7, 8,9};

 for ( int i =0; i<5;i++)
{swap ( bill[i] , Bill[i] );
 cout <<" bill["<<i <<"] = "<< bill [i] <<",  " ; }
 cout <<"\n";
 for (int j =0; j<5; j++)
 cout << "Bill["<<j<<"] = "<< Bill[j]<<",  " ;
return 0;
 }
```

The expected output of the program is given below.

```
bill[0] = 5,  bill[1] = 6,  bill[2] = 7,  bill[3] = 8,  bill[4] = 9
Bill[0] = 20, Bill[1] = 30, Bill[2] = 10, Bill[3] = 15, Bill[4] = 1245120
```

The Bill[4] is a garbage value. For swapping elements of arrays, take care that arrays are of equal size otherwise such potentially dangerous errors may happen.

Interactive Input for Several Arrays

The elements of more than one array may also be entered by user of the program in an interactive program. As illustrated above we use `cin` for the purpose. A *for* loop or *while* loop may be used for each array. For example let us name an array as data [50]. For interactive input the following code may be used.

```
for (int i=0;i<50;i++)
 cin>>data[i];
```

This has been already illustrated in the Program 8.6 wherein different types of data have been entered interactively by user. Also more than one array may be declared in same line if their elements are of same type.

PROGRAM 8.9 – Illustrates user interactive input of several arrays.

```
#include <iostream>
using namespace std;
int main()
{
int Bill[4], bill[5];   // both arrays are of type int
char Myname[7];
 cout<<"Write values of array Bill ; ";
 for ( int i = 0; i<4; i++)
 cin >> Bill[i];

cout<<"Write values of array bill ; ";
 for ( int k = 0; k<5; k++)
  cin >> bill[k];

 cout<<"Write values of array Myname ; ";
  for ( int n = 0; n<7; n++)
   cin >> Myname[n];

 cout<<"The Bill elements are: ";
  for (int j=0;j<4;j++)
   cout<< Bill[j]<<"  ";
    cout<<"\n" ;
 cout << "The bill elements are ";
  for (int m=0;m<5;m++)
   cout <<bill[m]<<"  " ;

 cout<<"\n ";
 cout<< "Myname is : ";

for (int p=0;p<7;p++)
 cout <<Myname[p];
  cout<<"\n";
return 0; }
```

While running the above program, the following line will first appear on the monitor.

```
Write values of array Bill ;
```

Type four integers each separated by a space from the previous one, say, 10 20 40 30 are typed. Next press enter-key. The second line as given below will then appear on the monitor.

```
Write values of array bill ;
```

As done before for array Bill, type five integers each separated by space and press enter-key. Then the third line given below will appear.

```
Write values of array Myname ;
```

Type a name consisting of 7 characters and each letter separated by a space. Then press *enter-key*. The following output will appear on monitor. In this the first three lines are of input and last three lines are of output.

```
Write values of array Bill ; 10 20 40 30
Write values of array bill ; 15 30 50 40 60
Write values of array Myname ; N a t a s h a
The Bill elements are: 10  20  40  30
The bill elements are 15  30  50  40  60
Myname is : Natasha
```

8.4 SEARCHING A VALUE IN AN ARRAY

Often it is required to search a value in an array. This may be carried out by comparing the key value with each element of array. It is illustrated in the program given below.

PROGRAM 8.10 – Illustrates searching a value in an array.

```
#include <iostream>
using namespace std;
int main()
 {
 int sum=0;
  int bill[ ] = {20,30,10,15, 50,40 ,30, 70,95};

int x ;
  int Size = sizeof (bill)/sizeof(int);
   cout<<"Write the number to be searched:";
cin >>x; // x is the value to be searched in the array

for(int i =0; i<Size;i++)
 if( x == bill[i])
{cout<< "Yes, the number is in bill- bill["<<i <<"]= "<<bill[i]<<endl;

goto End;}
 cout <<"The number is not in bill" <<endl;
End:
return 0;
}
```

The output is as under. First we enter the number 50 and the output is below.

```
Write the number to be searched:50
```

```
Yes, the number is in bill- bill[4]= 50
```

In the second trial we enter the number 75 and the output is as below.

```
Write the number to be searched:75
The number is not in bill
```

Binary Search for Ordered Arrays

In the above search method every array element is compared with the key. In case of ordered arrays the search may be shortened considerably by binary search which applies only to sorted arrays. In this method first determine the number of elements in the array. Then determine in which half of the array the key value (the value we wish to search) lies. This is easily done by comparing with the element at middle because the array is an ordered array. Then search only that half in which the value lies. This half may again be divided into two halves and again it is determined in which half (¼ the of original array) the key lies. In this way the search continues till the value is found. For large ordered arrays this method is very efficient. The following code illustrates the method. If the value is not in the array the following code displays it in the output Also C++ Standard Library has an algorithm **binary_search**() (see Chapter 25) and a programmer may use it by including the header file <algorithm> in the program.

PROGRAM 8.11 – Binary search of an array for a value.

```
#include <iostream>
using namespace std;
int main()
{ int sum=0;
 int bill[ ] = {20,30,40, 50,60 ,70, 80,95, 102, 166, 175,200 };
 int x ;
 cout<<"Write the number you want to find :"; cin>>x;
 int Size = sizeof (bill) / sizeof(int);
 int Low =0;
 int High = Size -1 ;
 while ( Low <= High)
 {
     if(Low ==High && bill[High] != x)
     { cout<<"The number is not in the array.\n";
     break;}
     int Mid = (Low + High)/2;
if ( bill[Mid] == x)
     {cout<< "Value found. It is bill ["<<Mid <<"]"<< endl;
     break;}
else
if ( bill[Mid] > x )
  High = Mid-1;
else
Low = Mid+1;}
 return 0;
}
```

The first trial gives the following output.

```
Write the number you want to find :70
Value found. It is bill [5]
```

The second trial with element not in array gives the following.

```
Write the number you want to find :103
The number is not in the array.
```

8.5 ADDRESS OF AN ARRAY

With the declaration of array as `int Bill[4];` four blocks of memory are allocated by the compiler for the array elements, i.e. one block for each element for storing its value. The array is initialized as given below. Figure 8.4 shows the memory blocks and the values expressed in binary in each block.

```
int Bill[4] = {20,30,10,15};
```

The size of blocks depends on the type of data in the array. For the present case, the type of elements is int so 4 bytes are allocated for each block. The value of each element is stored in binary as illustrated in Fig. 8.4 below.

Array element	0	1	2	3
	10100	11110	1010	1111
Memory address	0012FF 70	0012FF 74	0012FF 78	0012FF 7C

Fig. 8.4: An illustration of array address and addresses of array elements. The values inside the blocks are values of array elements in binary

Here 10100, 11110, 1010 and 1111 are binary equivalents of 20, 30, 10 and 15 respectively, and the memory addresses written below the blocks are in hexadecimal.

The address of an array is the address of first element of the array which is the number of the first byte of the memory block allocated to the first element of the array. It may be extracted by simply calling the name of array as illustrated in the following code. Thus for array Bill[4] the code for getting address of the array is

```
cout << Bill;
```

The output will be the address of the array. The address of any element of an array may also be extracted by calling array (name + offset). The offset is equal to the subscript or index value of the element. Thus for getting the address of the second element of array Bill[4] we can call Bill+1 as illustrated below.

```
cout << Bill+1 ;
```

Similarly, for obtaining the address of third element code is as below.

```
cout << Bill+2;
```

One can write similar codes for other elements as well.

The following program determines the address of an array and addresses of individual elements of the array.

PROGRAM 8.12 – Addresses of an array and its elements.

```
#include <iostream>
using namespace std;
int main()
 { int Bill[4] = {20,30,10,15};

 cout<< "The address of the array is  ";
 cout<< Bill <<"\n";
 cout<< "The addresses of the four elements are as below."<<endl;
 cout<<" "<<Bill <<" , "<<Bill+1 <<" , "<<Bill+2<<
 " , "<<Bill+3<<endl;
return 0;
}
```

The expected output of the above program is as under.

```
The address of the array is  0012FF70
The addresses of the four elements are as below.
0012FF70, 0012FF74, 0012FF78, 0012FF7C
```

The above output shows that elements of array Bill[4] are stored in computer memory starting from byte number 0012FF70 (in hexadecimal). Each element of array in this case occupies four bytes. **The address of an array is the address of the first element of the array.** Therefore, the address of array is 0012FF70. The subscript values of elements are 0, 1, 2 and 3. The addresses of elements are 0012FF70, 0012FF74, 0012FF78 and 0012FF7C. These are the byte numbers or addresses of the first bytes of the memory blocks allocated for each array element. Each element, in this case, is allocated a memory block of 4 bytes.

In the above programs we have written the individual elements of the array Bill [4]as Bill[0], Bill[1], etc. Also, we could as well write them as 0[Bill], 1[Bill], etc. This is illustrated in the following program. As already mentioned above the numbers 0, 1, 2 and 3 are called subscripts. You should note that subscripts start from 0. The starting element of array is the 0th element, that's why the array of 4 elements has the subscripts 0, 1, 2 and 3. This is true for all arrays. *The programmers generally make mistake by taking the starting element as 1.*

Also remember that a subscript value represents the position of an element in the array. It is not the value of the array element.

8.6 ARITHMETIC OPERATIONS ON ARRAY ELEMENTS

Individual array element can be treated as any other variable of the same *type*. Therefore, all the operators which can be applied on other variables of same *type* can also be applied to the elements of the array. The arithmetic operators, i.e. +, –, *, / and % may be used on individual array elements just like these operators are used on other variables. Program 8.13, given below illustrates the arithmetic operations on array elements. The program determines the average value and standard deviation of a sample of data presented as elements of an array. In quality control we often take a sample of measurements of objects and find out the average value and the standard deviation.

PROGRAM 8.13 – Illustrates arithmetic operations on array elements.

```
#include <iostream>
#include<cmath>
using namespace std;
int main()
 {
int m,n,p ;
double Sum = 0 ,Average = 0 , Sigma = 0;
int Sample[] = {20,16,10,15,11,12,15,22,14,13,14};

m =sizeof(Sample[1]); // gives number of bytes for one element
 p = sizeof(Sample);
      //p is the total number of bytes used for array.
  n = p/m;
       // n = number of elements in the array.

for(int i=0;i<=(n-1);i++)
 Sum += Sample[i];  // Calculates the sum of all elements.
  Average = Sum/n;
double Var =0;
for ( int j =0; j<n;j++)
 Var += ((Sample[j]-Average)*(Sample[j]-Average));
Sigma = sqrt(Var/(n-1));
        // Here sigma is the standard deviation
 cout<<"Sum of elements = "<<Sum<<"\nNo. of elements = "<<n <<endl;
cout <<"Sample average = "<<Average <<endl;
cout<<"Var = "<<Var <<endl;
cout<< "Sample std. deviation = "<< Sigma<<endl;
 return 0;
  }
```

The expected output is given below.

```
Sum of elements = 162
No. of elements = 11
Sample average = 14.7273
Var = 130.182
Sample std. deviation = 4.65717
```

The following program illustrates the general arithmetic operations on array elements.

PROGRAM 8.14 – Another illustration of arithmetic operations on array elements.

```
#include <iostream>
using namespace std;
int main()
 {
 float B[4] = {2.5 ,3.4 ,6.0,12.2};
 float C[4] = {4.0,2.0,3.6,6.4};
 float R[4];
 double S[4],a,b,c,d, sum =0;
 a = B[2] + C[3];
 b =B[3]- C[1];
 c= B[2] * C[1];
 d = (B[3]+C[2]) /(C[1]*B[1]);
  cout<< "a = "<<a<<",\tb = "<<b <<"\n";
  cout<<"c = "<<c<< ",\t\td = "<<d<<"\n";
 for (int i=0;i<=3;i++)
 {S[i] = B[i] /C[i];
  R[i] = B[i] * C[i];
cout<< "S["<<i<<"] = "<< S[i]<< ",\tR["<<i<<"] = "<< R[i]<<endl; }

for (i=0;i<=3;i++)
 sum += (B[i] +C[i]);
  cout << "Sum of B and C array elements = " <<sum <<endl;
return 0;
}
```

The expected output of above program is given below.

```
a = 12.4,         b = 10.2
c = 12,           d = 2.32353
S[0] = 0.625,     R[0] = 10
S[1] = 1.7,       R[1] = 6.8
S[2] = 1.66667,   R[2] = 21.6
S[3] = 1.90625,   R[3] = 78.08
Sum of B and C array elements = 40.1
```

Operation of Functions on Array Elements

In the following program two functions are defined, one returns the square of a number and other returns square-root of the number. The functions operate on the array elements and return the square and square root of the array elements.

PROGRAM 8.15 – Application of C++ Standard Library functions on array elements.

```
#include<iostream>
#include<cmath>
using namespace std;
 int F1(int x)
  {return pow(x,2);
  }

 double F2(int n)
 {return sqrt(n);}

main()
{int A[4] = { 2,3,4,5};
  int B[4];
   double S[4];

 for(int i=0;i<=3;i++)
 {B[i] = F1(A[i]);
   S[i] = F2(A[i]);

cout<<"A["<<i<<"] = "<<A[i]<< "\tB["<<i<<"] = "<<B[i]<<",\tS[" <<i<<"] =
"<<S[i]<<"\n";}
return 0;
}
```

The expected output is given below.

```
A[0] = 2        B[0] = 4         S[0] = 1.41421
A[1] = 3        B[1] = 9         S[1] = 1.73205
A[2] = 4        B[2] = 16        S[2] = 2
A[3] = 5        B[3] = 25        S[3] = 2.23607
```

8.7 SORTING OF ARRAYS

In many cases it is required to sort an array in the ascending or descending order. For example you may want to arrange the marks obtained by students in a descending order so that the student who scores highest is at the top and the one with lowest marks is at the bottom, or you may like to arrange a list of names in an alphabetical order, etc. The Program 8.16 illustrates the code for sorting out a list of numbers entered by user.

If the list is to be arranged in ascending order the element with lowest value should be the first. Let kim [j] and kim [j+1] be the two adjacent members of the array kim[]. Now the two are compared and if kim [j] > kim [j+1] the two are swapped. The comparison then shifts to next element and so on to the end of array. In this way the element with highest value goes to the end.

But if kim [j] is less than kim [j + 1] then no swapping is done and comparison shifts to next, i.e. kim[j + 1] and kim[j + 2]. This process of comparison and swapping is successively carried out with all the elements of the array. Thus if n is the number of elements in the array the process of comparison will be repeated n – 1 times. And this will have to be carried out (n –1) times to complete the sorting. The following program is coded to illustrate the process of sorting in an ascending order.

PROGRAM 8.16 – Illustrates sorting of an array of characters.

```
#include <iostream>
 using namespace std;

int main()
 {
 const int p = 5;
 char kim[10] ;

 cout <<"Enter 5 characters: ";
  for(int i=0;i<p;i++)
    cin>> kim[i];

 cout<<"\nyou have entered the following characters:\n ";
 for(int k =0;k<p;k++)
  cout<<" "<<kim[k]<<" ";

  cout<<"\n";
  for ( int n = 0 ; n<p; n++)

 {for(int j =0;j<p-1;j++)  //for explanation of p-1 see output
  {if(kim[j]>kim[j+1])
    swap( kim[j],kim[j+1]); }

  for ( int r =0 ; r<5; r++)
   cout<< kim[r]<< "  ";
    cout << "\n";}
 return 0;
}
```

The expected output is as below. The first line of output depicts that five characters, i.e. E D C B and A are entered. The next line shows that the first character E is successively compared with the other characters and is placed at the end of array. The third line of output shows that the new first element D is similarly compared and placed at a position before E. We see that in

4th round that is 1 less than the size of array all are sorted. Notice that two *for* loops have been used in the program. One for comparing the values and placing the element with higher value at appropriate place. The second *for* loop is for repeating the above process a number of times.

```
Enter 5 characters: E D C B A
you have entered the following characters:
 E D C B A
D C B A E      // E goes to the end in first round.
C B A D E      // D goes to position one less than the end.
B A C D E     // the C is placed in its position, i.e. on left of D.
A B C D E     // B is placed after A , Total 4 cycles of sorting.
A B C D E
```

The following program illustrates the sorting of a list of numbers in ascending order.

PROGRAM 8.17 – Illustrates sorting of a list of integers.

```
#include <iostream>
using namespace std;
 main()
 {
 int kim[10] ;
  cout <<"Enter 10 integers: ";
   { for(int i=0;i<10;i++)
     cin>> kim[i]; }

 cout<<"The sorted list is given below \n ";
   {for (int i=0;i<10;i++)
     for(int j =0;j<9;j++)
       if (kim[j]>kim[j+1])
          swap(kim[j],kim[j+1]); }

 for(int i=0;i<10;i++)
   cout <<" "<< kim[i]<<" ";
     cout<<"\n";

 return 0;
     }
```

The output is given below.

```
Enter 10 integers: 23 11 43 56 78 65 43 22 88 37
The sorted list is given below
11 22 23 37 43 43 56 65 78 88
```

8.8 FINDING THE MAXIMUM/MINIMUM VALUE IN AN ARRAY

Often it is required to find the maximum and minimum values in a list. For instance, in a list of marks obtained by students it is often needed to find out the topper. The listing of the following program determines the maximum value in an array of values of elements. It also finds which element has the maximum value. The values of the array elements are entered by the user of the program.

The scheme of the program is that let the first elements be assumed as the maximum value. This is compared with the second element. If the second element is greater than the first, the second element is designated as maximum and compared with the third and same process is repeated. If the first element is greater than second, the comparison shifts to third without doing anything. The process is carried out with all elements and maximum value is thus found.

PROGRAM 8.18 – Finding the array element with maximum value in an array.

```
#include <iostream>
using namespace std;
int main()

{int kim[10] ={0},max ;
 cout <<"Enter 10 integers: ";
  {for(int i=0;i<10;i++)
   cin>> kim[i];
  }
cout<<"\nyou have entered the following numbers: \n";
 for(int i =0;i<10;i++)
  cout<<" "<<kim[i]<<" ";
    cout<<"\n ";

max = kim[0];
 {for(int j =0;j<9;j++)
  if(kim[j]>max)
   max=kim[j];
    else max = max; }

 cout <<"max = "<< max<<endl;
  {for(int k=0;k<10;k++)
   if ( max ==kim[k])
    cout<<"kim["<<k<<"] = " << kim[k] <<endl; }
return 0;
 }
```

The expected output is as under.

```
Enter 10 integers: 65 34 23 87 68 97 64 32 10 45
you have entered the following numbers:
```

```
65  34  23  87  68  97  64  32  10  45
max = 97
kim[5] = 97
```

The output gives the maximum value and the index value of element. The index values start from 0 in arrays, so 97 is 6th element with index value 5.

8.9 PASSING AN ARRAY TO A FUNCTION

Just like a variable, an array may also be a parameter of a function. For declaration of a function with array as parameter we have to mention data type of the array and an unsigned integer which stands for number of elements in the array. Please note that ***the array elements cannot be functions.*** Thus the prototype of a function with an array as a parameter may be written as below.

```
int Func(int [], size_t );        // Prototype
```

In the above expression size_t is the typedef of unsigned int. And for the function definition, one may write as below.

```
int Func(int A [], size_t n)
{statement;
__________
 __________;}
```

PROGRAM 8.19 – Illustrates passing of an array to a function.

```
#include <iostream>
using namespace std;
double Average (double[], size_t ); // Prototype of the function
//Average

int main()
{int n=10;
 double kim[10];
  cout <<"Enter 10 floating point numbers: ";
   for(int i=0;i<10;i++)
     cin>> kim[i]; // entering the array elements
cout <<"You have entered the following numbers"<<endl;
 for(int j=0;j<10;j++)
  cout<< kim[j]<<" ";
   cout << "\n Average = " << Average(kim,n)<< endl;
return 0;
}

double Average(double kim[], size_t n)
          // definition of function
{ double Total = 0;
```

```
  for (int i =0; i<n; i++)
   Total += kim[i];
  return Total / n;
}
```

The expected output is given below.

```
Enter 10 floating point numbers: 6.5 4.6 5.8 5.9 6.1 6.7 6.4 5.3 4.6 5.0
You have entered the following numbers
6.5 4.6 5.8 5.9 6.1 6.7 6.4 5.3 4.6 5
 Average = 5.69
```

In the following program two arrays are passed to a function. The function evaluates the products of their respective elements and calculates the sum.

PROGRAM 8.20 – Illustrates passing of more than one array to a function.

```
#include <iostream>
 using namespace std;
double Product (double [], double[], size_t, size_t);
                   //function prototype
int main()
 { int n =4, m=4;
   double kim[4];
    double Bill[4];
 cout <<"Enter 4 decimal numbers for kim: ";
   for(int i=0;i<4;i++)
    cin>> kim[i];
 cout<<"\nEnter 4 numbers for Bill: ";
   for(int j=0;j<4;j++)
     cin>> Bill[j];    // Entering array elements
 cout <<"You have entered the following numbers for kim."<<endl;
   for(int k=0;k<4;k++)
    cout<< kim[k]<<" ";
cout<<"\nYou have entered the following numbers for Bill "<<endl;
  for(int s=0;s<4;s++)
    cout<< Bill[s]<<" ";
cout<<"\n Sum of Product of array elements = " <<   Product(kim, Bill, n,
m)<< endl;
 return 0;
 }
double Product(double kim[],double Bill[], size_t n, size_t m )
 {double Product[] ={0,0,0,0};
```

```
  double Total=0;

for ( n =0; n<4; n++)
 {Product [n]= kim[n] * Bill[n];
  Total += Product[n]; }
return Total;
}
```

The expected output is given below.

```
Enter 4 decimal numbers for kim: 1 2 3 4

Enter 4 numbers for Bill: 5 6 7 8
You have entered the following numbers for kim.
1 2 3 4
You have entered the following numbers for Bill
5 6 7 8
 Sum of Product of array elements = 70
```

8.10 TWO DIMENSIONAL ARRAYS

The elements of an array may be arrays. Such arrays are called multi-dimensional arrays. Thus an array having elements which are one dimensional arrays, is a two dimensional array. Similarly, an array whose elements are two dimension arrays is a three dimensional array. The declaration and initialization of multi-dimensional arrays have already been illustrated in the beginning of this chapter. A two dimensional array may be declared as given below.

```
int bill[2][4];
```

The array may be taken as having two rows of 4 columns each like in a matrix.

There are many applications of two dimension arrays in mathematic, in science, in engineering and even in making list of names, etc. The following program illustrates the input and output of a two dimensional array. For input or output nested *for* loops may be used. Say for bill[2][4], for the outer loop the subscripts vary from 0 to 1 for the two rows and for the inner loop the subscripts vary from 0 to 3 for the four columns. For each value of outer subscript the inner one has values 0, 1, 2 and 3. See the following program.

PROGRAM 8.21 – Illustrates input/output of two dimensional arrays.

```
#include <iostream>
using namespace std;
 void read(int bill[2][3]);

 int main()
 {
 int bill[2][3];
 read(bill);
```

```
    for(int i=0;i<2;i++)
    { cout << "Row "<<i+1<<endl; ;

    for(int j=0;j<3;j++)
    cout<<"bill["<<i<<"]["<<j<<"] = "<< bill[i][j]<<" ";
    cout<< "\n";}
     return 0;}

   void read(int bill[2][3])  // definition of function read()
   {cout<< "Enter 6 integers , 3 per row;\n";

    for(int k=0;k<=1;k++)
     {cout<<"Row "<<k+1<<" ; ";
      for(int j=0;j<3;j++)
      {
         cin>>bill[k][j]; }}}
```

The expected output is given below.

```
Enter 6 integers , 3 per row;
Row 1 ; 11 12 13
Row 2 ; 21 22 23
Row 1
bill[0][0] = 11  bill[0][1] = 12  bill[0][2] = 13
Row 2
bill[1][0] = 21  bill[1][1] = 22  bill[1][2] = 23
```

The initialization of a two dimensional array may also be done as it is carried out for one dimensional array illustrated in Program 8.1 or with *cin* as illustrated in the above program. The elements in all types of arrays are stored in the computer memory in consecutive memory blocks. Each element occupies one block of memory. The size of memory block depends on the type of array elements. In the following program the address of each element of a two dimensional array has been called. The output shows how a two dimensional array is stored in computer memory.

PROGRAM 8.22 – Addresses of elements of multidimensional arrays.

```
  #include <iostream>
  using namespace std;
   int main()
   {
   short bill[2][3];
   cout << "Enter 6 small numbers : " ;
   /*you may write in any groups, the program will read left to right. The
numbers must be separated by white space and not by comma.*/
   for(int i=0;i<2;i++)
    {for(int j=0;j<3;j++)
```

```
   cin>>bill[i][j];
   }
  cout<<"/n Address of the Array is "<<bill<<endl;
  cout<<"\n ";
  cout<<"Addresses of members of 2 dimension array are :\n"<<endl;
   {for(int i=0;i<2;i++)

  {for(int j=0;j<3;j++)
    cout<<"bill["<<i<<"]["<<j<<"] = "<< &bill[i][j] <<"\n"; }
   }
   return 0;
    }
```

The expected output is viven below.

```
Enter 6 small numbers : 3 4 5 6 7 8
Address of the Array is 0012FF74

Addresses of members of 2 dimension array are :

bill[0][0] = 0012FF74
bill[0][1] = 0012FF76
bill[0][2] = 0012FF78
bill[1][0] = 0012FF7A
bill[1][1] = 0012FF7C
bill[1][2] = 0012FF7E
```

From the output it is clear that elements of first row are stored first in adjacent memory blocks followed by elements of second row. The array may as well be written as

$$\text{Bill [2][3]} = \begin{bmatrix} 3 & 4 & 5 \\ 6 & 7 & 8 \end{bmatrix}$$

8.11 TWO DIMENSIONAL ARRAYS AND MATRICES

An important application of two dimensional arrays is in representation and operations on matrices. For example, a matrix A = a_{jk} with 'j' rows and 'k' columns may be represented by a two dimensional array A [j][k].

ADDITION OF TWO MATRICES

Let A =(a_{ij}) and B = (b_{ij}) be the two matrices. The addition and subtraction of A and B are illustrated below.

Addition

C = A + B

Or $C_{ij} = a_{ij} + b_{ij}$

Subtraction

D = A − B

Or $D_{ij} = a_{ij} - b_{ij}$

In both addition and subtraction the corresponding components of the matrices are added and subtracted. When presented in form of arrays the codes for addition/subtraction of matrices having n rows and m columns may be written as follows.

```
for( int i = 0 ; i<n ; i++)
 for(int j = 0; j<m; j++)
  {C{i] [j] = A[i] [j] + B[i] [j];
   D[i] [j] = A[i] [j] - B [i] [j];}
```

PROGRAM 8.23 – Illustrates addition/subtraction of matrices.

```
# include <iostream>
using namespace std;
 int main()
 {int C[2] [3] , D[2] [3];

 int A[2] [3] = {20,30,40,50,60,70};
 int B [2] [3] = {10,20,20,30,20,10};

 for ( int i =0; i<2; i++)
  for ( int j = 0; j<3; j++)
   {C[i] [j] = A[i] [j] + B[i] [j]; // addition
    D[i] [j] = A[i] [j] - B[i] [j];} //subtraction

 for ( int n =0 ; n<2; n++)
 {for ( int m = 0; m<3; m++)
  cout<<C[n] [m] <<" " ;
   cout << "\n";}

 cout<<endl;

for ( int p =0 ; p<2; p++)
 {for ( int s = 0; s<3; s++)
  cout<<D[p] [s] <<" " ;
   cout << "\n";}
 return 0 ;
  }
```

The expected output is given below.

```
30 50 60
80 80 80

10 10 20
20 40 60
```

MULTIPLICATION OF TWO MATRICES

Let A and B be the two matrices in which number of columns of A equals number of rows of B, i.e.

$A = (a_{ij})$

$B = (b_{j\,m})$

$C = AB$

Or $c_{im} = a_{ij} \,.\, b_{j\,m}$

The repetition of subscript j indicates summation of terms for the range of values of j. For sake of illustration let us take A be 2 × 3 matrix and B be as 3 × 1 matrix and let

$$A = \begin{pmatrix} a_{11} & a_{12} & a_{13} \\ a_{21} & a_{22} & a_{23} \end{pmatrix}$$

and

$$B = \begin{pmatrix} b_{11} \\ b_{21} \\ b_{31} \end{pmatrix}$$

The product is a 2×1 matrix which is given as below

$$C = \begin{pmatrix} c_{11} \\ c_{21} \end{pmatrix} = AB = (a_{2m})\ (b_{m1})$$

$$\begin{pmatrix} c_{11} \\ c_{21} \end{pmatrix} = \begin{pmatrix} a_{11} & a_{12} & a_{13} \\ a_{21} & a_{22} & a_{23} \end{pmatrix} \begin{pmatrix} b_{11} \\ b_{21} \\ b_{31} \end{pmatrix} = \begin{pmatrix} a_{11}\ b_{11} + a_{12}\ b_{21} + a_{13}\ b_{31} \\ a_{21}\ b_{11} + a_{22}\,b_{21} + a_{23}\ b_{31} \end{pmatrix}$$

The following program illustrates the above product.

PROGRAM 8.24 – Illustrates product of matrices.

```
#include<iostream>
using namespace std;
int main()
{
int S[2][3] = {1,2,3,4,5,6 };
 int P[3][1] = { 6,5,4 };
 int C[2] = {0} ;

 for ( int i =0 ; i<2; i++)
 for ( int j = 0; j<1; j++)
  for (int k = 0; k<3; k++)
```

```
{ C[i] += S[i][k] * P[k][j] ;}

for ( int m =0 ; m<2; m++)
cout<<C[m] <<"\n";
return 0;
}
```

The expected output is as below.

```
28
73
```

8.12 THREE DIMENSIONAL ARRAYS (ARRAYS OF MATRICES)

A 3-dimensional array can be taken as an array whose elements are two dimensional arrays. In practice it may be taken as an array of matrices. An array with int elements may be declared as below.

```
int A[m][n][p];
```

The following program illustrates the input and output of a three dimensional array.

PROGRAM 8.25 – Illustrates input / output of three dimensional arrays.

```
#include <iostream>
using namespace std;
 int main()
 {
 int bill[2][3][4];
 cout << "Write 24 integers separated by white space ;\n";

//you may write in any groups, the program will read left to right.

 for(int i=0;i<2;i++)
 {for(int j=0;j<3;j++)
  {for (int k = 0; k<4;k++)
   cin>>bill[i][j][k];
 }
  }
 cout<<"\n\n";

 for(int n=0;n<2;n++)
 {for(int j=0;j<3;j++)
 {for (int k =0;k<4;k++)
 cout<<"bill["<<n<<"]["<<j<<"]["<<k<<"] = "<< bill[n][j][k];
  cout<<"\n"; }}
  cout<<"\n\n";
```

```
for(int m=0;m<2;m++)
{for(int p=0;p<3;p++)
 {for (int k =0;k<4;k++)
  cout<< bill[m] [p] [k];
   cout<<"\n";}
cout<<"\n"; }

return 0;
 }
```

The output is given below.

```
Write 24 integers separated by white space ;
1 1 1 1 2 2 2 2 3 3 3 3 4 4 4 4 5 5 5 5 6 6 6 6

bill[0] [0] [0] = 1 bill[0] [0] [1] = 1 bill[0] [0] [2] = 1 bill[0] [0] [3] = 1
bill[0] [1] [0] = 2 bill[0] [1] [1] = 2 bill[0] [1] [2] = 2 bill[0] [1] [3] = 2

bill[0] [2] [0] = 3 bill[0] [2] [1] = 3 bill[0] [2] [2] = 3 bill[0] [2] [3] = 3
bill[1] [0] [0] = 4 bill[1] [0] [1] = 4 bill[1] [0] [2] = 4 bill[1] [0] [3] = 4
bill[1] [1] [0] = 5 bill[1] [1] [1] = 5 bill[1] [1] [2] = 5 bill[1] [1] [3] = 5
bill[1] [2] [0] = 6 bill[1] [2] [1] = 6 bill[1] [2] [2] = 6 bill[1] [2] [3] = 6

1111
2222
3333

4444
5555
6666
```

The output has also been tabulated in the form of two 3×4 matrices.

EXERCISES

1. How do you declare a single dimensional array?
2. How can array be initialized?
3. What will happen if the initialization has fewer elements than the number of elements of an array?
4. What will be the output if the initialization has more number of elements than the declared number of elements of an array?
5. How do you initialize a two dimensional array?
6. How would you access the first and last elements of the array A[6]?

7. How do you initialize a three dimensional array?
8. Write a user interactive program to record 5 weights in floating point numbers as an array with name Weights?
9. How do you determine the address of an array?
10. How do you determine the address of each element of an array?
11. Write code for sorting a list of integers in descending order.
12. Write code for sorting the following array in ascending order, i.e. A to Z.

    char Myarray [10] = { 'B', 'A', 'H', 'T', 'R', 'D', 'Z', 'S', 'N', 'L'};
13. Write code for determining the maximum value in an array of integer numbers and to determine the subscript value of array element with the maximum value.
14. Write code for determining the array element with the minimum value in an array of floating point numbers.
15. Write code for determining maximum value and minimum value in an array of integers. It should also determine the corresponding array subscripts.
16. What is the physical interpretation of a 3-dimensional array?
17. What is typedef and how it is coded?
18. Make a program which reads a sample of 11 values in floating point numbers entered by user and calculates the average value and standard deviation of the sample.
19. Make a user interactive program in which user is asked to enter four integers as elements of an array, and displays them on the monitor.
20. Make a program in which a function is defined to return the square of elements of an array of integers.
21. Write a program in which a function is defined to return the dot product of two vectors A and B having 3 components each, i.e. A1, A2, A3 and B1, B2 and B3. The magnitudes of vector components are integers which are entered by the user of the program.
22. Make a program to determine the average value and standard deviation of a sample of 10 measurements of diameters of jobs in floating point numbers and entered by user.
23. Make a program which reads 4 names typed and entered by a user and displays the names on the monitor.
24. Make program which asks the user to enter 5 quotations for price of an item in floating point numbers. The program calculates the average of the five and displays it on monitor.
25. For the following two dimensional array, write a program to carry out the output in rows and columns.

```
Myarray[3] [4] = { 1,2,3,4,11,12,13,14,21,22,23,24};
```

26. Make a program to carry out the product of two matrices.
27. Make a program to carry out the addition and subtraction of two matrices.

❍❍❍

CHAPTER

9 Pointers

9.1 INTRODUCTION

Pointer is a variable which holds (or whose value is) the memory address of another variable. As already discussed in Chapter1, the basic unit of memory is a bit. The bits are grouped into bundles of eight each. These bundles are called bytes. The main memory (RAM) of computer consists of bytes which are numbered sequentially. Each byte is numbered and this number is its address. When we declare a variable we mention its *type* and its *name*, and the compiler along with operating system allocates a block of memory and location for storing the value of the variable. The number of bytes allocated to a variable for storing its value depends on its *type*. For example, generally 4 bytes are allocated for storing the value of an int (integer). **The address of a variable is the address (byte number) of the first byte of the memory block allocated to the variable.** Thus the variable gets an address where its value is stored. You may say it is the house number where the variable resides in computer memory. We can dig out the memory address of a variable by using **address-of operator** (&) also called **reference operator**. For instance, if n is a variable, its address is given by &n. We may declare another variable for storing &n which is the address of n. That variable is called pointer to n.

9.2 DECLARATION OF POINTERS

Declaration of a pointer variable is done by mentioning the *type* of the variable for which it is the pointer, followed by **indirection operator**, which is also called **dereference operator** (*), and the name of the pointer variable. The operator (*) tells the compiler that the variable being declared is a pointer. Name of a pointer variable may be decided as it is done for any other variable. The illustrations of pointer declarations for int variables are given below.

```
int m, n,;      // m and n are integer variables
int *ptr ;  // ptr is pointer to any integer number
int* ptr = &n ;   // ptr now points to n.
int *ptr = &m;   // ptr now points to m
int* ptr = 0 ;     // now ptr is initialized to 0.
```

Also note that it is immaterial whether pointer is declared as **int* ptr** or as **int *ptr,** i.e. the asterisk (*) is attached to int in first case and to ptr in the second case. It is, however, a good programming practice to initialized the pointers when they are declared. Pointers may be initialized to an address or otherwise to 0 or NULL which is a symbolic constant defined in C and inherited by C++. NULL is also defined in <iostream> and other C++ header files. It is equivalent to 0. A NULL pointer does not point to any valid data.

Here in this chapter, we shall deal with pointers to variable, arrays, strings and functions. Pointers to classes, class members and class objects, etc., are discussed in Chapter 12.

A pointer to a variable with value in floating point decimal number such as *PI* = 3.14159; and to a character variable may be declared as illustrated below. Let pf be the name of pointer to a float variable, pd be the name of pointer to a double variable and pc be the name of pointer to a character variable. These are defined below and illustrated in Fig.(9.1).

```
float  PI = 3.14159;
float *pf = &PI;

char ch = 'A';
char *pc = & ch;

double D = 4328.6543
double * pd = &D ;
```

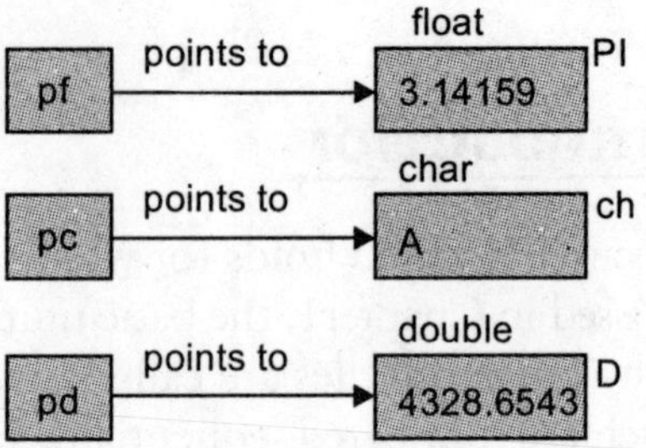

Fig. 9.1: Pointers to different data types

The pointers to two or more variables of same *type* may be declared in the same line as carried out in the following code.

```
int n,y , *ptrn, *py;  // n and y are integers variables
                        // ptrn and py are pointers
ptrn = &n;    // initialization of pointer ptrn by &n
py =&y;     // initialization of pointer py by &y
```

In the above declarations, ptrn is pointer to n and py is pointer to y. We may also use typedef as illustrated below to declare a number of pointers of same type.

```
typedef double* ptd;
double x,y,z;
ptd px = &x, py = &y, pz = &z ;
```

Indirection or Dereference Operator

The value of a variable may be obtained from its pointer by using **indirection operator** also called **dereference operator** (*). It is called indirection because it obtains the value indirectly. An application of dereference operator is given below.

```
int n = 60, *ptrn ;
ptrn = &n ;
*ptrn = 60;       // use of dereference operator.
```

Program 9.1, given below, illustrates the declaration of pointers and application of *address-of operator* (&). A pointer is also a variable and is allocated a block of memory for storing its value which is address of another variable. The *address-of operator* (&) may also be used to get the address of the pointer.

PROGRAM 9.1 – Illustrates declaration of **pointers** and use of **address-of operator (&)**

```
#include <iostream>
using namespace std;
 int main()
{ int n = 60 ;
 double B = 8.56;

  int* ptrn = &n;   //ptrn is pointer to int variable n.
  double *pB = &B;   //pB is pointer to a double variable B
  cout<<"n = "<<n<<", B = "<< B<<endl;
 cout<<"The address of n is = "<<&n<<" , ptrn = " << ptrn <<endl;
 cout<< "*ptrn = "<<*ptrn<< ",   *pB = " <<*pB <<endl;
 cout <<"The address of B = " << &B << ", pB = " << pB << endl;
 cout << "Address of ptrn = " <<& ptrn<<endl;
 return 0;
  }
```

The expected output is given below.

```
n = 60, B = 8.56
The address of n is = 0012FF7C , ptrn = 0012FF7C
*ptrn = 60,  *pB = 8.56
The address of B = 0012FF74, pB = 0012FF74
Address of ptrn = 0012FF70
```

From the output of the above program it is clear that n and *ptrn have the same value, i.e. 60. Similarly B and *pB are both equal to 8.56. Thus it shows that use of dereference operator (*) on pointer variables ptrn and pB gives the values stored at the respective addresses. The program also gives the address where ptrn is stored. Here we have attached *ptr* or *p* to the name of variable to indicate that it is a pointer. But you can put any other name which is legal in C++. The following program illustrates some more pointer declarations and the use of typedef.

PROGRAM 9.2 – Illustrates use of **typedef** in pointer declaration.

```
#include <iostream>
using namespace std;
int main()
{char ch = 'S';
char* pc = &ch;
cout << "*pc = "<< *pc<<endl;
double x = 4.5, z;
typedef double* pd;
```

```
pd px = &x; // here pd stands for double*
cout<<"px = "<<px<<endl; //display value of px
cout <<"&x = " << &x<<endl; // display address of & x

pd pz = &z;
pz = px; // px (address of x) is assigned to pz

cout << "*pz = " <<*pz<<endl;
cout<< "*px = "<<*px <<endl;
return 0;
}
```

The expected output is given below. Output shows that address of x is same as value of px and by equating pz = px we make pz also to point to value of x as illustrated below in Fig. 9.2.

```
*pc = S
px = 0012FF70
&x = 0012FF70
*pz = 4.5
*px = 4.5
```

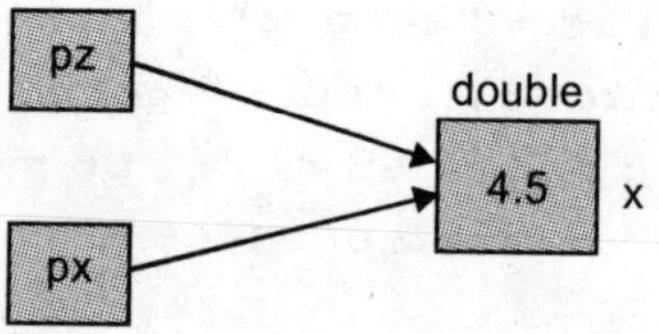

Fig. 9.2: Two pointers pointing to same value

The pointers to all *types* of data occupy the same size of memory because value of a pointer is the memory address – an unsigned integer. However, the variables to which the pointers point to, of course, occupy different sizes of memory blocks according to their *types*. This is illustrated in Program 9.3 given below. From the output of the program we find that the sizes of memory blocks allocated to pointers for different *types* of variables are equal to 4 bytes.

On most of 32 bit systems, a pointer is allocated 4 bytes of memory space, (see the following program)

PROGRAM 9.3 – Illustrates that **size of pointers** to all data types is same.

```
#include <iostream>
using namespace std;
int main()
{ int n = 60,*pn;
double PI = 3.14159 ,*pPI;
pPI = &PI;
pn = &n;
char ch = 'M',*sam; // sam is the name of pointer
sam = &ch; // initializing by &ch.
cout<< "Size of the pointer to int n = " <<sizeof(pn)<<endl;
cout <<"Size of the pointer to double PI = "<<sizeof(pPI)<<endl;
```

```
cout<< " Size of the pointer to char ch = "<<sizeof(sam) <<endl;
cout<<"Variables are "<<*pn <<", "<<*pPI<<" and "<<*sam<< endl;
return 0;
 }
```

The expected output of the program is given below.

```
Size of the pointer to int n = 4
Size of the pointer to double PI = 4
Size of the pointer to char ch = 4
Variables are 60, 3.14159 and M
```

The output shows that size of memory allocated to a pointer is 4 bytes irrespective of the fact whether the variable to which it points to is integer, double or character. Program 9.4 given below also illustrates that actions of dereference operator and that of address-of operator (&) are opposite to each other.

PROGRAM 9.4 – Illustrates the **address-of operator (&)** and **dereference operator (*)**

```
#include <iostream>
using namespace std;
main()
{ int n = 60;
 int* ptrn , *ptrm ; //declaration of pointers to int
  ptrn = &n;
    ptrm = ptrn;  // assigning a pointer
 cout<<"n = "<<n<< "\t&n = "<<&n <<"\t *&n = "<< *&n<<endl;
cout<< "ptrn = " <<ptrn<< "    " << "ptrm = " << ptrm <<endl;
cout<< "The value pointed to by ptrn = " << *ptrn<<"\n" ;
   // *ptrn is the value pointed to by pointer ptrn

cout << "The value pointed to by ptrm = " <<*ptrm <<endl;
cout << "Address of ptrn = " <<&ptrn<<endl;

double PI = 3.141592;
double *pPI;  // declaration of pointer for PI
pPI = &PI;
cout<<"PI="<<PI<<",\t &PI = " <<&PI<<"\n";
cout <<"*&PI = " <<*&PI<< " ,\t *pPI = " << *pPI<<"\n";
return 0;
 }
```

The expected output is given below.

```
n = 60     &n = 0012FF7C     *&n = 60
ptrn = 0012FF7C   ptrm = 0012FF7C
The value pointed to by ptrn = 60
The value pointed to by ptrm = 60
```

```
Address of ptrn = 0012FF78
PI=3.14159,     &PI = 0012FF6C
*&PI = 3.14159 ,    *pPI = 3.14159
```

From the output of the above program it is clear that *n* is an integer with value 60. The address of *n* is 0012FF7C. The value of *ptrn* which is pointer to *n* is also 0012FF7C. The value of ptrn is assigned to ptrm to creat another pointer to x. The address of *ptrn* can also be determined by the operator &. Thus the address of ptrn is determined as 0012FF78 which is 4 bytes away from 0012FF7C. The value of variable *n* may be determined by dereference operator (*). It is determined in the first line of output as 60. The memory blocks allocated for storing the value of n and its pointer are illustrated in Fig. 9.3a.

The second part of the output of the program similarly deals with a double number PI= 3.14159. The pointer for PI has been given the name pPI. The address of PI is 0012FF6C. The value of PI may be obtained by calling PI or by *&PI or by *pPI. This shows that actions of operators * and & are opposite to each other. The action of dereference operator (*) is illustrated in Fig. 9.3b.

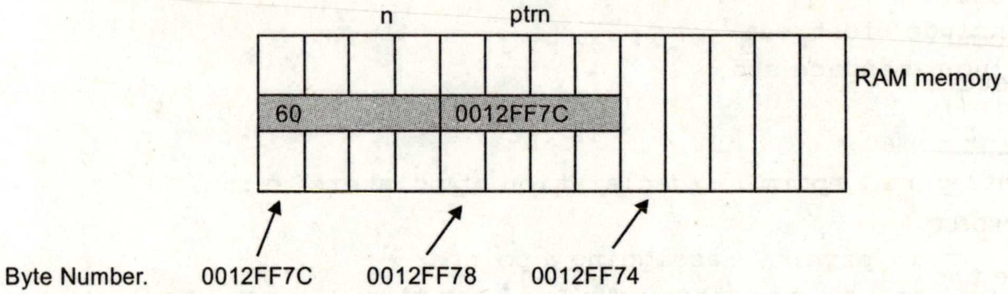

Fig. 9.3a: An integer and its pointer in memory

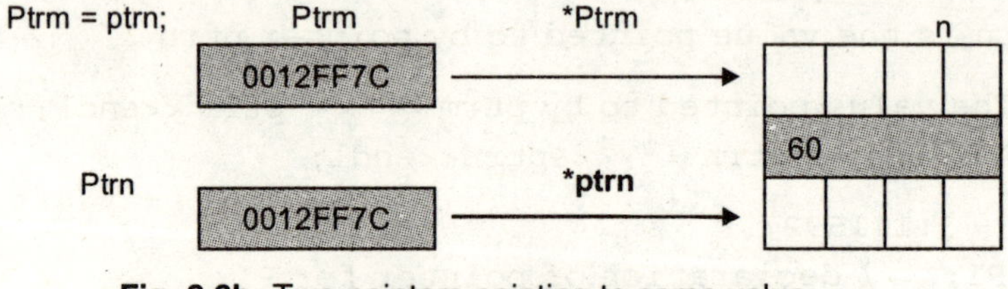

Fig. 9.3b: Two pointers pointing to same value

9.3 PROCESSING DATA BY USING POINTERS

The pointers may be used in place of the variables they point to. We have already seen in the above program that n and *ptrn have the same value. Now if there is a change in value of *ptrn the n will also change accordingly.

The following program computes the circumference and area of a circle having diameter D. Instead of D and PI = 3.14159, we make use of pointers to D and PI. The value of PI is given in the program while the diameter value is entered by the user. The two functions, i.e. area and circumference are written in terms of pointers.

PROGRAM 9.5 – The program illustrate the **application of pointers** in computations.

```
#include <iostream>
using namespace std;
int main()
{ int D , *ptrD = &D ; //declaration of D and pointer to D
 double PI= 3.14159;
 double* ptrPI = &PI;  //pointer to PI
 cout<<"Write the diameter of the circle: ";
 cin>>*ptrD;

 cout<<"Diameter = "<<*ptrD <<endl;
 double Circumference = *ptrD * *ptrPI;  // = PI*D
 double Area = *ptrPI* *ptrD **ptrD/4;  // = PI*D *D /4
  cout<<"Circumference = " <<Circumference <<endl;
  cout<< "Area of circle = " << Area<<endl;
return 0;
}
```

The expected output of the program is as under.

```
Write the diameter of the circle: 20
Diameter = 20
Circumference = 62.8318
Area of circle = 314.159
```

9.4 POINTER TO POINTER

Just like we have a pointer to a variable we can also define a pointer to a pointer which keeps the address of the pointer to the variable. In the following program, *n* is an integer variable with value 57, *ptrn* is the name of pointer to *n* and *pptrn* is the name of pointer to *ptrn*. The pointer ptrn to a variable *n* and pointer to pointer pptrn are declared and initialized as illustrated below.

```
int* ptrn = &n ; // ptrn is pointer to n
int** pptrn = & ptrn ; // pptrn is pointer to ptrn
```

Note that both for pointer and pointer to pointer the *type* is *int* because *n* is integer. Also note that for getting the value of variable we use one dereference operator (*) to pointer while for getting the value of variable from pointer to pointer, we have to use two dereference operators (**). But there is no change in the application of address-of operator (&). **Also note that we cannot use &&n** because & requires an l-value whereas &n is a r-value. The object that is placed on left side of assignment operator (=) is **l-value** and the one placed on right side is **r-value.**

PROGRAM 9.6 – The program illustrates operations with pointer to pointer.

```
#include <iostream>
using namespace std;
int main()
{ int n = 57 ;
int* ptrn = &n;  //Pointer to n
 cout<<"n = "<<n <<", Address of n = " <<&n <<endl;
 cout<<"ptrn = "<< ptrn<<endl;

 cout << "Address of ptrn = " << &ptrn<<endl<<endl;
 int** pptrn = &ptrn; // Pointer to the pointer to n
 cout << "pptrn = "<<pptrn<<endl;

 int*** ppptrn = &pptrn; //Pointer to pointer to pointer to n
 cout << "Address of pptrn = " << &pptrn <<endl;
  cout << "ppptrn = " << ppptrn <<"\n";
cout<<"*ptrn = "<<*ptrn<<endl;
 cout<<"*pptrn = " << *pptrn<<endl;
  cout<<"**pptrn = " << **pptrn<<endl;
  cout << "***ppptrn = " << ***ppptrn <<endl;
return 0;
  }
```

The output is given below.

```
n = 57, Address of n = 0012FF7C
ptrn = 0012FF7C
Address of ptrn = 0012FF78

pptrn = 0012FF78
Address of pptrn = 0012FF74
ppptrn = 0012FF74
*ptrn = 57
*pptrn = 0012FF7C
**pptrn = 57
***ppptrn = 57
```

The above output is self explanatory and is partly illustrated in Fig. 9.4 given below.

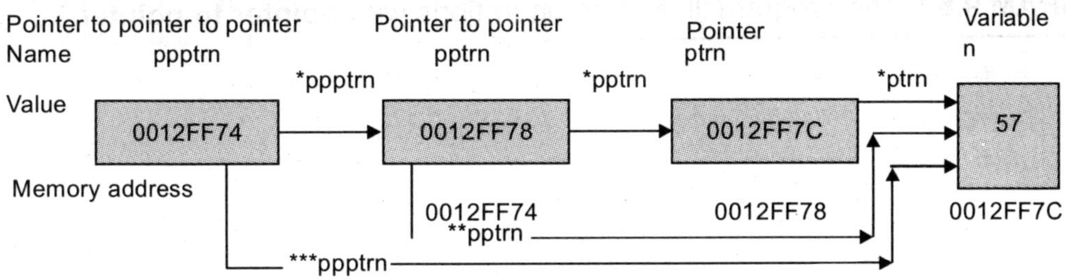

Fig. 9.4: The numbers written within the memory blocks are the values stored in the memory blocks. The addresses of the blocks are written below the blocks

In the declaration of pointers to floats and double objects the two types should not be intermixed as it is illustrated below.

```
 float m ;    // variable of type float
float* ptrm = & m; // pointer to float, do not use double.
float** kptrm = & ptrm; // pointer to pointer, type float
double n ;       // variable double
double* ptrn = &n; // pointer to double, do not use float.
double** kptrn = &ptrn // pointer to pointer to double
```

Do not mix float and double in pointers. Rather do not mix *types* when dealing in pointers.

Constant Pointers

The attribute modifier **const** may be used with pointers as well. However, the declaration should be done carefully keeping in view the following.

```
const int* ptr ;   // Here ptr is a non-constant pointer to a constant int
int* const ptr ;   // Here ptr is a constant pointer to a non-constant int.
const int* const ptr ;  // Here ptr is a constant pointer to a constant int.
```

9.5 POINTERS AND ARRAYS

When we declare an array, its identifier (name) is a **const pointer** to the first element of array. The pointer to array also carries the address of first element of array. Thus the pointer to an array has same value as the name of the array. The difference is that the name of an array is a **const pointer**, i.e. it cannot be incremented or changed while the pointer to an array which carries the address of first element of the array may be incremented. If pointer to an array is incremented by 1 it would point to the next element of the array. Thus the value of the pointer would increase by the number of bytes allocated to one array element. The declaration of a pointer to an array is illustrated below.

```
int A[] = {12, 25, 36 ,50}; // A is the name of array
int *ptrA ;
ptrA = A ;          // Notice there is no & operator before A
```

The above definition may also be written as below.

```
int *ptrA = A;
```

and also as,

```
int* ptrA = &A[0];
```

It is so because the address of A[0] is same as value of A. The elements of array are A[0], A[1], A[2], and A[3] have respective values as 12, 25, 36 and 50 which may also be obtained from pointers as illustrated below.

```
A[0] = *ptrA;
A[1] = *(ptrA+1);
A[2] = *(ptrA+2) ;
A[3] = *(ptrA+3);
```

The above discussion shows that array subscript and pointer offset are equal. If we call array A without a subscript it will give the address of first element of array. A +1 gives the address of second element, A+2 gives address of third elements and so on. Therefore, we can also get the values stored at these addresses by using dereference operator (*). Thus for the above declared array we may get the values of array elements as given below.

```
*A = 12
*(A+1) = 25
*(A+2 ) = 36
*(A+3) = 50
```

Note that expression *A++ is not legal because A is a **constant pointer** to array and a constant cannot be incremented. Also note that array subscripts are equal to pointer offset in traversing of array elements.

PROGRAM 9.7 – Illustrates declaration of **pointer to an array.**

```
#include <iostream>
using namespace std;
int main()
{ int A [] = {80,40,20,10}; // A is an array of integers

int *ptrA = A; //ptrA is pointer to A. Note that & is not used.

 cout <<"*ptrA = "<<*ptrA <<" , \tptrA = "<<ptrA<<endl;
 cout <<"*(ptrA+1) = " << *(ptrA+1)<< " ,\tptrA+1 = " <<ptrA+1<<endl;
cout<<"*(ptrA+2) = "<<*(ptrA+2)<< " , \tptrA + 2 = " <<ptrA+2 <<endl;
cout<<"*(ptrA+3) = "<<*(ptrA+3)<< " , \tptrA+3= " << ptrA+3<<"\n\n";
 cout << "A = " << A<<endl;
cout<< ptrA[0]<<"\t"<<ptrA[1]<<"\t"<<ptrA[2]<<"\t"<<ptrA[3]
<<endl;
cout << *(A+0) <<"\t"<<*(A+1) << "\t"<<*(A+2) << "\t" << *(A+3)<<endl;
// These will display the values of array elements.
return 0;
}
```

The expected output is as below.

```
*ptrA = 80 ,      ptrA = 0012FF70
*(ptrA+1) = 40 ,      ptrA+1 = 0012FF74
```

```
*(ptrA+2) = 20 ,        ptrA + 2 = 0012FF78
*(ptrA+3) = 10 ,        ptrA+3= 0012FF7C

A = 0012FF70
80      40      20      10
80      40      20      10
```

From the output given above note that value of A is same as that of pointer ptrA to the array. Both give the address of first element of array. A = ptrA = 0012FF70.

Now ptrA+1 has the value 0012FF74 which is 4 bytes away from the address of first element and at that address the value stored is *(ptrA+1) = 40; also *(A+1) = 40; which is the second element of the array. Therefore, when a pointer to an array is incremented by 1 it points to the next element in the array. Its value is, in fact, incremented by the number of bytes allocated to one element of array. Similarly ptrA+2 is pointer to the third element, ptrA+3 is the pointer to the fourth element of the array. The following program illustrates traversing of array with pointers.

PROGRAM 9.8 – Illustrates **traversing an array** by pointers.

```
#include <iostream>
using namespace std;
int main()
{ int kim [ ] = {50, 86, 90, 12} ;

int* pkim = kim; // defining the pointer to array kim
for ( int i=0 ; i<4;i++) // for loop for output of array
cout<<"kim["<<i<<"] = " << *(pkim +i) <<" , ";
  //*(pkim +i)is the value of kim[i]element of array
return 0;
 }
```

The expected output of the program is given below.

```
kim[0] = 50 , kim[1] = 86 , kim[2] = 90 , kim[3] = 12 ,
```

In case of arrays the increment in pointer by unity, in fact, increases the value of pointer equal to size of one array element, thus if pkim points to first element of array, pkim+1 points to the second element of array. In the following program the array elements are subjected to arithmetic operations with the help of pointers.

PROGRAM 9.9 – Manipulating **array elements** with **pointers.**

```
#include <iostream>
using namespace std;
int main()
{
```

```
int kim [ ] = {6,8,5,4} ; //4 element array
int* pkim = kim;   // Declaration of pointer

for ( int i=0 ; i<4;i++)
cout<<"kim2 ["<<i<<"] = "<< *(pkim +i)**(pkim +i) <<", ";
   // creating kim2 array from elements of kim
cout <<"\n";
for(int j= 0; j<4; j++) // creating kim3 array
cout<<"kim3 ["<<j<<"]= "<<*(pkim+j)**(pkim +j)-*(pkim+j)<<", ";

return 0;
}
```

The expected output is as below. The output is explained by comments.

```
kim2 [0] = 36, kim2 [1] = 64, kim2 [2] = 25, kim2 [3] = 16,
kim3 [0]= 30, kim3 [1]= 56, kim3 [2]= 20, kim3 [3]= 12,
```

9.6 ARRAY OF POINTERS TO ARRAYS

In the following program an array of pointers int *pAB[2] is declared for two arrays. The first element of the pointer array, i.e. pAB[0] points to array A with four elements 80, 70, 60, 50 and the second element, i.e. pAB[1] points to array B with elements 10, 20, 30 and 40. The program illustrates how to carry out the output of the elements of A and B.

PROGRAM 9.10 – Illustrates an **array of pointers** to arrays.

```
#include <iostream>
using namespace std;

int main()
{ int A [] = {80,70, 60,50} ;   // Array A
 int B [] = {10, 20, 30, 40};  // Array B

 int* pAB[] = {A, B} ;
  //Array of pointers initialized by names of arrays A and B

cout<< "Address of A = " << A <<endl;
cout << "Address of B = " << B <<"\n\n";

cout << "Address of first element of pAB[0] = "<< pAB <<endl;
cout << "Address of second element of pAB[1] = "<< pAB +1<<endl;
cout <<"*pAB = "<<*pAB <<",\t**pAB = "<<** pAB <<"\n\n";
 // Here *pAB = A and **pAB = A[0], see the output below.

cout <<"A[0] = *(*pAB) = "<< * (* pAB) << endl;
cout<<"A[1] = *(*pAB+1) =" << *(*pAB+1)<< endl;
cout<<"A[2] = *(*pAB+2) = "<< *(*pAB +2) << endl;
cout<<"A[3] = *(*pAB+3) = "<<*(*pAB +3)<<endl<<endl;
```

```
    cout<<"*(pAB+1)= " <<*(pAB+1) <<"\t **(pAB+1) = " <<**(pAB+1)<< endl;
// Here *(pAB+1) = B and **(pAB +1) = B[0], see output.

     cout<< "B[0]= *(*(pAB+1)) = "<<*(*(pAB+1)+0) << endl;
     cout<<"B[1] = *(*(pAB+1)+1) = "<<*(*(pAB+1)+1)<<endl;

     cout<<"B[2]= *(*(pAB+1)+2) = "<<*(*(pAB+1)+2)<<endl;
     cout<<"B[3] = *(*(pAB+1)+2) ="<<*(*(pAB+1)+3 )<<endl;
     return 0;
     }
```

The expected output is given below. If you carefully go through the output it is self explanatory.

```
    Address of A = 0012FF70
    Address of B = 0012FF60

    Address of first element of pAB[0] = 0012FF58
    Address of second element of pAB [1] = 0012FF5C
    *pAB = 0012FF70,       **pAB = 80

    A[0] = *(*pAB) = 80
    A[1] = *(*pAB+1) =70
    A[2] = *(*pAB+2) = 60
    A[3] = *(*pAB+3) = 50

    *(pAB+1) = 0012FF60        **(pAB+1) = 10
    B[0]= *(*(pAB+1)) = 10
    B[1] = *(*(pAB+1)+1) = 20
    B[2]= *(*(pAB+1)+2) = 30
    B[3] = *(*(pAB+1)+2) =40
```

In the code of the above program you would notice that initialization of pointer array has been carried out by array names because they are constant pointers to the arrays. In the following program we have three arrays and we declare an array of pointers for them. The initialization of pointer array is carried out by the names of arrays.

PROGRAM 9.11 – Another illustration of **array of pointers** to arrays.

```
    #include <iostream>
    using namespace std;
    int main()
    { int Kim [] = {6,8,5,4} ;  // 4 element array
     int Bill [] = {2, 3, 7 }; // 3 element array
      int Sim[] = {10, 11, 12, 13,14 }; //5 element array

    int* pKBS [] = { Kim , Bill, Sim};
      // Array of pointers, initialization done by array names
    cout<<"Kim : "<<**pKBS<<"\t"<<*(*(pKBS)+1) <<"\t"<<*(*(pKBS)+2) << "\t"
<< *(*(pKBS)+3)<<endl; // Getting elements of Kim
```

```
   cout<<"Bill : "<<*(*(pKBS+1))<<"\t"<<*(*(pKBS+1)+1)<<"\t"<< *(*(pKBS+1)+2)
<<endl; // Getting elements of Bill

   cout<<"Sim : " << *(*(pKBS+2))<< "\t" << *(*(pKBS+2)+1) << "\t" <<*(*(pKBS
+2)+2) <<"\t" <<*(*( pKBS+2)+3)<< "\t" << *(*( pKBS+2)+4) <<endl;
 // Getting elements of Sim
   return 0 ;
   }
```

The expected output is given below.

```
Kim : 6        8        5        4
Bill : 2        3        7
Sim : 10        11        12        13        14
```

9.7 POINTERS TO MULTI-DIMENSIONAL ARRAYS

Pointers to Two Dimensional Array

Program 9.11 is in fact an example of two dimensional array, because, an array whose elements are one dimensional array is a two dimensional array. In declaration of pointer to two dimensional array also we assign the address of array by its name which is the address of the first element of the array. The declaration is done as follow.

```
int A[n] [m] ;    // A is a two dimensional array
int (*pA) [m] = A ; // pointer to two dimensional array
```

An element of two dimensional array with subscripts i and j may be accessed as given below.

```
A [i] [j]
```

In pointer notation the element may be accessed by the following expressions.

```
*(*(A+ i) + j)
```

Or by a pointer pA as under.

```
*(*(pA +i)+j)
```

The following program illustrates the declaration and output of a two dimensional array.

PROGRAM 9.12 – Illustrates **pointers to two dimensional arrays** and output of arrays.

```
#include <iostream>
using namespace std;
int main()
{ int KBS [3] [4] = {6,8,5,4, 2,3,7,9, 10,11,12,13};
int(*pKBS ) [4] = KBS ; // declaration of pointer to KBS
cout<<**pKBS<<"\t"<<*(*(pKBS)+1)<<"\t"<<*(*(pKBS)+2)<<"\t"
<<*(*(pKBS)+3)<<endl;
cout<<*(*(pKBS+1))<<"\t"<<*(*(pKBS+1)+1)<<"\t"<<*(*(pKBS+1)+2)<<"\t"<<
*(*(pKBS+1)+3) <<endl;
cout<<*(*(pKBS+2))<<"\t"<<*(*(pKBS+2)+1)<<"\t"<<*(*(pKBS+2)+2)
<<"\t"<<*(*( pKBS+2)+3)<<endl;
 return 0 ; }
```

```
The expected output is given below.
6         8         5         4
2         3         7         9
10        11        12        13
```

From the output it is clear that A[i][j] and in the pointer notation *(*(pA+i)+j) are equivalent expressions. So we may as well use the expression like *(*(A+i)+j)for traversing a two dimensional array or a matrix.

Declaration of Pointer to Three Dimensional Array

A three dimensional array is an array of matrices. Let A be a 3 dimensional array. The pointer declaration and initialization is carried out as below.

```
int A[2] [3] [4] ;
int (*pA) [3] [4] = A ;  // pointer to array A
```

Here (*pA) [3][4] is the pointer to A[2][3][4]. An element of array with subscripts values i, j and k may be accessed by the following expression.

```
A[i] [j] [k]
```

And in pointer notation an element with subscripts i, j and k may be accessed by expression given below.

```
*(*(*(A +i) + j) + k)
```

In the following program a 3 dimensional array is declared. Its output is carried out in pointer notation as an array of two matrices.

PROGRAM 9.13 – Illustrates **pointer to three dimensional array** and array output.

```
#include <iostream>
using namespace std;

int main()
{int KBS [2] [3] [4] = {6,8,5,4, 2,3,7,9, 1 ,2,3,4, 21,22,23,24, 31,32,33,34,
41, 42, 43, 44} ; // 3 dimensional array

int(* pKBS ) [3]  [4] = KBS;  // Declaration of a pointer

for (int i =0; i<2; i++)
{for ( int j =0; j <3; j++)
{for ( int k =0; k<4; k++)
cout << *(*(*(pKBS +i) + j) +k)<<"  ";
cout<<"\n";}

cout<<"\n";}
 return 0 ;
}
```

The expected output is given below.

```
6  8  5  4
2  3  7  9
1  2  3  4

21  22  23  24
31  32  33  34
41  42  43  44
```

9.8 POINTERS TO FUNCTIONS

In the previous section we have seen that name of an array carries the value of address of first element of array and is a constant pointer to the array. Similarly the name of a function also carries the address of function and is a constant pointer to the function. Therefore, we can declare a pointer to a function and initialize it with the name of the function. The pointer to a function may be declared as below.

```
type ( *identifier_for_pointer ) ( types_of_parameters_of_ function);
```

Here type refers to the type of data returned by the function, in the first parentheses is the indirection operator followed by name of pointer. The next pair of parentheses contains the types of parameters. Let Fptr be name of pointer to a function Func of type int and which takes two integer parameters, i.e. int Func(int, int). The pointer to this function is declared as,

```
int (*Fptr) (int, int) ;
```

The above declaration is, in fact, for any function which has return value of *type* int and has two int parameters. Let int Func1(int, int) and int Func2(int, int) be any two functions which satisfy the above criteria. The above declaration of pointer applies to both these functions. Hence, if we may assign the following value to Fptr,

```
Fptr = Func1;    // Fptr points to Func1
```

The pointer Fptr points to Func1. The function Func1 may be called by dereference operator.

```
int a , b;
(*Fptr)(a, b ); // calling the function
```

In fact the dereference operator is not required and function may simply be called as below.

```
Fptr(a, b);
```

Now we may as well initialize Fptr with address of Func2.

```
Fptr = Func2;    // Pointer Fptr now points to Func2
```

With the above definition, the pointer Fptr now points to Funct2. The function Funct2 may be called by the expression (*Fptr)(i,d); or by Fptr(i,d); where i and d are integers. This gives the facility to the user of the program to choose any one of the functions provided in the program that matches the pointer declaration and user's requirement.

In the above declarations *Fptr has been enclosed in parentheses because otherwise there would be only one parentheses that encloses the parameter, and which will have higher precedence to (*) operator. Thus an expression such as int *Fptr(int, int); would mean that function Fptr takes two int arguments and returns a pointer to an integer. Therefore, it is necessary to enclose *Fptr in parentheses. The following program illustrates the use of pointers to functions. The user has a choice of four functions and choice is facilitated by switch statement.

PROGRAM 9.14 – Illustrates pointers to functions.

```
#include <iostream>
using namespace std;

int F1(int n){ return n   ;}           // returns argument
int F2( int n){ return n*n;}        // returns square of argument
int F3(int n ){ return n*n*n;}      // returns cube of argument
int F4( int n){ return n*n*n*n;}    //returns 4th power of argument


int main()
{ int m;
 int (*Fptr)(int m);  // pointer to above functions
 cout << "Writ an integer number ";
 cin >> m ;
 int userchoice ; // For user to choose the function
 cout << "Give your choice between 1 to 4 :";
 cin >> userchoice;
 switch (userchoice) // switch condition for multiple choice
 {
 case 1:
 Fptr = F1 ;   // selects function F1
 cout << m << "raised to power 1 = " << F1(m)<< endl ;
 break;

  case 2 :
  Fptr = F2 ;  // selects function F2
  cout << m << "raised to power 2 = " << F2(m)<<endl;
  break;

 case 3 :
 Fptr = F3 ; // selects function F3
 cout << m << "raised to power 3 = " << F3(m)<<endl;
  break;
 case 4 :
 Fptr = F4 ; // selects function F4
 cout << m << "raised to power 4 = " << F4(m)<<endl;
 break;
default :
 cout << "Make a second choice between 1 to 4 "<<endl;
 }
 return 0;
  }
```

The expected output to first choice with m = 5 and user choice equal to 3.

```
Writ an integer number 5
Give your choice between 1 to 4: 3
5 raised to power 3 = 125
```

The second trial was done with m = 6 and user choice = 5 which is not there, so it goes to default.

```
Writ an integer number 6
Give your choice between 1 to 4: 5
Make a second choice between 1 to 4
```

9.9 ARRAY OF POINTERS TO FUNCTIONS

Functions cannot be elements of an array, however, we can have an array of pointers which point to different functions. The functions may be called in the main ( ) through the pointers. In the following program we declare an array of pointers to three functions which are of type int. The functions are defined out side the main ( ) , because a function cannot be defined in side another function. The first function returns the argument, the second returns square of argument and third returns the cube of argument.

PROGRAM 9.15 – Illustrates an **array of pointer to functions.**

```
#include<iostream>
using namespace std;

 int func1(int);     // function prototype of Func1
 int func2(int) ;    // function prototype of Func2
 int func3(int);     // function prototype of Func3

int main()
{
 int P;
 int (*F[3])(int)={func1,func2,func3}; // Array of three pointers
       // initialization done by names of functions

 cout << "Enter a number ";
 cin>> P;
 cout<<"You entered the number "<<P<<endl;
for(int i=0;i<3;i++)    //for loop for calling different functions.
cout<< "Power "<<i+1<<" of the number = "<<(*F[i])(P)<<endl;
 return 0;
 }
 int func1(int a)   // Definition of func1
 {return a ; }

 int func2(int a)  // Definition of func2
 {return a*a; }

 int func3(int a)  // Definition of func3
 {return a*a*a;}
```

The *for* loop used in the above program, selects different functions which return the corresponding values. These are given in the output of the program which is given below.

```
Enter a number 5
You entered the number 5
Power 1 of the number = 5
Power 2 of the number = 25
Power 3 of the number = 125
```

One of the applications of pointers to functions is in interactive programming in which the user has a choice to make. The different choices can lead to different subroutines to execute the choice.

9.10 POINTER TO FUNCTIONS AS PARAMETER OF ANOTHER FUNCTION

The name of a function holds the address of the function. A function may have another function as one of its parameters. Thus a function may be passed on to another function as its argument either by its name or by its pointer which also holds the address of the function parameter. With pointer to function as parameter there is facility of choice of functions. And we can get more than one value out of a function.

In the following program a function by name Function is of *type* double, i.e. returns a double number. Pointer to other functions, i.e. double(*)(double, double, double), is one of its parameters. The other three parameters are double, double, double. The pointer is used to call two functions, i.e. volume and surface area of a cubical prism.

PROGRAM 9.16 – Illustrates **pointer to functions as a parameter of a function.**

```
#include <iostream>
using namespace std;

double Function(double (*) (double, double, double ),double, double, double);
// prototype of Function ()

double volume(double, double, double);     // Function prototype
double surface(double, double, double );    // Function prototype

int main()
{ cout<<"Surface area and volume of a cubiod of sides 4.0,5.0,6.0:"<<endl;
cout<<"Surface area = " <<Function(surface , 4.0,5.0,6.0)<<endl;
cout<< "Volume = " <<Function(volume,4.0,5.0,6.0) <<endl;
return 0;
}
    // definition of functions
double Function(double(*pF) (double k, double m, double n ),double p, double
q, double r)   // Definition of Function
{ return (*pF)(p,q,r) ; }
```

```
    // Below is definition of function surface
double surface(double k, double m, double n)
{ return 2*(m*k+ n*k+ m*n) ; }
    // Below is definition of function volume
double volume(double k, double m, double n)
{return k*m*n; }
```

The output of the program is given below.

```
Surface area and volume of a cubiod of sides 4.0,5.0,6.0:
Surface area = 148
Volume = 120
```

9.11 THE new AND delete

In many implementations of programs it is not known how much memory would be needed for the successful execution. In such cases memory has to be allocated during the execution of program. Such an allocation of memory is called dynamic allocation. In C language the function **malloc()** is used for allocation of memory and function **free()** (header file <stblib.h>) is used to free the memory so allocated. In C++ the operators **new** and **delete** are defined in the header file **<new>** for the same purpose. However, just for memory allocation we need not include the header file **<new>** in a program. But for special operators such as **placement new** the header file has to be included. The operator **placement new** enables you to create an additional object at predetermined memory location. For arrays, the **new[]** and **delete[]**are defined. If new[] is used for creation of a new array, then delete[]should be used for its removal. If only delete is used it will remove only the first element of the array and would result in memory leak.

The operator **new** allocates memory for the additional object and returns pointer to it. For variables of types int, float, double and char the application of new is illustrated below. However, **new** can also be used for objects of user defined *types* as well. The applications for user defined types are dealt in Chapter 12. Declaration of a pointer for a new variable may be done as below.

```
int* k ;   // k is pointer to an integer
k = new int; //k is pointer to an integer
*k = 15;   //assigning a value to new integer.
```

Note that in the above declaration name of variable is not declared, only pointer name is declared. The value of variable is obtained by dereference operator. The declaration and initialization may be done in the same code line as well. It is illustrated below.

```
int* k = new int(15);
double *d = new double (40.8);
char*pc = new char ('H') ;
```

For arrays we may use the operator **new** as illustrated below.

```
char* ch ;
ch = new char[6];
```

The following program illustrates the application of **new** and **delete**. Notice that variable name is not used. The value of variable is obtained by dereference operator (*).

PROGRAM 9.17 – Illustration of application of new and delete for fundamental types.

```
#include <iostream>
using namespace std;
main()
{ int* k ;
 k = new int;  // k is name of pointer.
 *k = 8;   // assigning value to new integer but without a name
  float *D ;
   D = new float (4.0); // Here D is name of pointer
cout<< "Address of k = " << k <<endl;
cout << "Area of circle of diameter 4.0 = " << 3.14159**D**D/4 <<endl;
delete k;
delete D;
return 0;
 }
```

The output is as given below.

```
Address of k = 004800D0
Area of circle of diameter 4.0 = 12.5664
```

The following program illustrate the application of **new**[] for creating new arrays.

PROGRAM 9.18 – Illustration of application of new [ ] and delete [ ].

```
#include <iostream>
using namespace std;

int main()
{
 int* k ;
 k = new int[5];
cout<< "Enter 5 integers : " ;

for (int i =0;i<5;i++)
cin >> k[i];   // user input of array elements
char *ch ;

ch = new char[6] ;
cout<<"Enter a name of 6 characters: ";

 for (int m = 0 ; m<6;m++)
 cin >> ch[m]; // ch is similar to name of array. So ch[m]
   // represents element at index value m
 cout<< "Address of k = " << k <<endl;

 for (int n = 0 ; n<5; n++)
 cout << k[n]<<"  "; // here k is similar to name of array
```

```
cout<<"\n";
for (int j = 0 ; j<6; j++)
cout << ch[j]<<"" ;   // for output of array elements

 cout<<"\n";
 delete []k; //notice the code for deletion of new array
 delete []ch;

return 0;
 }
```

The expected output of the program is as below.

```
Enter 5 integers : 4 5 6 7 8
Enter a name of 6 characters: MANALI
Address of k = 004900D0
4  5  6  7  8
MANALI
```

9.12 REFERENCES

Often people give alternative name to a person, may be out of love or it is simply easier to pronounce. For example, the family members and friends of Parminder may call him Pummy. Both Parminder and Pummy refer to the same person called Parminder. Here Pummy is a reference to Parminder.

Reference for a variable is also an alias or just another name for the same variable. The variable name and its reference-name both point to the same block of memory where the value of variable is stored. You must note that **any change in the value of reference also changes the value of variable.**

For creating a reference first write the *type* of the variable for which the reference is being created then write *reference operator* (&) followed by the name or identifier for the reference. Name of reference may be decided in the same way as it is done for any variable. For example, let there be an integer by name *n*. Reference to *n* with name *Count* may be defined as illustrated below.

```
int n = 100;
int &Count = n;     // Count is declared a reference to n.
```

Here *Count* is a reference to *n*. Let Weight be a floating point variable. We may define a reference to it with name W as illustrated below.

```
double Weight ;
double &W = Weight ;
```

Similarly the reference by name T for a char variable ch may be defined as below.

```
char ch = 'S';
 char & T = ch ;
```

In the following program we declare three variables. One integer by name n, second a double by name Weight and third a char by name ch. They have the values 100, 35.6 and 'S' respectively. For each of these variables we create a reference. The name of reference for n is Count, the name of reference for Weight is W and name of reference for ch is T. In the program the values of the three references are changed. From the output we find that values of the variables are also changed to the values of the corresponding references. Also note that the address of n and Count is same, i.e. `0012FF7C`. Also the variable Weight and its reference W have the same address where the value is stored.

PROGRAM 9.19 – Illustrates **declaration of references** to variables.

```
#include <iostream>
using namespace std;
int main()

{int n = 100 ;
double Weight = 35.6;
char ch = 'S';

int& Count = n ;    // Count is a reference to n.
double& W =Weight;   // W is a reference to weight.
char& T = ch;     // T is reference to ch.
cout<<"n = "<<n<<" \t&n = " <<&n <<"\n";
cout<<"Count = "<<Count<<" \t &Count = " <<&Count << endl;

cout<< "Weight = " <<Weight << ", &Weight = "<< &Weight<<"\n";

cout<< "W = " << W<< " \t &W = "<< &W<<"\n\n";
cout<<"ch = "<<ch <<"\t  T = " << T <<endl;
T = 'Z';
n = 50;   //The value of reference n is changed to 50
W = 12.5;  // The value of reference W is changed to 12.5

cout<< "n = "<<n << " \tCount ="<< Count <<endl;
cout << "W = "<< W<< " \tWeight =" << Weight << endl;

cout << "ch = " << ch <<" \t T = " << T << endl;
return 0;
 }
```

The output is given below.

```
n = 100         &n = 0012FF7C
Count = 100         &Count = 0012FF7C
```

```
Weight = 35.6, &Weight = 0012FF74
W = 35.6        &W = 0012FF74

ch = S          T = S
n = 50          Count =50
W = 12.5          Weight =12.5
ch = Z          T = Z
```

The output of the program shows that the address of the variable n and its reference *Count* is the same. If the value of reference *Count* is changed from 100 to 50, the value of n is also changed to 50. So dealing with a reference is as good as dealing with the variable. Similar results are obtained with double. Weight and the char ch.

In the following program it is shown that any number of references may be created and dealing with any of the references is as good as dealing with variable. A reference may be defined from another reference or a pointer as well.

PROGRAM 9.20 – Illustrates **multiple references** to a variable.

```
#include <iostream>
using namespace std;

int main()
{ int n = 60 ;   // variable n = 60
 int* ptrn = &n;   // ptrn is pointer to n
 int& Count = *ptrn ; // Count- a reference to n created from
      // pointer to n
int &m = n;     // m is another reference to n
int& T = Count;   // T is reference created by a reference

cout<<"Count = "<<Count<<"\t&Count = " <<&Count<<endl;
cout<<"*ptrn = "<<*ptrn<<" , \tptrn = " <<ptrn <<"\n";
cout<<"T = "<<T<<" , \t&T = "<<&T<<endl;

cout<<"n = "<<n<<" , \t&n = " <<&n <<"\n";
cout<<"m = "<<m<<" , \t&m = " <<&m <<"\n";

T = 80;    // value of T changed to 80
cout << "T = "<<T<<" \t*ptrn = "<<*ptrn<<endl;
cout<< "n = "<<n << ",   Count ="<< Count << ",    m = " << m <<endl;

return 0;
 }
```

The expected output is given below.

```
Count = 60          &Count = 0012FF7C
*ptrn = 60 ,      ptrn = 0012FF7C
T = 60 ,          &T = 0012FF7C
```

```
n = 60 ,            &n = 0012FF7C
m = 60 ,            &m = 0012FF7C
T = 80              *ptrn = 80
n = 80,     Count =80,      m = 80
```

In the above program Count, m, T are references to n. Count is created by the pointer to n while T is created by another reference Count. The reference m is created directly by n. In all these cases, the references behave in the same manner. All of them have the same address, i.e. 0012FF7C. If the value of any of the reference is changed, the value of all references including the variable changes. Manipulating any one reference is as good as manipulating the variable.

9.13 PASSING ARGUMENTS BY VALUE AND BY REFERENCE

Passing Arguments by Value

The arguments to a function may be passed on by values or by references. This topic has already been dealt briefly in Chapter 7 on Functions. When the arguments are passed on by values, the copies of the values of the variables are passed on to the function. The function may operate on these copies, i.e. may change their values, but the function does not get to the variables and so it cannot change their values. The benefit of this is that the function cannot change the original data. However, when the values are passed on by reference or by pointers, in fact, we pass on the variables to the function. Now if the function changes their values, the changed values get stored in the memory blocks allocated to variables. So the values of variables are also changed. It is explained by an example below. Let us define a function F() which has two integer parameters a and b as given below.

```
int F ( int a, int b)  // Function definition
{ a +=3;
b +=2;
return a*a + b*b; }

int main()
{ int P = 3, Q =2;
Z = F(P,Q);
cout<<Z << endl; }
```

In the above code a function with parameters `int a` and `int b` changes the values of *a* and *b* in its definition body and then function is evaluated taking changed values of a and b. In the *main*() when this function is called as F(P, Q) the copies of values of two integer variable P and Q are passed to it. The variable *a* takes the value of P and *b* that of Q. So *a* becomes 3 and *b* becomes 2. But variables themselves, i.e. P and Q are not passed on to the function, only their copies are passed to the function. The function in fact does not know where the variables P and Q are stored. The function as defined above changes the values of these copies which are passed on to it. The values of *a* and *b* are changed in the function to 6 and 4 respectively and function is evaluated. But values of variables P and Q do not change. *This is called passing arguments by value.* Passing the arguments by value has the advantage that the original data is not changed, but the disadvantage is that when data is very large the process would occupy more memory space as well as the execution of program will take more time. In some functions it is desired to change the values of variables, such as in swapping of values, in such cases we will have to pass on the arguments by reference.

Program 9.20 is an illustration of passing arguments by values. In the program a function Sum() has two integer parameters a and b. When the function is called in the main () the *values* of P and Q are passed on to function as *a* and *b* respectively. The values of *a* and *b* are changed in the function Sum () as explained above but the values of P and Q are not changed at all.

PROGRAM 9.21 – Illustrates passing of arguments by values.

```
#include<iostream>
using namespace std;
 int Sum(int a, int b )
 {a +=3;
 b+=2;
 return a*a + b*b ;
 }
int main()

{ int P,Q,Z ;
 P = 3;
 Q= 2;
 cout<<"Before calling function the values are: "<<endl;
 cout<< "P = " <<P<<", Q = " <<Q<< endl;
 Z = Sum(P,Q);

 cout<<"After the first call the values are :"<<endl;
 cout << " Z = " <<Z<<", P = " << P<<", Q = " <<Q <<endl;
 cout<<"After the 2nd call the values are:"<<endl;
 Z = Sum (P,Q);
 cout << "Z = " <<Z<<", P = " << P<<", Q = " <<Q <<endl;
 return 0;
 }
```

The expected output is given below.

```
Before calling function the values are:
P = 3, Q = 2
After the first call the values are :
Z = 52, P = 3, Q = 2
After the 2nd call the values are:
Z = 52, P = 3, Q = 2
```

PASSING ARGUMENTS BY REFERENCE

Now, for passing the variable by reference the same function is defined as given below.

```
int F( int &a, int &b)
{ a +=3;
b +=2;
return a*a + b*b;
}
```

In such a case *a* and *b* are references to P and Q. Since the values of a and b are changed in the body of the function the values of P and Q will also get changed. In Program 9.22 given below, the variables are passed to the function through references. So change in the value of references will change the value of variables also. Thus we see from the output of following program that values of P and Q after the call of the function are changed. See carefully the method of defining the function. In the following listing the function has been called twice. Each time a different result is obtained, because the values of P and Q get changed in every call of function.

PROGRAM 9.22 – Illustrates **passing arguments by reference.**

```
#include<iostream>
using namespace std;

int Sum(int &a, int &b) //&a and &b are references of variables.
 {a +=3;
 b+=2;
 return a*a + b*b ;
 }
int main()
{
 int P,Q,Z ;
 P = 3;
 Q= 2;
 cout<<"Before calling function."<<endl;
 cout<< "P = " <<P<<", Q = " <<Q<< endl;

 Z = Sum(P,Q); // first call of function
 cout<<"After the first function call"<<endl;
 cout << "Z = " <<Z<<", P = " << P<<", Q = " <<Q <<endl;

 Z = Sum(P,Q);  // second call of function
 cout<<"After the second function call"<<endl;
 cout << "Z = " <<Z<<", P = " << P<<", Q = " <<Q <<endl;
 return 0;
  }
```

The expected output of the program is as under.

```
Before calling function.
P = 3, Q = 2
After the first function call
Z = 52, P = 6, Q = 4
After the second function call
Z = 117, P = 9, Q = 6
```

The output of the above program shows that before the function call the values of variables are P =3 and Q =2. After the first call P becomes 6 and Q becomes 4. The value of the function Sum (P, Q) is = 52. After the second call of the function the values of P and Q are changed again. P is now equal to 9 and Q is equal to 6. The value of Sum () now becomes 117.

9.14 PASSING ARGUMENTS THROUGH POINTERS

Pointers keep the actual address of the variables, therefore, passing arguments through pointers is as good as passing on the variables to the function. Program 9.23 illustrates this fact.

Swap() Function

Here we define Swap function which exchanges the values of two int variables (this Swap () function is different from template function swap () of C++ Standard library, because S is in upper case. The function is defined so that values are passed on by pointers. The values are exchanged as expected.

PROGRAM 9.23 – An illustration of **passing arguments by pointers.**

```
#include <iostream>
using namespace std;

void Swap(int *px, int*py) // Definition of Swap function
{int temp;
 temp = *px;
  *px = *py;
   *py = temp; }

int main()
{
 int m ,n ;   // Declaration of two integers.
 cout<<"Enter two integers : m = "; cin>> m ; cout<< "n = " ;
 cin >>n;   // values of m and n are entered by user.
Swap (&n , &m );
cout <<"After swapping the values are :";
cout<<" m ="<<m<< ", n = " << n<<endl;
return 0;
}
```

The expected output is given below.

```
Enter two integers : m = 50
n = 120
After swapping the values are : m =120, n = 50
```

SORTING AN ARRAY WITH POINTERS

The Swap () function as defined above has been used to sort an array of integers in descending order. See the following program for illustration.

PROGRAM 9.24 – Illustrates **sorting of array** using pointers.

```
#include <iostream>
using namespace std;

void Swap(int *px, int *py) // Declaration and
 { int temp ;    // definition of Swap() we are
  temp = *px;  // not using swap() of C++ std Lib.
  *px = *py;
   *py = temp;}

int main()
{
int kim [ ] = { 60,50,86,90,120,67,89 } ;

int* pkim = kim; /* declaration and initialization of pointer to array kim[] */

 for ( int j = 0; j<=6;j++)
 for ( int k =0; k<6-j ; k++)
  if (*(pkim +k)< *(pkim +k+1))
  Swap((pkim+k), (pkim + k+1));

 for ( int i=0 ; i<=6;i++)
 cout << *(pkim +i) <<"  ";
 return 0;
  }
```

The sorted list is given in the output as under.

```
120  90  89  86  67  60  50
```

Application of pointers in selecting greater of two numbers

The following program is another example of using pointers for selecting greater of the two numbers.

PROGRAM 9.25 – An application of pointers in finding greater of two numbers

```
#include <iostream>

using namespace std;

 int Max(int *px, int*py)   // definition of Max()
{ return (*px>*py ? *px:*py); }
int main()
{
 int m ,n ;

 cout <<"Enter two integers :"; cin>> m>>n;
 int Maxnum = Max (&n,&m);

 cout<<"Maximum of the two numbers is " << Maxnum<<endl;

return 0;
}
```

The expected output is as below.

```
Enter two integers :65 32
Maximum of the two numbers is 65
```

9.15 POINTER ARITHMETIC

It has already been illustrated in Program 9.2 that a pointer may be assigned if the *type* of both is same. The assignment would result in having two pointers pointing to same value stored in memory. The other operators that may be applies to pointers are +, – and increment (++) and decrement (– –) operators

The relational operators, in general, have no meaning for pointers pointing to unrelated objects. However, they may be used when dealing with elements of same array, in which case, the pointer values (addresses) of different elements may be compared. The pointers may be incremented or decremented to access different elements of the array. The pointer increment, however, increases the value of pointer by the number of bytes occupied by one element of array. Thus if we are dealing with an array of integers, each element occupies 4 bytes. Let us declare a pointer as below.

```
int A[5] = { 6,8,9,8,4};
int * ptrA = A ;
```

In the above declaration ptrA points to the first element of array i.e. A[0]. Now ++ptrA points to the next element of array. Similarly (ptrA + 3) will point to A[3], i.e. the 4th element of array. The actual value of pointer increases by 4*3 = 12 bytes. The value of array element may be obtained by dereference operator. Thus *(ptrA + 3) gives the value of A[3]. Please note that the expression *(ptrA + 3) should not be written as *ptrA+3, which will be equivalent to addition of 3 to value of first element (A[0]) of array.

9.16 VOID POINTERS

As explained above, the pointers may be assigned if both are of same type. Otherwise, we need to convert the pointer on the right side to the *type* of pointer on the left side of equality sign (=). The void pointer (void *) can, however, represent any pointer type. Thus any type of pointer may be assigned to a void pointer. But the reverse is not valid. A void pointer cannot be assigned to any other type of pointer without first converting the void pointer to that type.

Also the void pointer cannot be directly dereferenced, because it is pointer without a type. The compiler does not know the number of bytes occupied by the variable to which the void pointer is pointing. It is illustrated in the following program.

PROGRAM 9.26 – Illustrates the application of **void pointers**.

```
#include<iostream>
using namespace std ;

int main()
{
int x = 8, *px; // declaration of int and pointer for int
double D = 5.8, * pd; // declaration of double and
      // pointer for double
    px = &x;
    pd = &D;
cout<<"x = " << *px<<endl;
cout <<"D = " << *pd<<endl;
void* pv ;   // declaring a void pointer
pv = &x ;   // assigning address of int to void pointer
cout<< "Now getting values through void pointers"<<endl;
cout <<"x =" << *(int*)pv << endl ;
    // pv is cast to type int for dereferencing

pv = &D; // assigning address of double to void pointer
 cout<<"D = " << *(double*)pv<< endl;
   // pv is cast to type double for dereferencing.
return 0 ;
}
```

The output is given below.

```
x = 8
D = 5.8
Now getting values through void pointers
x =8
D = 5.8
```

9.17 SUMMARY OF POINTER DECLARATIONS

Table 9.1 – Summary of useful declarations in pointers

Declaration	Description	Example
`int *ptr;`	Pointer to an integer.	`int y ;` `int *ptry = &y;`
`double *ptrd;`	Pointer to a double.	`double* ptrPI = &PI;`
`char *ptrc;`	Pointer to a character.	`char ch = 'A';` `char*ptrc= & ch;`
`void* ptr;`	Pointer to void.	`void *memset(void *S, int c, size_t n)`
`const int *ptr;`	Pointer to a const integer.	`const int n ;` `const int* ptrn = &n;`
`int* const ptr ;`	Constant pointer to an integer. The pointer cannot be changed.	`int n;` `int* const ptr = &n;`
`const int* const ptr ;`	Constant pointer to a constant integer. Both cannot be changed.	`const int n ;` `const int*const ptr = &n ;`

`int ** pptrn ;`	Pointer to pointer to an integer.	`int n ;`
		`int* ptrn = &n;`
		`int**pptrn= &ptrn;`

`int& Count = n ;`	Count is reference to n.	`int& Count = n ;`
`int A[4];int* ptrA = A ;`	Pointer to single dimensional int array A.	`int A[4];` `int* ptrA = A;`
`int (*ptr)[];`	Pointer to two dimensional array.	`int B[3][4];` `int (*ptrb)[4]= B;`
`int *A[6];`	Array of 6 pointers to integers.	`int *A[6];`
`int(*Function)(int,int);`	Pointer to function returning an int value and with two int parameters.	`int(*Funct)(int, int);`
`double(*Function[])(int, int );`	An array of pointers to functions returning double and having two int parameters.	`double(*Funct[])(int,int);`
`void (*function)(void);`	Pointer to a void function with void arguments.	`void(*function) (void);`

EXERCISES

1. What is a pointer? How is it declared for an integer?
2. An integer variable x has the value 50. Write the code for declaration of the variable, its reference by name myx and pointer by name ptrx.
3. Write a test program to declare a float variable y, initialize it to zero. Create a reference by name refy. Now change y to 3.675. Find the value of refy and its memory location.
4. What are the sizes (in bytes) of memory spaces allocated for pointers to (i) a character variable, (ii) a long int, (iii) a float number, (iv) double number.
5. Write code for declaring pointer to (i) one dimensional array, (ii) a two dimensional array.
6. How do you get the value of variable from its pointer to pointer?
7. Write a program to declare an int variable and its pointer and to determine its square and cube using its pointer.
8. How do you declare pointer to pointer for (i) int variable, (ii) for double variable.
9. What is wrong with the following codes.

   (i) int* ptrn = n;

   (ii) double ptrnPI = 3.14159;

   (iii) char * ch = A ;
10. What is difference between a reference and a pointer?
11. Declare a reference with name ref_grade for character grades like A, B, etc.
12. What do you understand by the following.

    (i) int (*Function)(int, int) ;

    (ii) double(*Function[])(int, int, double)
13. Explain the difference between following two declarations.

    (i) int (*A)[6];

    (ii) int *A[6];
14. What is the difference between following declarations?

    (i) const int*ptr ;

    (ii) int * const ptr;

    (iii) const int * const ptr;
15. PA is a pointer to an array A[10]. Which of the following codes are correct to get the next element of the array?

    (i) *PA +1;

    (ii) *(PA+1) ;

    (iii) *A++
16. Write a program for illustrating the use of pointers for traversing an array.
17. Write a test program to illustrate the application of oprators **new** and **delete** for int variables and for character variable.

18. When **new[]** is used to declare an array of integers, how do you initialize the elements and write code for their output and their deletion.
19. Write code of a program for preparing lists of names by user of program wherein the total number of entries are unknown. Make use of pointers.
20. Write a program to illustrate the application of **new[]** and **delete[]**

❍❍❍

CHAPTER

10 C-Strings

10.1 DECLARATION OF A C-STRING

A C-string is a sequence of characters stored in sequential memory blocks like an array and it is terminated by Null character ('\0'). Unlike arrays, a string is treated as a single unit. String characters may include letters, digits and special symbols such as +, –,*, [],(), etc., but not the escape characters. The strings based on class **<string>** are called C++ strings and are dealt separately in Chapter 17. The C++ Standard Library has many useful functions for manipulation of C-strings as well. Here in this chapter we shall deal with C-strings, however, we shall refer to them as strings. A C-string may be declared and initialized as illustrated below.

```
char Name [8] = "John";
```

Here `Name` is the identifier (name) of string . The names of strings are decided as we do for any other variable. The number 8 in square bracket indicates that there could be 8 characters in the string including the Null character ('\0') which is appended by the system to mark the end of string. This string is initialized as *John.* In assignment like this it is required to enclose the sequence of characters between double quotes as `"John"`. When a string is initialized with a string of characters in double quotes the system appends the null character at the end of string. In this case system would allocate 8 memory blocks (each of size one byte). Since the string Name[8] is also an array the different elements of this array are as below.

```
Name[0] = 'J';
Name[1] = 'o';
Name[2] = 'h';
Name[3] = 'n';
Name[4] = '\0';
```

The remaining three memory blocks are empty. The last character Null ('\0') marks the end of string. Thus if we determine the size of Name we would get 8 because it has been declared so. However, if the string is declared and initialised as

```
char Name[] = "John";
```

we would get the size as 5, i.e. 4 characters of John and one Null character ('\0').

PROGRAM 10.1 – Illustrates **declaration and initialization** of C-strings.

```
#include <iostream>
using namespace std;
int main()
 {
 char Name1[8] = "John";
 char Name2[]  = "John";
 char Symbols[] = "@ ! # $ % 5 , ~ ^ & * () _ + = \ ;: {} () [] \t\n\a";
 cout<<Name1<<endl ;
 cout<<Name2<<endl;

 cout<<sizeof(Name1)<<endl;
 cout<<sizeof(Name2)<<endl;

 cout<<"Name1 is "<<Name1<<endl;
 cout<<"Name2 is " << Name2<< endl;
 cout<< "Symbols are "<< Symbols<< endl;

 for(int i =0; i<8;i++)
    cout<<Name1[i] <<" ";
    cout<<endl;
 return 0 ;
 }
```

The expected output is given below.

```
John
John
8
5
Name1 is John
Name2 is John
Symbols are @ ! # $ % 5 , ~ ^ & * () _ + = ;: {} () []
John
```

From the output statements and the output it is clear that the strings *Name1*, *Name2*, and *Symbols* have been treated as single units. The size of *Name2* is 5 because it also includes the null character besides the 4 characters in John. Many symbols have been put in the string Symbol simply to show that these could also be part of string. You would notice that the **escape sequences are not part of strings.** These are not there in the 7th line of output. It should be noted that the characters in string Symbols are only characters, these do not have the usual meaning. For example, here in string Symbol the character '5' does not have the usual value five but is equal to 53 as per ASCII code (see Appendix A). The output of Name1, character by character shows only 4 characters of John, the remaining 4 characters are not shown in output. Out of these one is '\0' character which does not show up in output and the other 3 memory blocks are empty. In the computer memory string characters are stored in adjacent memory blocks of one byte each as an array of characters terminated by a Null character ('\0') as illustrated in Fig. 10.1.

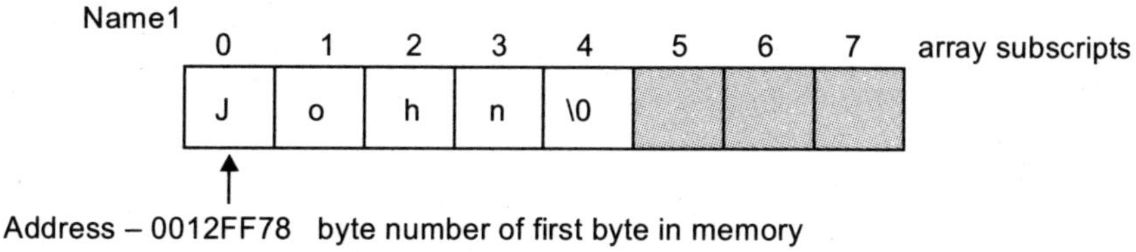

Fig.10.1: The string Name1[8] = "John"; is stored as an array in computer. The shaded bytes are empty. Array subscripts are shown above the blocks

The following program illustrates some differences between the normal arrays and character arrays and strings.

PROGRAM 10.2 – Illustrates differences between arrays and strings.

```
#include <iostream>
using namespace std;

int main()
 {
int Array [] = { 5 , 6 , 7 , 8 }; // int array
char B[] = { 'U', 'V', 'X','Y'}; // char array

char Name[] = "John";     // string
char* S = "You are Welcome to C++!" ; // string pointed to by S

 cout<<"Name = "<<Name<<endl;
 cout<<"*Name = " << *Name<<endl;
cout<<"S = "<<S<<endl;
cout<<"*S = "<<*S<<endl;
cout << "Array = " <<Array<<endl;
cout << "*Array = "<< *Array<<endl;
cout<<"B = "<< B<<endl;

cout<<"*B = " <<*B<<endl;
    return 0 ;
  }
```

The expected output is given below.

```
Name = John
*Name = J
S = You are Welcome to C++!
*S = Y
Array = 0012FF70
*Array = 5
B = UVXY?
*B = U
```

The array Array is an int array. When its name is called for output it gives the address of first element of the array. And when *Array is called for output it gives the value of the first element of the array. These are usual with arrays. Similarly when *Name is called for output it gives the first element of string Name that is J. So is the case with *S and *B. The output of *S is the Y the first character of string pointed by S and *B gives U the first element in the char array. However, when name of character array or name of string is called for output instead of giving address of first element it gives the complete string as output. Similarly when pointer S to a string is called for output it gives the full string as output while in other arrays it would give the address.

10.2 INPUT/OUTPUT OF C-STRINGS

The object *cin* of <istream> along with extraction operator >> may be used for input of strings if there is no white space between the characters because *cin* takes the white space as the end of string. However, there are other functions like `cin.get()` and `cin.getline()` which may also be used for input of strings. These functions read white spaces as well. The `cin.get()` reads character by character while `cin.getline()` reads the whole line.

In the following program only cin is used. The input string consists of two words Mona Lisa, but cin extracts only the first word Mona and stops reading on encountering white space.

PROGRAM 10.3 – Illustrates **string input by cin.**

```
#include <iostream>
using namespace std;
int main()
 {
 char S[15] ;
 cout<<"Write a short name : " ;

 cin >> S ;
 cout <<"You have written : "<< S<<endl;
 return 0 ;
  }
```

The expected output is below.

```
Write a short name : Mona Lisa
You have written : Mona
```

From the output it is clear that cin stopped reading after encountering the white space, i.e. after Mona. Now if the same string is extracted by cin character by character as an array, the complete name is read but the white space is not read as space. This is illustrated in the following program. The two words Mona and Lisa are merged together.

PROGRAM 10.4 – Illustrates **limitations of cin** in reading string.

```
#include <iostream>
using namespace std;
int main()
 { char S[15];

  cout<<"Write a short name : ";

  for (int i =0; i<=15;i++) // Use of for loop for reading
  { cin>>S[i] ;    // It does not read the white space
   cout<<S[i] ;
  }
  return 0 ;
 }
```

The expected output is given below.

```
Write a short name : Mona Lisa
MonaLisa
```

From the 2nd line of the output it is clear that the white space has not been read and included in the string. So in the output the two parts of name are merged together.

FUNCTION CIN.GET()

The above mentioned problem is not there if we use function cin.get() and function cin.getline (). The use of `cin.get()` is illustrated below. It has three arguments.

```
cin.get(identifier, n, ch);
```

Here identifier is the name of string, the function reads a maximum of n–1 characters and ch is the name of character on encountering which the reading would stop. The following three programs illustrate the application of cin.get() function with different number of arguments. Below in Program 10.6 the function call is coded as,

```
cin.get (S, 15);
```

Here S is the name of the string, n = 15. This program limits the number of characters for input by cin.get() to 14 even though the string may have more characters (the 15th character is

'\0' character). If the input is user interactive as in online filling of forms etc., the number *n* should be sufficiently large so that user input data is not lost.

PROGRAM 10.5 – Illustrates **cin.get()** function for reading strings up to specified number of characters.

```
#include <iostream>
using namespace std;
void main()
{char S[15];
 cout<<"Enter a name :" ;
  cin.get(S,15) ;
  cout <<"you have written :"<< S<<endl;
 }
```

The output given below shows that full name along with white space has been read. Compare this output with that of the last program in which only *cin* has been used.

```
Enter a name :Mona Lisa
you have written :Mona Lisa
```

PROGRAM 10.6 – Illustrates action of **cin.get()** when specified number is too small.

```
#include <iostream>
using namespace std;
void main()
{char S[15];
 cout<<"Enter a name :" ;
  cin.get(S,5) ;
  cout <<"you have written :"<< S<<endl;
 }
```

The output given below shows that only the first part of name, i.e. Mona has been read because it was specified to read only five characters in the statement cin.get (S, 5);.

```
Enter a name :Mona Lisa
you have written :Mona
```

As mentioned above, we can as well specify a character in `cin.get()` on encountering of which the reading would stop. In the following program we specify a character 's' in the function `cin.get ()` on encountering of which `cin.get()` stops reading.

PROGRAM 10.7 – Illustrates action of **cin.get()** with a delimiting character.

```
#include <iostream>
using namespace std;
void main()
```

```
{ char ch = 's';
int i =0;
 char B[20];
  cout<<"Enter a name : " ;
  cin.get(B,20,ch);

cout <<"You have written : "<< B <<endl;
 }
```

The expected output is given below.

```
Enter a name : Johnson
You have written : John
```

The above output shows that `cin.get()` has read only up to John. On encountering character 's' it has stopped reading. The delimiting character 's' has not been taken in.

The function `cin.get()` reads the string character by character. One benefit of reading character by character is that you can also operate on any particular character. You may count the number of characters or count the number of occurrences of a particular character in a string or replace a particular character with another character while the characters are read. The following program counts the total number of characters in a statement and the number of times 'o' occurs in a statement.

PROGRAM 10.8 – Illustrates that while reading with **cin.get()** the characters read may be counted.

```
#include <iostream>
using namespace std;
int main()
 {
 int n =0, m = 0;
 char para;

 cout<<"Enter a few words : \n" ;

 while (cin.get(para))
 {if ( para !=' ')
  ++ n ;
  if ( para == 'o')
   ++m;
 if ( para == '.')
  break; }

 cout <<"n = "<<n <<", m = "<<m <<endl;
 return 0;
 }
```

The expected output is as below.

```
Enter a few words :
Mohan and Sohan are going to market.
n = 30,  m = 4
```

The output of the program shows that the total number of characters are 30 and 'o' occurs four times. The white spaces are not counted. In the above program the while loop is not limited by white space so program does not come to an end. It is an endless loop. So we have put the statement break; to exit from the loop on encountering full stop.

Function cin.getline ()

The function `cin.getline()` reads all the characters in a line until the limiting number of characters is reached or it encounters a delimiting character. It takes maximum of three arguments. The syntax for function call is as below.

```
cin.getline( identifier, size_t n, ch);
```

The first argument in the bracket is the name of string we want to put in. The integer n is used to limit the number of characters to be read. The function stops reading when (i) n–1 characters have been read or (ii) a new line or end of file is encountered or (iii) the delimiting character ch is encountered. It will not produce an error even if ch is not specified because *n* , end of line or EOF can do the same job. In the following, Programs 10.9, 10.10 and 10.11 illustrate the applications of this function with different number of arguments.

PROGRAM 10.9 – Illustrates use of **cin.getline()** to read input from keyboard.

```
#include <iostream>
using namespace std;
int main()
 {
 char B[50];

 cout <<"Enter a long name: ";
 cin.getline(B,50) ; // It specifies to read up to read 50-1
  // characters from string. The last character is Null (\0).

 cout<<"You have written = "<<B <<"\n" ;
 return 0 ;
 }
```

The expected output is given below.

```
Enter a long name: Mohan Dass Karamchand Gandhi
You have written = Mohan Dass Karamchand Ghandhi
```

PROGRAM 10.10 – Illustrates application of **cin.getline()** function.

```
#include <iostream>
using namespace std;
```

```
int main()
{
char B[20];
cout <<"Enter a name: ";
cin.getline(B,5) ;   // read first 5 characters of B

cout<<"You have written = "<<B <<"\n" ;

return 0 ;
}
```

The name entered was Mona Lisa but the function has read only first five characters, i.e. Mona as given in the output given below, because, it was specified so in getline() function.

```
Enter a name: Mona Lisa
You have written = Mona
```

In the following program a delimiting character has been put in the cin.getline() function to stop reading on encountering the character.

PROGRAM 10.11 – Illustrates use of **cin.getline()** to read up to specified character.

```
#include <iostream>
using namespace std;

int main()
{
char B[20];

cout <<"Enter a name: ";

  char ch = 's';
  cin.getline(B,20, ch) ; //read up to character 'S'
   cout<<"You have written = "<<B <<"\n" ;
return 0 ;
  }
```

The output is given below. It stopped reading on occurrence of letter 's'. So only Mona Li is read as given in the output below.

```
Enter a name: Mona Lisa
You have written = Mona Li
```

10.3 STANDARD FUNCTIONS FOR MANIPULATING STRING ELEMENTS

Function cin.putback( )

With the help of this function a character may be replaced by another character in a string. See the following program in which the *if (expression)* examines if the character is 'M' and the statement cin.putback('S'); replaces it with character 'S'.

PROGRAM 10.12 – Illustrates the action of function **putback().**

```
#include <iostream>
using namespace std;
void main()
 {
 char ch;
 cout<<"Enter a sentence : " ;

 while (cin.get(ch))
  { if (ch =='M')
   cin.putback('S');
  else
   cout<<ch;
 }}
```

The expected output is given below. 'M' has been replaced by 'S'.

```
Enter a sentence : Mona and Madu went to Madras.
Sona and Sadu went to Sadras.
```

Functions cin.peek() and cin.ignore ()

The function cin.peek() takes note of a character, i.e. if the desired character is encountered it will give a signal but the function itself does not do anything, however, the signal may be used by other functions to carry out the desired process. In the following program cin.peek() has been used to notice the character 'n' while cin.ignore() function has been used to ignore it. The function call for cin.ignore() is coded as below.

```
cin.ignore(n, ch) ;
```

Here *n* is the maximum number of characters to ignore and ch is the termination character.

PROGRAM 10.13 – The program illustrates functions **cin.peek(), cin.ignore().**

```
#include<iostream>
 using namespace std;
int main()
 { int m =0 ;
  int k = 0;
  char ch ;
 cout<<"Enter a sentence :\n" ;
while (cin.get(ch))    // unending loop
 { ++k;
  if (ch =='M')
  {++m;
   cin.putback('S');}
else
```

```
    cout<<ch;
    while (cin.peek()=='n')
     cin.ignore(1,'n');

   if (ch == '.') break;} // break statement
    cout << "\nTotal number of characters read = " << k <<endl;
    cout<<"Number of M are = " << m <<"\n" ;
    return 0;
     }
```

The expected output is given below.

```
Enter a sentence :
Madhu , Malti and Mamta all will come on Monday.
Sadhu , Salti ad Samta all will come o Soday.
Total number of characters read = 49
Number of M are = 4
```

In the above program, in the first while loop, it finds if the character is 'M', if so, it replaces it with 'S'. In the second while loop the function peek() notices for the character 'n' and the function cin.ignore() ignores it. The variable k counts the total number of characters read while m counts the number of M occurring in the sentence.

10.4 CONVERSION OF C-STRING CHARACTERS INTO OTHER TYPES

FUNCTIONS ATOI(), ATOL(), ATOF()

In some programs strings may contain digits or digits with a decimal point etc. In a string the digits are stored as characters and not as the values that the digits represent. The functions `atoi()`, `atol()`, `atof()` of the general utilities header file **<cstdlib>** convert the character digits into digital values. The individual details of these functions are given below.

atoi() It converts its argument consisting of a string of digits into *int* type number and returns int value. However, if the first character is not a digit the string may not be converted, in that case, it returns 0. The syntax is given below. In this the chptr is pointer to character constant.

```
int atoi ( const char *chptr)
```

atol() It converts its argument consisting of a string of digit characters into *long* type number and returns the number. However, if the first character is not a digit the string may not be converted and in that case it returns 0.The syntax is,

```
int atol ( const char *chptr)
```

atof() It converts string of digit characters with decimal point representing a floating point number into *double* type number and returns the double number. However, if the first character is not a digit the string may not be converted and in that case it returns 0.The syntax is given below.

```
int atof ( const char *chptr)
```

The following program illustrates application of the three functions.

PROGRAM 10.14 – Illustrates use of **atoi()**, **atol()** and **atof()** on strings.

```
#include <iostream>
# include <cstdlib>
using namespace std;
void main()
 {
 char ch1 []= "6444";
    char ch2[] = "21.66";
     char ch3[] = "Absent45";
       char ch4[] = "45Absent";

          char chL1[] = "Delhi45676548";
            char chL2[] = "45676548Delhi";

cout<<"Number represented by ch1 divided by 2 = " << atoi(ch1)/2 <<endl;
 cout << "Number ch2 /3= " << atof (ch2)/3<<endl;
  cout << "Number ch3 = " << atoi (ch3)<<endl;
cout << "Number represented by ch4 = " << atoi (ch4)<<endl;
cout << "Number represented by chL1 = " << atol (chL1)<<endl;
cout << "Number represented by chL2 = " << atol (chL2)<<endl;
  }
```

The expected output is as below.

```
Number represented by ch1 divided by 2 = 3222
Number ch2 /3= 7.22
Number ch3 = 0
Number represented by ch4 = 45
Number represented by chL1 = 0
Number represented by chL2 = 45676548
```

Six strings ch1, ch2, ch3, ch4, chL1 and chL2 are declared and initialized. The functions atoi(), atof () and atol() are called to convert the strings into corresponding digits. The strings which begin with non digit characters are not converted and 0 is returned while those which begin with digit characters are converted. To show that the converted digits represent number, the numbers obtained in first two cases have been divided by 2 and 3 respectively. The trailing ends of strings consisting of non-digital characters are ignored.

FUNCTIONS `strtod (), strtol () and strtoul()`

In case of functions `atoi()`, `atol()` and `atof()` we saw that if the digits are followed by non-digital characters, the non-digital characters are ignored. This is not the case with the functions `strtod()`, `strtol()` and `strtoul()` which are explained below.

`strtod()` The function converts the digital part of string to double number and returns the double value. The second part is extracted by the pointer to the substring. The function arguments comprise pointer to string and **address of pointer** to substring. The syntax is given below.

```
double strod(const char* chptr, char** subptr)
```

`strtol()` The function strtol() takes three arguments, the first is the string name/pointer to string, the second is the **address of the pointer** to non-digital substring and the third is an integer which specifies the base of the value being converted. The code is given below.

```
long strol(const char* chptr, char** subptr, int base)
```

`strtoul()` The function converts the digits and returns unsigned long number. The function strtoul()also takes three arguments, the first is the pointer to string, the second is the **address of the pointer** to the non-digital sub-string and the third is the base (8 for octa, 10 for decimal and 16 for hexadecimal) of the value being converted. The code is as below.

```
unsigned long stroul(const char* chptr, char** subptr, int base)
```

The application of strtol() is illustrated in the following program.

PROGRAM 10.15 – Illustrates functions strtol().

```
#include <iostream>
# include <cstdlib>
using namespace std;
void main()
 { long n ;
 int m ;
 char ch1 []= "100 Delhi 110016 ";
 char ch3 [] = "D64";
 char *psubstring1;
 char *psubstring2;
 m = strtol(ch3, &psubstring2,10);
 n = strtol(ch1, &psubstring1, 10);
  cout<<"Converted digital (base 10) = n = " <<n<<endl;
  n = strtol(ch1, &psubstring1,16);
  cout <<"n ( base 16) = "<<n<<endl;
 cout<<"Original string = " <<ch1<<endl; // the original string

 cout<<"The remainder substring = "<<psubstring1<<endl<<endl;
 cout<<"Original string = " <<ch3<<endl;
 cout<<"Converted string part = m = " <<m<<endl;
 cout<<"The remainder substring = "<<psubstring2<<endl;
  }
```

The expected output is given below.

```
Converted digital (base)10 = n = 100
n ( with base16) = 256
Original string = 100 Delhi 110016
The remainder substring = Delhi 110016
Original string = D64
Converted string part = m = 0
The remainder substring = D64
```

In the above program two strings ch1 and ch3 are declared. String ch1 starts with digits while ch3 starts with letter D. In case of ch1, in the first conversion the base is taken 10 so 100 gets converted into 10 × 10 = 100, in the second conversion the base is 16 (hexadecimal) so in this case 100 gets converted to 16 × 16 = 256 that is square of 16. Similarly, other numbers may be taken as base. It would be better to consult the compiler document. The substring Delhi 110016 is also recovered. From output it is clear that ch3 has not been converted and 0 is returned because it does not start with a digit. The complete string is recovered as unconverted sub-string (D64).

10.5 ARRAYS OF C-STRINGS

If it is desired to make a list of statements such as list of names, list of quotations, list of books, etc., we would be dealing with arrays of strings. An array of strings is a two dimensional array of type char and may be declared as illustrated below.

```
char identifier [n] [m];
```

Here identifier is the name of the array, *n* is the number of strings and *m* is the number of characters in each string including the null character. The value of *m* may be decided so that a string having the maximum characters is covered. The Fig. 10.2a shows an array of strings in which a list of four names is displayed. Here *n* = 4 and *m* = 9. In this arrangement each string is allocated 9 bytes and can have 9–1 characters of string and the terminating null character. If a string has fewer characters than 8 characters the remaining memory blocks remain empty, and is wasteful for memory space. A better method of declaration is

```
char* identifier [n]
```

It is an array of pointers of type char. It is illustrated in the following program.

PROGRAM 10.16 – Illustrates an **array of strings**.

```
#include <iostream>
using namespace std;
int main()
{
char Name [4] [9] = {"Sun", "OurEarth", "Sky", "Mars"};
cout <<"Size of Name = " << sizeof(Name)<< endl;
char * name[4] = {"Sun", "OurEarth", "Sky", "Mars"} ;
```

```
   cout<<" The actual sizes of strings are: ";
   cout<<sizeof("Sun")<< " "<<sizeof ("OurEarth")<<" "<<sizeof("Sky") << " "<<sizeof("Mars")<<endl;
   return 0;}
```

The expected output is given below.

```
Size of Name = 36
The actual sizes of strings are: 4 9 4 5
```

The four names when written as a two dimensional array Name[4][9] occupy a total of 36 bytes.

In the second case, the names are stored by an array of pointers char* [4]. The array elements are stored one after another separated by end of string null character ('\0'). Thus the total size is equal to 22 bytes. It is illustrated in Fig.10.2b below.

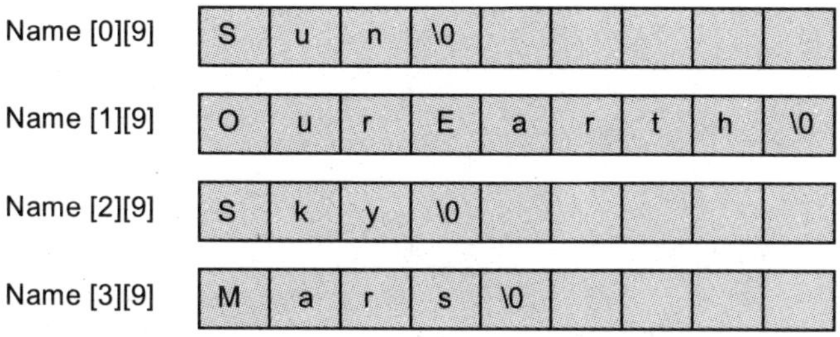

Fig. 10.2 (a): An array of strings. A two-dimensional array

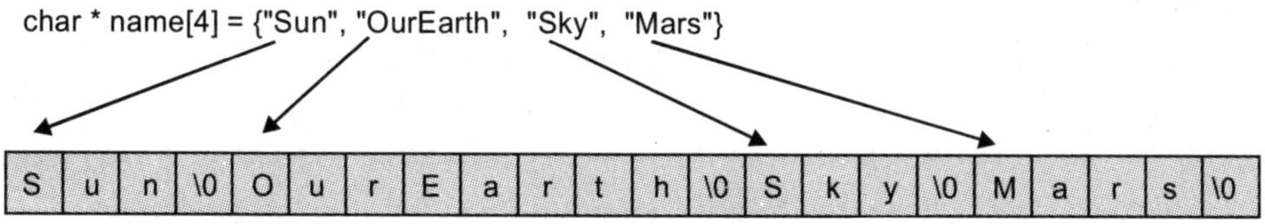

Fig. 10.2 (b): An array of pointers to strings. There is no empty block

In programs which make a list of objects as elements of an array, remember that the first entry is the 0th element in an array. If the output is also serially numbered starting from one, do not forget to add 1 for printing of serial numbers.

10.6 STANDARD FUNCTIONS FOR HANDLING C-STRING CHARACTERS

C++ Standard library has a number of useful character handling functions which are listed and explained in Table 10.1. The functions may be used for manipulations and tests on characters. The applications of some of these functions are illustrated in Programs 10.17 to 10.20. All these functions are of type int and receive a single integer argument. As per ASCII code characters are also integers and in C++ they may be treated as constants with values as per ASCII code (see Chapter 3) . Thus these functions manipulate characters as integers. If the functions are declared as char the return value is of type char. See the following program for `islower()` and `toupper()` functions.

PROGRAM 10.17 – Illustrates application of **islower()** and **toupper()**.

```
#include<iostream>
 using namespace std;

void main()
 { char ch;
  cout<<"Enter a sentence :\n" ;
   while (cin.get(ch))

{ if ( islower(ch) )
 cout<< char ( toupper (ch));
 else
 cout<<ch; }
  }
```

The expected output is given below.

```
Enter a sentence :
Go to your class.
GO TO YOUR CLASS.
```

Table 10.1 – Standard functions for handling string characters

Function	Description
`int isalnum(int c)`	It returns true if c is a digit or alphabet, otherwise returns false.
`int isalpha(int c)`	It returns true if c is a letter, otherwise returns false.
`int isdigit(int c)`	It returns true if c is digit character, otherwise false.
`int islower(int c)`	It returns true if c is lower case letter, otherwise it returns false.
`int isupper(int c)`	It returns true if c is upper case letter, false otherwise.
`int tolower(int c)`	It returns lower case letter if c is upper case letter.
`int toupper(int c)`	It returns upper case letter if c is lower case letter.
`int isspace(int c)`	It returns true if c is any one of the white space character such as ' ', '\f', '\n', '\r', '\t', '\v' (see Chapter 2 for the descriptions) otherwise returns false.
`int isgraph(int c)`	It returns true if c is a printing character other than blank space ' ', otherwise returns false.
`int isprint(int c)`	It returns true if c is a printing character or space ' ' otherwise it returns false.
`int ispunct (int c)`	It returns true if c is a printing character other than a digit, a letter or a space , otherwise it returns false.
`int iscntrl(int c)`	If c is a control character such as '\n ', '\t ', '\r' , ' \f ', '\a', '\b' the function returns true otherwise false.

Program 10.18 given below illustrates some of the above described functions.

PROGRAM 10.18 – Illustrates application of **isalpha(), isdigit() and isalnum()** functions.

```
#include<iostream>
using namespace std;

void main()
{ char ch;
int count =0;
int m =0, k = 0, n =0;

cout<<"Enter a sentence :\n" ;

while (cin.get(ch))
{ count ++;
if ( isalpha(ch) )
++m;
if( isdigit(ch))
k++;
if ( isalnum( ch))
n++;
if ( count ==25) break; }
cout<< "Number of letters = " << m<<endl;
cout <<"Number of digits = "<<k <<endl;
cout <<"Number of digits + letters = "<<n <<endl;
}
```

The expected output is given below.

```
Enter a sentence :
Your number is 657876897.
Number of letters = 12
Number of digits = 9
Number of digits + letters = 21
```

10.7 STANDARD FUNCTIONS FOR MANIPULATION OF C-STRINGS

C++ Standard Library contains many useful functions for manipulation of strings. Table 10.2 gives the description of these functions. The manipulation of strings generally involves replacing a string or substring with another string or substring, comparison of the two strings, appending one string or substring to the front or back of another string, replacing n characters of one string with n characters of another string etc. The applications of these functions are illustrated in the programs given after the following table.

Table 10. 2 – Standard C-string functions (header file **<cstring>**)
For the sake of being brief we shall refer to strings pointed to by S1 and by S2 as strings S1 and S2.

Name of function and function arguments and description
`char*strcpy (char *S1, const char *S2);` It copies S2 into S1 and returns S1. S1 becomes a copy of S2.
`char*strncpy (char*S1, const *S2 , size_t n);` The function replaces the first *n* characters of S1 with first *n* characters of S2 and returns S1. If n >= strlen(S2) then it behaves as strcpy(). size_t is the typedef of unsigned int.
`char* strcat(char *S1, const char *S2);` The function appends the characters of S2 at the end of S1, returns S1. The terminating null character of S1 is replaced by first character of S2.
`char *strncat(char *S1, const char *S2, size_t n);` The function appends first n characters of S2 at the end of S1 and returns S1. The terminating null character of S1 is replaced by first character of S2.
`int strcmp(const char *S1,const char *S2);` Compares lexicographically string S1 with string S2 and returns – 1, 0, 1 if S1 is less than , equal to or greater than S2 respectively.
`int strncmp(const char*S1, const char *S2, size_t n);` Compares lexicographically the first n characters of S1 with first n characters of string S2 and returns – 1, 0, 1 if the substring of S1 is less than , equal to or greater than that of S2 respectively.
`size_t strlen (const char *S);` The function returns the length of string S ignoring the Null character at end of string.
`char* strstr (const char *S1, const char * S2);` This function returns the address of first occurrence of S2 as substring of S1. It return 0 if S2 is not in S1.
`char *strchr (const char *S , int C);` The function return pointer to first occurrence of C in S1, returns 0 if C not found.
`char *strrchr (const char *S1, int C);` The function return pointer to the last occurrence of C in S1, returns 0 if not found.
`size_t strspn (char *S1, const char* S2);` The function returns the length of substring of S1 that starts with the first character of S1 and contains the characters of S2 only.
`size_t strcspn ( char * S1, const char *S2);` The function returns the length of longest substring of S1 which begins with character S1[0] and does not contain any character of S2.
`char *strtok( char *S1, const char *S2);` S1 is tokenized into tokens delimited by characters of S2. It requires a number of calls for complete tokenization. The first call is strtok(S1, S2); and in subsequent calls the first argument is NULL. The subsequent call returns a pointer to the next token of S1.

APPLICATIONS OF STRING MANIPULATING FUNCTIONS

strlen ( ) AND strcpy ()

The function strlen () returns the length of string (its argument), it includes white space but ignores the end of string character ('\0').

The function call for strcpy is coded as below.

```
strcpy(S1, S2 );
```

where S1 and S2 are name of two strings. The function copies S2 into S1. In other words S1 becomes a copy of S2. If S1 is longer than S2, it reduces it to the size of S2.

PROGRAM 10.19 – Illustrates `strlen()` and `strcpy()` functions.

```
#include<iostream>
# include <cstring>
using namespace std;

void main()
 {
 char Str1 [] = "Mona";
 char Str2 [] = "Learn C++";
 char Str3[] = "Lisa";

  cout<<"Lengths of Str1= " <<strlen(Str1)<<endl;
  cout<<"Length of Str2 = " << strlen(Str2)<<endl;

  cout<<"Contents of Str1 are = "<<Str1<<endl;

  cout<<"Contents of Str2 are = "<<Str2<<endl;

strcpy(Str1, Str2);

 cout << "Now contents of Str1 = "<<Str1<<endl;
 cout << "Now contents of Str2 = "<<Str2<<endl;
  }
```

The expected output is given below. The output is self explanatory.

```
Lengths of Str1= 4
Length of Str2 = 9
Contents of Str1 are = Mona
Contents of Str2 are = Learn C++
Now contents of Str1 = Learn C++
Now contents of Str2 = Learn C++
```

STRNCPY()

The function is called as illustrated below.

```
strncpy ( S1, S2, size_t n);
```

Here S1, S2 are names of the two strings and n is a positive integer. The function replaces the first n characters of S1 with first n characters of S2 and returns S1. If n is greater than the length of S2 then the function behaves as `strcpy()`. The size_t is the typedef of unsigned int. The following program illustrates its application.

PROGRAM 10.20 – Illustrates application of **strncpy ()** function

```
#include <iostream>
# include <cstring>
using namespace std;
void main()
 { char Str1 [] = "John";
char Str2 [] = "Mona Lisa";
cout<<"Lengths of Str1 and Str2 are "<<strlen(Str1)<<" and "<<
strlen(Str2)<<endl;
 strncpy (Str1,Str2,4);

cout<<"After strncpy, contents of Str1 are = "<<Str1<<endl;
cout<<" After strncpy, Contents of Str2 are ="<<Str2<<endl;
cout <<"Length of str1 = " <<strlen (Str1) << endl;
cout <<"Length of str2 = " <<strlen (Str2) << endl;
 }
```

The expected output given below shows that John in S1 has been replaced by Mona by the operation of `strncpy (Str1,Str2,4)`;.

```
Lengths of Str1 and Str2 are 4 and 9
After strncpy, contents of Str1 are = Mona
After strncpy, contents of Str2 are =Mona Lisa
Length of str1 = 4
Length of str2 = 9
```

FUNCTIONS STRCAT() AND STRNCAT()

The first function is called as below.

`strcat(S1,S2 );`

Here S1 and S2 are names of the two strings. The function appends the characters of S2 at the end of S1. The application of this function is illustrated in the following program.

The second function is called as illustrated below.

`strncat ( S1, S2, unsigned int n);`

Here S1and S2 are the names of two strings and n is a positive number. The function appends first n characters of S2 at the end of S1. However, if n is negative integer, some compilers may show error while others may convert `strncat()` into `strcat()` and append the complete S2 at the end of S1. If n is greater than the length of S2 then the function behaves as strcat(). The following program illustrates the two functions.

PROGRAM 10.21 – Illustrates application of **strcat()**and **strncat()** functions.

```
#include<iostream>
# include < cstring >
using namespace std;

void main()
 {
  char Str1 [10] = "Mona" ;
  char Str2 [14] = "Lisa Singh";
  char Str3 [10] = "Kirtika";
  char Str4 [10] = "Malhotra";

 strncat(Str1, Str2, 4);

 cout<<Str1<<endl;
 cout<<Str2<<endl;

 strcat( Str3, Str4);
 cout << Str3<<endl;
 cout<<Str4 <<endl;
  }
```

The expected output is given below.

```
Mona Lisa
Lisa Singh
Kirtika Malhotra
Malhotra
```

The first line of output is of Str1 after the operation of `strncat(Str1, Str2, 4);`. The first 4 characters of S2 (Lisa) are appended to end of Str1. The string Str2 is not affected by this operation. The third line of output is the result of `strcat(Str3,Str4);`. The complete string Str4 is appended to the end of string Str3. The string Str4 remains intact.

Function strncmp()

The function `strcmp()` is called as below.

`strcmp(S1, S2);`

It compares two strings S1 and S2 lexicographically and returns 1 if S1>S2 , returns 0 if S1 is equal to S2 and returns –1 if S1<S2. The following program illustrates the application of the function.

PROGRAM 10.22 – Illustrates application of function **strcmp()**

```
#include<iostream>
# include < cstring >
using namespace std;
int main()
```

```
{
 char *Str1 = "XYZ" ;
  char *Str2 = "ABC";
   char *Str3 = "XYZ";
 cout << strcmp(Str1, Str2)<<endl;
   cout << strcmp(Str2, Str1)<<endl;
     cout << strcmp(Str3, Str1)<<endl;
        cout << strcmp(Str2, Str3)<<endl;
 return 0 ;
  }
```

The expected output is given below. Str1 is lexicographically greater than Str2 and Str1 is lexicographically equal to that Str3. So the following output is obvious.

```
1
-1
0
-1
```

FUNCTION STRNCMP()

The function takes three arguments and is called as below.

```
strncmp(S1, S2, size_t n);
```

The function compares character by character the first n characters of string S1 with first n characters of string S2. This is illustrated in the following program by making the two strings different only by one character.

PROGRAM 10.23 – Illustrate application of function strncmp().

```
#include<iostream>
# include < cstring >
using namespace std;

int main()
{ char *Str1 = "You are making a drawing" ;
 char *Str2 = "Xou are making a portrait"; // Y replaced by X
 char *Str4 = "You are making a drawing" ;
 char *Str3 = "Zou are making a picture"; // Y replaced by Z
  cout << strncmp(Str1, Str2,15)<<endl;
  cout << strncmp(Str2, Str1,15)<<endl;
  cout << strncmp(Str3, Str1,15)<<endl;
  cout << strncmp(Str2, Str3,15)<<endl;
  cout << strncmp(Str4, Str3, 15)<<endl;
 return 0 ;
  }
```

The expected output is given below. The output is obvious.

```
1
-1
1
-1
-1
```

FUNCTION STRSTR()

Function strstr() is called as strstr(S1, S2). The function returns the first occurrence of a substring S2 in string S1. If S2 is not found it returns Null.

PROGRAM 10.24 – Illustrates application of **strstr ()** function.

```
#include<iostream>
#include < cstring >
using namespace std;
void main()
{
char Str1 [ ] = "Lajpat Nagar" ;
char* ptr = strstr(Str1, "pat" ); //pat - sub string of Str1
cout<< ptr- Str1 <<endl; //pointer to pat minus pointer to
  // to beginning of string. It will give index value.
cout << "Str1 ["<<ptr-Str1<<"]"<<endl;
cout<<Str1 <<endl;
}
```

The expected output is given below. See the above comment for explanation.

```
3
Str1 [3]
Lajpat Nagar
```

FUNCTIONS STRCHR() AND STRRCHR()

Functions are called as strchr(Str ,int C); and strrchr(Str , int C); Here Str is the name of string. The function strchr () returns a pointer to the first occurrence of C in string Str while the function strrchr() returns the pointer to the last occurrence of C. In the following program the pointer to string which is the address of first element of string has been subtracted from the pointer values given by the function so that it gives the index values where the C occurs.

PROGRAM 10.25 – Illustrates **strchr()** and **strrchr()**

```
#include<iostream>
# include < cstring >
using namespace std;
void main()
{
```

```
    char Str1 [ ] = "Ganga Nagar";
    cout << "Index value because of function strchr(Str1,'g' ):\n";

    char* ptr = strchr(Str1, 'g'); //Application of strchr()

    cout<< ptr - Str1 <<endl;
    cout << "Str1 ["<<ptr-Str1<<"]"<<endl;
    cout<<Str1 <<"\n\n";

    cout << "Index value due to function strrchr(Str1,'g' ):\n";
    char* ptrr = strrchr(Str1, 'g' ); //Application of strrchr()
    cout<< ptrr - Str1 <<endl;
    cout << "Str1 ["<<ptrr-Str1<<"]"<<endl;
    }
```

The expected output is given below. The first occurs at index value 3 while the last occurrence happens at index value of 8.

```
Index value because of function strchr(Str1,'g' ):
3
Str1 [3]
Ganga Nagar

Index value due to function strchr(Str1,'g' ):
8
Str1 [8]
```

FUNCTION INT STRSPN( )

Function is called as int strspn(S1, S2). Here S1 and S2 are the names of two strings. The function `strspn()` returns the length of the longest substring of S1 that starts with S1[0] and contains only the characters found in S2.

FUNCTION STRTOK( )

An illustration of function call is given below.

```
char* T = strtok( Str2, " ");
```

According to this the function splits or breaks the string str2 into tokens. The splitting is done at locations where a specified character or a substring is located or starts. In the above declaration the tokenisation would occur at locations of white spaces. In other words the first token is made on occurrence of first white space, i.e. after the first word. For continuing the process we have to have NULL ('\0') as the first argument. This is illustrated in the following program. For complete splitting the entire string into tokens we have to use a loop (while or *do—while*, etc). In the following program a *do – while* loop is used.

PROGRAM 10.26 – Illustrates application of int strspn() and strtok ()

```
#include<iostream>
# include < cstring >
using namespace std;
void main()
 { char Str1 [ ] = "I am making a picture " ;
 char Str2 [ ] = "He is making a portrait?";
 char S3 [] = "I am making a drawing" ;
 char S4 []= "You are doing portrait?" ;
 cout << "Str1 = " <<Str1 <<endl;
 cout<<"Str2= "<<Str2 <<endl;
  int N13 = strspn(Str1, S3);
  cout<<"N13 = "<<N13<<endl;
  int N14 = strspn(Str1, S4);
  cout << "N14 = " << N14<<endl;
 char* K = strstr(S3,"a" );
 cout << "K = " << K<<endl;
 char* T = strtok( Str2, " ");
 int n =0;
 do
 { ++n ;
  cout << "\nToken "<<n<<" = " << T ;
  T = strtok( '\0' ," "); }
 while ( T != '\0'); // do tokenize till the end of string
  }
```

The expected output is given below.

```
Str1 = I am making a picture
Str2 = He is making a portrait?
N13 = 14
N14 = 0
K = am making a drawing

Token 1 = He
Token 2 = is
Token 3 = making
Token 4 = a
Token 5 = portrait?
```

10.8 MEMORY FUNCTIONS FOR C-STRINGS

These functions, in fact, deal with blocks of memory spaces which are treated as arrays of bytes.

Therefore, any type of data stored on the bytes can be dealt with. The return values of functions are void pointers. The arguments are also void pointers so that they can receive pointers to any data *type*. In a way, these are templates. The different functions are described below. The return pointer has to be cast into appropriate type before dereferencing because void pointers cannot be dereferenced.

(i) void *memchr(const void * S, int C, size_t n);

Searches the first n characters of string pointed to by S for first occurrence of C. Returns pointer to C in the string, if not found it returns 0.

(ii) void *memcpy (void * S1, const void* S2, size_t n);

Copies n characters of string pointed to by S2 on to string pointed to by S1 and returns pointer to resulting string. The area from where the characters are copied and the area where the characters are deposited are not allowed to overlap.

(iii) void *memcmp (const void* S1, const void *S2, size_t n);

Compares lexicographically the first n characters of S1 with those of S2. Returns 0 if characters of S1 are equal, –1 if less and +1 if greater than those of S2 .

(iv) void *memmove (void *S1, const void *S2, size_t n)

Copies n characters of S2 into S1 and returns pointer to the resulting string. The area from where the characters are copied and the area where these are copied to are allowed to overlap.

(v) void *memset (void *S, int C, size_t n)

Copies (unsigned char) C into first n characters of string pointed to by S, returns pointer to resulting string.

The following two program illustrate the application of some of the above functions.

THE FUNCTION MEMCPY()

In the following program the function is called as below.

```
memcpy(Str1, Str2, 4);
```

In the operation of function, the first four characters of Str2, i.e. Mona are copied on to first four characters of Str1 which is Lisa Lisa, so after the operation of the function Str1 becomes Mona Lisa. The string Str2 is unchanged.

PROGRAM 10.27 – Illustrates application of **memcpy()** function.

```
#include<iostream>
# include < cstring >
using namespace std;
void main()
 { char Str1 [10] = "Lisa Lisa" ;
 char Str2 [10] = "Mona" ;
 memcpy(Str1, Str2 , 4);
 cout<<Str1<<endl;
```

```
cout<<Str2<<endl;
}
```

The expected output of the above program is given below.

```
Mona Lisa
Mona
```

The following program illustrates application of other memory functions.

PROGRAM 10.28 – Illustrates **memchr (),memcmp(), memset(), memcpy () and memmove ().**

```
#include<iostream>
# include < cstring >
using namespace std;
void main()
{
   char S1[32], S2 [] = "Learn C-strings.";
   char S3 [] = "Learn at proper time";
   char S4[] = "ABCDEFGH";
   char S5[] = "XYZ";
/* Below static_cast<char*> is used to convert void pointer
into appropriate type.*/

cout << static_cast<char*>( memchr(S4, 'D',5))<<endl;
cout<<"memcmp( S2, S3 ,5) = " <<memcmp( S2, S3 ,5) <<endl;

cout<< "memcmp ( S5, S4) = " <<memcmp ( S5, S4, 5) <<endl;

cout<< " String S4 after memset( S4, 'R', 4) is below.\n ";
cout<< static_cast<char*> ( memset( S4, 'R', 4))<<endl;
   // copies the character 'R' into first 4 places of S4.
   memcpy ( S1, S2, 33);
   cout<<"\n";
   cout << S1 <<endl;
   char S6[] = "Good morning John!";
   cout <<"S6 = " << S6 <<endl;
cout<<"memmove( S6, &S6 [5], 12) is given below."<<endl;
cout<<static_cast<char*> ( memmove( S6, &S6 [5], 12))<<endl;
cout <<"S3 = " << S3<<endl;
cout<< "S1 = " <<S1<<endl;
cout <<"memmove( S3, &S1[6], 20)) = ";
cout << static_cast<char*> (memmove( S3, &S1[6], 20))<<endl;
}
```

The expected output is given below.

```
DEFGH
memcmp( S2, S3 ,5) = 0
memcmp ( S5, S4) = 1
String S4 after memset( S4, 'R', 4) is below.
RRRREFGH

Learn C-strings.
S6 = Good morning John!
memmove( S6 , &S6 [5], 12) is given below.
morning John John!
S3 = Learn at proper time
S1 = Learn C-strings.
memmove( S3, &S1[6], 20)) = C-strings.
```

In the first line of output the substring after the letter 'D' is printed. For the second line of output, the first 5 letters of S2, S3 are identical, so output is 0. For the third line, 'X' is lexicographically greater than 'A' , therefore the output is 1. In the 4th line of output, 4 copies of 'R' are copied on to S4 replacing ABCD. The result is obvious. In the 8-9 lines of output the 12 letters of S6 starting from sixth element are copied and placed on first 12 characters. So resulting string is **morning John John!**. In the last line of output the 20 characters of S1 starting from seventh element are copied and placed on first 20 characters of S3, so resulting string is **C-strings.**

EXERCISES

1. What are similarities and differences between arrays and C-strings?
2. What is the difference between "A" and 'A' in C++?
3. Declare a pointer to a string.
4. What is difference between `cin.get()` and `cin.getline()`?
5. How do you code the above two functions in a program to read up to 20 characters?
6. Make a program that reads user's message like "Madan Mohan went to Mangalore on Monday." and counts the number of 'e', 'M' and number of total characters.
7. What is the difference between `cout.put()` and `cin.putback()`?
8. What does the function `cin.peek()` do?
9. Explain the differences between functions `strchr()` and `strrchr()`.
10. What do you understand by the function `strncat(S1, S2, unsigned int n)`?
11. What do you understand by function `strncpy(S1, S2,n)`?
12. What does the following codes do with two strings with names S1 and S2 ?
    (i) `memcpy (S1, S2, size_t n);`
    (ii) `strcpy (S1, S2);`
    (iii) `strcat (S1, S2);`
13. Give any two functions belonging to standard character handling library. How do you use them?

14. How do you convert a string of digits into an integer value?
15. What the functions `atol()` and `atof()` do to a string of digits?
16. What is the difference between the functions `strchr(Str, int C)` and `strrchr (Str, int C)`?
17. What do you understand by functions `isupper( )` and `tolower ( )`?
18. Explain the working of function `cin.ignore()`. Make a program with cin.ignore (4) to illustrate its working.

Answer:

PROGRAM 10.29 – An exercise to illustrate **ignore()**.

```
#include<iostream>
using namespace std;

void main()
 {char ch;
cout<<"Enter alphabets :\n" ;

 while (cin.get(ch))
   {cin.ignore(4);
    cout<<ch;}
}
```

The expected output is as below.

```
Enter alphabets :
ABCDEFGHIJKLMNOPQRSTUVXYZ
AFKPU
```

19. Make a small program to illustrate the application of *strlen()* .
20. Make a program in which a user is asked to enter his/her name. The program should get it verified by displaying the name and asking the user to enter yes if correct and no if incorrect.
21. Make a program which asks the user to enter one or more sentences and counts the numbers of 'e' in the sentence.

Answer:

PROGRAM 10.30 – Counts the characters while reading.

```
#include <iostream>
using namespace std;
void main()
 {
 int count =0;
  char para[150];
  cout<<"Enter a sentence :\n" ;
   cin.get(para,150) ;
```

```
cout<<"you have written the following.\n"<<para<<endl;
 for (int i = 0; i<150;i++)
  if ( para[i] =='e' ) ++count;
cout<<"There are "<<count<<"'e' letters in it."<<endl;
 }
```

The expected output is as under.

```
Enter a sentence :
Here every thing is at higher price.
you have written the following.
Here every thing is at higher price.
There are 6 'e' letters in it.
```

22. Make a Program asking the user to write a sentence with digits. The program counts the number of digits in the sentence.

Answer:

PROGRAM 10.31 – Illustrates counting only digits in characters read.

```
#include <iostream>
using namespace std;
void main()

{
int count =0;
char para[150];
 cout<<"Enter a sentence with digits: \n" ;
 cin.get(para,150) ;

cout<<"\nyou have written the following sentence.\n" <<para <<endl;
 for (int i = 0; i<150;i++)
 if ( para[i] >='0' && para[i]<='9') ++count;

 cout<< "\n There are " <<count <<" digits"<<" in this."<<endl;
 }
```

The expected output is as under.

```
Enter a sentence with digits:
Add number 564 to 342 and subtract 64 from sum.

you have written the following sentence.
Add number 564 to 342 and subtract 64 from sum.

There are 8 digits in this.
```

❍❍❍

CHAPTER

11 Classes and Objects–1

11.1 INTRODUCTION

A major feature which distinguishes C++ from C is the concept of classes and object oriented approach to programming. A class is a method of organizing the data and functions in the same structure which describes the properties or characteristics of real life objects. It is an extension of *structure* of C, but C-structures (discussed at the end of this chapter) have many limitations. One limitation is that it has only public members. The classes of C++ have the provision of categorizing the members into private, protected and public and thus they allow information hiding. Besides, the classes support inheritance, i.e. new classes may be derived from an existing class. The derived class uses the existing class as it is, besides, it may add new data and functions which add new features to the objects of the derived class. The process of inheritance is endless. You may derive newer classes from derived classes. Thus a very big program may be thought of consisting of several classes with objects that serve the purpose of the program. Each class may be developed independently, debugged and tested before putting in the big program. In this chapter, we shall introduce the concept of classes, constructor, destructor functions, local classes, structures etc., while the advanced topics are discussed in Chapter 12.

We can think of a class as a blueprint or a design in programming with abstract data variables and the relevant functions that describe the common characteristics of a group of objects. The functions of class operate on object data to yield useful information about the object of the class. The class by itself does not do anything. The class functions cannot be called on their own. They are called by linking them with the objects of class on whose data they operate. For instance, you cannot ride a car which is just a design on the paper. You can ride only when a car is built. Similarly a class program works only when we create an object or objects of the class. Also, once the car design is done, same design can be used to produce a large number of cars. In the same way, once a class code is perfected one can create as many objects of the class as desired and they can all co-exist in the memory. A class contains data variables and functions which are called **data members** and **function members** respectively.

The various class functions operate only when linked with an object of that class. That is why the name object oriented programming (OOP). There are, however, different opinions on what comprises the object oriented programming. The other attributes of classes are also part of OOP. The majority of programmers agree that OOP includes data abstraction, encapsulation of data and function members, information hiding, inheritance, polymorphism and dynamic binding. While some are of the opinion that OOP also includes generic programming. All these terms would be explained in this and subsequent chapters. The function members of a class generate information relevant to the particular object with whose identifier the functions are called. For example, in a computerised company the employees are allowed to check the entries in their pay accounts on their terminals. Let `display_pay()` be a function of the class program which the employee can invoke to get to their pay accounts. The employee is an object of the class and has an identifier in form of employee code, we call it `employee_identifier`. The employee would enter employee code and would ask for display as illustrated below.

```
employee_identifier.display_pay();
```

Notice that dot operator (.) provides link between the employee code and the function `display()`. If the employee simply calls the function without the employee identifier and the dot operator, i.e. `display_pay();` it will not operate, i.e. it will not display the pay entries of any employee. In a class, the operation of a function member is tied to the objects of the class.

The characteristics of objects of the physical world may be described by class programs. We all know cats belong to a different class of animals from that of dogs but both belong to the class animal. Let us name these classes as *class Cat*, *class Dog* and *class Animal*. Evidently, *class Cat* and *class Dog* may be inherited from *class Animal*, because, both the cats and dogs have some characteristics which are common with other animals as well. Also any one dog say *mydog* is one **object** or **instance** of the *class Dog*. In the same way if we think of manufactured goods, we can easily make a class for cars another for scooter, still another for vehicle. We may prepare data and functions to describe their characteristics. That is to say there are some common characteristics among all the scooters, similarly cars have common characteristics among themselves. Also some characteristics may be common with all other vehicles. For instance all vehicles have an engine, a registration number, etc. So it is possible to have a base class which we may call *class Vehicles* and the *class Cars* and the *class Scooters* as derived classes as illustrated in the figure below. That explains **inheritance**.

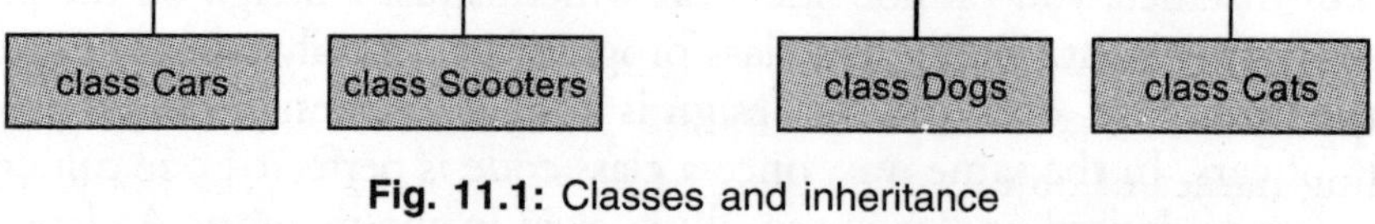

Fig. 11.1: Classes and inheritance

11.2 DECLARATION OF CLASS AND CLASS OBJECTS

The word *class* is a keyword of C++ and for declaring a class it is essential to write *class* followed by identifier or name of the class. In the declaration *class Car* for cars, *class Scooters* for scooters and *class Vehicles* for vehicles the word *class* is the keyword and *Cars, Scooters* and *Vehicles* are names of the respective classes. A short outline of a class declaration is given below.

```
class identifier
 {access specifier: // Body of class having data members
 statements;   //and functions members enclosed by curly braces {}.
 }; //The class declaration ends with the semicolon.
```

The class body comprises data members and function members. The data members comprise abstract data that applies to all the object of class and is relevant to the aim of the program. The common characteristics of objects of class are described by the function members of the class.

For the *class Car,* a particular car say *mycar* becomes an instance or an object of the *class Cars* if it is so declared. It (*mycar*) will have particular set of data. Similarly other cars may be declared as objects of the *class Car* and will have their own but similar sets of data. The objects of a class carry individual copies of their data unless data is declared **static** in which case all objects share same copy of data. The data of *mycar* becomes the arguments for the function members of the program *class Cars* when they are called for the object *mycar.* But before an object say *mycar* can call a function of *class Cars* we have to declare that *mycar* is an object of the class - *class Cars.* You remember when we declare a variable we first mention its *type* such as int, float, double or character. Similarly the ***type* of an object of a class is the *name* of its class.** For instance, *mycar* is an object of *class Cars,* therefore, its *type* is Cars. With declaration of class no memory is allocated. Memory is allocated when class objects are defined. Now an object belonging to the *class Cars* may be defined as below.

```
class Cars mycar; //declaration of object
```

Or we may simply write it as below.

```
Cars mycar;   //Cars is the type for the objects of Cars.
```

Name of class   name of object

If more than one objects belonging to same class say *class Cars* such as car1, car2, car3 are to be declared it may be done as below,

```
Cars  car1, car2, car3 ;
```

Name of class Names of objects separated by comma

With the above definition of the objects, each object will be allocated memory of same size which is appropriate according to declarations in the class. Objects may also be declared by simply adding names of objects after the closing right brace of class body and before the semicolon.

The class contains data members and function members which apply to all the objects of the class. The choice of the functions and data is done according to the purpose of the class program. For example, a class program called *class CarM* for a car manufacturer may have different data and functions from that of the *class CarD* for the dealer of car, though both the classes may deal with same cars. The detailed declaration of class is illustrated below.

DECLARATION OF CLASS

The form of code used for declaring a class is illustrated below.

```
class X            // class is keyword, X is the name of class
{
private:               //access label private
memberA;                  // memberA is a private member of class X.
protected:                  // access label protected
memberB;                  // MemberB is protected member
......          // dotted line stands for other data or functions
public:                //access label public
......
memberC;              //memberC is a public member
___
private:                        //a access label may be repeated
memberD;            // memberD is also a private member of class X
};                              // end of class
```

Starting from the top of the above declaration, *class* is the keyword of C++ and is must for every class declaration. The identifier *X* is the name of the class. Name may be chosen as we do for any other variable (see Chapter 3). The body of class begins with left brace '{' after the class name and ends with the right brace '}' followed by semicolon (;) at the end. Three access labels are permitted. These are **private, protected** and **public.** These access labels along with their respective functions may be written in any order in the class body. Also any access specifier may appear more than once in the class body. You may write first the access label private: followed by private data and functions members, the second may be *public:* followed by public data and function members. **Note that every access label ends with a colon (:).**

If there is no access specifier at the start, it is taken that the data members and functions up to next access label are private by default. The function members of a class may be defined inside or outside the class body. If functions are defined outside the class body their prototypes must be declared in the body of class.

The initialization of data declared private is carried out through public functions which may also be the constructor functions of the class. The constructors are discussed in Section 11.8.

11.3 ACCESS SPECIFIERS – private, protected and public

PRIVATE:

The class members written under the access label **private** are accessible by class function members or *friend functions* and the functions of *friend classes.* The keyword **friend** provides this special privilege to the function or class declared as *friend* in the class body. In Chapter 12 we shall deal with *friend functions* and *friend classes.* The data or functions declared *private* cannot be accessed from outside the class. The objects of the class can access the private members only through the public function members of the class. This property of class is also called information hiding. However, with the help of pointers one can indirectly access private data members provided the class contains at least one public data member. Generally data members are declared private. The intention is to hide as much information about data and implementation of class as possible. This also helps against accidental change in object data members. The functions members are in general declared public.

PROTECTED:

The class members declared **protected** are accessible by the function members of same class and *friend functions* and *friend classes* as well as **by functions of derived classes.** For all other operations protected members are similar to private members.

PUBLIC:

The class members declared **public** are accessible from inside or outside the class. Some of the public functions of class provide interface for accessing the private and protected members of the class. For instance, initialization of a class object with private or protected data is always carried through public functions. Some public function also provide interface for other classes. Figure 11.2 below gives a physical picture of private, protected and public members of a class. Program 11.1 given below, illustrates a simple class with only one public function.

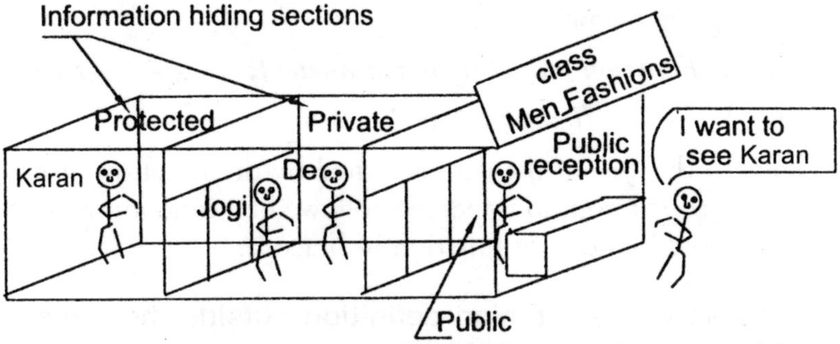

Fig.11.2: A physical illustration of public and private members of a class

PROGRAM 11.1 – Illustrates a **class declaration** and **function definition** in the class.

```
#include <iostream>
using namespace std;

class Market                    // Market is name of class.
{                  //The '{' marks beginning of class declaration.
public:                        // Access label public
 void Display()      // Definition of a public function Display ()
  { cout<< "Welcome To This Market" << endl;
      cout << "Here is the price List" <<endl;}

 };     //Semicolon after '}' marks end the of class declaration.
```

```
void main()                    // start of main program.
{Market L1;     // declaration of object L1 of class Market
L1.Display();                  // Function linked with object L1
}                              // dot(.) is  selection operator
```

The expected output is as under.

```
Welcome To This Market
Here is the price List
```

Note that class declaration is separate from the main program which, in the above case, starts with *void main()*. There is only one function void display () defined in the class body. In the main program we first declare an object of class by name L1, i.e. *Market L1*; . The function `display()` is called by writing `L1.Display ();` The dot operator (.) links the function display with object data of L1. In this example there is no data but below you will have more examples.

11.4 DEFINING A MEMBER FUNCTION OUTSIDE THE CLASS

The above program is repeated below with the prototype of member function declared in the class but function is defined outside the class body. The output is of course the same as given above. For defining a function outside the class body one has to use the scope resolution operator (::). An illustration is given below.

type class_name :: Function_name (type parameter1, - - -, - - -, type parameter n)

{ statements ; } // function body

Here *type* refers to the *type* of the data returned by the function, it is followed by name of the class, then the scope resolution operator followed by function name and parameters in brackets. This is followed by body of function in braces{}.

PROGRAM 11.2 – Illustrates **function definition outside the class**.

```
#include <iostream>
using namespace std;
class Market
{         // start of class declaration
public:
 void Display();          // function prototype
};        // end of class
 /*In the following function definition, void is type of function, Market
is class name, :: is the scope resolution and Display is name of function, there
are no parameters*/

void Market::Display () //function definition outside the class
{cout<< "Welcome To This Market" << endl;
 cout << "Here is the price List" <<endl;}
```

```
void main()          //main program
{Market L1;      // L1 is declared an object of class market
L1.Display();     // L1 calls function display
}
```

11.5 INITIALIZING PRIVATE DATA MEMBERS

An object of a class is constructed when its data members are initialized. If data is declared private, the initialization is carried by a public function which may be a constructor function (described in Section 11.8). In Program 11.3 given below, a class has both the public members and private members. The data members x, y and z are declared private. For accessing the private data members we need a public function. This is provided as Setprice (). In the class body, it is defined as below.

```
void Setprice (int a, int b, int c)
  {x = a,y = b, z = c;}
```

For defining the same function outside the class body, first we have to declare its prototype in the class as,

```
void Setprice (int , int , int );
```

and put the definition outside the class as given below.

```
void Market ::Setprice (int a , int b , int c )
   {x = a, y = b , z = c ;}
```

The general practice is to declare the function prototype inside the class and to define the same outside the class. The difference between the two is that functions defined inside the body of class are taken as **inline functions** while the ones defined outside the class body are called at the time of execution. The functions defined outside may also be declared inline by keyword **inline**.

PROGRAM 11.3 – Illustrates **initialization of private data** with a public function.

```
#include <iostream>
using namespace std;
class Market
{
private :
int x,y,z;
public:
 void Display1()
 {cout<< "Welcome! Here is the price List " << endl;}

 void Setprice (int a, int b, int c) // function defined in class
 {x = a, y = b, z = c;}

 void Display2 ()
 {cout<<" Price of item1 = "<< x<<endl;
```

```
cout<<" Price of item2 = "<< y<<endl;
cout<<" Price of item3 = "<< z<<endl;
}
};    // End of class

void main()
{
Market L1;
L1.Setprice (4,6,2); // Object L1 is initialized by function
    // setprice()
L1. Display1(); // Functions called by using dot operator.
L1.Display2();
}
```

The expected output is given below. The output is self explanatory.

```
Welcome! Here is the price List
Price of item1 = 4
Price of item2 = 6
Price of item3 = 2
```

In the Programs 11.4 and 11.5 we try to bring out the significance of declaring the data private. In Program 11.4 we declare a class Rect which deals with rectangles. It has one public function by name Area which finds area of rectangle if sides are given. The data variables are declared public. The function area is also public. R1 is an object of class Rect. You would see that R1 can directly access the data variables and can assign values as done in the main() by the following statements.

```
R1.x = 8;
 R1.y = 5;
```

The program illustrates that the public data members are directly accessible by objects of class.

PROGRAM 11.4 – Illustrates initializing public data members from outside the class.

```
#include <iostream>
using namespace std;
class Rect {    // beginning of class
 public:
 int x ,y;    // data declared public
 int Area( )
 {return x*y; }
 };      // End of class

int main()
 {
  Rect R1;  //R1 is an object of class Rect
```

```
    R1.x = 8;  // accessing data members directly
    R1.y = 5;
   cout << "Area = "<< R1.Area()<<endl;
   cout << "Length = " << R1.x <<endl;
   cout<< "Width = " << R1.y << endl;
   return 0 ;
    }
```

The expected output given below shows that object can directly access the data declared public.

```
Area = 40
Length = 8
Width = 5
```

Accessing Private Data Members

The above program is repeated below, now with the data x, y declared private. Now x and y are not accessible by the object directly and we have to create a public function to initialize the object data so that rectangle is realised. This is done by public function `void setsides ()`. In this function we declare two int variables L and W and we equate x = L and y = W. Since L and W are declared in the public domain they are accessible to the objects of class as already shown in Program 11.4 above. So in the main () we create an object R1 of the class and in next line the function `setsides()` is called and the values 8 and 5 are put in as its arguments. These are the values of L and W which are passed on to x and y through the function `setsides()`. These values of x and y are used to calculate the area. The Program runs to give the area 40.

Now if you try to access the data of the rectangle by calling R1.x or R1.y as done in the previous Program 11.4 you would get the following error message.

```
'x' : cannot access private member declared in class 'Rect'
'y' : cannot access private member declared in class 'Rect'
```

This is so because data is private. If it is required to display data you have to have another function in public domain to display the length and width of rectangle. This is carried out in the following program for sake of illustration. The following program shows that private data can be extracted through public functions.

PROGRAM 11.5 – Illustrates **accessing private data** with public function.

```
#include <iostream>
 using namespace std;

class Rect {
 private :
 int x ,y;

 public:
 void setsides ( int L, int W){ x = L, y = W;}
```

```
 int Area( ){return x*y;} // definition of function Area ()
  // public function to get object data
void Dimension (){cout <<"Length = "<< x <<",\tWidth = "<<y << endl; }
 };    // End of class
 int main()
 {
 Rect R1;
 R1.setsides (8,5) ; //Calling setside () to initialize x,y
 cout << "Area = "<< R1.Area()<<endl;
 R1.Dimension (); // calling function Dimension ()
 return 0 ;
  }
```

The expected output is given below.

```
Area = 40
Length = 8,     Width = 5
```

An important feature of class programming is its ability to hide private data and private functions. Therefore, in general, the intention is to hide as much as is feasible without impairing the normal execution of the program.

11.6 CLASS WITH AN ARRAY AS DATA MEMBER

The class data or functions may have arrays. In the following program the private data is an array. The functions `void Display1()` and `void Display2()` are defined inside the class while the function `Setprice()` is defined outside the class. As required, its prototype (given below) is declared inside the class.

```
unsigned int n;
void Setprice (int x[], n);
```

PROGRAM 11.6 – Illustrates how to access private array data member.

```
#include <iostream>
using namespace std;
class List {
private :   //Access label private
int x[4];   // Array data
public:
 void Display1() // Definition of function Display1()
 {cout<< "Welcome To This Market" << endl;
  cout << "Here is the price List" <<endl;}
 void Setprice (int x [4] );
 void Display2()  // Definition of function Display2()
```

```
{for (int i = 0; i<4; i++)
 cout<<" Price of item " "<<i+1<< " = "<< x[i] <<endl; }
 } ;     // End of class

void List ::Setprice (int a[4] ) // Definition of Setprice ()
{ for ( int j = 0; j< 4; j++)
 x[j] = a [j] ; }

void main()
{
List L1;     // L1 is an object of class List
 int P[4] = {6,5,4,8} ;

  L1.Setprice(P) ;  // P is const pointer to the array
   L1. Display1();
    L1.Display2();
 }
```

The expected output is given below.

```
Welcome To This Market
Here is the price List
Price of item 1 = 6
Price of item 2 = 5
Price of item 3 = 4
Price of item 4 = 8
```

11.7 CLASS WITH AN ARRAY OF STRINGS AS DATA MEMBER

In the following program the private data includes an *int* array which represents marks obtained by students and an array of C-strings for entering the names of students. The aim is to prepare a list in which marks are written against individual student name.

PROGRAM 11.7 – Illustrates how to access private array and string data.

```
#include <iostream>
#include<string>
using namespace std;

class List
{
private :

 int x[4];    // Array data
 char Names [4] [20] ;  // two dimensional array

public:
 void Display1 ()
 {cout << "Here is the Marks List" <<endl;}
```

```
    void Setmarks(int x [4] );   // Declaration of function
    void Setnames (char Names[4][20] ); // Declaration of function

    void Display2()   // Function defined inside the class.
    {for (int i = 0; i<4; i++)
    cout<<" Marks obtained by "<<Names [i]<<" = "<< x[i]<<endl;}
};                            // End of class

   void List :: Setmarks (int a[4] ) //Definition of setmarks ()
    {for ( int j = 0; j< 4; j++)  // outside the class
     x[j] = a [j] ;}

   void List:: Setnames(char b[4][20] ) //Definition of Setnames
    {for ( int m = 0 ; m<4; m++)   // outside the class

     {for (int p = 0 ; p<20; p++)
      Names[m][p] = b[m][p] ;}
    }
   void main()
   {
    List L1;
    char Students [4] [20] ;

    cout<<"Enter the names of 4 students: ";

    for( int i =0; i< 4;i++)
    cin.getline ( Students[i],20); // Reading names from keyboard

    cout<<"Enter Marks."<< endl;

   int P [4];
   for (int k =0; k<4;k++)
   cin>> P[k];

          //L1 is an object of class
    {L1.Setmarks(P) ;   // Putting in an array parameter
    L1.Setnames (Students);} // Putting in string parameter

     L1.Display1();
      L1.Display2();
    }
```

The program output is given below.

```
Enter the names of 4 students: Anjali
Sujata
Sunita
Mohan
Enter Marks.
76 68 87 75
```

```
Here is the Marks List
Marks obtained by Anjali = 76
Marks obtained by Sujata = 68
Marks obtained by Sunita = 87
Marks obtained by Mohan = 75
```

The scheme of the program 11.7 is extended in the following program. Here marks obtained in 4 subjects are listed against student names. The data members for the marks and names of students are declared private and are accessed through the member functions Setmarks() and Setnames () respectively. The program handles an array of strings in Setname() and four int arrays in Setmarks().

In this program the array MA [4] represents marks in mathematics, PH[4] represents marks in physics, CH[4] stands for marks in chemistry, ENL[4] for marks in English and Total represents the total of marks in mathematics, physics, chemistry and English for each student.

The student names are represented by an array of strings Names[4][20] which is used to represent 4 names each having a maximum of 20 characters, this includes the null character. The output gives the students name and marks obtained in different subjects and total in a single row.

PROGRAM 11.8 – Illustrates the **preparation of mark list** in 4 subjects and total marks.

```
#include <iostream>
#include<string>
using namespace std;
class List
{ int MA[4], PH[4], CH[4],ENL[4], Total[4]; // private by default
char Names[4][20] ;
public:
 void Display1()
 {cout << "Here is the Marks List" <<endl;}

void Setmarks(int MA [4], int PH[4], int CH[4], int ENL[4], int Total[4]);
 void Setnames (char Names[4][20]);

 void Display2()
{cout<< "Students/Subjects     Math     PHYS    CHEM     ENGLISH    Total
"<<endl;
for (int i = 0; i<4; i++)
      {Total[i] = MA[i] + PH[i] + CH[i] + ENL[i];
cout <<Names [i]<<"   \t        \t" << MA[i]<<" \t "<<PH[i]<<" \t "<<
CH[i]<<" \t   "<<ENL[i]<<" \t      " << Total[i]<<endl;
    } } };     // end of class

void List::Setmarks(int a[4],int b[4],int c[4],int d[4],int e[4])
 {for (int j = 0; j< 4; j++)
  { MA[j] = a [j];
  PH[j] = b[j];
```

```
    CH[j] = c[j];
    ENL[j] = d[j];
    Total[j] = e[j];} }

   void List:: Setnames(char b[4] [20] ) // definition of Setnames
   { for ( int m = 0 ; m<4; m++)
    {for (int p = 0 ; p<20; p++)
    Names[m] [p] = b[m] [p] ;}
   }
  void main()    // start of main program
  {
   List L1;
   char Students [4] [20] ;

   cout<<"Enter the names of 4 students: ";

   for( int i =0; i< 4;i++)
   cin.getline ( Students[i],20);

  int M[4];
     cout <<"Enter Marks in Math"<<endl;
     for ( int k =0; k<4 ; k++)
      cin>>M[k];

   int P[4] ;
   cout <<"Enter Marks in Physics"<<endl;
     for ( int m =0; m<4 ; m++)
      cin>>P[m];

   int C[4] ;
   cout <<"Enter Marks in Chemistry"<<endl;
     for ( int s =0; s<4 ; s++)
      cin>>C[s];

   int E[4] ;
   cout <<"Enter Marks in English"<<endl;

     for ( int n =0; n<4 ; n++)
      cin>>E[n];
   int T[4];
  {L1.Setmarks(M, P, C, E, T ) ;
   L1.Setnames (Students);}

  L1. Display1();
  L1.Display2();
  }
```

The expected output is given below.

```
Enter the names of 4 students: Sujata
Sunita
Namrita
Aakriti
Enter Marks in Math
67 76 65 87
Enter Marks in Physics
67 87 66 96
Enter Marks in Chemistry
88 76 85 76
Enter Marks in English
65 67 68 75
Here is the Marks List
Students/Subjects   Math    PHYS    CHEM    ENGLISH    Total
Sujata                67      67      88       65        287
Sunita                76      87      76       67        306
Namrita               65      66      85       68        284
Aakriti               87      96      76       75        334
```

The above program may be extended to any number of students and any number of subjects or tests by making corresponding changes in the number of elements in the arrays.

In the following example, we declare a class with name Cubicle. The name stands for any rectangular prismatic solid body having three dimensions, i.e. length, width, and height. The program calculates the surface area and volume of cubic prisms. Two instances or objects are created by names cube1 and cube2. Since their type is Cubicle, so in the declaration they are written as `Cubicle cube1;` and `Cubicle cube2;` The functions are called by the objects with the help by selection dot operator (.). The link between the object and the function is through the pointer **this** which is generated by compiler for every object that is created for a class. The dot operator passes on the pointer to the function and thus the function operates on object data. (for more details on pointer *this* see Chapter 12)

PROGRAM 11.9 – Illustrates another application of class program.

```
#include <iostream>
using namespace std;
class Cubicle {   // Cubicle is name of class
 private:
 int x,y,z;

public:
 void set_sides( int , int, int );
 int volume (); // declaration of function volume ()
 int surface_area (); // declaration of function surface_area ()
 };    // End of class
```

```
void Cubicle:: set_sides (int width, int height, int length )
{ x = width , y = height, z = length ; }

int Cubicle::surface_area() //Function surface_area defined
{ return 2*(x*y+x*z+y*z);} //outside the class

int Cubicle::volume ()  //Function volume defined outside
{ return x*y*z;}   // the class

int main()
{ Cubicle cube1; //cube1 is an object of the class Cubicle.
Cubicle cube2 ; // cube2 is another object of the same class.
cube1.set_sides (3,4,5); // The dot (.) is a selection symbol.
cube2.set_sides (2,4,6); // set_sides initializes the object

cout << "Volume of cube1 = " <<cube1.volume()<<"\n";

cout<<"Surface area of cube1 = "<<cube1.surface_area()<<"\n";
cout<< "Volume of cube2 = " <<cube2.volume()<<"\n";
cout<<"Surface area of cube2 = "<<cube2.surface_area()<<"\n";
return 0 ;
}
```

The expected output is as below.

```
Volume of cube1 = 60
Surface area of cube1 = 94
Volume of cube2 = 48
Surface area of cube2 = 88
```

In the above example, `class Cubicle`, the dimensions x, y and z are declared private while the functions `set_sides ()`, `volume()` and `surface_area()` are declared public members of the class. Also notice that these functions are defined outside the class, therefore, they are prefixed with name of class and scope resolution operator (::). For example, for defining volume function, the first line of code is `int Cubicle ::volume()`. In the `main()` two instances are declared as `Cubicle cube1;` and `Cubicle cube2 ;` Both are preceded by `Cubicle` because it is their type. Both the objects may be declared in single line, in that case it is coded as `Cubical cube1, cube2;`It is just like we declare two integers as `int x, y;`. The data members are accessed through the public function set_sides (). For cube1 it is coded as `cube1.set_values(3,4,5);`. A similar statement is written for cube2 which is another object of the class. In the output statements also we have to use selection symbol (.) for calling the class functions, for instance, `cube1.volume()` and `cube2.volume()` etc. to indicate that here we want to have the volume of cube1 and here we want to have volume of cube2, etc. The output is easily verified by manual calculations.

11.8 CLASS CONSTRUCTOR AND DESTRUCTOR FUNCTIONS

In the previous programs the private data members of the classes have been accessed through a public member functions such as *void set_sides ()* of Program 11.9. These functions are called after the objects have been created. It is not instantaneous initialization of the object at the time of declaration of object in the way we declare and initialize a variable like `int x = 6;`. In case of objects also the same may be achieved with a **constructor function** which is a **special public function** of the class.

A constructor function is a public function and has same name as that of the class. It is used to initialize the object data variables or assign dynamic memory in the process of creation of an object of the class so that the object becomes operational. Whenever a new instance or an object of the class is declared the constructor is automatically invoked and allocates appropriate size of memory block for the object. The constructor function simply initializes the object. It does not return any value. It is not even void type. So nothing is written for its *type*. The general characteristics of constructor functions are given below.

(i) Constructor function has same name as that of the class.
(ii) It is declared as a public function.
(iii) It may be defined inside the class or outside the class. If it is defined outside the class its prototype must be declared in the class body.
(iv) It does not return any value, nor it is of *type* void. So no *type* is written for it.
(v) The constructor is automatically called whenever an object is created.

The **destructor** function removes the object from the computer memory after its relevance is over. For a local object the destructor is called at the end of the block enclosed by the pair of braces { } wherein the object is created and for a static object it is called at the end of main() function. It releases the memory occupied by the object and returns it to heap. The destructor function also has same name as class but it is preceded by the tilde symbol (~) and has no parameters. It is a good programming practice to provide a destructor explicitly. If it is not provided explicitly in the program it is provided by the system.

The following program illustrates the parametric constructor. In such cases, objects are declared along with the object data values which are passed on as arguments of functions.

PROGRAM 11.10 – Illustrates a **class constructor.**

```
#include <iostream>
using namespace std;

class Cubicle {

private:
 int x, y, z;
public:

Cubicle ( int , int, int ); //constructor prototype
```

```
   int volume() {return ( x*y*z);}
   } ;      // End of class
    Cubicle::Cubicle(int a, int b, int c ) // Constructor
    {x = a, y = b, z = c ;  // defined outside class
     cout<<"constructed called"<<endl;}

   int main()
   {Cubicle cube1(3,3,3) ; // object 1 with arguments 3,3,3
    Cubicle cube2(4,5,6); //object 2
     Cubicle cube3 (2,4,5); //object 3

   cout << " Volume of cube1 = " <<cube1.volume()<<"\n";
    cout << " Volume of cube2 = " <<cube2.volume()<<"\n";
     cout << " Volume of cube3 = " <<cube3.volume()<<"\n";
   return 0 ;
   }
```

The expected output is given below.

```
constructed called
constructed called
constructed called
Volume of cube1 = 27
Volume of cube2 = 120
Volume of cube3 = 40
```

From the output it is clear that every time an object is created the constructor function is invoked. In the above program three objects cube1 and cube2 and cube3 are created. For the three objects the constructor has been called three times. The destructor function is called when the object goes out of scope.

11.9 TYPES OF CONSTRUCTORS

A program may have more than one constructor functions provided their arguments are different. At least one parameter should be different or at least of different type. The different types of constructors are listed below.

(i) Constructor with default values
(ii) Constructor with parameters
(iii) Copy constructor

The parametric type of constructor has already been illustrated in the Program 11.10 described above. The following program illustrates default constructor, parametric constructor, copy constructor and destructor functions.

In the following program we illustrate the different types of constructors and how these are invoked when objects with different type of arguments are called.

PROGRAM 11.11 – Illustrates types of constructors and destructor.

```
#include <iostream>
using namespace std;
class Cubicle {
private:
 int x, y, z;
public:
 Cubicle () { x = 3, y = 4, z = 2 ; // default constructor
   cout << "Default constructor called.";}
 ~ Cubicle () {cout<< "Destructor called to remove object.\n";}
  //Following is the parametric constructor definition
 Cubicle (int a, int b, int c ){x = a, y = b , z= c;
 cout << "Parametric constructor called. ";}

Cubicle (Cubicle & cubeA)  // copy constructor definition
{ x = cubeA.x , y = cubeA.y , z = cubeA.z ;
cout << "\nCopy constructor called." ;}
int volume() {return ( x*y*z);} // definition of function volume
} ;      // End of class

int main()
 {{ Cubicle cube1;  //scope of cube1 is this program block{}
 cout << "\nVolume of cube1 = " <<cube1.volume() <<"\n" ;}
  Cubicle cube2(6,5,4) ; // Scope main()
  cout << "\nVolume of cube2 = " <<cube2.volume();

 { Cubicle cube3 (cube2) ; //Scope of cube3 is this block {}
 cout << "\nVolume of cube3 = " << cube3.volume( )<<"\n";}
return 0 ;
}
```

The expected output is given below.

```
Default constructor called.
Volume of cube1 = 24
Destructor used to remove object.
Parametric constructor called.
Volume of cube2 = 120
Copy constructor called.
Volume of cube3 = 120
Destructor called to remove object.
Destructor called to remove object.
```

In the above program object cube1 is declared without any argument so the compiler chooses the default constructor for its construction. The object is created in a block contained within curly brackets. The scope of this object is that block of program in which it was created. At the end of block destructor was called to remove it from the memory. See third line of output.

Object cube2 is created in main () so its scope is up to end of main(). Object cube3 is a copy of cube2, so copy constructor is called to initialize it. The scope of object cube3 is also up to the end of block in which it is created. So at end of block the destructor is called to remove it from the memory. At the end of main the destructor is again called to remove the object cube2.

In case of default constructors some values may be by default while others may be parametric. So there could be variety of constructor types. Thus there could be constructors with all default argument, constructors with one parametric argument and other default, constructors with two parametric arguments and other default and so on. The following program illustrates the application of some of these constructor functions.

PROGRAM 11.12 – Illustrates types of constructors.

```
#include <iostream>
using namespace std;

class Cubicle {
private:
 int x, y, z;

public:
 Cubicle () { x = 3, y = 4, z = 2 ;}
    //above is constructor with default values
 ~ Cubicle () {cout<< "Destructor called to remove object.\n";}
Cubicle (int a){x = a, y = 2 , z= 3; //one parameter constructor
 cout << "\nConstructor with one parameter used. ";}
    // below is two parameter constructor
Cubicle (int m,int k){x = 3,y = m, z= k;
 cout<<"\nconstructor with two parameters used."; }

 Cubicle (Cubicle & cube2) // copy constructor
 { x = cube2.x , y = cube2.y , z = cube2.z ;
cout << "\nCopy constructor used." ;}

 int volume() {return ( x*y*z);}
} ;       // end of class

int main()
 {
 Cubicle cube2(3) ;

{Cubicle cube1;
  cout << "Volume of cube1 = " <<cube1.volume() <<"\n" ;}
cout << "Volume of cube2 = " <<cube2.volume()<<"\n ";
```

```
{Cubicle cube3 (4,5);
cout << "Volume of cube3 = " <<cube3.volume()<<"\n"; }

{ Cubicle cube4;
 cube4 = cube2;
cout << "Volume of cube4 = " << cube4.volume( )<<"\n"; }

return 0 ;
}
```

The expected output is as below. The output is self explanatory.

```
Constructor with one parameter used.
Volume of cube1 = 24
Destructor used to remove object.
Volume of cube2 = 18
Constructor with two parameters used.
Volume of cube3 = 60
Destructor used to remove object.
Volume of cube4 = 18
Destructor called to remove object.
Destructor called to remove object.
```

Also observe that destructor is called when the scope of the object is over.

11.10 ACCESSING PRIVATE FUNCTION MEMBERS OF A CLASS

Carefully see the following program, in which, the data members as well as functions `volume()` and `surface_area()` are declared private. The private functions cannot be accessed directly from outside. However, they can be accessed through other public member functions and friend functions of the class. In order that the objects could access private functions, first we have to introduce public functions which return the values of private functions. The objects can access these public functions. This is one reason that functions are generally declared public. But the functions which are used only by class members, and, if it is desired that these should not be visible to users of the program, may be declared private.

PROGRAM 11.13 – Illustrates that private member functions cannot be accessed directly.

```
#include <iostream>
using namespace std;

class Cuboid {

 private:
 int surface_area( );   // function declared privte
 int volume( );     // function declared private
 int x , y, z;    // data declared private
```

```
public:
Cuboid(int L,int W,int H ):x(L),y(W),z (H){} // Constructor
};   // End of class

int Cuboid::surface_area()
{return 2*(x*y +y*z +z*x);}

int Cuboid::volume()
{return x*y*z ;}

int main()
{
Cuboid C1(5,6,4);
cout << " Volume of cuboid C1 " << C1. volume()<<"\n";

cout<<" surface area of C1 = "<< C1. surface_area()<<"\n";
return 0 ;
 }
```

The expected output is as follows.

```
error : cannot access private member declared in class 'Cuboid'
error : cannot access private member declared in class 'Cuboid'
```

The remedy of the above situation is that either to make the functions public in which case the nature of processing is no longer hidden. However, we can also have public functions which just pass on the return values of the private functions. In this case the process still remains hidden, so this is a better option. This method is illustrated in the following program.

PROGRAM 11.14 –Illustrates **accessing private function** member through a public member function.

```
#include <iostream>
using namespace std;
 class Cuboid {
private:

int surface_area( );  // private member function
int volume( );   // private member function

int x , y, z;   // private data

public:
Cuboid( int L,int W,int H ):x(L),y(W),z (H){} // Constructor

int Surface_area () { return surface_area ();}
 //A public function to just pass on the return values.
int Volume () { return volume();}
```

```
//The public function for passing on the return value
// Volume and volume are different because of different case of
//first letter. So are the Surface_area and surface_area
}; // End of class

int Cuboid::surface_area() // Definition of surface_area()
{return 2*(x*y +y*z +z*x);}

int Cuboid::volume() // Definition of volume
{return x*y*z ;}

int main()
{
Cuboid C1(5,6,4);

cout << "Volume of cuboid C1 " << C1. Volume()<<"\n";

cout<<"Surface area of C1 = "<< C1. Surface_area()<<"\n";

return 0 ;
}
```

The expected output is as below.

```
Volume of cuboid C1 120
Surface area of C1 = 148
```

The above program illustrates that for accessing a private function one has to have a public function. In the above example the public function just passes on the value and nothing is revealed about the function. So it does not dilute the information hiding property of the class.

11.11 LOCAL CLASSES

A class may be declared inside a function, in which case it is called **local class**. The scope of a local class is up to the function definition. In the following program two classes are declared inside a function. The return value of function is calculated from object data of the classes. The objects are initializes inside the function definition. Such a scheme of programming is not a popular one.

PROGRAM 11.15 – Illustrates **classes local to a function.**

```
#include <iostream>
using namespace std;

int Function ( ) // function definition

{class X // class X declared inside the function
{ private:
int x ;
```

```
    public:
       X (int a ) {x = a;}
       int getx () { return x ;}

       } x_object (5) ; // object of class declared

    class Y  // Another class declared inside the function
   {
   private:
       int y;
   public :
    Y(int b ) {y = b;} // constructor function
    int gety (){return y ;} // function to access private data
   } y_object (10) ;  // object definition
       // Below is function return value
    return (x_object.getx()*(y_object.gety()));

    }
   void main()
   {
    cout<<Function ( ) <<endl;
   }
```

The expected output is given below.

```
50
```

11.12 STRUCTURES

Structures (a legacy from C language) also give facility to organize related data items in a single unit. It is a user defined data type containing logically related data but which may be of different *types* like int, double, char, arrays or strings. All of them are encapsulated in a unit. For example, suppose it is required to prepare list of students along with their data like name, registration number, age, address, etc. This can be done easily by designing a structure of relevant data. Each student is related to his/her structure, in fact, a structure represents a student. The data items are called members of the structure. The classes are in fact generalization of structures. A class with only public members is like a structure. **All members of a structure are by default public.** However, in a class declaration, if there is no access specifier, the members are by default private. **But in C++ structures the access specifier as well as functions may be used.** This is illustrated in Program 11.19. Below is an illustration of declaration of a structure like that in C. It starts with the keyword **struct** followed by its name and statements are enclosed between curly braces { } and a semi-colon after the closing right brace (}). The declaration does not contain any access specifier. The structure is made for employees of a company.

```
struct Employee  // Employee is name of struct
{ char Name [30];
```

```
int Age;
char Designation [25];
int Pay ;
};
```

Each employee may have an employee-code number such as E1, E2, E3, etc. The code may be used to represent the structure of a particular employee. In a program the codes E1, E2, etc., may be defined as an object of type Employee. It is illustrated below.

```
Employee E1, E2, E3 ;
```

The above definition allocates enough memory for each of E1, E2 and E3 for storing their respective data. Note that the declarations of E1, E2, E3 etc., are preceded by the name of structure *Employee* because that is their *type* (user defined type). It is just like we declare an object of a class. The name of class is the *type* of its objects. In same way *Employee* is the *type* for E1, E2, E3, etc.

Accessing Structure Members

The members of a structure are public by default and hence can be accessed by objects or instances directly. In the above structure, for instance, the relevant data about an employee may be extracted by using dot (.) operator as it is done for a class object. For instance, if the name, designation and pay of the employee with the code E3 are to be obtained, it is coded as illustrated below.

```
E3.Name ;  // The dot ( . ) operator provides the link.
E3.Designation ;
E3.Pay ;
```

Initialization

Initialization cannot be done inside the structure declaration because that is a kind of blue-print or design. The particular instances may be initialized as illustrated below for the case of struct Employee. The method of accessing the individual structure is illustrated above. If it is desired to initialize the name of employee for instance, we can write

```
E1.Name = " Ram Dass";
```

The whole structure may be initialised as illustrated below.

```
Employee E1, E2, E3;
E1 = {" Ram Dass", 30, "Engineer", 20000};
E2 = {"Dinesh", 25, "Jr-Engineer", 15000};
E3 = {"Priti", 20 , "Office Manager", 1500};
```

A structure may be assigned to another structure.

PROGRAM 11.16 – Illustrates a structure.

```
# include <iostream>
using namespace std;
```

```
struct Employee  // declaration of structure Employee.
{ char Name [30];
 int Age;
char Designation [25];
int Pay ;};    // End of structure

 int main ()
 { Employee E1 = {" Ram Dass", 30, "Engineer", 20000};
  Employee E2 = {"Dinesh", 25, "Jr-Engineer", 15000};
  Employee E3 = {"Priti", 20 , "Office Manager", 1500};
cout<< "The data of employee E2 is :\n";
cout<< "Pay " <<E2.Pay<<endl;
cout<< "Name " << E2.Name<<endl;
cout << "Age "<< E2.Age <<endl;
cout<< "Designation " << E2.Designation<<endl;
return 0;
}
```

The expected output is given below.

```
The data of employee E2 is :
Pay 15000
Name Dinesh
Age 25
Designation Jr-Engineer
```

A structure may be assigned to another structure. This is illustrated in the following program.

PROGRAM 11.17 – Illustrates that **structures may be assigned.**

```
# include <iostream>
 using namespace std;
 struct Employee
{ char Name [30];
 int Age;
 char Designation [25];
 int Pay ;};    // end of declaration
 int main ()
 { Employee E1 = {" Ram Dass", 30, "Engineer", 20000};
  Employee E2 = { "Dinesh", 25, "Jr-Engineer", 15000};
  Employee E3 = { "Priti", 20 , "Office Manager", 15000};
cout<< "The data of employee E2 is :\n";
cout<< "Pay " <<E2.Pay<<endl;
cout<< "Name " << E2.Name<<endl;
cout << "Age "<< E2.Age <<endl;
```

```
cout<< "Designation " << E2.Designation<<endl;
 E1 = E3;    // assignment of structure
cout<< "Pay " <<E1.Pay<<endl;
cout<< "Name " << E1.Name<<endl;
cout << "Age "<< E1.Age <<endl;
cout<< "Designation " << E1.Designation<<endl;
return 0;
 }
```

The expected output is given below.

```
The data of employee E2 is :
Pay 15000
Name Dinesh
Age 25
Designation Jr-Engineer
Pay 15000
Name Priti
Age 20
Designation Office Manager
```

DECLARATION OF A STRUCTURE IN MAIN()

A structure may be declared inside a function or inside of another structure. The following program illustrates declaration inside main (). It may contain functions just like classes.

PROGRAM 11.18 – Illustrates declaration of structure in main ().

```
#include<iostream>
 using namespace std;
 int main ()
 {

struct Employee
 { char Name [30];
 int Age;
 char Designation [25];
 int Pay ;};

Employee E1 = {"Ram Dass", 30, "Engineer", 20000};
Employee E2 = {"Dinesh", 25, "Jr-Engineer", 15000};
Employee E3 = {"Priti", 20, "Office Manager", 1500};
 cout<< "The data of employee E2 is :\n";
 cout<< "Pay " <<E2.Pay<<endl;
 cout<< "Name " << E2.Name<<endl;
 cout << "Age "<< E2.Age <<endl;
 cout<< "Designation " << E2.Designation<<endl;
return 0;
 }
```

The expected output is given below.

```
The data of employee E2 is :
Pay 15000
Name Dinesh
Age 25
Designation Jr-Engineer
```

C++ STRUCTURES

In C++ structures, the access specifier as well as functions may be used. There is little difference between a class and a structure. We may use a constructor function as in classes. This is illustrated in the following program.

PROGRAM 11.19 – Illustrates that **access specifiers in C++ structures** like in classes.

```
#include<iostream>
#include <string>
 using namespace std;
 struct Employee

{
private :
 int Pay, Employee_code ;

public:
    Employee ( int E,int P ) { Employee_code =E , Pay = P ;}
          // constructor function
  int getpay ( ) {return Pay ;}   // functions
  int getcode (){return Employee_code ;}
};

int main ()
 {
 Employee E1 (22, 10000);
 Employee E2 (32, 15000);
cout<< "Employee_code of E1 = " << E1.getcode ()<<endl;
cout<< "Pay of E1 =" <<E1.getpay()<<endl;
cout<< "Employee_code of E2 = " << E2.getcode ()<<endl;
cout<< "Pay of E2 =" <<E2.getpay()<<endl;
return 0;
  }
```

The expected output is given below.

```
Employee_code of E1 = 22
Pay of E1 =10000
Employee_code of E2 = 32
Pay of E2 =15000
```

EXERCISES

1. Give an outline of class declaration.
2. How is an object of a class declared?
3. What makes class program an objected oriented programming?
4. In what way procedural programming is different from object oriented programming?
5. What is the role of a constructor and destructor functions in a class?
6. Can the constructor and destructor functions be declared constants?
7. What is the function of dot (.) operator?
8. What is the difference between the class members declared as private and those declared public?
9. What is the difference between a private member and a protected member?
10. Why should some members of class be declared as private and others as public?
11. Why member functions of a class are generally declared public and data members as private?
12. Give an example of code for a function prototype declared in class body and function definition outside the class body.
13. Can you declare an object of a class inside the body of its own class?
14. Can a class definition body include objects of other classes? If so how will you declare the object in the class?
15. How is, a function declared private in a class, accessed by an object of the same class?
16. How is a function of a class called?
17. What do you understand by following terms.
    (i) Information hiding
    (ii) Encapsulation of data and functions
18. Make a class program to illustrate the following types of constructors.
    (i) Default constructor
    (ii) Parametric constructor
    (iii) Copy constructor
19. Make a class program with private data members. How can the objects of class access the same?
20. Make a class program for student registration in which the student is required to enter his/her name, age and address. The entries should be displayed on monitor so that they can be verified by the user.
21. Make a class program with a name Polygon for determining the area and periphery of any regular polygon. Verify the program by determining the area and periphery of following.
    (i) Square
    (ii) Equilateral triangle
22. Make a class program for determining the area and periphery of ellipses for which the major and minor axes are declared as private.

23. Make a class program which prints the list of grades of a group of 10 students. The list includes names of students and grades in five subjects.
24. What is the function of destructor function of class?
25. Make a class program with name Rectangle with a constructor function. The class functions determine the area and circumference of the objects of class. Illustrate the working of class with an object.
26. What is a structure? How do you define a structure?
27. What are the differences between a class and a structure?
28. Make a program to illustrate an array of structures. Also illustrate input/output for structures.

Answer:

PROGRAM 11.20 – Illustrates an array of structures.

```
# include <iostream>
using namespace std;

struct Employee

{ char  Name [30];
  int Age;
  char Designation [25];
  int Pay ;};
  void Display (Employee E )
{
 cout<<"Name  : "<<E.Name<< "\t Age "<<E.Age <<"\n";
 cout<< "Designation   " <<E.Designation<< " \t\nPay : "
 <<E. Pay<<endl; }

 int main ()
 {
   Employee employee [] = {

 { " Ram Dass", 30, "Engineer", 20000},
 { "Dinesh", 25, "Jr-Engineer", 15000},
 { "Priti", 20 , "Office Manager", 1500},
 { " Madhu" , 22, "Office Assistant", 10000}};

  Display (employee [2] );
  return 0;
  }
```

The expected output is given below.

```
Name  : Priti     Age 20
Designation   Office Manager
Pay : 1500
```

❍❍❍

CHAPTER

12

Classes and Objects–2

12.1 FRIEND FUNCTION TO A CLASS

A friend function to a class has access to all the members of the class whether these are private, protected or public and this characteristic makes it useful in many applications, particularly, in overloading of operators. However, the free access to all the members of a class goes against its frequent use, because, it dilutes the information hiding capability of the class. Since friendship is granted by the class, therefore, the class declaration should contain the declaration that the function is friend of the class. Also a friend function is not a member function of the class in which it is declared as friend, and hence **a friend function is defined outside the class body**. The declaration of prototype of a friend function in the class body is illustrated below. It starts with keyword *friend* followed by the *type* of function and identifier (name) for the function which is followed by a list of *types* of parameters of the function enclosed in parentheses (). It ends with a semicolon.

```
friend type identifier (type_parameter1,type_parameter2, ..);
```

For instance, a function with name `Area()` is declared a friend function of class Rect which is a class for rectangular figures having sides x and y as under.

```
friend int Area(const Rect &b);
```

In the above declaration the data of the object b of class Rect are the only parameters of the function, however, a friend function may have other parameters as well. The definition of the friend function has to be done outside the class body. The function declared above is defined below.

```
int Area (const Rect & b)
{return b.x * b.y ;}
```

In the above definition the scope resolution operator (::) is not used because Area function is not a member function of the class.

The following points should be noted about friend functions to classes.

1. If a function F is friend to class B, then F can access all the members of class B.
2. The friendship is granted by the class and not extracted by the function. Therefore, the friend function has to be so declared in the body of the class as illustrated above.
3. Function prototype of friend function preceded by keyword *friend* is declared inside the class body but the function is defined outside the class body.

4. Friend function is not a member function of the class to which it is friend. Therefore, the scope resolution operator is not required while defining the friend function outside the class body.
5. A class may have any number of friend functions. And a function may be friend to any number of classes.
6. A friend function may be declared any where in the class. The access specifiers, i.e. public, protected or private do not affect a friend function.

The following program illustrates the declaration and definition of a friend function.

PROGRAM 12.1 – Illustrates definition of a **friend function** to a class.

```
#include <iostream>
using namespace std;

 class Rect {
 friend int Area(const Rect &a);  // friend function Area
  int x,y;  // private by default
 public:
  Rect (int L, int W){ x = L,y = W;}  // constructor function
  };      // end of class

  int Area (const Rect &b)  // definition of friend function
 {return b.x*b.y;};  // scope resolution operator not needed

int main()
 {
  Rect R1(5,6), R2(3,4) ; //declaration of two objects R1 and R2
  cout << "Area of R1= " << Area ( R1 ) <<"\n";

  cout << "Area of R2 = " << Area ( R2 )<<"\n";
  return 0 ;
  }
```

The expected output is given below.

```
Area of R1= 30
Area of R2 = 12
```

In the above program the friend function takes all the arguments from the data of objects of the class. One of the object R1 has the dimensions 5 and 6, the friend function gives the area 30 while the second object R2 has the dimensions 3 and 4 and its area is given out as 12. The output shows that friend function can access the private data members of the class.

A class can have any number of friend functions. In the following program two friend functions are declared to a class *Rect* which deals with rectangles. The first friend function calculates the area taking the private data of the object. The second friend function calculates the cost of surface treatment of area of rectangle.

PROGRAM 12.2 – Illustrates a class with more than one **friend functions**.

```
#include <iostream>
using namespace std;
class Rect {
 friend int Area(const Rect &a);    // a friend function
 int x,y; // private by default

public:
  Rect (int L,int W){ x = L, y = W;} // constructor function
  friend double cost(const Rect &a, double);
              //second friend function
 }; // end of class

int Area (const Rect &b) // definition of Area Function
 {return b.x*b.y;}

double cost(const Rect &b, double s) //definition of cost ()
 {return b.x*b.y * s ;}

 int main()

 { double A = 4.5 , B = 5.2;  // A and B are for data for cost
  Rect R1(10,5), R2(20,5) ; // R1, R2 are two objects

  cout << "Area of R1= " << Area (R1) <<"\n";
  cout << "Area of R2 = " << Area (R2)<<"\n";
  cout << "cost  = " <<cost (R1,A) <<"\n";
  cout << "cost  = " <<cost (R2,B) <<"\n";
 return 0 ;
}
```

The expected output is given below.

```
Area of R1= 50
Area of R2 = 100
cost  = 225
cost  = 520
```

One Function Friend of Many Classes

A function may be friend to many classes. This is illustrated in the following program in which a function Display() is declared friend to two classes, i.e. class Sqr and class Rect.

PROGRAM 12.3 – Illustrates a function friend to more than one class.

```
#include <iostream>
using namespace std;
class Sqr;     //pre-declaration of class
```

```
class Rect {      // class Rect
 int x,y; // private by default
public:
 Rect ( int A, int B) { x = A, y = B;}
 int area ( )
 {return x*y;}
friend void Display ( Rect R, Sqr S ); // friend function to Rect
 };

class Sqr {          // class Sqr
 int side;           // private by default
public:
 Sqr (int C){ side = C;}
 int Area ( )
 {return side*side;}
 friend void Display (Rect R , Sqr S ); // friend function to Sqr
 };               //end of class

void Display ( Rect R, Sqr S)  // Definition of friend function
 {cout <<"Area of rect = " << R.area()<<endl;
 cout <<"Area of Square = " << S.Area()<< endl;}

int main()
 {Rect R1(10,5);

 Sqr S1 (10);
 Display ( R1, S1 );
 return 0 ;
 }
```

The expected output is given below. The result is self explanatory.

```
Area of rect = 50
Area of Square = 100
```

12.2 FRIEND CLASSES

When all or most of the functions of a class need access to data members and function members of another class, the whole class may be declared friend to the class. For instance, if the functions of a class say *class A* need to access the public, private and protected members of another class say *class B*, the *class A* may be declared as **friend class A** ; in the body of class B. As you know *friend* is a keyword of C++. The declaration is illustrated below.

```
Class B
{friend class A;   //declaration that class A is friend of B
private:
```

```
statements
friend class C; //declaration that class C is friend of B
public:
Other_statements;
};
```

Characteristics of Friend Classes

The following characteristics of friend classes should be noted.

1. If a *class A* is a friend of *class B*, then functions of *A* can access all the members of B.
2. If *class A* is a friend of *class B*, it does not mean that *class B* is also friend of *class A*. **The C++ friendship is not reciprocal.**
3. **Friendship is granted by the class whose members are to be accessed.** If a *class A* is friend of *class B*, it has to be so declared in the definition of *class B*.
4. If *class A* is friend of *class B* and *class B* is friend of *class C*, it does not mean that *class A* is also friend of *class C* or *class B* is friend of *class A* or *class C* is friend of *class B* or *class A*.
   The C++ friendship is neither transmitted nor it is reciprocal.
5. A class may be friend to more than one class. And a class may have more than one class as friends. **There is no limit on the number of friends of a class.**

In the following program we define a class *Cuboid* for prismatic components with rectangular base. The class has two functions to calculate the volume and external surface area of cubicle elements. A second class with name *paint* is defined. This class has a function to calculate the cost of painting the external surface of objects of *class Cuboid*. The *class paint* is declared friend of *class Cuboid*.

PROGRAM 12.4 – Illustrates declaration of a **friend class** to a class.

```
#include <iostream>
using namespace std;
class Cuboid {
friend class paint;   // Declaration of friend class
public:
void sides(int , int, int);
int Area();
int volume();
int x , y, z;
};    //end of class Cuboid

void Cuboid:: sides (int L, int W, int H )
{x = L, y = W,z = H; } // Setting the sides of Cuboid

int Cuboid::Area()    //Definition of area
{return 2*(x*y +y*z +z*x);}
```

```
int Cuboid::volume()   // definition of volume
 {return x*y*z ;}

class paint{  //declaration of friend class paint
private:
 int R;
public:
 paint () { R = 1;}   // default constructor
 paint ( int S) { R = S;} // parametric constructor

Cuboid C;    // C is the object of class Cuboid
 int area (){return C.Area ();}
int cost(int R , Cuboid C ) // R is the rate and C is object
{return R* C.Area () ;} // of Cuboid. cost() is a function
};
int main()
{Cuboid C1 ;    // C1 is object of class Cuboid

C1.sides (5,6,5 );
 paint P1 ;   // P1 is object of class paint
 int k = 4;
 cout << "Volume of C1 = " <<C1.volume()<<"\n";

cout<<"Surface area of C1 = "<<C1.Area()<<"\n";

cout<<"Cost of painting P1 = "<< P1.cost(k, C1)<<"\n";
return 0 ;
}
```

The expected output is given below. See carefully the definition and calling of function cost () of class paint. P1 is an object of class paint.

```
Volume of C1 = 150
surface area of C1 = 170
cost of painting P1 = 680
```

12.3 POINTER TO A CLASS

Pointer to a class may be declared in the same way as it is done for integer or double numbers. Let us have a class by name List and let L1 be an object of this class. Let ptr be the pointer to the class. For declaration of pointer to List we may write the code as below.

```
List L1 ; // declaration that L1 is an object of class List
List *ptr;   // declaration of pointer to List
ptr = &(List) L1;  // assignment of value to ptr
```

The last line may as well be written as **ptr = &List (L1);**

The following program gives an illustration of pointer to class.

PROGRAM 12.5 – Illustrates definition of a **pointer to a class**.

```
#include <iostream>
using namespace std;
class List
{
private :
  int x,y;   //let x = the no of items, y = price of one item.
public:

void Setdata (int a, int b )   //A public function to access x,y.
  {cout << "Enter number of items : "; cin >>a ;
  cout <<"Enter price of one item : " ; cin >> b ;
    x = a, y = b; }
 void Display1 ( )
  {cout<<"Number of items = " <<x <<endl; }

void Display2 ()

 {cout<<"Price of each item = "<<y <<endl ; }

void Display3 ()
{cout<<"Cost of "<<x<<" items at the rate of "<<y<<"per item = "<<x*y<<endl;}
 };     // End of class

void main()
{
 List L1 ;
 List *ptr;     // pointer to List
 ptr = &(List) L1; // assigning address of class object

 int i,j;
 (*ptr).Setdata (i,j); //values to be assigned by user

 ptr -> Display1 (); // (*ptr) and ptr-> are equivalent.
 ptr -> Display2();

 (*ptr).Display3();
 }
```

On running the program, the following text will appear on monitor.

```
Enter number of items :
```

Type the data say 50 and enter. Then the text of second line of output will appear on the monitor, type price say 20 and enter. The following output would appear on the monitor.

```
Enter number of items : 50
Enter price of one item : 20
Number of items = 50
```

```
Price of each item = 20
Cost of 50 items at the rate of 20 per item = 1000
```

The above program also shows that for calling a function of class in the *main ()* through a pointer ptr, either of the following two codes may be used.

```
    ptr -> Display3();
or
    (*ptr).Display3();
```

Both the above statements are equivalent. In the second statement *ptr has to be enclosed in brackets because the dot (.) operator has higher precedent than the dereference operator (*). The following program illustrates, how the functions relating to the second object of the same class may be called by the use of increment operator (++) on pointer of class pointing to the first object of the class. Both the objects should be declared before the increment operator.

PROGRAM 12.6 –Illustrates that an **increment to pointer** to a class points to second object of class.

```
#include <iostream>
using namespace std;

class List{
private :
 int x,y,z;

public:
 void Display1()
 {cout<< "Welcome To This Market" << endl; }

 void Setprice (int a, int b, int c)
 {x = a, y = b, z = c;}

 void Display2 ()
 { cout<<" Price of item1 = "<< x<<endl;
  cout<<" Price of item2 = "<< y<<endl;
  cout<<" Price of item3 = "<< z<<endl; }
 };      // End of class

void main()
 { List L1;
 List *ptr;    //pointer to List
 ptr = &(List) L1; // Assignment of address of L1 to pointer

 ptr -> Setprice( 6,8,10); // Function relating to L1
 ptr -> Display1();

 cout << "Price List 1"<<endl;
 ptr ->Display2();
```

```
List L2;    // L2 is second object of the class
*ptr++; // Increment of pointer of L1 gives pointer to L2.

ptr -> Setprice(32,27,38); // Function relating to L2.
ptr -> Display1();

cout<< " Price List 2"<<endl;

ptr -> Display2();
}
```

The expected output of the program is given below.

```
Welcome To This Market
Price List 1
Price of item1 = 6
Price of item2 = 8
Price of item3 = 10
Welcome To This Market
Price List 2
Price of item1 = 32
Price of item2 = 27
Price of item3 = 38
```

In the above program the pointer ptr is declared as pointer to class List with L1 as one of its object. The functions `Setprice()` and `Display()` are called. Obviously these calls are for L1. Then a second object L2 is declared and ptr is incremented. The incremented value of ptr points to L2. The functions `Setprice()` and `Display()` for L2 are called using this pointer.

12.4 POINTERS TO OBJECTS OF A CLASS

Let L1 be an object of class list, the pointer to L1 may be declared and assigned as below.

```
List *ptr = &L1;
```

PROGRAM 12.7 – Illustrates definition of a **pointer to an object of class.**

```
#include <iostream>
using namespace std;
class List{
private :
 int x,y,z;
public:
 List (int a,int b,int c) {x = a, y = b, z = c;} //Constructor
 void Display ()
  {cout<<" Price of item 1 = "<< x<<endl;
  cout<<" Price of item 2 = "<< y<<endl;
```

```
    cout<<" Price of item 3 = "<< z<<endl; }
  };     // End of class definition

  void main()
  { int n = 0;
  List L1 (12, 15,27) ;
   cout << "List "<<++n <<endl;
  List *ptr = &L1;  // The (*ptr) and ptr-> are equivalent
  ptr -> Display () ;

  cout<< "\nList"<< ++n <<"\n";
  List L2 (30, 54,60);
   ptr = & L2 ;
    (*ptr).Display();
   }
```

The expected output of the program is as below. In this case, the ptr++ does not automatically point to L2. Therefore, address of L2 is assigned to ptr.

```
List 1
Price of item 1 = 12
Price of item 2 = 15
Price of item 3 = 27

List2
Price of item 1 = 30
Price of item 2 = 54
Price of item 3 = 60
```

12.5 POINTERS TO FUNCTION MEMBERS OF A CLASS

A declaration and assignment of pointer to member function of class is illustrated below.

type (class_name ::*pointer_name)(types_parameters) = & class_name :: Function_name;

In the above illustration the first word *type* denotes the *type* of return value of the function, this is followed by, in parentheses, the class identifier, scope resolution operator and indirection operator (*) and pointer identifier. And in second pair of parentheses, the *types* of parameters of the function are listed, each separated by comma. The assignment (the right hand side of =) comprises address-of operator & followed by class name, scope resolution operator followed by name of function and it ends with a semicolon. In Program 12.7 given below we have a function by name `Setsides()` a public function of `class Rect` for initialization of sides of rectangle. It is defined as follows.

```
void Setsides ( int L, int W ){ x = L ,y = W ;}
```

The pointer *ptrSet to this function is declared and assigned as below.

```
void (Rect:: *ptrSet)(int, int) = &Rect :: Setsides;
```

For calling this function for an object R1 with length 20 and width 15 we write the code as below.

```
(R1.*ptrSet)(20, 15);
```

The following program illustrates the use of pointer to a member function of the class.

PROGRAM 12.8 – Illustrates definition of a **pointer to member function of class.**

```
#include <iostream>
 using namespace std;

class Rect {
 int x ,y;    // private by default
 public:

 void Setsides ( int L,int W ){ x = L ,y = W ;}
 int Area( )    // Definition of function Area
 {return x*y;}
 };      // end of class

int main()
 { Rect R1,R2,R3;
  void (Rect:: *ptrSet)(int,int) = & Rect :: Setsides;

 (R1.*ptrSet) (20,15);
  cout << "Area of R1 = "<< R1.Area()<<endl;

 (R2.*ptrSet) (20,30); //object R2 calls function by its pointer
  cout << "Area of R2 = "<< R2.Area()<<endl;
 Rect *ptr3 = &R3; // declaring pointer to object R3 of class

(ptr3 ->*ptrSet)(16,10); //calling function by pointer to object

  cout << "Area of R3 = "<< R3.Area()<<endl;
 return 0 ;
  }
```

The expected output of this program is as below.

```
Area of R1 = 300
Area of R2 = 600
Area of R3 = 160
```

12.6 POINTER TO DATA MEMBER OF A CLASS

The syntax for declaration and assignment of pointer to data members is as follows.

*type class_name :: *pointer_name = & class_name :: data_name;*

For example, a class with name Rect has data members int x and int y, the pointers ptrx and ptry to the two data members are declared as below.

```
int Rect :: *ptrx = &Rect :: x;
int Rect :: *ptry = &Rect :: y;
```

The application is illustrated in a friend function in the following program.

PROGRAM 12.9 – Illustrates definition of pointers to data members and objects of a class.

```
#include <iostream>
using namespace std;
class Rect {
friend int Area(Rect a); // friend function
int x, y;    // data members private by default

public:
friend double cost(Rect a, double); // another friend function

Rect (int L,int W){ x = L,y = W;} // constructor
};    // end of class

int Area (Rect b)   // Definition of area using pointers
{ int Rect :: *ptrx = &Rect :: x;  //ptrx is pointer for x
int Rect :: *ptry = &Rect :: y;  // ptry is pointer for y

Rect *ptrb = &b;   // ptrb is pointer to object b
return b.*ptrx * b.*ptry ;};

double cost(Rect b , double m)
{return b. x* b. y * m ;}

int main()
{ double n = 4.5;
 Rect R1(5,6), R2(3,4) ;
 cout << "Area of R1= " << Area (Rect (R1)) <<"\n";
  cout << "Area of R2 = " << Area (Rect (R2))<<"\n";
 cout << "Cost for R1 = " <<cost (Rect (R1),n) <<"\n";
return 0 ;
 }
```

Expected output is given below.

```
Area of R1= 30
Area of R2 = 12
Cost for R1 = 135
```

12.7 ACCESSING PRIVATE DATA OF AN OBJECT THROUGH POINTERS

The private data of an object may be accessed through pointers if there is one public data member. This is possible because the public data members and private data members of an object are stored in sequential blocks of memory. If we know the address of one member data we can determine the values of other data members by increment or decrement of the pointer. It is illustrated in the following program. In the program we also find the addresses of the public and private data by obtaining the values of decremented pointer. However, if you try to determine address of private data directly by the using &L1.z in the following program the result will be an error message, "cannot access private member declared in class".

PROGRAM 12.10 – Illustrates **accessing private data of an object through pointers.**

```
#include <iostream>
using namespace std;

class List{

 private :
 int x,y,z;

 public:
 int Alpha ;
List (int a, int b, int c ){x = a, y = b, z = c;} //Constructor
};      // End of class definition
void main()
{
 List L1( 10, 20, 30);
 int *pAlpha ;   // pointer to an integer
 L1. Alpha = 50;
 pAlpha = & L1.Alpha; // assignment of value to pointer
  cout<<"Alpha = "<<*pAlpha<< endl;
   cout <<"Address of Alpha = "<<pAlpha<< endl;

pAlpha--;   // decrement of pointer value for getting z
 cout <<"The z data of L1 = "<< *pAlpha <<endl;
 cout << "Address of z = "<< pAlpha<<endl;

pAlpha--;  // further decrement of value of pointer for y.
 cout << "The y data of L1 = "<< *pAlpha <<endl;
  cout << "Address of y = "<< pAlpha<<endl;

pAlpha--;   // Third decrement to value of pointer for x
 cout << "The x data of L1 = "<< *pAlpha <<endl;
  cout << "Address of x = "<< pAlpha<<endl;
  }
```

The expected output is given below.

```
Alpha = 50
Address of Alpha = 0012FF7C
The z data of L1 = 30
```

```
Address of z = 0012FF78
The y data of L1 = 20
Address of y = 0012FF74
The x data of L1 = 10
Address of x = 0012FF70
```

From the values of addresses you can easily find out that the data members of the class are stored in the sequential blocks of memory. Each block is 4 byte wide as it is allocated to integers, this is illustrated in Fig.12.1 below.

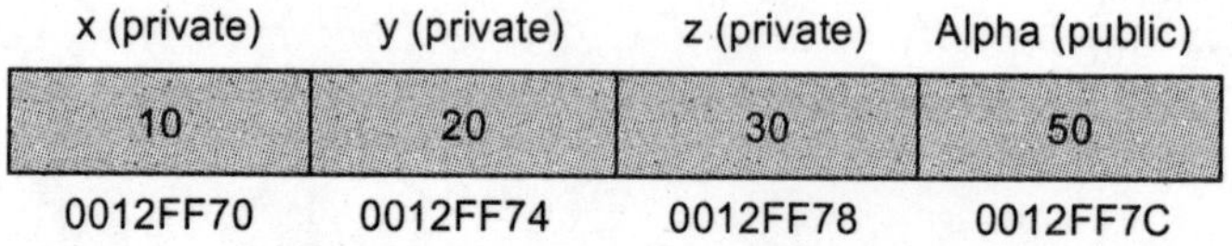

Fig. 12.1: Addresses of object data

In the following program we start from the address of object. Address of object is also the address of first data of the object.

PROGRAM 12.11 – Accessing the private data members from **address of object.**

```
#include <iostream>
using namespace std;
class List{
 private :
 int x, y, z;

public:
 int s ;

List (int a, int b, int c ) {x = a, y = b, z = c;} //Constructor

 };    // End of class

void main()
{
 List L1( 10, 20 , 30); ;
 L1.s = 40;

 int *ptrL1 ;
  ptrL1 = (int*)& L1 ;

cout << "Value of x = "<< *ptrL1<< endl;
 cout<<"Address of x = "<<ptrL1<<endl;
  ptrL1++;
  cout <<"The y data of L1 = "<< *ptrL1 <<endl;
   cout << "Address of y = "<< ptrL1<<endl;
```

```
ptrL1++;
 cout << "The z data of L1 = "<< *ptrL1 <<endl;
 cout << "Address of z = "<< ptrL1<<endl;

ptrL1 ++;
cout << "The s data of L1 = "<< *ptrL1 <<endl;
 cout << "Address of s = "<< ptrL1<<endl;
 }
```

The value of pointer ptrL1 is the address of first data that is address of x. The increment of this pointer gives pointer which points to second data that is y. Similarly we get to the third data that is z. The expected output is given below.

```
Value of x = 10
Address of x = 0012FF70
The y data of L1 = 20
Address of y = 0012FF74
The z data of L1 = 30
Address of z = 0012FF78
The s data of L1 = 40
Address of s = 0012FF7C
```

12.8 THE this POINTER

The word ***this*** is a keyword of C++ and is the name of pointer to an object of a class. When an object is created, the compiler creates ***this*** pointer which keeps the address of the object. Pointer ***this*** is not a part of object but object has access to it or we can say an object has access to its own address. When the object calls a member function of the class, ***this*** pointer becomes implicit argument of the function and the function processes the data of the object.

In the following program ***this*** as well as ****this*** have been used in the constructor of a class. Also we find that values of ***this*** pointer for two objects C1 and C2 of the class. We also find the addresses of the objects C1 and C2 by using of address-of operator &. The values of this pointer for the two objects are equal to their addresses.

PROGRAM 12.12 – Illustrates application of pointer **this.**

```
#include <iostream>
using namespace std;

class Cuboid {
 public:
 Cuboid(int L,int W,int H ){this ->x=L , (*this).y=W ,this->z=H;}
     // the above function is constructor
 int surface_area( );
  int volume( );

void Display1()  // Displays private data of object.
```

```
{cout <<"x = "<<this->x <<", y = " <<this->y << ", z = "<< (*this).z <<endl;}
  void Display2 ()
   {cout << this<<endl; }  // gives value of this
  private:
   int x ,y, z;     // private data
   };    // end of class
  int Cuboid::surface_area()   // definition of surface area
   {return 2* (x*y +y*z +z*x) ;}

   int Cuboid::volume () // definition of volume
   {return x*y*z ;}

  int main ()
   { Cuboid C1 (5,6,4), C2 (7,8,5) ; // C1 and C2 are two objects
    C1.Display1 ();
    C1.Display2 ();   // value of this pointer for C1

   cout <<&C1<<endl;  // Address of C1
   C2. Display1 ();
   C2. Display2 ();   // value of this for C2
   cout << &C2<<endl;  // Address of object C2

   cout << "Volume of cuboid C1 = "<<C1.volume ()<<"\n";
   cout<< "Volume of cuboid C2 = "<< C2.volume ()<<"\n";
    cout<<"Surface area of C1 = "<< C1.surface_area()<<"\n";
   cout<<"Surface area of C2 = "<< C2.surface_area()<<"\n";
  return 0 ;
    }
```

The expected output is given below.

```
x = 5, y = 6, z = 4
0012FF74
0012FF74
x = 7, y = 8, z = 5
0012FF68
0012FF68
Volume of cuboid C1 =120
Volume of cuboid C2 = 280
Surface area of C1 = 148
Surface area of C2 = 262
```

From the output of the program it is clear that value of *this* pointer and address of respective objects are equal. Also the statement `(*this).z` has been used to determine the value of z data of object. The **this** pointer points to the object of class.

12.9 STATIC DATA MEMBERS OF A CLASS

Objects of a class keep their own copy of data members of class. In certain situations a part of data may be same for all objects of a class. In such cases instead of every object keeping an individual copy of this data, it would be prudent if one copy of the data is shared by all the objects of class, because, this would save memory space, particularly, when the common data is large. For such applications the common data may be declared static. The static data may be declared under any one of the three access specifiers, i.e. public, protected or private. A public static data member may be accessed directly through any object of the class because it is same for all the objects. The code comprises the object name followed by dot operator followed by name of data member. Static data member declared private or protected may be accessed through the corresponding public functions of the class.

For declaration of static data the usual declaration of a variable is preceded by the keyword **static**. This is illustrated in the following program.

PROGRAM 12.13 – Illustrates declaration of **static members in a class.**

```
#include <iostream>
using namespace std;

class Cuboid {
public:
static int x;    // x declared static
Cuboid( int W ): y(W) {} // constructor

static void Display ( )  // static function
{cout <<" Height of all objects is = " << z <<endl;}

int surface_area( );
int volume( );

private:
int y;
static int z ; // static variable
};   // end of class

int Cuboid :: x = 10;
 int Cuboid :: z = 5;

int Cuboid::surface_area()
  {return 2*(x*y +y*z +z*x);}

int Cuboid::volume()
{return x*y*z ;}
```

```
int main()
{
Cuboid C1(6), C2(3) ;
cout << "C1.x = "<< C1.x << ", C2.x = "<<C2.x <<endl;

Cuboid :: Display( ); // function call without an object
cout << "Volume of cuboid C1 " << C1.volume()<<"\n";
cout<< "Volume of cuboid C2 = " << C2.volume()<<"\n";
cout<<"surface area of C1 = "<< C1.surface_area()<<"\n";
cout<<"surface area of C2 = "<< C2.surface_area()<<"\n";
return 0 ;
}
```

The expected output is as below.

```
C1.x = 10, C2.x = 10
Height of all objects is = 5
Volume of cuboid C1 300
Volume of cuboid C2 = 150
surface area of C1 = 280
surface area of C2 = 190
```

In the above program two data members x and z are declared static. The int x is declared static under public domain while the int z is declared static under access label private. The data x (a public member) may be accessed directly by an object of the class. See the output C1.x =10 and C2.x = 10, in the first line of output. The static data declared private cannot be accessed directly by an object. It has to be accessed through a public function like any other private data member. In the above program it is illustrated by function Display () which displays value of z.

In case of fundamental type static data members, they are by default initialized to 0 at the time of declaration. Putting any other value in the declaration may give error. Static members are defined at file scope. The x and z in the above program are defined outside the main () in file scope as below.

```
int Cuboid :: x = 10;
int Cuboid :: z = 5;
```

12.10 STATIC FUNCTION MEMBER OF A CLASS

A function member of a class may also be declared static provided its arguments are also declared static or if it does not access any non-static member of the class. The pointer `this` associated with every object of class is applicable only to non-static function members of the class. The static function members of class do not have `this` pointer. The following program illustrates the application of a static function with static parameters.

PROGRAM 12.14 – Illustrates **static member function** of a class.

```
#include <iostream>
using namespace std;

class Cuboid {

public:
Cuboid(int H):z(H) {} //constructor
static int Base_area (){ return x*y;} // static function

int surface_area( );
int volume( );

private:
static int x , y;  // x and y declared static
int z ;
};     // end of class

int Cuboid :: x = 5;    // static data member
int Cuboid :: y =8 ;    // static data member

int Cuboid::surface_area() // definition of surface_area ()
{return 2*(x*y +y*z +z*x);}

int Cuboid::volume()  // definition of function volume()
{return x*y*z ;}
int main()
{
Cuboid C1(5), C2(8) ;
cout<<"Base area of all objects = "<< Cuboid::Base_area()<<endl;

cout << "Volume of cuboid C1 " << C1.volume()<<"\n";
cout<< "Volume of cuboid C2 = " << C2.volume()<<"\n";

cout<<"Surface area of C1 = "<< C1.surface_area()<<"\n";
cout<<"Surface area of C2 = "<< C2.surface_area()<<"\n";

return 0 ;
}
```

The expected output is given below.

```
Base area of all objects = 40
Volume of cuboid C1 200
Volume of cuboid C2 = 320
Surface area of C1 = 210
Surface area of C2 = 288
```

12.11 DYNAMIC MEMORY MANAGEMENT FOR CLASS OBJECTS

OPERATORS NEW AND DELETE AND NEW[] AND DELETE[]

The operator **new** allocates memory from the free store called heap while the operator **delete** does just the opposite, it releases the memory by deleting the object. The released memory is added to heap for other uses. For allocation of memory for an array we have the operator **new**[] and corresponding operator **delete**[] for removing the array and releasing the memory. For fundamental types we have already discussed these operators in Chapter 9. For class objects **new** may be used for allocating memory for single object while **new**[] may be used for creating an array of class objects. Similarly single object is removed from memory by operator delete and array of objects are removed by **delete**[] operator. It must be noted that when **new** [] is used for allocation of memory, for releasing the memory we must use **delete** [] and not simply **delete.** For example if you have created an array of objects by **new**[] and if you use simply delete to remove the array, it will only delete the first object of the array, the remaining objects would not get deleted. So it will be only partial release of memory. The following program illustrates the application of new and delete for class objects.

PROGRAM 12.15 – Illustrates application of **operators new and delete** for class objects.

```
#include <iostream>
using namespace std;

class List {
 private :
 double x ; // x = weight in kg, y = price of one kg.
 double y;

public:
 void Setdata (double a, double b )
 {x = a; y = b; }

void Display ( )
 {cout<<" Weight = "; cin >> x;
  cout<<" Price = "; cin >>y;
cout<<" Cost of "<<x<<"kg at the rate of "<<y<<" per kg = "<<x*y<<endl;}
};
 void main()
{double i,j;
 List *ptr= new List ;  // use of new operator
 (*ptr).Setdata (i,j);
 ptr -> Display (); // (*ptr) and ptr-> are equivalent.
 delete ptr;
}
```

The expected output is given below. By now the reader should be able to follow the implemention of the program.

```
Weight = 8.45
Price = 10.0
Cost of 8.45kg at the rate of 10 per kg = 84.5
```

The following program illustrates the application of `new[]` and `delete[]`.

PROGRAM 12.16 – Illustrates the operators **new[]** and **delete[]** for an array of objects.

```
#include <iostream>
using namespace std;
class List {
 private :
 int x,y; // x = the no of items, y = price of one item.
public:
 void Setdata (int a, int b )
{x = a;
 y = b;
 }
void Display ( )
 {cout<<" Number of items = "; cin >> x;
 cout<<" Price of each item = " ; cin >>y;
 cout<<" Cost of "<<x<<" items at the rate of "<<y<<" per item = "<<x*y<<endl;}
}; 	// End of class
void main()
{
 List *ptr= new List[3]; //pointer to List
for (int k=0; k<3; k++)
 {cout<< " For item Number " <<k+1<<endl;
  int i=0,j=0;  //for user input of data
  (*ptr).Setdata (i,j);
  ptr -> Display ();} // (*ptr) and ptr-> are equivalent.
  delete[]ptr;
  }
```

The expected output of the above program is given below.

```
For item Number 1
Number of items = 20
Price of each item = 50
Cost of 20 items at the rate of 50 per item = 1000
For item Number 2
```

```
Number of items = 30
Price of each item = 10
Cost of 30 items at the rate of 10 per item = 300
For item Number 3
Number of items = 40
Price of each item = 60
Cost of 40 items at the rate of 60 per item = 2400
```

In the above programs, we have been having the class and the main program in continuity. The class programs may be stored in a separate file and included in the program by the header #include "class_name" (see Appendix E for more details.)

Besides, the operator new may be used in the constructor function itself so that memory is allocated at run time. The following program illustrates a class program for matrices.

12.12 A MATRIX CLASS

The following class deals with the input/output of matrices. The functions such as addition, subtraction or multiplication are included in the main program. However, another class may be developed for carrying out these operations and the following class may be inherited.

PROGRAM 12.17 – Illustrates addition, subtraction and product of matrices.

```
# include <iostream>
using namespace std;
class Matrix
{
private:
int m, n;
public :
 int** Ptr;

Matrix ( int R , int C )
{ m = R, n = C ;  // R stands for row and C stands for column

Ptr = new int * [m] ;
for( int i =0; i<m; i++)
Ptr[i] = new int [n] ;}
     // E_Val stands element value
void Read_Elements ( )
{ cout <<"Enter the elements of "<<m <<"x"<<n << " matrix: ";
 int E_Val =0;
  for( int r =0; r< m; r++)
  for ( int k =0; k<n;k++)
   { cin >> E_Val;
    Ptr [r][k] = E_Val; } }

void Write_Elements ( )
{
```

```
   for(int s =0; s<m; s++)
    {for ( int p =0; p<n ; p++)
     cout<< Ptr[s] [p]<<"\t ";
     cout<<endl;}}
  };

  int main()
  {
  Matrix A (3,3), B (3,3), C(3, 3), D(3,3), E(3,3);
  cout <<"Enter elements of matrices A and B. \n";

  A.Read_Elements( );

   B.Read_Elements ( );
   cout <<"For matrix A you have entered the elements as below.\n";
   A.Write_Elements( );
   cout <<"For matrix B you have entered the elements as below.\n";

   B.Write_Elements( );
   cout << "A.Ptr[1] [0] = " << A.Ptr[1] [0]<< endl;

  for ( int k = 0; k<3; k++ )
   for ( int p =0; p<3; p++)
   {C.Ptr[k] [p] = A.Ptr[k] [p] + B.Ptr[k] [p]; // Matrix addition
  D.Ptr[k] [p] = A.Ptr[k] [p] - B.Ptr[k] [p];} //Matrix Subtraction

  for(int J =0;J<3 ; J++)    // Multiplication
   for (int K =0; K<3;K++)
   { E.Ptr[J] [K] =0;
    for ( int S =0 ; S<3 ; S++)
     E.Ptr[J] [K] += A.Ptr[J] [S] * B.Ptr[S] [K];}
       // Below are output statements
  cout<< "Matrix C = Matrix A + Matrix B :"<<endl;
  cout << "The elements of matrix C are as below "<<endl;
  C.Write_Elements();

  cout<< "For Matrix D = Matrix A - Matrix B :"<<endl;
  cout << "The elements of matrix D are as below "<<endl;
  D.Write_Elements();

  cout<< "For Matrix E = Matrix A * Matrix B :"<<endl;
   cout << "The elements of matrix E are as below "<<endl;
  E.Write_Elements();
  return 0;
   }
```

The expected output is given below. The output is quite obvious.

```
Enter elements of matrices A and B.
```

```
Enter the elements of 3x3 matrix: 1 2 3 4 5 6 7 8 9
Enter the elements of 3x3 matrix: 10 20 30 40 50 60 70 80 90
For matrix A you have entered the elements as below.
1         2         3
4         5         6
7         8         9
```

For matrix B you have entered the elements as below.

```
10        20        30
40        50        60
70        80        90
 A.Ptr[1][0] = 4
Matrix C = Matrix A + Matrix B :
```

The elements of matrix C are as below

```
11        22        33
44        55        66
77        88        99
For Matrix D = Matrix A - Matrix B :
```

The elements of matrix D are as below

```
-9        -18       -27
-36       -45       -54
-63       -72       -81
For Matrix E = Matrix A * Matrix B :
```

The elements of matrix E are as below

```
300       360       420
660       810       960
1020      1260      1500
```

12.13 LINKED LISTS

A linked list is a data structure in which the items are linked together through pointers. A linked list consists of nodes. In case of singly linked lists, each node contains the data items which may be fundamental type or class/structure object and a pointer to the next node. Such a list can be traversed only in the forward direction. In a doubly link lists, each node contains the data item, a pointer to next node and a pointer to previous node. Such a list can be traversed in both directions, i.e. forward as well as backward. Figures.12.2 (a and b) illustrate the node structures of singly linked lists and doubly linked lists respectively.

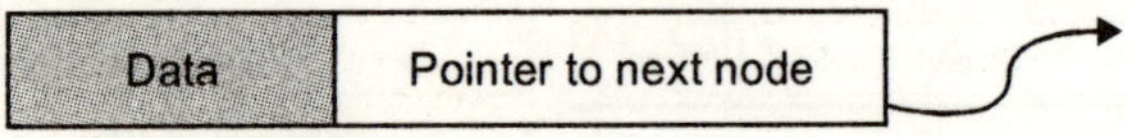

Fig. 12.2(a): A node of singly linked list

Fig. 12.2(b): A node of doubly linked list

The nodes may be stored anywhere in the memory. In case of arrays the data items are stored in a linear way, in adjacent memory locations and the elements are linked because of their location. If the address of one array elements gets known addresses of all the elements can be determined. In case of linked lists, however, the items are not stored in adjacent memory blocks but a node knows the address of the next node but not of next to next. Therefore the traversal is possible only from one node to the next node. Random access is not possible. Figure 12.3 illustrates a singly linked list and Figure 12.4 illustrates a doubly linked list.

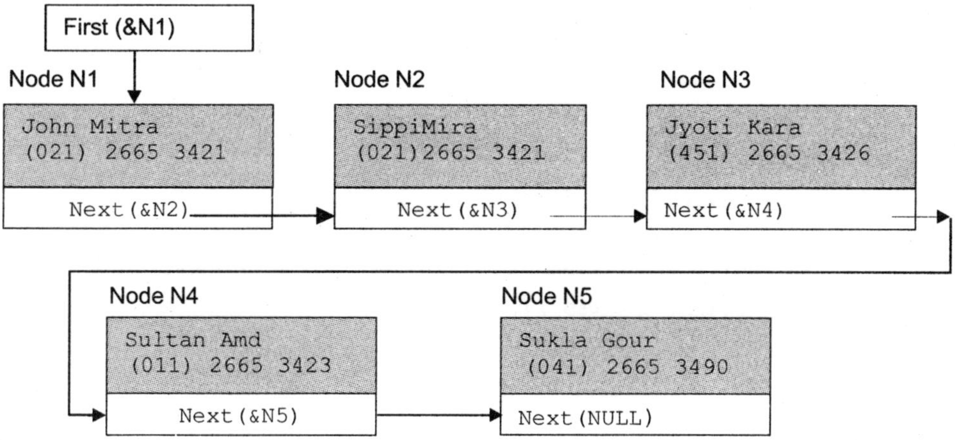

Fig. 12.3: Singly linked list—The data item is in shaded rectangle and pointer in the other

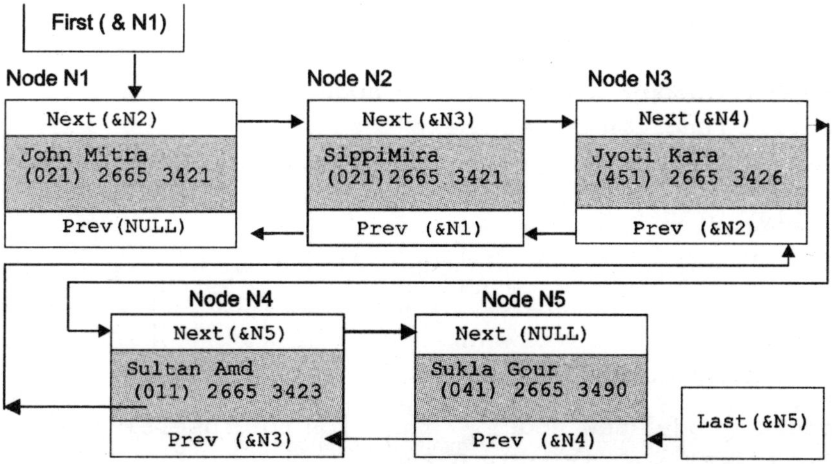

Fig. 12.4: Doubly linked list—Data items are in shaded rectangle, pointers in other two

The following two programs which are developed from ideas of illustrations in references [1, 2, 5 and 8] illustrate a singly linked list and a doubly linked list respectively. In Program 12.18, a list of students roll numbers and grades is made. The entries done at random are inserts in appropriate places in the list so that it makes a sorted list. In Program 12.19 a doubly linked list of persons is made, the data item is the telephone numbers.

PROGRAM 12.18 – Illustrates singly linked list

```
# include <iostream>
#include < string>
using namespace std;
class Student
{
int Roll_Number;  // private by default
int Grades ;

public:
Student() {Grades = 0;}
~ Student(){};  // destructor function, below is constructor
Student ( int N , int Marks) { Roll_Number = N, Grades = Marks;}
int getRN ( ) { return Roll_Number;} // for accessing private
int getGrad () { return Grades ;} // data
};

class Node
{
Student * Pstudent;  //pointer to student
Node * Pnext;    // pointer to next node

public:
Node (Student *);
~Node () {} ;
void setnode ( Node * node) {Pnext = node;}
   // public function to set Pnext
Student * getStudent() const{return Pstudent;} // for access

void Display_Grades(void)
{ if ( Pstudent ->getGrad() >= 0) // display if grades >=0
cout <<"  " << (*Pstudent).getRN() <<" \t \t "<< Pstudent -> getGrad()<<"\n";

if ( Pnext)
Pnext-> Display_Grades();}

void Insert ( Node* new_node) // function for inserting new_node
{ if (Pnext ==0 )    // if it is first
Pnext = new_node;
 //if it is not the first determine, place to insert new_node
```

```
// by comparing values of previous node, new_node and next node
else
{ int next_Grades = Pnext->getStudent() ->getGrad();
int new_Grades = new_node->getStudent()->getGrad();
int Current_Grades = Pstudent->getGrad ();
if ( Current_Grades < new_Grades && next_Grades >new_Grades )
 // if new_node is between current_node and next_node
{new_node ->setnode( Pnext); // new_node = Pnext and
Pnext = new_node;}   // Pnext = new_node
else
  // if above two options are not there, it is last node
Pnext -> Insert(new_node);}
}
};

Node :: Node ( Student * Pst ):Pstudent ( Pst),Pnext (0){}

int main()
{
int Marks;
int rollnumber;
Node * pnode =0;
Student *Pstudent = new Student(0,0);

Node *Start= new Node(Pstudent); // defines the start of list
while ( true)
{cout<<"Enter rollnumber : "; cin >> rollnumber;
 if ( rollnumber == 0)
   // condition for getting out of endless loop
break;
cout<< "Enter Marks :"; cin >> Marks; // get data Marks

Pstudent = new Student( rollnumber,Marks); // new student points
 pnode = new Node(Pstudent);    // new node
Start -> Insert(pnode );} // insert new node

cout << "Roll-Number Marks" <<endl; // top line of display
Start -> Display_Grades();   //Display values
delete Start;
return 0;
}
```

An example of its application is given below.

```
Enter rollnumber : 21   // Entry of data
Enter Marks :76
Enter rollnumber : 23
```

```
Enter Marks :57
Enter rollnumber : 24
Enter Marks :87
Enter rollnumber : 32
Enter Marks :95
Enter rollnumber : 33
Enter Marks :65
Enter rollnumber : 0
Roll-Number Marks    //output of program
0            0
23           57
33           65
21           76
24           87
32           95
```

The various comments given in the program help explain the output. It places the nodes such that it makes a sorted list as illustrated in the output.

The following program illustrates doubly linked list using structures. Each node contains the address to the next node as well as to the previous node. It is also illustrated in Fig. 12.5. After entries of names and numbers, a search is made for the number of a certain person. Two trial searches are made one for person in the list and one for person not in the list. See the output.

PROGRAM 12.19 – Illustrates doubly linked list by using structures.

```
# include <iostream>
#include <string>
using namespace std;
struct Node
{string Name ;
string Tnumber ;
Node * Next;    // pointer to next node
Node* Prev ;   // pointer to previous node
};     // end of structure

void Display1(Node *next)
{while (next != NULL )
{ cout << next -> Name<<" \t "<<next ->Tnumber<<endl;
next = next->Prev;}}

void Search(Node *S , string Str)
{while ( S != NULL)
if ( S->Name == Str )
 {cout << "Result of search is;\n";
 cout<< S->Name <<" \t "<< S->Tnumber<<endl;
 break;}
```

```
else S = S->Next;
if( S == NULL)
 { cout << "Result of search is;\n";
 cout<<"The name "<< Str<< "is not in the list\n";}}

int main()
{ Node N1, N2,N3,N4,N5;
N1.Name = "John Mitra" ;
N1.Tnumber = "(021) 2665 3421" ;
N2.Name = "SippiMira";
N2.Tnumber = "(013) 2665 3434";

N3.Name= "Jyoti Kara";
N4.Name= "Sultan Amd";
N5.Name= "Sukla Gour" ;
 N3.Tnumber = "(451) 2665 3426";
 N4.Tnumber = "(011) 2665 3423";
 N5.Tnumber ="(041) 2665 3490" ;

Node *Last =&N5;
N5.Prev = &N4;
N4.Prev = &N3;
N3.Prev = &N2;
N2.Prev = &N1;
N1.Prev = NULL;

Node *First = &N1;
N1.Next = &N2;
N2.Next = &N3;
N3.Next = &N4;
N4.Next = &N5;
N5.Next = NULL;

 Display1 (Last);
 Search(First, "SippiMira");
Search ( First, "Gurmeet");
return 0; }
```

The entries and expected outputs are given below.

```
Sukla Gour        (041) 2665 3490
Sultan Amd        (011) 2665 3423
Jyoti Kara        (451) 2665 3426
SippiMira         (013) 2665 3434
John Mitra        (021) 2665 3421
Result of search is;
SippiMira         (013) 2665 3434
Result of search is;
The name Gurmeet is not in the list
```

12.14 NESTED CLASSES

A class may be declared inside another class. The access specifiers work on nested class in the same way as they act on other functions. In the following illustrative program class Z is declared in class Y in the public domain and class Y is in turn is declared in class X in public domain. All the three classes have private data for which appropriate constructor functions are provided in each class. The objects of each of these are declared in the main() and values assigned to them.

PROGRAM 12.20 – Illustrated nested classes.

```
#include <iostream>
using namespace std;
class X
{private:
 int x ;

public:
X (int a ) {x = a;}
int getx () { return x ;}

class Y    // nested class Y declared in class X
{private:
int y;
public :
Y( int b ) {y = b;}
int gety (){return y ;}

class Z    // class Z declared in class y
{ private:
int z ;
public :
Z (int c ) { z = c;}

int getz () { return z;}
};      // end of class Z
};      // end of class Y
};      // end of class X
int main()
{ X x_object (5);
X::Y y_object (10);
X::Y::Z z_object (20);
cout<<"x_object = "<<x_object.getx() <<endl;
cout << "y _object = "<< y_object.gety()<<endl;
cout<< "z_object = " <<z_object.getz()<<endl;
return 0 ;
}
```

The expected output is given below.

```
x_object = 5
y _object = 10
z_object = 20
```

EXERCISES

1. What is a friend function to a class?
2. What are the privileges of a friend function with respect to the class?
3. How is a friend function declared and defined?
4. How to declare a friend class?
5. What are characteristics of a friend class?
6. What is a static data member of a class?
7. What is a static function member of a class? Write an illustrative code for declaration of a static function member of a class.
8. What is the difference between the static data member of class and constant data member of a class?
9. How do you declare and initialize a static data member of a class?
10. What is `this` pointer? How is it related to the object of class?
11. Give an example of code in which *this* pointer is explicitly used.
12. Give an example of code which declares a pointer to member function of a class.
13. How would you declare a pointer to object of a class?
14. How do you declare pointer to data member of a class? Write an illustrative code.
15. Which function of class is called when an object of a class is created and which function is called to destroy it?
16. What for we use the pointer **new** and pointer **new[ ]**? Write the corresponding destructors.
17. What do you understand by 'dynamic memory management'. Which operators/functions are used for the purpose?
18. Make a class program to illustrate declaration of pointer to the object of class.
19. Make a class program for regular polygons with number of sides and length of side as private data. Declare two friend functions one for calculation of area of polygon and the other for circumference of polygon.
20. Make a class program for ellipses with major axis and minor axis as private data. Make a friend class to this program to calculate the circumference and area of ellipses.
21. Make a class program and illustrate the declaration and use of pointer to a member of class.
22. Make a class program to illustrate the declaration and use of pointer to the class.
23. Make a program to register the applicant names and their addresses. Make use of pointer *new* to register the next applicant. The program should also display the information on the monitor.
24. Fill in the blanks with the appropriate words given in brackets.
    (a) A friend function is defined ——— of class. (inside or outside)
    (b) A class C is declared as friend of class B in the body of class B. With this declaration class B ——— friend of class C. (becomes, does not become).
    (c) The pointer —— enables to call multiple functions in the same statement. (*this* or *new*)
    (d) A friend function to a class has access to ——— members of a class. (only public members, only private members, all members)

❍❍❍

CHAPTER

13

Operator Overloading

13.1 INTRODUCTION

The operators such as + , –, * etc. are used to carry out certain operations and are frequently used in program statements. C++ has a rich store of such operators which are defined for the fundamental types such as *int, float, double, char* variables. For example let us consider the following statements.

```
int z = int x + int y;

bool( y == z );
```

In execution of first statement the value of int x is added to the value of int y and the result is assigned to int z. The actions of operator + and operator = are already defined in C++. The operations are automatic in the sense that the programmer does not have to write any additional code except to write the above statements in a program and run it. Similarly in the second statement the value of y is compared with the value of z and if they are equal the outcome is true or 1 and if they are not equal the output is 0. The mode of comparison is already defined for fundamental types. In the above case each of objects x, y and z has only one value at a time.

For user defined types such as class objects in which case an object may comprise several items of data, how can you compare whether one class object is equal to another class object or assign the values connected with one object to another object of the class. For example let us consider a class graph and let Graph1 and Graph2 be the two objects of the class (Figure 13.1a). Now if it is desired to compare the two graphs in order to find if Graph1 is equal to Graph2 how do we write code for this comparison. Figure 13.1b shows another example – two vectors V1 and V2 as objects of a class Vector. As you know a vector has magnitude as well as direction. Now it is desired to compare the two vectors to check if the two are equal or add the two vectors or assign a vector to another vector, just like we often do for int, float and char variables. Also C++ does not allow invention of new operators. We have to use the operators that we use for the fundamental types. Straight away we cannot write V1 = V1 as we write for int variables unless we redefine how the operator = is going to work in this particular case. C++ does allow us to redefine the functionality of these operators so that they can perform the operations as we expect them to do for objects of a particular class. The redefinition of the functionality of operators for class objects is called **operator overloading.** It is not only elegant to use the same operators to do similar operations with class objects, it also makes the class objects on par with the fundamental types as far as operators are concerned.

In case of graph (Fig. 13.1a) we may code that if the lengths of lines in their respective order are equal and the lines are similarly placed in the two graphs then the two graphs are equal. For instance, starting from left if the line on the extreme left of Graph1 is equal to the line on the extreme left of Graph2, and similarly if all other lines are equal in the two graphs and they are similarly placed we can take the two graphs as equal. For dealing with vectors, in algebra we take components of vectors along chosen directions represented by axes of a coordinate system. Addition of two vectors involves addition of respective components, i.e. add x-component of vector V1 to x-component of vector V2 and repeat the same for other components. The comparison of two vectors also involves the comparison of respective components. For example, the two vectors are equal, if x-component of one is equal to x-component of the other and y-component of one is equal to y-component of the other and so on. In C++ the number of vector elements or components are not limited by the number of axes of co-ordinates. Like arrays there may be any number of elements in a vector. However, the same algebraic concepts are applied for operations like assignment, addition, comparison etc. For example the two vectors are equal if their elements in the respective positions are equal.

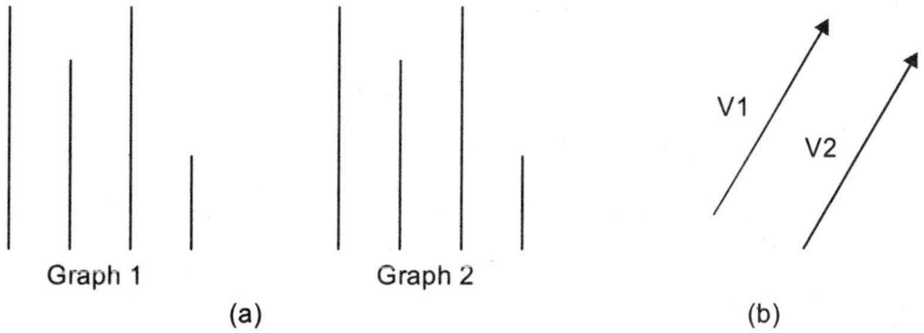

Fig. 13.1

The functionality of all the operators of C++ except a few may be redefined for user defined types (class objects) to carry out the operations as user wants them to do. This is called **overloading of operators. Remember operator overloading is applicable only to user defined *types*, or to a mix of user defined *types* and the fundamental *types*.** For the fundamental types the operations of different operators are already defined in C++ Standard Library and these cannot be altered by operator overloading.

The overloading of operators is a very important aspect of C++ and is highly useful in object oriented programming. It gives us the facility to assign one class object to another, or compare two class objects and carry out several conditional statements using the same operator symbols as they are used for fundamental types. Thus operator overloading gives a vast extension to C++. The overloading of operators, however, is not an exclusive property of C++. Other object oriented computer languages also provide this facility. For instance, the concept of operator overloading was first used in Fortran, though then the scope was very much limited. C++ provides a much more general tool which is highly important in OOP. In this chapter we shall discuss the operators that may be overloaded, the methods to carry it out and the over-riding conditions.

13.2 OPERATORS THAT MAY BE OVERLOADED

Most of the operators of C++ except a few may be overloaded. Table 13.1 gives the list of operators which can be overloaded and there are only 5 operators given below the table which cannot be overloaded.

Table 13.1 – Operators that can be overloaded

+	–	*	/	%	=	&	|	~	^
==	>	<	!=	<=	>=	+=	–=	*=	/=
%=	&=	^=	|=	>>	<<	>>=	<<=	&&	||
!	unary++	Unary – –	Unary +	unary –	,	[]	()	–>	–>*
new	new[]	delete	delete[]						

Among the operators listed in the table above, the following operators may be overloaded both in their unary and binary form.

+ – * &

The Operators that cannot be Overloaded

The following operators cannot be overloaded.

. .* :: ?: sizeof

Restrictions on Overloaded Operators

The overloading of operators is subject to following restrictions or conditions.

1. Operators can be overloaded only for user defined types or a mix of user defined types and fundamental types.
2. The number of operands that an operator takes (arity) cannot be changed.
3. The operator precedence cannot be changed in overloading.
4. The operator associativity (left to right or right to left) cannot be changed in overloading.
5. There is no restriction on defining the functionality (behaviour) of overloaded operator.

However, it is desirable and advisable that an overloaded operator should carry out similar operation on class objects as it does for the fundamental types. For instance, if operator + does addition for fundamental types, it should do same for class objects.

13.3 OPERATOR OVERLOADING FUNCTIONS

For overloading of an operator, we define a function which redefines the functionality of the operator being overloaded, i.e, the overloading function defines what the operator will do and how it will do that operation when it is applied to objects of a particular class. The operator overloading function is a non-static function (because it has to operate on non-static arguments). The overloading function is declared with first word **type** (type of data it returns) followed by the keyword **operator** which is followed by the operator symbol which is desired to be overloaded followed by argument in parentheses (see the declaration below). The operator overloading function may be a class function member, it may be a friend function of class or it may be a global function. The choice of function is discussed below. For example for overloading operator (+) we may have it as class member function. In class body the overloading function is defined in the following way.

```
type operator + (arguments)
        { function_ body }
```

Here *type* refers to the type of data it returns. If it returns a class object then name of class is the *type.* Should the function be a class function, a friend function or a global function? Both the class function and friend function have access to all the members of a class, i.e. private, protected and public. A global function cannot have direct access to private and protected members of a class, therefore, additional public functions will have to be included for accessing private and protected members of class. This impairs the information hiding capability of class as well as it is an additional load on the performance. Therefore, either a class function or friend function should be used as far as possible. For overloading the function call operator, i.e. (), subscript operator, i.e. [], indirection operator i.e. -> and assignment operator, i.e. = , the operator overloading function should be a class member.

Overloading Functions and Arguments

In case of friend functions and global functions a unary operator overloading function will have one argument and a binary operator overloading function will have two arguments. However, for class member functions, the class object is the argument which is implicitly available to the operator overloading function. Therefore, for overloading functions which are class members only one argument is required for binary operators and none is required for unary operators. For selecting between the class member function and global/ friend function the following guideline may be used.

(a) In the application of the operator, if the leftmost operand is an object of the class for which the overloading function is being defined, the function may be a class member. However, friend functions or global functions may also be used.

For example, let V1 and V2 be the two objects of a class Vector, for operators like = we write V1 = V2 ; In this code, the left most operand VI is a class object therefore, overloading function may be a class member function.

(b) If the leftmost operand is not an object of the class for which the overloading function is being defined then a global or a friend function is needed [2]. For example, suppose we want to redefine the functionality of operators << and >> for vectors having more than one values. For output/input we wrote the code *cout << class object* or *cin>> class object.* Here cout and cin are not objects of the class for which the overloading functions are to be defined. For such cases friend functions or global functions may be used. Considering the performance, friend functions are superior to global functions, hence friend functions are preferred.

In the following program the operator + is overloaded to perform addition of two vectors.

PROGRAM 13.1 – Illustrates overloading of operator + for addition of two vectors.

```
#include <iostream>
using namespace std;
class Vector{
 private:
 int x, y, z ;          // three components of a vector
 public :
 Vector(int a,int b,int c){ x =a ; y = b; z =c;} //constructor
 Vector (){};           // Empty or default constructor
 Vector operator+ (const Vector&S) //for overloading binary operator +
 {                 //only one argument needed.
  x =x +S.x;
  y = y + S.y;
  z = z + S.z;          //The leftmost operand is class object
 return Vector (x,y,z);}     // so class member function is used.

 void Display() {
 cout << "x component = "<< x << endl;
  cout << "y component = "<< y << endl;
   cout << "z component = "<< z << endl;}
 };                // End of class
int main()
 { Vector V1 ( 2,4,5), V2( 6, 5, 8), V3;
  V3 = V1 +V2;
  V3.Display( ) ;
  return 0;
  }
```

The expected output is given below. The overloaded operator adds the respective components of the two vectors, i.e. 2+6 =8, 4+5 = 9 and 5 + 8 = 13.

```
x component = 8
y component = 9
z component = 13
```

If the operator overloading is defined outside the class, the function prototype must be declared inside the class body. For the above case, in the class body we write function prototype as given below.

```
    Vector operator + (Vector);
```

The function definition placed outside the class would be coded as below.

```
Vector Vector :: operator+ (const Vector&S)

x = x +S.x;
y = y + S.y;
z = z + S.z;
return Vector (x,y,z); }
```

This is illustrated in Program 13.2 below. The last line in the above could also be written as

```
  return *this ;
```

OPERATOR + DEFINED TO CARRY OUT MINUS OPERATION

In overloading, the functionality of the operator is redefined, so it is possible that + operator may be defined to carry out minus (see Program 13.2) or multiplication or division (/). But it is a not a good practice. It is advised that the native functionality of operator should not be changed in overloading. Because, after some time the programmer may forget the redefinition of the operator and it can lead to serious errors in use of the program as well in debugging the program. However, it is for the sake of illustration that following program is included.

PROGRAM 13.2 – The operator + is overloaded to carry out minus operation.

```
#include <iostream>
using namespace std;

class Number {
private:
 int x, y ;
public :
 Number (int a, int b ){ x = a ; y = b;} // constructor
 Number(){}; // empty or default constructor

Number operator+(const Number & m); // function prototype
void Display()
 {cout << "The x component = "<< x << endl;
 cout << "The y component = "<< y << endl; }
  } ; // End of class

Number Number :: operator+ (const Number & m) // function definition
{                                              // outside the class
 x =x - m.x;
 y =y - m.y;
 return Number (x,y); }
int main()
{
Number N( 16, 21 ), M( 5,6 ), D, E;  //N, M, D, E are objects
 D = N + M;
  D.Display( ) ;
  int A = 10;  // A and B are fundamental type integers
   int B =5;
 cout << "A + B = " << A+B <<endl;
 return 0;
  }
```

The expected output is given below:

```
The x component = 11
The y component = 15
A + B = 15
```

The output shows that on class objects the operator + has carried out minus operation, i.e. x =16–5=11, in the first line and 21–6 =15 in the second line of output. However, the native functionality (addition) of operator + for fundamental types is not lost by overloading which is for a class objects only. This is shown in third line of output by addition of two integers A and B in which case it is doing addition while for class objects it is doing minus operation. The program also illustrates how to define the overloading function outside the class.

13.4 ADDITION OF COMPLEX NUMBERS

A similar case is that of addition of complex numbers. In algebra we write a complex number as x + y i. Here x is the real part, and yi where i = $\sqrt{-1}$ is the imaginary part. Suppose we want to add two complex numbers such as (6 + 5i) + (4 + 8i). The result in algebra is 10 + 13i, that is the real part is added to real part and imaginary part is added to imaginary part. The operator + in C++ with its native functionality defined for fundamental types cannot do such an addition. However, C++ allows us to overload the operator + such that it does the same type of addition as it is carried out in algebra for complex numbers.

PROGRAM 13.3 – Illustrates addition of two complex numbers.

```
#include <iostream>
using namespace std;

class Number
{
 int x, y ;  //complex number is x + yi, private by default

public :
 Number (int a, int b ) { x =a ; y = b;} // constructor
 Number (){};   // empty or default constructor

 Number& operator+(const Number & m)  //redefinition of operator +
  {
  x = x + m.x;
  y = y + m.y;
  return* this; }

void Display(){
cout<<"The resultant number is = "<< x <<" + "<< y <<"i"<< endl;}
  } ; // End of class

int main()
{ Number N( 16, 21 ), M( 5,6 ), D ;
 D = N + M;
 D.Display( ) ;
return 0;
 }
```

The expected output is given below. The program is similar to that for vector additions.

```
The resultant number is = 21 + 27i
```

13.5 OVERLOADING OF += AND -= OPERATORS

In the following program combination operators += and −= are overloaded.

PROGRAM 13.4 – Illustrates overloading of **+=** and **−=** operators.

```
#include <iostream>
using namespace std;
class Vector
{
 private:
 int x, y, z ;  // three components of vector

 public :
void setvalues (int a, int b, int c) { x =a ; y = b; z =c;}

 void operator += (Vector P) // Definition of overloading
 { x = x + P.x ;    // function
 y = y + P.y ;
 z = z + P.z ; }

 void operator -= ( Vector P)  // definition of overloading
 {x = x - P.x ;     // function
 y = y - P.y ;
  z = z - P.z ; }

 void Display( )
 { cout << "x = "<< x <<"\ty = "<<y << "\tz = "<< z <<endl;}
 };   // End of class

int main()
{ Vector V1, V2, V3;
 V1.setvalues ( 12,4,6);
  V2.setvalues( 2, 5, 7);
   V3.setvalues (4,5,6) ;
 V1 += V2;
 V3 -= V2;
 cout<<" Components of V1 are : ";
  V1.Display() ;
  cout<<" Components of V3 are : ";
   V3.Display();
    cout<<" Components of V2 are : ";
     V2.Display();
 return 0;
  }
```

The expected output is given below.

```
Components of V1 are : x = 14      y = 9       z = 13
Components of V3 are : x = 2       y = 0       z = -1
Components of V2 are : x = 2       y = 5       z = 7
```

The components of V1 are obtained by adding components of V2 to components of V1 and assigning the sum to components of V1, so in the output we get component of V1 as 14, 9 and 13. In case of V3 the components of V2 are subtracted from the components of V3 and result is assigned to components of V3. So, we get components of V3 as 2, 0 and –1.

13.6 OVERLOADING OF INSERTION (<<), EXTRACTION (>>) AND /= OPERATORS

Since the left side operands of << and >> are not the objects of class for which the overloading function is being defined, therefore, we have to use either a global function or a friend function. The friend function can access all the members of a class, therefore, in the following program we use a friend functions for overloading << and >> operators. Program also illustrates overloading of /= operator for an array.

PROGRAM 13.5 – Overloading of **insertion (<<), extraction (>>)** and **/= operators.**

```
 #include <iostream.h>
 const int n = 5;
 class List {
 friend ostream & operator << ( ostream & , List & ) ;
 friend istream & operator >> ( istream & , List & ) ;

float x[n] ; // private by default
public :
List(){}; // empty or default constructor
List (float a[n])   // constructor
{for ( int i =0; i<5; i++)
x[i] = a[i];}

float operator /=(int m)   // overloading of /= operator
{ for ( int i =0; i<5; i++)
 x[i] = x[i]/m;
 return x[i];}
 } ;    // End of class
istream & operator>> ( istream &In, List&L)  // Friend
 { for ( int i = 0 ; i< n ; i++)    // function definition
  In >> L.x[i]; // In is an object of istream so type is
  return In;}  //istream. L is an object of List

ostream & operator<< ( ostream &Put, List &L )   //friend
 {Put<<"("<<L.x[0];    //function definition.
```

```
for ( int i = 1; i<n; i++) //Put is defined an object of ostream
 Put<<", "<< L.x[i] ; // so type is ostream
  Put<<")";
 return Put ;}

int main()
{List L1 , L2;
float B[n] ={2.2,3.3,4.4,5.5,6.6};
 cout<<"Put in "<<n<<" elements of L2: ";
 cin>> L2;
  L1 = B ;
  L1 /=2;

cout<<L1<<"\n";
L2 /=3;
cout<<L2 <<endl;
 return 0;}
```

The expected output is as below. The output is self explanatory.

```
Put in 5 elements of L2: 3.6 6.6 9.9 12.66 15.99
(1.1, 1.65, 2.2, 2.75, 3.3)
(1.2, 2.2, 3.3, 4.22, 5.33)
```

13.7 OVERLOADING OF INCREMENT AND DECREMENT OPERATORS (++ AND – –)

The unary operator ++ can be prefixed before a name of variable or class object or postfixed after the name of variable or object. In the first case, it first increments the value of variable or object and then the value is used for evaluation of following expression. In postfix the initial value is used for evaluation of expression and then the increment is carried out. The unary operator – – behaves in a similar fashion with decrement of values.

PROGRAM 13.6 – Illustrates overloading of **++ and – –**

```
#include <iostream>
using namespace std;
class Vector
{
   private:
   int x, y, z ;          // three components of vector
  public :

  Vector(int a, int b,int c) { x =a ; y = b; z =c;}
  Vector (){}
Vector operator ++(int)      // Postincrement operator ++
```

```
{ x +=1;
y += 1;
z +=1;
return Vector( (x-1), (y-1), (z-1));}

Vector operator ++()                    // Preincrement operator++
{ x +=1;
y += 1;
z +=1;
return Vector (x,y,z);}
Vector operator -- ()                   // Predecrement operator--
{ x -=1;
y -= 1;
z -=1;
return Vector (x,y,z);}
Vector operator --(int)       // Postdecrement operator --
{ x -=1;
y -= 1;
z -=1;
return Vector( (x+1), (y+1), (z+1));}

 void Display( )
   {  cout << "x = "<< x <<", y = "<<y <<", z = "<< z <<endl;}

    }; // End of class B

int main()

{ Vector V1 (4,5,6), V2(21,22,23), V3 ( 1,2,3), V4(11, 12, 13) ;

cout<< "Initial V1-components are: ";
   V1.Display();

cout<< "After post increment V1-components are: ";
(V1++).Display();
cout<<"Now V1 components are : " ;
 V1.Display();


cout<< "Initial V2-components are: " ;
  V2.Display();

cout<< "After preincrement V2-components are: ";
  (++V2).Display () ;

cout<< "Initial V3-components are: ";
    V3.Display();
```

```
cout<< "After post decrement V3-components are : " ;
   (V3--).Display();
cout<<"Now components of V3 are : " ;
  V3.Display();

cout<< "Initial V4-Components are :" ;
  V4.Display();

    cout<< "After predecrement V4-components are :";
   (--V4).Display () ;
 return 0;
 }
```

The expected output is given below. The three components of the vector V1 are 4, 5 and 6 and after post increment these values are same. However, the vector is incrementd as is clear from the next line of output. Same is true for post decrement for vector V3. See the 6th, 7th and 8th lines of output. The initial components 21, 22, 23 of V2 become 22, 23 and 24 after pre-increment. In case of predecrement of vector V4 its components 11, 12 and 13 become 10, 11 and 12 after the operation of overloaded pre-decrement. The detailed output is given below.

```
Initial V1-components are: x = 4, y = 5, z = 6
After postincrement V1-components are: x = 4, y = 5, z = 6
Now V1 components are : x = 5, y = 6, z = 7
Initial V2-components are: x = 21, y = 22, z = 23
After preincrement V2-components are: x = 22, y = 23, z = 24
Initial V3-components are: x = 1, y = 2, z = 3
After postdecrement V3-components are : x = 1, y = 2, z = 3
Now components of V3 are : x = 0, y = 1, z = 2
Initial V4-Components are :x = 11, y = 12, z = 13
After predecrement V4-components are :x = 10, y = 11, z = 12
```

In the above program the actions of preincrement and predecrement as well as postincrement and postdecrement for class objects are illustrated.

13.8 DOT PRODUCT OF VECTORS

In vector mathematics the dot product involves multiplication of corresponding components (components with same index value) of two vectors and adding the results of multiplications. The following program illustrates it.

PROGRAM 13.7 –Overloading (*) using friend function in order to carry out the inner product of two vectors.

```
#include <iostream>
using namespace std;

class Vector{
```

```
  private:
   int x, y, z ;  // three components of vector
  public :
   Vector (int a, int b, int c) { x =a ; y = b; z =c;}
   Vector (){};
  friend int &operator*(const Vector &, const Vector & ); // two parameters
  }; // End of class
 int & operator* (const Vector &S, const Vector &P ) // function definition
  { int Innerproduct;
   Innerproduct= S.x * P.x + S.y * P.y + S.z *P.z ;
   return Innerproduct;}
  int main()
  { Vector V1 ( 3,5,5);
  Vector V2( 10,6,8);

  int dotproduct = V1 * V2;
  cout << "dotproduct of V1 and V2 = "<<dotproduct<<endl;
  return 0;
   }
```

The expected output is as below.

```
dotproduct of V1 and V2 = 100
```

The output of the above program gives the dot product of two vectors each having three components. The program can be easily extended for n components. The following program overloads operator == for two vectors with class member function.

13.9 OVERLOADING OF EQUALITY OPERATOR (==)

When we are dealing with quantities like vectors, complex numbers, etc., the comparisons whether two vectors are equal, involves comparison of each component of vector V1 with the corresponding component of vector V2. The two vectors are equal if the components of one vector are equal to the corresponding components of the other vector. So we have to redefine the functionality of == operator. This is illustrated in the following program.

PROGRAM 13.8 – Illustrates overloading of operator (==) for vectors.

```
#include <iostream>
using namespace std;
class Vector
{
 int x, y, z ; // private by default

public :
 Vector (){x = 3, y = 2, z =1;} // default constructor
```

```
 Vector (int a, int b,int c) { x =a ; y = b; z =c;}

void operator== ( Vector S)
 {if ( x==S.x && y == S.y && z== S.z)
 cout << "true"<< endl ;

 else
 cout<<"false"<< endl; }

void Display ()
 {
cout << "Vector = ("<< x << ",  " <<y << "  " <<z<<")"<< endl;}
 } ;   // End of class

int main()
{
 Vector V1 ( 2,4,5), V2( 6, 5, 8) ,V3 ( 6,5,8);
  V1 == V2;
  V2 == V3;
  V1.Display ();
  V2.Display();
  V3.Display ();
 return 0;
  }
```

The expected output is given below.

```
false
true
Vector = (2,  4,  5)
Vector = (6,  5,  8)
Vector = (6,  5,  8)
```

13.10 OVERLOADING OF INDEX OPERATOR []

In C++ there is no provision to check whether the index or subscript value of an array element called is within the number of elements of the array or not. If it is greater than the number of elements in the array, a garbage value may return leading to errors. The following program, by overloading [] operator provides a check for this and gives a message if the subscript value is out of bounds.

PROGRAM 13.9 – Illustrates overloading of [ ] operator.

```
#include <iostream.h>
#include <cstdlib>
```

```
const int n = 5;
class List {
 friend ostream & operator << ( ostream & , List & ) ;

int x[n] ;    // private by default
 public :

void Setvalues (int a[n] )
 {for ( int j = 0; j< n; j++)
  x[j] = a[j] ; }

 int operator [] (int k)
 { if (k <0 || k > n)

 { cout << "Array index k is out of bound";
 exit (0);}
 return x[k];}
 };  // End of class List

 ostream & operator<< (ostream &Put , List &L )
  {Put<<"The components are :("<<L.x[0];
  for ( int i = 1; i<n; i++)
   Put<<", "<< L.x[i] ;
   Put<<")";
    return (Put) ;}

int main()
{
 List L1 ;
 int B1[] = {11, 12, 13, 14,15};
  L1.Setvalues (B1);
 cout<< L1 <<endl;
 cout << L1[2] << endl;

cout<< "The following result is for L1[7] "<<endl;
 cout << L1[7]<<endl;
return 0;
 }
```

The expected output is given below.

```
The components are : (11, 12, 13, 14, 15)
13
The following result is for L1[7]
Array index k is out of bound
```

The output given above is self explanatory. The first line of output is a normal output of an array. In the second line the third component of array has been called. This is 13. Remember that the subscripts start from zero. Next the eighth component has been asked while the array contains only 5 elements. So the overloaded subscript operator gives the message that the index is out of bound and terminates the program.

EXERCISES

1. What is operator overloading?
2. What is the need for operator overloading?
3. Which operators cannot be overloaded?
4. How do you define an overloading function?
5. How do you decide whether overloading function should be a class function, a friend function or global function?
6. How many arguments a class function would take for overloading following operators?

   (i) + (binary) (ii) +=
   (iii) – unary (iv) ==
7. What kind of function (class, friend or global) may be used for overloading following operators?

   (i) + operator (ii) >> operator
   (iii) += operator (iv) ++ or -- operator
8. How many arguments friend functions would take for overloading following operators.

   (i) << operator (ii) ++ operator
   (iii) *= operator (iv) == operator
9. Can the operator overloading be used for fundamental type data?
10. Which of the following operators can not be overloaded?

    (i) == (ii) .
    (iii) :: (iv) .*
    (v) /=
11. What are the conditions (or restrictions) on overloaded operators?
12. Give instances of practical class objects and operations for which the following overloaded operators may be used.

    (i) >> and << (ii) ==
    (iii) ( )
13. Which type of function (class member or friend function) be used for overloading the following operators?

    (i) << (ii) [ ]
    (iii) >> (iv) –>
    (v) /= (vi) ==
14. Make a program to illustrate the overloading of operators << and >>.
15. Make a program for overloading operator (*) for multiplication of two complex numbers.
16. Make a program for overloading operator (+) for adding two strings.
17. Make a program for overloading operators `new` and `delete`.

18. Make a program for overloading new [ ] and delete [ ].
19. Make a program to illustrate the overloading of || (OR) and && (AND) operators.
20. Make a program to illustrate the inner product of two vectors each having 10 components.

Answer:

PROGRAM 13.10 - Inner product of two10 dimension vectors.

```
#include <iostream>
using namespace std;
const n =10 ;
class Vector
{
 int x [n] ;  // n components of vector/ array
 public :
Vector (int A [n]) {for (int i = 0 ; i < n ; i++)
  x[i] = A[i] ;}
 Vector (){};
friend int operator* ( Vector P , Vector S );
} P,S ;  // End of class
int operator* ( Vector P , Vector S )
 {int IP =0;
  for ( int j =0; j< n; j++)
   IP = IP + P.x[j] * S.x[j] ;
    return IP;}
int main()
{
int C1[ ] = { 4,3,2,3,2,5,3,1,2,3 };
 int C2[ ] = {4,2,1,3,2,1,3,1,4,2};
 Vector V1 (C1);
 Vector V2(C2);
 int dotproduct = V1 * V2 ;

cout << "dotproduct of V1 and V2 = "<<dotproduct<<endl;
 return 0;
 }
```

The expected output of the program is given below.

```
dotproduct of V1 and V2 = 66
```

21. Change the Program 13.4 by changing the function void operator +=() to Vector operator +=(), Make other required changes.

❍❍❍

CHAPTER

14

Inheritance

14.1 INTRODUCTION

Inheritance is an important feature of software reuse and object oriented programming (OOP). Suppose you have already made a class program for describing some features of a group of objects. And you also know that a subgroup of them possesses some special features over the others. Instead of making a complete class program starting from scratch to describe the special features along with the ones for which you have already made the class program, you can better make a new class program which inherits the existing class as it is with all its functions and data members and adds the additional features that you wish to describe for the special group of objects. You are thus reusing the existing class program which has already been debugged and tested without doing any modification to it. The new class is called **derived class** and the existing class is called **base class.** The process does not end here, you may have another derived class which inherits the features of the derived class or features of the derived class as well as features of some other classes. When a class inherits a single class, it is called **single inheritance**. This is illustrated in Fig.14.1. Say class D is the derived class and class B is the base class, in case of single inheritance, the derived class is declared as below.

```
class D : access_specifier B
```

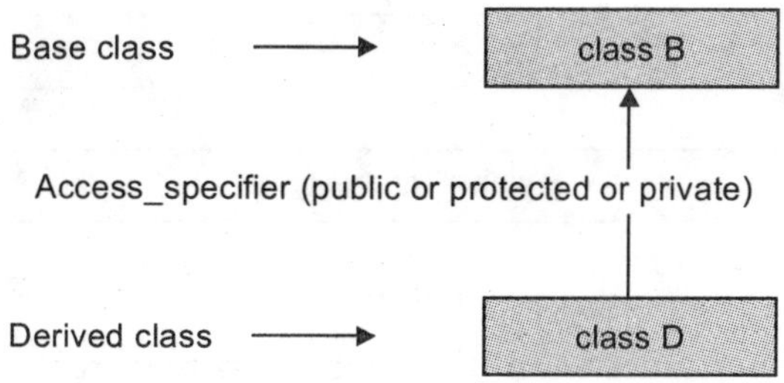

Fig. 14.1: Single inheritance, example of declaration (`class D: public B`)

The access specifier is either **public** or **protected** or **private**. For example for public inheritance the code for declaration of class D would be

```
class D : public B
```

C++ also supports inheritance from more than one class in many different ways as illustrated in Fig.14.2 below. The classes from which a class is derived may or may not be related to one another.

In real life also, objects derive several of their characteristics from the characteristics of other objects. Thus a garment is as good as the fabric from which it is made. Similarly, the characteristics of wooden furniture are related to the type of wood it is made from. The following figures illustrate some more examples of inheritance in real life objects.

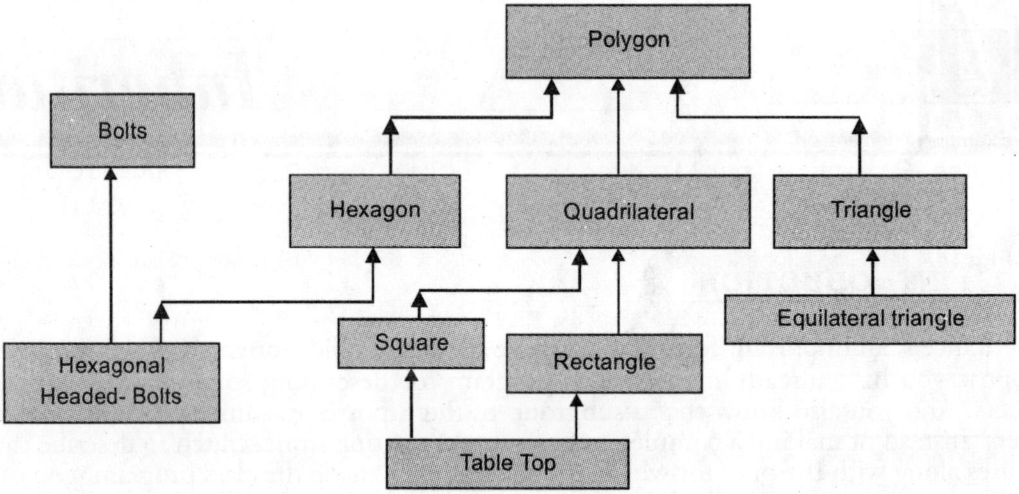

Fig. 14.2: The figure shows the shapes and their connection with physical objects

Figure14.2 shows the complex way in which the polygonal shapes are related to one another and to industrial products. Even the design of industrial products like cars, etc., are influenced by customer's perceptions (Fig. 14.3). This shows that real life products are interconnected in a complex way.

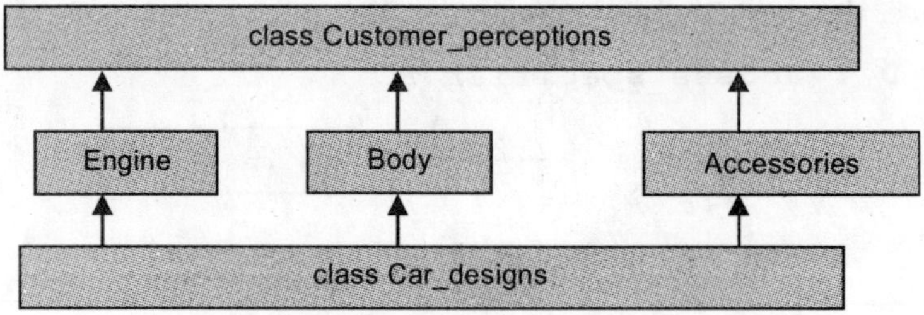

Fig. 14.3

As explained above, inheritance is an important feature of real life objects. It is also a very important feature of C++ because it is instrumental in reusing the existing software and in building really big programs. Thus a big program may be subdivided into suitable base class, derived classes and objects.

14.2 FORMS OF INHERITANCES

The base classes and derived classes may be related in a number of ways as illustrated in the Fig.14.4 (a – e). Codes for declaration of derived classes are also given below each figure.

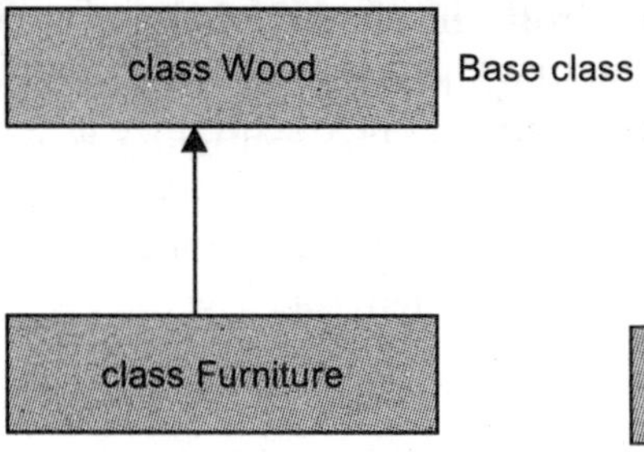

Example of declaration

```
class Furniture: public Wood
```

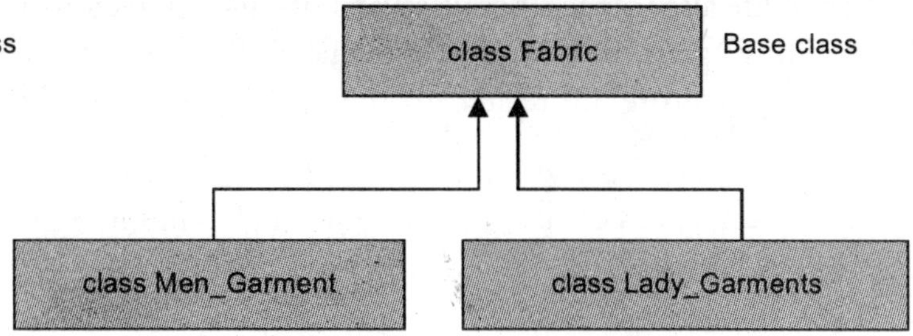

Example of declaration of derived classes

```
class Men_Garment: public Fabric
class Lady_Garment: public Fabric
```

Fig. 14.4 (a): Single inheritance

Fig. 14.4 (b): Hierarchical inheritance

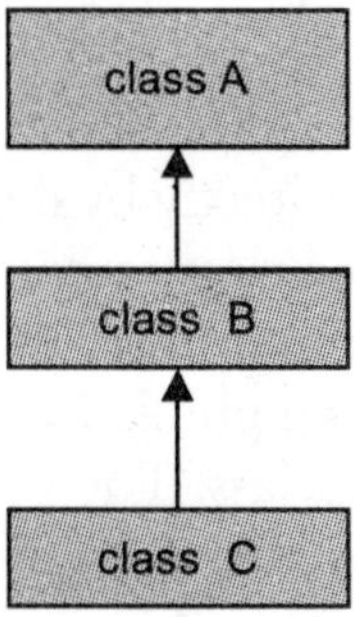

Example of declaration

```
class A
{ – };

class B : public A
{---};
class C: public B
{---} ;
```

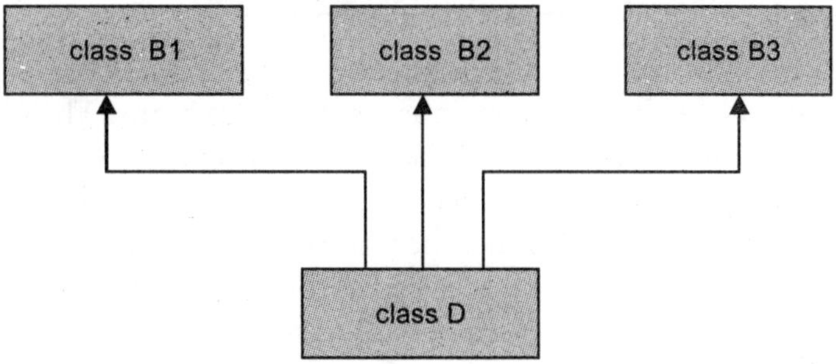

Example of declaration

```
class D: public B1,public B2,private B3
```

Fig. 14.4 (c): Multilevel inheritance

Fig.14.4 (d): Multiple inheritance

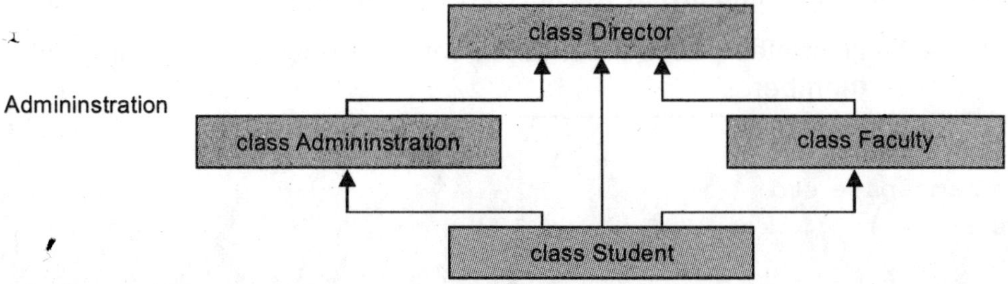

Example of declaration of class Student

```
class Student : public Faculty, public Admin, public Director
```

Fig.14.4 (e): Multi-path inheritance

As illustrated in the above figures, the inheritance may be declared public, private or protected. However, in all the declarations of derived classes the first word is *class* – a keyword. This is followed by name of derived class, followed by colon (:) and then followed by access specifier and name of base class. In case of more than one base class, the access specifier has to be mentioned individually with each class. Let class B be the base class and class D be the derived class. The declarations of class D in case of single inheritances may be coded as below.

```
class D : public B      // public inheritance
class D : protected B   // protected inheritance
class D : private B     // private inheritance
class D : B   //No access specifier, private by default
```

Figures 14.4(a–e) also show the codes for declaration of derived class in several different types of inheritances.

14.3 SINGLE PUBLIC INHERITANCE

In this kind of inheritance the public functions of base class may be accessed directly by derived class members, i.e. derived class inherits these functions. The objects of derived class can directly access the public functions of base class. Out of the private and protected members of base class, only protected members may be accessed by derived class through its own public function members while the private members of base class are not visible in derived class. The private members of base class can be accessed through public and protected function members of base class. However, friend functions of base class also have access to all the members (public, private, protected) of base class but friend functions are not inherited. **Objects of derived class are also objects of base class but objects of base class are not the objects of derived class.**

If the base class has only public members and inheritance condition is also public then all the members of the base class can be directly accessed by member functions as well as by objects of derived class. Programs 14.1 to 14.3 illustrate the public inheritance with base class having the following categories of members.

(i) Base class has only public members, (Program 14.1).
(ii) Base class has public and protected members, (Program 14.2).
(iii) Base class has public and private members, (Program 14.3).

PROGRAM 14.1– Illustrates public inheritance with the base class having only public members.

```
#include <iostream>
using namespace std;
class B
{
public :
 int m ,a ;
 int Product1 () { return a*m;}
} ;           // End of base class B
```

```
class D : public B    // Declaration of derived class D
{
public:
  int n ;
  int Product2 () { return n* Product1 () ;}
} ;                // End of class D

int main()
{ D C1;       // C1 is an object of class D
 C1.m = 5;      // data directly accessed by object
  C1.a = 4 ;
   C1.n = 3 ;

 cout<< "Product1 = "<<C1. Product1 ()<< endl;
 cout << "Product2 = "<< C1.Product2()<<endl;
return 0;
 }
```

The expected output is given below.

```
Product1 = 20
Product2 = 60
```

In the above program, the object C1 of derived class D has direct access to the public functions of base class. This is illustrated by the statement C1.m = 5; and the statement C1.Product1(),etc.

If the base class has public as well as protected members, all the members of base class can be accessed by members of derived class. The protected members of base class cannot be directly accessed by objects of derived class, however, they may be accessed though public member functions of the derived class.

PROGRAM 14.2–Illustrates public inheritance with base class having only public and protected members.

```
#include <iostream>
using namespace std;

class B       // declaration of class B
{
protected :
  int m;       // protected member of class B
public:
  int k;
  int Square (){return k*k ;}
  int Product () { return k*m;}
  };           // End of class B
```

```
class D : public B  //class D inherited from class B
{
public:
 void setvalue1(int a) // public function to access m of B
 {m = a;}
 };        // End of class D.

int main()
 { D C;        // C is declared an object of D
 C.k = 9;       //Direct access to k of class B
 C.setvalue1(6); //Access to m through public member of D

cout<< "Square = " << C.Square()<< ",  Product = "<< C.Product() <<endl;
return 0;
 }
```

The expected output is given below.

```
Square = 81,  Product = 54
```

In the above program the protected data member of class B has been accessed via a public function member of class D, i.e. `void setvalue1(int a){m = a ;}`

The private members of base class cannot be accessed by public functions of derived class. A private member of base class when accessed by members of derived class would result in an error signal as illustrated in the output of the following program.

PROGRAM 14.3 – Illustrates public inheritance with base class having private data.

```
#include <iostream>
using namespace std;
class B
{
private :        // private access
 int m ;
} ;            // End of class B

class D : public B     // Declaration of class D
{
public:
 int a;
 void setvalue( )   // Function for accessing m of class B
 {m = a;}
 int n ;
} ;            // End of class D

int main()

 { D C;     // C is an object of class D
```

```
    C.a = 5 ;
    C.n = 4 ;
    int product= C.a* C. n;

  cout<< " Product of members of B and D = "<< product<< endl;
  cout << " Sum of squares of members of B & D = "<< C.n*C.n + C.a*C.a<<endl;
   return 0;
    }
```

The expected output is an error message of the type given below.

```
cannot access private member declared in class B
```

If it is required to access the private data members or private function members of base class, corresponding public functions which provide access to private members have to be included in base class. These functions provide the interface. These are like brokers in trade. **The private members of a base class can only be accessed through public and protected functions of base class or by friend functions of base class. But friend functions are not inherited.**

However, protected member of base class may be accessed by public member function of derived class. This has already been illustrated in Program 14.2. Also see the following program.

PROGRAM 14.4 – Illustrates public inheritance when base class has private data members and function members.

```
#include <iostream>
using namespace std;

class B {            // base class B
private :
 int x;               // private member of B
 int Square (){ return x*x ;}  // private member of class B
public:
 void setvalue (int p );  //setvalue()-a public member for
// accessing the private member x of B
 int Psquare(){return Square ();} // A public member of B to
              //access private member Square()
 int m ;
 };          // End of class B

void B::setvalue (int p){x = p;}; // Definition of setvalue()

class D : public B //declaration of D with public inheritance
{
public:
 int n ;
 };          // End of class D

int main()
```

```
{ D C;           // C is an object of class D
 C.setvalue(5) ;   // accessing x of B through setvalue ()
 C.m = 4 ;      // accessing public member of B directly.
 C.n = 3 ;      // accessing public member of D directly.
 cout<< "Product of m and n = " << C.m*C.n<< endl;
 cout<< "Square = " << C.Psquare() << endl;
 return 0;
 }
```

The expected output of the program is given below.

```
Product of m and n = 12
Square = 25
```

In class B of the above program there is a private data member `int x`; and public data member `int m`; and a private function member `int square(){return x*x ;}`. The private data of class B is accessed by defining a public function `void setvalue (int p)`; in class B and the `int square()` is accessed by declaring another public function in class B, i.e.

```
int Psquare(){return Square ();}
```

and this public function is accessed directly by objects of derived class D. Also note that we cannot write as below.

```
C.m*C.setvalue(5)
```

This is because the function `setvalue()` is declared `void` (no return value) and hence use of arithmetic operators is not legal with `void` functions.

14.4 SINGLE PROTECTED INHERITANCE

In case of protected inheritance the public members and the protected members of base class become protected members of derived class. The private members of base class are not visible to derived class. They can only be accessed through public and protected member functions of base class. The following program illustrates the protected inheritance with base class having protected and public members.

PROGRAM 14.5 – Illustrates protected inheritance when base class has protected and public data as well as function members.

```
#include <iostream>
using namespace std;
class B {
protected :       // Access protected
 int m;
 int Square () {return m*m;}
public :        // Access public
 int k ;
```

```
  product () {return k*m;}
};          // End of class B
class D : protected B   // Inheritance protected
{ public:
  void setvalue1(int a ) // public member to access m
  {m = a;}
void setvalue2( int p) { k = p;} // public member to access k
int dsquare( ){ return B:: Square () ;} //For accessing Square()
int dproduct(){ return B:: product();} //For accessing product()
};          // End of class D, C is an object

int main()
{ D C;          // C is an object of D

 C.setvalue2(10);
 C.setvalue1(5);

 cout<<"Product of m and k = " << C.dproduct() <<endl;
 cout<<"Square = " << C.dsquare( ) <<endl;

 return 0;
 }
```

The expected output of the above program is given below.

```
Product of m and k = 50
Square = 25
```

In case of protected inheritance the public and protected members of base class become protected members of the derived class. These may be accessed by public member functions of derived class.

But the private members cannot be accessed by members of the derived class directly. They can only be accessed through public and protected member functions of base class itself. In the following program we have a base class with private data members as well as private function member. For accessing these two members we have to create public functions in the base class itself. For private data m we have the public function `set_value()` and for private function `Square()` we have the public function `bSquare()` which returns the *return value* of `Square()`.

PROGRAM 14.6 – Protected inheritance with base class having private members.

```
#include <iostream>
using namespace std;
class B {           // base class
private :
 int m;           // private member data
 int Square(){return m*m ;} // private member function
```

```
public :
void setvalueb(int a ) {m = a;} // public member to access m
int bSquare(){return Square ();}  // for accessing Square
 int k ;            //public member of B
 int product (){return k*k;}
};              // End of class B
class D : protected B    // protected inheritance
{
 public:
 void setvalued (int n) { setvalueb(n);}
 void setvalue2(int p) { k = p;}  // For accessing k,
 int dbsquare(){return bSquare ();} // For accessing bSquare,
 int dproduct(){return product ();}  //for accessing product
 };        // End of class D.
int main()
{ D C;        // C is an object of class D
 C.setvalue2(10);
 C.setvalued(5) ;
cout<<"Product = " << C.dproduct() <<endl;
cout<<"Square = " << C.dbsquare( ) <<endl;
 return 0;
}
```

The expected output is given below. The output is self explanatory.

```
Product = 100
Square = 25
```

14.5 SINGLE PRIVATE INHERITANCE

With private inheritance the public and protected members of base class become private members of derived class. Hence they cannot be accessed directly by an object of derived class. However, they can be accessed through public function members of the derived class. The private members of base class are not visible in the derived class, they can be accessed only through public and protected member functions of the base class.

PROGRAM 14.7 – Illustrates that in private inheritance public and protected members of base class become private members in derived class.

```
#include <iostream>
using namespace std;
class B {
protected :
 int m ;
```

```
public:
 int k;
};          // End of class B

class D : private B    // private inheritance
{
public:         // access specifier in class D
 int a;

 void setvalue( ) {m = a;}

 int n ;
};
           // End of class D
int main()
{ D C ;         // C is an object of class D
 C.k = 6;
  C.a = 5 ;
   C.n = 4 ;

int product= C.a* C. n;
cout<< " Product of members of B and D = "<< product<< endl;
cout << " Sum of squares of members of B & D = "<< C.n*C.n +  C.a*C.a<<endl;
 return 0;
 }
```

The expected output is an error message that k cannot be accessed directly.

`'K'; cannot access public member declared in class B`

In the following program the inheritance condition is private. The base class has one protected data member m, one public data member k and a public function Square (). For the derived class all these become private. Therefore, public functions are developed in the derived class so that these can be accessed by the objects of derived class.

PROGRAM 14.8 – In private inheritance the public and protected members of base class are accessed through public functions of derived class.

```
 #include <iostream>
using namespace std;

class B{
 protected :
 int m;

 public :
 int k;
 int Square () {return k*k;}
```

```
    int msquare () {return m*m;}
    };            // End of class B

    class D : private B     // private inheritance
    {
    public:
     int a;
     void setvalue1()    // public member of D to access
     {m = a;}        //protected member of B
     void setvalue2 (int b) { k = b;}

    // public member of D required to access public member of B.
    //Because of private inheritance. Same applies to following also.
     int dmsquare () {return msquare () ;}
    int Dsquare(){ return B:: Square () ;}
    } ;             // End of class D

    int main()
    { D C;      // C is an object of class D
     C.setvalue2(6);
     C.a = 5 ;
     cout<<" Square = " << C.Dsquare() <<endl;
    cout <<"square of m = "<<C.dmsquare ()<<endl;
    return 0;
     }
```

The expected output is given below.

```
Square = 36
Square of m = 25
```

From the results of above programs the access condition in the three types of inheritances have been summarised below in Table 14.1. Here D is the name of derived class and B is the name of base class.

Table 14.1 (A) – Public inheritance **(class D: public B)**

Base class access specifier	Access in the derived class
public	Public.Directly accessible by member functions and objects of class D and its friend functions.
protected	Protected. These can be accessed by member functions of derived class and its friend functions.
private	Not accessible directly by members in derived class. Private members of base class can be accessed, only through public and protected member functions of base class, by member functions and friend functions of derived class.

Table 14.1 (B) – Protected inheritance **(class D: protected B)**

Base class access specifier	Access in the derived class
public	Protected. These can be accessed only by member functions and friend functions of derived class.
protected	Protected. These can be accessed only by member functions and friend functions of derived class.
private	Not visible in derived class. These can be accessed only through public and protected members of base class.

Table 14.1(C) – Private inheritance **(class D: private B)**

Base class access specifier	Access in the derived class
public	Private. These can be accessed by member functions and friend functions of derived class.
protected	Private. These can be accessed by member functions and friend functions of derived class.
private	Not visible in derived class. These can be accessed only through public and protected member functions of base class.

From the above table it is clear that **class members which are desired to be inherited should be declared either public or protected in the base class.**

14.6 MULTIPLE INHERITANCE

The following figure illustrates the multiple-inheritance in which a class is derived from several base classes.

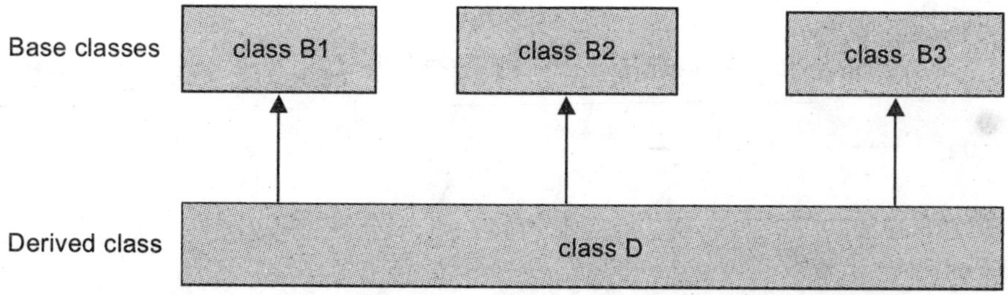

Fig. 14.5: Multiple-inheritance—Class D derived from three base classes B1, B2, B3

In the following program the class D is derived from two base classes B1 and B2. The rules of inheritance have already been discussed above. The same rules apply to multiple inheritances as well.

PROGRAM 14.9 – Illustrates multiple-inheritance from more than one base class.

```
#include <iostream>
using namespace std;

class B1 {
private :
 int m ;
public :
 int a;
 void setvalue( )
{m = a;}
 } ;            // End of class B1

class B2
{ public :
 int k;
};          //End of class B2

class D : public B1,public B2
    // Declaration in multiple in heritance
{
public:
 int n ;
 };
        // End of class D
int main()
{ D C;      // C is declared an object of class D
 C.k = 5;  // C accesses directly the public member of B2
  C.a = 4 ;  // C accesses directly the public member of B1
  C.n = 3 ;
int product= C.a* C.n*C.k;

cout<<"Product of data members of B1, B2 and D = "<< product<< endl;

 return 0;
 }
```

The expected output is as follows.

```
Product of data members of B1, B2 and D = 60
```

14.7 MULTILEVEL INHERITANCE

The multilevel inheritance is illustrated in Fig.14.4c. The figure shows that class A is the base class for class B and class B is the base class for class C. The rules of inheritance as discussed above apply to this as well. This is illustrated in the following program in which class B is the base class to derived class D1 which in turn is the base class for class D2. All the three classes contain a function with same name Display. In the main () these functions are called. In order to remove the ambiguity as to Display function of which class is called, the scope resolution operator is used for the Display() functions of class B and class D1. For Display function of class D2 the scope resolution operator is not necessary because the function call of object of D2 would go to the function of class D2.

PROGRAM 14.10 – Illustrates multilevel inheritance.

```
#include <iostream>
using namespace std;
 class B
{ public :
 void Display () { cout << "It is class B Display" <<endl;}
    };

class D1 : public B
 {
 public :
 void Display () { cout << "It is class D1 Display" << endl;}
 } ;

class D2 : public D1
 { public :
  void Display () { cout << "It is class D2 Display"<< endl;}
 };

int main ()
{
 D2 d2 ;              // d2 is an object of class D2.
  d2.B::Display();
    d2.D1::Display() ;
   d2.Display();

return 0 ;
}
```

The expected output is given below. The above code also shows that objects of derived class are also objects of base class.

```
It is class B Display
It is D1 Display
It is D2 Display
```

The following example is another instance of multilevel inheritance. In this, instead of constructor function another public function is used to initialize the objects of different classes. The constructors and destructors in inheritance are discussed in Section 14.8 of this chapter.

PROGRAM 14.11 – Illustrates multilevel inheritance.

```
#include <iostream>
using namespace std;

class B
 { protected :
  int bx ;
  public :

  void Bset( int m) { bx = m ;}
  void Display (){cout<< "Display of class B "<<endl;}

 } ; // End of class B

 class D1 : public B
 {
 protected :
  int D1x ;
 public :
    void D1set(int n){ D1x = n;}
    void Display (){cout << "Display of class D1"<<endl;}
 } ; // End of class D1

class D2 : public  D1
{
 protected :
   int D2x ;
 public :
  void D2set( int p ) { D2x = p ;}
   void Display (){ cout << "Display of class D2"<<endl;}
 } ;        // End of class D2

class D3 : public D2
{
private :
   int D3x;

public :
   void D3set ( int q) { D3x = q;}
int Product ( ) { return D3x * D2::D2x * D1::D1x * B::bx ;}
void Display (){ cout << "Display of class D3 "<<endl;}

 } ;
  // End of class D3

int main ()
{
D3 d3;
```

```
d3.D3set (10);
d3.D2::D2set(4);
d3.D1::D1set(3);
d3.B::Bset(2);

cout << "Product = "<< d3.Product()<<endl;

d3.Display();
d3.D2::Display();
d3.D1::Display();
d3.B::Display();
return 0 ;
}
```

The expected output of the program is as below.

```
Product = 240
Display of class D3
Display of class D2
Display of class D1
Display of class B
```

14.8 CONSTRUCTORS AND DESTRUCTORS IN INHERITANCE

In the illustrative examples mentioned above we have used public functions other than constructors to initialize the class objects. If base classes do not have constructor functions or their constructors do not take any argument then the derived class need not have a constructor function. However, if any of the base class has constructor function that takes an argument then derived class has to have its constructor function because it is the responsibility of derived class constructor to initialize the base class or supply arguments to base class constructor. Therefore, the derive class constructor carries data for its own initialization as well as for base class constructors. An illustration of derived class constructor is given below. Let the classes B1 and B2 be the two base classes and let class D be the derived class. The class B1 has a private data member `int x` and B2 has a private data member `int y`. The constructors of the base classes are as below.

```
B1(int n) { x = n ;}            // constructor of B1
B2(int m ) { y = m ;}           // Constructor of B2
```

The constructor of derived class D in which `int z` is a private data member, would be coded as,

```
D ( int i, int j ,int k ) : B1(i), B2(j) {z = k;}
```

See carefully the above expression. The constructor is declared for class D , so the first word is the name of class, i.e. D. This is followed by the names of parameters preceded by their *types* individually in parentheses. Then there is a colon (:) which is followed by name of the first base class with the parameter (i) in parentheses. The integer i is for the constructor of B1. Similarly this is followed by comma and then by name of second class B2 and the j in parentheses for constructor of B2. The int k is meant for class D and is assigned to z in braces {}.

In the constructor of class D, the `int i` and `int j` are for the constructors of base classes and `int k` is for the private member of class D. The order of execution of constructors and destructors of base and derived classes are listed in Table 14.2. It is obvious that the constructors of base classes should be called first in the order in which they are declared in declaration of derived class. Thus if the declaration is as below.

```
class D : public B1, public B2
```

the constructor of B1 will be called first followed by that of B2 and in last the constructor of class D. For destructors this order is reversed. First the destructor of derived class D is called then that of class B2 and then destructor of class B1. The following program illustrates the above discussion.

PROGRAM 14.12 – Illustrates definition of constructor in derived class.

```
#include <iostream>
using namespace std;
class B1{
 private :
   int x;

 public :
   B1() { x =1;}                    // default constructor of B1
 B1(int a ) { x = a;}          // parametric constructor of B1
   int getx(){return x ;}      // another public function of B1
   ~ B1 () { }                  // destructor for B1
  };                          // End of class B1

  class B2 {
   int y ;              // private by default

public :
   B2(){y=2;}
   B2(int b ) { y = b;}                // Parametric constructor of B2
   ~ B2(){ }               // Destructor for B2
 int gety(){ return y;}
  } ;                                // End of class B2

class D : public B1 , public B2
{
  private :
    int z;
  public :
    D ( int i, int j ,int k ) : B1(i), B2(j) { z = k;}
                         // Constructor for D
    ~ D () { }            // Destructor of D
  int Product () {return  getx()* gety()*z;}  // A function of D
  };                                     // End of class D

int main()
```

```
  { D  d (4, 5 , 6);      //d is an object of class D
     cout<< "Product = " <<d.Product()<<endl;
   return 0; }
```

The expected output is given below.

```
Product = 120
```

The order in which the constructors and destructors are executed is illustrated in the following program.

PROGRAM 14.13 –Illustrates the order of execution of constructors and destructors in inheritance.

```
#include <iostream>
using namespace std;

class B1 {                        // start of class B1
 private :
     int x;

 public :
     B1  ( ) {x = 4;
     cout << "Constructor of B1 called\n";}  // constructor

 ~ B1(){cout<<"Destructor of B1 called\n";} //Destructor of B1
 };                       // End of class B1

class B2                       // start of class B2
  {
private:
  int y ;
public :

  B2 (   ) { y = 5;
   cout  <<  "Constructor  of  B2  called\n";}  //default  constructor
~  B2(){cout<<"Destructor  of  B2  called\n";}  //Destructor  of  B2}  ;
// End of class B2

class D : public B1, B2      // class D derived from B1 and B2 { private :
  int z;
public:
    D ( int c ) { z =c ; cout<< "Constructor of D called\n" ;}
   ~ D () { cout<< "Destructor of D called\n";}
 } ;              // End of class D

int main()
{
```

```
    D d (10);     // d is declared an object of class D
    return 0;
    }
```

The expected output is as under.

```
Constructor of B1 called
Constructor of B2 called
Constructor of D called
Destructor of D called
Destructor of B2 called
Destructor of B1 called
```

In case there is only one base class, the constructor of base class is called before the constructor of derived class. If there are several base classes but no virtual base class, the constructor functions of base classes are called in the order in which the base classes are declared in the declaration of derived class but before the constructor of derived class.

If one of the base class is a virtual class, its constructor is the first to be called followed by constructors of other base classes in the order in which they are declared. For example let the derived class be declared as

```
class D : public B1, public B2 , public virtual B3
```

The constructors would be called in the following order.

```
B3( )  Constructor of virtual class B3
B1( )  Constructor of base class B1
B2( )  Constructor of base class B2
D( )  Constructor of derived class D
```

The Table 14.2 also gives the order of calling of constructor and destructor functions for a number of cases.

Table 14.2 – Order of execution of constructors and destructors in inheritance

Category of inheritance	Priority in execution of constructor/ destructor in base and derived classes	
class D : public B	B( ) D( ) ~ D( ) ~B( )	Constructor of base class B Constructor of derived class D Destructor of derived class D Destructor of base class B
class D: public B1, public B2	B1( ) B2( ) D ( ) ~D( ) ~B2 ( ) ~B1 ( )	Constructor of base class B1 Constructor of base class B2 Constructor of derived class D Destructor of derived class D Destructor of base class B2 Destructor of base class B1

Contd...

class D: public B1, public virtual B2	B2( )	Constructor of virtual class B2
	B1( )	Constructor of base class B1
	D( )	Constructor of derived class D
	~D( )	Destructor of derived class D
	~B1 ( )	Destructor of base class B1
	~B2 ( )	Destructor of base class B2

Copy Constructor and Inheritance

The following program is an example of copy constructor and inheritance.

PROGRAM 14.14 – Illustrates copy constructor in inheritance.

```
#include <iostream>
using namespace std;

class B
{ protected:
int x;
public:
B () { x = 4;}
B(int a) {x = a;
cout<< "Base constructor called"<<endl;}
B( const B &b) { x = b.x;
cout<< "copy constructor of B called."<<endl;}
};
class D : public B
{
int y;   // private by default

public:
D () { y = 5;}
D ( int k ){ y = k;
cout<< "Derived class constructor called."<<endl;}
int Display () { return y ;}
};

int main()
{
D d1 (10); // d1 is defined an object of class D

D d2 = d1; // d2 is defined as a copy of d1.

cout << "d2 = "<<d2.Display() <<endl;
return 0 ;
}
```

The expected output is given below.

```
Derived class constructor called.
copy constructor of B called.
d2 = 10
```

The following program is yet another example of declaration of derived class constructor. In this example the program class Cubicle calculates the surface area of prismatic bodies having three integer dimensions. This class is a base class to the class Cube which uses the surface area for finding the cost of painting the surface. Examine the constructor by name Cube in the following program.

PROGRAM 14.15 – Illustrates constructors of base and derived classes.

```
#include <iostream>
using namespace std;

class Cubicle {

private:
 int x, y, z;
 public:

 Cubicle (){}
 Cubicle (int a, int b, int c )  // Constructor
 {x = a;
 y = b ;
 z = c ;

cout<<"constructor of Cubicle called"<<endl;}
 int surface_area() { return 2*(x*y +y*z +z*x);}
 } ;     // end of class Cubicle

 class Cube : public Cubicle
 {
 public:
 int Rate;
  Cubicle C;
   // below is the constructor function of class Cube
Cube(int L, int W, int H, int A): Cubicle (L, W, H) { Rate = A;}

int cost(int Rate, Cubicle C ){return Rate * C.surface_area() ;}
};     // end of class Cube

int main()
{
 int x =2;
Cubicle C1 (3, 3, 3);
Cubicle C2 (4, 5, 6);
```

```
 Cube cube1(3,3,3, x);
 Cube cube2(4,5,6,3);
cout<<"Surface area of cube1 = "<<cube1.surface_area()<<"\n";
cout << "Cost for cube1 = "<< cube1.cost(x, C1 )<<"\n";

cout<<"Surface area of cube2 = "<<cube2.surface_area()<<"\n";
cout<<"Cost for cube2 = " << cube2.cost(3,C2)<<"\n";
return 0 ;
}
```

The expected output is given below.

```
Constructor of Cubicle called
Constructor Cubicle called
Constructor of Cubicle called
Constructor of Cubicle called
Surface area of cube1 = 54
Cost for cube1 = 108
Surface area of cube2 = 148
Cost for cube2 = 444
```

14.9 CONTAINMENT AND INHERITANCE

For many real life problems we have classes that contain objects of other classes as their members besides having their own function members and data members. This is a form of nesting called **containership or container class.** The other form of nesting is that a class is declared inside another class. The container class will have characteristics of contained classes through their objects. C++ also supports such a relationship. In a way, this provides an alternate method to inheritance. Thus if a class D has objects of class B and class C as its members we say *D has a relationship* with C and B. Here we shall discuss how to define the constructor of the container class. Let the three classes B , C and D be defined as below. Class D contains objects of class B and class C.

```
class C{
 int x;          // private by default
public:
C ( int a ) { x=a ;} // Constructor of class C
———
  } ;                    // End of class C
class B
  int y;          // private by default
Public:
B ( int b ) { y = b;} // constructor of class B
————
};                       // end of class B
class D{
int z;
public:
 C object_C;
B object_B;
          // Constructor of class D is given below.
```

```
D(int i, int, j, int k) : object_C (i), object_B(j){z = k;}
 —
  } ;              // end of class D
```

In the above definition, the constructor for D has three integers in parentheses followed by colon (:) for the three constructors. The constructors of class B and class C are called by their objects, i.e. object_B and object_C which follow the colon and contain the arguments in parentheses for their constructors, this is followed by constructor body for class D, i.e. { z = k ;}. The following program illustrates this.

PROGRAM 14.16 – Illustrates constructor of a class containing objects of other classes.

```
#include <iostream>
using namespace std ;

class C
{
private :
 int x;
public :
 C(int a) {x = a;
 cout << "Constructor of C called.\n";}            // Constructor
 ~ C () { cout<<"Destructor of C called\n";}          //destructor
 int getx( ) { return x;}
 };    // End of class C

 class B {
 private:
  int y ;

public :

  B (int b) { y = b;
 cout << "Constructor of B called\n";} // Constructor
 ~ B () { cout<<"Destructor of B called\n";} // Destructor
 int gety(){return y;}
 };     // End of class B

class D
{
private :
 int z;
public:
 C objC ; // objC is declared an object of Class C
 B objB ; // objB is declared an object of class B
```

```
    D ( int i, int j, int k ) : objB (i) , objC(j) { z =k ; cout<< "Constructor of
D called\n" ;}
          // Constructor of class D
    ~ D () { cout<< " Destructor of D called\n";} //Destructor
    int Product (){return objC.getx()* objB.gety()* z;}
    } ;     // End of class D

    int main()
    {
     D objD(5, 20, 4 );
     cout << "Product = " << objD.Product () <<endl;
     return 0;
     }
```

The expected output is as under.

```
Constructor of C called.
Constructor of B called
Constructor of D called
Product = 400
Destructor of D called
Destructor of B called
Destructor of C called
```

A derived class may contain objects of other classes, thus presenting a case of inheritance as well as containment. The derived class constructor feeds arguments to the constructors of base class as well to those classes whose objects are contained by derived class. For the contained class the name of its object is used while for base class the name of class is used to feed arguments to the corresponding constructor. The following program illustrates this.

PROGRAM 14.17 –Illustrates constructor of derived class having a base class and containing object of another class.

```
#include <iostream>
using namespace std;

class C
 {
 private :
 int x;
 public :

 C (int a) {x = a;
 cout << "Constructor of C called.\n";} //constructor of class C
 ~ C () { cout<<"    Destructor of C called\n";}
 int getx( ) { return x;}
 };    // end of class C
```

```
class B {
 private:
  int y ;
 public :
  B (int b) { y = b;

 cout << "Constructor of B called\n";} // constructor of class B
  ~ B () { cout<<"   Destructor of B called\n";}

  int gety(){return y;}
 } ;      // End of class B

 class D : public B  // class D derived from class B
 {
 private :
  int z;
 public:
  C c ;    // Object c of class C in class D
   // Below is the constructor of class D.
 D ( int m, int n, int k ) : B(m) , c(n) { z =k ;
 cout<< "Constructor of D called\n" ;}

  //constructor of B called by class name B.
  // constructor of C called through name c of its object

  ~ D () { cout<< "   Destructor of D called\n";}
  int Product () { return c.getx()* gety()* z;}
 } ;  // End of class D

 int main()
 {
  D d (10, 20,5); // object of class D
  cout << "Product = " << d.Product () <<endl;
  return 0;
   }
```

The expected output is shown below. Examine the priority in which the constructors and destructors are called.

```
Constructor of B called
Constructor of C called.
Constructor of D called
Product = 1000
   Destructor of D called
   Destructor of C called
   Destructor of B called
```

Program 14.18, given below, is yet another example of declaration of constructor function in a multilevel inheritance. The method of constructing the constructor function is similar to the class having both the base class as well as objects of other classes.

PROGRAM 14.18 – Illustrates constructor function for a derived class in a multilevel inheritance.

```
#include <iostream>
using namespace std;

class B {
 protected :
  int bx ;

 public :
  B (){}
  B( int m) { bx = m ;}
  int getbx(){ return bx;}

} ; // End of class B

 class D1
 {
 protected :
 int D1x ;
public :
 D1(){}
 D1( int m ) { D1x = m;}
 int getD1x () { return D1x;}
 } ;

class D2 :public D1
{
protected :
  int D2x ;
public :
  int getD2x(){return D2x;}
  D2 (){}
  D2( int e ) { D2x = e ;}
 } ;

class D3 : public D2
{
private :
 int D3x;
public :
 B b ;   // b is an object of class B
```

```
D1 d1;  // d1 is an object of class D
  // The constructor of D is defined below.
D3 (int i, int j, int k, int s ) : b(i), d1(j), D2(k) { D3x = s;}

int Product () { return D3x * D2x * d1.getD1x() * b.getbx() ;}
void Display (){ cout << "Display of class D3 "<<endl;}

};

int main ()
{
 D3 d3 ( 10, 5, 4, 2);
 cout << " Product = "<< d3.Product( )<<endl;
 return 0 ;
}
```

The expected output is as below.

```
Product = 400
```

14.10 OVERLOADED OPERATOR FUNCTIONS AND INHERITANCE

The overloaded function of base class is inherited by derived class. This is illustrated by the following program in which the overloaded operator function += is defined in the base class. The function is invoked when it is applied to objects of derived class.

PROGRAM 14.19 – Illustrates inheritance of overloaded function +=.

```
 #include<iostream>
using namespace std;
class Vector
{
 protected:
  int x, y, z ;  // three components of vector
 public :
  Vector (){ x=1,y=2,z=3;}
  Vector (int a, int b,int c) { x =a ; y = b; z =c;
  cout<< "constructor of class Vector called."<<endl;}

  Vector operator += (constVector & P)
 {
 x = x + P.x ;
 y = y + P.y ;
 z = z + P.z ;

 cout << "overloaded function of Vector called."<<endl;
 return *this;}

void Display() {
```

```
cout << "x component = "<< x << endl;
  cout << "y component = "<< y << endl;
   cout << "z component of = "<< z << endl;}

} ; // End of class Vector

class D : public Vector
{
public :
      // constructor function
D ( int a, int b, int c ): Vector (a,b,c) {
cout<<"constructor of D called."<<endl;}
};

int main()
{
D V1 ( 12,4,6), V2( 3, 5, 7) ;
V1 += V2;
V1.Display( ) ;

return 0;
}
```

The expected output given below shows that overloaded functions are inherited.

```
constructor of class Vector called.
constructor of D called.
constructor of class Vector called.
constructor of D called.
overloaded function of Vector called.
constructor of class Vector called.
x component = 15
y component = 9
z component of = 13
```

Friend Functions and Inheritance

The friend functions are not inherited by the derived class.

EXERCISES

1. What is inheritance? How is it useful in object oriented programming?
2. What are the different types of inheritances?
3. What is the difference between single inheritance and multiple inheritance. Explain with diagram and class declarations.
4. With the help of a diagram show the multi-path inheritance. Also give an example of derived class declaration.

5. In case of single inheritance distinguish between public and private inheritances?
6. In a single inheritance how the public inheritance and protected inheritances are different?
7. What is the difference between multiple inheritance and multilevel inheritance? Explain with diagrams and class declarations.
8. How do you access the public and protected members of base class in a public inheritance?
9. In Fig. 14.2 how would you declare the class Hexagonal_headed_bolts as a derived class?
10. How can an object of derived class access the private function of base class?
11. A derived class D is derived from two base classes B1 and B2 which have one private data member each and constructor functions. The derived class D also has a private member. How would you define the constructor function for class D.
12. What will be the order of execution of constructors in following class declarations?
    (i) class D : public class B1, public B2
    (ii) class D : public virtual class V, private class B1, public class B2
    (iii) class D : public B1, public B2, public virtual V.
13. Give an example of constructor of derived class for a single public inheritance in which the base class has one integer private data member and derived class has one private data member of *type* double.
14. For a multilevel inheritance, construct the constructor function of class D2 which is derived from class D1 which in turn is derived from class D which in turn is derived from class B. All the classes except D2 have one protected data member each while D2 has a one private data member.
15. Write a program to declare a derived class by name Grades from the base class Student. The base class has roll numbers and names while the grade class has roll numbers and grades. The derived class displays the marks list giving students' names, roll numbers and grades.
16. What is containment? How would you define the constructor function of a class which contains objects of two other classes?
17. A class D is derived from a class B and contains the object of another class C. If all the classes have constructor functions how would you define the constructor function of class D?
18. Do you need a constructor function if the base and derive class have only public function?
19. What is the order of calling of destructor function in a multilevel inheritance?
20. Do you need a constructor function in the derived class if the constructor functions of base classes do not take arguments.
21. Give an illustration of a constructor function of a class which is derived with single public inheritance and has objects of other two classes as its members.

❍❍❍

CHAPTER 15

Virtual Functions and Polymorphism

15.1 INTRODUCTION

Polymorphism is a combination of two Greek words, i.e. poly and morphism, which means the ability to acquire different forms or shapes according to the environment. We have already got acquaintance with two forms of polymorphism which are function overloading and operator overloading. In operator overloading the same operator carries out different forms of operations according to the *type* of data presented to it. In function overloading several functions have the same name but they differ in their number of arguments or *types* of arguments. So the same function name is called to carry out different actions. Templates (see Chapter 16) is still another form of polymorphism. All these cases are examples of **static binding** or **early binding** because the choice of the appropriate function gets decided at the compile time itself that is before the execution of program starts.

The polymorphism in which the choice of function is done during the execution of the program is called **run time binding** or **late binding** or **dynamic binding**. This is achieved through virtual functions and pointer to the base class. All these are illustrated in Fig. 15.1 below.

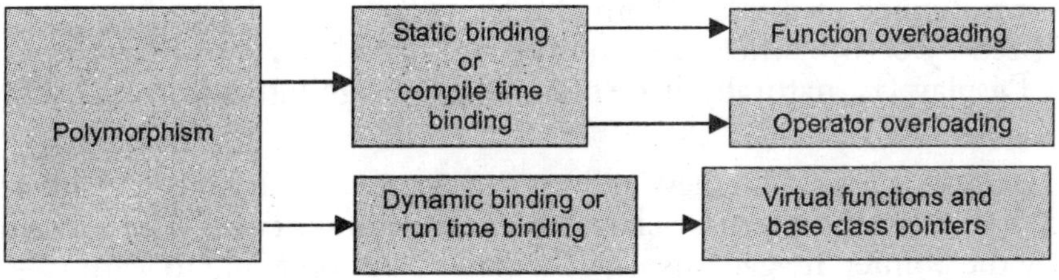

Fig. 15.1: Polymorphism

15.2 VIRTUAL FUNCTIONS

The run time polymorphism is realised through virtual functions. But the application of virtual functions is through the base class pointer. The reason for using base class pointer is illustrated in the Fig. 15.2(a, b). A base class pointer can be made to point to objects of base class as well as to objects of derived classes. But a derived class pointer can point to objects of the derived class only. It cannot point to objects of base class because a base class object is not an object of derived class. If another class is derived from a derived class, i.e. class Derived2 from class

Derived1 as shown in the figure below, then the class Derived1 is in fact a base class to class Derived2. In that case the pointer to class Derived1 can point to objects of class Derived1 and objects of class Derived2. But pointer to class Derived2 cannot point to objects of class Derived1. However, the class Base pointer (see Figure15.2b) can point to objects of Base class as well as to objects of class Derived1 and to objects of class Derived2. Thus with pointer of a base class we can access the objects of the whole hierarchy of objects on the down stream.

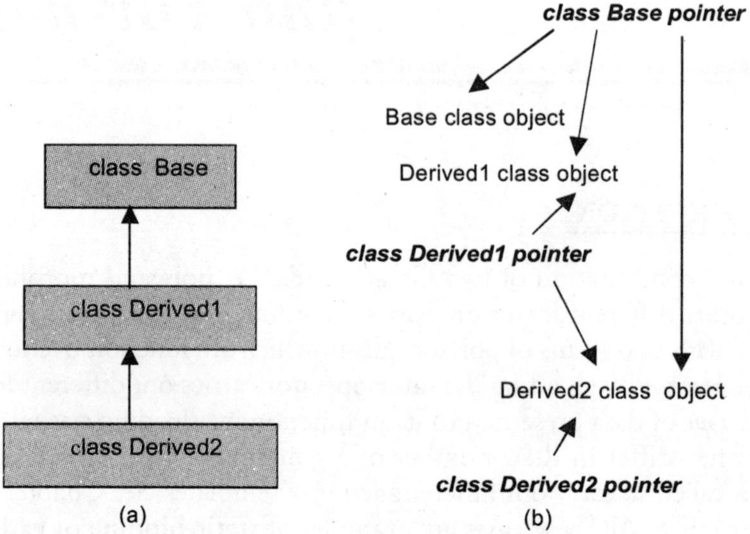

Fig. 15.2: Class pointers and their reach

In order to clearly bring out the characteristics of virtual functions, the following four programs have been designed. In Program 15.1 a base class with name B and a derived class with name D have been defined (class D : public B). Both the classes have got a public function by name Display( ). In the base class it is defined to display "Are you going to learn C++?" and in derived class it is defined to display "I am also learning C++.". Pointer bptr is pointer to class B. It is initialized by &(B)b where b is an object of class B. When this pointer is used to call the function Display () , naturally it displays "Are you going to learn C++?", i.e. base class definition.

Now the pointer is assigned a new address &d where d is an object of the derived class D. The object d is also an object of base class B because of inheritance. The function Display() is again called by the pointer. It again displays the same "Are you going to learn C++?" and not the definition given in class D. See the following program for illustration.

PROGRAM 15.1 – Illustrates that if a function is not declared virtual the base class pointer will point to base class function definition even though it is assigned the address of derived class object.

```
#include <iostream>
using namespace std;
class B
{
```

```
public:
 void Display ()
 {cout<< "Are you going to learn C++?"<<endl;}
  };  // End of class B

class D : public B
{
 public :
  void Display( )
  {cout<< "I am also learning C++."<<endl;}
  };  // End of class D

int main()
{ B b;    //b is an object of base class B
 D.d;   // d is an object of derived class D
 B *bptr;  // pointer to class B

 bptr = &(B)b; //pointer initialization of pointer to B
 bptr -> Display(); // Function called by pointer

 bptr = & d;  //the pointer is assigned address of d.
 bptr -> Display (); //the pointer is used to call the function
return 0;
 }
```

The expected output is given below.

```
Are you going to learn C++?
Are you going to learn C++?
```

From the output it is clear that even though the pointer bptr of class B has been assigned the address of object d of derived class D, the function displayed through the pointer is the function of base class.

Now if the pointer is defined for class D and initialized by value & (D) d and if we try to assign to it the address of base class object, i.e. &b, the compiler will show an error because b is not an object of class D. **The objects of derived classes are also objects of base class but objects of base class are not the objects of derived class.** In fact, a base class does not know the existence of any class derived from it. This is illustrated in the following program.

PROGRAM 15.2 – Illustrates that pointer of derived class cannot point to an object of base class.

```
#include <iostream>
using namespace std;

class B
{
public:
```

```
void Display ()
 { cout<< "Are you going to learn C++?"<<endl;}
  }; // End of class B

class D : public B
{
public :
 void Display( )
  {cout<< "I am also learning C++."<<endl;}
   };  // End of class D

int main()

{ B b;    // b is declared an object of class B
 D d;   // d is declared an object of class D
 D *dptr = &(D)d; // pointer to class D
 dptr -> Display();

 dptr = & b;  // dptr is assigned address of base class
    // this would generate an error message.
 dptr -> Display ();
 return 0;
  }
```

The expected output is the following error message.

```
cannot convert from class B* to class D*
```

The above result is due to the fact that **objects of base class are not objects of derived class.** Therefore, a derived class pointer cannot call a function of base class.

Program 15.3 given below shows that the appropriate form of function Display () may be obtained by defining separate pointers for class B and class D. Though we get the relevant functions but that is not what is desired. We wish to point to object of the derived class by pointer of base class so as to get the form of function `Display()` defined in derived class D.

PROGRAM 15.3 – Illustrates the actions of separate pointers of base class and of derived class.

```
#include <iostream>
using namespace std;
class B
{
 public:
  void Display ()
   { cout<< "Are you going to learn C++?"<<endl;}
    } ;  // End of class B
```

```
class D : public B
{
 public :
 void Display( )
  {cout<< "I am also learning C++."<<endl;}
  } ;  // End of class D

int main()
{ B b ;    //b is an object of base class B
 D d ;   // d is an object of derived class D
 B *bptr = & (B) b ; //pointer to B
 D *dptr = &(D) d ;   // pointer to class D

  bptr -> Display ();

   dptr -> Display();
   return 0;
  }
```

The expected output is as under.

```
Are you going to learn C++?
I am also learning C++.
```

The above output is obtained by defining two different pointers, i.e. one for base class and the other for derived class. It is natural to get the respective form of function Display (), but it not our aim. Aim is to get the corresponding derived class functions by base class pointers. This can be achieved only by declaring the function Display() a **virtual function** in the base class. The word **virtual** is a keyword in C++. In the derived class the word virtual may or may not be used but the prototype of the virtual function in the base class should be identical with the prototypes of the function in the derived classes. In the following program the function `void Display()` has been declared virtual. The definition of function Display () is modified to following type.

```
virtual void Display () { statement; }
```

Now the same function is called in derived class through base class pointer. The definition given in the derived class overrides the base class definition, and in each derived class its own definition is carried out.

This is illustrated in Program 15.4 given below. In the derived class the function should have same name and same parameter types as that of base class virtual function. If the type or number of parameters are changed it would be taken as overloaded function and it would lose the property of virtual function. One may or may not use the keyword virtual in the derived class. But the corresponding function in derived class should have the same name and same parameter types, i.e. the prototypes of the function in the base class and in the derived classes should be identical.

PROGRAM 15.4 – Illustrates application of virtual function.

```
#include <iostream>
using namespace std;
class B
{
 public:
  virtual void Display ()
   { cout<< "Are you going to learn C++?"<<endl;}
   };     // End of class B

class D : public B
{ public :
 void Display( )
  {cout<< "I am also learning C++."<<endl;}
   };  // End of class D
int main()
{
 B b;
 D d;
 B *bptr = &(B) b ;    // Base class pointer
 bptr -> Display();   // statement for base class function
 bptr = & d; // base class pointer assigned address of d
 bptr -> Display (); // calling function Display ()
 return 0;
  }
```

The expected output is given below. Note that the function Display() has been declared virtual. The base class pointer has been assigned the address of object of derived class and then the pointer is used to call the function Display(). In this case the derived class definition of the function Display () overrides the base class definition of the function and the result is shown in the output given below.

```
Are you going to learn C++?
I am also learning C++.
```

CHARACTERISTICS OF VIRTUAL FUNCTIONS

(1) A virtual function should be defined in the class in which it first appears (base class). It is defined as a public member function with the keyword **virtual** preceding the definition. Exception to this is the pure virtual function, in which case, there is no definition of the function in the base class. See Section 15.4 below.

(2) A virtual function cannot be a static member.

(3) A virtual function may be declared an inline function.

(4) A virtual function may be declared a friend of another class.

(5) Apart from the same name, the virtual function prototypes in the base and derived classes should match exactly in terms of *type*, *number* of arguments and respective *types* of arguments. Any deviation from this will make the compiler to take it as an overloaded function and it will lose the status of virtual function.

(6) A constructor function cannot be a virtual function.

(7) A destructor function may be a virtual function.

(8) The virtual function definition in base class is overridden by the respective definitions in the derived classes. If in the derived class the function is not redefined, then the base class definition is invoked.

(9) The virtual functions are inherited to any depth of hierarchy.

(10) A class containing one or more virtual functions is often called **polymorphic class.**

The following program illustrates the application of a virtual function.

PROGRAM 15.5 – Illustrates polymorphism.

```
#include <iostream>
using namespace std;

 class B
 {public :
 virtual void Display(){cout<<"Display of class B called"<<endl;}
 } ;    // End of class B

 class D1 : public B
 { public :
 void Display(){cout << "Display of class D1 is called"<<endl;}
 } ;    //End of class D1

class D2 : public B
{
public :
void Display (){ cout << "Display of class D2 is called"<<endl;}

 } ; // End of class D2

int main ()
{
 B b;   // b is an object of class B
  B *bptr = &b; // base class pointer
    D1 d1;   // d1 and d2 are objects of classes D1
    D2 d2;  // and D2 respectively.

bptr ->Display() ;

bptr = &d1;    // base class pointer assigned address
     // of derived class object
 bptr -> Display ();
```

```
  bptr = &d2;
   bptr ->Display() ;

return 0 ;
}
```

The expected output is given below.

```
Display of class B called
Display of class D1 is called
Display of class D2 is called
```

15.3 ARRAYS OF BASE CLASS POINTERS

When there are several derived classes which redefine and use the virtual function of a base class, it is convenient to declare an array of pointers to the base class. The elements of array are the addresses of respective class objects. Let the classes such as D1, D2, D3, etc., be derived from a base class B. Let b, d1, d2, d3, etc. be the objects of classes B, D1, D2, D3, etc. For such a situation we may declare and initialize an array of base class pointers as below.

```
B *bptr[] = {&b, &d1, &d2, &d3};
```

where &b is the address of base class object and &d1, &d2 and &d3 are the addresses of the objects of derived classes D1, D2 and D3 respectively. The application is illustrated in the following program.

PROGRAM 15.6– Illustrates an array of base class pointers to base and derived class objects.

```
#include <iostream>
using namespace std;

 class B
{
public :
virtual void Display(){cout<< "Display of class B called"<<endl;}
} ;    // End of class B

 class D1 : public B
 { public :
void Display (){ cout << "Display of class D1 is called"<<endl;}
 } ;       //End of class D1

class D2 : public B
{
public :
void Display (){ cout << "Display of class D2 is called"<<endl;}
 } ;     //End of class D2

class D3 : public B
```

```
{ public :
void Display (){ cout << "Display of class D3 is called"<<endl;}
 } ;      //End of class D3
int main ()
 {B b;
 D1 d1;
  D2 d2;
   D3 d3;
B *bptr[] = { &b , &d1, &d2, &d3}; // Array of pointers of B
  for ( int i = 0; i<4; i++)
   bptr[i] ->Display() ;
return 0 ;
}
```

The expected output is given below.

```
Display of class B called
Display of class D1 is called
Display of class D2 is called
Display of class D3 is called
```

In the above program the elements of an array of pointers to the base class are assigned the values which are the addresses of the objects of base class and derived classes. In the output we see that the function definitions of the respective classes are called.

15.4 PURE VIRTUAL FUNCTIONS AND ABSTRACT CLASS

A pure virtual function is not defined in the base class in which it first appears but is defined in the derived classes. In the base class it has no function body and its declaration is followed by = 0. The declaration of a pure virtual function in base class is illustrated below.

```
virtual type Identifier (type parameters, –,–) = 0 ;
```

Here virtual is a keyword of C++, *type* is the *type* of return data and identifier is the name of function. There is no definition of the function in the base class. The prototype of the function is equated to zero. But the virtual function is defined in derived classes in their own way. A class containing a pure virtual function is called **abstract class**. An abstract class cannot have objects of its own. The following are the consequences of declaration of pure virtual function.

(i) A pure virtual function cannot be used for any action in the base class. In fact, the base class with a pure virtual function cannot have objects and hence is not initialized.

(ii) The class in which one or more pure virtual functions are declared is known as **abstract class** or **pure abstract class.**

(iii) An abstract class cannot have any objects of its own.

(iv) The derived classes have their own definitions of the pure virtual function in the respective classes.

(v) If a derived class does not define the pure virtual function declared in its base class, it also becomes an abstract class.

The following program gives an illustration of abstract class and the compiler gives an error message if objects to the abstract class are declared.

PROGRAM 15.7 – Illustration of pure virtual function.

```
#include <iostream>
using namespace std;
class B
{ public :
 virtual void Display () = 0;
 } ;                              // End of class B
class D1 : public B           // Derived class
{ public :
void Display (){ cout << "Display of class D1 is called"<<endl;}
} ;

int main()

{ B b ; // object b of B declared but it will result in
   // an error message.
B *bptr = &b;
bptr -> Display();
return 0 ;
}
```

The output is an error message that an abstract class cannot have an object. It shows that an attempt to declare objects of abstract class would result in compiler error given below.

```
cannot initiate abstract class.
```

The following program illustrates an application of pure virtual function. A class dealing with regular shapes has a pure virtual function Area. The function Area is defined in class Circle and in class Square which are the derived classes of class Regularshapes.

PROGRAM 15.8 – Illustrates another application of pure virtual function.

```
#include <iostream>
using namespace std;
class Regularshapes {
 int side;                // private by default
public:
 void set_side( int a )
 { side = a;}
int getside () { return side;}
virtual double Area (void) =0;
};                        // end of class Regularshapes
```

```
class Circle : public Regularshapes
{
public:
 double Area (void)
 {return (3.14159*getside()*getside()/4) ;}
};                        // end of class Circle

class Square : public Regularshapes
{
public:
 double Area (void)
 {return (getside()*getside()) ;}
};                   // end of class square

int main ()
{ double A1, A2;
Square S1;
Circle C1;
Regularshapes* RS1 = & S1;
Regularshapes* RS2 = & C1;

(*RS1).set_side ( 10);
RS2 -> set_side (10);
A1 = (*RS1). Area(); // (*RS1).Area() and RS1 ->Area() are
     // equivalent
A2 = RS2 -> Area ();
cout << "A1 = " << A1 << "\t A2 = "<< A2<<endl;
return 0;
}
```

The expected output is given below.

```
A1 = 100        A2 = 78.5397
```

15.5 VIRTUAL DESTRUCTORS

Destructor function may be declared virtual while constructor function cannot be declared virtual. It is natural to ask, what is the benefit of declaring destructor function a virtual function? In case of dynamically created objects of a derived class through base class pointer, if the base class pointer is deleted only the base class destructor is invoked. This is illustrated in the following program.

However, if the base class destructor function is declared virtual, on deletion of base class pointer the destructor functions of derived class as well as related classes (classes contained in derived class) would also get invoked. The following two programs illustrate it.

PROGRAM 15.9 – Illustrates behaviour of destructor functions when base class destructor is not declared virtual.

```
#include <iostream>
using namespace std;
class B
 {
protected :
 int bx ;
public :
 B () {} // empty constructor of base class
 B (int m) { bx = m ;    // constructor of base class
  cout<< "Constructor of B called" <<endl;}
 virtual int Product ( ){return 2*bx;}
   // The destructor function not declared virtual
 ~ B () { cout << "Destructor of class B called"<<endl;}
} ;  // End of class B
class D1
 {
 protected :
     int D1x ;
public :
  D1 () {} // empty / default constructor of D1
  D1(int n){ D1x = n;  // constructor of class D1
     cout<< "Constructor of D1 called. "<<endl;}
     int getD1x(){ return D1x;}
  ~ D1 () { cout<<"Destructor of D1 called"<<endl;}
 } ;
class D2
{
protected :
    int D2x ;
 public :
     D2(){}
 D2 ( int p ) { D2x = p ;
  cout << "Constructor of D2 called " << endl;}
    int getD2x(){ return D2x;}
 ~ D2 () { cout <<"Destructor of D2 called."<<endl;}
 } ;
class D3 : public B
{
 int D3x;  // private by default
```

```
public :
D3 () {}
    D1 d1;   // d1 is declared object of class D1
 D2 d2;  // d2 is declared object of class D2

D3 ( int p, int q , int r, int s) : B(p), d1(q), d2(r) { D3x = s;
    cout << "Constructor of D3 called."<< endl;}

int Product (){ return D3x * d2.getD2x() * d1. getD1x() * bx ;}

~ D3 () { cout<<"Destructor of D3 called."<<endl;}
} ;

int main ()
{
B *Bp ;
Bp = new B(10); // dynamic object created by new

cout << "Product of B = " <<Bp ->Product ()<< endl;
Bp = new D3 ( 2,3,4,5);
cout<< "Product = "<<Bp -> Product() << endl;

delete Bp;   // deletion of base class pointer

return 0 ;
}
```

The expected output is given below.

```
Constructor of B called
Product of B = 20
Constructor of B called
Constructor of D1 called.
Constructor of D2 called
Constructor of D3 called.
Product = 120
Destructor of class B called
```

In the output of above program it is clear that destructor of only base class is called. In the following program the destructor function of base class is declared virtual. With this, on deletion of base class pointer the destructor functions of derived as well as of related classes (D1 and D2 in the above case) are also invoked. The output of following program illustrates it.

PROGRAM 15.10 – Illustrates the effect of declaring base class destructor virtual.

```
#include <iostream>
using namespace std;

class B
 { protected :
  int bx ;

 public :
 B () {}
    B ( int m) { bx = m ;

 cout<< "Constructor of B called" <<endl;}
     virtual int Product ( ){return 2*bx;}
virtual ~ B (){ cout << "Destructor of class B called"<<endl;}

   // Destructor function declared virtual
} ;  // End of class B

 class D1          // class D1 is not derived from class B but it is a
 {              // related class because its object is used in class D3
 protected :
    int D1x ;

 public :
    D1 () {}
    D1(int n){ D1x = n;
     cout<< "Constructor of D1 called. " <<endl;}
      int getD1x(){ return D1x;}

 ~ D1 () { cout<<"Destructor of D1 called"<<endl;}
 } ;
 class D2          // it is also a related class like class D1
{
protected :
   int D2x ;
 public :
   D2(){}

 D2 ( int p ) { D2x = p ;

cout << "Constructor of D2 called " << endl;}
 int getD2x(){ return D2x;}

 ~ D2 () { cout <<"Destructor of D2 called."<<endl;}
 } ;

class D3 : public B
{
private :
   int D3x;
```

```
public :
    D3 () {}          // empty/default constructor
  D1 d1;             // d1 is object of class D1
   D2 d2;            // d2 is object of class D2

 D3(int p, int q , int r, int s): B(p), d1(q), d2(r) { D3x = s;
 cout << "Constructor of D3 called."<< endl;} // constructor

int Product (){return D3x * d2.getD2x() * d1. getD1x() * bx ;}

 ~ D3 () { cout<<"Destructor of D3 called."<<endl;}
 } ;

int main ()
{
 B *Bp ;
 Bp = new B(10);

 cout << "Product of B = " <<Bp ->Product ()<< endl;
 Bp = new D3( 2,3,4,5);
   cout<< "Product = "<<Bp -> Product() << endl;
 delete Bp;
 return 0 ;
}
```

The expected output is given below. The destructor functions of base class, derived class and related classes are called.

```
Constructor of B called
Product of B = 20
Constructor of B called
Constructor of D1 called.
Constructor of D2 called
Constructor of D3 called.
Product = 120
Destructor of D3 called.
Destructor of D2 called.
Destructor of D1 called
Destructor of class B called
```

15.6 VIRTUAL BASE CLASS

Figure15.3 below shows a case of inheritance in which two classes D1 and D2 are derived from a base class B. Another class D3 is derived from these two derived classes. Now an object of class D3 calls a function of class B. The compiler shows an error that there is ambiguity. Because, both the classes D1 and D2 have a copy each of class B. Thus D3 has two copies of B. The compiler cannot decide which of the two copies of B to invoke. The ambiguity can be resolved if the base class is declared virtual in the definitions of class D1 and class D2. In that case there would be only one copy of the base class in D3 and hence there is no ambiguity. This is taken up in programs 15.11 and 15.12. In Program 15.11 the ambiguity is illustrated and in Program 15.12 it is resolved.

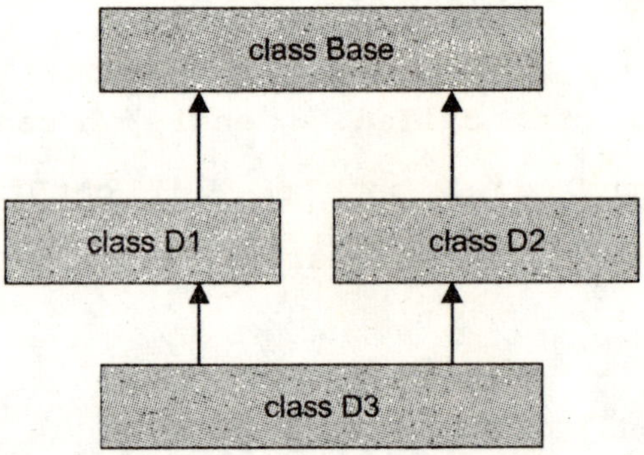

Fig 15.3: Multi-path inheritance from same base class

PROGRAM 15.11 – Illustrates ambiguity created in class derived from multi-path derived classes from same base class

```
#include <iostream>
using namespace std;
 class B
{ public :
void Display () { cout << " It is B class Display"<< endl;}
     };
class D1 : public B
 { } ;

class D2 :  public B
 { };
class D3 : public D2, public D1
 { };

int main ()

{ D3 d3;
 D3.Display();
  return 0 ;
  }
```

The expected output is as below.

`'D3::Display' is ambiguous`

The above ambiguity is resolved by declaring the base class virtual in the declaration of derived classes.

PROGRAM 15.12 – Illustrates virtual base class.

```
#include <iostream>
using namespace std;

class B
 {
public :
 void Display () { cout << "It is B class Display"<< endl;}
     };

class D1 : virtual public B
 { } ;

class D2 : virtual public B
 { };

class D3 : public D2, public D1
 { };

int main ()
{
 D3 d3;
 d3.Display();
  return 0 ;
  }
```

The expected output is given below. The ambiguity is resolved by declaring the base class virtual.

```
It is B class Display
```

15.7 RUN-TIME TYPE INFORMATION (RTTI)

As explained in the above sections the pointer to base class can be made to point to objects of any derived class on the down stream, even to object of classes derived from derived classes. However, the pointer does not carry any information as to which class object it is pointing to. In some programs this information is required if we want to apply a special function to objects of a particular class only. This involves distinguishing the types of objects and finding objects of the desired class to which the function can be applied.

One solution is to define a member function in each class to supply the *type* information and which may be used to select the *type* of object desired. When the number of classes is large the coding for selection may become cumbersome with if-else chains or switch expressions. The virtual functions may also be used to do this job. The following program uses virtual function Type () to have run time type information.

PROGRAM 15.13 – Obtaining run time type information.

```
#include <iostream>
using namespace std;
class B
```

```
{ public:
 virtual char Type() { return 'B';}
};

class C : public B
{ public:
char Type (){ return 'C';}
};

class D : public B
{public:
char Type (){ return 'D';}
};

int main()
{ B b;
 C c ;
  D d ;

B* pb = &b;
 cout <<"Type of pb now is : "<< pb -> Type()<<endl;

pb = & c;
 cout<< "Type of pb now is : "<<pb -> Type()<<endl;

pb = & d;
 cout <<"Type of pb now is : "<<pb -> Type()<<endl;
return 0 ;
}
```

The expected output is given below. The type information is obtained at run time.

```
Type of pb now is : B
Type of pb now is : C
Type of pb now is : D
```

The C++, however, offers direct support to RTTI with two operators, i.e. dynamic_cast () and typeid (). The operator typeid ( ) allows its application to polymorphic classes as well to non-polymorphic classes (see application of typeid in Chapter 2). It determines and returns a reference to the exact *type* of the object. The name of the class of the object may also be obtained by function name(). Figure 15.4 gives a physical illustration of typeid( ) operator.

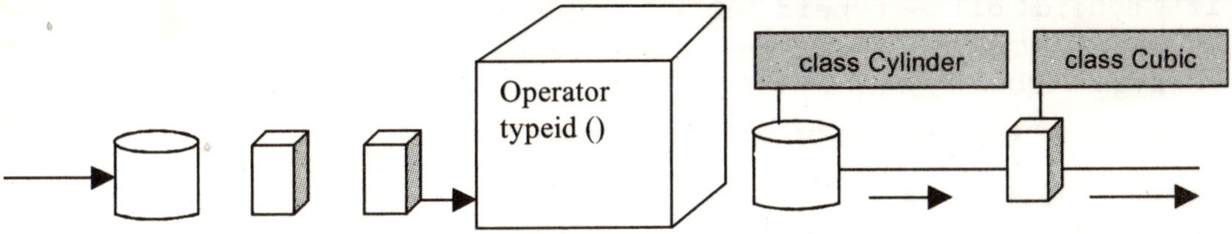

Fig. 15.4: Identification of class of objects

The classes relating to typreid () are contained in the header file **<typeinfo>** and this header file should be included in the program if its objects are to be used in the program. The syntax for typeid () is as follows.

```
typeid (d) ;
```

where d is an object of a class. The code gives reference to the *type* of object d. The header file **<typeinfo>** also defines two relational operators, i.e. == and != for comparing the *types* of two objects say d1 and d2. The syntax is illustrated below.

```
if(typeid (d1) == typeid (d2))
```

or

```
if (typeid(d1) != typeid(d2))
```

The header file <typeinfo> also defines function name() which gives the name of the *type* or name of class to which an object belongs. The syntax for using name() is given below.

```
typeid(d1).name( );
```

The function returns the name of the type of object d1. For display, it may be coded as below.

```
cout << typeid(d1).name( );
```

The application of operator typeid () is illustrated in the following program.

PROGRAM 15.14 – Illustration of application of **typeid()**on non-polymorphic classes.

```
#include <iostream>
# include <typeinfo>  // header file for typeid()

using namespace std;

class B
 { };
class D1 : public B
 { };
class D2 : public D1
 { };

int main ()
{ D2 d2 ;
 D1 d1 ;
```

```
if ( typeid( d1) == typeid (d2))
    cout<< "The two are of same type "<<endl;
    else
    cout<< "The two are of different type"<<endl;

cout << "Type of d1 is " <<typeid(d1).name( )<<endl;
cout << "Type of d2 is " <<typeid(d2).name( )<<endl;
return 0;
}
```

The expected output is given below. It is self explanatory.

```
The two are of different type
Type of d1 is class D1
Type of d2 is class D2
```

15.8 NEW CASTING OPERATORS IN C++

THE DYNAMIC_CAST <> ()

The operator is used to cast *types* of objects at run time and is applicable only to polymorphic classes, i.e. the base class should have at least one virtual function. The operator dynamic_cast<> () is applicable to pointers as well as references. For pointers it is coded as below

```
dynamic_cast < derived_type*> (ptr_base);
```

The dynamic_cast converts the base class pointer (ptr_base) to the derived class pointer (derived_type*) subject to the condition that the object to which the ptr_base is pointing belongs to the desired derived class or to a class derived from the desired derived class, otherwise it returns 0. So it is a convenient way to select the objects of the desired derived class from objects belonging to several derived classes. Its physical illustration is shown in the Fig. 15.5 below. The pointers to several objects from which we wish to select objects of a particular class, are all cast by dynamic_cast. The pointers which point to objects of desired class will be converted while others would return 0, so they would be out of list. The following figure gives a physical illustration.

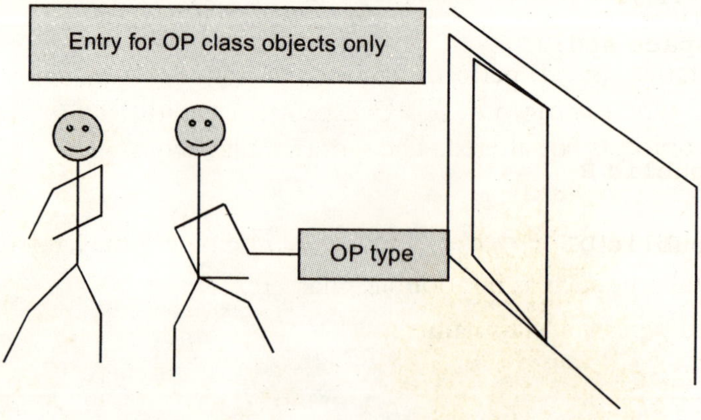

Fig. 15.5: An illustration of **dynamic_cast <> ()**

An illustration of code for dynamic_cast <> () is given below.

Application of dynamic_<>()cast

```
#include <iostream>
using namespace std;
class B
{ public:
B () {}
virtual void Function (){}
};
class D1 :public B
{ };
class D2 : public B
{ };
class D3: public B
{};
int main ()
{ B* Ab[3];
 Ab[0] = new D1 ;
   Ab[1] = new D2 ;
   Ab[2] = new D3 ;
 for ( int i =0; i<3; i++)
 {D2 *ptrd2 = dynamic_cast<D2*>(Ab[i]);
 if (ptrd2 != 0 )
    cout << "D2 object found \n" ; }
 return 0; }
```

The header file <typeinfo> also defines two functions bad_typeid and bad_cast. If the operator typeid () is not successful it throws an exception bad_typeid. If dynamic_cast <>() is not successful the bad_cast is thrown and it may lead to termination of the program.

THE STATIC_CAST<>()

The operator static_cast<>() performs conversion from one type to another in a way similar to conventional C-type casting, i.e. (T) U except for the difference that in static_cast the constantness of an object is not altered. The syntax is illustrated below.

```
static_cast<T>(object)
```

The expression converts the *type* of object to T. The type T may any one of the following.

(i) Fundamental type such as int, double, char, etc.

(ii) User defined types, i.e. class name.

(iii) Pointers.

(iv) References.

(v) The enum type – int and double may be cast to enum.

As the name static implies the operator is applicable to static type checking and non-polymorphic cases. The object of one class may be changed to object of another class provided the appropriate construction functions are there. The following program provides an illustration of application of static_cast <>() for pointers (from that of base class to derived class) and references.

PROGRAM 15.15 – Illustrates application of static_cast<>()

```
#include <iostream>
using namespace std;
class Base
{ public :
int x;
int y;
void Speak () { cout << "I am class Base. \n" ;}
};    // end of Base class

class D : public Base
{ public:
   void speak () { cout << "I am class D. \n";}
Base B;    // B is object of class Base.
   int Area (Base B )
   {return B.x*B.y;}
};
int main()
{
 Base B ;
 B.x =5;
 B.y = 20;
 Base * basep = &B; // pointer to base class.
 cout<< "Function Speak() called by basep."<<endl;
 basep -> Speak();
 cout<< "After static cast the function of D called."<<endl;
 D * dp = static_cast<D*>(basep) ; // basep cast to D type
 dp->speak(); // Function speak() of D called by pointer dp
 D* dp1 = (D*)basep; // C-type conversion

cout<<"After C-type conversion function call to speak()."<<endl;
 dp1 ->speak();
 D d;   // d is declared an object of class D
cout <<"Area = "<< d.Area(B)<<endl; // call to function Area()
cout<< "After casting an object to reference by C-type conversion" << endl;
 D &dp2 = (D&) B; // casting a reference by C-type casting
 dp2.Speak(); // calling a function of class B
```

```
 dp2.speak(); // calling a function of class D
D &dp3 = static_cast<D&>(B); //casting a reference by static cast
cout<< "After the static cast the functions are again called."<< endl;
dp3.Speak();    //Speak() and speak() are Two different functions.
dp3.speak();
return 0 ;
}
```

The output is given below. The comments given above have made the output self explanatory.

```
Function Speak() called by basep.
I am class Base.
After static cast the function of D called.
I am class D.
After C-type conversion function call to speak().
I am class D.
Area = 100
After casting an object to reference type by C-type conversion
I am class Base.
I am class D.
After the static cast the functions are again called.
I am class Base.
I am class D.
```

THE REINTERPRET_CAST <>()

The operator is coded as below.

`The reinterpret_cast <T>(object)`

The operator returns a reinterpretation of its operand which is quite different from that of the operand. For instance, it can cast an int into a pointer type and a pointer into an int *type* or change a pointer to an integer into a pointer to char, etc. Both the dynamic cast and reinterpret_cast are prone to errors and should be used with caution. Some compilers also give a warning to this aspect.

The reinterpret_cast can be used on pointers as well as references. It is applicable to static as well as to dynamic objects. Like static_cast it also preserves the constantness of an object. The following program illustrates the application of the reinterpret_cast for conversion of pointers and references. The operator can be applied to objects of incomplete classes as well without getting an error message from compiler. Some of these applications are illustrated in the following program.

PROGRAM 15.16 – Illustrates application of **reinterpret_cast<>()**

```
#include <iostream>
#include <string>
using namespace std;
```

```
class A;   // incomplete class
class B;   // incomplete class
class Base
{ public :
void Speak () { cout << " I am class Base. \n" ;}
};
 class D : public Base
 { public:
   void speak () { cout << " I am class D. \n";}
 };

int main()
{ int x = 65;
 int * px = &x;  // px is pointer to int x
 char* chp = (char*) px; //px converted into pointer char* chp
     // by C-type casting
cout << "*chp = " << *chp << endl; // output statement for *chp
cout << *px <<endl;
 // below similar conversion done by reinterpret_cast<>()

char* ptrx = reinterpret_cast<char*> (px);

cout <<"*ptrx = " << *ptrx<<endl;
D* ptrd = reinterpret_cast< D*>( px); //px converted into type D
 ptrd ->speak();
 B * bp ;  // It also applies to incomplete classes
 A* ap = reinterpret_cast<A*>(bp);
}
```

The expected output is given below. The output demonstrates the successful conversion of the pointers.

```
*chp = A
65
*ptrx = A
I am class D.
```

In the following program the **reinterpret_cast <>()** is used with pointers to functions.

PROGRAM 15.17 – Illustrates application of reinterpret_cast <>() with functions

```
 #include <iostream>
using namespace std;

void Funct1 ( )
{ cout<< "This is void function with void argument \n";}

void Funct2(int m, int n)
{ cout<<"This is void function with two arguments.\n";}
```

```
int Funct3 (int x, int y )
 {return x*y;}

int main()
{ int x = 65;
 int * px = &x;  // px is pointer to int x
 typedef void (*PF) ( ); // typedef of pointers to void functions

PF function1 = (PF)Funct1; // conventional C-type cast
   function1() ;  // function call
PF function2 = reinterpret_cast<PF>(Funct1);//by reinterpret_cast
  function2 ();   // function2 called
  int y = 2;
PF Function2 = reinterpret_cast<PF>(Funct2);
  Function2();
typedef int(*pF)(int, int); //type definition of pointers to
    // int functions having 2 int parameters

pF function3 = (pF) Funct3 ; // conventional C-type cast
 cout << function3(x,y )<<endl; // function call
 //below similar conversion is done by reinterpret_cast<>()
pF function4 = reinterpret_cast<pF>(Funct3);

cout << function4 (x,y)<< endl;
return 0;
 }
```

The output is given below.

```
This is void function with void argument
This is void function with void argument
This is void function with two arguments.
130
130
```

In the above out put, the first two lines are due to function calls function1() and function 2(). The third line of output is due to function call of *function2(x,y)*. The pointer of funct3 is again converted to pointer of *function3(x,y)* and into pointer to *function4 (x,y)*. The last two lines of out put are due to call of these two functions.

THE CONST_CAST<>()

The operator provides an access to a variable with the attributes **const** or **volatile**. The objects declared volatile may be modified from outside the control of the program. The operator const_cast<>()does not change the basic attribute of the variable. The syntax of the operator is as follows.

```
const_cast <T*> ( ptr_object)
```

The following program tries to bring out the action of const_cast.

PROGRAM 15.18 – Illustrates the application of **const_cast<> ().**

```
#include <iostream>
using namespace std;
void F ( char* M )
 { cout<< M <<endl;}
int main()
 { const char * S= "Delhi";
 //F (S); Error, cannot convert from const char* to char*
 F ( const_cast<char*> (S)); // it is alright

 const int n = 10;
 const int *ptrn = &n;
// n= n+5; Error, the n is const. But the following is alright

 *(const_cast<int*>(ptrn) ) = n + 5;
 cout <<*(const_cast<int*>(ptrn) )<<endl;

//const_cast<int>(n) = n+8; This gives error, const_cast
//cannot convert from const int to int.
cout << n <<endl;
return 0 ;
}
```

The expected output is given below.

```
Delhi
15
10
```

EXERCISES

1. How do you declare pointer to a class?
2. How do you make the base class pointer point to object of derived class?
3. What is the benefit of declaring a base class function a virtual function?
4. What is a virtual base class?
5. What is the difference between a virtual function and an overloaded function?
6. What are abstract classes? How are they useful?
7. What do you understand by the term dynamic binding?
8. What do you understand by polymorphism?
9. Why constructors are not declared virtual while the destructors are declared virtual?
10. What is the benefit of declaring destructors virtual?
11. Make a program for illustrating pure virtual function Speak() in the base class Animal. The derived classes are class Dog, class Cat, class EMan for Englishman and class HMan for Indian. The function Speak() displays their respective mother tongue.

Answer:

PROGRAM 15.19 – Another example of abstract class and pure virtual function.

```
#include <iostream>
using namespace std;
class Animal {
public:

virtual void Speak() =0;
};

class Dog : public Animal
{ public:
 void Speak ( )
{cout<<" BHOO BHOO" <<endl;}
};
class Cat : public Animal
{
public:
void Speak (void)
 {cout<< " Miewn Miewn" << endl;;}
};
class EMan : public Animal
{ public :
void Speak(){ cout << "I speak English."<<endl;}
};
class HMan : public Animal
{ public :
void Speak(){ cout << "I speak Hindi."<<endl;}
};
void main ()
{
Dog D ;
Cat C ;
EMan EM;
HMan HM;

 D.Speak();
 C.Speak();
 EM.Speak();
 HM.Speak();
 cout<<"\n";
 }
```

The expected output is given below.

```
BHOO BHOO
Miewn Miewn
I speak English.
I speak Hindi.
```

❍❍❍

CHAPTER

16 Templates

16.1 INTRODUCTION

There are a large number of programs which carry out similar operations on different *types* of data. For example, sorting of lists, whether the list consists of integers or floating point numbers or characters the operational code is similar. Similarly in swap of two quantities the code is identical except for the type of variables. Same is true in the case of finding the greater of two quantities whether they are integers, floating decimal point numbers or characters. In C++ whenever a variable is declared, its *type* has to be mentioned before its name. Therefore, even though the codes are similar, for making them applicable to different data types, i.e. `int`, `double` or `char`, etc., the programmer has to write a number of programs one for each data type. Templates give the facility that you need not write a number of programs. With template we need write only one program that is equally applicable to all types of data — the fundamental types as well as user defined types. In case of templates the program is made with a place holder in place of *type*. When the type is substituted or referred to, the compiler substitutes the specified *type* in place of the place holder and compiles the program. Now if another *type* is specified, the compiler generates another template specialization for that *type* and compiles the program. So template is like a mould which allows different *types* to be cast for generating the corresponding programs.

Template programming is also called generic programming. The function templates and class templates are also called generic functions and generic classes respectively. There are other methods also to achieve the same end such as use of macros, # define and void pointers, etc. Such programs were used by programmers before the implementation of templates, however, these methods have disadvantages which are not there in templates. For instance, macros do not allow strict type checking while the templates do.

Use of templates started around 1991. The greatest advantage of generic programming is that it is applicable to any type of data, i.e. the fundamental types as well as to user defined types.

In the following we first discuss the functions templates and then the class templates.

16.2 FUNCTION TEMPLATES

A function template declaration in which the function and its parameters are of same *type* is illustrated below. A function template is declared with keyword **template** followed by angular brackets which contain the keyword **typename** or **class** followed by an identifier or name of the *typename* or *class*, i.e. the name of place holder for the *type.* After the angular brackets the function is defined. See illustration below.

template *<typename type_identifier > type_identifier function_name (type_identifier* **parameter1, – , –***)*

{ *statements;* }

Or it may be coded with keyword *class* in place of *typename* as below.

template < class *type_identifier* > *type_identifier function_name* (*type_identifier* **parameter1, – , –**)

{ *statements;* }

In the above declarations the words *template, typename* and *class* are keywords of C++. Both the above declarations are equivalent. A *type_identifier* is any valid identifier in C++ which is used as a place holder for *type*. The *type_identifier* used for *class* or *typename* has to be placed before the function name as well as before the name of every parameter of the function. For instance, let T be the *type_identifier* or name of the *typename* or *class*, a function template for calculation of area of a rectangle with sides represented by x and y may be defined as given below.

```
template <typename T> T Area (T x, T y) // function head
   { return x * y ; }           // function body
```

Here T is the *type_identifier.* The T placed before the name area is its return type. The above function may also be defined with the keyword *class* as below.

```
template < class T > T Area ( T x, T y )
 {return x * y;}
```

Both the function definitions given above are equivalent and any one may be used. Here T is the *type_identifier*, in fact, it is a place holder for the *type* which is still not specified and will be substituted later. Area is the name of function. The sides x and y are the two parameters of function Area (). The variable x may be length of rectangle and y may be width of rectangle and Area is the area of rectangle. Note that the name T appears before Area as well as before x and before y in the head of the function. The first line in the above definition may be written in two lines as illustrated in program 16.3.

CALLING A FUNCTION TEMPLATE

The function template is called by mentioning the name of function followed by the actual *type* in angular brackets, followed by list of arguments in parentheses ( ). It is illustrated below.

```
Function_name <type> (arguments);
```

An example of calling template function is given below.

```
 int x = a, y = b;   // a and b are arguments
Area<int>(a,b); // calling the function Area
```

Now if the sides and Area are *double* numbers, the function call would become,

```
   double x = A, y = B ;  //A and B are arguments
Area <double> (a, b);   // function call
```

The following program illustrates the use of function template which calculates area of rectangle whose sides are either in integers or *double* numbers.

PROGRAM 16.1 – Illustrates definition and calling of a function template.

```
#include <iostream>
using namespace std;
template <typename T > T Area (T x, T y ) //function template
{return x*y ; }        // definition
int main()
{
int n = 4 , m = 3;
double j = 6.5 , k = 4.1 ;
cout<<"Area1 = "<<Area<int>(n, m)<<"\t Area2 = " << Area <double> (j,k) <<
endl;
return 0;
}
```

The expected output is given below. Area1 represents the area for rectangle with sides (4, 3) and Area2 represents the area for rectangle with sides 6.5 and 4.1.

```
Area1 = 12        Area2 = 26.65
```

In the above program T is in fact place holder for the *type.* The template program is compiled only when the actual *type* of variables is substituted for T. In Program 16.1, in the call `Area<int>(n,m)` the type of variable area is int and in the call `Area <double>(j,k)` the type of return value is double. Both types of return values, i.e. *int* and *double* are obtained with the same function definition.

Another example is provided in Program 16.2. In this program we have not mentioned the *type* in the angular brackets at the time of function call. The compiler, in fact, can know the type of variables it is dealing with because the *type* is mentioned at the time of declaration of the variables. Even if the type `<int>` or `<double>` is not included in the function call the compiler can find out the type from declarations of variables, for instance, when it encounters integers like `int m, n;` the T is replaced by `int` and the program is generated for integers. When it comes across floating point numbers declared as `double j, k ;` in the program the compiler regenerates the template specialization for *double* numbers. Moreover, you may use any valid identifier (name) in place of T. However, it is better to explicitly mention the type of return value, particularly, when the function template contains more than one type of parameters.

Below we define a function template for determining the maximum of two numbers with the declaration `<class T>` instead of `<typename T>`. The variables may be integers, floating point numbers or characters. Characters also have integral values as per ASCII code. For instance 'A' = 65 and 'B' = 66 and so on. The function template definition is given below. This function determines greater of the two numbers.

```
template <class T> T max(T x, T y)
{ return x > y ? x:y ;}
```

In case a template function is defined below the main (), the template prototype or template declaration of function should be given above main (). As explained above for Program 16.1, T is the identifier or name for *type*, max is the name of function, x and y are the two parameters of max(). Note that max is preceded by identifier T and the two parameters are also individually preceded by identifier T. This is very similar to the usual declaration of function except for the *type* which is now represented by T. The following program illustrates the declaration of a function template which finds the greater of the two variables which may be of type *int* or *double* or *char.*

PROGRAM 16.2 – Illustrates function template for finding greater of two numbers.

```
#include <iostream>
using namespace std;
template <class T> T max(T x, T y) // function definition
{return x>y ? x : y;} // if(x>y) return x else return y

int main()
{ int n = 64 , m = 67 ;    // int variables
char ch1 = 'S' , ch2 = 'R';  // char variables
double D1 = 6.87, D2= 8.34;  // double variable
cout << "max (n,m) = "<<max <int>(n,m)<<endl;
cout<< "max (ch1,ch2) = " << max <char>(ch1,ch2)<<endl;
cout<< "max(D1,D2) = " << max<double>( D1, D2)<< endl;
return 0;
}
```

The expected output is given below. The program and the results are self explanatory.

```
max (n,m)= 67
max (ch1,ch2) = S
max(D1,D2) = 8.34
```

The following program makes a function template for Swap function which exchanges the values of two variables. The quantities involved may be integers, double numbers, characters or strings. Strings are objects of class string (C++ strings) and hence a user defined type. Same function template can be used for all the types of data. You should note that Swap() is user defined function and is different from swap() of C++ Standard Library because S is in this is in upper case.

PROGRAM 16.3 – Illustrate a function template for swapping two quantities.

```
#include <iostream>
# include <string>
using namespace std;
template <class T>  // Template definition of Swap()
void Swap (T &x , T &y) // values passed on by reference
{ T temp;
temp = x;
```

```
x = y;
y = temp;}

void main()
{ int n =60, m=30;
char ch1= 'A', ch2 = 'D';
double a = 2.45 , b = 4.76;

string S1 = "Morning";  //S1 and S2 are string objects
string S2 = "Evening";  // their type is string

Swap <double>(a,b);
Swap<char>(ch1,ch2);
Swap<int>(n,m);
Swap<string>(S1,S2 ); // swapping user defined data

cout <<"a = "<<a<<"\tb = "<<b<<"\n";
cout<< "ch1 = "<<ch1<<"\tch2 = " << ch2<< endl;
cout <<"n = "<<n <<" \tm = "<<m<<"\n";
cout << "S1 = "<< S1 << " ,  S2 = "<< S2<< endl;
}
```

The expected output is given below.

```
a = 4.76        b = 2.45
ch1 = D        ch2 = A
n = 30         m = 60
S1 = Evening ,  S2 = Morning
```

Before the implementation of Swap function, the initial values are a = 2.45, b = 4.76, ch1 =A, ch2 = D, n = 60, m = 30 and string S1 = "Morning" and S2 = "Evening". The values have been interchanged by implementing Swap function. Also note that the variables are passed by reference in the declaration of Swap function. As we have already discussed earlier (in Chapter 7 on functions and in Chapter 9 on pointers and references) in passing variables by values, only copies of variable values are passed on and variables do not get changed. For a change in the values of variables they have to be passed on to functions by references or pointers.

16.3 FUNCTION TEMPLATE WITH ARRAY AS A PARAMETER

The following program illustrates a function template for output of an array. The function template Display () is declared as below.

```
template <class T>
void Display(const T*A, unsigned int size)
```

Here size stands for number of elements in the array, T is the name of place holder for *type* and A is the name of array which is a constant pointer to the first element of array. The application of code is illustrated in the following program,

PROGRAM 16.4 – Illustrates a function template for output of an array.

```
#include <iostream>
using namespace std;

template <class T>
void Display(const T*A, unsigned int size)// function declaration
{ for( int i =0 ; i<size; i++ )  // and definition
  cout<< A[i] <<" ";
  cout<<endl;}

 int main ()
 {const int K = 6,M =15, J = 4 ;
  int Bill[J] = {20, 30, 40, 50}; // an array of integers
// Below is an array of doubles
  double Kim[K] = { 4.5, 5.6, 7.8, 8.9, 1.2, 3.4};
   char Name[M] = "B.L.Juneja"; // a string of characters

 Display (Bill, J);
 Display (Kim , K);
  Display (Name , M);

return 0;
}
```

The expected output is given below.

```
20 30 40 50
4.5 5.6 7.8 8.9 1.2 3.4
B . L . J u n e j a
```

Below the Program 16.5 is extended to include strings along with characters, int and double numbers. The same function template Display() is used to display on the monitor an array of integers, an array of double numbers, an array of characters and an array of strings.

PROGRAM 16.5 – Illustrates a function template for displaying arrays and strings.

```
#include <iostream>
using namespace std;

template <class T>
void Display(T A[],unsigned int size)

{ for ( int i =0 ; i<size;i++ )
  cout<< A[i] <<" ";
  cout<<endl;}

 int main ()
 {
  const int K = 6,M =5, J = 7, N = 4 ;
```

```
int Bill[J] = {20,30, 40,50,60,70,80};
char ch [N] = { 'D', 'E', 'X', 'S'};
double Kim[K] = { 4.5, 5.6, 7.8, 8.9 , 1.2 , 3.2};
char* S[M] ={"Malini" , "Sneha" , "Sunita" , "Pushkar", "Alka"};
Display( Bill , J); // calling template function
Display (Kim , K);
Display (ch,N);
Display ( S, M);
return 0;
}
```

The output is as under.

```
20 30 40 50 60 70 80
4.5 5.6 7.8 8.9 1.2 3.2
D E X S
Malini Sneha Sunita Pushkar Alka
```

Sorting of lists is very common in programming. The list may be of elements of type int, doubles or characters, the codes for sorting are similar. Therefore, in the following program a template function is developed for sorting the elements of an array in ascending order.

PROGRAM 16.6 – Illustrates a function template for sorting of lists.

```
#include <iostream>
using namespace std;
template <class T>  // sorting function template
void Listsort (T A[], const int n)
 {for ( int i = 0 ; i<n;i++)
  {for(int j =0;j<n-1;j++)
   if(A[j]>A[j+1])
   swap( A[j],A[j+1]);}}

template <class T>

void Display( T A[] , unsigned int size)

{ for ( int i =0 ; i<size; i++ )
 cout<< A[i] <<" ";
 cout<<endl;}

int main ()
{ const int K = 6,M =4, J = 7, N = 4 ;
 int Bill[J] = {20,30,70, 80,40,50,60};
```

```
 char ch [5] = { 'D', 'E', 'X', 'S', 'Z'};
  double Kim[K] = { 4.5, 5.6, 1.2 ,7.8, 8.9 , 3.2};

 Listsort(Bill,J);
 Display( Bill , J);

 Listsort(Kim,K);
 Display <double>(Kim , K);

 Listsort (ch,5);
 Display<char> (ch,5);

return 0;
}
```

The expected output is given below.

```
20 30 40 50 60 70 80
1.2 3.2 4.5 5.6 7.8 8.9
D E S X Z
```

Template Function for Swapping Specified Number of Elements of Arrays

In Program 16.7 given below a Swap template function is developed which swaps the specified number of elements of two arrays which may be of type int, double or character etc. The name genric has been used as the class name.

PROGRAM 16.7 – Illustrates a function template for swapping a specified number of elements of two arrays.

```
#include <iostream>
using namespace std;

template <class genric> // declaration and definition of Swap
void Swap ( genric x[ ], genric y[ ],int m )
{
 genric temp ;  // type identifier is genric in place of T
 for (int i = 0; i<m;i++)
 {temp = x[i];
  x[i] = y[i];
   y[i] = temp ; }
 }     // end of template function

void main()
 { double Bill[ ] = { 11.1, 12.2, 13.3,14.4 ,15.5};
 double Kim [] = { 30.5, 31.1, 32.2, 33.3, 34.4};
  char Ch[ ] = { 'A', 'B', 'C','D','E' };
   char Kh [] = { 'S', 'T','U','V','X'};
```

```
    int K[5] = {1 ,2 , 3, 4,5};
    int M[5] = {50,60,70,80,90};

     cout << "Before swap the arrays are as below\n";
     cout <<"Bill\tKim\tCh\tKh\tK\t M " << endl;

    for ( int k = 0; k <5; k++)
   cout <<Bill[k] <<"\t"<<Kim[k]<<"\t"<<Ch[k]<<"\t"<<Kh[k] <<"\t" <<
K[k]<<"\t"<<M[k] <<endl;
    Swap (Bill, Kim,1 );

    Swap ( K , M ,3 );
    Swap ( Ch, Kh,5 ) ;

    cout << "After swapping the arrays are \n";
    cout << " Bill\tKim\tCh\tKh\tK\tM " << endl;

   for ( int j = 0; j <5; j++)
   cout <<Bill[j] <<"\t"<<Kim[j]<<"\t"<<Ch[j]<<"\t"<<Kh[j]<< "\t"<<
K[j]<<"\t"<<M[j]<<endl;
    }
```

The expected output is given below.

```
Before swap the arrays are as below
Bill      Kim      Ch      Kh      K      M
11.1      30.5     A       S       1      50
12.2      31.1     B       T       2      60
13.3      32.2     C       U       3      70
14.4      33.3     D       V       4      80
15.5      34.4     E       X       5      90
```

After swapping the arrays are

```
Bill      Kim      Ch      Kh      K      M
30.5      11.1     S       A       50     1
12.2      31.1     T       B       60     2
13.3      32.2     U       C       70     3
14.4      33.3     V       D       4      80
15.5      34.4     X       E       5      90
```

As specified in the program between Bill and Kim only one element has been exchanged, between Ch and Kh all the five elements have been exchanged and between K and M only 3 elements have been exchanged as instructed in the code.

16.4 FUNCTION TEMPLATES WITH MULTIPLE TYPE ARGUMENTS

Up till now we have discussed function templates which involved only one *type* of variables. For instance, all the function parameters are either integers only or only double numbers or only char, etc., and return values are also of same type. But there are ample situations wherein the functions parameters are of more than one *type* like int and double and you may like to have the return value either in integers or double number. The illustrations of template declarations for such cases are given below. The template function selects greater of the two values which may not be of same *type*. Therefore, two place holders are declared for class name.

```
template <class T, class E >
T max ( T x , E y)
{return x > y ? x : y ; }
```

In this declaration the output will be of type T because we have taken max of type T. If it is desired to have output of type E we may declare the above expression as below.

```
template< class T, class E>
 E max ( T x , E y)
 {return x > y ? x : y ;)}
```

The following program gives an illustration of above function template in finding out the greater of two values whether they are of *type* char, int or a double, etc.

PROGRAM 16.8 – Illustrate functions template for more than one data types.

```
#include <iostream>
using namespace std;

template <class T , class E> E max(T x, E y)
 {return x>y ? x : y;}

int main()
 {
 int n = 88 ;
 double m = 80.4 ;
  int ch1 = 67 ;

 char ch2 = 'A';
 double D1 = 76.87 ,D2= 90.3;

 cout << "max (n, m)= "<<max (n,m)<<endl;
 cout<< "max (ch1,ch2) = " << max (ch1,ch2)<<endl;

  cout<< "max (D1,D2) = " << max ( D1, D2)<< endl;
  cout<< "max (n,D2) = " << max (n,D2)<<endl;
 return 0;
  }
```

The expected output is given below

```
max (n, m)= 88
max (ch1,ch2) = C
max (D1,D2) = 90.3
max (n,D2) =90.3
```

From the output it is clear that the output is of the type of the second variable in the function because we specified it so in the function declaration, i.e. `E max(T x, E y)`. If the function head is declared as given below,

```
T max(T x, E y)
```

the output would be of type T.

16.5 OVERLOADING OF TEMPLATE FUNCTIONS

The template function overloading is similar to non-template function overloading. In overloaded function the function name is same while the arguments are different in number and or in type. The following program illustrates overloaded template functions.

PROGRAM 16.9 – Illustrates overloading of template functions with parameters of single *type*.

```
#include <iostream>
using namespace std;
 template <class T>
  T Product (T x, T y)
   {return x*y;}

template <class T>
 T Product ( T x, T y, T z)
    {return x*y*z;}
int main ()
{ int a (2), b(3), c(4);
 double A(2.0), B(5.5), C(1.5);
 cout<<"Product (A,B,C) = "<< Product (A,B,C)<< endl;;
 cout<<"Product ( A,B ) = "<< Product ( A,B )<< endl;
 cout << "Product ( a,b,c ) = "<< Product ( a,b,c)<<endl;
 return 0;
}
```

The expected output is given below.

```
Product (A,B,C) = 16.5
Product ( A,B ) = 11
Product ( a,b,c ) = 24
```

Every function in the above program has one type of variable. It is either int, or double. In the following, we take the functions with multiple type arguments.

PROGRAM 16.10 – Illustrates overloaded template functions with parameters of multiple *types*.

```
#include <iostream>
using namespace std;
```

```
template <class T, class U>
 U Product ( T x, U y)
  {return x*y;}

template <class T, class S, class U>
 S Product ( T x, S y, U z)
  {return x*y*z;}

int main ()
{ int a (1);
    double B(1.5);
     char Ch('D');

cout<<"Product (a,B,Ch) = "<< Product (a,B,Ch)<< endl;
cout<<"Product (a,B) = "<< Product (a,B)<< endl;
cout<<"Product( 'A', 4.5, 6) = " <<Product ( 'A', 4.5, 6)<< endl;
return 0;
}
```

The expected output is given below.

```
Product (a,B,Ch) = 102
Product (a,B) = 1.5
Product ( 'A', 4.5, 6) = 1755
```

16.6 CLASS TEMPLATES

We have already got some experience with function templates. Different data types may be used for the evaluation of the function. The class template has similar properties. Class objects having different types of data can use the same class template. A class template is declared as below.

template < class *type_identifier* > class *identifier_for_class*

For example the class template Cuboid of the following program is declared as below.

```
template <class T> class Cuboid
```

Here *Cuboid* is the name of class while *T* is the name of place holder for *type*. You may use any valid name in place of *T*. Also wherever the variables are declared in the class, they would be preceded by type identifier *T*. The class object is declared as below.

Class_name <type> object_name;

The following program is a class template for the class Cuboid which calculates the surface area and volume of rectangular prismatic bodies. The dimensions may be in *int* or *float*, *double*, *long* or *short*. In this program the member functions are defined inside the class.

PROGRAM 16.11 – Template class with member functions defined inside the class.

```
 #include <iostream>
  using namespace std;

template <class T>
```

```
class Cuboid {
T x , y , z ;  // The variables x , y, z are of same type
public:
Cuboid(T L, T W, T H){x = L; y = W; z = H ;}

T surface_area( )
 {return 2* (x*y +y*z +z*x);

T volume( ) { return x*y*z ;}
};
     // end of class
int main()
{Cuboid <int> C1(3,8,5);   // dimensions in int
Cuboid < double> C2(3.5,5.5,4.5) ; // dimensions in doubles

cout << "Volume of C1= "<< C1.volume()<<"\n";
cout<< "Volume of C2 = " << C2.volume()<<"\n";

cout<<"surface area of C1 = "<< C1.surface_area()<<"\n";
cout<<"surface area of C2 = "<< C2.surface_area()<<"\n";
return 0 ;
 }
```

The expected output is given below.

```
Volume of C1= 120
Volume of C2 = 86.625
surface area of C1 = 158
surface area of C2 = 119.5
```

Defining Function Template Outside The Class Template

In the above program all the function are defined inside the class template. The code for defining a function template outside the class template is illustrated below.

T class_identifier <T> :: function_identifier (***type_identifier*** **parameter1, ..)**

{ statements ;}

An illustration of this, the declaration of function volume class cuboid is given below. An application is illustrated in Program 16.12.

```
template <class T>
T Cuboid <T> ::volume()
{return x*y*z ;}
```

PROGRAM 16.12 – Illustrates definition of template member functions outside the class template. Constructor is defined inside the class.

```
#include <iostream>
using namespace std;
template <class T>   // Declaration of class template
```

```
class Cuboid {
 public:
  T x , y , z ;
 Cuboid (T L, T W, T H){x = L; y = W; z = H ;} // constructor
 T surface_area( ); // function prototype in the class body
 T volume( );  // function prototype in the class body
 };    // end of class
 template <class T > // definition of function surface area
 T Cuboid <T>::surface_area()
  {return 2*(x*y +y*z +z*x);}
 template <class T >   // definition of function volume
 T Cuboid <T>::volume()
  {return x*y*z ;}
int main()
 {Cuboid <int> C1(5,6,4); // Object with int dimensions
  Cuboid <double> C2(2.2,3.5,4.5) ; // An object with dimensions
      // in floating point numbers.
 cout << "Volume of C1= " << C1.volume()<<"\n";
 cout<< "Volume of C2 = " << C2.volume()<<"\n";
 cout<<"surface area of C1 = " << C1.surface_area()<<"\n";
 cout<<"surface area of C2 = " << C2.surface_area()<<"\n";
 return 0 ;
  }
```

The expected output of the above program is given below.

```
Volume of C1= 120
Volume of C2 = 34.65
surface area of C1 = 148
surface area of C2 = 66.7
```

The class object C1 has integer type data while object C2 has data of type double. The class template processes both types of data.

In the following program dealing with class template, all the function prototypes including the constructor function are declared in the class template and defined outside the class template.

PROGRAM 16.13 – Illustrates class template with all functions defined outside the class.

```
#include <iostream>
 using namespace std;
 template <class T>
 class Cuboid {
 public:
```

```
Cuboid (T , T, T ); // constructor prototype

 T surface_area( ); // prototype of surface_area ()
 T volume( );    // prototype of volume () function

private:
T x , y, z;
} ;

template < class T> // definition of constructor function
Cuboid <T>::Cuboid <T> ( T L, T W, T H ) { x = L; y= W; z=H ;}

template < class T>  // definition of surface_area ()
T Cuboid <T>::surface_area()
{ return 2*(x*y +y*z +z*x);}

template < class T>  // definition of function volume
T Cuboid <T>::volume()
{ return x*y*z ;}
 int main()
{
Cuboid <int> C1(5,6,4);
 Cuboid <double> C2(2.5,3.5,4.5) ;

cout << "Volume of C1= " << C1.volume()<<"\n";
cout << "Volume of C2= " << C2.volume()<<"\n";

cout << "surface area of C1 = "<< C1.surface_area()<<"\n";
cout << "surface area of C2 = "<< C2.surface_area()<<"\n";
 return 0 ;
 }
```

The expected output of the program is given below.

```
Volume of C1= 120
Volume of C2= 39.375
surface area of C1 = 148
surface area of C2 = 71.5
```

16.7 FRIEND FUNCTION TEMPLATE TO CLASS TEMPLATE

The declaration of friend function template in the class is similar to the non-template function declaration. The definition of friend function is done outside the class without the scope resolution operator.

The following program illustrated the declaration of a friend function template with name Area in a class template called Rect which deals with rectangles. The class template includes private data i.e., sides of rectangle, constructor function and declaration of friend function which is defined outside the class. The class object is the argument of the friend function.

PROGRAM 16.14 – Illustrates friend function template to class template.

```
#include <iostream>
using namespace std;

template <class T>
class Rect {
friend T Area (const Rect &R); //declaration of friend function
      // template
private :
 T x;  // x and y are sides of rectangle
 T y;
public :
   Rect (T A, T B) { x = A , y = B; } // constructor
 };        // end of class template
template <class T>      // definition of friend function
 T Area( const Rect <T> &R){ return R.x* R.y ;} // R is an object

int main ()
 {
 Rect<int> myrect(6, 2); // myrect is an object of Rect
 cout<<"Area = " << Area(myrect) << endl;;
 return 0;
  }
```

The expected output is given below.

```
Area = 12
```

PROGRAM 16.15 – Illustrates friend function template to a class template with data of multiple *types*.

```
#include <iostream>
using namespace std;

template <class T, class U> //class template with multiple types
class Rect
{
private :
 T x;
 U y;
public :
 Rect (T A, U B) { x = A , y = B; }
 friend U Area (const Rect &R); // Friend function template
};

#include <iostream>
```

```
using namespace std;

template <class T, class U>
 U Product ( T x, U y)
  {return x*y;}

template <class T, class S, class U>
 S Product ( T x, S y, U z)
  {return x*y*z;}

int main ()
{ int a (1);
    double B(1.5);
     char Ch('D');

cout<<"Product (a,B,Ch) = "<< Product (a,B,Ch)<< endl;;
cout<<"Product (a,B) = "<< Product (a,B)<< endl;

cout <<"Product ( 'A', 4.5, 6) = " <<Product ('A', 4.5, 6)<<endl;
return 0;
}
```

The expected output is given below.

```
Product (a,B,Ch) = 102
Product (a,B) = 1.5
Product ( 'A', 4.5, 6) = 1755
```

The following program is another example of a friend function template to a class template.

PROGRAM 16.16 – Illustrates another application of friend function template to class a template.

```
#include <iostream>
 using namespace std;

template <class T>   // type declaration
class Cuboid {    // beginning of class template
 private:
 T x , y, z;
 public:
 Cuboid ( T, T, T); // constructor prototype
 T surface_area( );

 T volume( );
      // Friend function template
 friend T costpaint ( T, const Cuboid <T> &C);

 } ;   //end of class Cuboid
```

```
template < class T> // definition of constructor outside class
 Cuboid <T> :: Cuboid<T>( T L, T W, T H) { x = L ;y = W ; z =H ;}

template <class T>  // definition of function surface area
 T Cuboid <T>::surface_area()
 {return 2*(x*y +y*z +z*x);}

template <class T>   // definition of volume
 T Cuboid <T>::volume()
 {return x*y*z ;}

 //Below is the definition of friend function template

template <class T >
 T costpaint (T Rho, Cuboid<T> &C )
  {return Rho * C.surface_area() ;}

int main()
 {Cuboid <int> C1 (4, 5, 6 ) ;
  Cuboid <double> C2 ( 2.5, 3.0, 4.0 );

 int D1 = 3 ;
 double D2 = 2.0;

cout << "Volume of C1 = " <<C1.volume()<<"\n";
cout<< "Volume of C2 = " <<C2.volume()<<"\n";

cout<<"surface area of C1 = " <<C1.surface_area()<<"\n";
cout<<"surface area of C2 = " <<C2.surface_area()<<"\n";

cout <<"cost of painting P1 = " <<costpaint ( D1 ,C1 )<<"\n";
cout<<"cost of painting P2 = " <<costpaint (D2 , C2 )<<"\n";

return 0 ;
}
```

The expected output is given below.

```
Volume of C1 = 120
Volume of C2 = 30
surface area of C1 = 148
surface area of C2 = 59
cost of painting P1 = 444
cost of painting P2 = 118
```

16.8 FRIEND CLASS TEMPLATE TO A CLASS TEMPLATE

The process of declaration of friend class template is similar to that for non template classes except for the type of variables involved. It is illustrated in the following program in which a friend class template is declared by name paint. The class paint is declared as friend to class Cuboid. The declaration of the class paint is illustrated below.

```
template <class U > class paint ;
```

In the body of class Cuboid, the class paint is declared as

```
friend class paint;
```

PROGRAM 16.17 – Illustrates friend class template to a class template.

```
template <class U> class paint;

#include <iostream>
using namespace std;

template <class T>
class Cuboid {
friend class paint; // declaration of class paint as friend
public:
Cuboid ( T, T, T); // constructor protoype of class Cuboid

T surface_area(); //Prototypes of area() and volume()
T volume();

private:
T x, y, z;   // x , y and z are of same type
} ;    // End of class Cuboid

template < class T> // constructor definition for class Cuboid
Cuboid <T> :: Cuboid<T>( T L, T W, T H) { x = L ;y = W ; z =H ;}

template <class T>  // definition of function area()
T Cuboid <T>::surface_area()
  {return 2*(x*y +y*z +z*x);}

template <class T>  // Definition of function volume
T Cuboid <T>::volume()
  {return x*y*z ;}

template <class U>  // class paint
class paint {   //definition of class paint

private:
U Rho;
public:
paint (U);  // prototype of constructor
paint(){Rho =2;}; // default constructor
U cost( U Rho,U surface_area ) // Definition of cost().
{
U CP; // CP = cost of paint
CP = Rho* surface_area ;
return CP;}
};    // end of class paint
```

```
template < class U>  // constructor for class paint.
paint<U>:: paint<U>( U D ) { Rho = D;}
int main()
{ Cuboid <int> C1 (4, 5, 6 ) ;
Cuboid <int> C2 ( 2, 3, 4);
paint <int> P1;
paint <int> P2;
int R1 =2;
int R2 = 3;
cout << "Volume of C1 = " <<C1.volume()<<"\n";
cout<< "Volume of C2 = " <<C2.volume()<<"\n";
cout<<"surface area of C1 = "<<C1.surface_area()<<"\n";
cout<<"surface area of C2 = "<<C2.surface_area()<<"\n";
cout <<"cost of painting P1 = "<<P1.cost(7 ,C1.surface_area())<< "\n";
cout<<"cost of painting P2 = "<< P2.cost (7 , C2.surface_area() )<<"\n";
return 0 ;
}
```

The expected output is given below.

```
Volume of C1 = 120
Volume of C2 = 24
surface area of C1 = 148
surface area of C2 = 52
cost of painting P1 = 1036
cost of painting P2 = 364
```

16.9 TEMPLATE CLASS FOR COMPLEX VARIABLES

The header file <complex> contains the template class for manipulation of complex type variables. The following program illustrates some arithmetic operation on complex variables by including this file in the program. A variable consists of a pair of values, i.e. the real and the imaginary values.

PROGRAM 16.18 – Illustrates manipulation of complex variables.

```
#include<iostream>
#include<complex>
using namespace std;
int main ()
{ complex <double> a(4.5, 5.5)  ;
complex <int> b(2,3) ;
complex <int> g(3,4) ;
complex<double> e (1.4, 3.4);
complex <double> C = a + e ;
```

```
 complex <int>D = g - b;
 complex<int> Product = b*b ;
cout<<"a = " <<a<<"\t"<<"b = "<<b <<"\n";
cout<<"C= "<<C<<"\t"<<"D = "<<D <<"\n";
cout << "Product b*b = "<< Product<<endl;
return 0;
}.
```

The expected output is given below

```
a = (4.5,5.5)  b = (2,3)
C= (5.9,8.9)   D = (1,1)
Product b*b = (-5,12)
```

EXERCISES

1. What is a function template?
2. What is a class template?
3. What do you understand by generic programming?
4. How do you declare a function template?
5. How would you declare a function template for displaying an array?
6. How do you define a function template when all the parameters are of same type?
7. What is a function template specialization?
8. What is a class template specialization?
9. How do you declare function template which involves more than one type parameters?
10. Can a function template be overloaded? If so how can it be done?
11. How do you define a friend function template for functions having more than one type of parameters?
12. How do you define a class template for multiple type object data?
13. Give an example of declaration of a friend function template to a class template.
14. How do you declare a class template as friend to another class template?
15. Why is class template called parameterized type?
16. Make a program for a function template for calculation of area of regular polygons. Make a test program and calculate areas of a square and hexagon having side =10 units.
17. Make a template program to determine greater of two numbers of different types.
18. Make a function template program which can swap two variables which may be int, floats or characters.
19. Make function template program to swap elements of arrays which may be arrays of integers, arrays of characters or arrays of double numbers.
20. Make program for display function template for output of integers, floating point numbers, characters and strings.
21. Make a program for function template to find out and display the smaller of the two numbers which may be integers or floating decimal point numbers or characters.
22. Make a program for class template by name Cubic which finds out the surface area of rectangular prismatic components.

❍❍❍

CHAPTER

17 C++ Strings

17.1 INTRODUCTION

Standard Template Library (STL) has defined three types of containers, i.e. first class containers, adapters and near containers (see Chapter 21). There are three near containers which have some functions similar to other containers and thus some aspects of their behaviour are similar to those of containers. For instance, these containers support **iterators** and have functions like **begin** () and **end** (), etc. The near-containers are bitsets, valarray and C++ strings. We have already discussed the C-strings in Chapter 10 which are pointer based arrays terminated by Null character. C++ strings belongs to a class template string. Its header file is **<string>**. C++ strings are functionally an improvement over C-strings. For example, many of the operators commonly used on fundamental type variables cannot be used on C-strings, though the individual elements of a C-string may be treated as elements of an array. Above all, a C-string is a fixed length string. Its length cannot be changed after its declaration. All these limitations are not there in C++ strings. The C++ strings can be assigned as a whole and can be modified during execution of program. The operators =, !=, ==, >, <, >= , <=, +, << and >> can be applied to C++ strings in the same way as we apply them on variables of fundamental types. A C++ string is a dynamic string, i.e. the length (number of elements) may be changed during execution of the program. For working with C++ strings we have to include the header file **<string>** in the program. A C++ string is declared as below.

```
string identifier ;
```

Here `string` is the name of class or *type* of string object and *identifier* is name of object.

17.2 CONSTRUCTION OF C++ STRINGS

A number of constructors are provided in the string class. C++ string may be constructed by any of the following methods.

(i) By declaring an empty string.
(ii) By declaring and initializing with string of characters in double quotes.
(iii) By assigning a number of copies of a character to the string.
(iv) As a copy of another string.
(v) As substring of current string by specifying index location and number of characters.
(vi) A substring of current string by specifying the iterator start to iterator end.

The methods mentioned above are illustrated in Program 17.1 below. In this program the string S is not initialized so it is string without any element. This is tested with function `empty()`. The string Str1 is declared and initialized by a string of characters in double quotes. String Str2 is declared to have 6 elements each equal to 'B'. String Str3 is copy of string Str1. Str4 is a substring of Str1. It contains 7 characters of string Str1 starting from its 8th character. String 5 is a substring of Str1 and has elements starting from element at the location iterator `(Str1.begin()+3)`, i.e. from 4th element to iterator Str1.end(), i.e. to end of Str1. String Str6 is constructed by the first 8 characters of another string given in double quotes.

PROGRAM 17.1 – Illustrates methods of constructing C++ strings.

```
#include <iostream>
#include <string>          //include header file <string>
using namespace std;
int main(){
string S ;
if(S.empty())          // Test if the string S is empty
cout<< "S is empty"<<endl;
string Str1;
Str1 = "YOU ARE WELCOME!"; /* Initialization by characters in double quotes
(" ") */
string Str2 (6,'B');     // Str2 is constructed by 6 'B's
string Str3 (Str1);     // Str3 is a copy of Str1
string Str4(Str1,8, 7);  // Str4 is constructed by 7 characters
                    //of Str1 starting from 8th character.
  string Str5 (Str1.begin()+3, Str1.end()); /*Str5 constructed by iterator
(begin()+ 3) i.e., 4th element of Str1 to end.*/
string Str6  ( "YOU ARE WELCOME!", 8);
//Str6 is constructed by first 8 characters of string in double quotes
cout<<"Str1 = "<<Str1<<endl;
cout<<"Str2 = "<<Str2<<endl;;
  cout<<"Str3 = "<<Str3<<endl;
  cout<<"Str4 = "<<Str4<<endl;
  cout<<"Str5 = "<<Str5<<endl;
  cout<<"Str6 = "<<Str6<<endl;
  return 0;
    }
```

The expected output is given below. The output is made self explanatory with the comments included in the program.

```
S is empty
Str1 = YOU ARE WELCOME!
Str2 = BBBBBB
Str3 = YOU ARE WELCOME!
Str4 = WELCOME
Str5 =  ARE WELCOME!
Str6 = YOU ARE
```

17.3 C++ STRING CLASS FUNCTIONS

A number of functions supported by the C++ strings along with brief description of each are listed in Table 17.1. Below in Program 17.2 we illustrate the application of one of the functions, i.e. `compare()` which is used to compare two strings or substrings. The function returns –1, 0 and 1 respectively if the string being compared with the current string is lexicographically (dictionary style) is greater than, equal to or less than the current string. For example Z is lexicographically greater than any alphabet between A to Y. Similarly S is greater than K. See the following program.

PROGRAM 17.2 – Illustrates application of function **compare()** to strings.

```
#include <iostream>
#include <string>
using namespace std;

int main()
 {string Str1, Str2, Str3, Str4 ;
   Str1 = "Calcutta";
    Str2 = "Delhi";
      Str3 = "Delhi";
        Str4 = "ZA";

 cout<< "Str1 = " << Str1 <<",  Str2 = " << Str2 <<endl;
 cout<<"Str3 = " << Str3 <<", Str4 = " << Str4  <<endl;
 cout << "Str1.compare (Str2) = "<< Str1.compare (Str2)<<endl;

 cout << "Str2.compare (Str3) = " <<Str2.compare (Str3)<<endl;
 cout << "Str4.compare (Str2) = " <<Str4.compare (Str2)<<endl;
 cout << "Str3.compare (Str4) = " <<Str3.compare (Str4)<<endl;
 return 0;
 }
```

The expected output is given below.

```
Str1 = Calcutta,  Str2 = Delhi
Str3 = Delhi,  Str4 = ZA
Str1.compare (Str2) = -1
Str2.compare (Str3) = 0
Str4.compare (Str2) = 1
Str3.compare (Str4) = -1
```

Among the above three strings, ZA is greatest of all, Z is greater than all other alphabets in upper case. Similarly Delhi is greater than Calcutta, because D is greater than C. So the result is quite obvious.

Table 17.1 – C++ string class functions and their description

Function	Description
append()	The function is used to append a substring at the end of current string. For details see Program17.3.
assign()	The function assigns (i) a string or (ii) a specified number of characters of a string or (iii) a substring to the current string. For details see Program 17.3.
at()	The function returns reference to an element at the indexed location. See Program 17.3 for illustration.
begin()	Returns iterator to the first element of the string. See Programs 17.1& 17.4
C_str()	Returns a const pointer to a C-string which is identical to the current C++ string. C-strings are terminated by Null character.
capacity()	Returns the maximum number of elements that the current memory allocation can hold. See Program 17.3 for its application.
clear()	The function deletes all elements of the string.
compare()	The function returns –1, 0 and 1 respectively if the string being compared *lexicographically* (i.e. dictionary style) is bigger than, equal to or smaller than the current string. For illustration see Program 17.2 and 17.4.
copy()	The function copies specified number of characters of current string. For illustration see Program 17.6.
data()	Function returns a pointer to the first element of current string. See Program 17.6 for illustration.
empty()	Returns true if there are no elements in the string. Returns false if string is not empty. See Program 17.1 and Program 17.4 for illustration.
end()	It returns iterator pointing to just past the end of string. See Program 17.1 and Program 17.4 for illustration.
erase()	The function erases specified elements of the string. For illustration see Program 17.4.

Contd...

Function	Description
`find()`	Returns location of first occurrence of a string/substring in the current string. For illustration see Program 17.6.
`find_first_not_of()`	It returns index of the first occurrence of a character of current string which does not match any character of specified string.
`find_first_of ()`	The function returns index of first occurrence of a character that matches a character of given string.
`find_last_not_of()`	The function returns index of the last occurrence of a character of current string which does not match any character of given string.
`find_last_of()`	The function returns index of last occurrence of a character that matches a character of given string.
`getline()`	The function is used to read strings from I/O stream.
`insert()`	Function is used to insert characters or substring in various ways in a current string.
`length()`	It returns the number of elements in the string without Null character.
`max_size()`	Returns the maximum number of elements that can be held in the presently allocated memory for the string.
`rbegin()`	It returns a reverse iterator to end of string.
`rend()`	It returns a reverse iterator to beginning of string.
`replace()`	Function is used to replace elements in various ways.
`reserve()`	It sets the capacity of string to minimum size.
`resize()`	Function changes the size of string to specified size. If the value of elements is also specified the newly created elements are initialized to that value.
`rfind()`	Function returns the first occurrence of string in the current string by reverse search from given index.
`size()`	Function returns current number of elements in the string. See Program 17.3 and Program 17.4 for application.
`substr()`	It returns substring of specified number of elements (n) out of the current string from the specified location. (Program 17.4).
`swap()`	It exchanges (swaps) the elements of two strings.

17.4 APPLICATIONS OF SOME C++ STRING CLASS FUNCTIONS

The application of functions `append()`, `assign ()`, `at()`, `capacity()` and `size()` is illustrated in the following program. The function size() gives the actual number of elements in the string while capacity gives the maximum number of elements that may be held in the current allocation of memory for the string.

PROGRAM 17.3 – Illustrates application of functions **append(), assign (), at(), capacity()** and **size ()**.

```
#include <iostream>
#include <string>
using namespace std;
int main()
 {string Str1, Str2, Str3 ;
Str1 = "you are welcome!";
Str2 = "If you want to learn C++,";
Str3 = "If you want to join this college,";

 cout<< "Size of Str1 = "<<Str1.size ()<<endl;
 cout<< "Capacity of Str1 = " << Str1.capacity()<<endl;
 cout<<"Before appending \nStr1 ="<< Str1;
 cout<<"\nStr2 = " << Str2<<"\nStr3 = "<< Str3<<endl;

 Str2.append(Str1);     // Str1 is appended at back of Str2
 Str3.append (Str1);      // Str1 is appended at back of Str3

cout<<"After appending\nStr2 = "<< Str2 <<"\n"<<"Str3 = "<< Str3 <<endl;

 Str1.assign (Str2);  // Str2 is assigned to Str1
 cout<< "After assigning \nStr1 = "<<Str1<<endl;
cout<<"The element at location 5 of Str2 is "<<Str2.at(5)<< endl;
 return 0 ;
  }
```

The expected output is as under.

```
Size of Str1 = 16
Capacity of Str1 = 31
Before appending
Str1 = you are welcome!
Str2 = If you want to learn C++,
Str3 = If you want to join this college,
After appending

Str2 = If you want to learn C++, you are welcome!
Str3 = If you want to join this college, you are welcome!
After assigning
Str1 = If you want to learn C++, you are welcome!
The element at location 5 of Str2 is u
```

The output given above is self explanatory. The output shows the difference between `size()` and `capacity()`. The statement `Str1.size()` gives the current number of elements in Str1 as 16 while it has capacity for 31 elements.

FUNCTION ERASE()

The function may be used for the following.

(i) To erase the entire string the code is given below and an illustration is given in Program 17.4.

```
Str.erase();
```

(ii) To erase a specific number of characters starting from a specified location. Say we want to erase 3 characters of string Str starting from index 4. The code is as below.

```
Str.erase(4,3);
```

(iii) To erase all character of string Str starting from a position (say 10) to end of string. The code is given below.

```
Str.erase (10);
```

PROGRAM 17.4 – Illustrates **substr(), begin(),end(),compare()**and **erase().**

```
#include <iostream>
#include <string>
using namespace std;

int main()
 {
string Str1, Str2, Str3 ;
Str1 = "You are welcome to this meeting";
Str3 = "Mahrashtra";

  cout << "Size of Str1 = "<<Str1.size ();
  cout << "\nSize of Str3 = "<<Str3.size();

  cout<<"\nInitial Str1 = "<<Str1<<endl;
  cout<<"Str1.substr(4,11 ) = "<<Str1.substr(4,11)<<endl;

  Str2 = "You are going to learn C++" ;
  cout<<"Str2 = "<<Str2<<endl;

 string :: iterator itr1 =Str2.begin() ;  // for iterators see
 string :: iterator  itr2 = Str2.end(); //Chapter21, Section 21.3

 Str2.erase (itr1+3, itr1+16);
 cout<<"After  Str2.erase ( itr1+3, itr1+16) = "<<Str2<<endl;
 Str2.erase (4);
 cout<<"After Str2.erase(4) = " <<Str2<<endl;

 Str2.erase();
```

```
if ( Str2.empty ())
 cout<<"After Str2.erase() Str2 is empty."<<endl;
  return 0;
 }
```

The expected output is given below.

```
Size of Str1 = 31
Size of Str3 =10
Initial Str1 = You are welcome to this meeting
Str1.substr(4,11 ) = are welcome
Str2 = You are going to learn C++
After Str2.erase (itr1+3, itr1+16) = You learn C++
After Str2.erase(4) = You
After Str2.erase() Str2 is empty.
```

The first two lines of output give the size of string Str1 and string Str3. The fourth line of output consists of a substring of Str1 which contains 11 characters starting from 4th character. In the next line of output the effect of erasing from 4th element to 17th element of Str2 leaves You learn C++. It is erased again from 4th element to end, so only You is left. It is again erased by erase() which erases it completely.

17.5 STRING CLASS OPERATORS

The following operators are supported by class string.

```
= , ==, !=, < , > , <=, >= , + , << and >>
```

Let us have three strings S1 , S2 and S3 as declared below.

```
string S1 ("welcome!") ;
string S2 ("You are") , S3 ;
```

The operator + may be used as it is used with fundamental types (See Prog.17.5). Thus we can write

```
S3 = S2 + S1;
```

The above operator + appends S1 at back of S2 and we get the following.

```
S3 = "You are welcome!";
```

Similarly we may add a character to a string. Thus, let string S be given as

```
string S = orange;
```

The operation S +'s' will add s at end of string S. After the addition S = "oranges".

FUNCTION GETLINE()

The function getline() for a string is coded as below,

```
string Str;
getline (cin, str) ;
```

The application of the function is illustrated in the following program. The program also illustrates application of some operators on strings.

PROGRAM 17.5 – Illustrates action of operators on strings.

```
#include <iostream>
#include <string>
using namespace std;
int main()
{
string Str1(" YOU ARE WELCOME!"), Str2("Nikita,") ;
 cout << "Str1 = "<<Str1<<endl;
   string Str3;
     Str3= Str2+Str1;
      cout<<"Str3 = "<< Str3 << endl;

string S1 = "Orange";
 string S2 = "ointer";
   string S3 = "P";
     char ch = 's';
       string S4=  S1 + ch;

S2 = S3+S2;
   cout<<"S1 = "<< S1<<"\tS4 ="<<S4 <<"\tS2 = "<<S2 <<endl;
     string S5;
       cout<<"Write a small sentence\n";

getline(cin, S5);
 cout<<"S5 = "<<S5<<endl;

if ( Str1> S5)
   cout<< "Str1 is greater than S5"<<endl;
else
   cout <<"Str5 is bigger than S1."<<endl;
if (S1==Str1)
   cout<< "S1 and Str1 are equal"<<endl;
else
   cout<< "S1 and Str1 are not equal"<<endl;
if (S4>S1)
   cout << "S4 is greater than S1"<<endl;
else
   cout << "S1 is greater than S4"<<endl;
 return 0;
 }
```

The expected output is given below. The output is self explanatory.

```
Str1 =  YOU ARE WELCOME!
Str3 = Nikita, YOU ARE WELCOME!
S1 = Orange    S4 =Oranges    S2 = Pointer
```

```
Write a small sentence
He is going to office.

S5 = He is going to office.
Str5 is bigger than S1.
S1 and Str1 are not equal
S4 is greater than S1
```

Functions data(), find(), copy()

The code `Str.data ()` returns pointer to the first element of the string Str. Function find() returns the position of first occurrence of a string/substring in the current string. The function `copy ()` makes a copy of specified number of characters of a string. The following program illustrates the application of the two functions along the function compare used in if condition.

PROGRAM 17.6 – Illustrates the application of functions **data(), find()** and **copy().**

```
#include <iostream>
#include <string>
using namespace std;
int main()
 {
string Str1, Str2, Str3, Str4 ;

Str1 = "You are welcome!";
Str2 = Str1;                    // assignment
cout<<"Str2 = "<<Str2;

Str3 = "If you want to join this college,";
cout<<Str3;
cout<< "\ndata = "<< Str2.data();

 if ( (Str1.compare(Str2)) ==0)
   cout << "\nStr1 and Str2 are equal"<<endl;
 else
   cout << "Str1 and Str2 are not equal" <<endl;
cout<<"In Str1 substring com occurs at "<<Str1.find("com")<<endl;
  char S[12];         // C-type string or array of characters
   memset(S,'\0',12) ;  //The function memset()fills the 12
              //elements of array S with Null character

Str3.copy( S, 11);   //copy first 11 characters of Str3
```

```
cout<<"Number of characters copied = "<< Str3.copy( S ,11)<<endl;
// Display number of characters copied
  cout<<S<<endl;        // Display the C-string S
  cout<<Str3<<endl;      // Display Str3
  return 0;
}
```

The expected output is given below.

```
Str2 = You are welcome!
If you want to join this college,
data = You are welcome!
Str1 and Str2 are equal
In Str1 substring com occurs at 11
Number of characters copied = 11

If you wan

If you want to join this college,
```

FUNCTION **find_first_not_of( ) , find_last_not_of( )**

find_first_of( ), find_last_of() and replace()

The code for the first function for Str1 and Str2 would be coded as

Str2.find_first_not_of(Str1);

The return value of the function is the index value of the first element of Str2 which is not an element of Str1. The second function may be coded as

Str2.find_last_not_of(Str1);

This function returns the index value of the last element of Str2 which is not a member of Str1. The application of these and the other two functions mentioned above are illustrated in the following program.

PROGRAM 17.7 – Illustrates the application of functions **find_first_not_of()**, **find_last_ not_of()**.

```
#include <iostream>
#include <string>
using namespace std;
int main()
 {
 string Str1, Str2, Str3(6,'B') ;
 Str1 = "YOU ARE WELCOME!";
 Str2 = "Are you going to DELHI";

 cout<<( Str2.find_first_not_of(Str1))<<endl;
 cout<<( Str2.find_last_not_of(Str1))<<endl;
```

```
    cout<<( Str2.find_first_of(Str1))<<endl;
    cout<<( Str2.find_last_of(Str1))<<endl;

    Str3.replace( 1,5 ,"B.L.Juneja");
          //replace 5 elements Str3 starting from index 1.
    cout<< "Now Str3 = "<< Str3<<endl;
    return 0; }
```

The expected output is as under.

```
1       //Comments: the first element is r with index value 1
21            // The last element is I with index value 21.
0             // The first element is A with index value 0
19            // The last element is L with index value 19.
```

Now Str3 = B.L.Juneja //The 0th element is B other Bs are replaced

17.6 ARRAY OF C++ STRINGS

An array of strings may be declared as

```
string S[n];
```

Here *string* is the *type* (name of class), S is the name of array and *n* is the number of strings in the array. Each element of the array is accessed by its index value in the array. The application is illustrated in the following program.

PROGRAM 17.8 – Illustrates array of strings.

```
#include <iostream>
#include <string>
using namespace std;
int main()
{ string S1, S2[4] ,S3;
 string Name[4] = { "Nimi", "Malti", "Narayani", "Shanti"};
   for (int i =0; i < 4; i++)
      S2[i] = Name[i];   // assigning array elements to S2

 for( int k=0; k<4; k++)
 cout<<S2[k]<<" ";          // output of array elements of S2
  S1 = " , You are welcome to C++! ";
 string Msg [4];
 cout<<"\n";

 for( int j =0; j<4; j++)
 {Msg[j] = S2[j]. append (S1); // append S1 to elements of S2
             // and assign the result to elements of Msg[]
 cout << "Msg ["<<j<<"] = " <<Msg[j]<<endl; }

 return 0;
  }
```

The expected output is given below.

```
Nimi Malti Narayani Shanti
Msg [0] = Nimi , You are welcome to C++!
Msg [1] = Malti , You are welcome to C++!
Msg [2] = Narayani , You are welcome to C++!
Msg [3] = Shanti , You are welcome to C++!
```

The output is self explanatory. The program takes an array of names and appends a message at the end of each element (name) of string array. The program also illustrates the assignment of strings.

EXERCISES

1. What is the difference between C-string and C++ string?
2. Do the C++ strings have null character at the end?
3. What are the methods of constructing C++ strings?
4. Which operators can be applied to C++ strings?
5. Do the C-strings also support the operators that are supported by C++ strings?
6. What is the difference between function sizeof() and function capacity ()?
7. What action the following C++ string functions perform?
   (i) append () (ii) assign ()
   (iii) capacity () (iv) size ()
8. What actions the following C++ string functions perform?
   (i) at () (ii) compare ()
   (iii) copy ()
9. What do the following functions of C++ string do?
   (i) data () (ii) find ()
   (iii) find_first_of () (iv) find_last_of()
10. Make program to illustrate the action of following functions of class string.
    (i) reserve () (ii) replace ()
    (iii) max_size()
11. Make a program to illustrate following functions for C++ strings.
    (i) getline () (ii) insert ()
    (iii) length ()
12. Make a program to compare the action of function `length()` of C++ string and function `sizeof()` of C-string.
13. How do you convert a C++ string into a C-string?
14. Make program to illustrate the application of following functions of class string.
    (i) clear () (ii) resize ()
    (iii) refind ()

15. What do you understand by the following statement involving the function erase(). Str is the name of string.
    (i) Str.erase (4,3); (ii) Str.erase (12);
    (iii) Str.erase ()
16. What action takes place when code `str. append (Str2);` is executed.
17. Make a program to illustrate the functions `length()` and `size()`.
18. What is the difference between the string class function size() and the C++ Standard Library function `sizeof()`?
19. Make a program to illustrate the action of operators ==, != and = on strings.

    Answer: The following program illustrates the operators.

PROGRAM 17.9: Illustrates use of relational operators on strings.

```
#include <iostream>
# include<string>
using namespace std;
int main()
 {
string Str1 = "Hello! Good Morning" ;
string Str2 = "Same to you";
string Str3 = "Let us learn C++";
 if( Str3 !=Str2)
cout<<"Str3 and Str2 are different."<<endl;
cout << ( Str1 ==Str2 ? "True ": "False" )<<"\n";
cout << " Before assignment \n Str1 = "<<Str1<<endl;
cout << " and \n Str2 = "<<Str2 <<endl;
Str3 = Str2 = Str1;
cout << "After the assignment"<<endl;
cout<< " Str1= "<<Str1<<"\n Str2 = "<<Str2 <<"\n Str3 = " <<Str3 <<endl;
 return 0 ;
 }
```

The output is given below.

```
Str3 and Str2 are different.
False
Before assignment
Str1 = Hello! Good Morning
and
Str2 = Same to you
After the assignment
Str1= Hello! Good Morning
Str2 = Hello! Good Morning
Str3 = Hello! Good Morning
```

❍❍❍

CHAPTER

18 Exception Handling

18.1 INTRODUCTION

The present day society is increasing becoming dependant on computer systems. Whether it is reservation and ticketing for travel by air, train or bus, telephonic communication by land lines and mobiles, transactions in banks, transactions in stock exchanges, keeping of records by companies as well as government agencies, raising and collection of bills, the systems of credit cards and ATMs, internet system, admission of students in universities, etc., are all controlled by computer systems. So much so that even in sports the decisions of winner or loser in split second finishes are decided by replaying the computer records made during the event. In such an environment it is absolutely necessary that the computer systems (hardware and software) handling these tasks should be highly reliable and should function as expected continuously. However, exceptions do happen either due to failure of a component of hardware system or due to failure of a portion of software/program or due to some unexpected circumstance created during running of the program. The exceptions created due to causes which are unrelated to the program such as hardware problems, usually called *asynchronous exceptions* are not in the scope of present chapter. In this chapter we shall deal with *synchronous exceptions* which are caused in a program which otherwise runs normally, but due to some exceptional input or exceptional conditions like non-availability of computer memory, division by zero etc., runs into problems which may lead to aborting the program.

In C++ language, there is provision to deal with many of the known types of exceptions. A programmer may add exception handling code at the places in the program, where it is feared that problems may arise. If an exception occurs the exception handling code takes care of the problem. Normally the exception handling provision informs the user about the exception (error) when it occurs and also prompts the user for a proper corrective action. For instance, if an improper input is the cause of problem it will ask the user to correct the input data. For other problems remedial measures are provided in the exception handling code included in the program. For some types of errors, the program may also be made fault tolerant. In such cases the program may run normally though in a part, faults have occurred. However, if the exception cannot be handled the exception handling code would call the function **abort()** to terminate the program. In this process, however, there are functions which may be used to inform the user about the type of error that has occurred and that the program is being aborted.

Aborting a program is an extreme step which normally should not be resorted to if it can be managed otherwise. You can think of the problems if the software of a bank fails. In C++ there are provisions to deal with the known exceptions. Below we discuss the types of exceptions and how to deal with them.

18.2 THE try, throw and catch

In C++ the exception handling is managed through three keywords, i.e. **try**, **throw** and **catch**. The programmer has to identify the portions of program where an exception is most likely to occur. For example, user input portion can be one such region where it is likely that a user may enter wrong data. Provision is made so that the user can correct the input data. Another example is that in an integer division in which the denominator may become zero or in floating point numbers the denominator may become a very small quantity leading to overflow problem. The statements for such a portion are placed in a **try** block. A try block starts with keyword **try** which is followed by the statements which are placed in curly braces {}. The try block, generally comprises selection conditions for the values of variable that may lead to an exception. That is the detection mechanism. If an exception is detected it is thrown by using the keyword **throw** as illustrated in the sample code below.

```
try
{statements;        // try and throw block
throw type_exception; //if exception is detected, throw the type
}
catch (type1_exception)   // first catch block
{
statements;
}
catch(type2_exception)   // second catch block
{
statements;
}
```

Note that the throw segment is immediately followed by one or more **catch** blocks. Each catch block starts with the keyword **catch** followed by parentheses () which contains the type of the catch block, this is followed by statements of the block which are enclosed between curly braces {}. **Each catch block has a different *type* to catch.** Here *type* refers to either one of the fundamental data types such as *int, float, double* or *char* or the user defined types, i.e. the name of *class* of the object thrown. The selection of a particular catch block depends on the result of matching the *type* of the throw with the *type* of catch block. Obviously there should not be two catch blocks with same *type.* The whole process is illustrated in the Figure 18.1.

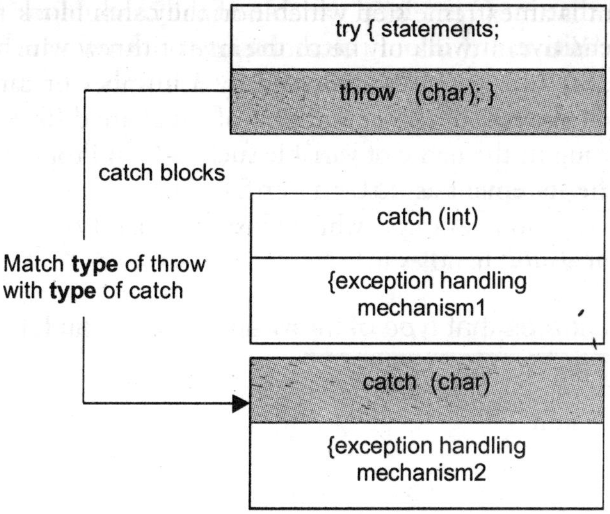

Fig. 18.1: Illustration of try, throw and catch mechanism

The following program illustrates the exception that may occur if division by zero is tried.

PROGRAM 18.1 – Illustrates application of try, throw and catch.

```
#include<iostream>
 using namespace std;
int main ()
 { int A, B ;
  double D;
   cout<<"Enter two numbers ";
    cin>> A>>B;

try        // try block
 { if( B == 0)
    throw B;        // throw
  else
  { D = A/double(B);
   cout << "D = " << D <<endl; }} // End of try block

catch (int C )      // exception handling block starts
 { cout << "You have entered B = 0, enter another number"<<endl;
 }
return 0;
}
```

The expected output when B is put as 0 is given below.

```
Enter two numbers 5 0
You have entered B = 0, enter another number
```

Second trial with the same program in which B = 15 is entered is given below.

```
Enter two numbers 6 15
D = 0.4
```

It should be noted that int C is a local variable of the catch block mentioned above. **The catch process is type sensitive.** It will only catch the *type* of throw which matches with the *type* declared in catch. The try block may be followed by a number of catch blocks each with a different *type* to catch. If the *type* of throw and that of catch are different, the catch block will be skipped. In fact, putting in the name of variable such as C in Program 18.1, is not necessary. We may as well write the statement as `catch(int)`. That is the *type* of the variable thrown. The following program is another example which illustrates that if *type* of object thrown is *double* the catch with argument *double* handles it.

PROGRAM 18.2 – Illustrates that *type* of throw and *type* of catch block should match.

```
 #include<iostream>
 using namespace std;
int main ()
{ int A  ;
 double B , D ;
   cout<<"Enter two numbers ";
    cin>> A>>B;
try          // try block
 { if(B == 0.0)
  throw B;        // throw statement B is double
else
 { D = A/B;
   cout << "D = " << D <<endl; }} // End of try block
catch (int)     // exception handling block for "int" throw
 { cout << "The throw \"int \" is caught"<<endl; }

catch( double) // exception handling block for "double" throw
   { cout <<"The throw \"double\" is caught."<<endl;}
return 0;
}
```

The expected output is shown below. The output shows that the catch *type* which matches with the *type* of throw will handle the exception.

```
Enter two numbers 6 0
The throw "double" is caught.
```

PROGRAM 18.3 – Illustrates that if none of the catch blocks' *types* provided in the program matches the *type* of throw, the program will be aborted.

```
 #include<iostream>
 using namespace std;

int main ()
 {
  int A ;
   double B , D ;
```

```
  char ch = 'C';

cout<<"Enter two numbers ";
cin>> A>>B;

try         // try block
{
 if(B == 0.0)
  throw ch;         // throws a char type
else
 { D = A/B ;
 cout << "D = " << D <<endl; }} // End of try block

catch (int)      // exception handling block for int
 { cout << "The throw \"int \" is caught"<<endl; }

catch( double)  // exception handling block for double
 { cout <<"The throw \"double\" is caught."<<endl;}

return 0;
}
```

None of the catch *types* matches the *type* of throw, i.e. char. So the program is aborted. The following is shown on monitor.

```
abnormal program termination.
```

In the above program, the *type* of throw is *char* while the catch *types* provided are *int* and *double*. So neither of the two catch *types* match thus none of them would work. In such a case the function abort () is called to close the program. The program also shows that the *type* of throw need not be the *type* of variable involved in the exception. The following program shows that the exception thrown may be a class object. In that case the *name of class* is the *type* of exception thrown. When a class object is thrown its *type* is the name of class to which it belongs.

PROGRAM 18.4 – Illustrates that throw is a class object.

```
#include<iostream>
using namespace std;
class Base      // class Base defined
{ };

int main ()
{ Base base_obj ;   //base_obj is an Object of class Base

int A ;
 double B , D ;
 char ch = 'C';
  cout<<"Enter two numbers ";
   cin>> A>>B;
```

```
try    // try block
{
 if(B == 0.0)
  throw base_obj;  // throws an object of class Base
else
 { D = A/B ;
 cout << "D = " << D <<endl; }} // End of try block

catch (int)  // exception handling block for int
 { cout << "The throw \"int \" is caught"<<endl; }
catch(Base)  // exception handling block for class Base
 { cout <<"The throw \"Base\" is caught"<<endl;}

 return 0;
}
```

The expected output is given below.

```
Enter two numbers 6 0
The throw "Base" is caught
```

If the exception thrown is a derived class object, the catch block with base class type can handle it. It is illustrated in Program 18.17 in the exercise 15.

In the following program a class with name Except is defined. It is different from the C++ Std. Library class except. The throw is used with an object Exc of class Except. In the catch statement the *type* is same, i.e. Except, however the object now is Exd. The exception is caught because *type* is same. If more than one exceptions of the same *type* are thrown, then only one catch block is needed for them. In order to differentiate the two exceptions the selection statements are provided in the catch block so that appropriate exception handler may be invoked.

PROGRAM 18.5 – Illustrates that multiple exceptions may be thrown from same try block.

```
# include<iostream>
 using namespace std;

class Except {
 public:
 void Display1( )
{cout<<"There is an exception.\nValue entered for A is negative\n ";
 cout <<"Enter a positive value.\n"; }

void Display2 ()
 {cout<<"The number B entered is zero. \n";
  cout << "Enter a number more than zero.\n" ;}
 };

int main ()
{ Except Exc;
```

```
int A, B ;
double D;
cout<<"Enter two numbers ";
cin>> A>>B;

try
{
if (B == 0)
throw Exc ;
else
if ( A < 0 )
throw Exc;
else
{D = A/ double(B);
cout << "D = " << D <<endl;
}}
catch (Except Exd )
{if ( A < 0)
Exd.Display1();
if ( B == 0 )
Exd.Display2();
}
return 0;
}
```

Two trial runs are carried out. In the first case both the exceptions are thrown and in the second case none of the exceptions is thrown. The expected outputs in the two cases are shown below. Output of first trial is given below.

```
Enter two numbers 4 0
There is an exception.
Value entered for A is negative
Enter a positive value.
The number B entered is zero.
Enter a number more than zero.
Output of second trial is given below.
Enter two numbers 10 5.0
D = 2
```

The try block may have more than one throw statements. Also try block may be followed by more than one catch blocks but their arguments should of different *type*. One catch block can not have two different *types* as arguments, for example the code like `catch (int A, double B)` will result in compiler error. In the following program two different *types* are thrown in the same try block, but it needs two separate catch blocks, one for each *type*.

PROGRAM 18.6 – Illustrates more than one throw from same try block, needing different catch blocks.

```
#include<iostream>
 using namespace std;

int main ()
{ int A ;
 double D, B;
  cout<<"Enter two numbers ";
   cin>> A>>B;
try
{
 if (B == 0)
 throw B;
  if (A > 50)
  throw A;

else
 {D = A/ B;
cout << "D = " << D <<endl;
 }}

catch (double C )

{cout << "You have entered B = 0, enter another number"<<endl;}
catch (int E )
 {cout<< "Enter another number less than 50 for A. "<<endl; }

return 0;
}
```

The expected output is given below.

```
Enter two numbers 60 5
Enter another number less than 50 for A.
```

In the same try block, one may have multiple throws. If the throws are of same type only one catch block is needed. For the information of the user as to which exception is caught, a set of selection statements may be included in the catch block. As is normal with selection statements if one statement is selected the others are neglected.

18.3 CATCH ALL TYPES OF EXCEPTIONS

For catching all *types* of exceptions thrown, the code **catch (…)** may be used. Note that there are only three points in the parentheses. With more or less number of these the compiler may show error. The following program illustrates **catch (…)** .

PROGRAM 18.7 – Illustrates catch(...), i.e. catch all types of exceptions.

```
#include<iostream>
using namespace std;

class Base
{ };

int main ()
{ Base base_obj ;

int A ;
double B , D ;
char ch ;
cout<<"Enter an integer, a double and a character: ";
cin>> A>>B>>ch;

try
 { if(B == 0.0)
  throw base_obj;

 if (A > 50)
     throw A;

 if(ch != 'Z')
     throw ch;
else
 { D = A/double(B);
  cout << "D = " << D <<endl; }} // End of try block

catch (...)   // exception handling block starts
 {
 if ( A >50)
     cout << "The exception on int is caught"<<endl;
 if (B==0)
  cout <<"The exception on Base is caught."<<endl;

 if( ch != 'Z')
  cout <<"The exception on char is caught."<<endl; }
return 0;
}
```

The program has been run twice to test it. In the first trial all the variables are in the range so the program runs normally and following is the output.

```
Enter an integer, a double and a character: 40 6.0 Z
D = 6.66667
```

In second trial all the variables are out of range and following output is obtained.

```
Enter an integer, a double and a character: 56 0 H
The exception on int is caught
The exception on Base is caught.
The exception on char is caught.
```

18.4 EXCEPTION HANDLING FUNCTION

The try-throw and catch sequence may be put in a function. It is convenient to call the function in the main program. The following program illustrates the same.

PROGRAM 18.8 – Illustrates application of exception handling function.

```
#include<iostream>
 using namespace std;
 void Test(int A ,double B, char ch)
 { try

{
 if ( A > 50.0)
 {cout << "A not in range"<<endl;
  throw A; }
 if (B == 0)
 {cout <<"B is equal to zero"<<endl;
  throw B; }
 if (ch != 'D')
 {cout<< "ch is not equal to D"<<endl;
  throw ch; }
 else
 cout<< "All in range. No exception thrown:" <<endl; }

 catch (...)
 { cout<< "Caught an exception "<<endl; }
 }

int main ()
{ int A;
 double B;
 char ch;
 cout<< "Write values of A, B and ch :";
 cin >> A>>B>>ch;
  Test (A,B,ch); // Test function for try, throw and catch
return 0;
}
```

The above program has been run 4 times in order to test its operation for different types of exceptions. The first trial is for a case when all variable are in range and no exception is thrown. The output of this is given below.

```
Write values of A, B and ch :40 6.0 D
All in range. No exception thrown :
```

The second case relates to when only A is not in range, so exception thrown is of type integer. The output is as under.

```
Write values of A, B and ch :60 5.0 D
A not in range
Caught an exception
```

In the third case only B is equal to 0 while other two are in range. So exception thrown is double. The output is as under.

```
Write values of A, B and ch :40 0.0 D
B is equal to zero
Caught an exception
```

In the fourth case the error is in value of character. So an exception of type character is thrown and caught as illustrated in the following output.

```
Write values of A, B and ch :40 5.0 C
ch is not equal to D
Caught an exception
```

18.5 EXCEPTION SPECIFICATION

C++ allows the user to declare a set of exceptions that a function may throw. The exception specification is in fact is a suffix to the normal function head. The suffix comprises the keyword *throw* followed by, in parentheses, the list of exception *types*. A function definition with an exception specification is of the following general form.

type function_identifier (***argument_List***) **throw** (***exception_type_list***) // function head
(***statements***;} // function body

In the above definition the first word *type* is the type of data returned by the function. This is followed by the function name which is followed by arguments list in parentheses and then the suffix which comprises the keyword *throw* followed by a list of exception *types* in parentheses. The function *type* is not affected by the suffix. The exception_type_list as well as the argument_list are optional and hence we may have the following three cases.

(i) **void Function1() throw ()** // Empty exception_type_list, cannot throw an exception.
(ii) **void Function2 () throw (X, Y, Z)** // Can throw X, Y and Z *types* of exceptions only.
(iii) **void Function3 ()** // Can throw any type of exception.

If the function throws an exception which is not in the exception_type_list the function **unexpected()** is called. The default action of the function unexpected is to call the function `abort ()` which terminates the program.

The function with suffix `throw()` cannot throw any exception and if it does the function unexpected is called and the program is aborted. Similarly if the second function with exception_type_list (X, Y , Z) throws an exception other than X, Y or Z the program would be terminated. In the third option (void Function3()), the function can throw any type of exception.

PROGRAM 18.9 – Illustrates exception specification.

```
#include<iostream>
 using namespace std;
void Fexcep (int j ) throw ()  // cannot throw an exception
{
   if ( j== 1)
         throw j;

   if ( j == 2)
  throw char () ;
if ( j==3)
throw double ();}

int main ()
{
int n;
cout << "Enter a number from 1 to 3: ";
cin >> n ;
   try{
   Fexcep(n);
   }   // End of try block

catch (int )  // exception handling block starts
{ cout << "The throw int is caught"<<endl;
 }
catch(double)
{ cout <<"The throw double is caught."<<endl;}

return 0;
}
```

On execution a number 2 is entered, and this throws an exception of *type* char. But the function is with empty exception list. Therefore, the program is terminated. The output is given below.

```
Enter a number from 1 to 3: 2
abnormal program termination
```

PROGRAM 18.10 – Program illustrates that if an exception of the *type* thrown is not in the exception specification list of the function, the program is terminated.

```
#include<iostream>
 using namespace std;
```

```
//The following function can throw int or double
void Fexcep (int j ) throw (int, double)
{
   if (j== 1)
   throw j;

   if (j == 2)
 throw 'D' ;

if(j==3)
throw 0.8;}

int main ()
{ int n;

cout << "Enter a number from 1 to 3: ";
cin >> n ;
   try
 {
 Fexcep(n);
 }   // End of try block

catch (int )  // exception handling block starts
{ cout << "The throw int is caught"<<endl;
 }
catch(double)
{ cout <<"The throw double is caught."<<endl;}

return 0;
}
```

The program is run and number 2 is entered. This corresponds to throwing a char which is not in the specification list. Therefore the program is terminated. The output is given below.

```
Enter a number from 1 to 3: 2
```

On entering 2, the program is terminated with following message.

```
abnormal program termination
```

In the following the exception thrown are implemented because they are in the specification list.

PROGRAM 18.11 – Illustrates implementation of specified exceptions.

```
#include<iostream>
 using namespace std;

void Functspecify ( int j ) throw ( int, double, char)
 {
 if ( j == 1)
  throw j;
```

```
  if ( j ==2)
   throw 0.6;

  if ( j == 3)
   throw 'H';}
 int main ()
 {
 try
 {
 int A (4);
 if ( A != 3)
 Functspecify (1);}

  catch (int )   // exception handling block starts
 { cout << "The exception on int is caught"<<endl;
  }
  try {     // try block
 double B (6.6) ;
 if ( B!=7)

 Functspecify ( 2 );}
  catch (double )   // exception handling block starts
  { cout << "The exception on double is caught"<<endl;
  }

 try {
  char ch = 'C';
  if ( ch != 'H')
  Functspecify ( 3 ) ;}
 catch(char)
  { cout <<"The exception on char is caught."<<endl;}
  return 0;
 }
```

The expected output is given below.

```
The exception on int is caught
The exception on double is caught
The exception on char is caught.
```

18.6 RETHROW AN EXCEPTION

An exception may be caught by a handler and partly dealt with. The programmer may like to rethrow the exception so that it can be dealt again by an outer catch mechanism. For such a case the following code may be included in the catch block, i.e. throw without parentheses.

```
throw ;
```

This code will rethrow the same type of exception so that it can be dealt by outer catch block. The rethrown exception is not caught by the same catch block. It is caught by an outer catch block.

The following program illustrates the rethrow done twice.

PROGRAM 18.12 – Illustrates re-throw of exception.

```
#include<iostream>
using namespace std;

void Rethrow(int A )  //definition of Function Rethrow()
{
try
 { int B;
  cout<<"Enter a positive number : "; cin>> B ;
  if ( B<=0)
  throw B;}

catch (int)
 { cout<<"This catch is inside function."<<endl;
  throw;    // first rethrow
 }}

int main ()
{
 try{

    try {
          Rethrow (6);
    }

 catch(int)
    { cout << "This catch is inner catch inside main."<<endl;
  throw; // second rethrow
    }}

 catch(int)
    {
    cout << "This catch is the outer catch in the main."<<endl;
    }
  return 0;
  }
```

The expected output is given below.

```
Enter a positive number : -10
This catch is inside function.
This catch is inner catch inside main.
This catch is the outer catch in the main.
```

18.7 C++ STANDARD LIBRARY EXCEPTION CLASSES

There are a large number of classes in C++ Standard Library which deal with exceptions. Figure 8.2 shows the hierarchy of prominent exception handling classes in C++. The header file <exception> defines the base class exception. A number of classes are derived from the base class. These include classes on logic_error , runtime_error , bad_alloc, bad_cast, bad_typeid and bad exception. The classes derived from runtime_error are the overflow and underflow errors. Three classes are derived from logic_error class. These are out_of_range, length_error and invalid_argument. The classes on runtime error and logic error are defined in header file <stdexcept>. The four classes, i.e. bad_alloc, bad_cast, bad_typeid and bad_exception are the ones in which exceptions are thrown by operators. The class except also defines a virtual function what() which is overridden by every derived class to convey an appropriate message.

The different classes dealing with exceptions and their inherited classes are illustrated in Fig. 18.2 below. Table 18.1 elaborates the various exception classes.

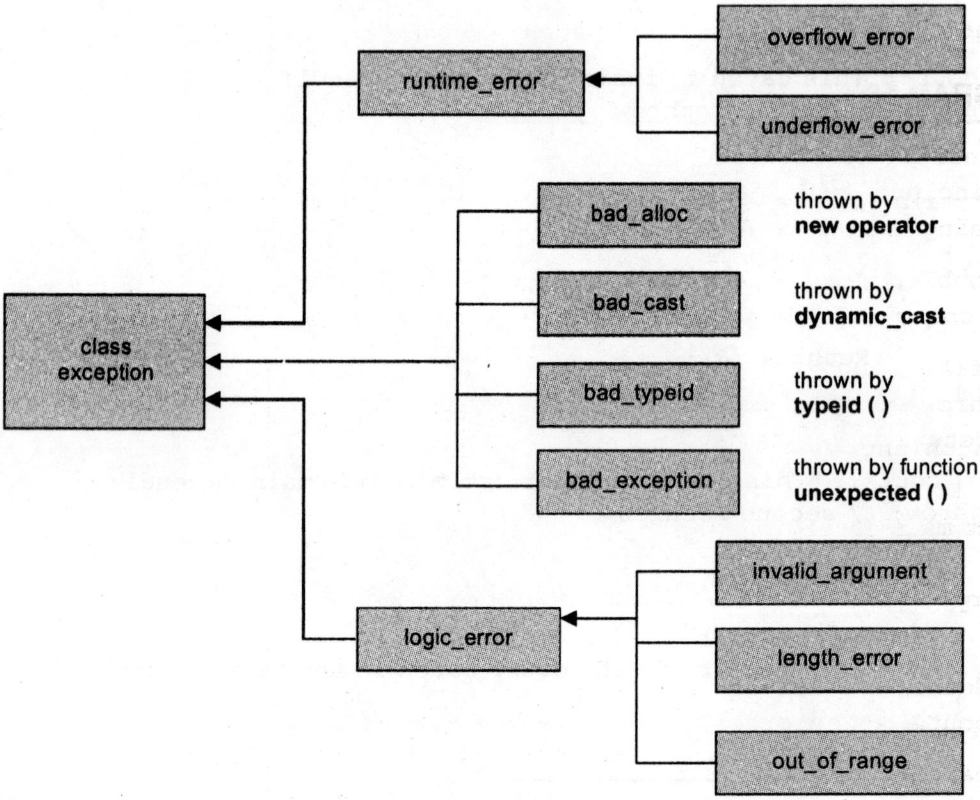

Fig.18.2: Exception classes of C++ Standard Library

Table 18.1

Class	Description
overflow_error	Deals with overflow of a number if it is too big for the computer.
underflow_error	Deals with underflow of number. Number is too small for the computer to store.
bad_alloc	Exception thrown by operator **new** in case of bad allocation of memory (memory not available).
bad_cast	This exception is thrown by **dynamic_cast** if it is unsuccessful.
bad_typeid	Exception thrown by operator **typeid()** if it is unsuccessful.
bad_exception	If an exception, not listed in exception specification occurs the exception bad_exception is thrown by function unexpected(). This may be managed by registering function set_unexpected ().
invalid_argument	For example a negative number for a square root is invalid argument.
length_error	It indicates that a length larger than the one specified for the object is used.
out_of_range	Indicates when a value exceeds the allowed range of values.

The following program is an illustration of application standard exception class.

PROGRAM 18.13 – The program illustrates the application of **overflow_error**.

```
#include <iostream>
#include <stdexcept>
using namespace std;

double Reciprocal(double A) throw (overflow_error)
{ cout<< "Write a small number "; cin>> A ;

if(A < 0.000001)
throw overflow_error ("Reciprocal is too large.");
 return 1/A ;
}

int main ()
{
 try
  {

  double B =0.0;
  cout << "Reciprocal of B = " << Reciprocal(B) <<endl; }

  catch ( exception & x)
  { cout<< "Exception -> " << x.what() <<endl; }

return 0;
}
```

The output when the numbered entered is 0.00000001 is given below.

```
Write a small number 0.00000001
Exception -> Reciprocal is too large.
```

The output, when the number entered is 0.00004, is given below.

```
Write a small number 0.00004
Reciprocal of B = 25000
```

The following program illustrates the throwing of invalid_argument of class exception.

PROGRAM 18.14 – Illustrates standard functions of class <exception>.

```
#include<iostream>
using namespace std;
#include <cmath>
#include <exception>
double Square_root ( int n) throw ( invalid_argument)
{
if ( n < 0)
throw logic_error ("invalid_argument in square root");
 return sqrt (n);}
int main ()
{
   int m;
    cout<< "Enter an integer number ";
  cin >> m ;
try
 {double Square_root (m);
 cout<<"The square root of "<<m<<" is "<<Square_root(m)<< endl;}
catch ( exception& exc)
 {cout << exc.what()<<endl; }
return 0;
 }
```

The output of first run when m =16 is given below.

```
Enter an integer number 16
The square root of 16 is 4
```

The second run with m = –16 gives the following output.

```
Enter an integer number -16
invalid_argument in square root
```

18.8 FUNCTION terminate() and set_terminate()

When an exception is thrown and there is no corresponding catch block or is not caught, the default action is that function `terminate()` is called which by default calls function `abort()` to terminate the program. However, the programmer can have a second option by defining the function `terminate()` and by registering it in the program by the function `set_terminate()`. See the following program for illustration.

PROGRAM 18.15 – Illustrates **terminate()** and **set_terminate()** functions.

```
#include<iostream>
#include<stdexcept>

using namespace std;

void Terminate ()
{ cout<< "An exception has occurred."<<endl;
 cout<<"The program is being terminated."<<endl;
  exit (1);}

int main ()
 { set_terminate (Terminate);
try
{
int A;
cout<< "Enter a number less than 60 : "; cin >> A;

if ( A > 60)
 throw A;
 cout<<"The number entered is "<< A <<endl; }

catch (double)
{ cout<<"Number out of range."<<endl;}
return 0;
}
```

The expected output is given below.

```
Enter a number less than 60 : 70
An exception has occurred.
The program is being terminated.
```

18.9 FUNCTION unexpected() and set_unexpected()

If a function throws an exception which is not listed in the exception specification, the function `unexpected()` is called which by default calls the function `terminate()`, and which in turn calls abort() to terminate the program. The function set_unexpected gives a second option to programmer. Instead of having the default output, the programmer can define his/her own function `unexpected()` which will be called when an unexpected exception occurs. The user defined function `unexpected()` is registered by making the function an argument of the function `set_unexpected()`. One such code is illustrated below.

```
void Unexpect(){ cout<<"Unexpected called"<<endl;
exit(1);}
```

```
void F() throw ( ) // the function cannot throw an exception
{
   throw 4.0 ;} // but it throws double

int main ()

{set_unexpected(Unexpect);

try
{ F();
 }
catch (double)
{ cout<<"double caught"<<endl;}
 return 0;
}
```

18.10 THE auto_ptr CLASS

We have already dealt with dynamic memory allocation through the operator **new**. The operator new allocates memory and returns a pointer and **delete** is used to delete the object and clear the memory. If the memory allocation is not successful it throws an exception bad_alloc. However, if the memory has been successfully allocated then it would not throw an exception bad_alloc. But if an exception happens after the memory has been allocated but before the delete, the allocated memory would not be recovered. The provision of auto_ptr in C++ tries to solve this situation. C++ Standard Library contains the class auto_ptr in the header file **<memory>**. The class provides the facility to allocate memory to objects through a pointer and when the pointer goes out of scope or is removed the object that it points to is also removed.

PROGRAM 18.16 – Illustrates auto_ptr for class objects.

```
# include<iostream>
# include<memory>
using namespace std;
class Rect
{ public:
   Rect (){cout<< "Constructor function called.\n";};
~ Rect(){}
void Func(){ cout <<"It is Rect class function."<<endl;}
};
int main ()
{
   Rect R1;
 Rect* ptrR1 = &R1 ;
 ptrR1 -> Func();

   auto_ptr<Rect> ptr(new Rect), ptr2;
   ptr-> Func();
```

```
    ptr = ptr2;
    ptr2 -> Func();

    return 0;
}
```

The output is given below.

```
Constructor function called.
It is Rect class function.
 Constructor function called.
It is Rect class function.
It is Rect class function.
```

EXERCISES

1. What is an exception in C++?
2. What are the provisions to deal with exceptions?
3. Explain the `try`, `throw` and `catch` method of dealing with exceptions.
4. What do you understand by exception specification?
5. Give an example of a try block.
6. What should match between a throw and catch so that the exception is handled?
7. What are uses of functions `terminate ()` and `set_terminate ()` functions?
8. When do we use the functions `unexpected ()` and `set_unexpected()`?
9. Which exception is thrown by operator `new`?
10. Make a small program to illustrate the working of try, throw and catch mechanism.
11. What is the code for catching all types of exceptions?
12. What types of exceptions the following functions can throw?
    (i) void Function ()
    (ii) void Function(int) throw(int ,double)
    (iii) void Function() throw ()
13. Write a program to illustrate the working of `terminate ()` and `set_terminate()` functions.
14. Write a program to illustrate the function `unexpected()` and the function `set_unexpectd()`.
15. Make a program to show that if derived class object is thrown the catch block with base class *type* would also work.

    Answer:

    PROGRAM 18.17 – Illustrates that throw of derived class object can be handled by a catch block with base class type.

```
#include<iostream>
using namespace std;
```

```
class Base    // class Base defined
{};

class Derived : public Base // Derived class defined.
{};

int main ()
{ Base base_obj ;  //base_obj is an Object of class Base
 Derived D_object;      // D_object is object of derived class

int A ;
 double B , D ;
 char ch = 'C';

cout<<"Enter two numbers ";
cin>> A>>B;

try    // try block
{
 if (B == 0.0)
 throw D_object;  // throws an object of Derived class
 else
 { D = A/B ;
 cout << "D = " << D <<endl; }} // End of try block

catch (int)  // exception handling block for int
{ cout << "The throw \"int \" is caught"<<endl; }

catch(Base)  // exception handling block for class Base
{ cout <<"The throw \"Base \" is caught."<<endl;}
return 0;
}
```

The expected output is given below.

```
Enter two numbers 6.0 0.0
The throw "Base" is caught.
```

The above program illustrates that if the derived class object is thrown in the try block, it can be handled by the catch block with base class *type*.

❍❍❍

CHAPTER

19

Input/Output Streams and Working with Files

19.1 INTRODUCTION

Most of the programs involve some kind of input and output. There are several devices for doing input to a program, for instance, it may be from keyboard connected to computer, it may from a file on the hard disc, on CD ROM, floppy disc, from an internet file or from a control device connected to computer. Similarly the output may be displayed on monitor connected to the computer, it may be directed to printer, to a file on hard disc/floppy disc/CD ROM or to any other device connected to computer. Of all these devices keyboard is regarded as **standard input device** and monitor is regarded as **standard output device**. In the previous chapters we have frequently used **cin** and **cout** for performing input and output. These two objects are defined in the header file **<iostream>** (input/output stream). The cin is meant to do input from the standard input device, i.e. keyboard and cout carries out output to standard output device which is the monitor connected to the computer.

In C++ the input/output (I/O) operations are carried out by member functions of relevant template classes. Therefore, the I/O operations are object oriented and are type sensitive. The I/O of a particular data type is carried out by corresponding member function of the class. If the compiler cannot find a function for the type of data presented, it will give an error signal. For fundamental types the overloaded functions for **insertion operator** (<<) for output, and **extraction operator** (>>) for input are already defined in the header files **<ostream>** and **<istream>** respectively and are inherited by the class **<iostream>** which takes care of both input and output.

Working with files is an important feature of almost all computer applications. The present days applications deal with very large numbers of files. For instance, the computers for mobile service providers may have millions of customer files, the records of calls for more than at least two months may have to be kept which come to trillions of entries. Similarly the central computer for a big bank may have to deal with several million account files. The input/output operations with files are facilitated by header file **<fstream>** which is derived from **<ifstream>**, **<ofstream>** and **<iostream>** header files.

The first part of this chapter deals with input/output streams for console operations and the second part deals with the input/output streams for files.

19.2 I/O STREAMS FOR CONSOLE OPERATIONS

In C++ the I/O operations are carried out by streams (Fig.19.1). A stream is a sequence of bytes. In case of input, the input stream flows from the external device to the main memory of computer and in case of an output, a stream of bytes flows out of main memory to the output device. In case of standard input the stream comes from keyboard and for standard output the stream flows from main memory to the monitor. However, the stream may be redirected from devices other than keyboard in case of input and can be directed to devices other than monitor in case of output. The input and output streams are illustrated in Fig.19.1 below.

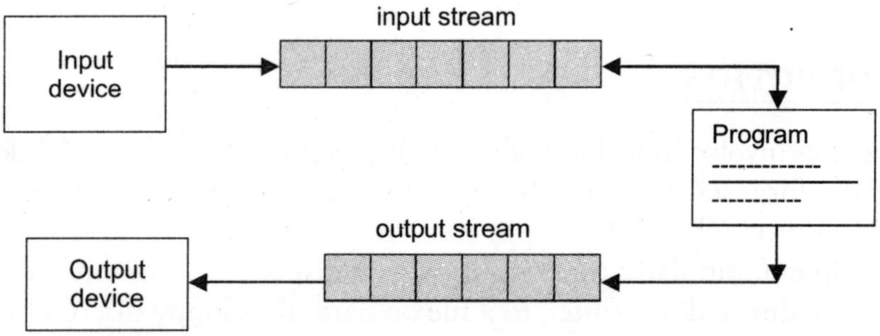

Fig. 19.1: Input/output streams

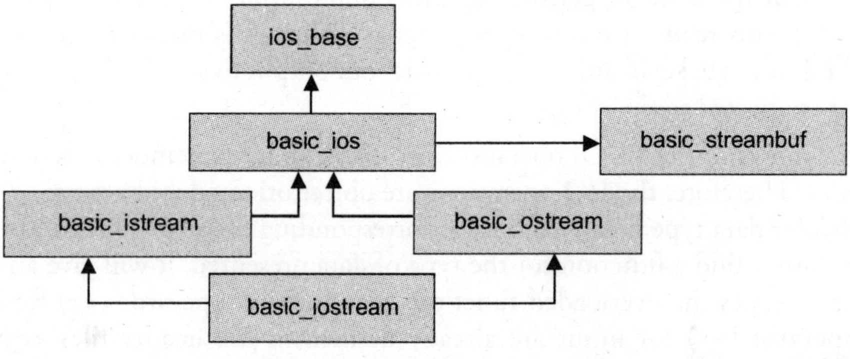

Fig. 19.2: Stream classes for input/output with console

Figure19.2 shows the different classes associated with I/O operations and their hierarchy. The class basic_ios derived from ios_base supports both formatted and unformatted I/O operations. The class **<iostream>** that we have used in all the programs is a typedef of basic_iostream for char. The details of various classes are given below.

ios_base and basic_ios The class **ios_base** is the base class which has functions common to both input and output of formatted as well as unformatted data. The class basic_ios is derived from class ios_base. The classes basic_istream and basic_ostream are derived from basic_ios. The typedef of basic_ios, i.e. **ios,** is used for implementing basic_ios for using char and **wios** is used for implementing it for **wchar_t.**

basic_istream The class basic_istream supports input operations. It is derived from class basic_ios using virtual inheritance. It is implemented by its typedef **istream** for using char. It also defines three functions **get**(), **getline**()and **read**()besides the other functions. Some of these are discussed below. It contains the overloaded stream extraction operator (>>) for C++ fundamental types. The wchart_t is supported by the typedef **wistream.**

basic_ostream The class basic_ostream supports all output operations. It is derived from basic_ios and hence inherits the functions of this class. It defines the function **put**() for writing single character and function **write**() for output of a number of bytes from memory to output device. For implementing it for char its typedef **ostream** is used. For wchar_t the corresponding typedef is **wostream.**

basic_iostream The class basic_iostream supports all input/output operations. It is inherited from basic_istream and basic_ostream through multiple inheritance. Thus it inherits the functions of basic_ios, basic_istream and basic_ostream. For its implementation, its typedef **iostream** is used for using char. For wchar_t the name is **wiostream**. The class **iostream** is contained in header file **<iostream>**. The **iostream** defines four objects **cin, cout** , **cerr** and **clog** which are discussed below. For wchar_t the corresponding objects of **wiostream** are **wcin, wcout, wcerr** and **wclog.**

basic_streambuf The class basic_ios contains the pointer for basic_streambuf . This class provides buffer interface between data and the memory and other physical devices. Its typedef **streambuf** is used for implementing it for char. It supports low level methods of handling streams in which negligible formatting is required. The classes basic_filebuf and basic_strstreambuf are derived from basic_streambuf . The typedefs for char and wchar_t are **streambuf** and **wstreambuf** respectively.

19.3 PREDEFINED STANDARD I/O STREAMS

The following four stream are defined for standard I/O. The extraction operator (>>) and insertion operator (<<) are defined for fundamental types. For user defined types the user has to overload the extraction and insertion operators for a particular class objects.

cin	for input from standard input device-keyboard.
cout	for output to standard output device-monitor
cerr	for standard error output on monitor
clog	for buffered error output on monitor.

Standard Input Stream

The class istream supports methods for input of formatted as well as unformatted data. Its object **cin** along with extraction operator (>>) is used for the input of fundamental types. For user defined types the extraction operator >> is overloaded for the class of input object. In fact the operator >> is the right shift operator which is overloaded to do the extraction operation. After each extraction, the extraction operator sends reference back to cin. This allows cascading operation and we are able to extract a number of values written one after another and each of them preceded by extraction operator. For instance, if it is required to extract values of n, m, A and B we may write the input statement as

```
cin >> n >> m >> A >> B ;
```

The reference sent back by extraction operator may also be used in a loop. The following program illustrates the application of cin.

PROGRAM 19.1 – Illustrates application of cin.

```
#include<iostream>
 using namespace std;
void main()
{ int A ;
 double B ;
   char ch ;
     char Name [10] ;
 cout <<"Enter value of A : "; cin >>A;
 cout <<"Enter the value of B : "; cin >>B ;
 cout <<"Enter the value of ch : "; cin>>ch ;
 cout<<"Enter a short name : "; cin >> Name ;
 cout <<"You have entered the following data."<<endl;
 cout <<"A = "<<A <<" , B = "<<B <<" , ch = "<<ch <<" ,    Name = " <<Name <<
endl;
}
```

The expected output of the program is given below.

```
Enter value of A : 8
Enter the value of B : 5.5
Enter the value of ch : K
Enter a short name : Madhuri
You have entered the following data.
A = 8 , B = 5.5 , ch = K ,  Name = Madhuri
```

Standard Output Stream

For standard output stream we use the object **cout** of class ostream along with overloaded insertion operator <<. The operator << is the left shift binary operator which is overloaded to do the insertion operation for data of fundamental type. For user defined data the overloading functions for operator << are defined by the programmer for the class of the objects being dealt. The return value of insertion operator is the reference to the object of class ostream, which invoked it i.e., cout. This allows the cascading of stream objects. Thus a number of outputs may be written in the same output statement as illustrated below.

```
cout << n << m << A << B;
```

The following program illustrates the application of cout and insertion operator for different types of data.

PROGRAM 19.2 – Illustrates output with object **cout** and insertion operator **<<.**

```
#include<iostream>
 using namespace std;
void main()
{
 int A =4;
  double B =2.5;
   char ch = 'T';
     char Name [] = "Mona";
 cout << A<<endl;
 cout << B <<endl;
 cout << ch<<endl;
 cout<< Name <<endl;
cout<<Name<<" paid rupees "<<B<<" for "<< A <<" apples." <<endl;
}
```

The expected output is given below. The output is self explanatory.

```
4
2.5
T
Mona
Mona paid rupees 2.5 for 4 apples.
```

THE CERR AND CLOG

The cerr and clog are also objects of ostream. The cerr is generally used for handling errors. The cerr does unbuffered (immediate) output on the standard output device, i.e. monitor. The clog is also an object of ostream for carrying out output to standard device, however, the output is buffered. It is also used for error handling.

PROGRAM 19.3 – Illustrates application of **cerr** and **clog** objects of class ostream.

```
#include <iostream>
#include <cmath>  //included for mathematical Functions
using namespace std;

int main()
{
```

```
double x ;
cout<<"Enter a double number: "; cin>>x;

 if ( x<0)
  {cout<<"The sqrt argument is negative"<<endl;
  cout<< "Enter a positive number.\n";
    exit(0);
  }

cout<<sqrt(x)<<endl;

cerr.width(20);
 cerr.fill('*');
  cerr.precision(7);
   cerr<<sqrt(6.0)<<endl;

clog << "The square root of 16 is : "<<sqrt(16)<<endl;
return 0;
}
```

In the first trial the number entered is –10. The expected output is given below.

```
Enter a double number: -10
The sqrt argument is negative
Enter a positive number.
```

In the second trial the number entered is 12 and the expected output is given below.

```
Enter a double number: 12
3.4641
*************2.44949
The square root of 16 is : 4
```

19.4 FUNCTIONS OF <istream> AND <ostream>

Below we discuss the commonly used functions of istream and ostream.

Functions get() and put()

The function `get()` is a member function of class istream and the function `put()` is a member function of class ostream. Both the functions are meant to deal with single character. Thus `get()` is used to read single character from an input device and function `put()` is used to write a character to output device. The arguments for the two functions are discussed below.

The function get()

The function `get()` fetches a single character which includes white space characters and eof. It has to be used with an object of class istream, for example, `cin.get()`. It may be used with void argument such as `cin.get()` or with one argument such as `cin.get(char*)`, with two arguments or three arguments. All these cases are discussed below.

```
cin.get();
char ch;
ch = cin.get()
```

In this case the function get() reads a character and returns the value which is assigned to ch. Program 19.4 illustrates its application in this form. The function get() with single argument is illustrated below.

```
cin.get(char*);
```

In this case the function assigns the input character to its argument. The code is illustrated below.

```
char ch;
cin.get(ch);
```

Program 19.5 illustrates the application in this form. The function get() with two arguments is illustrated below.

```
cin.get(char* buffer, size_t n );
```

In this form the function get() reads one after another the first n – 1 characters into buffer. The last character is the NULL(\0) character which marks the end of string and is appended by the system. The application is illustrated in Program 19.6 below.

```
cin.get(char* buffer, size_t n, char delim );
```

In this form of the function, the number of characters to be read into the buffer is limited either by the number (n – 1) or by the delimiting character *delim* or EOF whichever occurs first. On encountering delimiting character the function stops reading. Even delimiting character is not included. Programs 19.6 and 19.7 illustrate the application of this function.

PROGRAM 19.4 – Illustrates application of **cin.get()**

```
#include<iostream>
using namespace std;
int main ()
{
char ch ;
 cout <<"Write a character :";
  ch = cin.get();
   cout <<"The character ch = "<< ch << endl;
 return 0;
}
```

The expected output is given below.

```
Write a character :B
The character ch = B
```

The following program illustrates the second version `cin.get(ch)`.

PROGRAM 19.5 – Illustrates application of function **get()** in the form **cin.get(ch).**

```
#include<iostream>
using namespace std;
int main ()
{
char ch ;
cout <<"Write a character : ";

cin.get(ch);
cout <<"Character ch = "<< ch;
cout<<"\n";
return 0;
}
```

The expected output is given below.

```
Write a character : B
Character ch = B
```

The following program illustrates the function cin.get () with two arguments.

`cin.get(char*buffer, size_t n);`

In this form the function reads into buffer the characters one by one till the total number is n – 1 or it is end of file. The nth character is the Null character appended by the system.

PROGRAM 19.6 – Illustrates the function **cin.get()** with two arguments.

```
#include <iostream>
using namespace std;
void main()
{
int i =0;
  char B[20];
   cout<<"Enter a name : " ;
          cin.get (B,6); // reads only 5 -one less than 6
// The last character is '\0'appended by system.
cout <<"You have written ; "<< B <<endl;
}
```

The expected output is given below. The output shows that 5 characters have been read.

```
Enter a name : Madhuri
You have written ; Madhu
```

The following program illustrates the function cin.get() with three arguments, i.e. in the following form.

```
cin.get( char* buffer, size_t n, char delim )
```

Here (n – 1) is the maximum number of characters that may be read. It also includes a delimiting character, i.e. char *delim*. If this character is encountered the function stops reading even though the number (n – 1) is not reached. See Program 19.7 below for illustration.

Function getline()

The function is used with istream object for reading complete line, for instance, cin.getline(). It can take two or three arguments as illustrated below.

```
char Buffer [ ]= "Learn C++";
cin.getline( Buffer, size_t n);
cin.getline( Buffer, size_t n, char delimit);
```

The application of the function is already demonstrated in Chapter 10 in programs 10.9, 10.10 and 10.11. Also see the following program.

PROGRAM 19.7 – Illustrates the function `cin.get()` and `cin.getline()`.

```
#include <iostream>
using namespace std;
void main()
 { char ch = 'r'; //below 'r' is used as a delimiting character.
 char C[30] ;
    cout << "Enter a name : ";
    cin.getline(C,30);
  cout<<"You have entered the name : ";
    cout<<C;
 char B[20];
  cout<<"\nEnter a name : " ;
    cin.get (B,20, ch );   // reads only up to r
  cout <<"You have written ; "<< B <<endl;
  }
```

The expected output is given below.

```
Enter a name : Adity Malhotra
You have entered the name : Adity Malhotra
Enter a name : Madhuri
You have written ; Madhu
```

The output shows that in case of cin. get() reading stopped on encountering the character 'r'.

Function ignore()

The function is used with input streams. The function is coded as below.

```
cin.ignore (streamsize n, int delimit)
```

The function reads and discards up to n characters or up to the reading of delimit character or end of file whichever occurs first. The default value of n is 1. The application of function is illustrated in Program 10.13 in Chapter 10.

FUNCTION PEEK()

This function is used with input stream. The function takes note of the specified character, i.e. its argument, but it does not take any action. It is coded as below.

```
cin.peek('D');
```

The application is illustrated in Chapter 10 in Program 10.3.

FUNCTION PUTBACK()

It is a member function of istream. It returns the previously read character to input stream. The code is illustrated below.

```
char ch = 'M';
cin.peek('S');
cin.putback (ch);
```

According to the above code when the character 'S' is noticed it is replaced by M. The application is illustrated in Programs (10.12 and 10.13) in Chapter 10.

FUNCTION PUT()

The function put is used with an object of class ostream such as **cout.put(ch);** It puts the argument ch – a single character to output stream. The following program illustrates its application.

PROGRAM 19.8 – Illustrates the applications of function **put().**

```
#include <iostream>
using namespace std;
int main()
{ cout.put('D').put('E').put('L').put('H').put('I'). ut('\n');
 char* Name = "Calcutta";
  cout<<Name<<endl;    // the output is Calcutta

 cout.put(*Name);  // Output is one character C
 cout<<"\n";
  char string [] = "Delhi";
   for ( int i = 0; i<5;i++)
    cout.put(string [i]);
      cout.put('\n');
cout.put(70)<<endl; // the output is a character F
return 0;
}
```

The expected output is given below.

```
DELHI
Calcutta
C
Delhi
F
```

The function `put ()` writes only single character. In the first output statement the function is used repeatedly to write DELHI. In the second output statement the object cout along with insertion operator << are used for writing a string "Calcutta". When the same is tried by `cout.put ()` the output is only C of Calcutta. The output Delhi is managed by writing character by character through a *for* loop and function `cout.put ()`. The last but one line of program `cout.put (70);` results in the output of `'F'` because according to ASCII the equivalent value of F is 70 and the function put () writes it as a character.

THE FUNCTION READ() AND WRITE()

The functions **`read ()`** is a member function of istream and is used with input streams such as `cin.read ()`. The function **`write ()`** is a member function of ostream and hence it is used with output streams such as `cout.write ()`. The function `write ()` does output of a number of bytes from the character array in the memory without any formatting. Similarly the function **`read ()`** does input into the memory some bytes without any formatting. Both the functions `read ()` and `write ()` take two arguments as illustrated below.

```
char Name [15] ;
cin.read(Name ,15);
cout.write (Name, 15)
```

The following program illustrates the application of the two functions.

PROGRAM 19.9 – Illustrates the function **write()** and **read()**

```
#include <iostream>
using namespace std;

int main()
{
 char sentence [] = "Go to school";

 cout.write(sentence , 13).put('\n'); // put('\n')is used
        // in place of endl
char ch[] = "A";
cout<<"ch = ";
cout.write(ch,1)<<endl; // asked to write one byte of ch.

char CH[] = "ABCDEFGHIJC" ;
cout.write(CH, 5)<<endl; // asked to write 5 bytes/characters
```

```
char Name[9];
cout<< "Type a name ";
cin.read(Name ,9);   // asked to read 9 bytes /char
cout.write( Name,9)<<endl; // asked to write 9 bytes from Name
return 0;
}
```

The expected output is given below. The output shows that white spaces are also read by function read().

```
Go to school
ch = A
ABCDE
Type a name Mona lisa
Mona lisa
```

19.5 FORMATTED I/O OPERATIONS WITH MANIPULATORS

Formatted I/O operations are needed in several applications such as preparations of lists, tables, alignment of digits in arithmetic manipulations or for better presentations. In C++ there are a number of predefined manipulators and class member functions which may be used to control the format. The user defined functions may also be used for formatting. Thus formatted I/O may be achieved by following three methods.

(i) By standard manipulators.
(ii) By member functions of class ios.
(iii) By user defined functions.

STANDARD MANIPULATORS

The manipulators are like function-type operators defined in header files<iostream> and <iomanip>. Some of manipulators are non parameterized while others are parameterised. Table 19.1 given below describes the non-parameterized manipulators such as dec, endl, ends, flush, hex, oct, and ws. These are defined in header file iostream. The parameterized manipulators given in Table 19.2 are defined in header file <iomanip>.

Table 19.1 – Non parameterized manipulators

Manipulator	Affected stream	Description
`dec`	Input/output	Decimal conversion base (base 10).
`endl`	Output	Insert new line in output and flush an output stream.
`ends`	Output	Insert Null character ('\0') at end of string.
`flush`	Output	Flush an output stream.
`hex`	Input/output	Hexadecimal conversion base (base 16).
`oct`	Input/output	Octal conversion base (base 8).
`ws`	Input	Skip leading white space characters from input stream.

Some of the above manipulators are illustrated in the following program.

PROGRAM 19.10 – Illustrates the application of **manipulators hex, oct and dec.**

```
#include <iostream>
using namespace std;
int main ()
{ int n= 183;
 cout<<"n in hexadecimal base is = " <<hex<<n <<endl;
 cout<<"n in octal base is = " <<oct<<n <<endl;

 cout<<"n in decimal base is = " <<dec<<n <<endl;
 return 0;
}
```

The expected output is given below. The number 183 is converted into hexadecimal and octal numbers.

```
n in hexadecimal base is = b7
n in octal base is = 267
n in decimal base is = 183
```

The parameterised manipulators given in Table 19.2 are member functions of header file <iomanip>.

Table 19.2: Parameterized manipulators, header file <iomanip>

Manipulator	Affected stream	Description
setbase(int n)	I/O	It sets conversion base format flag to n.
setfill(int C)	output	It sets fill character to C .
setiosflags (long F)	output	Sets (turns on) format flags specified by F.
resetiosflags(long R)	output	Resets (turns off) format flags specified by R.
setprecision (int P)	output	Sets precision for floating point numbers to P.
setw(int w)	output	Sets the field width to w.

The following program illustrates some of the manipulators listed in Table19.2

PROGRAM 19.11 – Illustrates the application of **manipulators for formatting**.

```
#include <iostream>
 #include <iomanip>
  #include <cmath>
  using namespace std;
int main()
{ double root;
cout<<setw(6)<<"Number"<<setw(20)<< "root(Scientific)" <<setw(15) <<
"root(normal)\n"<< endl;
```

```
    for ( int i =0; i<6;i++)
    { root = sqrt(i);
    cout.setf(ios::left);
    cout<<setprecision (8);

    cout<<setw(10)<<i<<setw(20)<<setiosflags(ios::scientific) <<root <<
setw(20);
   // sets width to 10 for i and 20 for root, sets ios::scientific
   cout<<setprecision(4)<<resetiosflags(ios::scientific)<<root<< endl;}
    // sets precision to 4, unsets ios::scientific flag
   return 0 ;
   }
```

The expected output is given below. The output is self explanatory.

```
Number root(Scientific) root(normal)

0       0.00000000e+000       0
1       1.00000000e+000       1
2       1.41421356e+000       1.414
3       1.73205081e+000       1.732
4       2.00000000e+000       2
5       2.23606798e+000       2.236
```

Besides the above mentioned manipulators the class ios has member functions which may also be used in formatting. Some of these are listed in Table 19.3.

Table 19.3 – ios class functions

Function	Description
`fill()`	Sets the character for filling unused field width.
`precision()`	Sets the number of digits for output of floating point numbers.
`setf()`	Sets the flag that controls the output format.
`unsetf()`	Turns off the specified flag.
`width()`	Sets the width of field for output.

A number of the functions listed in Table 19.3 have already been illustrated in Chapter 2 in Programs (2.9 to 2.13).

19.6 FORMATTING BY SETTING FLAGS AND BIT FIELDS

Some formatting operations are accomplished by setting formatting flags through the function `setf()`. For example, when the width is set, the number of characters may be less than the set width. By default the empty spaces will be on the left side. For having the output on left and empty spaces on right, we may set the formatting flags by the function `setf()` which has the following two forms

```
setf( argument1, argument2);
setf (argument1);
```

The argument1 is for setting formatting flag and the argument2 is the bit field to which the formatting flag belongs. In the case of using setf() with only one argument, the argument1 is used. The different flag setting codes for various formatting settings are listed in Table 19.4. For un-setting the flag the function `unsetf()` is used and it takes only one argument. The setting and un-setting are illustrated below.

The flag setting instructions belong to different bit fields. Therefore, while putting in two arguments care should be taken that the first argument corresponds to the bit field specified by second argument. This is illustrated below. For having output in scientific notation one may write either of the following two codes.

```
cout.setf(ios::scientific, ios::floatfield);
cout.setf(ios::scientific);
```

But for un-setting the flag only one argument, i.e. the first one is required. For example the following code un-sets the above setting.

```
cout.unsetf(ios::scientific);
```

Table 19.4 – Arguments of `setf(argument1, argument2)` and resulting effect.

argument1 Flags value	argument2 Related bit-field	Description
ios::dec	ios::basefield	Conversion to decimal base (10).
ios::hex	ios::basefield	Conversion to hexadecimal base (16).
ios::oct	ios::basefield	Conversion to octal base (8).
ios::fixed	ios::floatfield	Normal float notation.
ios::scientific	ios::floatfield	Scientific notation.
ios::left	ios::adjustfield	Output left justified.
ios::right	ios::adjustfield	Output right justified.
ios::internal	ios::adjustfield	For internal padding between sign or base indicator and the number when the number does not fill full width.

The following program illustrates the application of some of the above flag setting codes.

PROGRAM 19.12 – Illustrates the ios functions **fill(), width(), precision(), scientific, setf (ios::left)** and **setf(ios::right), unsetf()**

```
#include <iostream>
 using namespace std;
int main()
{
cout.width(20);
cout.fill('-');
cout<<"Good morning!\n";

  /*Good morning! will be written in 20 spaces
  the empty spaces will be filled with dash(-) */
```

```
cout.width(40);
cout.fill('*');

  //the output will be written in 40 spaces,
  //the empty spaces will be filled with star *.

cout<<" Welcome to programming in C++!\n";

int n = 4500600;
cout.width(25);
cout.setf(ios::left); // left justification
cout<<n<<endl;

 cout.width(25);
cout.setf(ios::right);  // right justification
cout<<n<<endl;
double m = 344.567585435656;
cout. width(5);
cout.precision(10);  // precision is set to 10 digits.

cout.setf(ios::scientific);  // scientific notation
 // This could also be coded as
  // cout.setf(ios::scientific, ios::floatfield);
cout<< m<<endl;

cout.unsetf(ios::scientific); // unsetting the scientific
   // notation. unsetf()takes only one parameter
cout<<m <<endl;
return 0;
}
```

The expected output is given below.

```
------Good morning!
******** Welcome to programming in C++!
4500600******************
******************4500600
3.4456758544e+002
344.5675854
```

The scientific and normal notation is illustrated by the last two lines of output. The other function `width()` sets the field width in which the output should be printed. The default justification is right. So if nothing is specified about justification, the empty spaces if any would be on the left side. The justification may be changed to left by the following code so that the empty spaces are on the right.

```
cout.setf(ios::left);
```

FORMATTING FLAGS WITHOUT BIT FIELDS.

The formatting flags for the function setf(), which do not have bit fields are listed in Table 19.5 along with brief descriptions against each.

Table 19.5 – Arguments of setf() which do not have related bit field

Flags	Description
ios::showbase	Show base indicator on output.
ios::showpoint	Show decimal point and trailing zeros.
ios::showpos	Show + sign before integers.
ios::skipws	Skip white space characters.
ios::unitbuf	Use unit buffer size.
ios::uppercase	Use uppercase for indicators e and x in scientific and hexadecimal.

The following program illustrates some of the above flag settings.

PROGRAM 19.13 – Illustration of **ios::uppercase** and **ios::showbase**

```
#include<iostream>
using namespace std;
void main()
 { int A = 206;
 cout.setf(ios::showbase );

 cout.setf(ios::uppercase);

 cout<<"Number A is presented in different bases."<<endl;
 cout<< "A in hexadecimal = "<<hex <<A<<endl;
 cout<< "A in octal = " <<oct<< A<<endl;
 cout << "A in decimal = "<<dec<<A<<endl;
  }
```

The expected output is given below. In the output, the base for hexadecimal and octal is shown in upper case (see 0X and 0 in last two lines of the output.)

```
Number A is presented in different bases.
A in hexadecimal = 0XCE
A in octal  = 0316
A in decimal  = 206
```

DISPLAYING TRAILING ZEROS

In normal outputs the trailing zeros are omitted. However, by including the following code the trailing zeros are also included up to the set precision.

```
cout.setf(ios::showpoint);
```

This is illustrated in the following program.

PROGRAM 19.14 – Use of ios::showpoint for showing trailing zeros.

```
#include<iostream>
using namespace std;
void main()
 {
 double A = 60.35, B= 50.0, C= 36.80, D = 79.450;
 cout.setf(ios::showpoint);
 cout<< "A = " <<A<<endl;
  cout<< "B = " <<B<<endl;
   cout<< "C = " <<C<<endl;
   cout<< "D = " <<D<<endl;
 }
```

The output is given below. The default precision is 6 digits, so trailing zeros up to 6 digits are included in output.

```
A = 60.3500
B = 50.0000
C = 36.8000
D = 79.4500
```

WORKING WITH FILES

19.7 INTRODUCTION TO FILES

The present day computers are used to store a very large amount of data. You can imagine the amount of data stored in railway bookings, in bank transactions of large banks, in computers managing mobile communications and their billing which may aggregate to trillions of bytes. All this data is stored in files. In some cases such as in banks or telephone service providers, the number of files may run into millions. The story does not end with just storage. The data has to be retrieved also. In case of a travel booking agency, for instance, the customer needs instant answers to his inquiries. So is the case in banks. In such cases the data should be accessible at random. Such files are called **random access files.** Others are **sequential files** in which data is stored sequentially. In a sequential file if you wish to find some data you have to start looking from the beginning till you find your data. In such files also, the programmer can create a structure of file which helps in fast retrieval of the data.

Files are stored on permanent storage devices such as hard disc, tapes or floppy discs which are magnetic storage devices and CD ROM and DVD which are optical storage devices. The floppy disc is relatively small storage device (1.41 Mb). Its main use is for moving data from one computer to another. Use of floppy discs is gradually decreasing because these are easily corrupted and there are better options available in the form of portable solid state memory devices and CD ROM. Some computer companies discourage the provision of floppy disc drive on their personal computers.

The other memory in a computer is RAM which is a volatile memory. The moment you switch off the computer all the data on RAM is lost. So it cannot be used for permanent storage, besides its capacity is also very small. Its main use is to fulfil the memory needs of a running program.

The above discussion shows that storage and retrieval of data are very important features of all computer operations. The programs and data are stored in files which are often required to be created, opened for writing and reading and for updating (reading and writing). C++ has no restrictions on the form or structure of a file. It may be a free form text file or it may be formatted. It may contain program and data or only data which may be numeric data or alphanumeric data. In short a file may be used to store any type of information and there is no restriction on its form or size if enough memory space is available. It is the creator of file who decides its contents, form and structure. The computer recognises a storage space in memory through its name. So a file must also have a distinct name in its directory.

No two files can have the same name in the same directory because it will introduce an ambiguity. However, you can have extensions to a name to create several related files with same *primary name* but with different *extensions*.

File Identifier or Name

A file identifier (name) is a sequence of characters, which may be declared as a sequence of characters or a string. Besides, the name may consist of a single string of characters or two strings connected by dot operator. The first string is the **primary name** and the second string is called **extension**. The maximum number of characters in a file name depends on the operating system. In most of the modern operating systems there is no limit on the numbers of characters in the name though some compilers take the first 31 characters as significant. However, in MS-DOS the file name is limited to eight characters and extension is limited to three characters. Below are some examples of file names.

```
Student.Grades     // primary name Student. Extension - Grades
Employee_data      // it is a single name
Employee.salary    // primary name Employee, extension salary.
```

Operations with a File

The different file operations are listed below.

(i) **Assigning an identifier or name to the file** – Every file has to have a distinct name or identifier in its directory.

(ii) **Opening the file** – It may involve opening a new file if it does not exist, or opening an existing file.

(iii) **File processing** – A file is opened for different purposes i.e. for reading only or for writing only or for both reading and writing or to append some data or delete some data or modify some data. The purpose of opening a file is called **mode of file or file open mode.**

(iv) **Detecting errors** – Sometimes the intended operation is not carried due to some cause. The cause must be determined so that it can be rectified. For instance, a new file may not open due to lack of memory space, etc.

(v) **Closing the file** – After processing, the file is closed. The closure is carried out by calling member function `close()` of the file stream classes which are described below. The function does not take any argument.

19.8 FILE STREAM CLASSES

In C++ three template stream classes are defined for carrying out various operations with files. These are

(i) basic_ifstream
(ii) basic_ofstream
(iii) basic_fstream

The typedef for char specializations of these are respectively called **ifstream, ofstream** and **fstream**. These classes are derived from the istream, ostream and iostream as illustrated in Fig. 19.3 below. The files manipulations are done through **input stream** and **output stream.** These streams are governed by the three classes, i.e. ifstream, ofstream and fstream, which are contained in header file **<fstream>.** Therefore, any program which deals with files has to include the header file <fstream>. It is better to include the header <iostream> as well if standard I/O operations are also desired through the file is contained in <fstream>.

For standard input and output operations we use cin and cout along with extraction and insertion operators respectively. However, for file input/output operations there are no such predefined standard streams. The input/output stream are defined by the programmer in the program itself by creating objects of files <ifstream> for input steam and class <ofstream> for output stream. The file <fstream> may be used for both input and output streams. The streams get linked to the particular file if the file name is assigned.

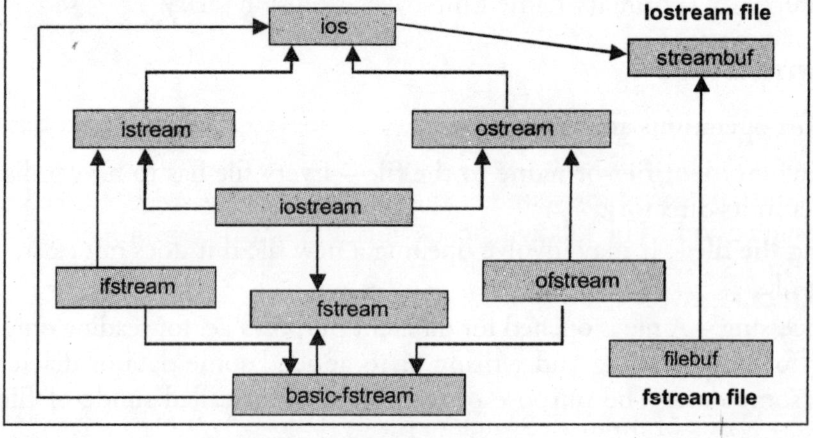

Fig. 19.3

ifstream – This class supports **input operations from a file to a program**. As shown in the Fig.19.3 the class ifstream is derived by multiple inheritances from class istream and class basic_fstream which has one constructor with void arguments and another with two arguments i.e. *file_name* and open *mode*. Besides it defines three functions as given below.

```
  (i) bool is_open();
 (ii) void open(file_name, mode);
(iii) void close();
```

The first function is used to test whether the file is open or not. The second function can open an existing file but does not open a new file by default. The third function is used to close the file. This function has no arguments. The modes are described in Table 19.6.

ofstream – This class supports output operations from program to file. The class is derived in multiple inheritance from classes ostream and fstream. In this class also there are two constructors – one constructor with void arguments and another constructor with two arguments, i.e. file_name and mode. The default mode is **out**. The various modes are described in Table 19.6. The object of this class opens an existing file or opens a new file by default if the file name is assigned to it. This class also defines three functions as given below.

```
bool is_open();
void open(file_name, mode);
void close();
```

fstream – This class supports both input and output operations with files. The class is derived from class iostream. Any program dealing with I/O with files and standard devices should include the header files <fstream> and <iostream>. The file <fstream> also defines the three functions mentioned above in ifstream and ofstream.

19.9 FILE INPUT/OUTPUT STREAMS

As already mentioned above, the file processing is carried out with the help of constructors and class functions of the three classes ifstream, ofstream and fstream. The class ifstream is used for input operations, i.e. input from file to program, the class ofstream is used for output operations, i.e. output from program to file, while fstream is useful for both input operation and output operation. A file may be opened by following two methods.

(i) Using the constructor function of the concerned class.
(ii) Using the member function open () through an object of the concerned class.

The constructor function constructs the object of the class. The objects of class ifstream and ofstream may be constructed by the name of the stream. The stream gets linked to the file if the file name is assigned to it. The following code illustrates the declaration of input stream.

INPUT STREAM DECLARATION

```
ifstream      infile      ("Myfile");
```

ifstream	infile	("Myfile");
Name of class	Name of input stream or class object	Name of file

In the above declaration `infile` is the name of an object of class ifstream just like `cin` is an object of class istream. It is initialized with the file name "`Myfile`" and this attaches the stream to the file `Myfile`. The file name is a string of characters and hence is enclosed in double quotes. The terms 'instream' and 'outstream' are with respect to program and not with respect to the file. Thus here `infile` is the name of an input stream which extracts data from the file and feeds it to the program. You can put any other name for this as well. The class ifstream is used for input files, i.e. for reading the files or for extracting data from files by the program. Similarly for out stream we create an output stream object of the file ofstream as illustrated below.

OUTPUT STREAM DECLARATION

An illustration of declaration of output stream is given below.

```
ofstream        outfile        ("Myfile");
   |               |               |
 Name      Name of output    Name of file
of class       stream
```

Here `outfile` is an object of class ofstream and because of initialization with "`Myfile`" the output stream gets attached to Myfile. Figure 19.4 illustrates input and output streams for files.

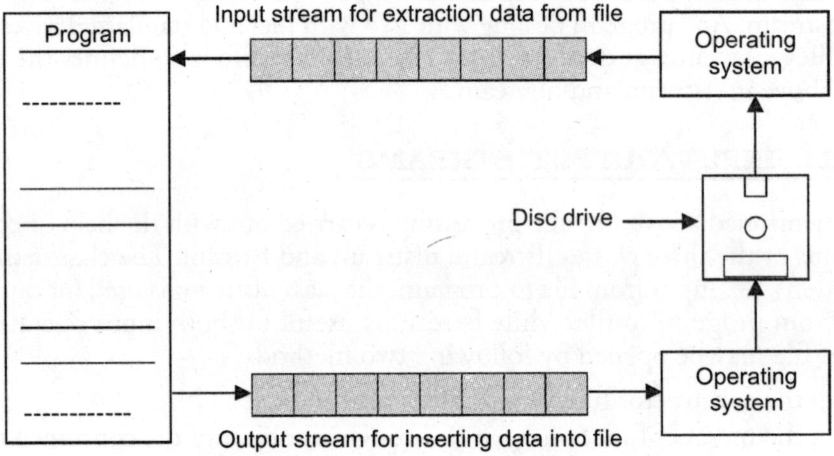

Fig.19.4: Input and output streams for files

If a file does not already exist, the ifstream objects do not open a new file by default with the given name. However, if a file does not already exist, the ofstream objects open a new file with the specified name. This is illustrated by the following two programs. In the following program the ofstream object by name out_to_file is declared and is initialised with the file name "Myfile". The stream name out_to_file clearly indicates that data flows from program to the file. The file does not exist, so it opens a new file with name "Myfile". However, if the file already exists this statement will open the file but the existing data in the file will be wiped off. In the following program we open a file and write two sentences into it.

PROGRAM 19.15 – Illustrates **opening a new file** for writing in to file.

```
#include <fstream>
#include <iostream>
using namespace std;

int main ()
{
ofstream out_to_file ("Myfile"); // declaration of output stream

   out_to_file <<"Let us learn C++.\n"; // writing into file
   out_to_file <<"You need a compiler to practice.\n";
    // writes another sentence in file
   out_to_file.close(); // closes the file
   return 0;
 }
```

In the following program we open a file for reading its contents. The file was created in Program 19.15. An input stream by name *in_from_file* is declared and is initialized by name Myfile same as used in Program 19.15. The contents are extracted with the help of function `getline()`. We are already well acquainted with this function and have used it in standard input stream as `cin.getline()`. Here we use it with a user defined input stream as illustrated below.

`in_from_file.getline(str,80);`

Name of stream	dot operator	Name of function	Name of string	Number of characters to read

PROGRAM 19.16: Illustrates **opening an existing file** for reading into program.

```
#include <fstream>
#include <iostream>
using namespace std;

int main ()
{ char str [80];
ifstream in_from_file ("Myfile");
  in_from_file.getline(str,80);
cout<<str <<endl;
   in_from_file.getline(str,80);
cout << str<<endl;
   in_from_file.close();
   return 0;
}
```

Output consists of following two lines of text which were written into the file in Program 19.15.

```
Let us learn C++.
You need a compiler to practice.
```

In the above program we have used the function `getline()` twice because we have to read two lines. We could as well use a loop. After reading a line, it is displayed on monitor by the following output statement.

```
cout << str<<endl;
```

Also notice that we also declared the character array str as `char str[80];` before using it. With this declaration the compiler allocates 80 byte of memory for it. The function `getline()` reads the line which is stored in this memory and is copied for display by standard output statement. If a number of lines are to be read it is better to use a *while loop* because, in general, we do not know how many lines are there in the file. This is illustrated in Program 19.17.

PROGRAM 19.17 – Illustrates reading a number of lines from a file.

```
#include <fstream>
#include <iostream>
using namespace std;
int main ()
{char str [80];
   ifstream in_from_file ("Myfile");

while(in_from_file)   // while loop
 {in_from_file.getline(str,80);
  cout<<str <<endl;}
     in_from_file.close();
   return 0; }
```

The expected output is given below.

```
Let us learn C++.
You need a compiler to practice.
```

In Program 19.15 we observed that if a file does not exist the output stream opens a new file. But the same thing cannot be done by an input stream. Obviously it cannot read a non-existing file. See the following program for illustration.

PROGRAM 19.18 – Illustrates that if file does not exist then object of class ifstream does not open a new file.

```
#include <fstream>
#include <iostream>
using namespace std;

int main ()
{
ifstream infile ("Myfile");
```

```
if(!infile)
 cout<< "The file with name Myfile does not exist."<<endl;

   return 0; }
```

The expected output is given below.

```
The file with name Myfile does not exist.
```

The file input/output may be carried out in the same program. Besides the file may be opened for reading any number of times. However, for writing you have to be careful because by opening with default mode will wipe out the existing contents of the file. If the file contents are to be preserved, then a proper open mode should be specified (see Table 19.6).

PROGRAM 19.19 – Illustrates **input from and output to file** in the same program.

```
#include<iostream>
#include<fstream>
using namespace std;

main()
{
char Name[40];
char RegNo[11];
int Age;

ofstream To_file ;
To_file.open("Student"); // To_file is the name of stream,
    // it opens a file with name "Student"
cout<< "Enter name of student: ";
cin.getline(Name , 40);

To_file<<Name<<"\n";   // record Students name in file

cout << "Enter Registration Number of student:";
cin.getline (RegNo , 10)
To_file<< RegNo<<"\n";  // record the registration number

cout<< "Enter age of student :";
cin >> Age;
 To_file << Age<<"\n";   //record the age of student
To_file.close();

ifstream From_file ("Student"); // input stream from file
From_file >> Name ;    // extracting name from file

cout<< " Output from file is :"<<endl;
cout<<"Name = "<<Name<<endl;

From_file >>RegNo ;   // extracting registration number
```

```
cout<<"Reg.No = "<<RegNo<<endl;
cout<<"Age = "<<Age<<endl; // extracting age of student
From_file.close();
return 0 ;
 }
```

The expected output is given below.

```
Enter name of student: Madhuri
Enter Registration Number of student:21007
Enter age of student :21
Output from file is :
Name = Madhuri
Reg.No = 21007
Age = 21
```

19.10 FUNCTIONS is_open(), get() and put() for FILES

In a big program it is sometimes not readily known whether a file is still open or if it was opened and then closed. Besides the opening and closing of files is quite error prone, so it better to check if the file is still open or not. The function **is_open**() is provided in all the three classes ifstream, ofstream and fstream for this purpose. The return value of function is 1 if the file is open and 0 if it is not open. Its application both for open files and closed files is illustrated in the following program.

We have already used the function **get**() with istream object cin. This function reads one character at a time. The function can also be used with ifstream objects as well. Similarly the function **put** () which writes one character at a time can also be used with objects of class ofstream.

Both the functions, i.e. get() and put(), deal with single character at a time. This characteristic can be used to count the number of characters read or written or a particular character may be replaced by another character, etc. Its application is illustrated in the following program.

PROGRAM 19.20 – Illustrates functions **get(), put()** and **is_open**().

```
#include <fstream>
#include <iostream>
using namespace std;
int main ()
{ ofstream outfile("Myfile");
   outfile<<"I find you have keen interest in C++.\n" ;
   outfile <<"You need a compiler to practice.\n";

outfile.put('D'); // write character D
 outfile.put('E').put('L').put('H').put('I').put('\n');
 outfile.close();
```

```
if (outfile.is_open())    // use of is_open
 cout<< "The file is open."<<endl;
else
 cout<<"The file is closed."<<endl;
  char kh;
  ifstream infile ("Myfile");
  while (infile)
   {infile.get(kh); // read the file character by character
   cout << kh ;} // display it on monitor
    infile.close();

 if(!(outfile.is_open()))
  cout<< "The file is closed"<<endl;
  return 0 ;
  }
```

The expected output is given below. It is self explanatory.

```
The file is closed.
I find you have keen interest in C++.
You need a compiler to practice.
DELHI
The file is closed
```

19.11 THE FUNCTION open() AND FILE OPEN MODES

The public member functions `open()` and `close()` are provided in each of the three classes basic_ifstream , basic_ofstream and basic_fstream for opening and closing of files. Both are of type void. The function `close()` has no arguments. We have already used this function in the previous examples.

The function open has two arguments, i.e. the first is the name of file and second is the mode. For example, if the file is to be opened for reading only the mode is `ios::in`, for writing only the mode is ios::out, for appending something at the end of file, the mode is ios::app, etc. The different modes are listed in Table 19.6 below. The function open() is coded as illustrated below.

```
ifstream-object.open ( "Name_of_file", mode)
```

Let `infile` be an object of class `ifstream`. The function `open()` may be called in append mode as below.

```
infile.open("Myfile", ios::app);
```

Table 19.6 – File opening modes

Mode code	Description
ios::app	Mode for appending at the end of file.
ios::ate	Mode for opening at end of file.
ios::binary	Mode for opening as binary file.
ios::in	Open for reading mode (default for ifstream objects).
ios::nocreate	In this mode the open () function fails if file does not exist.
ios::noreplace	In this mode the open () function fails if the file exists.
ios::out	Mode for opening the file for writing. (default for ofstream objects)
ios::trunc	Mode for deleting the contents of the file if it exists.

The following program illustrates the use of ios::app for appending more information at the end of the file created in Program 19.19.

PROGRAM 19.21 – Illustrates the application of mode **ios::app.**

```
#include<iostream>
#include<fstream>
using namespace std;

int main()
 {
 char Name[40];
 char RegNo[11];
  int Age;
   char Grade [2];

 ofstream outfile ;
 outfile.open("Student", ios::app); // To_file is name of stream
       // "Student" is the name of file
 cout<< "Enter the grade of student: ";
  cin>> Grade;
  outfile << Grade;
   outfile.close();
  ifstream infile ("Student"); // input stream from file
 cout<< "Output from file is :"<<endl;
  infile>>Name; // extracting name from file
   cout<<"Name = "<<Name<<endl;
   infile >>RegNo ; // extracting registration number
    cout<<"Reg.No= "<<RegNo<<endl;

infile >> Age;
 cout<<"Age = "<<Age<<endl; // extracting age of student
  infile>> Grade;
   cout << "Grade = " << Grade<<endl;
   infile.close();
return 0;
  }
```

The expected output is given below in which the grade is appended.

```
Enter the grade of student: A+
Output from file is :
Name = Madhuri
Reg.No= 21007
Age = 21
Grade = A+
```

19.12 FILE POINTERS

Whenever a modification of file contents is required is, it is necessary to reach the spot where the modification is desired. A file is sequence of bytes with the first byte as the 0th byte. For a reaching a particular spot you have to know how many bytes it is away from the beginning of file or from the end of file in a backward motion. A file pointer points to a position in a file, which is determined by the offset (number of bytes) from the beginning or from the end. You would have understood that file pointer is different from the pointers we have used in arrays and classes in which case the pointer value is the address (the byte number of the start byte) in allocated memory in RAM. The file pointer is not the address, it is simply an offset in bytes from the beginning of file or end or from current position. When a file is opened in the read mode the file pointer is positioned at the beginning of the file. Similarly when file is opened in write mode the pointer is again at the beginning of file because opening in write mode deletes the existing contents of the file, so the pointer is positioned at the beginning of file. In case of append mode (ios::app) the pointer is at the end of file ready to add the additional data. In the append mode the existing contents remain intact. The Figure 19.5 illustrates the pointer positions for read, write and append modes.

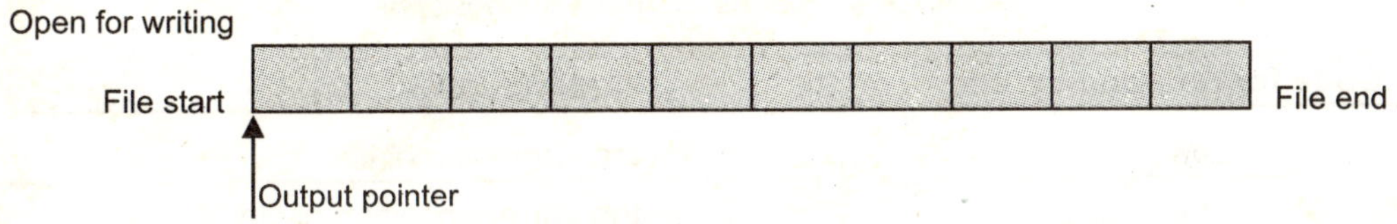

(a) `infile.open("Myfile", ios::out);`

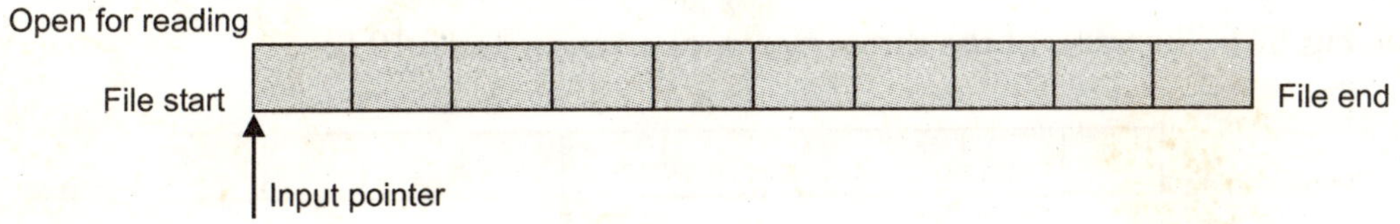

(b) `infile.open("Myfile", ios::in);`

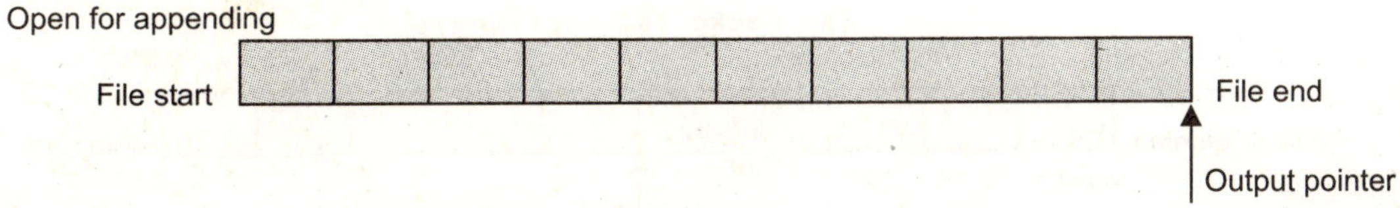

(c) `infile.open("Myfile", ios::app);`

Fig.19.5: Position of file pointer when file is opened for writing, reading and append modes

Two pointers, i.e. input pointer and output pointer are associated with every file. The input pointer which is used for reading the file from a particular location is called **get pointer**. The output pointer which is used for writing in the file is called **put pointer**. The four functions listed in Table 19.7 are used to shift the pointer to a location in the file.

Table 19.7 – Functions for file pointers

Function	Header file	Description
`seekg()`	<ifstream>	It moves the file get pointer to location specified by its arguments which are discussed below. Used for reading.
`seekp()`	<ofstresm>	It moves the file put pointer to specified location by its arguments which are discussed below. Used for writing.
`tellg()`	<ifstream>	It returns the current position of the get pointer.
`tellp()`	<ofstream>	It returns the current position of put pointer.

THE FUNCTIONS SEEKG() AND SEEKP()

Both the functions have two arguments. The first is an integer number which specifies the offset and the second is the `seek_dir` which specifies the reference position from where the offset is measured, i.e. from file beginning, from the current position of pointer or from file end. The codes for the three references are given in Table 19.8 below. The codes for calling the two functions are illustrated below.

```
Seekg( int offset, reference_position);
Seekp( int offset, reference_position);
```

Table 19.8 – Codes for reference positions

Code for reference point	Description
`ios::beg`	From the beginning of file.
`ios::cur`	From the current position of file.
`ios::end`	From the end of file.

The Fig.19.6 illustrates of the three references given in Table 19.8.

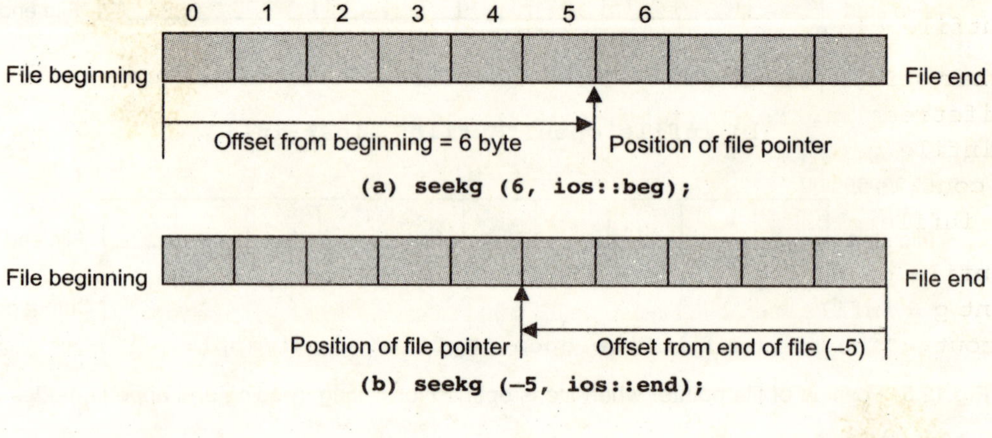

(a) seekg (6, ios::beg);

(b) seekg (–5, ios::end);

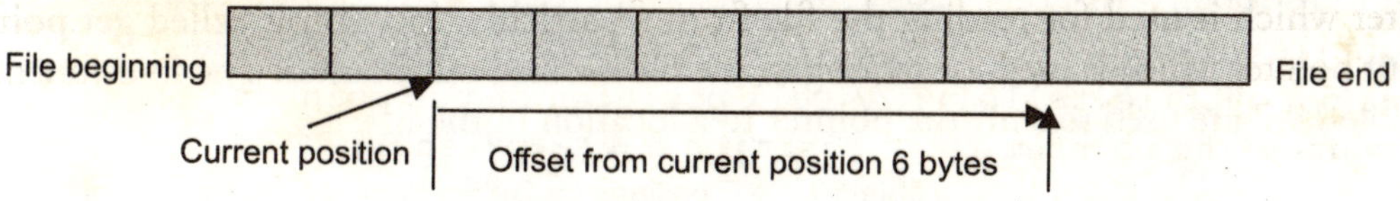

(c) seekg (6, ios::cur);

Fig. 19.6: Reference points for file pointers

Table 19.9 – Codes for seekp() arguments and the file pointer position

seekp() function option	Description of action
`infile.seekp(0,ios::beg)`	Go to the begin of file for writing.
`infile.seekp(0,ios::cur)`	Stay at the current position for writing.
`infile.seekp(0,ios::end)`	Go to the end of file for writing.
`infile.seekp(n,ios::beg)`	Move forward by n bytes from the beginning for writing.
`infile.seekp(n,ios::cur)`	Move forward by n bytes from the current position for writing.
`infile.seekp(-n,ios::end)`	Move back by n bytes from the file end for writing.

The functions tellp() and tellg() return an integer which indicates the current position of the pointer for writing and reading respectively. The following program illustrates the application of these functions along with the function seekp(). The comments included at various points have made the program self explanatory.

PROGRAM 19.22 – Illustrates application of functions **seekp(), tellp(), tellg(), ios::in and ios::app**

```
#include <fstream>
#include <iostream>
using namespace std;
int main ()
{ ofstream outfile("Mfile");
outfile<<"Bela! Learn C++ file pointers\n"; // write into file
outfile.close();

 char str [80];
  ifstream infile ("Mfile")
  infile.getline(str,80); // read the file
   cout<<str <<endl<<endl;     // display it on monitor
    infile.close();    // close the file

 infile.open ("Mfile", ios::in); // open file for reading
 int g = infile.tellg(); // tell position of get pointer
  cout<<"The pointer is at position g = "<<g<<endl;
                          // display the pointer position
```

```
outfile.open("Mfile", ios::app); // open for writing at end
outfile<<"which depict position in file"; // add this line
int p = outfile.tellp(); // tell position of put pointer.
cout<<"The pointer is at position p = "<<p<<endl;

infile.getline(str,80);  // read first line
cout<<str<<endl;
infile.getline(str,80);  // read the next line
cout<<str<<endl;

outfile.seekp(5, ios::beg ); //move 5 bytes from beginning
int n = outfile.tellp();  // tell position of pointer

cout<<"The pointer is at position n = "<<n<<endl;
outfile.seekp(-3, ios::cur ); // move the back 3 bytes
int m = outfile.tellp();  // now tell the position
cout<<"The pointer is at position m = "<<m<<endl;
outfile.close();
infile.seekg(-6, ios::end ); // move back 6 from file end
int a = infile.tellg(); // tell pointer position
cout<<"The pointer is at position a = "<<a<<endl;
outfile.close();
infile.close();
return 0;
}
```

The expected output is given below.

```
Bela! Learn C++ file pointers

The pointer is at position g = 0
The pointer is at position p = 60
Bela! Learn C++ file pointers
which depict position in file
The pointer is at position n = 5
The pointer is at position m = 2
The pointer is at position a = 54
```

19.13 BINARY FILES AND ASCII CHARACTER CODES

We all know that computer stores all types of data in the binary sequences of zeros and ones. However, the binary forms will differ if we store a digit as a character or store it as its numerical value that it represents. This is so because value as a character, as per ASCII code, is different from numerical value that the digit represents. For instance, the number 1242 has the numerical value twelve hundred forty two. If it is stored as short int it would be allocated two bytes and its binary representation is 10011011010 which is called **binary format** stored as illustrated below.

					1	0	0	1	1	0	1	1	0	1	0

Fig.19.7 (a): Number 1242 stored in binary

Storing the same number as digit characters takes 4 bytes. One character is allocated 1 byte.

	1110	1111	10001	1111
ASCII code	'1' = 14,	'2' = 15,	'4' = 17,	'2' = 15

Fig. 19.7 (b): Storing the same number 1242 as digits (characters format)

On a display system (monitor) or a printer it is the characters that are displayed or printed. So the numerical value stored in the memory as a value of digit is converted into character format and displayed. Similarly when we enter the numerical value of a variable from keyboard we enter as a character and the character format of a digit is converted to the numerical value and stored as value of the variable in the computer memory.

19.14 FUNCTIONS write() AND read() FOR FILE OPERATIONS

We have already discussed above the **binary format** and the **character format** of representing the numerical values. The functions write() and read() process the files in the binary format. This is the format followed for storage in computer memory. The functions get() and put() discussed earlier in this chapter process the file in character format.

PROGRAM 19.23 – Illustrates functions `read()` and `write()` for files operations.

```
#include <fstream>
#include <iostream>
using namespace std;

int main ()

{ int Bill [5] = { 5, 6, 7, 8, 9};

ofstream outfile ("Myfile");
 for ( int i=0 ; i<5 ; i++)
    outfile.write((char*) &Bill, 5);

outfile.close();

ifstream infile ("Myfile");
infile.read( ( char *) &Bill, 5);

for ( int k =0;k<5 ; k++)
cout << "Bill ["<<k<<"] = "<< Bill[k]<<" and size in bytes = "
<<sizeof(Bill[k])<< endl;
   return 0;
}
```

The expected output is as below. The size of elements is 4 bytes, same as for int.

```
Bill [0] = 5 and size in bytes = 4
Bill [1] = 6 and size in bytes = 4
Bill [2] = 7 and size in bytes = 4
Bill [3] = 8 and size in bytes = 4
Bill [4] = 9 and size in bytes = 4
```

19.15 FILE OPERATIONS FOR CLASS OBJECTS

The functions write () and read ( ) illustrated above can be used to store object data into file and read the same from file when required. Since the object data members are stored sequentially, the object may be treated a single unit occupying a number of bytes equal to its size. The size of object, which is required in these functions, can be obtained by sizeof( ) function. The input and output of data is carried out in the form it is stored in the computer memory. However, the object data consists of the data members only and not the class function members. In the class program all the objects share the same copy of class function members. So the function members are not stored with anyone object. Even the *type* of object is not there when the object data is stored in a file. This gives rise to a serious problem when objects of several classes are stored in same file. If the program knows the *type* of data it is reading from the file it can construct object from it. Otherwise, the information about object *type* should be incorporated by overloading insertion operator. The following program illustrates the write() and read() functions for writing and reading the objects of single class.

PROGRAM 19.24 – Illustrates file operations with class objects.

```
#include <fstream>
#include <iostream>
using namespace std;

class Grades
{
private:
char Name [30];
int Reg_No ;
char grade;
public:
    void Read()
    {cout<<"Enter name of student: ";
     cin>>Name;

cout<< "Enter the registration number: ";
 cin >> Reg_No;
    cout<<"Enter the grades : ";
     cin >> grade;}

void Write()
```

```
{cout.width(27);
cout.setf(ios::left);
 cout<<Name;
 cout.width(10);
 cout.setf(ios::left);

 cout<<Reg_No;
    cout.width(2);
  cout.setf(ios::left);
    cout<<grade<<endl;}
};

int main ()
{
 ifstream infile ("STDfile");
 ofstream outfile ("STDfile");
    cout<< "Enter the names, Reg_No and grades \n" ;

Grades Grad [4];

for (int j=0; j<4; j++ )
 {Grad[j].Read();
 outfile.write( (char*) & Grad[j], sizeof(Grad [j]));
  }

outfile.close();
 cout<< "\nStudent's Grade List \n";
  cout << "Name \t\t Reg_No\t Grade"<<endl;
  for (int i =0; i<4;i++)
   { infile.read((char*)& Grad[i], sizeof( Grad[i]));
    Grad[i].Write();
 }
 infile.close();
 return 0;
}
```

The program output is given below.

```
Enter the names, Reg_No and grades
Enter name of student: Sunita
Enter the registration number: 21007
Enter the grades : A
Enter name of student: Madhuri
Enter the registration number: 22007
Enter the grades : B
Enter name of student: Nagacharji
Enter the registration number: 23007
```

```
Enter the grades : C
Enter name of student: Mamtani
Enter the registration number: 24007
Enter the grades : A

Student's Grade List
Name                           Reg_No     Grade
Sunita                           21007       A
Madhuri                          22007       B
Nagacharji                       23007       C
Mamtani                          24007       A
```

19.16 RANDOM ACCESS FILES

Often it is required to update the data in a file which may involve insertion or deletion of data in the middle of file or at ends of a file. A **sequential file** is a continuous record in which every byte is occupied. For example, let there be an entry "Mohan has not paid his bills." If there are many such entries scattered in the file you have to see the file from the beginning to this particular entry to get its location. Say the name Mohan is a wrong entry and you want to change the name to 'Mohan Katwala. After the correction it will read "Mohan Katwala paid his bill." The additional bytes (space) required for the new name have eaten the subject matter and has changed the entire case. However, the correct correction may be made but in tedious way, i.e. by putting the contents after the name in a separate file, correcting the name and then appending the separated part of the file to the name.

A better solution to such problems is to have random access file. In such a file each object occupies a specified number of bytes. If each object is allocated m bytes then to read nth object you have to have an offset of (n – 1)*m bytes. You can easily reach the required object. Within the object space every entry is allotted a specific memory space. Say you may put 50 bytes for name (limiting the name to 49 characters) etc. Within the allocated space any correction may be performed without affecting any other entry for that object as well as for the other objects. Figure 19.8 illustrates a random file.

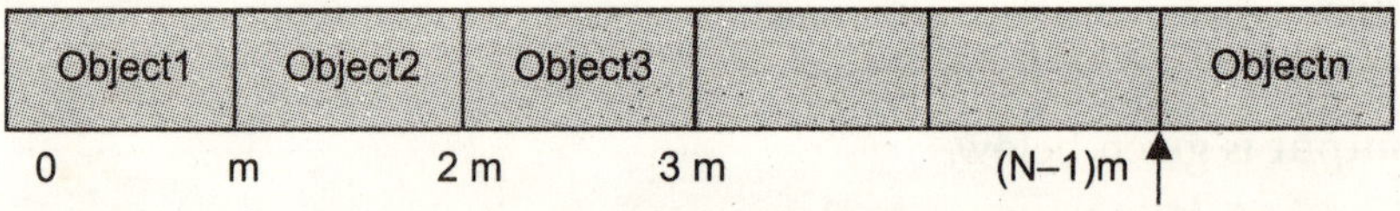

Fig. 19.8: A random access file

19.17 ERROR HANDLING FUNCTIONS

The stream 1/O oprations like any other computer operation are prone to errors which may be due to programmer or due to constraint of the hardware such as insufficient memory or due to user. The errors may be of following types.

(i) Using an invalid or wrong file name.
(ii) The user attempts to read a file which does not exist.
(iii) Attempt to write on a file which is opened for read only.
(iv) An attempt to open a read-only file for writing.
(v) An attempt to open a new file with a name which already exists.
(vi) An attempt to read the file when file pointer is already set at end of file.
(vii) Insufficient disc space.
(viii) Hardware problem.

STREAM STATUS FLAGS

To deal with stream error conditions the class ios_base declares an enumerated type (anum io_state) with following members. These are explained in Table 19.10.

```
goodbit = 0x00
badbit = 0x01
eofbit = 0x02
failbit = 0x04
```

Table 19.10 – Status bit is set according to the condition

Bit	Description
`goodbit`	The bit is set when non of other bits are set. It is detected by `cin.good();`
`badbit`	It is set when an error results in loss of data. It may be detected by `cin.bad();`
`eofbit`	End of the file bit is set for an input stream when end of file is encountered. It can be detected by `cin.eof();`
`failbit`	The bit is set when format error occurs in the stream. The data is not lost in such error. It is detected by `cin.fail();`

The functions listed in Table 19.11 check the status of the error bits and return values as dessribed in the table.

Table 19.11 – Error handling functions

Function	Action and return value
`bad()`	Returns true if error has occurred, false otherwise.
`good()`	Returns true when no error has occurred, false otherwise.
`clear()`	It clears error states.
`eof()`	Returns true when end of file is detected.
`fail()`	Returns true if an operation, i.e. read or write has failed. The function checks the bits for the purpose.
`rdstate()`	Returns the stream state data.

PROGRAM 19.25 – Illustrates **stream status functions.**

```
#include<iostream>
using namespace std;
int main()
{
   double D;
   cout<< "Initial stream state:"<<endl;
   cout<<"cin.bad = " << cin.bad()<<endl;
   cout<<"cin.good = " << cin.good<<endl;
   cout<<"cin.fail= " << cin.fail()<<endl;
   cout<<"cin.eof = " << cin.eof()<<endl;
cout<< "Enter value of D.";
cin>> D;
cout<<"User put a string \"Sham\" for D."
<<"The stream state after input"<<endl;

cout<<"cin.bad = " << cin.bad()<<endl;
cout<<"cin.good = " << cin.good<<endl;
cout<<"cin.fail= " << cin.fail()<<endl;
cout<<"cin.eof = " << cin.eof()<<endl;
cin. clear();
cout<<"After application of function clear():"<<endl;

cout<<"cin.bad = " << cin.bad()<<endl;
cout<<"cin.good = " << cin.good<<endl;
cout<<"cin.fail= " << cin.fail()<<endl;
cout<<"cin.eof = " << cin.eof()<<endl;
return 0;
}
```

The expected output is given below.

```
Initial stream state:
cin.bad = 0
cin.good = 1
cin.fail= 0
cin.eof = 0
Enter value of D.Sham
User put a string "Sham" for D.The stream state after input
cin.bad = 0
cin.good = 1
cin.fail= 1
cin.eof = 0
After application of function clear():
cin.bad = 0
cin.good = 1
cin.fail= 0
cin.eof = 0
```

EXERCISES

1. What are the input/output streams?
2. What do you understand by low level I/O and high level I/O ?
3. What are the stream classes for managing I/O with console?
4. To which I/O stream class do the following objects belong?

   (i) cout (ii) cin
   (iii) cerr (iv) clog

5. What is the difference between the function put() and the function write()?
6. Elaborate the difference between function get() and getline().
7. What is a file pointer? Why can't we use ordinary pointer in case of files?
8. Which header filed is included for working with parameterized manipulators?
9. For which data-type the function precision () is applicable?
10. What are the left and the right justifications? How are these set?
11. What does function ignore () do?
12. Elaborate the action of the function peek ().
13. What for are the following manipulators used?

    (i) oct (ii) hex
    (iii) dec

14. How do you declare the file out_stream and file in_stream?
15. Which stream classes are included for carrying out file input and file output?
16. What are the formatting flags? For what actions the following flags are set?

    (i) `ios::fixed` (ii) `ios::scientific`
    (iii) `ios::left` (iv)) `ios::oct`

17. What do you understand from the following code lines?

```
infile.seekp(n,ios::beg)
infile.seekp( n,ios::cur)
infile.seekp(-n,ios::end)
```

18. What are the file opening modes?
19. What do you understand by following file opening modes?

```
ios::binary
ios::in
ios::nocreate
```

20. Show the output for the following statements.

    (i) cout.width (20) << " Ram Chander "<< endl;
    (ii) cout << scientific << 3543.14159 ;

(iii) cout << "Good\nMorning"<< "\nKim\n";

(iv) cout << setw(20) <<setprecision (4) << 53426.87566;

(v) cout << hex << 484 << oct<< 400;

21. Show the output for the following statements.

(i) cout.fill('*');

cout.width(10);

cout<< 8546<<endl;

(ii) cout<<"Hello! \t Good morning\n;"

22. What do you understand by following?

(i) failbit

(ii) badbit

(iii) goodbit

23. What do the following function do ?

(i) good() (ii) clear ()

(iii) eof() (iv) fail()

24. What is the structure of a random access file?

25. What is the difference between character format and binary format?

❍❍❍

CHAPTER 20

Namespaces and Preprocessor Directives

20.1 INTRODUCTION TO NAMESPACES

The concept of namespace is an important addition to C++. The need was felt after 1990 when C++ was gaining popularity and several organizations began offering reusable programs. It is natural to expect name clash problem if one program is bought from one vendor and the second from another. Name clash refers to same name being used for different variables. Similar problems may occur in development of a big program if several programmers are engaged to write code for different parts of the program. It is quite likely that some names may be common in different sub-programs though they point to different variables, constants or functions. Naturally when these sub-programs are put together in a single program, it is not likely that the program will work or give desired results because of the ambiguities in names. The remedy is (i) either to change the common names or (ii) to compartmentalize the names under different namespaces. The first option is a tedious task as well as time consuming. The second option involves putting the names in different namespaces. The concept of namespace was introduced in C++ in 1995. It is explained below.

In order to illustrate the concept, let us consider that there are several fruit baskets containing nearly identical fruits. Say apples are in all of them. If we simply say apples it can refer to apples contained in any of the baskets. However, if we number the baskets or give them names like basket1, basket2, basket3, etc. then we can easily identify the apples in basket1 from the apples in basket3, etc. In C++ code we may refer to apples in different baskets as,

```
basket1 :: apples ;        // this refers to apples in basket1
basket3 :: apples ;        //this refers to apples in basket 3
```

In two or more sub-programs, if *apple* is a common name of different variables and basket1, basket2 and baskets3, etc., are the names of namespaces declared in the programs or even in the different sections of same program, the different sets of names can be easily identified with the help of scope resolution operator and identifiers for namespaces. Alternatively, if we want to examine or deal with all the fruits in a basket, we say take basket1, or take basket3, etc. The equivalent code in C++ would be *using namespace NS1* where NS1 is the name of namespace.

20.2 APPLICATION OF NAMESPACES

We have to first declare the namespace at file scope for a program or subprogram. This is similar to giving names to baskets or numbering the baskets as discussed in the above example. The namespace may be declared as below.

namespace *NS1 { Declaration_of_variables ; }*

The first word is the keyword *namespace*, it is followed by the identifier NS1 which is in turn is followed by braces{} in which the names of a set of variables are declared. For calling the variable in the program we have to make use of scope resolution operator as illustrated above in case of apples and baskets. The following program illustrates the concept. We declare some variables under the namespace S1. Same names are used for different variables under another namespace S2. The compiler can identify which name belongs to which namespace. Wherever we use a particular variable we have to first write its namespace identifier followed by scope resolution operator (::) and then the name of variable. That is also called ***fully qualified name.***

PROGRAM 20.1 – Illustrates application of namespaces.

```
#include <iostream>
using namespace std;

 namespace S1                    // name of namespace S1
 {int  a = 8;    //int variable defined under namespace S1.
   char ch = 'X';
     double b = 10.5;  // variable defined under namespace S1.
        char E[] = "John!"; }

namespace S2
 {double a = 5.4;        // 'a' is now double in namespace S2
   char ch = 'Y';        //ch is now 'Y' was 'X' under S1
     int E = 5;        // E is now int was string in S1

char b[] = "Go to school";} // b is now string was double in S1
 void main ()
 {double A = S1::a * S2::a; //the scope resolution identifies
                           // whether it belongs to S1 or S2
    double B = S1:: b + S2::E ;
      cout << "A = " << A <<" , " << "B = "<< B << endl;

 cout << S1::ch <<" , " <<S2 :: ch<<endl;
   cout << S1::E <<" "<< S2::b<< endl;
   }
```

The expected output is as below.

```
A = 43.2,  B = 15.5
X , Y
John! Go to school
```

We have already been using the declaration `using namespace std;` for simplifying the writing of std::cout to simply cout, etc. The C++ header files and functions are written under the **namespace std.**

20.3 DIRECTIVES `using` AND `using namespace`

In the above program we have used scope resolution operator (::) preceded by the identifier for namespace to access the desired variable. This may also be done by using the keyword **using** followed by namespace identifier and scope resolution operator to reach a single name whether it is for variable or function. If several names declared under one namespace are to be used in the section of a program then we may use the following directive.

`using namespace` ***`identifier_of_namespace;`***

The following program illustrates the above option.

PROGRAM 20.2 – Illustrates application of namespaces with **using namespace** directive.

```
#include <iostream>
using namespace std;
namespace doll        // Here doll is identifier for namespace
   { int  a =  8;
    char E[] = "John!"; }
namespace ball   // Here ball is identifier for namespace
   {double b = 4.5;
    char E[] = "Go to school";}
 void main ()
    {using namespace doll;   // application of using directive
      cout << a*a<< endl;   // now scope resolution not needed
                     //for variable of namespace doll but
               //it is needed for variables of namespace ball
cout << E <<" "<< ball:: E<<endl;
                   // use of scope resolution operator for E
          }
```

The expected output is given below.

```
64
John! Go to school
```

The following program illustrates application of keyword **using** for name of one variable.

PROGRAM 20.3 – Illustrates the use of keyword **using.**

```
#include <iostream>
using namespace std;

 namespace NS1
{ int n = 3;
  float m = 2.5;}
 namespace NS2
```

```
{float n = 4.0;
int m = 2 ;}
namespace NS1
{
 int k = 2;
 double R = n*m*k;}

namespace NS2
{double k = 3.0 ;
 double R = n*m*k;
}
int main()
{
using NS1::R;                      // Application of using
 cout<< "R of NS1  = "<< R <<endl;
  using NS1::k;                      // Application of using
    cout << "k of NS1 = "<< k << endl;

cout<< "m of NS2 = " <<  NS2::m<< endl;

using NS1::m;                          // Application of using
 cout << "m of NS1 = "<<  m <<endl;
   cout << "R of NS2 = " << NS2::R<< endl;
return 0 ;
 }
```

The expected output is given below.

```
R of NS1 = 15
k of NS1 = 2
m of NS2 = 2
m of NS1 = 2.5
R of NS2 = 24
```

20.4 NAMESPACE ALIASES

Aliases for namespace identifiers may be used wherever it is convenient. With short names there is greater likelihood of name clash. So it is better to have a big name to start with and then declare a short name as alias for frequent use. This is illustrated in the following program.

PROGRAM 20.4 – Illustrates **aliases for namespaces**.

```
#include <iostream>
using namespace std;

namespace myspace_program
 { int n = 3;
```

```
    float m = 2.5;
      int k = 2;

         double R = n*m*k;
  }
 namespace Myspace
  {float n = 4.0;
     int m = 2 ;
        double k = 3.0 ;
           double R = n*m*k;
            }
 int main()
 {
 namespace  NS1= myspace_program ;
                         //NS1 is alias for myspace_program
 namespace  NS2 = Myspace ;  // NS2 is alias for Myspace

 cout<< "R in myspace_program= "<< NS1:: R << " , \tn in NS1 = " <<NS1::n<<endl
 cout <<"R in Myspace = " <<NS2::R<< " , \tn in NS2 = " << NS2::n <<endl;
 cout<<"m in myspace_program  = " <<NS1::m<< " , \tm in NS2 =" <<NS2::m <<
endl;
 return 0 ;
 }
```

The expected output is given below.

```
R in myspace_program = 15 ,        n in NS1 = 3
R in Myspace = 24 ,                n in NS2 = 4
m in myspace_program = 2.5 ,       m in NS2 = 2
```

The following program is yet another instance of aliases for namespaces.

PROGRAM 20.5 – Another illustration on aliases to namespaces.

```
#include <iostream>
using namespace std;

 namespace NS1
 { int n = 3;
    float m = 2.5;}
 namespace NS2
  {float n = 4.0;
     int m = 2 ;}

 namespace NS1
  {

  int k = 2;
     double R = n*m*k;}

 namespace NS2
  { double k = 3.0 ;
```

```
    double R = n*m*k;
   }
 namespace Myspace = NS1;
 namespace Space = NS2;

 int main()
 {
cout<< "R of Myspace  = "<< Myspace:: R <<endl;
  cout << "k of Myspace  = "<< Myspace::k << endl;
    cout << "k of namespace NS2 = " <<  NS2::k << endl;

cout<< "m of Space  = " <<  Space::m<< endl;
  cout << "m of Myspace  = "<< Myspace::m <<endl;
    cout << "R of Space = " <<Space::R<< endl;

 return 0 ;
  }
```

The output of the program is given below.

```
R of Myspace  = 15
k of Myspace  = 2
k of namespace NS2 = 3
m of Space  = 2
m of Myspace  = 2.5
R of Space = 24
```

20.5 EXTENSION OF NAMESPACES

The namespaces may be defined in parts in the same program or may span over several files. The following program is an illustration of extending namespaces in same program.

PROGRAM 20.6 – Illustrates extension of namespaces.

```
#include <iostream>
using namespace std;

 namespace NS1
 { int n = 3;
   float m = 2.5;}

  namespace NS2
   { float n = 4.0;
      int m = 2 ;}

  namespace NS1    // using NS1 again
   { int k = 2;
      double R = n*m*k;}
```

```
namespace NS2        // Using NS2 again
  {double k = 3.0 ;
     double R = n*m*k; }

int main()
{  cout<< "R of NS1  = "<< NS1:: R <<endl;
     cout << "k of NS1 = "<< NS1::k << endl;
       cout<< "m of NS2 = " <<  NS2::m<< endl;
         cout << "m of NS1 = "<< NS1 ::m <<endl;
           cout << "R of NS2 = " << NS2::R<< endl;
return 0 ;
 }
```

The expected output is given below.

```
R of NS1  = 15
k of NS1 = 2
m of NS2 = 2
m of NS1 = 2.5
R of NS2 = 24
```

20.6 NESTING OF NAMESPACES

The namespaces may be nested, i.e. a namespace is declared inside another namespace. For instance, the following is an illustration of nested namespaces.

```
namespace NS1
{ namespace NS2    //namespace NS2 is declared inside NS1
   {int x = 2;}}
```

With above declaration the variable x may be accessed given below.

```
NS1::NS2::x;
```

The following program illustrates the nested namespaces.

PROGRAM 20.7 – Illustrates nested namespaces.

```
#include <iostream>
using namespace std;
 namespace NS1
 { int n = 3;
    float m = 2.5;
  namespace NS2          // NS2 declared inside NS1
   { float n = 4.0;
      int m = 2 ;}}
  namespace NS3
   { int k = 2;
  double R = NS1::n*NS2::m*NS3::k;  // using variables of
                                    // different namespaces
```

```
    namespace NS4      // NS4 declared inside NS3
      {double k = 3.0 ; }}

    int main()
  {  cout<< "R of NS1  = "<< NS3:: R <<endl;
  cout << "k of NS4 = "<< NS3::NS4 ::k << endl;
  cout<< "m of NS2 = " <<  NS1::NS2::m<< endl;
  cout << "m of NS1 = "<< NS1 ::m <<endl;
  return 0 ;
    }
```

The expected output is given below.

```
R of NS1  = 12
k of NS4 = 3
m of NS2 = 2
m of NS1 = 2.5
```

20.7 THE namespace std

The various header files and names in C++ are now declared under the **namespace std.** As discussed above, the namespaces, in general, can be modified by additional declarations and definitions, however, this does not to apply to the **namespace std. The namespace std cannot be modified.** According to earlier convention the header files are written with the extension (.h) such as <iostream.h>. Now, under namespace std, the same is written as <iostream>, however, you have to include the statement **using namespace std;** in the program in global scope, i.e. above main().

The standard C header files which were earlier written with extension such as (<xxxx.h> are now written as <cxxxx> under the namespace std. The extension h is omitted and c is added before the name. For example, the name <assert.h> is now written as <cassert>. The compilers at present support both the conventions. More examples are given below.

Table 20.1

Earlier name	Name under namespace std
Examples of some C++ header files	
<algorithm.h>	<algorithm>
<bitset.h>	<bitset>
<iomanip>	<iomanip>
<set.h>	<set>
Examples of some ANSI C header files	
<assert.h>	<cassert>
<float.h>	<cfloat>
<limits.h>	<climit>
<math.h>	<cmath>
<stdio.h>	<cstdio>
<stdlib.h>	<cstdlib>
<time.h>	<ctime>

20.8 PREPROCESSOR DIRECTIVES

There are a number of preprocessor directives which C++ has inherited from C. These may be used for defining symbolic constants, macros and conditional directives. We are already well acquainted with `#include` and `#define`. A list of preprocessor directives is given in Table 20.2. All the preprocessor directives are preceded by the symbol #. For many of these, there are equivalent replacements in C++. For instance, an inline function does the same as a macro, i.e. it substitutes the code wherever the name of function appears. In fact, inline function is a better option than a macro because there is static type checking while a macro bypasses the type check. Similarly *const* in C++ does the same as a constant defined by directive `#define`.

Table 20.2 – Preprocessor directives and operators

Preprocessor directive	Description
`#`	# ignored if single on a line. It is Null directive.
`#define`	Used for defining a symbolic constant or a macro.
`##`	Used with # define, the operator concatenates two items.
`#error`	Stops compilation and displays error message.
`#include`	Includes the files names in <> brackets or in double quotes " " in source code. We have used this directive in all the programs.
`#line`	Allows to specify the line number in a file. It is coded as `#line Number_line<"Name_of_file">.`
`#pragma`	Directive specific to implementation.
`#undef`	Undefine the previously defined.

DEFINE

The preprocessor directive **#define** is used to create macros and symbolic constants. The directive #define may be used as illustrated below.

```
#define Pi 3.14159
```

Note that there no semicolon at the end of line and there is a space between define and Pi and between Pi and the value 3.14159. In the program using the above code, wherever Pi occurs, the value `3.14159` would be substituted. In fact, the above declaration is equivalent to the following statement.

```
const double Pi = 3.14159 ;
```

Macros may also be created by #define. For instance, see the following code.

```
#define          max(x,y)          (x >y ? x : y)
```

Pre-processor | Space | Function name and arguments | Space | Definition

In the above declaration the directive **#define** creates a macro — a function to obtain the greater of the given two values. The values may be integers or floating point numbers, or characters. There is no type checking. Note that in the definistion no space is allowed between max and the left bracket '('. Its application is illustrated in the following program.

PROGRAM 20.8 – Illustrates preprocessor directive **#define.**

```
#include<iostream>
using namespace std;

 # define max(x,y) (x >y ? x : y)  // definition of macro
int main()
{
  float x,y;
     char ch, kh;
         int A, B;

 cout<<"Write two integers " ; cin >> A >> B;
 cout << "Enter two floating point numbers ";cin >>x>>y;
 cout <<"Enter Two characters "; cin >> ch>>kh;

cout << "Greater of the two int = " <<max (A ,B ) << endl;
cout << "Greater of the two floats = " << max(x,y)<<endl;
cout<< "Greater of two characters is = " << max (ch,kh)<<endl;

return 0;
 }
```

The expected output of the program is given below.

```
Write two integers 4 8
Enter two floating point numbers 7.7 9.6
Enter Two characters S H
Greater of the two int = 8
Greater of the two floats = 9.6
Greater of two characters is = S
```

The following program is another illustration of defining a macro by preprocessor directive # define. None that both length and width are enclosed in brackets. This is to eliminate error that may occure if, for instance, length = 2+3 and width = 2+2 in which case it would compute as

2+3* 2+2 = 10

instead of 20. This is be cause (*) has higher precedence than +.

PROGRAM 20.9 – Illustrates another function definition with **#define.**

```
#include<iostream>
using namespace std;

 # define area ((length)*(width))
          // the macro defines area of a rectangle.
int main()
{
  int length, width;
     cout<<"Write the length & width of a rectangle: " ;
        cin >> width >> length;
 cout <<"Area = "<< area << endl;
```

```
 return 0;
}
```

The expected output is as below.

```
Write the length & width of a rectangle: 60 20
Area = 1200
```

OPERATORS # AND

The single # in its own line is neglected by compiler. Thus,

#

is of no consequence. When used with a variable such as `#x` in a `#define` statement, the # operator is replacement token, i.e. it replaces the value wherever x appears. The replacement is converted into a string with double quotes. For example, see the following code.

```
#define F(x) cout << "Good Morning" #x
```

When function `F(x)` is called as `F(Babu)` the above code is equivalent to the following statement.

```
cout << "Good Morning Babu";
```

The preprocessor operator ## is used along with `#define`, it puts together (concatenates) two tokens. For example the following code.

```
#define concat(m , n) m ## n
```

would give output as mn. See the following program for illustration.

PROGRAM 20.10 – Illustrates preprocessor **operator ##.**

```
#include<iostream>
using namespace std;

#define Funct(y) cout << "Good Morning " #y<<endl;

  # define CONCAT(a, b) a ## b

 void main()
 {
 Funct (Aparna!);
 cout << CONCAT (5, 7 )<< endl;
  cout << CONCAT ("O","K")<< endl;
    cout << CONCAT (  "Good", " Morning John!" )<< endl;
    }
```

The expected output is given below.

```
Good Morning Aparna!
57
OK
Good Morning John!
```

#UNDEF

The preprocessor `#undef` is used to discard or undefine the symbolic constants and macros created by `#define`. Thus the scope of macros and symbolic constants starts from the definition to the point where it is undefined by #undef or if not undefined to the end of file. There is no restriction on redefining the same macro or symbolic constant by `#define`. It is illustrated in the following program.

PROGRAM 20.11 – Illustrates **#define** and **#undef**

```
#include<iostream>
#define Length 40                // First define should be before main()
using namespace std;
int main()
{ cout << "Initial length = " << Length << endl;
 #undef Length
   #define Length 60
      cout << "New length = "<< Length << endl;
 return 0; }
```

The expected output is given below

```
Initial length = 40
New length = 60
```

20.9 CONDITIONAL PREPROCESSOR DIRECTIVES

The conditional preprocessor directives are provided to control the action of preprocessors and to control the compilation of the program. These are listed in Table 20.3 with the description in each case. Note that if an *#if* is used it ends with **#endif.** Program 20.11 illustrates the application of some of these.

Table 20.3 – Conditional preprocessor directives

Preprocessor directive	Description
`#if`	Conditional *if* directive. The #if is followed by # endif
`#elif`	*else if* conditional directive
`#endif`	end of if
`#else`	else
`#ifdef`	if defined
`#ifndef`	if not defined

Some of the above directives are illustrated below.

PROGRAM 20.12 – Illustrates application of **#if, #elif, #define** and **#undef.**

```
#include<iostream>
using namespace std;
#define width 40
 #define area (length*width)
#if 0
  #if length > 2*width
 #undef width    // discard the previous definition of width
   #define width length/2
#elif length < width      // Similar to else if
#endif
#undef width
#define width length/4  //redefinition. No semicolon at end
#endif
int main()
{   int length ;

cout<<"Write the length of a rectangle: " ;

 cin >> length;
cout << "Length = " <<length<< "\t Width = " << width<<endl;
cout << "area  = " << area << endl;

 return 0; }
```

The expected output is given below. The code between #if 0 and #endif is not compliled. This technique is used for debugging programs.

```
Write the length of a rectangle: 100
Length = 100      Width = 40
area  = 4000
```

PROGRAM 20.13 – Illustrates application of **#error, #if, #endif, #else**

```
#include<iostream>
using namespace std;

#define area (length*width)
#define length 100

#if (length>50)
 #error 1- Not according to plan
  #else

   #endif

int main()
{
 int width;
```

```
cout<< "Write the width of a rectangle: " ;
   cin >> width;

      cout << "Area= " <<width*length<<endl;
 return 0;
}
```

First run with length = 10

```
Write the width of a rectangle: 5
Area= 50
```

```
Second run when length =100.
#error :  1- Not according to plan
```

ASSERT ()

The function `assert()` is defined in header file `<cassert>`. It is used to test a value. For instance one may use it as below.

```
assert (k>0);
```

With such a statement if k happens to be 0 or less than 0 the program will be aborted and the error message will identify the line in which the error occurred. It is illustrated in the following program.

PROGRAM 20.14 – Illustrates application of **assert()** function.

```
#include<iostream>
#include <cassert>

using namespace std;

 void main()
 {
int A, B;
cout<< "Enter two integers "; cin >> A>>B;
assert(B > 0);

double C = A/B;
cout << "C = " << C <<endl;
    }
```

The output, when program was tested on Visual C++6 is given below.

```
Enter two integers 5 0
Assertion failed: B>0, file C:\Documents and
Settings\Administrator\Desktop\Prep
ro.Assert.cpp, line 7
```

The following program illustrates other preprocessor functions.

20.10 PREDEFINED MACROS

A list of six predefined macros is given in Table 20.4. The table also explains the expected output of these macros. Program 20.15 illustrates the application of some of them.

Table 20.4 – Predefined macros

Name of macro	Description
_cplusplus	C++ program.
DATE	Date month day year (mmm dd yyyy) mmm = three character for name, i.e. Oct.
FILE	Name of source code file.
LINE	The line number.
STDC	ANSI compliant.
TIME	Compilation time (hh: mm : ss).

The following program illustrates some of the predefined macros.

PROGRAM 20.15 –Illustrates pre-defined macros **_LINE_, _TIME_, _DATE_ , _FILE_** and **_cplusplus**

```
#include <iostream>
using namespace std;
int main()
{
 int sum = 0;
 for ( int i = 0 ; i<6; i++)
 sum +=i;
 cout <<"sum = " << sum<<endl;
 cout << "Line No = " << __LINE__ <<endl;
           // double underscore on each side
 cout << "Date of writing the program "<< __DATE__<<endl;
 cout << "The time of compilation is "<<__TIME__<< endl;
 cout <<"File No = "<<  __FILE__ << endl;
 cout<< "Value of cplusplus " << __cplusplus <<endl;
 return 0;
 }
```

The expected output obtained on Microsoft Visual C++ 6 is as under.

```
sum = 15
Line No = 9
Date of writing the program Oct  1 2006
The time of compilation is 19:27:31
File No = F:\C++ Prog\c++ All Programmes\Predefined.cpp
Value of cplusplus 1
```

EXERCISES

1. What is a macro?
2. How do you define a macro and undefined a macro?
3. What is a symbolic constant?
4. What does the macro *assert* do? Make a small program to illustrate its application.
5. Define a macro to find the greater of the two numbers.
6. Define a macro to find greatest of three numbers entered by a user.
7. Define a macro to determine area of a triangle when three sides are specified.
8. Write the expected output from the following program.

```
#include <iostream>
using namespace std;
void main()
{
cout<< _TIME_<<endl;
cout << _DATE_<< endl;
cout<< _LINE_ <<endl;
return 0;
 }
```

❍❍❍

CHAPTER 21

Standard Template Library

21.1 INTRODUCTION

Standard Template Library (STL) is an excellent collection of templatised reuseable software which deals with data structures and operations most commonly used by programmers in many diverse applications. The concept was developed by Alxender Stepanov and Meng Lee of Hewlett-Packard. The collection has contributions by many other researchers and experts in C++ programming. It is now a part of C++ Standard Library.

Use of STL components can save considerable time and effort of programmers, besides assuring a degree of efficiency and accuracy to the application programs because of their being based on well tested pieces of software written by experts. STL is a big collection of programs, however, the following three are its main components.

(i) Containers

(ii) Iterators

(iii) Algorithms

Containers are objects which store other objects which may be data of fundamental type or user defined type. The storage, retrieval and various operational functions to manipulate data are based on template classes, so containers allow storage and manipulation of any type of data.

Iterators are like pointers, however, iterators being based on template classes allow their use for diverse data types. The main function of iterators is to provide access to elements of containers and thus can be used to traverse the containers as well as for operation on any one element of a container. There are different types of iterators depending on their capability and hence their use is accordingly limited. All the containers do not support all types of iterators. The details are discussed below.

Algorithms are pieces of software which are used to manipulate the data in containers with help of iterators. The algorithms are not only for STL containers and hence can be used for operations on other types of containers like arrays, strings or variables in general. In this chapter all the topics mentioned above are introduced, while details on sequence containers, associative containers and algorithms are dealt separately in Chapters 22, 23 and 25 respectively.

21.2 THE CONTAINERS

The containers are categorised into following three main groups, i.e. (i) sequence containers, (ii) associative containers and (iii) container adapters as illustrated in the following diagram. These are further specialised into containers with special functions, so a programmer may choose the one best suited to the application on hand. Besides the above mentioned three containers there are three near containers. These are C++ strings, bit sets and valarray. The near containers have some functions similar to other containers. Figure (21.1) shows the relationships of various container classes.

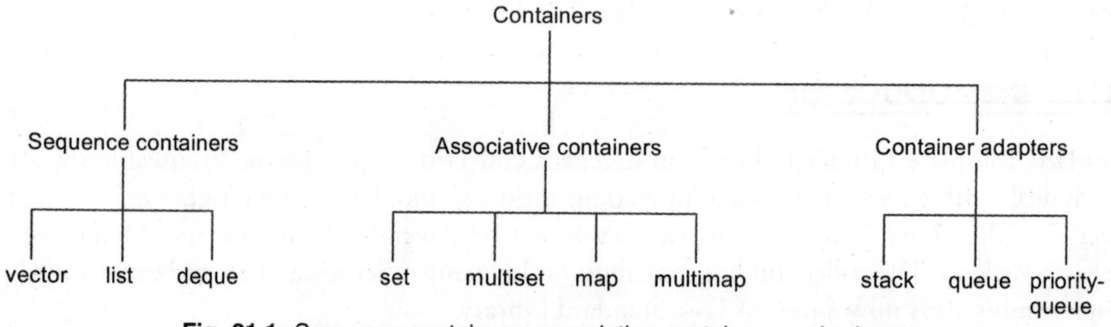

Fig. 21.1: Sequence containers, associative containers and adapters

Sequence containers and associative containers are collectively called first class containers because they store as well as have the capability to manipulate data with the help of iterators and have sets of predefined functions. The container adapters do not support iterators and hence cannot manipulate data. Adapter classes support only few functions which are mainly for pushing in or for removing data from front or back-end of the sequence.

Sequence containers are in fact linear sequences of data. The individual data element is linked to other elements by way of its position in the sequence. They allow insertion and deletion of data in the sequence as well as can allocate to themselves additional memory if the number of elements increases beyond the capacity (memory) initially allocated. In this respect they are dynamic, unlike C- arrays which are of fixed length right from the point they are declared. The sequence containers are of three types, i.e. (i) vector, (ii) deque (also called double ended queue and pronounced as 'deck') and (iii) list. Each has speciality of being efficient in some aspects over the other two. For instance vector allows fast random access to an element as well as addition and deletion of elements at the back-end only, but is slow in insertion or deletion in the middle. The list is fast in insertion and deletion in the middle and at front-end but does not support random access. The list supports only bidirectional iterators, therefore, are slow to access an element at random. Similarly deque is fast at random access as well as in insertion or deletion at both ends, but slow in insertion or deletion in the middle. The deque also supports random iterators. The individual data element may be accessed by iterators and can be manipulated. The salient features of each of these are given in Table 20.1 below.

Table 21.1 – Header files and brief description of containers

For details on sequence containers and associative containers see Chapters 22 &23.

Container	Header File	Brief Description
vector	<vector>	The container provides direct access to any element.Rapid addition and deletion at back. For the functions and operators supported by vector class see Chapter 22.
list	<list>	Rapid insertion and deletion at any location in the list. For the list of functions and operators supported by list class see Chapter 22.
deque	<deque>	Allows direct access to any element of deque container.Rapid addition and deletions at both ends of the queue.For list of functions and operators supported by deque see Chapter 22 .
set	<set>	Only unique values are allowed, duplicate copies ignored if inserted. Values are sorted in specified order such as increasing order or decreasing order, etc.(See Chapter 23)
multiset	<set>	Multiple copies of a value allowed.The elements are sorted in order as specified like in sets.
map	<map>	The container stores pair of values for each element, the first value is the key and the second is the associated value. The elements are sorted according to key and only unique keys are allowed. For details see Chapter 23.
multimap	<map>	The container stores pair of values for each element, the first value is the key and second is the associated value. The elements are sorted according to key. Multiple keys are allowed. (See Chapter 23 for details).
stack	<stack>	Stack of objects has input/output order as first in last out order (FILO) or in other words last in first out. For more details see Sect.21.6 of this chapter.
queue	<queue>	A queue of objects. The input/output order is first in first out (FIFO). For more details see Section 21.6.2 below.
priority queue	<queue>	A queue of objects. The element of highest priority is at top of queue and is first out. The details are given in this chapter in Section 21.6 below.

21.3 ITERATORS

Iterators are like pointers, they are used to access the elements of container classes. They are also used to traverse from one element to another of the container by increment and decrement operators. The iterators are of following types. However, all of them are not supported by all the container classes.

Iterator	Description
input_iterator	These can be used to read values. These can be incremented, i.e. can move only forward. Other operators supported by input_iterator are given in Table 21.2.
output_iterator	They can be used to write and can be incremented and dereferenced.
forward_iterator	They can do the functions of input as well as output iterators. However, these move in forward direction only. These support dereferencing and assignment operator.
bidirectional_iterator	These can be used to read or write. These can have forward or backward motion (can be incremented as well as decremented) and can be dereferenced.
random_iterator	These may be used for random access to an element, can be used for reading as well as writing. Random iterators encompass all the characteristics of all other iterators.

Declaration of an Iterator

The declaration of iterators for a `vector <int>` is illustrated below.

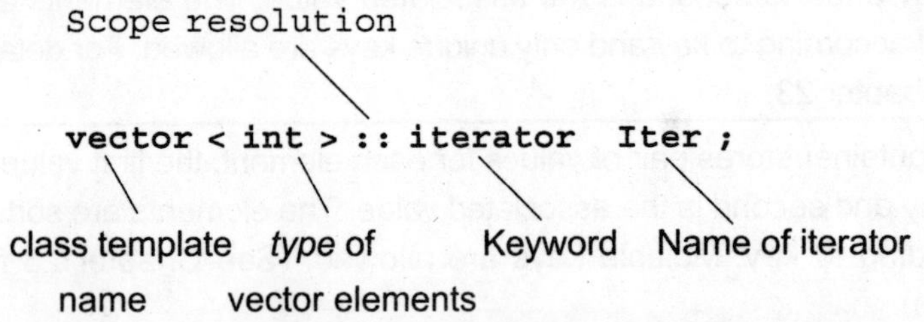


```
Iter = V1.begin();    // assigning a value to iterator Iter
                      // V1 is name of vector.
```

Fig. 21.2: Declaration and assignment of an iterator for vector class.

The declaration and assignment may be combined as given below.

```
vector <int> :: iterator Iter = V1.begin();
```

The value of the element to which the iterator is pointing may be obtained by dereference operator (*). For instance, the value of first element of the vector V1 from the above declaration is given by *Iter and value of second element is *(++Iter).

Operators Supported by Different Iterators

There are five types of iterators as already discussed above. Each type of iterator supports a set of operators as listed in Table 21.2.

Table 21.2 – Operators supported by different iterators

Input interator	Output interator	Forward interator	Bidirectional interator	Random interator	Description of operator
++itr	++itr	++itr	++itr	++itr	pre-increment
itr++	itr++	itr++	itr++	itr++	post-increment
*itr read only		*itr	*itr	*itr	Value = *itr See Program 21.1
	*itr write only	*itr	*itr	*itr	*itr = Value See Program 21.2
itr1 == itr2		itr1 == itr2	itr1 == itr2	itr1 == itr2	comparison for equality
itr1 != itr2		itr1 != itr2	itr1 != itr2	itr1 != itr2	comparison for inequality
				itr1 = itr2	assignment
			––itr	––itr	pre-decrement
			itr––	itr––	post-decrement
				itr + k	increase by int k
				itr – k	decrease by int k
				itr += k	increase by int k and assign
				itr –= k	decrease by int k and assign
				[k]	subscript operator
				itr1 < itr2	comparison less than
				itr1>itr2	greater than
				itr1<=itr2	less than or equal to
				itr1>=itr2	greater than or equal to

21.4 SEQUENCE CONTAINERS

Some of the features of containers have already been discussed in the Table 21.1. The sequence containers comprise three containers which are vector, list and deque (double ended queue). Here we take illustrative examples of each of the three, for more details see Chapter 22.

The Vector

The vectors are dynamic arrays. The number of elements may be changed during the program execution. Here a few features are illustrated. The following program gives an illustration of vector, iterators and functions like `push_back()`, `begin()`, `end()`, etc. For other functions and operators supported by vector class see Chapter 22.

PROGRAM 21.1 – Illustrates application of vectors and input iterator of istream.

```
#include<iostream>
#include<vector>
# include <iterator>
using namespace std;
vector<int> V;  // Declaration of a vector with int elements

int main()
 {
 cout<<"Enter 5 integers one after another."<<endl;
 istream_iterator <int> readit(cin);  // input iterator
 /*Below function push_back() is used to add elements at back of a vector
V. The function pushes back the value read by readit. Thus a vector with 5 elements
is created. For more details on constructors of vector class see Chapter 22.*/

 V.push_back (*readit++);
 V.push_back (*(readit++));
 V.push_back (*(readit++));
 V.push_back (*(readit++));
 V.push_back (*(readit));

 cout<<"Elements of V are : ";
 vector<int>:: iterator iter = V.begin();
/* vector is name of class, iterator is key word. iter is the name of iterator.
Function begin()returns iterator to first element of V. vector class supports
random iterator */
 while( iter != V.end())

 //end() returns iterator just past the last element of vector

 cout<< *iter++ <<" "; // display values of elements of vector

 return 0;
  }
```

The expected output is given below.

```
Enter 5 integers one after another.
30 40 50 60 70
Elements of V are : 30 40 50 60 70
```

Below is another program dealing with vectors and uses iterators for traversing the vector.

PROGRAM 21.2 –Example of a vector, input iterator of istream and iterator for traversing the vector.

```
#include<iostream>
#include<vector>
```

```
# include <iterator>
using namespace std;
 vector<int> V;  // Declaration of a vector with int elements

int main()
 {
 cout<<"Enter 5 integers one after another."<<endl;
 int count =0;
  while (count <=4)
   {istream_iterator <int> readit(cin); // input iterator

 V.push_back (*readit);
 ++count;}
/* vector is constructed by pushing back elements. The elements  are added
at the back of vector*/
 cout<<"\nElements of V are : ";

vector<int>:: iterator iter = V.begin(); // iterator defined

/*iter is name of iterator. In following it is used for traversing through
the vector*/

while( iter != V.end())
 {cout<< *iter <<" ";
  iter++;}
return 0;
  }
```

The expected output is given below.

```
Enter 5 integers one after another.
25
30
40
30
60

Elements of V are : 25 30 40 30 60
```

The Deque

The following program illustrates operations on a deque, i.e. declaration of deque, construction of deque and input, output iterators of iostream. The deque also supports random iterator and any element may be accessed directly. For more details and illustrations on deque see Chapter 22.

PROGRAM 21.3 – Illustrates input, output iterators and application to a deque.

```
#include<iostream>
#include<deque>
# include <iterator>
```

```
using namespace std;
deque <int> Dek; // declaration of deque of integers

int main()
 {
 cout<<"Enter 4 integers."<<endl;
 int count =0;
 while (count < 4)
 { istream_iterator <int> readit(cin);
  Dek.push_back (*readit);
   ++count; }
 int k=0;
 cout<<"\nElements of Dek are : ";

 while (k <4)
 {ostream_iterator <int> writeit(cout);
   * writeit= * (Dek.begin()+k );
    cout<<" ";
     k++;}
 return 0;
  }
```

The output of the program is given below.

```
Enter 4 integers.
45
30
20
60

Elements of Dek are : 45 30 20 60
```

THE LIST

The following program illustrates the list container. It is like a doubly linked list. The program illustrates declaration of list, its construction and its output. Below is a sample program. For more details on lists and functions and operators supported by class list see Chapter 22.

PROGRAM 21.4 – Illustrates declaration and construction of lists and input/output.

```
#include<iostream>
#include<list>
using namespace std;

list<char> Lc ; //declaration of a list with name Lc and type char
list<int> Li (7,60);  // declaration of list with name Li
     // it has 7 int elements each of value 60
```

```
int main()
{
for (int i=0; i<6;i++)
 Lc.push_back(65+i); // Adding elements at back of list Lc

cout <<"The first element of Lc is "<<Lc.front()<<" and last element is "
<<Lc.back()<<endl; // output of first and last

list<double>Ld(3,2.5); //List Ld has 3 elements each of value 2.5

 for ( int j =0; j< 3; j++)
  {Ld.push_back( 5.5);  // Add 3 elements each 5.5 at back
  Ld.push_front( 10.5);} //Add 3 elements each 10.5 at front

 cout<< "Lc = ";
 list<double>::iterator itrd; // iterator for a double list

 list<int> :: iterator itri; //declaration of iterator for int

 list <char>:: iterator itrc;  // iterator for char list

for(itrc= Lc.begin(); itrc!=Lc.end(); itrc++)
cout << *itrc <<" ";  // output of elements of list Lc

 cout<<"\n Li = ";
 for(itri= Li.begin(); itri!=Li.end(); itri++)
 cout << *itri <<" "; // output of elements of list Li

 cout<< "\n Ld = ";
 for(itrd= Ld.begin(); itrd!=Ld.end(); itrd++)
 cout << *itrd<<" "; // output of elements list Ld.

cout <<"\n First element of Ld = " <<*(Ld.begin())<<endl;
cout<<"\n Third element of Ld from beginning = " <<*(++(++ Ld.begin())) ;
// list class does not support random access

cout<<"\n Third element of Ld from end = " << * (--(-- Ld.end()))<<endl ;
return 0;
 }
```

The expected output is given below.

```
The first element of Lc is A and last element is F
Lc = A B C D E F
Li = 60 60 60 60 60 60 60
Ld = 10.5 10.5 10.5 2.5 2.5 2.5 5.5 5.5 5.5
First element of Ld = 10.5

Third element of Ld from beginning = 10.5
Third element of Ld from end = 5.5
```

21.5 ASSOCIATIVE CONTAINERS

The associative containers support fast retrieval of elements through keys. These comprise (i) sets, (ii) multisets, (iii) maps and (iv) multimaps. The container size may be varied during the program execution. The elements of an associative set are of type *value_type*. Each element is associated with a key of type *key_type*. In case of sets and multisets the element value itself is the key, i.e. key and the associated value is one and same while in case of maps and multimaps the keys are different from the associated values. Thus in sets and multisets an element comprises single value while in maps and multimaps an element is a pair comprising a key and a value.

The sets have only unique keys while multiset allows duplicate keys. Similarly, map allows only unique keys while multimaps allow duplicate keys. The following program illustrates the construction and input/output of a map. For more details on set and maps see Chapter 23. Here we take an illustrative program as given below on sets.

PROGRAM 21.5 – Illustration of construction and output of a map.

```
#include<iostream>
using namespace std;
#include<map>
#include<string>
typedef map <string, int> Mint ;
 /* typedef has been used to avoid writing of map<string, int> several times.
In the declaration key is a string and value int.*/
int main()
{
 string Name ;
 int Marks;
 Mint Grade; // Grade is the name of map

 for (int i = 0; i<4; i++)
 {cin>> Name ;
 cin >> Marks;

 Grade [Name] = Marks ;} // making pairs of values

 Mint :: iterator iter;   // declaration of iterator

 for( iter = Grade.begin(); iter != Grade.end(); iter++)
 cout<< (*iter).first<<" \t " <<(*iter).second<<"\n" ;

/*first is the key and second is the value. The dot operator selects first
and second.*/
return 0;
  }
```

The output of the program is given below. The first eight lines are data input and remaining four lines are output of program.

```
Sunita
85
```

```
Mamta
75
Adity
90
Pummy
70
Adity 90
Mamta 75
Pummy 70
Sunita 85
```

21.6 CONTAINER ADAPTERS: STACK, QUEUE AND PRIORITY QUEUE

The stack, queue and priority queue are the container adapters in STL. They do not support any iterator and do not have their own data implementation structure like vectors, lists, etc. However, they can adapt the data structures of other containers. Therefore, the programmer can choose the container that suits the program at hand.

STACK

Stacks allow the insertion and deletion of data at one end, i.e. last in first out (LIFO) or first in last out order (FILO). It is illustrated in Fig. 21.3 below. The figure shows that plates are stacked one over another. For taking out a plate it is picked from the top of the stack. So the plate that was placed last is picked up first. There are many applications of stacks, for instance, compiler makes a stack of machine code from the source code. The functions supported by stack class are listed in Table 21.3.

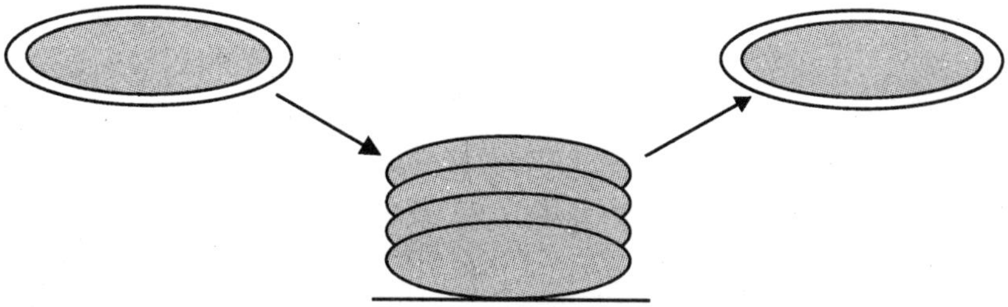

Fig. 21.3: Last in first out LIFO

Table 21.3 – Functions associated with stacks

Function	Description
`empty()`	The function returns true if stack is empty.
`pop()`	The function removes the top element of stack.
`push()`	The function adds an element at the top of stack.
`size()`	The function returns the number of elements in the stack.
`top()`	The function returns the top element of stack.

The following program illustrates implementation of a stack. The function push () is used to fill the stack. The applications of some of the above mentioned functions are illustrated with a stack thus formed.

PROGRAM 21.6 – Illustrates application of different functions on a stack.

```
#include<iostream>
#include<stack>
using namespace std;

void main()
 { stack<int> St1 ;  //St1 is declared a stack of integers

 for ( int i =1; i< 7; i++) // construction by push function
 St1.push (10* i);
    //The elements pushed are 10, 20, 30, 40, 50, 60
   // In stack it is last in first out order

 cout <<"Top element of St1 = " <<St1.top() <<endl;
 cout<<"Size of stack St1 is = " << St1.size() <<endl;

 cout<<"Elements of St1 are: ";

 while(!St1.empty()) // output statement for stack elements
  {cout<<St1.top()<<" " ;
   St1.pop() ; } // remove the top element
  }
```

The expected output is given below.

```
Top element of St1 = 60
Size of stack St1 is = 6
Elements of St1 are: 60 50 40 30 20 10
```

In the above program the stack is constructed by pushing values. In the output statement the top element is put to output stream first, then, the top element is removed by the function **pop()**. The next element comes to top and is put to output stream and then popped out (removed). The process continues till the last element is out. From the output it is clear that the first element in output stream is the one that was pushed in last. The following program presents another example of stack.

PROGRAM 21.7– Illustrates another example of stacks of elements of different types.

```
#include<iostream>
#include<stack>
#include <string>

using namespace std;

void main()
{
stack<int> Ski ; // declaration of stack of integers
 stack<char> Sch; // declaration of stack of char elements
  stack<string> Skt ; // declaration of stack of strings
```

```
string Name[4]={"Delhi", "Mumbai", "Kanpur", "Madras"};
 char ch[4] = { 'B','A', 'C', 'T'};
 int Array[5] = { 10, 40, 60,20,10 };

for ( int i = 0;i < 4; i++)
{Ski.push (Array[i]);  // push 4 elements in stack Ski
 Sch.push (ch[i]);  // push 4 elements in stack Sch
  Skt.push (Name[i]);} // push 4 elements in stack Skt

cout <<"Top element of Skt = " <<Skt.top()<<endl;

cout <<"Top element of Sch = " <<Sch.top()<<endl;
cout <<"Top element of Ski = " <<Ski.top()<<endl;

cout<<"Size of stack Skt is = " << Skt.size() <<endl;
cout<<"The elements of three stack are as below."<<endl;

for ( int j = 0;j < 4; j++)
{ cout<<Skt.top()<<"\t" << Sch.top()<<"\t" <<Ski.top() <<"\n";

Skt.pop() ;   // remove the top element of Skt

 Sch.pop();   // remove the top element of Sch

  Ski.pop();  // remove the top element of Ski
 }
 }
```

The expected output is as under.

```
Top element of Skt = Madras
Top element of Sch = T
Top element of Ski = 20
Size of stack Skt is = 4
The elements of three stack are as below.
Madras      T      20
Kanpur      C      60
Mumbai      A      40
Delhi       B      10
```

PROGRAM 21.8 – Illustrates stacks with underlying data structure of vector.

```
#include<iostream>
#include<stack>
using namespace std;

#include <vector>

int main()
 {
 stack <int, vector <int> > Stack1, Stack2, Stack3;
     // Declaration of Stacks of int
      // The underlying container is vector
```

```
int Array1[]={12 ,13 ,14 ,15 , 16 };
int Array2[] = { 40, 60,20,10,50 };

for ( int i = 0;i < 5; i++)
{Stack1.push (Array1[i]);
 Stack2 .push (Array2[i]); }

Stack3 = Stack2;  // Stack2 is assigned to Stack3

cout<<"Size of Stack3 is = " << Stack3 .size() <<endl;

if ( Stack2 == Stack3 ) // relational == operator
   cout<< "Stack3 and Stack2 are equal \n";
else
 cout<<"Stack3 and Stack2 are not equal \n";

Stack3.push(80); // add another element into stack
cout << "Now size of Stack3 = "<<Stack3.size()<<endl;

for ( int j = 0;j < 6; j++)  // for output of stack elements
{cout<<Stack3.top()<<" " ; //display the top element of Stack3

Stack3.pop();} // remove the top element of Stack3

return 0;
 }
```

The expected output is given below.

```
Size of Stack3 is = 5
Stack3 and Stack2 are equal
Now size of Stack3 = 6
80 50 10 20 60 40
```

QUEUE

In queue the data elements can be inserted at the back and removed from the front-end. The order is same as it happens in real life queues, i.e. first in first out (FIFO). It is illustrated in the following figure. Queue may be formed by pushing items by function `push()`.

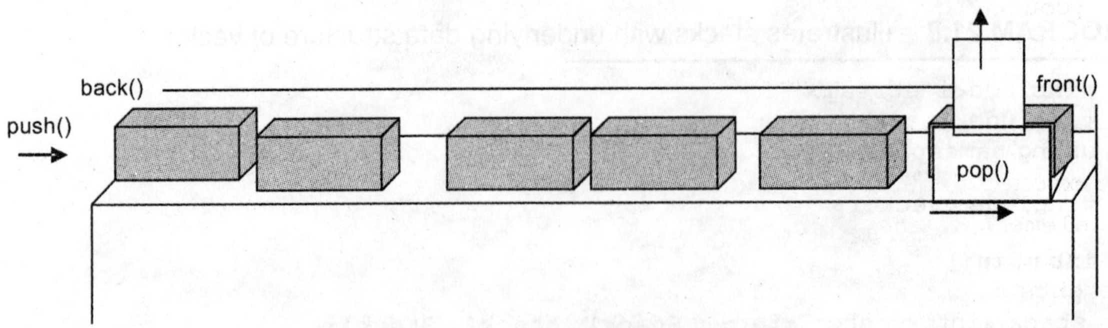

Fig. 21.4: An illustration of queue

The various functions associated with a queue are listed in Table 21.4

Table 21.4 – Functions associated with queues. Header file **<queue>**

Function	Description
back()	The function returns a reference to last element of queue.
empty()	The function returns true if queue is empty.
front()	The function returns a reference to the first element of current queue.
pop()	The function removes the front element of queue.
push ()	The function adds an element at the end of queue.
size ()	The function returns the number of elements in the queue.

The following program illustrates different operations on queues.

PROGRAM 21.9 – Illustrates application of some queue functions.

```
#include<iostream>
#include<queue>
using namespace std;

 void main()
{
queue <int> Q ;

 for ( int i =1; i<7; i++)
 Q.push (10* i);
 // in queue there is no function top() instead it is front()
 // the output of elements from the front of queue is
//illustrated below.
 cout<< "The element at the front = " <<Q.front()<<endl;
 cout<<"Size of queue Q is = " << Q.size() <<endl;
 cout<<"Elements of Q are: ";

 while(!Q.empty())   // output statement for queue
 {cout<<Q.front()<<" " ;
 Q.pop() ; }

   }
```

The expected output is given below.

```
The element at the front = 10
Size of queue Q is = 6
Elements of Q are: 10 20 30 40 50 60
```

The following program illustrates some of operators supported by queues.

PROGRAM 21.10 – Illustrates operators acting on queues.

```
#include<iostream>
#include<queue>
using namespace std;

int main()
{
 queue<int> q2,q3 ;
 queue<double> q1;

 for ( int i =0; i< 6; i++)
 {q1.push (1.5*i);
 q2.push (i*i);}

 q3 = q2; // assignment operator

 if( q2 == q3)
  cout<< "Now the queues q2 and q3 are equal"<<endl;
 else
  cout<< "Now the queues q2 and q3 are not equal"<<endl;

 cout<< "The elements of q2 are: ";

 while(!q2.empty())
  {cout<<q2.front()<<" " ;
   q2.pop() ;}

cout<<"\n";
cout<< "The elements of q3 are: ";
 while(!q3.empty())
 {cout<<q3.front()<<" " ;
 q3.pop() ;}

 cout<<"\n";

 if( q2 == q3)
  cout<< "The queues q2 and q3 are equal"<<endl;
 else
  cout<< "The queues q2 and q3 are not equal"<<endl;

  cout<<"push another element 10 into q3 \n";
  q3.push (10);

  cout<< "The elements of queue q3 are: ";

 while(!q3.empty())
  {cout<<q3.front()<<" " ;
  q3.pop() ;}

  cout <<"\n";
```

```
cout<< "The elements of q1 are: ";

while(!q1.empty())
{cout<<q1.front()<<" " ;

 q1.pop() ;}
 cout <<"\n";
return 0;
 }
```

The expected output is given below.

```
Now the queues q2 and q3 are equal
The elements of q2 are: 0 1 4 9 16 25
The elements of q3 are: 0 1 4 9 16 25
The queues q2 and q3 are equal
push another element 10 into q3
The elements of queue q3 are: 10
The elements of q1 are: 0 1.5 3 4.5 6 7.5
```

In the above program three queues are declared—two queues of int and one of double numbers. The queues q1 and q2 are constructed by push function while q3 has been made as a copy of queue q2. The elements are added at back while they are popped out (removed) at the front-end. The application of functions empty () and front () and operator ++ is illustrated. After the assignment q3 = q2 ; the two queues are equal. After the elements have been popped (removed) then also they are equal because there is no element left in both the queues. Then an element (10) is added to q3. Now the element in q3 is only 10. In the last line of output the elements of q1 are displayed. After the display there is now no element left in q1 because all are removed (popped out) during display.

PRIORITY_QUEUE

The priority queues are queues in which the elements are ordered by a predicate. By default the element with highest value is at the top. The various functions associated with priority queues are described in Table 21.5. Here the function top() is used to point to the element at the front-end in place of function front() which is used in queue.

Table 21.5 – Functions associated with priority_queue

Function	Description
`empty()`	The function returns true if priority_queue is empty.
`pop()`	The function removes the top element of priority_queue.
`push()`	The function adds an element into priority_queue.
`size()`	The function returns the number of elements in priority_queue.
`top()`	The function returns top element of the priority_queue.

The following program illustrates the application of some of these functions.

PROGRAM 21.11 – Illustrates priority queues.

```
#include<iostream>
#include<queue>
using namespace std;
void main()
 {
 priority_queue <int> PQ ; // declaration of priority queue
 int Array[6] = { 10, 80, 90, 20, 40,70};

 for ( int i =0; i<6; i++)
 PQ.push (Array[i]);

 // in priority _queue there is no front instead it is top()

 cout<< "The element at the top = " <<PQ.top()<<endl;
 cout<<"Size of queue PQ is = " << PQ.size() <<endl;

 cout<<"Elements of PQ are: ";

 while(!PQ.empty())
 {cout<<PQ.top()<<" " ;
 PQ.pop() ; }
  }
```

The expected output is given below.

```
The element at the top = 90
Size of queue PQ is = 6
Elements of PQ are: 90 80 70 40 20 10
```

The output is self explanatory. The unordered elements of an array are pushed into the priority queue. We see from the output that the items are ordered with the element having highest value at the top.

21.7 FUNCTION OBJECTS/PREDICATES

A function object is a class object which acts as a function and returns a bool value depending upon whether its argument, which may be a container element, satisfies the function or not. In several algorithms the elements of a container are selected subject to whether the element satisfies a predicate which is a function object. The algorithm is implemented subject to the return value of function object. If the return value is true the algorithm is implemented otherwise not. Before going to function objects, we shall examine an ordinary function acting as a predicate.

PROGRAM 21.12 – Illustrates a global function used as predicate in an algorithm.

```
#include<iostream>
#include<algorithm>
#include<functional>
```

```
using namespace std;

 bool Odd (int n) // definition of function for odd number
  {return n%2 ? true : false;}

 bool Even(int m ) // definition of function for even number
  {return !(m%2) ? true: false ;}

int main()
{
 int S[ ] = { 5,6,8,7,4,3,8,10,11, 12};
 int n = count_if(S, S+10, Even );
/* count_if()is an algorithm. Even is the address of (pointer to) the function
Even() defined above. The function count_if is implemented if the element
satisfies the function Even*/
cout<< "Number of even elements of S are = " <<n <<endl;

int K = count_if(S, S+10, Odd);
/* Odd is the address of function Odd defined above. The function count_if()
is implemented if the element satisfies the function Odd*/
cout<<"Number of odd elements of S are = " <<K<<endl;
return 0;
}
```

The expected output is given below.

```
Number of even elements of S are = 6
Number of odd elements of S are = 4
```

In the above case the elements are examined if they are divisible by 2 or not and according to the bool return value which is either true or false the element is counted or rejected. One of the functions (Odd) tests the elements for odd numbers while the second function (Even) tests the elements whether they are even. Though only one function is needed, the two are included to illustrate the form of the functions. The selection of even or odd depends on the return values of these functions. Similarly, one may define a function whether a particular integer is divisible by another integer or not. In such a case, if the divisor is required to be changed often, then for every new divisor the program has to be changed. It is better to define a class with the function as an object of the class. It is convenient because class object can hold the data (the divisor). In such a scheme the function is called **function object**. It is illustrated below.

PROGRAM 21.13 – Illustrates definition of a predicate as a template class.

```
#include<iostream>
# include<algorithm>
using namespace std;

 template <class T>
 class GTE {   // GTE = Greater than or equal to
    private :
    T x;
```

```
public :
 GTE (T A){ x = A;}  // constructor function
    bool operator() (T y)
     {return y >= x ? true :false;}
     };       // end of class

int main()
{ GTE <int> gte(30); //gte is declared an object of GTE for int

GTE <double> gted (25.0); // gted is an object for double 25.0

int S[] = { 10,20,30 ,36, 44, 60, 70 };
double SD [] = { 3.5, 27.5, 22.6, 56.7, 80.0, 90.7, 65.5, 35.5};
      //count_if() is a an algorithm

int m = count_if ( S, S+7, gte); // here gte is a predicate
cout << "Number of elements in S >= 30 are = "<<m<<endl;

int n = count_if( SD, SD+8, gted); //here gted is a predicate

cout<< "Number of elements in SD >= 25.0 are = "<< n<<endl;
return 0 ;
 }
```

The expected output is given below.

```
Number of elements in S >= 30 are = 5
Number of elements in SD >= 25.0 are = 6
```

In the above program the objects gte and gted behave like functions. The initialisation values of the objects, i.e. 30 and 25.0 become the arguments of the functions. It seems a better option than the predicate function of the previous program.

There are several predefined predicates in C++ as listed in Table 21.6 below. As illustrated above the user may as well develop his/her own predicates.

21.8 PREDEFINED PREDICATES IN C++

There are nine predefined relational and logical predicates defined in header file **<functional>**. Some of the predicates provided in the header file are listed in Table 21.6.

Table 21.6 – Predefined predicates in header file **<functional>**

Predicate	Arity (Unary/binary)	Equivalent operation
plus	binary	x + y
minus	binary	x – y
multiplies	binary	x * y
divides	binary	x / y
modulus	binary	x % y

Contd...

negate	unary	– x
equal_to	binary	x==y
not_equal_to	binary	x!=y
greater	binary	x>y
greater_equal	binary	x>=y
less	binary	x<y
less_equal	binary	x<=y
logical_and	binary	x&&y
logical_or	binary	x||y
logical_not	unary	!x

An illustration of use of some predicates is provided by Program 21.14 given below.

PROGRAM 21.14 – Illustrates application of **predicates less and greater** with algorithm **sort()**.

```
#include<iostream>
#include<algorithm>
#include<functional> // header file for predefined predicates

using namespace std;
int main()
{
int S[8] = { 5,6,8,7,4,3,8,9};
char ch [] = { 'A', 'Z', 'C', 'M', 'G', 'K', 'T'};

sort(S, S+8, less<int>()); // arrange in increasing order
sort( ch, ch+7, greater<int>()); // arrange in decreasing order
for ( int i =0; i<8;i++)
cout<<S[i]<<" ";
cout <<endl;

for ( int j =0; j< 7 ; j++)
cout << ch[j]<<" ";
cout<<endl;

return 0;
}
```

The expected output is given below.

```
3 4 5 6 7 8 8 9
Z T M K G C A
```

In the first line of output the array element are sorted in increasing order. In the second line the characters are sorted in decreasing order.

21.9 BINDER FUNCTIONS

When every element of a sequence is to be compared with a value for further action it is better to bind the value with which it is to be compared with the predicate by a binder function. Two functions are defined as given below. Let us have a comparison of type expression x >= y.

bind1st (x) // calls or binds the function with x as first argument.

bind2nd (y) // calls or binds the function with y as second argument.

The application of bind2nd() is illustrated in the following program.

PROGRAM 21.15 – Illustrates application of **bind2nd()**.

```
#include<iostream>
#include<algorithm>
#include<functional>
using namespace std;

template <class T >
 struct Greater: binary_function< T , T , bool > {
 bool operator () (const T & x, const T& y) const
  { return ( x >y ) ;}};

int main()
{
int S[10] = { 5,6,8,7,4,3,8,9,12, 14 };

int n = count_if ( S, S +10, bind2nd(Greater<int>(), 7) );

cout<<"The number of elements greater than 7 are : "<< n <<endl;
return 0;
}
```

The expected output is given below. Every element of array is compared if it is more than 7.

```
The number of elements greater than 7 are : 5
```

The following program uses the standard function objects greater than and less than.

PROGRAM 21.16 –Illustrates application of **predicates greater, less and binder function.**

```
#include<iostream>
#include<algorithm>
using namespace std;

#include<functional>

int main()
{
```

```
int S[ ] = { 5,6,8,7,8,3,8,10,8, 12};

int n = count_if(S, S+10, bind2nd(greater<int>(),7));
cout<< "Number of elements of S >7 are = " <<n <<endl;

int m = count_if(S, S+10, bind2nd(less<int>(),10));
cout<< "Number of elements of S < 10 are = " <<m <<endl;
return 0;
}
```

The expected output is as under.

```
Number of elements of S >7 are = 6
Number of elements of S < 10 are = 8
```

EXERCISES

1. What is STL all about?
2. What are the main components of STL?
3. What is an iterator?
4. Which of the containers are first class containers and why?
5. How are associative containers different from sequence containers?
6. How are iterators declared? Give examples of declaration of iterator for following cases.
   (i) vectors with int elements.
   (ii) deque with double elements.
   (iii) list of a names.
7. Do the stacks support iterators?
8. What is the difference between a queue and a priority queue?
9. Make a program to illustrate the application of following functions.
   (i) push()
   (ii) top()
   (iii) size()
10. Make a program to illustrate the application of following functions.
    (i) size()
    (ii) push()
    (iii) pop()
11. How is a stack different from a vector?
12. What is a predicate?
13. Define a function predicate for sorting an array in increasing order.
14. What is a binder function?
15. Make a test program to sort out even numbers in a sequence of integers.

❍❍❍

CHAPTER

22

Sequence Containers
vector, list and deque

22.1 INTRODUCTION

Some of the features of containers have already been discussed in the Chapter 21 on STL. The sequence containers comprise three containers which are vector, list and deque (double ended queue). The comparative features of the three are described in the Table 22.1 below.

Table 22.1 – Salient features of vector, list and deque containers.

vector Header file <vector>	list Header file <list>	deque Header file <deque>
Supports random iterator Rapid access to any element.	Supports bidirectional iterator. The iterator can be incremented or decremented.	Supports random iterator. Rapid access to any element in deque.
Because of random iterator, all STL algorithms can operate on vectors.	The STL algorithms that require input/output, forward and bidirectional iterators can operate on lists	Because of random iterator, all STL algorithms can operate on deques
Rapid insertions and deletions at the back-end of vector.	Rapid insertions/deletions anywhere in the list.	Rapid insertions and deletions at the both ends of deque.
Data stored in sequential memory locations like an array.	Doubly linked list like data structure.	Based on array like data structure. Direct access possible with index operator.
The commonly used functions are described in Table 22.2.	The commonly used functions are given in Table 22.3 and Table 22.4.	The commonly used functions are described in Table 22.5.

22.2 VECTOR CLASS

Declaration of Vectors

As mentioned above, the vector class is a container class and vector elements are stored in sequential memory locations like an array. A C++ vector is not the mathematical vector though some of the concepts are similar. The C++ vector can have any number of components. It may be taken as a more robust and dynamic array. Besides, the vector class supports many functions which cannot be directly applied to pointer based arrays such as insertion and deletion of elements. The vector is a dynamic array in the sense that it can allocate to itself additional memory if needed due to the addition of elements. To start with, the allocation is a small chunk of memory which is sufficient for a few elements. If the elements increase during execution of program, the vector can relocate itself with a bigger segment of memory. While an array is a fixed length sequence (number of elements is fixed at the time of declaration). In case of arrays, an individual element can be assigned, while the array as a whole cannot be assigned. A vector may be assigned as a whole. For working with vectors we have to include the header file **<vector>** and have to declare the *type* of elements of the vector, i.e. *int, double, char,* etc., in angular brackets (< >). Examples of vector declarations are given below.

```
#include <vector>      // Header file
vector <int> V1;       // V1 is vector with int elements
vector <double> V2;     // V2 has elements of type double
vector <char> Vect;     // Vect has elements of type char
```

In the above declarations V1, V2 and Vect are the identifiers or names of the vectors. The elements of vector V1 are of type *int*, elements of V2 are of type *double* and elements of Vect are of type *char*.

More than one vector may be declared in same line if their type is same, we need to write *type* in angular brackets only once after the class name *vector*. For instance, we may declare multiple vectors as below.

```
vector <int> V1, V3 ;
vector <double> A, B, C ;
```

Constructors and Destructors of Vector Class

The container class *vector* supports a number of constructors. Some methods of constructing vectors are illustrated below.

```
vector <double> V(5);  /* Constructs a vector with 5 elements of type double
and value 0*/
vector <int> V1(4,35);   /* Constructs  V1 with 4 elements of type int and
value 35*/
vector <int> V4 (V1);     // Constructs vector V4 as a copy of vector V1
vector <char> V2 ( 4, 'D') ;
                            /* Constructs vector V2 with 4 elements each of type
char and value 'D'*/
~vector ();          /* Destructor of the vector—it deletes all the components
of the vector.*/
```

The following program illustrates some methods of constructing vectors. The output of vector elements has been carried out by [ ] operator as it is used for array elements.

PROGRAM 22.1 – Illustrates construction of vectors and output of vector elements.

```
#include<iostream>
#include<vector>
using namespace std;

vector <double> V(4) ;      // size =4, value of each = 0
  vector <int> V1(4,35)  ;   // size =4, value of each =35

int main()
 {vector<double> V2 (4, 4.5); //size = 4, value of each = 4.5
   vector<char> V3 (4, 'B');
           // vector V3 has four elements each equal to 'B'.
     vector <int> V4 (V1);    // V4 is copy of V1

       vector<int> V5  ;

  for(int i =0; i<4;i++ )   // It constructs a vector with 4
   V5.push_back (5);    //elements. Each element is equal to 5.
    cout<<"V \tV1\tV2\tV3 \tV4"<<"\tV5"<<endl;

for ( int j = 0; j< 4; j++)      // for loop for output
cout <<V[j]<<"\t"<< V1[j]<<"\t" <<V2[j]<<"\t"<< V3[j] <<"\t"<<
V4[j]<<"\t"<<V5[j]<<endl ;
  return 0;
  }
```

The expected output is as under. The elements of vectors are printed from top to bottom.

```
V    V1   V2    V3   V4   V5
0    35   4.5   B    35   5
0    35   4.5   B    35   5
0    35   4.5   B    35   5
0    35   4.5   B    35   5
```

The output is self explanatory. The vector V has 4 elements each having a value 0, the vectors V1, V2 and V3 are similarly constructed. The values of their elements are 35, 4.5 and 'B' respectively. The vector V4 is a copy of V1. The vector V5 is constructed by the function push_back (). The function adds elements at the back. In this case, all the values pushed are 5.

22.3 FUNCTIONS OF VECTOR CLASS

There are a number of member functions of vector class which may be used for manipulation of elements in the sequence. Some of these are given below in Table 22.2.

Table 22.2 – Functions of class vector

S.No.	Function	Description
1.	`assign()`	The function assigns values to a vector from beginning to end. Function is also used to assign a number of copies of a value to a vector. The previous contents are removed.
2.	`at()`	This function returns a reference to an element in a vector at the specified location (written in brackets).
3.	`back()`	It returns reference to the last element of the vector.
4.	`begin()`	It returns iterator to first element of the vector.
5.	`capacity()`	It returns number of elements that a vector can hold in the current allocation of memory. It is not the actual number of elements of the vector.
6.	`clear()`	The function deletes all the elements of a vector.
7.	`empty()`	The function returns true if there is no element in the vector, false otherwise.
8.	`end()`	It returns iterator just past the end of vector.
9.	`erase()`	It deletes element at the indexed location or elements between start and end iterators. The start element is included but the end element is not included.
10.	`front()`	It returns reference to first element of the vector.
11.	`insert()`	It inserts elements in vector (i) one value or (ii) a number of copies of a value at a specified location, (iii) insert from start to end before a location.
12.	`max_size()`	Returns maximum number of elements that a vector can hold.
13.	`pop_back()`	Removes the last element of the vector.
14.	`push_back()`	Appends an element at the back of vector.
15.	`rbegin()`	Returns a reverse iterator to the end of the vector.
16.	`rend()`	Returns a reverse iterator to the beginning of vector.
17.	`reserve()`	Sets the capacity of vector to at the least size.
18.	`resize()`	Changes the size of vector to the size specified.
19.	`size()`	Returns the current number of elements in the vector.
20.	`swap()`	Exchanges the elements of two vectors.

22.4 DEFINITION AND APPLICATION OF ITERATORS

Iterators are like pointers. These are used to traverse through the elements of a vector. The declaration of iterator say for vector V1 of *type int* is illustrated below. In the following declaration it is also initialized to `V1.begin()`, i.e. the value corresponding to the first element of vector V1.

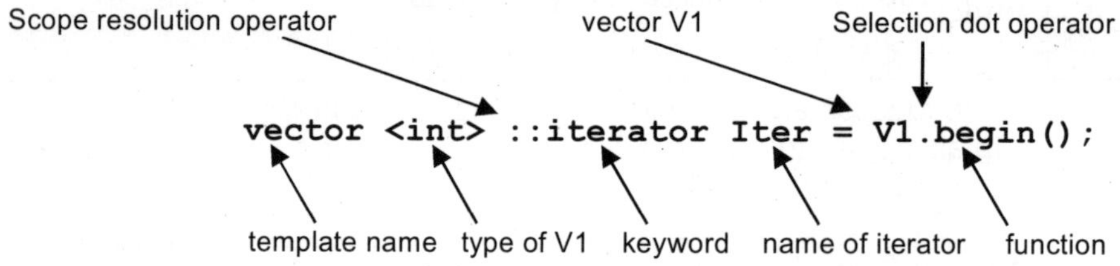

Fig. 22.1: Declaration and assignment of iterator

According to the above declaration, Iter is the name of iterator. It is initialized with value corresponding to the first element of the vector. The value may be incremented to reach the other elements of the vector. Thus Iter+1 will point to the second element of the vector. Similarly Iter+2 points to the third elements and so on. The V1.end() points to just past the last element of the vector. The values of respective elements may be obtained by dereference operator (*). Thus the value of first element is equal to *Iter , second element is equal to *(Iter+1), etc. See the following program for illustration.

PROGRAM 22.2 – Illustrates **iterators** and functions **push_back(), begin()** and **end().**

```
#include<iostream>
#include<vector>
  using namespace std;
  vector<int> V1 , V2 ; // declaration of two vectors
int main()
 {
  V1.push_back(10); // Use of function push back to construct V1
  V1.push_back(20);
  V1.push_back(30);

 vector <int> :: iterator iter = V1.begin(); // iterator for V1
 cout<< *iter <<"\t" << *(iter+1)<<"\t"<< *(iter +2) <<endl;

cout<< iter<<"\t"<< iter+1<<"\t" << iter+2 << endl;
cout << "Elements of vector V2 are as below.\n ";

 for (int i =0;i< 6; i++)
 V2.push_back (i*i);          // construction of V2
 iter  = V2.begin();          // iterator for V2
   while ( iter != V2.end())
      {cout <<*iter <<"  ";
          iter++;}
 cout<<endl;
 return 0;
 }
```

The expected output is as under.

```
10     20     30
00480070        00480074        00480078
Elements of vector V2 are as below.
 0  1  4  9  16  25
```

With the help of function push_back () three elements are pushed into V1. These are additions to the existing elements. The values of these elements are 10, 20 and 30 respectively. The output of these has been carried out by iterator iter which is initialized to V1.begin(). Thus `*iter` is the value of 1st element, `*(iter+1)` gives value of 2nd element and `*(iter+2)` gives value of third element and so on. The values of iter, iter+1 and iter+2 are the addresses of the elements. Similarly the elements of V2 are extracted with the help of while loop along with iterator `iter`.

22.5 OPERATORS SUPPORTED BY VECTOR CLASS

Two vectors may be compared with overloaded comparison operators such as `==`, `>`, `<`, `<=`, `>=`, `!=`. A vector may be assigned to another just like we assign the variables of fundamental type. This is illustrated below.

```
vector<int> V1 (5, 50) , V2 ;
V2 = V1;
```

In the above code two vectors are declared. The V1 has been initialized with 5 elements each equal to 50. The vector V1 is assigned to V2, so V2 becomes a copy of vector V1. The equality may be tested with the operator (==). Two vectors are equal if their sizes are equal and each element of vector one at location i is equal to the element at location i of the second vector. The arithmetic operations are possible on individual elements of a vector. The following program illustrates the application of some of the operators.

22.6 APPLICATION OF FUNCTIONS OF VECTOR CLASS

The different functions supported by vector class are listed in Table 22.2 along with the brief description about the action they can perform. Some of these are discussed below.

FUNCTION ASSIGN ()

Let V be a vector to which the values are to be assigned. If all the components are equal we may assign the values as below.

```
V.assign (6, 80);
```

According to the above code the vector V has been assigned 6 elements and each element has value 80. Thus the vector V has the elements 80, 80, 80, 80, 80 and 80. The function assign () removes the existing elements of the vector. The function `push_back()` is also used to put in values of vector elements. It appends the value written in the brackets at the back of the vector, i.e. it adds a new element at the back of the vector. Thus if it is intended to add a new element to V at its back, the syntax is given below.

```
V.push_back (35);
```

With the addition of 35, the vector V now has the elements 80, 80, 80, 80, 80, 80 and 35.

PROGRAM 22.3 – Illustrates functions **assign(), push_back()** and some operators.

```
#include<iostream>
#include<vector>
# include <string>
using namespace std;
   vector<int> V1, V2,V3 , V4;
   vector <string> V5;

int main()
 {
  V1.assign(5,5 ); //V1 is assigned 5 values each equal to 5.
  V2.assign(5,4); //V2 is assigned 5 values each equal to 4.

  V3 = V2;        // vector V2 is assigned to vector V3
  string Str [] = {"Nimi" ,"Simi", "Jimmy", "Ginny", "Pummy"};
  int Array [] = { 1,2,3,4,5};

 for (int j =0; j<5 ;j++)
  {V4.push_back (Array[j]);
     V5.push_back (Str[j]);}
                 //elements of array Str are pushed in V5
  if(V2 == V3)
  {cout <<"V2 and V3 are equal"<<endl;}

  else
  cout<<" V2 and V3 are not equal"<<endl;

  cout<<"V1 \tV2 \tV3 \tV4 \t V5"<<endl ;

 for ( int i = 0; i< 5; i++)
 cout<<V1[i] <<"\t"<<V2[i] <<"\t"<<V3[i]<< "\t"<< V4[i]<<"\t" << V5[i]
<<endl;

 cout<< "Address of V3 = "<< &V3 <<endl ;
   for ( int k=0;k< 5 ;k++)
     V2[k] *= V1[k] ;

  cout<< "Components of V2 now are = ";
   for (int m =0; m<5; m++)
     cout<<V2.at(m) <<"  ";
```

```
        cout<<"\n";
         return 0;
        }
```

The expected output of the program is given below.

```
V2 and V3 are equal
V1     V2     V3     V4      V5
5      4      4      1       Nimi
5      4      4      2       Simi
5      4      4      3       Jimmy
5      4      4      4       Ginny
5      4      4      5       Pummy
Address of V3 = 0047B780
Components of V2 now are = 20  20  20  20  20
```

In the above program we get an illustration of application of function `assign()` and the function `at()`. Also the program has a vector whose elements are strings. The output of vectors has been done by [] operator like an array rather than by iterators. The individual elements of a vector may be subjected to arithmetic operations like any other variable.

FUNCTIONS SIZE () AND FUNCTION CAPACITY ()

The function size() gives the actual number of elements in the vector while capacity gives the maximum number of elements it can hold in the current memory allocation. Vector is a dynamic array, as the number of elements increases beyond the allocated capacity, the vector is relocated with a bigger chunk of memory.

PROGRAM 22.4 – Illustrates **`iterators`** and functions **`size()`**, **`capacity()`**, **`end()`**,**`begin()`**, **`push_back()`** and **`pop_back()`**.

```
#include<iostream>
#include<vector>

using namespace std;
vector<int> V ;

int main()
 {
for ( int i =1; i<=5;i++)
  V.push_back (i*i);    // 5 values 1,4,9,16,25 are pushed into V

cout<<"Size of V = "<< V.size()<<endl;
  cout<<"Capacity of V = " << V.capacity()<< endl;
     cout<<"The elements of vector V are, "<<endl;

for (int j = 0; j<=4; j++)
```

```
    cout <<"  "<< V[j]<<"   " ;
      cout<<endl;

   V.pop_back(); //The last element (25) of V is removed
   cout<<"After pop_back the size of V is = "<< V.size()<<endl;
    cout<< " Capacity of V = " << V.capacity()<<endl;

   for ( int k =1; k< 6; k++)
   V.push_back (2*k);   // 5 values (2,4,6,8,10)are pushed in to V
   cout << "Now size of V is = "<<V.size();
   cout<<"\nNow capacity of V is = "<< V.capacity();

   vector <int> :: iterator itr;   // declaration of iterator itr
   cout<<"\nAfter pop_back the elements of V are,"<<endl;
   for ( itr  = V.begin() ; itr < V.end ()  ; itr ++)
   cout<<*itr <<"    " ; // output of values of elements with iterators
   cout<<endl;
   return 0;
     }
```

The expected output is given below.

```
Size of V = 5
Capacity of V = 8
The elements of vector V are,
 1   4   9   16   25
After pop_back the size of V is = 4
 Capacity of V = 8
Now size of V is = 9
Now capacity of V is = 16
After pop_back the elements of V are,
1   4   9   16   2   4   6   8   10
```

The program output given above illustrates the difference between function `capacity()` and the function `size()`. Capacity gives the maximum number of elements that the vector can hold in the current memory allocation while size gives the actual number of elements. Vectors are dynamic arrays. The number of elements may increase or decrease during the execution of the program. If the number of elements increases and the vector needs more than the memory allocated initially, the vector is relocated with bigger chunk of memory. The relocation is done automatically and the existing elements are copied to the new location. In the above output it shows that when the elements increase to 9 the capacity increases from 8 to 16.

The function push_back () adds the element after the end of the vector and pop_back() removes the last element from vector.

FUNCTION AT()

In case of arrays, there is no check to see that an index value does not exceed the number of elements of the array. It is quite possible that the index value may exceed the number of elements in the array and some garbage value may be substituted as its value. In vector class a guard is provided by the function **at()**. It is coded as `V.at(k)` where k is the index value and the function gives value of element of vector V at location k. If the value of index exceeds the number of elements it will give a warning and abort the program as illustrated in the following program.

PROGRAM 22.5 – Illustrates application of function **at().**

```
#include<iostream>
#include<vector>
using namespace std;
  vector<int> V ;
 int main()
  {
  V.assign(6,8 );     //assigns 6 values each equal to 8 to V
  for ( int i = 0; i< 6; i++)
  cout<<V[i] <<"   ";
  cout<<"\n\n";
for( int j=0;j< 6 ;j++)
 {V[j] = j*V[j]; //each element is multiplied by its index value
   cout <<V[j]<<"   " ;
   }
  cout<<"\n\n";
for (int k =0; k<8; k++)
  //Note that the maximum value of k is more than the number of elements
cout<<"The " <<k<< " element = " << V.at(k)<< endl;
 return 0;
  }
```

In the above program the vector V has 6 elements, each has value 8 and this is displayed in the first line of the output given below. The values are then multiplied by its position index value in the vector, so values are now 0, 8, 16, 24, 32 and 40 as displayed in the second line of the output. These value are programmed to be displayed with the function `at(k)`, where k varies from 0 to 7, i.e. 2 more than the number of elements. The program runs to display the first 6 elements after which it terminates the program because the index value is more than the number of elements in the vector. The complete output is given below.

```
8   8   8   8   8   8

0   8   16   24   32   40
```

```
The 0 element = 0
The 1 element = 8
The 2 element = 16
The 3 element = 24
The 4 element = 32
The 5 element = 40

abnormal program termination
```

PROGRAM 22.6 – Illustrates application of **erase()**, and **front()**.

```
#include<iostream>
#include<vector>
using namespace std;

 vector<int> V2(2);  // V2 has two elements each of value 0.
 vector< double > V4;

int main()
 {
 for ( int i = 1; i<6; i++)
 { V2.push_back (i*i); // 5 values( 1,4,9,16,25)are pushed in V2

   V4.push_back (i*2.5);} //5 values are pushed in V4
   cout<<"\n V4 = ";

   vector<double>:: iterator itr4;
   for( itr4 = V4.begin(); itr4 != V4.end(); itr4++)
   cout<< *itr4<<"  ";    //output of elements of V4

 vector<int> :: iterator itr;
 cout<<"\nNow V2 = ";

   for( itr = V2.begin(); itr != V2.end(); itr++)
   cout<<*itr<<"   " ;

   cout<<"\nAfter erasing first two elements  V2 = ";
   if ( V2.front() ==0)
   V2.erase(V2.begin(),V2.begin()+2);
  // erase 1st and 2nd element. The third element is not erased

 for( itr = V2.begin(); itr != V2.end(); itr++)
 cout<< *itr<<"  "; // output statement

 V2.pop_back( );
 V2.pop_back();

 cout<<"\nAfter two pop-backs V2 = ";
 for( itr = V2.begin(); itr != V2.end(); itr++)
```

```
cout<< *itr<<"   ";
cout<<endl;
return 0;
}
```

The expected output is given below. V2 had 2 elements each equal to 0, later 5 more elements are pushed into it.

```
V4 = 2.5   5   7.5   10   12.5
Now V2 = 0   0   1   4   9   16   25
After erasing first two elements V2 = 1   4   9   16   25
After two pop-backs V2 = 1   4   9
```

In the following program we carry out various operations with relational operators such as ==, <, >, >=, <=, etc., in the same way as we use these operators for fundamental types.

PROGRAM 22.7 – Illustrates use of relational operators with vectors.

```
#include<iostream>
#include<vector>
using namespace std;

vector<int> V1;
  vector <int> V2;
    vector <int> V3;
      vector<int> V4;
int main()

 {V2.assign (5, 65); //assigns 5 elements each equal to 65 to V2.
  V3.assign(5,70); //assigns 5 elements each equal to 70 to V3.

  V1.push_back(2);
  V1.push_back(4);   // push_back appends value 4 at the back of
              //the vector. A method of creating a vector.
  V1.push_back(5);
  V1.push_back(6);
  V1.push_back(7);

 if ( V2 == V1)   // test for equality
   cout<< "The vectors V1 and V2 are equal."<<endl;
 else
   cout<<"Vectors V1 and V2 are not equal"<<endl;

  V2 = V1;                  // V1 is assigned to V2
cout<<"After assignment," << endl;
if( V1!= V2)
  cout <<"Vector V1 is not equal to V2"<<endl;
```

```
else

  cout<<"Vector V1 and V2 are equal."<<endl;
  cout<< "The elements of V2 are as below"<<endl;

  for ( int i = 0; i< 5; i++)
  cout <<" V2["<<i<<"] = "<< V2[i]<<endl;

return 0;
 }
```

The expected output of the above program is as below.

```
Vectors V1 and V2 are not equal
After assignment,
Vector V1 and V2 are equal.
The elements of V2 are as below
V2[0] = 2
V2[1] = 4
V2[2] = 5
V2[3] = 6
V2[4] = 7
```

FUNCTION INSERT()

The function `insert()` takes three arguments, the first is the location where the insertion is desired, second is the number of insertions and the third is the value of each insertion. See the following program for illustration.

PROGRAM 22.8 – Illustrates insertion of additional elements at specified locations in a vector.

```
#include<iostream>
#include<vector>
#include<cmath>
using namespace std;
 vector<int> V1;
 vector<double> V2  ;
 vector<char> V3;

void main()
 { for ( int i =0; i<=4;i++)
  {V1.push_back (i+2 );      // creating a vector
  V2. push_back (sqrt(i+2));
  V3.push_back ( 65 + i); }

 vector<int>::iterator K1  = V1.begin();
 vector<double>::iterator K2  = V2.begin();
 vector<char>::iterator K3   = V3.begin();
```

```
cout <<"Before insertion."<<endl;
 cout << "V1\tV2\t  V3"<<endl;
   while ( K1  != V1.end() )
  {cout <<*K1 <<"\t"<< *K2 <<"\t  " << *K3<< endl;
K1++;
K2++;
K3++;
}
vector<int>::iterator A1  = V1.begin();
  vector<double>::iterator A2  = V2.begin();
   vector<char>::iterator A3   = V3.begin();

  V1.insert(A1 ,3,9); //insert three 9 at the beginning of V1.
  V2.insert(A2+2,3,10.5); /* insert three elements each of
                       value 10.5 at 3rd location.*/
  V3.insert (A3+3,3,'A'); /* insert 3 elements each equal to A
                      at the 4th location.*/
   cout<< " After insertion."<<endl;
   cout << "V1\tV2\t  V3"<<endl;
    while ( A1  != V1.end() )
  {cout <<*A1 <<"\t"<< *A2 <<"\t  " << *A3<< endl;
A1++;
  A2++;
    A3++;
  }}
```

Before the insertion V1 has elements 2, 3, 4, 5 and 6. V2 has elements which are square roots of elements of V1 and V3 has elements A, B, C, D and E. In V1 three elements each of value 9 have been inserted at the beginning, in V2 three elements each of value 10.5 have been inserted at the third location in V2. Similarly three A have been inserted at the fourth place in V4. The output is as below.

```
Before insertion.
V1        V2         V3
2         1.41421    A
3         1.73205    B
4         2          C
5         2.23607    D
6         2.44949    E
After insertion.
V1        V2         V3
9         1.41421    A
9         1.73205    B
9         10.5       C
2         10.5       A
```

```
3         10.5      A
4         2         A
5         2.23607   D
6         2.44949   E
```

CONTAINER CLASS LIST

22.7 FUNCTIONS AND OPERATORS SUPPORTED BY LIST CLASS

The list is another sequential container class in C++. The list class allows fast insertion and deletions anywhere in a list. List supports only bidirectional iterators. Many of the member functions of list class are similar to that of vector class with a few additions. The functions common to both vectors and lists are given in Table 22.3.

Table 22.3 – Functions common to the vector and list classes

`assign()`	`back()`	`begin()`	`clear()`
`empty()`	`end()`	`erase()`	`front()`
`insert()`	`max_size()`	`pop_back()`	`push_back()`
`rbegin()`	`remove()`	`rend()`	`resize()`
`size()`	`swap()`		

Table 22.4 – Additional Functions in class list

Function	Description
`merge()`	Merges a list with another.
`pop_front()`	The function removes first element of list.
`push_front()`	The function adds an element to the front of list.
`remove ()`	The function removes the element from the list.
`remove_if()`	Removes the element if a predicate is satisfied.
`reverse ()`	The function reverses the list.
`sort()`	Sorts the list in ascending order.
`splice()`	The function removes elements from one list to another.
`unique()`	The function removes consecutive duplicate elements. The list should first be sorted to bring make duplicate elements consecutive.

The codes for application of the functions given in Table 22.3 are similar to those already illustrated in case of vector class, however, the following programs give the illustrations of applications of the additional functions described in Table 22.4 along with some of the ones described in Table 22.3. The list supports the relational operators. A list can be assigned with operator = and compared with other lists with overloaded comparison operators >, <, == , !=, >=, <= , etc. The following program illustrates the construction of lists by different methods.

PROGRAM 22.9 – Illustrates the application of functions **assign(), push_back(), begin (), end ()**, and operators = and == for lists.

```
#include <iostream>
#include <list>
#include <string>
using namespace std;

  list <int> L1 , L2 ,L3 ;  // Declares three lists of type int.
  list <string> L4;        //Declares list of strings.

 void main()
 {
 for (int i=1; i<6;i++)
 L1.push_back(i*i );       // putting in values by push_back

 L2.assign (5, 75);       // Putting values by assignment
   L3 = L1;         // construction of list by assigning.

 const int n =5;
 string Name[n]={ "Kunti", "Sunita","Preeti", "Kamla", "Roshan"};
  for(int j=0; j<5; j++)
  L4.push_back( Name[j] );
                    // pushing values in form of strings

    cout<<"The original lists are as below."<<endl;
    cout<< "L1 = " ;
    list<int>::iterator itr ;   //Declaration of iterator
    for(itr  = L1.begin(); itr !=L1.end(); itr ++)
    cout<< *itr <<"  ";
  cout<<"\n";
  cout<<"L2 = ";

  for(itr  = L2.begin(); itr !=L2.end(); itr ++)
  cout<<*itr <<"  ";
  L3 = L2;
  cout<<"\n";
  cout<<"L3 = ";
  for(itr  = L3.begin(); itr !=L3.end(); itr ++)
    cout<<*itr<<"  ";
    cout<<"\nL4 = ";
```

```
    list<string>::iterator iter ;
    for(iter = L4.begin(); iter !=L4.end(); iter ++)
   cout<< *iter <<"  ";
   L3 = L1 ;           // L1 is copied on to L3
   cout<<"\nNew L3 = ";
   for(itr = L3.begin(); itr !=L3.end(); itr ++)
   cout<<*itr<<"  ";
  if ( L1 == L3)       // comparison of two strings.
  cout<<"\nL1 and L3 are now equal"<<endl;
  else
  cout<<"\nL1 and L3 are not equal\n";
    }
```

The expected output is given below.

```
The original lists are as below.
L1 = 1  4  9  16  25
L2 = 75  75  75  75  75
L3 = 75  75  75  75  75
L4 = Kunti  Sunita  Preeti  Kamla  Roshan
New L3 = 1  4  9  16  25  .
L1 and L3 are now equal
```

22.8 APPLICATION OF SOME FUNCTIONS OF LIST CLASS

Functions unique(), reverse() and remove()

The function unique removes the duplicate elements from the list. The function reverse() reverses the order of elements in the list, i.e. the first element becomes the last element with similar changes in other elements. See the following program for illustration.

PROGRAM 22.10 – Illustrates functions unique(), reverse() and remove() for list.

```
#include<iostream>
#include<list>
using namespace std;
  list<char> L1 ;
  void main()
{
  for (int i=0; i<6;i++)
   { L1.push_back(73 - i );
     L1.push_back(73 - i );
     }
cout <<"The original list is as below."<<endl;
   list<char>::iterator T1;
```

```
    for ( T1 = L1.begin() ; T1!=L1.end() ; T1++ )
  cout <<"  " <<*T1 ;
  cout <<endl;
    L1.unique();          // remove the duplicate copies.

  cout <<" After removal of duplicate copies the list is:"<<endl;
    for ( T1 = L1.begin() ; T1!=L1.end() ; T1++ )
  cout <<"  " <<*T1 ;
    L1.reverse();
  cout<<"\n After reversing the list it is \n";
    for ( T1 = L1.begin() ; T1!=L1.end() ; T1++ )
  cout <<"  " <<*T1 ;

  cout <<"\nAfter removal of F the list becomes \n";
    L1.remove ('F');
    for ( T1 = L1.begin() ; T1!=L1.end() ; T1++ )
  cout <<"  " <<*T1 ;
  cout <<endl;
    }
```

The expected output is given below.

```
The original list is as below.
I I H H G G F F E E D D
After removal of duplicate copies the list is:
I H G F E D
After reversing the list it is
D E F G H I
After removal of F the list becomes
D E G H I
```

The output of the above program is self explanatory. The second line of output is the original list which has duplicate elements. With function unique the duplicate elements are removed and the resultant list consists of unique values (4th line of output). The list is then reversed. In the reversed list the letter F is removed with function **remove()**. The last line of output is the resulting list.

PROGRAM 22.11 – Illustrates functions **begin()**, **end()** and functions **swap()** and **sort()** for list.

```
 #include<iostream>
#include<list>
using namespace std;

  list<char> L1 ;
  list<int> L2  ;
```

```
   list <int> L3;
void main()
 {
  int A  [] = {78, 58, 90, 44, 33,11} ;
 for (int i=0; i<6;i++)
   {L1.push_back(75 - i );
   L2.push_back (A [i]);
   L3. push_back(i*i);
   }
 cout<<"The original lists are as below."<<endl;
   list<char>::iterator  T1;
   list <int>::iterator T2;
 cout<< "List L1 = ";
   for ( T1 = L1.begin()   ; T1!=L1.end() ; T1++ )
 cout  <<" " <<*T1<<"  " ;
 cout<<"\nList L2 = ";
   for ( T2 = L2.begin()   ; T2!=L2.end() ; T2++ )
   cout <<" " <<*T2<<"  " ;
   cout<<"\nList L3 = ";
   for ( T2 = L3.begin()   ; T2!=L3.end() ; T2++ )
    cout  <<" " <<*T2<<"  " ;
 L3.sort();
 L2.sort();
 L2.swap(L3);      // swapping elements of two lists
 cout<<"\nThe sorted and swapped lists are as below."<<endl;
  cout<< "\nList L2 =" ;
  for ( T2 = L2.begin() ; T2!= L2.end() ;  T2++)
  cout  <<"  " <<*T2<<"  " ;
 cout<< "\nList L3 =" ;
 for ( T2 = L3.begin()  ; T2!= L3.end() ;  T2++)
 cout  <<" " <<*T2<<"  " ;
   }
```

The expected output is given below.

```
The original lists are as below.
List L1 = K  J  I  H  G  F
List L2 = 78  58  90  44  33  11
List L3 = 0   1   4   9   16   25
The sorted and swapped lists are as below.

List L2 = 0   1   4   9   16   25
List L3 = 11  33  44  58  78  90
```

In the above program the list L2 and list L3 are swapped and sorted. It is clear from the output of the program.

The following program declares a list of elements of *type char* and by name L1 and another by name L2 and of *type int.* The list L1 is constructed by function push_back (). L2 is assigned 5 elements each equal to 50 by the function `assign()`. The function `L1.front ()` and `L1.back()` give reference to the first and the last element of the list L1 respectively. The two lists are displayed with the help of iterators.

PROGRAM 22.12 – Illustrates functions **`front(),back(),begin(),end()`** for lists.

```
#include<iostream>
#include<list>
using namespace std;
 list <char> L1  ;

  list<int> L2;
   int main()
  {
   for (int i=0; i<5;i++)
{  L1.push_back(65+i);
   L2.assign( 5, 50 ); }
   list <char> ::iterator T1= L1.begin()  ;
   cout<<"The list L1 is."<<endl;

    while ( T1 !=L1.end())
    {cout  <<"  "<<*T1 <<"  ";
     T1++; }
    cout<<"\n";

  list <int> :: iterator T2 = L2.begin();
  cout<< "The list L2 is. " <<endl;

   while
    ( T2 !=L2.end())
    {
     cout <<"  "<< *T2 <<"  ";
        T2++;}
 cout<<"\n";
 cout <<"The first element of L1 is "<<L1.front()<<endl;
  cout<<"The last element of L1 is " <<L1.back()<<endl;
   return 0;
   }
```

The expected output of the program is given below.

```
The list L1 is.
A   B   C   D   E
The list L2 is.
50    50    50    50    50
The first element of L1 is A
The last element of L1 is E
```

FUNCTION MERGE()

If the list L2 is required to be merged with list L1, the code is written as below.

```
L1.merge(L2);
```

After the execution of the program the list L2 becomes empty. This is illustrated in the following program.

PROGRAM 22.13 – Illustrates application of function **merge()** for list.

```
#include<iostream>
#include<list>
using namespace std;
 list<int> L1,L2  ;

 void main()
 {
   for (int i=1; i<5;i++)
    { L1.push_back(i);
     L2.push_back(i*i);
     }
   cout<<"The lists are given below."<<endl;
      cout<<" List1\t List2 "<<endl;
         list<int>::iterator T1;
           list<int>::iterator T2;

  for(T1=L1.begin(),T2=L2.begin(); T1 != L1.end() ;T1++,T2++ )
  cout<<"  "<<*T1 <<" \t  "<< *T2  <<endl;

  L1.merge(L2);     // merge L2 with L1

   cout<<"New list1:"<< endl;
     for (T1=L1.begin() ; T1 != L1.end(); T1++  )
      cout<<"  " <<*T1 <<"  " ;

  if ( L2.empty())
  cout<< "\nL2 is now empty."<<endl;
   }
```

The expected output is given below.

```
The lists are given below.
List1  List2
1       1
2       4
3       9
4       16
New list1:
1   1   2   3   4   4   9   16
L2 is now empty.
```

DEQUE

The class deque, also called double ended queue, supports random iterator. The components are stored in adjacent memory blocks. Individual element may be accessed by random iterator or by [ ] operator like an array. Elements may be added or removed at both ends of a deque. The salient features of deque as compared with those of list and vector are given in Table 22.1. This container has a combination of some characteristics of both vectors as well as lists. The functions of class deque are listed in Table 22.5.

22.9 FUNCTIONS AND OPERATORS SUPPORTED BY DEQUE

Some of the commonly used functions supported by this class are listed in Table 22.5. The functions supported by deque in addition to those for vectors are `push_front ()` and `pop_front()` while some functions like `capacity()` and `reserve()` are not members of class deque.

Table 22.5 – Functions supported by deque class

assign ()	at()	back ()	begin()	clear ()
empty ()	end ()	erase ()	front ()	insert ()
max_size()	pop_back()	push_back ()	pop_front	push_front
rbegin()	rend()	resize ()	size()	swap()

Operators Supported by deque class. The deque class supports the relational operators such as == , != , >=, <= , >, < and = .

PROGRAM 22.14 – Illustrates **`iterator, push_back(), push_front()`** for deque.

```
#include<iostream>
#include<deque>
using namespace std;
deque<int> Q1, Q3;
deque <char> Q2;
```

```
int main()
 {for ( int i =0; i<4;i++)
  {Q1.push_back (i*i);
    Q2.push_back (65 +i);
    }
  Q3 = Q1;           // Q1 is assigned to Q3

 Q3.push_front (20);
     Q3.push_back (20*20);
 for ( int j = 0; j<4; j++)
  cout  << Q1[j]<<"\t"<<Q2[j]  <<endl;

 cout<< "\nSize of Q3 = " << Q3.size()<<endl;
 cout << "Elements of Q3 are : ";
 deque<int>:: iterator iter;
 for (iter = Q3.begin() ; iter < Q3.end(); iter++)
 cout<< *iter <<" ";
 return 0;
  }
```

The expected output is given below.

```
0        A
1        B
4        C
9        D

Size of Q3 = 6
Elements of Q3 are : 20  0  1  4  9  400
```

22.10 APPLICATION OF SOME FUNCTIONS SUPPORTED BY DEQUE

PROGRAM 22.15 – Illustrates application of **push_back()**, **pop_front()** and **pop_back()** and **size()** for deque.

```
#include<iostream>
# include <deque>
using namespace std;

int main()
{ deque <double> Q1;
    for ( int i =0; i< 7;i++)
     Q1.push_back (1.5*i);

 cout<<"The elements of queue  are, "<<endl;
  for ( int j = 0; j<6; j++)
```

```
  cout <<" "<< Q1[j]<<" " ;
     cout<<endl;

 cout << "The size of Q1 is " << Q1.size()<<endl;
 Q1.pop_back();

 Q1.pop_front();
        cout<<"Now size of Q1 is "<<Q1.size()<<endl;

 deque <double> :: iterator itr;   // itr is the name of iterator

  Q1.insert((Q1.begin() +2),2,50.5); ;
                                  // insert 2 elements of value 50.5.
    cout<<"Elements of Q1 are,"<<endl;
   for ( itr = Q1.begin(); itr < Q1.end() ; itr ++)
    cout<<*itr <<"   " ;

 cout<<endl;
 return 0;
 }
```

The expected output is as below.

```
The elements of queue are,
0    1.5    3    4.5    6    7.5
The size of Q1 is 7
Now size of Q1 is 5
Elements of Q1 are,
1.5   3   50.5   50.5   4.5   6   7.5
```

Since deque is double ended queue, elements may be added at the front-end as well as at the back-end of the queue. The following program illustrates it.

PROGRAM 22.16 –Illustrates application of functions **erase()**, **push_front()**, **push_back()** and **insert()** for deque.

```
#include<iostream>
# include <deque>
using namespace std;

int main()
 { deque <int> Q1;

 Q1.assign(4, 12)  ;
  cout<<"The elements of queue are, "<<endl;
```

```
for ( int j = 0; j<4; j++)
 cout <<"  "<< Q1[j]<<"  "  ;
 cout<<endl;

cout << "The size of Q1 is " << Q1.size()<<endl;
cout<< "Put two tens at front and two 20s at end."<<endl;

Q1.push_front(10 );
  Q1.push_front(10 );
  Q1.push_back(20);

Q1.push_back(20);
deque <int> :: iterator itr  ;
    // itr is the name of iterator

for ( itr= Q1.begin(); itr != Q1.end(); itr++)

cout << *(itr ) <<"  ";

cout << "\nElements 2nd to 4th are erased,"<<endl;
   Q1.erase ( (Q1.begin() +1),(Q1.begin() +4 )  );

cout<<"Insert two 50s at 3rd location."<<endl;
   Q1.insert((Q1.begin() +2),2,50 );
    cout<<"Now size of Q1 is "<<Q1.size()<<endl;
cout<<"Elements of Q1 are,"<<endl;
 for ( itr  = Q1.begin() ; itr < Q1.end ()  ; itr ++)

 cout<<*itr <<"   " ;
 cout<<endl;
 return 0;
 }
```

The expected output is as below.

```
The elements of queue  are,
12    12    12    12
The size of Q1 is 4
Put two tens at front and two 20s at end.
10  10  12  12  12  12  20  20
Elements 2nd to 4th are erased,
Insert two 50s at 3rd location.
Now size of Q1 is 7
Elements of Q1 are,
10   12   50   50   12   20   20
```

EXERCISES

1. What are the sequence containers?
2. What are similarities and differences between vectors and lists?
3. A vector has to have 5 elements. Each element has value 35. How do you construct the vector?
4. A list has to have 5 names as its elements. How will you declare and initialize the list?
5. What are the main differences between a list and a deque?
6. What is the difference between function `capacity ()` and function `size()`?
7. What are the arguments of the function `erase()` of vector class?
8. Which functions are supported by list but not supported by vector?
9. What are the iterators ?
10. How do you declare an iterator for a vector with int elements?
11. What do you understand by function `begin()` and `end ()`?
12. What is the difference between the functions `back ()` and `end ()`?
13. What is the difference between the function `begin ()` and function `rbegin ()`?
14. What is the difference between function `begin()` and `front()` when applied to list?
15. Give examples of code to illustrate function `remove ()` and function `remove_if` ().
16. What do you understand by function `max_size ()` when applied to deque?
17. Make a program to illustrate the function `sort()` for sorting a list of 10 characters entered by a user.
18. Make a program for deque in order to illustrate the functions `size()`, `resize()` and `insert()`.
19. Make a program for vectors to illustrate the different constructors.
20. Make a program in which two vectors of equal size are constructed and swapped and displayed on the monitor.
21. Make a program for list and illustrate the application of the function `insert()` any where in the list.
22. Make a list of characters in the decreasing order from Z to A and sort it in the increasing order A to Z and display the contents.

Answer:

PROGRAM 22.17 – Sorting a list consisting of characters from Z to A.

```
#include<iostream>
#include<list>
using namespace std;

list <char> L1;   // declaration of list
void main()
  {
for (int i=0; i<26;i++)
```

```
 L1.push_back(90 - i );    // construction of list
list<char>::iterator T;
 cout<<" The original list is: "<<endl;

for ( T = L1.begin(); T!=L1.end(); T++)
cout  <<" " <<*T ;        //output statement

cout<<"\n\n";
L1.sort() ;           // sort function
   {list<char> ::iterator IT;
cout<<" The sorted list is: "<<endl;
   for ( IT = L1.begin(); IT!=L1.end(); IT++)
   cout<<" " <<*IT ; //output statement after sorting
   }
cout<<endl;
   }
```

The expected output is given below.

```
The original list is:
Z Y X W V U T S R Q P O N M L K J I H G F E D C B A

The sorted list is:
A B C D E F G H I J K L M N O P Q R S T U V W X Y Z
```

23. Make a program which illustrates the application of function `at()` and shows that it is superior to calling the element by index operator [].

❍❍❍

CHAPTER 23

Associative Containers
set, multiset, map and multimap

23.1 INTRODUCTION

The associative containers support fast retrieval of elements of sets through keys. The container size may be varied dynamically. The elements of an associative set are of type *value_type.* Each element is associated with a key of type *key_type*. The associative containers comprise (i) sets, (ii) multisets, (iii) maps and (iv) multimaps. The header file for sets and multisets is <set> and for map and multimaps is **<map>.**

In case of sets and multisets the element value itself is the key, i.e. key and the associated value is one and same. While in case of maps and multimaps the keys are different from the associated values. Thus in sets and multisets an element comprises single value while in maps and multimaps an element is a pair comprising a key and a value. It is natural to expect that key associated with an element is immutable while the element value may be changed. Since in sets the element value and the key are same, therefore, set elements are not mutable.

The difference in sets and multisets is that in a set there are unique keys (or values because key and associated value is one and the same) while a multiset may have more than one element (key) with same value, i.e. multiple copies. Similarly in a map only unique keys are allowed while in multimaps two or more elements may have same key. However, in maps or multimaps there are no restrictions on the associated values. Two or more keys in a map or multimap may have same associated values.

Associative containers keep the keys in a specified order. The default order is ascending order. In case of sets and multisets the stored values are also the keys so the values are stored in ascending order by default. But this can be altered by specifying the mode of arranging the keys.

CONSTRUCTOR FOR ASSOCIATIVE CONTAINERS

The associative container classes have a default constructor, a copy constructor and a destructor. A default constructor does not take any argument. A copy constructor creates a copy of the given set. Destructor is called for removing all the elements of a container from the memory and free the memory.

23.2 FUNCTIONS SUPPORTED BY ASSOCIATIVE CONTAINERS

Functions supported by sets, multisets, maps and multimaps are described in the following table.

Table 23.1

S.No.	Function	Description
1.	`begin()`	It returns iterator to first element of the set.
2.	`clear()`	The function deletes all the elements of a set.
3.	`count()`	The function returns the number of elements that match a key.
4.	`empty()`	The function returns true if there is no element in the set, false otherwise.
5.	`end()`	It returns iterator just past the end of set.
6.	`equal_range()`	The function returns two iterators, one to the first element that matches *key* and second to the element just past the last element that matches the key.
7.	`erase()`	It deletes element at the indexed location or elements between start and end iterators or erases all the elements. The start element is included but the end element is not included.
8.	`find()`	The function returns an iterator to key if found, otherwise it returns iterator to end of set.
9.	`insert()`	Inserts a value (element) in a set if the value does not already exist (ii) inserts a number of elements from start to end.
10.	`key_comp()`	The function compares keys.
11.	`lower_bound()`	The function returns iterator to the first element that has value greater than or equal to key.
12.	`max_size()`	The function returns the maximum number of elements that the set can hold.
13.	`rbegin()`	The function returns a reverse_iterator to the end of the set.
14.	`rend()`	Return a reverse_iterator to the beginning of the set.
15.	`size()`	Returns the current number of elements in the set.
16.	`swap()`	Exchanges the content of one set with that of another.
17.	`upper_bound()`	The function returns iterator to the first element in the set with a key greater than specified key.
18.	`value_comp()`	The function compares values.

OPERATORS SUPPORTED BY ASSOCIATIVE CONTAINERS

All the associative sets support comparison operators == , != , > , < , >= , <= besides the assignment operator = . Thus associative containers can be assigned as well as compared.

23.3 THE SETS

General characteristics of sets and other associative containers have already been described above. In the following few programs the operation of some of the functions listed in Table 23.1 and operators supported by sets are illustrated. The iterators are used for output of elements of sets. The program given below is an illustration of construction and output of elements of sets.

PROGRAM 23.1 – Illustrates construction of sets and functions **`begin()`** and **`end()`**.

```
#include<iostream>
using namespace std;
#include <set>
#include <iterator>

const int n = 8,m = 5;

int main()
{ char ch [m] = { 'A','D','E' ,'C', 'B' };
 int AR1[n] = { 65, 72, 67, 69, 71, 68, 66, 70 };

 set <int> Set1( AR1, AR1+7); // set constructed with an array
 set <char> Set3 (ch, ch +5); // set constructed with an array
 set<int> Set2 (Set1); // Set2 is constructed as copy of Set1
set<int>:: iterator itr; // declaration of iterator for int set
cout<<"Set1 elements are: ";
    //below is the output statement for set1
for( itr = Set1.begin(); itr!= Set1.end(); itr++)
 cout<< *itr<<" ";
 cout<<"\nSet2 elements are :";
    // below is the output statement for set2
for( itr = Set2.begin(); itr!= Set2.end(); itr++)
  cout<< *itr<<" ";
 cout<<"\nSet3 elements are :" ;
  set<char>:: iterator iter; // declaration of iterator
   for( iter = Set3.begin(); iter!= Set3.end(); iter++)
    cout<< *iter<<" "; // output statement for set3
  return 0;}
```

The expected output is given below. The output is self explanatory.

```
Set1 elements are: 65 66 67 68 69 71 72
Set2 elements are :65 66 67 68 69 71 72
Set3 elements are :A B C D E
```

The output shows that the values have been ordered in an ascending order on entering a set. The corresponding array elements are not in any order.

The following program illustrates the application of functions **size()** which returns the current number of elements in the set, **lower_bound ()** which return iterator to a value just above the value specified in lower bound, **swap ()** which exchanges the values in the two sets, **clear()** which removes all the elements of a set and **empty()** which checks if there are any elements in the set.

PROGRAM 23.2 – Illustrates application of **size(), lower_bound(), swap()** and **empty()** functions for sets.

```
#include<iostream>
using namespace std;
#include <set>
int main()
{ int G[8] = { 100, 78, 34, 34, 34 ,20 ,104,78 };
 set <int> S1 ( G, G+8) ; // Elements G to G+8 are entered
 set <int> S2 (G, G+5) ;  // Elements G to G+5 are entered
cout << "Size of S1 = "<<S1.size()<<endl ;
cout << "Size of S2 = "<<S2.size()<<endl;
cout<<"number of element of value 34 = "<<S1.count(34)<<endl;
cout<<"Lower_bound of 35 in S1 = "<< *(S1.lower_bound(35))<<endl;

 cout <<"The elements of S1 are : ";
  set<int> :: iterator iter;
   for (iter = S1.begin(); iter != S1.end(); iter++)
    cout<<*iter <<" ";
 cout<< "\nThe elements of S2 are : ";
  for (iter = S2.begin(); iter != S2.end(); iter++)
   cout<<*iter <<" ";

 S2.swap(S1);     // swap S2 with S1
  cout <<"\nAfter swapping\n";
   cout <<" The elements of S1 are : ";

for ( iter = S1.begin(); iter != S1.end(); iter++)
  cout<<*iter <<" ";
   cout<< "\nThe elements of S2 are : ";
 for ( iter = S2.begin(); iter != S2.end(); iter++)
```

```
cout<<*iter <<" ";
S2.clear();
 if (S2.empty()) // test if there is any element in the set.
  cout<<"\nAfter operation of clear(), S2 is empty.\n";
 return 0;
}
```

The expected output is given below.

```
Size of S1 = 5  // Note that duplicate elements are removed
Size of S2 = 3
number of element of value 34 = 1  // duplicates are removed
Lower_bound of 35 in S1 = 78
The elements of S1 are : 20 34 78 100 104
The elements of S2 are : 34 78 100
After swapping
The elements of S1 are : 34 78 100
The elements of S2 are : 20 34 78 100 104
After operation of clear(), S2 is empty.
```

From the output it is clear the elements in a set are arranged in ascending order. That is the default setting. Also a set does not contain duplicate elements. The function lower_bound () returns iterator to an element just above the specified key. The value of lower_bound is obtained by dereference operator (*). In the following program the descending order is specified.

PROGRAM 23.3 – Illustrates arranging the set in a specified order.

```
#include<iostream>
using namespace std;
#include <set>
typedef std::set<int , std::greater <int> > Inset;
   // std:: greater <int> for descending order
   // std::less for ascending order.
int main()
 {int G[8] = { 100, 78, 34, 34, 34 ,20 ,104,78 };
  Inset S1( G, G+8) ;
   Inset S2 (G, G+5) ;
cout << "Size of S1 = "<<S1.size()<<endl ;
cout << "Size of S2 = "<<S2.size()<<endl;
cout<<"number of element of value 34 = "<<S1.count(34)<<endl;
cout<<"Lower_bound of 35 in S1 = "<< *(S1.lower_bound(35))<<endl;
cout <<" The elements of S1 are : ";
 Inset :: iterator iter;
```

```
  for ( iter = S1.begin(); iter != S1.end(); iter++)
   cout<<*iter <<" ";

 cout<< "\nThe elements of S2 are : ";
 for ( iter = S2.begin(); iter != S2.end(); iter++)
  cout<<*iter <<" ";   // for output of elements
 S2.clear();
 if (S2.empty())
  cout<<"\nS2 is empty after operation of clear().";
   return 0; }
```

The expected output is given below. S1 is now arranged in descending order.

```
Size of S1 = 5
Size of S2 = 3
number of element of value 34 = 1
Lower_bound of 35 in S1 = 34
The elements of S1 are : 104 100 78 34 20
The elements of S2 are : 100 78 34
S2 is empty after operation of clear().
```

The following program illustrates creating sets of strings (class objects). An array of strings consists of names. This array on putting into a set gets arranged in ascending order (A to Z) by the default setting.

PROGRAM 23.4 – Illustrates sets consisting of objects of class string and characters.

```
 #include<iostream>
 using namespace std;
 #include <string>
 #include <set>
  const int n =4;
  int main()
 {string Str[n] = {"Sunita","Asha", "Priti", "Kishor" };
  char ch[n] = { 'B', 'C', 'A', 'V'} ; // char array
 set <string> S1 ( Str, Str+n);
 set <char> S2 (ch, ch+n) ;
   cout << "Size of S1 = "<<S1.size()<<endl ;
   cout << "Size of S2 = "<<S2.size()<<endl;

   cout <<"The elements of S1 are : ";
   set<string> :: iterator iter;
  for ( iter = S1.begin(); iter != S1.end(); iter++)
  cout<<*iter <<" ";
  cout<<"\nAfter erase elements of S1 are: ";
```

```
S1.erase( S1.begin()); // erase the first element
for ( iter = S1.begin(); iter != S1.end(); iter++)
cout<<*iter <<" ";

set<char> :: iterator itr;
 cout<< "\nThe elements of S2 are : ";
 for ( itr = S2.begin(); itr != S2.end(); itr++)
 cout<<*itr <<" ";
 S2.clear();
 if(S2.empty())
 cout<<"\nS2 is empty"<<endl ;
 return 0;
 }
```

The expected output is given below. Note the names are arranged in alphabetical order in the set.

```
Size of S1 = 4
Size of S2 = 4
The elements of S1 are : Asha Kishor Priti Sunita
After erase elements of S1 are: Kishor Priti Sunita
The elements of S2 are : A B C V
S2 is empty
```

In the following program the function **erase()** is used to remove the first element in the set and function **insert()** is used to insert a character in the set.

PROGRAM 23.5 – Illustrates **erase()** and **insert()** functions for sets.

```
#include<iostream>
using namespace std;
#include <set>
#include <iterator>
 typedef std::set< char> Chrset; // typedef for avoiding
    // writing std::set< char> many times
int main()
{const int n =4;
char G[n] = { 'Z', 'S' , 'N', 'A' };
 Chrset Set1 (G , G+n); // construction of set
 Chrset Set2 (Set1);
 Chrset:: iterator itr; // declaration of iterator

 cout<<"Set1 elements are : ";
 for( itr = Set1.begin(); itr!= Set1.end(); itr++)
 cout<< *itr<<" ";
 cout<<"\n";
```

```
cout<<"Set2 elements are : ";
for( itr = Set2.begin(); itr != Set2.end(); itr++)
cout<< *itr<<" ";

Set1.erase( Set1.begin()); // erases the first element
cout<<"\n";
Chrset:: iterator iter;

Set1.insert('T'); // insertion of an element

cout<< "After insertion Set1 elements are: ";
for( iter = Set1.begin(); iter!= Set1.end(); iter++)
cout<< *iter<<" ";
return 0;
 }
```

The expected output is given below. It is easily compared with the code statements.

```
Set1 elements are : A N S Z
Set2 elements are : A N S Z
After insertion Set1 elements are: N S T Z
```

23.4 THE MULTISETS

Multisets allow multiple elements having same key. The keys are sorted according to the prescribed order, ascending order is the default order. The following program is an illustration of a multiset which also illustrates the functions **count()**, **size()** and **upper_bound()**. Also descending order is specified for sorting of the multiset. For multisets also we have to include the header file **<set>** in the program.

PROGRAM 23.6 – Illustrates multisets, specification of order of elements and operation of functions **count()**, **size()** and **upper_bound()**.

```
#include <iostream>
#include<set> // Header file is same for sets and multisets
using namespace std;
typedef std ::multiset<int, greater <int> > IntMset ;
 // greater for descending order and less for ascending order.
int main()
 { const int n = 8;
 int bill[n] = {20,50,10,15, 70,10, 40,10 };

 IntMset Xset( bill , bill+n); // construction of set
 IntMset ::iterator iter; // declaration of iterator.

 cout<< "Size of Xset = " << Xset.size()<<endl;
 cout<< "Elements in Xset are : ";
```

```
 for ( iter = Xset.begin(); iter != Xset.end(); iter++)
 cout<< *iter<<" " ;
 cout<<"\nUpper_bound = "<<*(Xset.upper_bound(50))<<endl;

cout<<"Number of copies of 10 in Xset are = "<< Xset.count (10)<<
endl;

 return 0;
}
```

The expected output is given below.

```
Size of Xset = 8
Elements in Xset are : 70 50 40 20 15 10 10 10
Upper_bound = 40
Number of copies of 10 in Xset are = 3
```

23.5 THE MAPS

In maps and multimaps an element comprises a pair of values. The first one is the key and the second is the associated value. The keys are sorted according to the prescribed order. The default order is ascending order. The map class has a default constructor, a copy constructor and a destructor. The header file is **<map>** for both maps and multimaps. As already mentioned in the introduction, keys are not mutable, however, the values associated with the keys may be changed. The following program is an illustration of map in which the keys are the names of three metals, i.e. steel, copper and brass, and the associative values are the prices per kg. After entering the data the prices are revised to new values, i.e. the associated values are changed.

PROGRAM 23.7 – Illustrates construction of a map.

```
#include<iostream>
using namespace std;
#include<map>
#include<string>
typedef map <string, int > Mint ;
     // typedef has been used to avoid the
   // the writing of map <string, int> several times
int main()
{
Mint Pricelist ;
 string Metal[3] = {"steel", "copper", "brass"};
 int Values [3] = { 20, 200, 180};
 for ( int j = 0; j<3; j++)

Pricelist [Metal[j]] = Values[j] ; // input to map
Mint :: iterator iter; // declaration of iterator.
```

```
cout << "The prices are as below"<<endl;
 for ( iter= Pricelist.begin();iter != Pricelist.end(); iter++)
  cout<< (*iter).first<<"\t"<<(*iter).second<<endl;

iter = Pricelist.begin();
(*iter).second = 250;   // Changing the associated value
 (*(++iter)).second = 350; // Changing the associated value
  (*(++iter)).second = 25 ; // Changing the associated value

cout<< "Prices after revision are as below"<<endl;
 for ( iter= Pricelist.begin();iter != Pricelist.end(); iter++)
 cout<< (*iter).first<<"\t"<<(*iter).second<<endl;

 return 0;
  }
```

The prices are as below

```
brass     180
copper     200
steel     20
Prices after revision are as below
brass     250
copper     350
steel     25
```

In the following program, the input from keyboard has been used to construct the map. It makes a grade list.

PROGRAM 23.8 – Illustrates input from keyboard to construct a map.

```
#include<iostream>
using namespace std;
#include<map>
#include<string>
typedef map <string, int > Map_Grade ;

int main()
{
string Name ;
int Marks;

Map_Grade Grade; // Grade is name of map

for (int i = 0; i<4; i++) // loop for entering names and marks
 { cout<<"Enter a name : ";cin>> Name ;
 cout<<"Enter the marks obtained : "; cin >> Marks;

 Grade [Name] = Marks ;}
```

```
   // below another name and marks are inserted.
Grade.insert (Map_Grade::value_type("Sujata", 85));
    // inserting an entry of name and value
cout<< " The grade list is as below.\n\n" ;

Map_Grade :: iterator iter; // declaration of iterator
 iter = Grade.begin();
    // below is loop for output
for( iter = Grade.begin(); iter != Grade.end(); iter++)
 cout<< (*iter).first<<"\t" <<(*iter).second<<"\n" ;
return 0;
 }
```

The expected output is given below.

```
Enter a name : Manjri
Enter the marks obtained : 80
Enter a name : Sunita
Enter the marks obtained : 79
Enter a name : Bandal
Enter the marks obtained : 85
Enter a name : Chanan
Enter the marks obtained : 80
 The grade list is as below.

Bandal     85
Chanan     80
Manjri     80
Sujata     85
Sunita     79
```

Note that in the output the names (keys) are arranged in alphabetical order. In the following program the application of functions **insert()** and function **size()** are illustrated.

PROGRAM 23.9 – Application of functions **insert()** and **size()**.

```
#include<iostream>
using namespace std;
#include<map>

#include<string>
typedef map <string, int > Map_Grade ;

int main()
 { string Name ;
```

```
 int Marks;
 Map_Grade Grade;

for (int i = 0; i<4; i++)
{cin>> Name ;
 cin >> Marks;
  Grade [Name] = Marks ;}

Grade.insert (Map_Grade::value_type ("Sujata", 85));
Grade.insert (Map_Grade ::value_type ("Mumta" ,90));

cout<<"\n"<< Grade.size ( )<<endl;  // number of elements
Map_Grade :: iterator iter;

 for( iter = Grade.begin() ; iter != Grade.end(); iter++)
 cout<< (*iter).first<<" \t " <<(*iter).second<<"\n" ;
 return 0;
 }
```

The expected output is as below.

```
Nany
90
Mini
88
Simi
77
Tiny
85

6
Mini      88
Mumta     90
Nany      90
Simi  77
Sujata    85
Tiny      85
```

In the following program map is created as a copy of another map.

PROGRAM 23.10 – Use of assignment operator (=) in order to get a **copy of map.**

```
#include<iostream>
using namespace std;
#include<map>
#include<string>

typedef map <string, int > Map_Grade ;
```

```
int main()
{
string Name ;
int Marks;

 Map_Grade Grade1 ;

 for (int i = 0; i<4; i++)
 {cin>> Name ;
 cin >> Marks;
 Grade1 [Name] = Marks ;}

 Map_Grade Grade2;
 Grade2 = Grade1 ; // Application of assignment operator
    // to maps
 Grade1.insert (Map_Grade::value_type("Sujata", 85));
  Map_Grade :: iterator iter;
  iter = Grade1.begin();
  cout<<"The Grade1 list is as below."<<endl;

for( iter = Grade1.begin(); iter != Grade1.end(); iter++)
cout<< (*iter).first<<" \t " <<(*iter).second<<"\n" ;

 Map_Grade :: iterator iter2;

 cout << "The Grade2 list is as follows."<<endl;
 iter2 = Grade2.begin();

 for( iter2 = Grade2.begin(); iter2 != Grade2.end(); iter2++)
 cout<< (*iter2).first<<" \t " <<(*iter2).second<<"\n" ;

 return 0;
 }
```

The expected output is as under.

```
Kumar
88
Nimi
90
Sunita
78
Trini
77
The Grade1 list is as below.
Kumar     88
Nimi      90
Sujata     85
```

```
Sunita     78
Trini     77
The Grade2 list is as follows.
Kumar      88
Nimi      90
Sunita     78
Trini     77
```

The element ("Sujata",85) was inserted in Grade1 after the assignment. Therefore, the output of Grade2 does not contain this name.

In the following program the function **`insert()`** is used to create a map.

PROGRAM 23.11 – It is another example of application of function **insert().** In fact the entire map is constructed by insert function.

```
#include<iostream>
using namespace std;
#include<map>
#include<string>
typedef std:: map < string ,int > Multigrade ;

int main()
 {
 Multigrade pairs;
 pairs.insert (Multigrade::value_type("Sunita", 80));

 pairs.insert (Multigrade::value_type("Sunita", 85));

 pairs.insert (Multigrade::value_type("Kunti", 96));

 pairs.insert (Multigrade::value_type("Punita", 70));

 pairs.insert (Multigrade::value_type("Punita", 65));
 pairs.insert (Multigrade::value_type("Bubita", 95));
 pairs.insert (Multigrade::value_type("Mumta", 60));

 pairs.insert (Multigrade::value_type("Mumtaz", 60)) ;

 cout<< "Present size of pairs is = " <<pairs.size()<<endl;

 Multigrade :: const_iterator itr= pairs.begin();
 cout<<" The contents of pairs are as below."<<endl;

 for(itr = pairs.begin(); itr != pairs.end(); itr++)
 cout<< itr-> first <<"\t"<< itr-> second<<"\n";

 pairs.erase (pairs.begin() ); // erase the first element
 cout <<"The size after erasing first pair is = "<< pairs.size() <<endl;
 cout << "The contents after erase are:"<<endl;
```

```
Multigrade :: iterator iter; // declaration of iterator
for(iter= pairs.begin(); iter != pairs.end(); iter++)
 cout<< iter-> first <<"\t"<< iter-> second<<"\n";
 return 0;
  }
```

Output is given below. The duplicate names have been ignored in construction of the map.

```
Present size of pairs is = 6
The contents of pairs are as below.
Bubita   95
Kunti   96
Mumta   60
Mumtaz   60
Punita   70
Sunita   80
The size after erasing first pair is = 5
The contents after erase are:
Kunti   96
Mumta   60
Mumtaz   60
Punita   70
Sunita   80
```

The following program illustrates the application of function **erase()**, function **size ()** and function **max_size ()**.

PROGRAM 23.12 –Illustrates the application of **size()**, **max_size()** and **erase()** in maps.

```
#include<iostream>
using namespace std;
#include<map>
#include<string>
 typedef std:: map < string ,int > Multigrade ;

int main()
 { Multigrade pairs;
 pairs.insert (Multigrade::value_type("Sunita", 80));
 pairs.insert (Multigrade::value_type("Sunita", 85));

 pairs.insert (Multigrade::value_type("Kunti", 96));
 pairs.insert (Multigrade::value_type("Punita", 70));
 pairs.insert (Multigrade::value_type("Punita", 65));
```

```
    pairs.insert (Multigrade::value_type("Bubita", 95));
    pairs.insert (Multigrade::value_type("Mumta", 60));
    pairs.insert (Multigrade::value_type("Mumtaz", 60)) ;

   cout<< "Present size of pairs is = " <<pairs.size()<<endl;
   cout<<"Maximum numbers that map can hold = "<<pairs.max_size() <<endl;

   Multigrade :: const_iterator itr= pairs.begin();
    cout<<"The pairs in the map are as below."<<endl;

    for( itr= pairs.begin(); itr != pairs.end(); itr++)
    cout<< itr-> first <<"\t"<< itr-> second<<"\n";

    pairs.erase (++pairs.begin(), --pairs.end() );
       // erase from 2nd to last but one element.
    cout <<"The size after erasing first pair is = "<< pairs.size() <<endl;

    cout << "The pairs now in map are given below."<<endl;

   Multigrade :: iterator iter;
    for( iter= pairs.begin(); iter != pairs.end(); iter++)
    cout<< iter-> first <<"\t"<< iter-> second<<"\n";
    return 0;
     }
```

The expected output is as under.

```
Present size of pairs is = 6
Maximum numbers that map can hold = 1073741823
The pairs in the map are as below.
Bubita    95
Kunti   96
Mumta   60
Mumtaz    60
Punita    70
Sunita    80
The size after erasing first pair is = 2
The pairs now in map are given below.
Bubita    95
Sunita    80
```

23.6 THE MULTIMAPS

As already discussed in introduction a multimap allows multiple copies of keys. The header file for multimaps is also **<map>**. The following program illustrates it.

PROGRAM 23.13 – Illustrates **construction of a multimap**.

```
#include<iostream>
using namespace std;
#include<map> // Header file is same as for maps.
#include<string>
typedef std::multimap < string ,int > Multigrade ;

 // With this typedef we need write only Multigrade instead of
// std::multimap < string ,int > many times

int main()
 {
 Multigrade pairs;
 pairs.insert (Multigrade::value_type("Sunita", 80));
 pairs.insert (Multigrade::value_type("Sunita", 85));

 pairs.insert (Multigrade::value_type("Kunti", 96));
 pairs.insert (Multigrade::value_type("Punita", 70));

 pairs.insert (Multigrade::value_type("Punita", 65));
 pairs.insert (Multigrade::value_type("Anita", 95));
 pairs.insert (Multigrade::value_type("Mumta", 60));

 for( Multigrade :: const_iterator itr = pairs.begin();
  itr != pairs.end(); itr++)
  cout<< itr-> first <<"\t"<< itr-> second<<"\n";

 return 0;
  }
```

The expected output is given below.

```
Anita    95
Kunti    96
Mumta    60
Punita    70
Punita    65
Sunita    80
Sunita    85
```

The following program illustrates the application of functions **count()**to find how many times a particular key appears in the map.

PROGRAM 23.14 – Illustrates the function `count()` to a multimap.

```
#include<iostream>
using namespace std;
#include<map>
```

```
#include<string>
typedef std::multimap <string ,int> Multigrade ;

int main()
 {
 Multigrade pair ;
 pair .insert (Multigrade::value_type("Sunita", 80));
 pair .insert (Multigrade::value_type("Sunita", 85));

 pair .insert (Multigrade::value_type("Kunti", 96));
 pair .insert (Multigrade::value_type("Punita", 70));
 pair .insert (Multigrade::value_type("Punita", 65));
 pair .insert (Multigrade::value_type("Anita", 95));
 pair .insert (Multigrade::value_type("Mumta", 60));

 cout<<"The number of times Sunita appears = "<< pair.count ("Sunita") <<endl;
 cout<<"The number of times Mumta appears = "<< pair.count ("Mumta")<<endl;

cout<< "The number of times Kanta appears = "<< pair.count ( "Kanta")<<endl;
cout<<"The names of students and grades are as below."<<endl;
for( Multigrade :: const_iterator itr= pair .begin();
  itr != pair.end(); itr++)
  cout<< itr-> first <<"\t"<< itr-> second<<"\n";

 return 0;
  }
```

The expected output is given below.

```
The number of times Sunita appears = 2
The number of times Mumta appears = 1
The number of times Kanta appears = 0
The names of students and grades are as below.
Anita    95
Kunti    96
Mumta    60
Punita    70
Punita    65
Sunita    80
Sunita    85
```

EXERCISES

1. What is difference between a set and a map?
2. What are the methods of constructing a set?
3. Are the values in a set ordered?
4. How would you write the code for the keys in a set to be ordered in descending order?
5. What is the difference between a set and a multiset?
6. How is a multimap different from a map?
7. If the keys in a multimap are the names of students, how would you make a code for making list of students with grades, listing names in alphabetical order?
8. In the program of Q.7 how would you add code to determine the first ranker?
9. What are the return values of functions `lower_bound()` and `upper_bound()`?
10. What does the function `equal_range()` do?
11. Make a program for arranging names of students in order of merit.
12. Make a program to construct a multimap from two arrays. Insert two more pairs in the set.
13. What operators may be used with sets? Make program to illustrate the action of operators = and >= on the sets.
14. Make a program to illustrate the working of functions `key_comp()` and `upper_bound()` on elements of maps.
15. Make a program to illustrate the functions `rbegin()` and `rend()`.
16. What does function `find()` do? Make program to illustrate the action of `find()` and function count () in a multimap.
17. What is the return value of max_size in a multimap? Make a program to illustrate the application of function `max_size()` and `value_comp()`.
18. Make a program for a multimap in which keys are roll numbers of 10 students from ME200401 to ME200410 and associated values are the marks obtained by students entered by user in the range from 0 to 100. The program determines the number of students who have marks between 0 to 40, between 41 to 60, from 61 to 80 and more than 80.

❍❍❍

CHAPTER

24 Bit Sets

24.1 INTRODUCTION

Bit sets are useful in many applications, particularly in real time control systems. In fact, the various processes in computer system itself are controlled by bit sets. Bit sets are particularly useful when a choice is to be made out of different hardware devices such as printer, keyboard, etc., connected to a computer or any other device. With a single bit one can choose one out of two devices. One device for bit = 0 and second for bit = 1. However, if 0 is taken as default value and neglected, we can connect to a device with one bit as illustrated in Table 24.1 below.

Table 24.1

Bit value (signal)	Device connection
0	default case, no device connected
1	connect device1

Similarly with two bits one can choose one out of four cases. However, if the condition when the two bits are zero is neglected as a default case, choice may be made for one out of three as given in Table 24.2 below.

Table 24.2

Bit1 value	Bit2 value	Device connection
0	0	default case, no device connected
1	0	connect device1
0	1	connect device2
1	1	connect device3

Similarly with 3 bits one can select one out of 8 devices and with 4 bits one out of 16 and so on. In bit sets the data structure comprises sets of bits which are sequences of 0s and 1s. This concept can be used in any other control system as well.

The class **bitset** has a number of functions for manipulation of bit sets. We have to include the header file **<bitset>** in the program for using functions of class bitset. The bitwise operators are listed in Table 24.3. The bitset functions are briefly described in Table 24.5.

24.2 CONSTRUCTION OF BIT SETS

Bit sets may be constructed by converting a signed or unsigned integer variable (short int, long or character) into binary representation as given below.

```
#include <bitset>          // Header file for bit sets
bitset();                  //an empty bit set
    unsigned int n = 384;
   bitset <16>   Bset1 ( n );       // bit set desired in 16 bits
```

Name of class — size of bit set — Name of bit set — Number to be converted into bits

Fig. 24.1: Construction of a bit set

In the following program we make use of the above code to convert integer numbers into bit sets.

PROGRAM 24.1 – Illustrates construction of bit sets.

```
#include<iostream>
#include<bitset>
using namespace std;
 void main ()
   {short int p =  75;
    short k = -75;
     unsigned int n = 285;
      unsigned long m = 24567854;

 bitset<8> Bitset1(p), Bitset2(k), Bitset3('B');
 bitset<16> Bitset4(n);
 bitset<24> Bitset5 (m);

 cout << "Bit set for  "<<p <<" is : " <<Bitset1<<endl;
  cout << "Bit set for "<<k <<" is : " <<Bitset2<<endl;
   cout << "Bit set for "<<'B' <<" is : " <<Bitset3<<endl;
    cout << "Bit set for "<<n <<" is : " <<Bitset4 <<endl;
      cout << "Bit set for "<<m <<" is : " <<Bitset5 <<endl;
   }
```

The expected output is given below.

```
Bit set for  75 is : 01001011
Bit set for -75 is : 10110101
Bit set for B is : 01000010
Bit set for 285 is : 0000000100011101
```

```
Bit set for 24567854 is : 0111011011100000000101110
```

The output of the above program shows how a negative integer is stored in computers. The bit on extreme left is for sign (0 for +ve and 1 for –ve). The remaining part is the compliment of bit set for 75 plus 1).

In the above case the bit sets are treated as strings of 0s and 1s. If the output is required as element by element the following code may be used. In a *for loop* we generally write the expression as `(int i = 0; i<n ;i++)`, however, for getting bits we have to reverse the limits, i.e. *for* (int i < Bitset_size `-1 ; i >= 0; i--`). The reason is explained in the program given below.

PROGRAM 24.2 – Illustrates output of bit set as elements of an array.

```
#include<iostream>
#include<bitset>
using namespace std;

void main ()
 { unsigned long n = 85;
   unsigned long m = 456;
   bitset<16> Bitset1(n);
   bitset<16> Bitset2(m);

  cout << "Bit set for "<<n <<" is: \n ";
  for (int i = (long) Bitset1.size()-1 ; i>= 0 ; i--)
  cout << Bitset1[i]<<" ";
  cout << "\nBit set for "<< m<<" is: \n ";

  for ( int j = (long) Bitset2.size()-1; j>=0 ; j--)
     cout << Bitset2[j] << " " ;
     cout <<"\n";
          }
```

The output is given below.

```
Bit set for 85 is:
0 0 0 0 0 0 0 0 0 1 0 1 0 1 0 1
Bit set for 456 is:
0 0 0 0 0 0 0 1 1 1 0 0 1 0 0 0
```

If the above *for loop* had been written as

```
for(i=0; i<(long) Bitset2.size() ; i++)
```

the output for 85 would have been,

```
 1 0 1 0 1 0 1 0 0 0 0 0 0 0 0 0
```

which is obviously wrong because of trailing zeroes which should have been on left hand side.

24.3 BITSET CLASS OPERATORS

The bitwise operators are also described in Chapter 4. Here these are included in Table 24.3 for ready reference. These are supported by **bitset** class.

Table 24.3 – Operators supported by bitset class

Operator symbol	Description
|	Bitwise OR.
&	Bitwise AND.
^	Bitwise XOR.
<<	Left shift.
>>	Right shift.
|=	Bitwise OR and assign.
&=	Bitwise AND and assign.
^=	Bitwise XOR and assign.
<<=	Left shift and assign.
>>=	Right shift and assign.
!=	Not equal to.
==	Equal to.
~	Complement operator, equivalent to function `flip()`.
[]	Returns reference to indexed bit.

Truth Tables for the Operators OR, XOR, AND and Complement

In all the operators described above the operations are carried out bit by bit. The truth tables for some of the operators such as complement `(~)`, `OR(|)`, `AND` (&) and `XOR(^)` are illustrated in Table 24.4 below.

Table 24.4 – Truth table for **OR, AND, XOR** and **complement** (~) operators

Bit1	Bit2	Complement ~ Bit1	BitwiseOR Bit1 | Bit2	Bitwise AND Bit1 & Bit2	Bitwise XOR Bit1 ^ Bit2
0	0	1	0	0	0
1	0	0	1	0	1
0	1	1	1	0	1
1	1	0	1	1	0

The following program illustrates the application of some of the operators described above.

PROGRAM 24.3 – Illustrates application of **bitwise operators.**

```
#include<iostream>
#include<bitset>
using namespace std;
int main ()
    {unsigned int n = 185;
     unsigned int m = 200;
 bitset<12> Bset1(( int ) n);
 bitset<12> Bset2(( int)  m);

 cout << "Bset1 for "<<n <<" is = "<<Bset1<<endl;
 cout << "Bset2 for "<< m<<" is = " <<Bset2<<endl;

 cout <<" Bset1 OR Bset2 = " <<(Bset1 | Bset2)<<endl;
 cout << " Bset1 AND Bset2 = "<<(Bset1 & Bset2 )<<endl;
 cout << " Bset1 XOR Bset2 = "<<(Bset1  ^ Bset2 )<<endl;

 cout << " Complement of Bset1 = "<< ~ Bset1 <<endl;
 return 0;
   }
```

The expected output is given below.

```
Bset1 for 185 is = 000010111001
Bset2 for 200 is = 000011001000
Bset1 OR  Bset2 = 000011111001
Bset1 AND Bset2 = 000010001000
Bset1 XOR Bset2 = 000001110001
Complement of Bset1 = 111101000110
```

In the above program bit sets are generated for two numbers 185 and 200. The third line of the output gives result of OR operation between the two sets. The operation is carried out bit by bit according to the truth Table 24.4. Similarly the 4th line of output gives the result of AND operation. The result of XOR operation is given in the fifth line of the output. The following program illustrates the application of operators |= , &= , ^= and ~ .

PROGRAM 24.4 – Illustrates application of **combination assignment operators** for bit sets.

```
#include<iostream>
#include<bitset>
using namespace std;
int main ()
{unsigned int n = 185;
```

```
int m = 200;
bitset<12> Bset1(( int ) n);
bitset<12> Bset2(( int) m);

cout << "Original Bset1 for "<<n <<" is = "<<Bset1<<endl;
cout << "Original Bset2 for "<< m<<" is = " <<Bset2<<endl;
cout <<"New Bset1= Bset1 |= Bset2 = " <<(Bset1 |= Bset2)<<endl;

cout <<"New Bset1= Bset1 &= Bset2 = "<<(Bset1 &= Bset2 )<<endl;
cout <<"New Bset1= Bset1 ^= Bset2 = "<<(Bset1 ^= Bset2 )<<endl;
cout << "Reversed Bset2 = ~ Bset2 ="<< ~ Bset2 <<endl;
return 0;
}
```

The expected output is given below.

```
Original Bset1 for 185 is = 000010111001
Original Bset2 for 200 is = 000011001000
New Bset1= Bset1 |= Bset2 = 000011111001
New Bset1= Bset1 &= Bset2 = 000011001000
New Bset1= Bset1 ^= Bset2 = 000000000000
Reversed Bset2 = ~ Bset2 =111100110111
```

The output given above is self explanatory. The reader should compare the program output with the manual calculations according to the truth table given in Table 24.4.

The operators left shift and right shift are illustrated in the following program.

PROGRAM 24.5 – Illustrates application of **shift operators** on bit sets.

```
#include<iostream>
#include<bitset>
using namespace std;
void main ()

{unsigned int n = 185 ,m = 221 ;
bitset<16> Bset1(n);
bitset<16> Bset2(m);

cout << "Bit set for "<<n <<" is = "<< Bset1 <<" \n" ;
cout <<"After right shift 4 digits"<<endl;
cout<<" Bset1 = "<<(Bset1>>=4)<<endl; // shift right and assign
cout <<"Bit set for "<< m<<" is = "<< Bset2<<endl ;

cout << "After left shift by 3 digits"<<endl;
cout<<"Bset2 = "<< (Bset2<<=3)<<endl; // shift left and assign

if (Bset1==Bset2)        //check for equality
cout<<" The Bset1 and Bset2 are equal"<<endl;
```

```
else
cout<<"The Bset1 and Bset2 are not equal"<<endl;
   }
```

The expected output is given below.

```
Bit set for 185 is = 0000000010111001
After right shift 4 digits
Bset1 = 0000000000001011
Bit set for 221 is = 0000000011011101
After left shift by 3 digits
Bset2 = 0000011011101000
The Bset1 and Bset2 are not equal
```

Shifting the bit set to right by one place has the effect of integer division by 2. Therefore, the 4 shifts to right of bit set for 185 is equivalent to integer division by $2^4 = 16$. Therefore, the division gives 185/ 16 = 11 (integer division). In binary, the result is 0000000000001011.

The bit set for 221 is shifted left by three places and zeroes are substituted in the places vacated by shift. This is equivalent to multiplying 221 by $2^3 = 8$. Therefore, the resultant bit set Bset2 represents a number $221 \times 8 = 1768$ which in binary is equal to 0000011011101000.

24.4 BIT SET CLASS FUNCTIONS

The class **bitset** in header file **<bitset>** supports the following functions.

Table 24.5 – Functions supported by class **bitset**.

Function	Description
any ()	The function return true if any of bits is set, false otherwise.
count ()	The function returns the number of set bits in a bit set.
flip ()	The function gives inverse bit by bit of the bit set.
none ()	The function returns true if none of bits is set.
reset ()	The function is used to reset a bit to 0.
set ()	The function is used to set a bit to 1.
size ()	The function returns the number of bits that the bit set can hold.
test ()	The function returns the value of a bit.
to_string ()	The function converts the bit set into a string of bits.
to_ulong ()	The function returns the integral value of bit set.

PROGRAM 24.6 – Illustrates application of functions **count(), any (), none()** and **reset().**

```
#include<iostream>
#include<bitset>
```

```
using namespace std;
void main ()
{unsigned int n = 125 ,m = 11765,p=0;

bitset<16> Bset1(n);
bitset<16> Bset2(m);
bitset<16> Bset3(p);

 cout <<"Bset3 = "<<Bset3<<endl;
 cout<<"Number of set bits in Bset3 = " <<Bset3.count()<<endl;

if (Bset3.any())

   cout<< "yes, some bits are set in Bset3"<<endl;
else
   cout<<" No bit is set Bset3"<<endl;

if (Bset3.none())
   cout<< "None of bits are set"<<endl;
else
   cout<<" Some bits are set." <<endl;

   cout << "Bit set for "<<n <<" is = "<< Bset1<<endl ;

Bset1.reset(5);
   cout << "After resetting 6th bit it is = "<< Bset1 <<" \n";
   cout << "Bit set for "<< m<<" is = "<<Bset2 <<endl ;

   cout<<"Number of set bits in Bset2 = " <<Bset2.count()<<endl;
   Bset2.set (3);
   cout <<"After setting 4th bit it is = "<< Bset2 <<endl ;
   }
```

The output of the program is self explanatory and is given below.

```
Bset3 = 0000000000000000
Number of set bits in Bset3 = 0
No bit is set Bset3
None of bits are set
Bit set for 125 is = 0000000001111101
After resetting 6th bit it is = 0000000001011101
Bit set for 11765 is = 0010110111110101
Number of set bits in Bset2 = 10
After setting 4th bit it is = 0010110111111101
```

FUNCTIONS SIZE(), TO_ULONG() AND ANY()

The function `size()` returns the number of bits that the bit set can hold. The function `to_ulong ()` returns the integral value of bit set. The function `any()` returns true if any of bit in the bit set is set otherwise it returns false.

PROGRAM 24.7 – Illustrates application of functions **size(), to_ulong()** and **any().**

```
#include<iostream>
#include<bitset>
using namespace std;

void main ()
{ unsigned int n = 1123 ,m = 12758;

bitset<16> Bset1(n);
bitset<16> Bset2(m);

 cout << "Bit set for "<<n <<" is \n";
 cout << Bset1 <<" \n";
 cout <<" size of bit set = "<< Bset1.size()<<endl;
 cout << Bset2 <<endl ;
cout<<"Number equivalent to Bset2 = " << Bset2.to_ulong()<< endl;
 cout<< Bset2.any()<<endl;
  }
```

The expected output is given below.

```
Bit set for 1123 is
0000010001100011
size of bit set = 16
0011000111010110
Number equivalent to Bset2 = 12758
1
```

Function flip () and none()

The function flip gives inverse of bit set bit by bit. A set bit is reset and an unset bit is set. The function none() returns true if none of the bits in a bit set is set otherwise it returns false.

PROGRAM 24.8 – Illustrates application of functions **flip()** and **none().**

```
#include<iostream>
#include<bitset>
using namespace std;

void main ()
  {
    unsigned int n = 1123 ,m = 12758;
    bitset<16> Bset1(n);
    bitset<16> Bset2(m);
 cout << "Bit set for "<<n <<" is \n";
```

```
cout << Bset1 <<" \n";
cout <<" Inverse of bit set = "<< Bset1.flip()<<endl;
cout<< Bset1.none()<<endl;
cout << Bset2 <<endl ;

 cout<<" Are the two bit sets equal?"<<endl;
if ( Bset1 == Bset2)
  cout << "Yes"<<endl;
else

  cout << "No"<<endl;
  cout<<"Are the two bit sets unequal?"<<endl;

if ( Bset1 != Bset2)
  cout << " Yes"<<endl;
else
  cout << "No"<<endl;
  }
```

The expected output given below is self explanatory.

```
Bit set for 1123 is
0000010001100011
 Inverse of bit set = 1111101110011100
0
0011000111010110
 Are the two bit sets equal?
No
Are the two bit sets unequal?
 Yes
```

FUNCTIONS TEST(), SET() AND RESET ()

The function `test()` returns the state of bit. The function `set()` sets the specified bit to 1. The function `reset()` sets off the bit to zero. See the following program for illustration.

PROGRAM 24.9 – Illustrates application of functions **`test()`**, **`reset()`** and **`set()`**.

```
#include<iostream>
 #include<bitset>
 using namespace std;

 void main ()
 {unsigned int n = 125 ,m = 11765;
 bitset<16> Bset1(n);
 bitset<16> Bset2(m);
```

```
    cout << "Bit set for "<<n <<" is Bset1 = "<< Bset1<<endl;
    cout<< "Test bit 5. The 5th bit = " <<Bset1.test(4)<<"\n";

   Bset1.reset(4);
    cout<<"After reset bit 5 = "<< Bset1.test(4)<<endl;
    cout << "Bit set for "<<11765 <<" is Bset2 = "<<Bset2 <<endl ;
    cout << "Test bit 10. The 10th bit = " << Bset2.test(9)<<endl;

   Bset2.set(9) ;
    cout<< "After setting the 10th bit  = " <<Bset2.test(9)<<endl;
      }
```

The expected output is given below.

```
Bit set for 125 is Bset1 = 0000000001111101
Test bit 5. The 5th bit = 1
After reset bit 5 = 0
Bit set for 11765 is Bset2 = 0010110111110101
Test bit 10. The 10th bit = 0
After setting the 10th bit  = 1
```

EXERCISES

1. What are the bit sets?
2. How are the bit sets useful?
3. How bit sets may be used to activate one out of 6 peripherial devices connected to a computer?
4. In a bit set which is 8 bit wide only, the 4th bit is desired to be set. Write code to set it?
5. Compare the bit sets for 246 and –246. Explain the method of storing –ve numbers in computer memory.
6. Make a program to illustrate the action of operators &, ^ and | for bit sets.
7. Make a program to illustrate the action of operators << and >> on bit sets. How do the above shifts change the values represented by the bit sets?
8. Make a program to illustrate the working of operators |= , &= and ^= on bit sets.
9. Make a program to illustrate the following function of bit set class.

   (i) any() (ii) count () (iii) flip()
10. Make a program to illustrate the action of following functions of bit set class.

    (i) set () (ii) reset () (iii) test ()
11. Make a program to illustrate the action of following functions. Explain their meaning.

    (i) none () (ii) size ()
12. What do you understand by function `to_ulong()` and `to_string()` as applied to bit sets? Make a program to illustrate the action of these functions.

❍❍❍

CHAPTER

25

Algorithms

25.1 INTRODUCTION

In this chapter we deal with templates functions and algorithms which may be reused by a programmer in application programs. These were briefly mentioned in the Chapter 21 on STL. Here we shall deal in some detail. The main advantage of using these algorithms is that the programmer does not have to invent the wheel again. It saves time and effort. Moreover, being based on template functions and classes, these can be used for any type of data, i.e. fundamental type as well as user defined type. Besides, these programs have been made by experts in C++ and thus assure a degree of robustness as well as efficiency.

The algorithms are independent of container classes, so these are applicable to objects of container classes as well as to arrays, strings and other data types. All the algorithms except the numeric ones, are contained in the header file **<algorithm>**. Therefore, we have to include header file <algorithm> in the programs in which we are using them. The numeric algorithms which deal with numerical manipulations are contained in the header file **<numeric>**. Hence for using these algorithms the header file **<numeric>** has to be included. In all there are about 75 algorithms. These are broadly classified into following categories. The actions of the different algorithms in each category are briefly described in Tables 25.2 to 25.9 and many of them are illustrated in the following pages.

Table 25.1

Algorithm category	Header file
Numeric algorithms	<numeric>
Comparison (relational) algorithms	<algorithm>
Non-mutating algorithms	<algorithm>
Mutating algorithms	<algorithm>
Searching and sorting algorithms	<algorithm>
Algorithms on sets	<algorithm>
Permutation algorithms	<algorithm>
Algorithms on heap	<algorithm>

25.2 CATEGORIES OF ALGORITHMS AND BRIEF DESCRIPTIONS

The different categories of algorithms are listed and briefly described in following tables.

RELATIONAL ALGORITHMS

Table 25.2 – Relational algorithms (Header file **<algorithm>**)

Algorithm	Description
`equal()`	Returns true if two sequences are equal else false.
`lexicographical_compare()`	Compares two sequences lexicographically. It returns true if the first is less than the second.
`max()`	Returns greater of the two values.
`min()`	Returns smaller of the two values.
`max_element()`	Returns iterator to the largest element in the range.
`min_element()`	Returns iterator to element with minimum value.
`mismatch()`	Finds the first position of mismatch between two sequences of same size.

NON-MUTATING ALGORITHMS

Table 25.3 – Non-mutating sequence algorithm (Header file **<algorithm>**)

Algorithm	Description
`adjacent_find()`	Finds the first adjacent pair of elements which have same value.
`count()`	Counts the number of elements that match the specified value.
`count_if()`	Counts the number of elements that satisfy a predicate.
`find()`	Finds the first element that matches the specified value.
`find_end()`	Finds the last occurrence of a subsequence.
`find_first_of()`	Finds the first occurrence of an element of a given sequence.
`find_if()`	Finds the first element that satisfies the specified predicate.
`for_each()`	Applies a given function to each element of the sequence.
`search()`	Searches for matching sub-sequences.
`search_n()`	Searches for matching sub-sequence of n consecutive elements.

Mutating Algorithms

Table 25.4 – Mutating algorithms (Header file **<algorithm>**)

Algorithm	Description
`copy()`	Makes a copy from start to end at a new location.
`copy_backward()`	Makes a copy at new location in backward direction.
`fill()`	Replaces elements of a sequence with copies of a value or object.
`fill_n()`	Replaces the first n elements of sequence with a given value.
`generate()`	Fills the sequence with values obtained by calling a function.
`generate_n()`	The generate () is applied to first n elements of the sequence.
`iter_swap()`	Swaps the values of elements at specified positions.
`iota()`	The iota assigns a value to first element, value+1 to second element and so on.
`power()`	power (x, n) returns x^n.
`random_sample()`	Randomly copies the elements of a sequence. Any one elements appears only once in output.
`random_sample_n()`	Randomly copies n elements of a sequence.
`random_shuffle ()`	It rearranges the elements in random fashion.
`remove()`	Removes elements having specified value in a sequence.
`remove_copy()`	Copies sequence without the elements having specified value. The original sequence is left intact.
`remove_copy_if()`	Copies sequence elements that do not satisfy a given predicate.
`remove_if()`	Removes the elements which satisfy a given predicate.
`replace()`	Replaces the values of elements with new values.
`replace_copy()`	Makes another sequence by replacing elements of a sequence.
`replace_copy_if()`	Makes new sequence by replacing values of elements whose old values satisfy a predicate.
`replace_if()`	Replaces element values whose old values satisfy a predicate.
`reverse()`	Reverses the order of elements of a sequence in a given range.
`reverse_copy()`	Makes a new sequence with elements of a sequence reversed.
`rotate()`	Rotates the elements of a sequence as if the two ends are connected.
`rotate_copy()`	Makes a new sequence by rotating the elements of a sequence.

Contd...

Algorithm	Description
`swap()`	Swaps values of two objects of same type.
`swap_ranges()`	Swaps elements in the specified ranges of two sequences.
`transform()`	The elements of a sequence are transformed as a result of user defined operation.
`unique()`	Removes adjacent duplicate elements in a sorted sequence.
`unique_copy()`	Makes a copy of sequence without adjacent duplicate elements.

SEARCH AND SORT ALGORITHMS

Table 25.5 – Search and sort algorithms (Header file **<algorithm>**)

Algorithm	Description
`binary_search()`	Carries out binary search for a value in a sorted sequence.
`equal_range()`	It searches a sorted sequence for a range of elements equal to a given value.
`lower_bound()`	The function searches sorted sequence for the first position where a given value may be inserted.
`merge()`	Produces a sorted sequence by merging two sorted sequences.
`inplace_merge()`	Merges two parts of same sequence.
`is_sorted()`	The function returns true if the sequence is sorted in ascending order.
`nth_element()`	Sorting is carried out as much as it is necessary to place nth element in its correct sorted position.
`partial_sort()`	Sorts a specified number of elements from the beginning of the sequence in ascending order.
`partial_sort_copy()`	Makes a copy of a number of elements of a sequence and sorts it.
`partition()`	Partitions a sequence such that the elements that satisfy a predicate are placed in the first part.
`stable_partition()`	The function while partitioning maintains the relative order of elements in both the parts.
`sort()`	It sorts the sequence in ascending order.
`stable_sort()`	In sorting the original order of equal elements is maintained.
`upperbound()`	The function searches a sorted sequence for the last occurrence of a given value.

Algorithms on Sets

Table 25.6 – Algorithms on sets (Header file **<algorithm>**)

Algorithm	Description
`includes()`	It returns true if all elements of second set are in the first set. Both the sets should be sorted.
`set_difference()`	Makes a set of elements of the first set which are not in the second set.
`set_intersection()`	Makes a set out of intersection of two given sets (common elements of the two sets).
`set_symmetric_difference()`	Produces a sequence of elements that are members of either set but not of both.
`set_union()`	Produces a set out of union of two sets.

Numeric Algorithms

Table 25.7 – Algorithms for manipulation of numeric values (Header file **<numeric>**)

Algorithm	Description
`accumulate()`	Sums up the values of the elements of a segment of sequence to the initial value.
`adjacent_difference()`	Creates adjacent differences (S[n] – S[n – 1]) and loads these on to another sequence.
`inner_product()`	Returns the inner product of elements of two sequences of same size.
`partial_sum()`	Makes a sequence by partial sum of range of elements in a sequence.

Permutation Algorithms

Table 25.8 – Algorithms for permutation (Header file **<algorithm>)**

Algorithm	Description
`next_permutation()`	Produces permutations of a sequence into next lexico-graphically greater permutation.
`prev_permutation()`	Produces permutations of a sequence into next permutation which is lexicographically smaller sequence.

Algorithms on Heap

Table 25.9 – Algorithms on heap (Header file <algorithm>)

Algorithm	Description
make_heap()	Elements of a sequence are rearranged into a heap.
pop_heap()	Removes the first element and rest are rearranged into heap.
push_heap ()	An element is added to heap.
sort_heap ()	Sorts the elements of a sequence into a heap.

25.3 ILLUSTRATIVE APPLICATIONS OF SOME ALGORITHMS

Simple typical applications of some of the algorithms are illustrated by the following programs which are listed in alphabetical order.

Algorithm accumulate()

The syntax for accumulate() is of the following type

T accumulate (iterator *start*, iterator *end*, T *initial_value*);

The function sums up the values of element between the start and end iterators. The sum is initialized by inititial_value. Program 25.1 illustrates it.

PROGRAM 25.1 – Illustrates **accumulate()** algorithm.

```
#include<iostream>
#include<numeric>
using namespace std;
int main()
{ int S[8] = {1,2,3,4,5,6,7,8};
  int sum_four = accumulate( S , S+4, 0); //initial value is 0
  cout<< "Sum of first 4 elements = " << sum_four<<endl;

  int sum_all = accumulate( S , S+8, 0);
  cout << "Sum of all the element = " << sum_all<<endl;
 cout<<"Sum of all elements + 100 = "<<accumulate(S,S+8,100)<< endl;
// initial value is 100.

 cout<<"Sum of all elements -100 = " <<accumulate(S,S+8,-100)<< endl;
// initial value is -100.
 return 0 ;
}
```

The expected output is given below.

```
Sum of first 4 elements = 10
Sum of all the element = 36
Sum of all elements + 100 = 136
Sum of all elements -100 = -64
```

ALGORITHM ADJACENT_DIFFERENCE()

Let there be a sequence (a, b, c, d, e,). The function adjacent_difference produces the sequence of adjacent differences (a, b – a, c – b, d – c, e – d) and loads it on another sequence.

PROGRAM 25.2 – Illustrates application of `adjacent_difference()` algorithm.

```
#include<iostream>
#include<numeric>
using namespace std;
int main()
{
 int S[5] = { 5,20,40, 80, 160};
 int A[5];
 adjacent_difference( S, S+5,A);    // A is another sequence.

 for (int i =0; i<5;i++)
 cout<< A[i]<<"  ";
 cout <<"\n";
 return 0 ;
}
```

The output given below is self explanatory.

```
5 15 20 40 80
```

ALGORITHM ADJACENT_FIND ()

The syntax of the function is

```
iterator adjacent_find( iterator start, iterator end );
iterator adjacent_find( iterator start, iterator end,
binary_predsicate BP);
```

The function searches from start to end for two consecutive elements having identical values. The function returns an iterator to the first of the two elements. If such an adjacent pair is not found the return iterator points to the end of sequence. In the second version if a predicate BP is provided to test then the predicate is used to determine equality of two elements.

PROGRAM 25.3 – Illustrates the application of `adjacent_find()` algorithm.

```
#include<iostream>
# include<algorithm>   // includes header file <algorithm>

#include<vector>    // includes header file <vector>
using namespace std;

int main()
{
vector<int> V;
int S[6] = { 10, 20, 40, 40, 50, 60};
for(int i =0; i < 6 ;i++)
V.push_back (S[i]);      // constructing the vector.

int *Find = adjacent_find ( V.begin(), V.end() );
  // Find is the iterator and *Find the value of element.

if ( Find == V.end())
 {cout<<" No match found"<<endl;    }

else
 cout<<"Found the match starting at "<<*Find <<endl;
 return 0 ;
}
```

Output is as under.

```
Found the match starting at 40
```

ALGORITHM BINARY_SEARCH()

The function binary_search () searches from start to end of a sequence for a specified value. The sequence must be a sorted sequence. The function returns true (1) if the value is found otherwise it returns false (0). See the following program for illustration.

PROGRAM 25.4 – Illustrates the function `binary_search()` algorithm.

```
#include<iostream>
# include<algorithm>
#include<vector>
using namespace std;
int main()
{
 vector<int> V;
  int S[7] = { 10,20,30 ,36, 44, 60, 70};
   for(int i = 0; i< 7 ; i++)
```

```
V.push_back (S[i]);

bool B = binary_search( V.begin(), V.end(), 36 );
   // here 36 is the value to be searched.

if ( B!=0)
 cout<<"The number "<<n<<" is contained in the vector V." <<endl;
else
 cout<<n<< "The number is not in the vector V."<<endl;
 return 0 ;
   }
```

The expected output is given below.

```
The number 36 is contained in the vector V.
```

Algorithm copy()

The syntax is

`iterator copy(iterator start, iterator end, iterator destination);`

The function copies the elements from start to end to the destination specified as an argument of the function. The return value of the function is iterator (or pointer) to the last element copied.

PROGRAM 25.5 – Illustrates **`copy()`** algorithm.

```
#include<iostream>
#include<algorithm>
using namespace std;
int main()
{
int S[11] = { 10,20,30 ,36, 44, 60, 70, 80, 90,100,110};
 int A[6];

  copy( S+2 , S+8, A ); // A is the destination
   cout<< "The elements of A are as below.\n";

for(int i =0; i< 6; i++)
  {cout << A [i] <<"  ";}
   cout<<"\n";

 return 0 ;
}
```

The expected output is given below.

```
The elements of A are as below.
30 36 44 60 70 80
```

The algorithm copies from element at index 2 to element at index 8. The S+8th element is not included.

ALGORITHMS COPY_BACKWARD()

The function is similar to copy(), the difference is that it starts depositing elements from back end.

PROGRAM 25.6 – Illustrates the application of copy_backward().

```
#include<iostream>
#include<algorithm>
using namespace std;
int main()
 { int S1[10] = { 1,2,3,4,5,6,7,8,9,10};
  int S2[10] = {0};
  int S3[10] = {0};
 cout << "S1 is : ";
 for (int i =0 ; i<10; i++)
 cout<<S1[i]<<"  ";

 cout <<"\nS2 is : ";
 copy(S1, S1+10, S2);

  for(int n =0; n<10; n++)
  cout <<S2[n]<<"  " ;

  copy_backward( S1, S1 + 6 , S3+10 );
  cout<<"\nS3 is : ";
  for ( int j = 0; j< 10 ; j++)
 cout<<S3[j]<<"  ";
 cout<<"\n";
  return 0;
   }
```

The expected output is as below. The output is self explanatory.

```
S1 is : 1  2  3  4  5  6  7  8  9  10
S2 is : 1  2  3  4  5  6  7  8  9  10
S3 is : 0  0  0  0  1  2  3  4  5  6
```

ALGORITHM COUNT()

The function returns the number of elements in the sequence that matches a specified value. The following program illustrates the application of the function.

PROGRAM 25.7 – Illustrates the algorithm `count()`.

```
#include<iostream>
#include<algorithm>
#include<vector>

using namespace std;
int main()
{
 vector<int> V;
 int S[8] = { 10,20,24 ,36, 24, 24, 70};
 for(int i =0; i < 6 ;i++)
 V.push_back (S[i]);
 int n = 24;
 int m = count( V.begin(), V.end(), n );
cout<<"The number of elements with value "<<n<<" in V are = "<< m <<endl;
  return 0 ; }
```

The expected output is given below.

```
The number of elements with value 24 in V are = 3
```

ALGORITHM COUNT_IF()

The application of this algorithm has already been illustrated in Chapter 21 on STL. Below is another application.

PROGRAM 25.8 – Illustrates application of `count_if()` algorithm.

```
#include<iostream>
#include<algorithm>
#include<functional>     //This is needed for predicates.
using namespace std;

int main()
{
int S[ ] = { 5,6,8,7,8,3,8,10,8, 12};
int n= count_if(S, S+10, bind2nd(greater<int>(),7));
     //n is count of elements greater than 7 in S
cout<< "Number of elements of S >7 are = " <<n <<endl;
int m = count_if(S, S+10, bind2nd(less<int>(),10));
     // m is count of elements less than 10
cout<< "Number of elements of S < 10 are = " <<m <<endl;
return 0;
}
```

The expected output is given below. For more details on predicates and binder functions see Chapter 21.

```
Number of elements of S >7 are = 6
Number of elements of S < 10 are = 8
```

ALGORITHM EQUAL()

The function equal() returns true if the elements in the two ranges are same, otherwise it returns false. The function takes three arguments, the first two are the start and end of the first sequence and the third is the start of second sequence.

PROGRAM 25.9 – Illustrates `equal()` algorithm.

```
#include<iostream>
#include<algorithm>
#include<vector>
using namespace std;
int main()
{
 vector<int> V1;
   int S1[6] = { 10,13,25 ,36, 25, 50};
   for(int i =0; i < 6 ;i++)
   V1.push_back (S1[i]);
vector<int> V2;
int S2[6] = { 10,13,25,36,25,25};
for(int j =0; j < 6 ;j++)
V2.push_back (S2[j]);
  int S3 [] = {11,12,13, 4,5,11,12,13};
  vector<int> V3;
  for ( int k =0; k<8 ; k++)
  V3.push_back ( S3[k]);
 if (equal( V3.begin(), V3.begin()+3, V3.begin()+5));
  cout << "The two subsets of three values are equal."<<endl;
 if(equal( V1.begin(), V1.end(), V2.begin ()))
  cout<<"The two vectors are equal." <<endl;
 else
 cout<<"The two vectors are not equal."<<endl;
 return 0 ;
}
```

The expected output is given below.

```
The two subsets of three values are equal.
The two vectors are not equal.
```

In the above program the function equal is tested on elements of two vectors (second line of output) as well on two segments of the same vector. See the first line of the output.

ALGORITHMS EQUAL_RANGE ()

The function equal_range returns the range of elements which are equal to a specified value in a sorted sequence. The following program illustrates the same.

PROGRAM 25.10 – Illustrates `equal_range()` algorithm.

```
#include<iostream>
#include<algorithm>
#include<vector>
using namespace std;
int main()
 {  vector<int> V;
      int S[8] = { 10,20, 24 ,24, 24, 36, 70};
    for(int i =0; i < 6 ;i++)
      V.push_back (S[i]);
  int n = 24;
  pair <vector<int>::iterator, vector<int>::iterator> Range;
  Range = equal_range ( V.begin(), V.end(), n );

 cout<<"The equal range starts after "<<*( Range.first -1) <<" and ends before"
<<*(Range.second )<<endl;
  return 0 ;
 }
```

The expected output is given below.

```
The equal range starts after 20 and ends before 36
```

ALGORITHMS FILL() AND FILL_N ()

The function assigns the specified value to all the elements from a start to an end. The function fill_n assigns values to the first n elements of the sequence.

PROGRAM 25.11 – Illustrates the `fill()` algorithm and `fill_n()` algorithm.

```
#include<iostream>
#include<algorithm>
#include<vector>
using namespace std;
int main()
```

```
{
 vector<int> V;
 int S[9] = { 15,20, 30 , 40, 50, 60, 70, 80, 90};
 for(int i =0; i < 9 ;i++)
 V.push_back (S[i]);
int m =5;
fill_n ( V.begin(), V.size()/3 , m );
for (int k =0; k<V.size(); k++)
cout << V[k] << " " ;
cout<< "\n";
int n = 10;
fill ( V.begin(), V.end(), n );
for (int j =0; j<V.size(); j++)
cout << V[j] << " " ;
cout<< "\n";
 return 0 ; }
```

The expected output is given below.

```
5 5 5 40 50 60 70 80 90
10 10 10 10 10 10 10 10 10
```

In the first line of output the value 5 replaces the previous values of first three elements of vector V. In the second line of output, all the elements of vector V are filled with a value 10 by function `fill()`.The previous values are removed.

ALGORITHM FIND()

The algorithm `find()` return iterator to the element that matches a specified value. If the value is not found, it returns iterator to end of sequence. The following program illustrates the same.

PROGRAM 25.12 – Illustrates application of `find()` algorithm.

```
#include<iostream>
#include<algorithm>
#include<vector>
using namespace std;
int main()
{ vector<int> V;
 int S[7] = { 10,20, 24 ,30, 35, 36, 70};
 for(int i =0; i < 7 ;i++)
 V.push_back (S[i]);
int n = 24;
vector <int> ::iterator iter;
```

```
 iter = find(V.begin(), V.end(), n);
 if (iter != V.end())
  cout << "The number "<<n<<" is an element of vector."<<endl;

 else
  cout<< "The number " << n<<" is not an element of vector.\n";

 return 0 ;
}
```

The expected output is given below.

```
The number 24 is an element of vector.
```

ALGORITHM FIND_END ()

The function searches for a sequence of elements in another sequence. If the sequence is found, the algorithm returns iterator to first element of the last sequence found. Otherwise it returns iterator to end of sequence.

PROGRAM 25.13 – Illustrates the algorithm `find_end()` algorithm.

```
#include<iostream>
#include<algorithm>
#include<vector>
using namespace std;
int main()
 { vector<int> V;
  int S[12] = { 10,20,25 ,26, 27, 36, 20,25 ,26,27, 70, 90};
  for(int i =0; i < 12 ;i++)
  V.push_back (S[i]);

 int Find_Seq1 [] = {20, 25,26,27};
 vector<int>:: iterator iter;
 iter = find_end( V.begin(), V.end(), Find_Seq1, Find_Seq1+3);
 if ( iter != V.end())

  cout<<"The last Find_Seq1 starts at "<< *iter <<endl;
 else
  cout<< "There is no Find_Seq1 in the vector."<<endl;

 int Find_Seq2 [] = {20, 4,26 };
 iter = find_end( V.begin(), V.end(), Find_Seq2, Find_Seq2+2);
 if ( iter != V.end())
  cout<<"The last Find_Seq2 starts at "<< *iter <<endl;
 else
  cout<< "There is no Find_Seq2 in the vector."<<endl;
 return 0 ;
}
```

The expected output is given below. The output is self explanatory.

```
The last Find_Seq1 starts at 20
There is no Find_Seq2 in the vector.
```

ALGORITHM FIND_FIRST_OF()

The function finds the first occurrence of an element of a sequence in a sequence.

PROGRAM 25.14 – Illustrates `find_first_of()` algorithm.

```
#include<iostream>
#include<algorithm>
using namespace std;
int main()
{
int * Find;
 int S[9] = { 1,6,2,3,4,5,6,7,8};
 int S2[] = { 5,6,7};
Find = find_first_of( S, S+9, S2, S2+3);

if(Find != S+9) //if no match is found the pointer points to end
cout<<"Found the match :" << *Find<<endl;
return 0 ;
}
```

The expected output is given below.

```
Found the match :6
```

ALGORITHM FIND_IF()

It searches for a value subject to satisfaction of a predicate. In the following program the search is for element greater than 7. Since all the elements have to be compared with the number 7, the number 7 is bound to the function greater<int>() by the binder function bind2nd. See Chapter 21 for details on function objects, predicates and binders.

PROGRAM 25.15 – Illustrates `find_if()` algorithm.

```
#include<iostream>
#include<algorithm>

#include<functional>
using namespace std;

int main()
{
int S[ ] = { 5,6,3,7,8,3,8,10,8, 12};
int* n = find_if(S, S+10, bind2nd(greater<int>(),7));
```

```
    cout<< "*n = "<< *n<<endl;

    cout << "The position of element = "<<n+1-S <<"th"<<endl;
    return 0;
    }
```

The expected output is given below.

```
*n = 8
The position of element = 5th
```

ALGORITHM FOR_EACH()

The algorithm applies the specified function to each element of a sequence.

PROGRAM 25.16 – Illustrates the application of **`for_each()`** algorithm

```
#include<iostream>
#include<algorithm>
#include<functional>
using namespace std;
 void Multiplies ( int &x)
 {cout<< 10*x <<"  ";}

int main()
{ int S1[ ] = { 5,6,8,7,4,3,8,10,11, 12};
 for_each ( S1, S1+10, Multiplies );
 cout<<"\n";
 return 0;
}
```

The expected output is given below.

```
50 60 80 70 40 30 80 100 110 120
```

Clearly the function multiplies each element by 10 and displays it.

ALGORITHMS GENERATE() AND GENERATE_N()

The two functions are used to generate values through the operation of a function. In the following program the `generate()` is used to generate 8 random numbers each of 2 digits. The second function `generate_n()` is used to generate a specified number of random numbers.

PROGRAM 25.17 – Illustrates **`generate()`** **and** **`generate_n()`** algorithms.

```
#include<iostream>
#include<algorithm>
```

```
using namespace std;
 void Display (int x)

{cout<<x<< " ";}
int main()
 { int S[8] = { 0 };
generate (S, S+8, rand );
for ( int i =0; i<8; i++)
 cout<< S[i]%100<<"  ";
 cout<<"\n";

  int B [6] = {0};
  generate_n( B , 6, rand);
  for(int j =0; j<6; j++)
  cout<< B[j] <<"  ";
 return 0 ;
}
```

The expected output is given below.

```
41 67 34 0 69 24 78 58
26962 24464 5705 28145 23281 16827
```

ALGORITHM INCLUDES()

The function returns a Boolean value if the elements of a set or specified segment of a set is included in another set. In the following program `includes()` is used to test if a segment of a set is included in another set.

PROGRAM 25.18 – Illustrates the **includes()** algorithm.

```
#include<iostream>
#include<algorithm>
using namespace std;
int main()
{  int S[8] = { 5,6,7,8,9,11,12,13 };
   int A [9] = { 5,6,7,8, 21,22,23,24,25};
   bool B ;
   B = includes (S, S+8, A, A+4); //test if A to A+4 are in S
   if (B)
cout << "The Sequence S includes A[0] to A[3]" << endl;
else
cout << "The Sequence S does not includes A[0] to A[3]" << endl;
 return 0 ;
}
```

The expected output is given below.

```
The Sequence S includes A[0] to A[3]
```

ALGORITHM INNER_PRODUCT()

This algorithm is part of header file <numeric>. So this header file must be included in the program. The algorithm `inner_product()` does the inner vector product of two vectors. For example if the two vectors have elements (2, 4, 5) and (1, 3, 6), the inner product = $2\times1 + 4\times3 + 5\times6 = 44$.

PROGRAM 25.19 – Illustrates `inner_product()` algorithm.

```
#include<iostream>
#include<numeric>
using namespace std;
int main()
{ int S[7] = { 6,4,8,9,10,20,10};
 int A[7] = { 2,2,2,2,2,2,2};
 int n = 20;
 // the value of n initializes the inner_product.

 int Innerproduct = inner_product ( S , S+7, A, n );
 cout<< "Innerproduct of elements S and A plus "<<n<<" = " <<
 Innerproduct<<endl;
 return 0 ;
}
```

The expected output is given below.

```
Innerproduct of elements S and A plus 20 = 154
```

ALGORITHM INPLACE_MERGE()

The function merges two parts of the same sequence and results in a sorted sequence.

PROGRAM 25.20 – Illustrates `inplace_merge()` algorithm.

```
#include<iostream>
#include<algorithm>
using namespace std;
int main()
{
   int S[8] = { 2,4,5,1,3,6,7,9 };
   int A [8] ={ 12,13,14,15, 5,6,7, 24} ;

 inplace_merge ( S, S+3, S+8);
 inplace_merge ( A, A+4, A+8);
```

```
for(int i =0; i<8; i++)
 cout << S[i] <<" ";

cout<<"\n";

   for ( int j =0; j<8; j++)
  cout<< A [j] <<" ";
   return 0 ;
}
```

The expected output is given below.

```
1 2 3 4 5 6 7 9
5 6 7 12 13 14 15 24
```

ALGORITHM ITER_SWAPS()

The function swaps the elements of two sequences at specified locations.

PROGRAM 25.21 – Illustrates `iter_swap()` algorithm.

```
#include<iostream>
#include<algorithm>
using namespace std;
int main()
{  int S[8] = { 2,4,5,1,3,6,7,9 };
   int A [8] ={ 12,13,14,15, 5,6,7, 24} ;
iter_swap ( S+4, A+3);
for ( int i =0; i<8; i++)
   cout << S[i] <<" ";

 cout<<"\n";
   for ( int j =0; j<8; j++)
 cout<< A [j] <<" ";
   return 0 ;
}
```

The expected output is given below. The value 15 of A has been exchanged with 3 of S.

```
2 4 5 1 15 6 7 9
12 13 14 3 5 6 7 24
```

ALGORITHM LEXICOGRAPHICAL_COMPARE()

The function compares two sets lexicographically, i.e. dictionary style. For such a function it is best to take strings for comparison. In the following program the string “AA” is compared with “ZZ” lexicographically. Evidently the first string is smaller than the second, hence, the output is 1 (true). If the second is compared with the first the result is 0. In the third case a string is compared with itself. The result is 0 because it cannot precede itself. In the third case a string "compute" is compared with string "computer". The output is obviously 1.

PROGRAM 25.22 – Illustrates `lexicographical_compare()` algorithm.

```
#include<iostream>
# include<algorithm>
using namespace std;
int main()
{
char S1[ ] = "AA";
char S2 [ ] ="ZZ" ;
char B[] = "compute";
char C[] ="computer";
bool b1 =lexicographical_compare ( S1, S1+1, S2, S2+1);
cout<<"b1 = " << b1<<endl;
bool b2 =lexicographical_compare (S2, S2+1 ,S1, S1+1 );
cout<< "b2 = " << b2<<endl;
 bool b3 = lexicographical_compare ( S1, S1+1, S1, S1+1);
 cout<<"b3 = " <<b3<<endl;
 bool b4 = lexicographical_compare ( B, B+7, C, C+8);
 cout<<"b4 = " << b4<<endl;
 return 0 ;
}
```

The expected output is as below.

```
b1 = 1
b2 = 0
b3 = 0
b4 = 1
```

The algorithms lower_bound() and upper_bound()

The functions are applied to sorted sequences. The `lower_bound` gives the position of first occurrence of a value in the sequence. The `upper_bound` gives the position of element next to last occurrence of a value in the sequence. The following program illustrates both the functions. First the function lower_bound is applied to an array of integers for a value 20. It is at index value 6. The upper_bound gives a value 9. That is index value of 22 in the array.

PROGRAM 25.23 – Illustrates application of `lower_bound()` and `upper_bound()`.

```
#include<iostream>
# include<algorithm>
```

```
using namespace std;

int main()
{ int S1[ ] = { 11, 12, 13 ,16, 16 , 19,20, 20, 20 , 22, 24 };
 int* ptr1 = lower_bound( S1, S1+11 ,20);
 cout <<"lower_bound for 20 = " <<ptr1 -> S1 <<endl;

 int* ptr2 = lower_bound( S1, S1+11 ,16);
   cout <<"lower_bound for 16 = "<< ptr2 -> S1 <<endl;
 int *uptr1 = upper_bound ( S1, S1+11, 16);

  cout <<"upper_bound of 16 is = " << uptr1 -> S1 <<endl;
 int* Uptr2 = upper_bound ( S1, S1+11, 20);
   cout << "upper_bound of 20 = " <<Uptr2 -> S1 <<endl;
   return 0 ;
}
```

The expected output is given below.

```
lower_bound for 20 = 6
lower_bound for 16 = 3
upper_bound of 16 is = 5
upper_bound of 20 = 9
```

ALGORITHM MAKE_HEAP()

The function turns a given sequence of elements into heap.

PROGRAM 25.24 – Illustrates `make_heap()` algorithm

```
#include<iostream>
#include<algorithm>
using namespace std;

int main()
{
 int S[13] = {10, 12, 22,24 ,34,51,71,13,16 ,177 ,106 ,6,7};
 make_heap( S,S+13);

for ( int i =0; i<13; i++)
 cout << S[i] <<" ";
 cout<<"\n";

return 0 ;
}
```

The expected output is given below.

```
177 106 71 24 34 51 22 13 16 10 12 6 7
```

ALGORITHM MAX_ELEMENT()

The function returns position of element with maximum value.

PROGRAM 25.25 – Illustrates application of **max_element()** algorithm.

```
#include<iostream>
# include<algorithm>
using namespace std;
int main()
{ int S1[ ] = { 11, 12, 113 ,216 , 19,20 };
 cout<< *max_element ( S1, S1+6) <<endl;
 const int * ptr= max_element ( S1, S1+6);
      // value of max_element
 cout<< ptr - S1 <<endl; // position of max element
 return 0 ;
}
```

The following output is obvious.

```
216
3
```

ALGORITHM MERGE()

The algorithm merges two sorted sequences to create a new sorted sequence.

PROGRAM 25.26 – Illustrates **merge()** algorithm

```
#include<iostream>
# include<algorithm>
using namespace std;
int main()
{ int S1[ ] = {10, 12, 40 };
 int S2[] = {34,51,71 ,106 ,177 };
 int A[8];
 int B[6];
merge ( S1, S1+3, S2, S2+5 , A);
for ( int i =0; i<8 ;i++)
cout<< A[i]<<" ";
cout<<"\n";

merge ( S2, S2+4,S1, S1+2, B);
for ( int k =0; k<6 ;k++)
 cout<< B[k]<<" ";
   cout<<"\n";
return 0 ;
  }
```

The expected output is given below.

```
10 12 34 40 51 71 106 177
10 12 34 51 71 106
```

ALGORITHM MIN_ELEMENT()

The function returns iterator to the element with minimum value.

PROGRAM 25.27 – Illustrates `min_element()` algorithm.

```
#include<iostream>
# include<algorithm>
using namespace std;
int main()
{
 int S1[ ] = { 19,20, 11, 12, 113 ,216};
 cout<< *min_element ( S1, S1+6) <<endl; // value of min. element

 const int * ptr= min_element ( S1, S1+6);
 cout<< ptr -> S1 <<endl; // gives index value of min. element
return 0 ;
}
```

The expected output is given below.

```
11
2
```

ALGORITHM MISMATCH()

The function returns a pair of iterators which give position of mismatch between two sequences. The following program illustrates the same.

PROGRAM 25.28 – Illustrates `mismatch()` algorithm

```
#include<iostream>
#include<algorithm>
using namespace std;
int main()
{
 char S1[] = "Computer, Computar, Computor";
 char S2[] = "Computer, Computer, Computer";

 int m = strlen(S1);

 pair<char*, char*> p = mismatch( S1, S1+m, S2);

 char* S1ptr= p.first;
```

```
 char* S2ptr= p.second;
cout<<"length = "<< m <<endl;
cout<< "First location of mismatch in string S1 is at "<<S1ptr - S1<<endl;
The pointers S1 and S2 are subracted to get index values.
cout<< "First location of mismatch in string S2 is at "<<S2ptr - S2<<endl;
return 0 ;
}
```

The expected output is given below. The result is obvious.

```
length = 28
First location of mismatch in string S1 is at 16
First location of mismatch in string S2 is at 16
```

ALGORITHM NEXT_PERMUTATION()

Gives another permutations of a sequence

PROGRAM 25.29 – Illustrates `next_permutation()` algorithm.

```
#include <iostream>
#include<algorithm>
using namespace std;
void main()
{
 char A[5] = "XYZ";
 for( int k =0; k<6;k++)
 { next_permutation (A, A+3);
 cout<<A<<" ";}
 cout<<"\n";
  }
```

The expected result is given below.

```
XZY YXZ YZX ZXY ZYX XYZ
```

ALGORITHM NTH_ELEMENT()

The function partitions the sequence into two and rearranges the sequence about the specified middle element. The elements with values less than that of the specified element are sorted and put before the element and those with values more than the specified value are put after the specified element. The following program illustrates the function.

PROGRAM 25.30 – Illustrates `nth_element()` algorithm.

```
#include<iostream>
#include<algorithm>
using namespace std;
int main()
{
int S[10] = {10, 12, 22,24 ,34,51,171,13,16 ,170};
nth_element(S, S+4, S+10);

 for ( int i =0; i<10; i++)
  cout << S[i] <<"  ";

 cout<<"\n";
 return 0 ;
}
```

The expected output is given below.

```
10 12 13 16 22 24 34 51 170 171
```

ALGORITHM PARTIAL_SORT()

The function sorts the sequence up to a specified position, the remaining elements are placed after the specified position. See the following program for illustration.

PROGRAM 25.31 – Illustrates `partial_sort()` algorithm.

```
#include<iostream>
#include<algorithm>
using namespace std;

int main()
{
 int S[12] = {10, 24,12, 22 ,34,51,171,13,16, 176, 56, 42};
 partial_sort(S, S+6, S+12); // sort up to s+6

 for ( int i =0; i<12; i++)
     cout << S[i] <<"  ";
 cout<<"\n";
return 0 ; }
```

The expected output is given below.

```
10 12 13 16 22 24 171 51 34 176 56 42
```

ALGORITHM PARTIAL_SORT_COPY

The function makes a copy of the partially sorted elements. The original sequence remains intact.

PROGRAM 25.32 – Illustrates `partial_sort_copy()` algorithm.

```
#include<iostream>
# include<algorithm>
using namespace std;
int main()
{ int S[12] = {10,24,12,22,34,51,171,115,20,176, 56, 42 };
 int A [6];

partial_sort_copy (S, S+12, A, A+6);
 cout<<" S = ";
 for ( int i =0; i<12; i++)
    cout << S[i] <<" ";

cout<<"\nA = ";
 for (int k =0; k<6; k++)
    cout << A[k] <<" ";
  cout<<"\n";
 return 0 ;
}
```

The expected output is given below.

```
S = 10 24 12 22 34 51 171 115 20 176 56 42
A = 10 12 20 22 24 34
```

ALGORITHM PARTIAL_SUM ()

The function creates a new sequence by adding the elements of existing sequence up to the element position. Thus if a, b, c, d are the elements of a sequence, the function partial sum makes the sequence a, a + b, a + b + c, a + b + c + d and loads it to the new sequence. The following program illustrates the same.

PROGRAM 25.33 – Illustrates `partial_sum()` algorithm.

```
#include<iostream>
#include<numeric>
using namespace std;
int main()
{
 int S[8] = {2,3,4,5,6,7,8,9 };
 int A [8];

 cout<< "S = ";
 for ( int i =0; i<8; i++)

cout << S[i] <<" ";
 partial_sum (S, S+8, A);
 cout<<"\nA = ";
```

```
for ( int k =0; k<8; k++)
cout << A[k] <<" ";
cout<<"\n";
return 0 ;
}
```

The expected output is given below.

S = 2 3 4 5 6 7 8 9
A = 2 5 9 14 20 27 35 44

ALGORITHM PARTITION()

The function partitions a sequence such that the elements which satisfy a predicate are put in the first part followed by the elements which do not satisfy the predicate. See the following program for illustration.

PROGRAM 25.34 – Illustrates the function `partition()`.

```
#include<iostream>
#include<algorithm>

using namespace std;

bool Even(int m ) // definition of function for even number
{return !(m%2) ? true: false ;}

int main()
{
int S[ ] = { 5,6,8,7,4,3,8,10,11, 12};
partition(S, S+10, Even );
    //partition and put even numbers first.
for ( int i =0; i<10 ; i++)
cout<< S[i]<< " ";
return 0;
}
```

The expected output is given below.

12 6 8 10 4 8 3 7 11 5

ALGORITHM PREV_PERMUTATION()

It is inverse of next_permutation. The following program illustrates it.

PROGRAM 25.35 – Illustrates `prev_permutation()` algorithm.

```
#include <iostream>
#include<algorithm>
using namespace std;
```

```
void main()
{
 char A[4] = "XYZ";
 for( int k =0; k<6;k++)
{ next_permutation (A, A+3);
 cout<<A<<" ";}
 cout<<"\n";
 for( int i =0; i<6;i++)
 {prev_permutation (A, A+3);
 cout<<A<<" ";}
  }
```

The output is given below.

```
XZY YXZ YZX ZXY ZYX XYZ
ZYX ZXY YZX YXZ XZY XYZ
```

ALGORITHM RANDOM_SHUFFLE()

The function performs a random shuffle of elements of a sequence.

PROGRAM 25.36 – Illustrates `random_shuffle()` algorithm.

```
#include <iostream>
#include<algorithm>
using namespace std;
void main()
{ char A[7] = "ABCDEF";
 for( int k =0; k<5;k++)

 {random_shuffle(A, A+6);
 cout<<A<<" ";}
 cout<<"\n";
  }
```

The output of the program is given below.

```
EDACFB CEFABD EDCBFA DABFEC BECADF
```

THE ALGORITHMS REMOVE() AND REMOVE_IF()

The function removes the specified element from the sequence. In case of remove_if the element is removed if it satisfies a given predicate. See following program for illustration.

PROGRAM 25.37 – Illustrates `remove()` and `remove_if()` algorithms.

```
#include<iostream>
#include<algorithm>
```

```
#include<functional>
#include <vector>
using namespace std;
vector <int> V;
int main()
 {
 int S[ ] = { 5,6,8,7,8,3,8,10,8,12};
 for (int i =0 ; i<10;i++)
 V.push_back (S[i]); //construct a vector V with elements of S
 cout<< "V = ";
vector<int>:: iterator iter; // declaration of iterator
for (iter= V.begin(); iter <V.end(); iter++)
cout<< *iter<<" "; // Display elements of V
cout<<endl;
int Count = count(V.begin(), V.end(), 8); // count number of 8s
cout<<"Number of digit 8 = "<<Count<<endl;
remove ( V.begin(), V.end() , 8 ); // remove the digit 8s
for ( int j = 0; j<Count; j++)
V.pop_back( ) ;
 cout<< " Now V = ";
 for (iter= V.begin(); iter <V.end(); iter++)
 cout<< *iter<<" "; // display elements after removing 8s
cout<<endl;
Count = count_if(V.begin(), V.end(), bind2nd(less<int>(),6) );
cout<<" Number of elements less than 6 = "<<Count;
remove_if(V.begin(), V.end(), bind2nd(less<int>(),6) );
 // remove the number if less than 6
for ( int k = 0; k<Count; k++)
V.pop_back( ) ;
cout<< "\nThe new vector after two removals is as below."<<endl;
cout<<"V = ";
    for (iter= V.begin(); iter <V.end(); iter++)
    cout<< *iter<<" ";
cout<<endl;
return 0;
}
```

The expected output is as below.

```
V = 5 6 8 7 8 3 8 10 8 12
Number of digit 8 = 4
Now V = 5 6 7 3 10 12
Number of elements less than 6 = 2
```

```
The new vector after two removals is as below.
V = 6 7 10 12
```

THE ALGORITHMS REPLACE()AND REPLACE_IF()

The following program illustrates the application of the two functions on a vector.

PROGRAM 25.38 – Illustrates the `replace()` and `replace_if()` algorithms.

```
#include<iostream>
#include<algorithm>
#include<functional>
#include <vector>
using namespace std;

vector <int> V;

int main()
{
int S[ ] = { 5,6,8,7,8,3,8,10,8, 12};
 for (int i =0 ; i<10;i++)
 V.push_back (S[i]);

 vector<int>:: iterator iter;
 for (iter= V.begin(); iter <V.end(); iter++)
    cout<< *iter<<" ";
  cout<<endl;
replace ( V.begin(), V.end() , 8 , 9 ); // replace 8 by 9
 for (iter= V.begin(); iter <V.end(); iter++)
    cout<< *iter<<" ";
  cout<<endl;

replace_if(V.begin(), V.end(), bind2nd(less<int>(),9), 5);
     // replace those less than 9 by 5
 cout<< "The new vector after replacement is as below."<<endl;
 for (iter= V.begin(); iter <V.end(); iter++)
    cout<< *iter<<" ";

return 0;
}
```

The expected output is as under.

```
5 6 8 7 8 3 8 10 8 12
5 6 9 7 9 3 9 10 9 12
The new vector after replacement is as below.
5 5 9 5 9 5 9 10 9 12
```

The output shows that elements with value 8 has been replaced by value 9 and then those less than 9 are replaced by 5.

ALGORITHM REVERSE()

It reverses the order of elements in the sequence. See the following program for illustration.

PROGRAM 25.39 – Illustrates `reverse()` algorithm.

```
#include <iostream>
#include<algorithm>
using namespace std;
void main()
{
char A [ ] = "ABCDEFGH";
 int n = strlen(A);
 reverse(A, A+4);
     cout<< A<<endl;
  }
```

The expected output is given below.

```
DCBAEFGH
```

ALGORITHM ROTATE()

The function rotates the elements as if it is endless chain.

PROGRAM 25.40 – Illustrates `rotate()` algorithm.

```
#include<iostream>
# include<algorithm>
using namespace std;
void main()
{
int S1[ ] = { 11, 12, 13 ,15 ,16,17, 18,19 ,20};
 cout<< "S1= ";
  rotate ( S1, S1+4,S1+9);
   for ( int j =0; j<9; j++)
      cout << S1[j]<<" ";
}
```

The expected output is given below.

```
S1= 16 17 18 19 20 11 12 13 15
```

THE ALGORITHMS DEALING WITH SETS

set_difference(),set_intersection(),set_symmetric_difference() and **set_union ()**

These algorithms concerning sets are illustrated below.

PROGRAM 25.41 – Illustrates **set_difference(), set_intersection(), set_symmetric_difference()** and **set_union()** algorithms.

```
#include<iostream>
# include<algorithm>
using namespace std;
int main()
{
char Set1[ ] = { "ACDGHIJKTUVZ" };
char Set2[] = { "BCDKMNPUV"};
char Setx[12];
char Setxy[15];
char SetA[20];
char SetU[25];

cout<<"Set1 = "<<Set1<<endl;
cout<<"Set2 = "<< Set2<<endl;

char* Sety = set_difference(Set1, Set1+12, Set2, Set2+9, Setx);
 *Sety =0;
 cout<<" set_difference = "<<Setx <<endl;
char* Setz = set_intersection(Set1, Set1+12, Set2, Set2+9,Setxy);

 *Setz =0;
cout <<"set_intersection = "<<Setxy<<endl;
char* Setm = set_symmetric_difference(Set1, Set1+12, Set2,Set2+9, SetA);
 *Setm = 0;
 cout <<"Set_symmetric_difference = "<< SetA<<endl;
 char* Setn = set_union(Set1, Set1+12 , Set2, Set2+9 , SetU);
 *Setn =0;
cout << "Union of Set1 and Set2 = "<<SetU <<endl;
return 0 ;
}
```

The expected output is given below.

```
Set1 = ACDGHIJKTUVZ
Set2 = BCDKMNPUV
set_difference = AGHIJTZ
```

set_intersection = CDKUV
Set_symmetric_difference = ABGHIJMNPTZ
Union of Set1 and Set2 = ABCDGHIJKMNPTUVZ

ALGORITHM SORT()

Sorts a sequence.

PROGRAM 25.42 – Illustrates `sort()` algorithm.

```
#include<iostream>
# include<algorithm>
using namespace std;
int main()
{
int S1[ ] = { 11, 12, 19 ,13 ,16 ,20,24 ,22};
sort (S1, S1+8);
for ( int i =0; i<8;i++)
cout << S1[i]<<" ";
cout<<"\n";
return 0 ;
}
```

The expected output is given below.

```
11 12 13 16 19 20 22 24
```

ALGORITHM SWAP_RANGES()

The function exchanges the elements in a range with the elements of an another range of same size.

PROGRAM 25.43 – Illustrates `swap_ranges()` algorithm.

```
#include<iostream>
#include<algorithm>
using namespace std;
void main()
{
int S1[ ] = { 11, 12, 19 ,13 ,16 ,20, 24 ,22};
 int S2[] = { 1, 2, 3, 4, 5, 6, 7, 8};

cout<< "S1= ";
swap_ranges ( S1, S1+4, S2+4);
  for ( int j =0; j<8; j++)
cout << S1[j]<<" ";
cout<< "\nS2= " ;
for ( int k =0; k<8; k++)
cout << S2[k]<<" ";
}
```

The expected output is given below.

```
S1= 5 6 7 8 16 20 24 22
S2= 1 2 3 4 11 12 19 13
```

ALGORITHM UNIQUE(), REVERSE() AND REMOVE()

The unique () removes adjacent duplicate elements in a sorted sequence. The remove () removes the elements having specified value in a sequence. The reverse () reverses the order of elements of a given range.

PROGRAM 25.44 – Illustrates **unique(), reverse()** and **remove()** algorithms.

```
#include<iostream>
#include<list>
using namespace std;
 list<char> L1 ;

 void main()
 { for (int i=0; i<6;i++)
  {L1.push_back(65 +i );
  L1.push_back(65 + i );
  }
 cout<<"The original lists is as below."<<endl;
 list<char>::iterator T1;
 for ( T1 = L1.begin() ; T1!=L1.end() ; T1++ )
 cout <<" " <<*T1 ;
 cout<<endl;

L1.unique();
 cout<<" After removal of duplicate the list is:"<<endl;
  for ( T1 = L1.begin() ; T1!=L1.end() ; T1++ )
  cout <<" " <<*T1 ;

L1.reverse();
 cout<<"\n After reversing the list it is \n";
  for ( T1 = L1.begin() ; T1!=L1.end() ; T1++ )
   cout <<" " <<*T1 ;

 cout<<"\nAfter removal of F The list becomes \n";
L1.remove ('F');
 for ( T1 = L1.begin() ; T1!=L1.end() ; T1++ )
  cout <<" " <<*T1 ;
  cout << endl;
  }
```

The output is given below.

```
The original lists is as below.
A A B B C C D D E E F F
After removal of duplicate the list is:
A B C D E F
After reversing the list it is
F E D C B A
After removal of F The list becomes
E D C B A
```

ALGORITHM UPPER_BOUND()

PROGRAM 25.45 – Illustrates `upper_bound()` algorithm.

```
#include<iostream>
# include<algorithm>
using namespace std;
int main()
{
int S1[ ] = { 11, 121, 19 ,122 ,260 ,203,240 ,22};
int* ptr = upper_bound (S1, S1+8, 122);
cout<< "The upper bound is "<< *ptr<< endl;
cout<< "Its subscript is "<< ptr - S1 << " in the array."<<endl;
return 0 ;
}
```

The expected output is given below.

```
The upper bound is 260
Its subscript is 4 in the array.
```

EXERCISES

1. What is an algorithm?
2. Which header file is included for using the alogrithm accumulate()?
3. What is the action of function `adjacent_difference()` on elements of a container?
4. Explain the action of algorithm `adjacent_find()`.
5. Explain the mechanism of binary_search.
6. What is a predicate?
7. How would you use the algorithm `find_if()`, if it is required to separate the even and odd elements of an int array?
8. Explain the difference between the algorithms `count()` and `count_if()`.
9. Explain the actions of algorithm `upper_bound()` and `lower_bound()`.
10. What does the algorithm `equal_range()` do?
11. Explain the difference between `fill()` and `fill_n()` algorithms.
12. Explain the action of algorithm `find_end()`.
13. Explain the difference between the algorithms `remove()` and the algorithm `remove_if()`.
14. Make a small program to explain the action of algorithm `remove_if()`.
15. Explain the action of algorithms `swap()` and `swap_ranges()`.
16. Make a small program to illustrate the action of algorithm `rotate()`.
17. Make a small program to illustrate the action of algorithm `for_each()`.
18. Explain the action of algorithm `partition()` on a sequence.
19. Explain the action of following algorithms on sets.
    (i) `set_difference()`
    (ii) `set_intersection()`
    (iii) `set_symmetric_difference()`
    (iv) `set_union()`
20. Make a program to illustrate `set_union()` and `set_difference()`.

❍❍❍

References

1. John R. Hubbard; *Programming with C++* (Second Edition); McGraw-Hill, International Editions, 2000.
2. Deitel H. M., Deital P. J.; *C++ How to Program*, Fifth Edition; Prentice-Hall of India Pvt. Ltd, New Delhi, 2005.
3. Venugopal K. R., Rajkumar Buuya and Ravishankar T.; *Mastering C++*; Tata McGraw-Hill Publishing Company Ltd., New Delhi, 2006.
4. Balagurusamy E.; *Object Oriented Programming*; Third Edition; Tata McGraw-Hill Publishing Company Ltd., New Delhi, reprint 2006.
5. Jesse Liberty and Jim Keogh; *C++: An Introduction to Programming*; Prentice-Hall of India, New Delhi, 1999.
6. Graham M. Seed; *An Introduction to Object Oriented Programming in C++*; 2nd Edition; Springer, Berlin, 2001.
7. Daniel W. Lewis; *Fundamentals of Embedded Software*; Prentice-Hall of India Pvt. Ltd., New Delhi, 2003.
8. Gary J. Bronson; *A First Book of ANSI C*; (Brook/cole) Thomson Asia Pte Ltd., Singapore, 2001.
9. A. N. Kamthane; *Object-Oriented Programming with ANSI & Turbo C++*; Pearson Education (Singapore) Pte. Ltd., 2003.
10. Bjarne Stroustrup; *The C++ Programming Language,* Special Edition; Addison-Wesley Publishing Company, 2000.
11. Meyers Scott; *More Effective C++*; Addison-Wesley Publishing Company, 1996.
12. Irv Englander; *The Architecture of Computer Hardware and Systems Software*; 2nd Edition, John Wiley & Sons, Inc., New York, 2000.
13. David J. Lilja; *Measuring Computer Performance. A Practitioner's Guide*; Cambridge University Press, 2000.
14. Arnold S. Berger; *Hardware and Computer Organization—The Software Prospective*; Elsevier, Amsterdam, 2005.

15. Internet Sources:–
    a. cppreference.com
    b. http://www. glenmccl.com/tmpl_cmp.html
    c. http://microsoft.toddverbeek.com/lang.html
    d. ttp://www.cplusplus.com/doc/tutorial
    e. http://www.gnu.org/
    f. http://gcc.gnu.org/
16. Peter Coad and Edward Yourdon; *Object-Oriented Analysis*; YourDoon Press, New Jersey, 1991.
17. Yashavant. P Kanetkar; *Visual C++ Programming*; BPB Publications, New Delhi, 1998.
18. Dimitris N. Chorafas; *Fourth and Fifth Generation Programming Languages*. Vol. II, McGraw-Hill Book Company, 1986.
19. A. P. Ershov, *Origins of Programming*; (Translated by Robert H. Silverman); Springer-Verlag, Berlin.
20. M. Ben-Ari; *Principles of Concurrent Programming*; Prentice-Hall.
21. Adele Goldberg; *Small Talk;* Addison-Wesley Publishing Company, California, USA, 1984.
22. Robert Lafore; *Object-Oriented Programming in Turbo C++;* Galgotia Publications Pvt. Ltd., 1993.
23. Martin Richards, Colin Whitby – Streven; *BCPL – The Language and its Compiler;* Cambridge University Press, London, 1980.
24. Michel Parent and Claude Laurgeau; *Logic and Programming*; Kogen Page, London.
25. Anthony J. Field and Peter G. Harrison; *Functional Programming*; Addison-Wesley Publishing Company, California, USA, 1989.
26. Peter Abel; *IBM PC Assembler Language and Programming*; Prentice-Hall International, Inc. 1987.
27. *The C++ Standard*; John Wiley Ltd., N.Y. 2003.
28. Danny Kalev; *ANSI/ISO C++– Professional Programmer's Handbook*; Prentice-Hall of India Pvt. Ltd., New Delhi-1999.
29. Paul E. Ceruzzi; *A History of Modern Computing*; The MIT Press, Cambridge, Massachusetts, USA, 2002.
30. Mark Allen Weiss; *Data Structures and Algorithm Analysis in C++*; Pearson Education (Singapore) Pvt. Ltd., Delhi-2005.

❍❍❍

Appendix–A

ASCII CHARACTER CODE SET

Decimal	Binary	Hexadecimal	Character	Description
0	0	0	NUL	
1	1	01	SOH	Start of heading
2	10	02	STX	Start of text
3	11	03	ETX	End of text
4	100	04	EOT	End of transmission
5	101	05	ENQ	Enquiry
6	110	06	ACK	Acknowledge
7	111	07	BEL	"\a", bell, system beep
8	1000	08	BS	"\b" , back space
9	1001	09	HT	"\t" , horizontal tab
10	1010	0A	LF	"\n", new line character
11	1011	0B	VT	"\v" , vertical tab
12	1100	0C	FF	"\f" , form feed
13	1101	0D	CR	"\r", carriage return
14	1110	0E	SO	Shift out
15	1111	0F	SI	Shift in
16	10000	10	DLE	Data link escape
17	10001	11	DC1	Device control 1
18	10010	12	DC2	Device control 2
19	10011	13	DC3	Device control 3
20	10100	14	DC4	Device control 4
21	10101	15	NAK	Negative acknowledgement
22	10110	16	SYN	Synchronous idle
23	10111	17	ETB	End of transmission block
24	11000	18	CAN	Cancel
25	11001	19	EM	End of medium
26	11010	1A	SUB	Substitute
27	11011	1B	ESC	Escape

Decimal	Binary	Hexadecimal	Character	Description
28	11100	1C	FS	File separator
29	11101	1D	GS	Group separator
30	11110	1E	RS	Record separator
31	11111	1F	US	Unit separator
32	100000	20	SPC	Space
33	100001	21	!	Exclamation mark
34	100010	22	"	Double quote
35	100011	23	#	Hash symbol
36	100100	24	$	Dollar sign
37	100101	25	%	Percent sign
38	100110	26	&	Ampersand
39	100111	27	'	Single quote
40	101000	28	(	Left parentheses
41	101001	29	)	Right parentheses
42	101010	2A	*	Asterisk
43	101011	2B	+	Plus sign
44	101100	2C	,	comma
45	101101	2D	-	Dash
46	101110	2E	.	Dot, Decimal point
47	101111	2F	/	Slash
48	110000	30	0	digits
49	110001	31	1	
50	110010	32	2	
51	110011	33	3	
52	110100	34	4	
53	110101	35	5	
54	110110	36	6	
55	110111	37	7	
56	111000	38	8	
57	111001	39	9	
58	111010	3A	:	Colon
59	111011	3B	;	Semicolon
60	111100	3C	<	Less than
61	111101	3D	=	Equal to
62	111110	3E	>	Greater than
63	111111	3F	?	Question mark
64	1000000	40	@	At the rate of symbol

Decimal	Binary	Hexadecimal	Character	Description
65	1000001	41	A	Capital letters
66	1000010	42	B	
67	1000011	43	C	
68	1000100	44	D	
69	1000101	45	E	
70	1000110	46	F	
71	1000111	47	G	
72	1001000	48	H	
73	1001001	49	I	
74	1001010	4A	J	
75	1001011	4B	K	
76	1001100	4C	L	
77	1001101	4D	M	
78	1001110	4E	N	
79	1001111	4F	O	
80	1010000	50	P	
81	1010001	51	Q	
82	1010010	52	R	
83	1010011	53	S	
84	1010100	54	T	
85	1010101	55	U	
86	1010110	56	V	
87	1010111	57	W	
88	1011000	58	X	
89	1011001	59	Y	
90	1011010	5A	Z	
91	1011011	5B	[	Left square bracket
92	1011100	5C	\	Backslash
93	1011101	5D	]	Right square bracket
94	1011110	5E	^	Caret Mark
95	1011111	5F	_	Under score
96	1100000	60	‘	Accent mark
97	1100001	61	a	lower case letters
98	1100010	62	b	
99	1100011	63	c	
100	1100100	64	d	
101	1100101	65	e	
102	1100110	66	f	

Decimal	Binary	Hexadecimal	Character	Description
103	1100111	67	g	
104	1101000	68	h	
105	1101001	69	i	
106	1101010	6A	j	
107	1101011	6B	k	
108	1101100	6C	l	
109	1101101	6D	m	
110	1101110	6E	n	
111	1101111	6F	o	
112	1110000	70	p	
113	1110001	71	q	Lower case letters
114	1110010	72	r	
115	1110011	73	s	
116	1110100	74	t	
117	1110101	75	u	
118	1110110	76	v	
119	1110111	77	w	
120	1111000	78	x	
121	1111001	79	y	
122	1111010	7A	z	
123	1111011	7B	{	Left curly bracket (brace)
124	1111100	7C	|	Pipe sign
125	1111101	7D	}	Right Curly bracket
126	1111110	7E	~	Tilde mark
127	1111111	7F	DEL	delete

Appendix–B

C++ KEYWORDS

Keyword	Description
and	A synonym for the Boolean operator AND
and_eq	Bitwise AND assignment. A synonym for &= operator
asm	Specifies that the code be passed on to assembler directly.
auto	Storage class that is used to define variables within a block{}, i.e. local variables
bitand	Bitwise AND. A synonym for & operator.
bitor	Bitwise OR. A synonym for | operator.
bool	bool type specifier. Can have values 1 or 0 (true or false)
break	Used to terminate a loop. Also used in switch statement for the same purpose.
case	Used in switch statement to specify a match.
catch	Catch (T) specifies a catch block for type T. The block takes action when the T type exception occurs.
char	Type used to define character objects.
class	Used for class declaration. It creates user defined type.
compl	A synonym for bitwise NOT
const	Specifies objects that do not change value for the lifetime of program.
const_cast	Provides access to an object with constant or volatile attribute.
continue	Used to transfer control to the beginning of loop.
default	Used in switch statement to handle the statement not dealt by any case.
delete	Releases the memory allocated by **new** operator.
do	Indicates the start of *do –while* loop
double	A fundamental data type used to define decimal point numbers with double precision.
dynamic_cast	Used to cast a pointer or reference type at run time.
else	Specifies an alternative choice in *if – else*
enum	Enumeration *type*
explicit	Declares explicit constructor
export	Makes a template definition accessible from another compiler unit
extern	Specifies a storage class object with external link to the block

Contd...

Key word	Description
false	One of the two values, i.e. (0) of bool type
float	A fundamental type for specifying floating point numbers
for	Specifies start of *for* loop
friend	A class or function specified as friend has access to private , protected and public members of the class.
goto	Used to transfer control to a label statement.
if	Specifies *if* expression for selective control
inline	Specifies a function for inline substitution instead of function call.
int	A fundamental type which specifies whole numbers.
long	A data modifier for int and double
mutable	Specifier for overriding constantness
namespace	Specifies a scope for names
new	Operator for allocating memory
not	A synonym for ! operator, i.e. NOT
not_eq	Not equal to. A synonym for !=.
operator	Used for operator overloading
or	OR operator. A synonym for ||.
Or_eq	Bitwise OR assignment. A synonym for |= operator
private	Specifies private members of a class
protected	Specifies protected members of class
public	Specifies class members which are accessible from outside the class
register	An **auto** specifier for objects to be stored in register
reinterpret_cast	Used to convert an int type to pointer type and vice versa
return	Specifies end of function with a return value.
short	A data type modifier for int numbers.
signed	A data type modifier for numbers which can be positive or negative.
sizeof	The sizeof() returns size of an object in number of bytes allocated for object.
static	Specifies objects that stay throughout the program
static_cast	Used for casting. static_cast respects the constantness of object while casting.
struct	Declares a user type
switch	Specifies switch statement for multiple choices.
template	Specifies a generic type

Contd...

Key word	Description
`this`	A class pointer by compiler that points to class object.
`throw`	Generates an exception
`true`	Specifies a bool condition with value 1
`try`	Indicates start of exception handling block.
`typedef`	Declares a synonym for a type (fundamental type or user defined type)
`typeid`	typeid ( ) returns the type of its argument
`typename`	Used as an alternative to word class in template.
`using`	Used as declaration or directive.
`union`	It specifies a structure in which the members occupy the same memory space.
`unsigned`	A type modifier which specifies that all the bits are to be used for the object, i.e. positive value.
`virtual`	Specifies a member function which will be redefined in derived class.
`void`	Signifies absence of type of function or absence of parameter list
`volatile`	Declares an object that may be modified outside the control of program (undetected by compiler)
`wchar_t`	Wide character type allocated 2 byte memory
`while`	Specifies start of while loop and end of *do – while* loop
`xor`	Bitwise exclusive OR operator
`xor_eq`	Bitwise exclusive OR assignment operator

Appendix–C

C++ OPERATORS

The operators are shown below in order of decreasing order of precedence. Those in the same group have same precedence. In case of multiple occurrences in same code line the associativity takes care of order of implementation.

Operator	Arity	Description	Associativity
::	Unary	Global scope	Right to left
::	binary	Class scope	Left to right
.	Binary	Object component selector	Left to right
( )	Not applicable	Function call	Left to right
( )	Not applicable	Brackets – grouping operator	Left to right
[ ]	Binary	Array index operator	Left to right
->	Binary	Access from a pointer	Left to right
!	Unary	Logical NOT	
~	Unary	Bitwise compliment	
++	Unary	Increment	
– –	Unary	Decrement	
–	Unary	Unary minus	
+	Unary	Unary plus	
*	Unary	Dereference	
&	Unary	Address_of operator	Right to left
Sizeof()		Size in bytes	
new		Dynamic memory allocation	
new[]		Dynamic memory allocation	
delete		Dynamic memory deallocation	
delete[]		Dynamic memory deallocation	
(type) conversion	Binary	C-type casting to given type	Right to left
–>*	Binary	Pointer to member via pointer	Left to right
.*	Binary	pointer to member via dot selector	

Contd...

Operator	Arity	Description	Associativity
*	Binary	Multiplication	Left to right
/	Binary	Division	
%	Binary	Modulus	
+	Binary	Addition	Left to right
–	Binary	Subtraction	
<<	Binary	Bitwise shift left	Left to right
>>	Binary	Bitwise shift right	
<	Binary	Less than	Left to right
>	Binary	Greater than	
<=	Binary	Less than equal to	
>=	Binary	Greater than equal to	
==	Binary	Equality	Left to right
!=	Binary	Inequality	
&	Binary	Bitwise AND	Left to right
^	Binary	Bitwise XOR	Left to right
|	Binary	Bitwise OR	Left to right
&&	Binary	Logical AND	Left to right
||	Binary	Logical OR	Left to right
?:	Binary	Conditional operator	Left to right
=	Binary	Assignment operator	Right to left
+=	Binary	Add and assign	
–=	Binary	Subtract and assign	
*=	Binary	Multiply and assign	
/=	Binary	Divide and assign	
%=	Binary	Modulus and assign remainder	
&=	Binary	Bitwise AND and assign	
^=	Binary	Bitwise exclusive OR and assign	
|=	Binary	Bitwise OR and assign	
<<=	Binary	Bitwise left shift and assign	
>>=	Binary	Bitwise right shift and assign	
,	Binary	Evaluation operator	Left to right

Appendix–D

COMMONLY USED HEADER FILES IN C++

S.No.	Name	Description
1	**<algorithm>**	Contains algorithms- functions for manipulation of element of C++ Standard Library containers.
3	**<bitset>**	Bitset classes
4	**<cassert>**	C-style assert () macro.
5	**<cctype>**	Testing character for certain properties.
6	**<cerrno>**	Error handling – C-style
7	**<cfloat>**	Floating point implementation classes
8	**<cheks.h>**	For diagnostic.
9	**<climits>**	Size limits for integral types of the system. It replaces <limits.h>
10	**<clocale>**	Country and language specific
11	**<cmath>**	Mathematical functions
12	**<complex.h>**	Complex number classes
13	**<constrea.h>**	Supports consol output
14	**<csetjmp>**	Contains setjump() and longjump() which enable immediate jump from deeply nested function call.
15	**<csignal>**	C-style processing of signals
16	**<cstdarg>**	Support for variable length function arguments
17	**<cstddef>**	C-style library support.
18	**<cstdio>**	Support C-style standard input/output. It replaces <stdio.h>
19	**<cstdlib>**	Definitions for commonly used functions and types
20	**<cstring>**	C-style string manipulation functions.
21	**<ctime>**	Time and date manipulating functions.
22	**<cwchar>**	Supports wide character
23	**<deque>**	Container classes for double ended queues.

Contd...

24	**<exception>**	Exception handling classes.
25	**<fstream>**	Contains classes and functions for file input/output streams
26	**<functional>**	Supports function objects.
27	**<iomanip>**	Contains functions for manipulation of input /output streams.
28	**<ios.h>**	Basic-stream input/output classes
29	**<iosfwd>**	Support for forward input/output declarations.
30	**<iostream>**	Supports standard input/output streams.
31	**<istream>**	Supports standard input streams.
32	**<iterator>**	Supports iterators used for traversing elements of a container.
33	**<limits>**	Classes for numerical data type limits
34	**<list>**	Container classes for doubly linked list of type T
35	**<locale>**	Comprises classes and functions to support stream processing for different languages.
36	**<map>**	Associative container classes for maps and multimaps
37	**<memory>**	Contains classes for memory allocation
38	**<new>** or **<new.h>**	Supports allocation and de-allocation of memory
39	**<numeric>**	Numerical manipulation algorithms
40	**<ostream>**	Supports output stream
41	**<queue>**	Container classes for queues and priority queues.
42	**<ref.h>**	Some classes for strings. Some compilers may not have it.
43	**<regexp.h>**	Supports regular expression search
44	**<set> or <set.h>**	Associative container classes for set and multiset .
45	**<sstream>**	Contains functions and classes for input/output of strings.
46	**<stack>**	Adapter class *stack*
47	**<stdexcept>**	Exception handling classes of C++ Standard Library
48	**<streambuf>**	Stream buffer classes
49	**<string> or <string.h>**	Deals with C++ string classes.
50	**<strstrea.h>**	Stream classes dealing with byte arrays.
51	**<typeinfo> or <typeinfo.h>**	Run time type identification classes.
52	**<utility>**	General utility templates used by many C++ std library classes.
53	**<valarray>**	For numerical manipulation of vectors
54	**<vector>**	Vector container classes

Appendix–E

GETTING STARTED

If you are using Microsoft Visual Studio 6.0, below is the step by step illustration of how to run a C++ program. In the first case we run a simple program without a class and in the second case we create a project, include a class and implement a program.

Load the Microsoft Visual Studio 6.0 on your computer. Restart your computer and click on Programs menu. Out of the list of programs select Microsoft Visual C++ 6.0. You will get the screen as shown below.

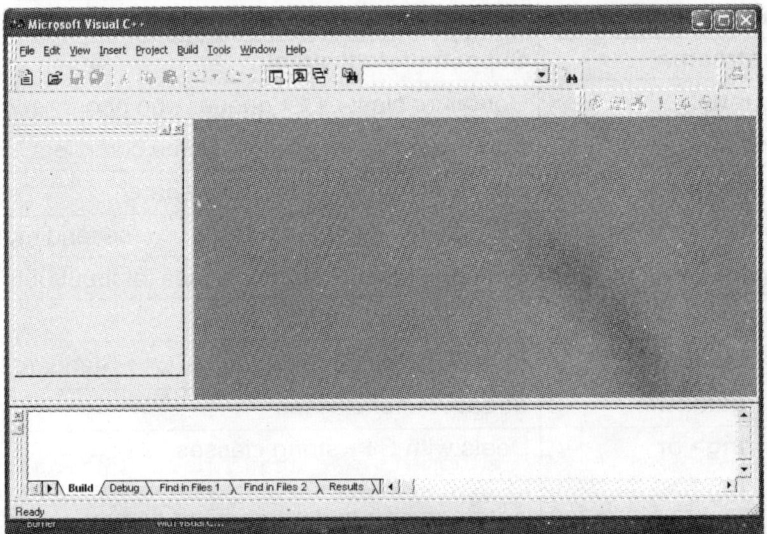

Fig.1

It has three compartments. A view pan on the left. A document window on the right and a message window at bottom. The message window is used for displaying error messages or warnings when the program is compiled. The document widow is used for typing the program. When a class program is run the left view gives option for viewing the class or file view by hitting on the appropriate button provided at its bottom (see Fig.9). For the first case, described below, we will not need it.

Case 1 – Running a Simple Program

Now open the file menu and select (click with mouse) on New. You will see the screen as demonstrated in Fig. 6 below. In the new window click on files. You would get the new window as shown in Fig. 2. Select (click) on C++ source file. It would get shaded as shown in Fig. 2. In the 'File name' window, type the name of file. In the present case it is typed Myprogram with extension .cpp. So complete name typed is Myprogram.cpp. In the location window in the present case, it is filled by default. Click/hit on OK. A dialog box will appear for creating a project. Click on 'yes'.

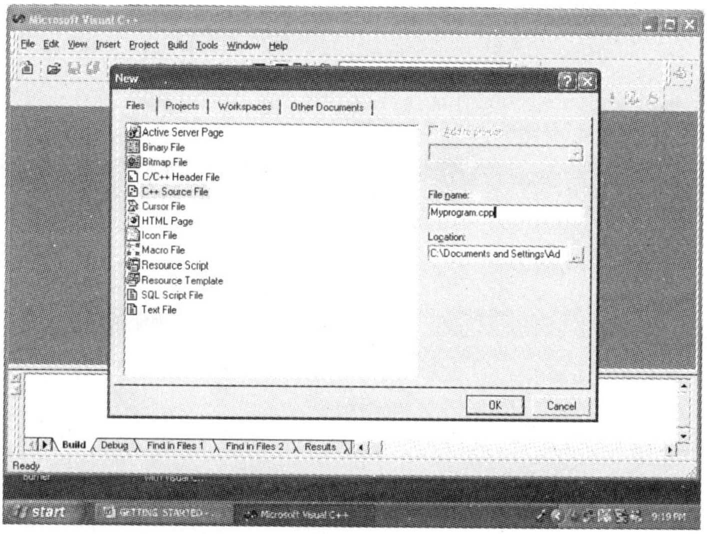

Fig.2

You will get a blank right document window on which you type the statements of your program as illustrated in Fig. 3. The following program has been typed. You may close the window pane by hitting (Clicking) on x on top right corner of view pane.

```
#include<iostream>
using namespace std;
int main()
{
cout<<"Welcome to C++!"<<endl;
return 0;
}
```

After typing the program, open the 'Build' menu and select (click on) 'Compile Myprogram.cpp'.

The program gets compiled and if there are any errors in the program, these would be shown in the bottom window. You can correct them and again compile the program.

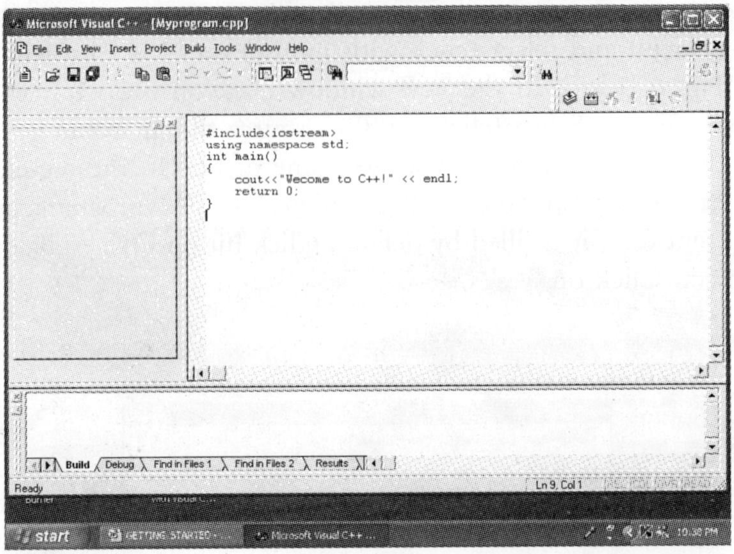

Fig. 3

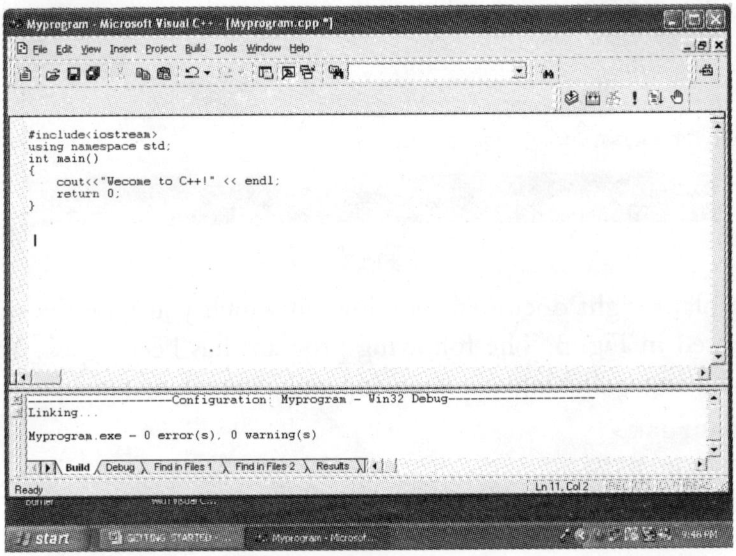

Fig. 4

When it becomes error free you would get the screen as illustrated in Fig.4, in which the bottom window shows,

```
0 error(s), 0 warning(s).
```

The next step is to execute the program. For this open 'Build' menu and click on 'Execute Myprogram.exe. The result of this is shown in the dark window in Fig.5

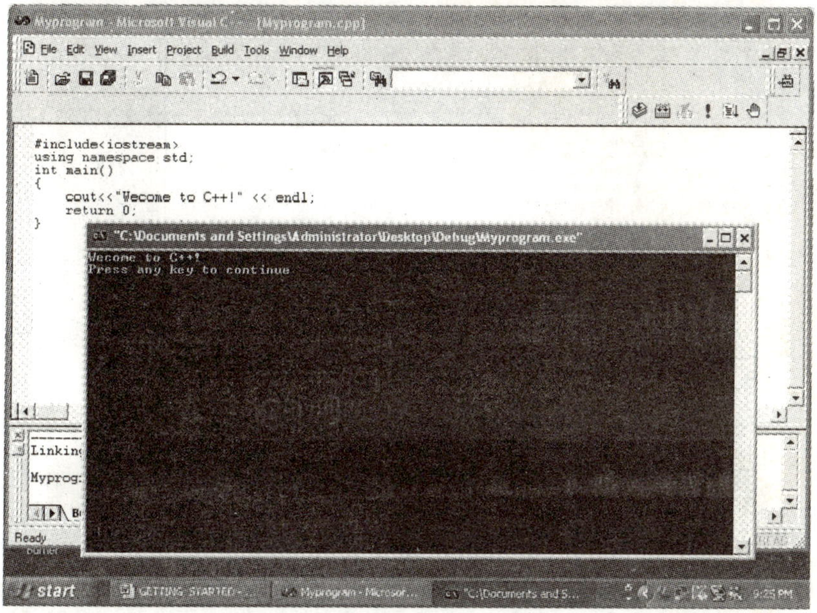

Fig. 5

The program with the output is shown below.

```
#include<iostream>
using namespace std;
int main()
{    cout<<"Wecome to C++!" << endl;
   return 0;
}
```

The output is given below.

```
Wecome to C++!
Press any key to continue
```

CASE 2 – MAKING A PROGRAM WITH A CLASS

As mentioned in Case 1, start your computer and click on Programs menu. Out of the list of programs select Microsoft Visual C++6.0. You will get the screen as shown in Fig.1. Open 'File' menu and click on New. You get a screen as illustrated in Fig.6. In the 'Project name' window type the name of project. In the present case the name is 'Training'. In the location window you may type the place and path where you want to store the project. In the present case it is a default site.

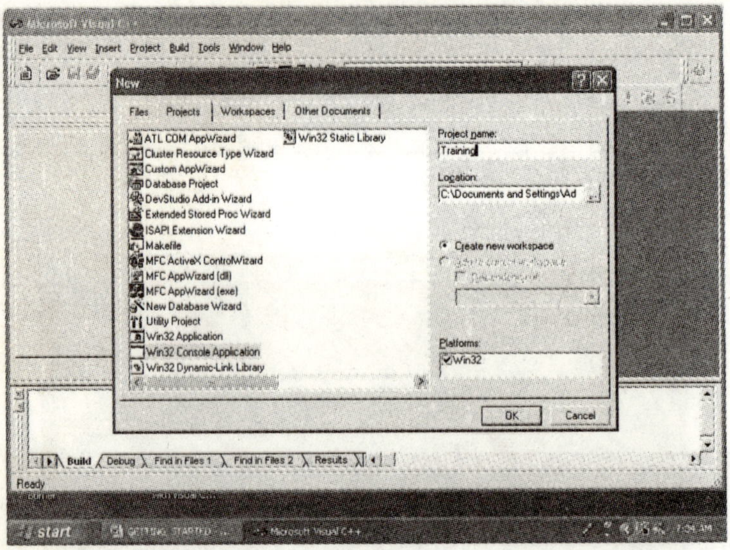

Fig. 6

Out of the list of options select 'Win32 Console Application' and the 'Create new workspace' is selected by default, if not, select it. After filling these click on OK. You get a screen as shown in Fig.7. Just click on 'Finish'. You may get a message page which tells you that you have created an empty project. Click on OK. Now you get a screen similar to the Fig.1 but with a difference that in the left view pane the name 'Training' appears. Our next step is to add a class to the project.

Again open File menu and click on New. You get a screen as shown in Fig.8. In this you will find that the name of project is already filled by default and 'Add to project' is also selected if not you can select it.

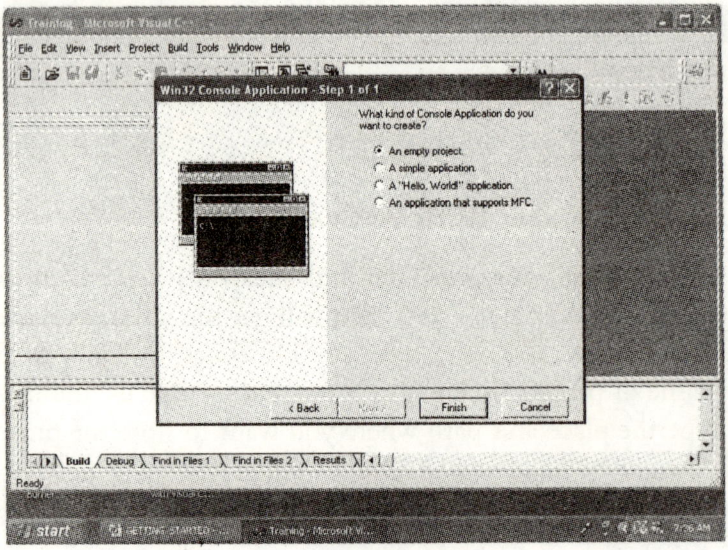

Fig. 7

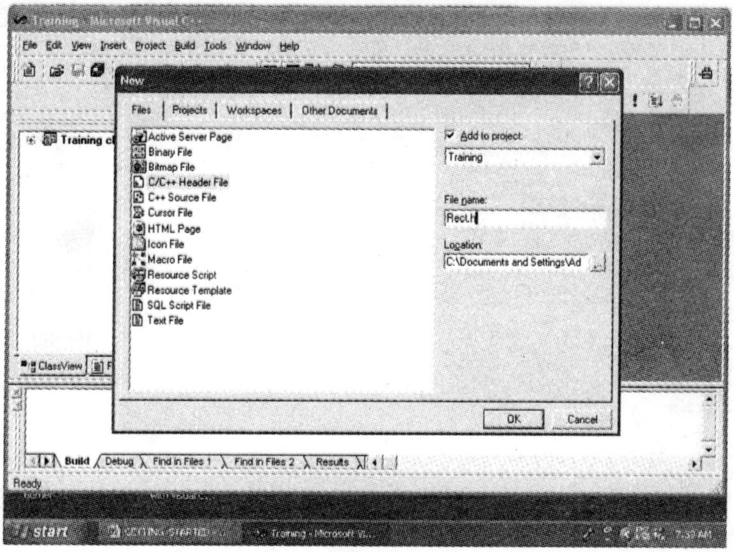

Fig. 8

Now we have to add a class to the project. A class needs a header file. So select 'C/C++ Header File' from the list of options. It is shown shaded in Fig.8. In the 'File name' window (Fig. 8) fill the name of class. In the present case it is typed as 'Rect.h' . The 'Location' window is filled by default. After filling the name click on OK. You get the screen in which the right window is blank. In this window type the statements of the class as illustrated in Fig.9.

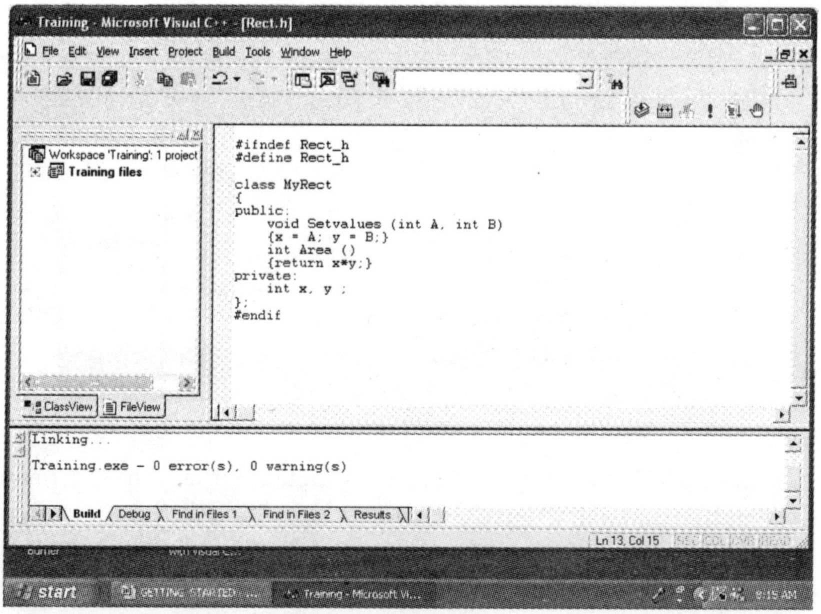

Fig. 9

The class entered is as below.

```
#ifndef Rect_h
#define Rect_h
class Myrect
{ pubic:
      void Setvalues(int A, int B)
           { x = A; y = B;}
      int Area ()
           {return x*y;}
private:
      int x, y;
};
#endif
```

Now save this. After typing the class statements the message window would be blank. The messages given in the third window at bottom of Fig.9 is in fact the result of next operation. So, there should be no confusion.

After typing and saving the next step in implementation of class. For this again open file menu and click on New. The screen is illustrated in Fig.10. Now select 'C++ Source File' from the list.

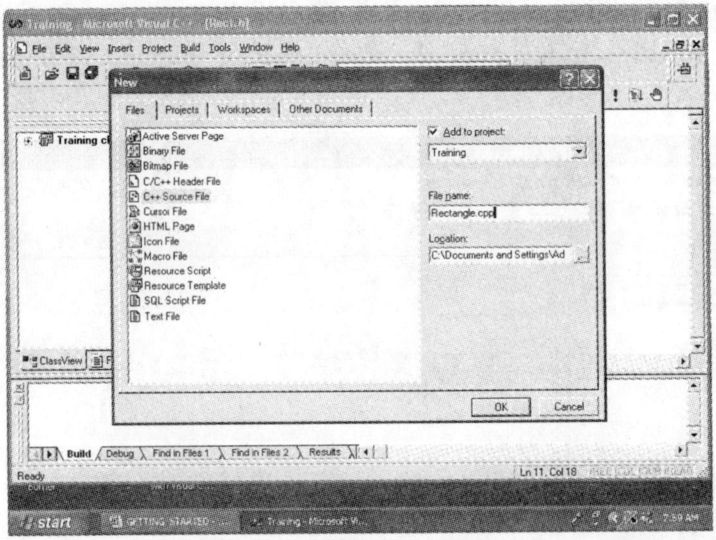

Fig. 10

You will find that 'Add to project' is selected by default, the name of project "Training" also appears by default. You have to give a name to this file. All the files must have distinct names. So for this file we type the name 'Rectangle.cpp' as illustrated in the figure. The window below Location is also filled by default. After writing the name click on OK. Again you will get screen with three segments and the blank right window. Here you type the main program for implementing the class. This is illustrated in Fig.11 which also illustrates the output which is the result of subsequent operations. The program typed in this window is given further.

```
#include<iostream>
using namespace std;
#include "Rect.h"
int main()
{MyRect  Rect1, Rect2;
Rect1.Setvalues(15,10);
Rect2.Setvalues(20,5);
cout<<"Area of Rect1 = "<<Rect1.Area()<<endl;
cout<<"Area of Rect2 = "<<Rect2.Area()<<endl;
return 0;
}
```

After typing the program, open the Build menu and click on Compile option. If there are errors these would be shown in the message window at the bottom, otherwise the message would be no error(s), no warnings. In the program Rect1 and Rect2 are two objects of MyRect. So they are declared as

```
MyRect  Rect1, Rect2;
```

Here Rect1, Rect2 are of type MyRect. The function Setvalues() is called by Rect1 and by Rect2 by the expressions

```
Rect1.Setvalues(15,10);
Rect2.Setvalues(20,5);
```

The Rect1 has dimensions 15 and 10 and Rect2 has dimensions 20 and 5. Next the Area () function for the two objects is called. Again open the Build menu and now click for execution of the program by clicking on Execute Rectangle.exe . You would get the result as shown on the dark window in Fig. 11. The output shows the areas as 150 and 100.

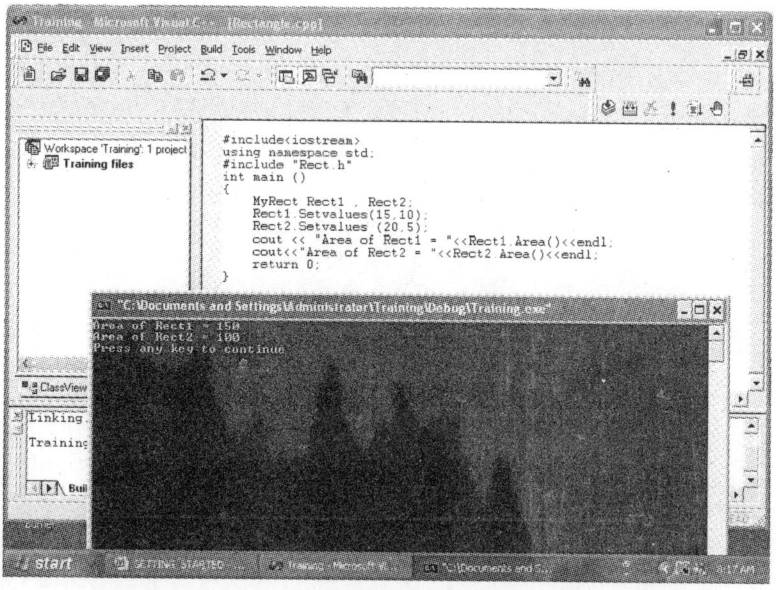

Fig. 11

The execution is now over and program may be closed. Later if you want to go back to this project select Visual C++6.0 and open the File menu. And click on 'Open'. You would get the screen as given in Fig.12. You may open the class Rect.h or the file Rectangle.cpp as desired.

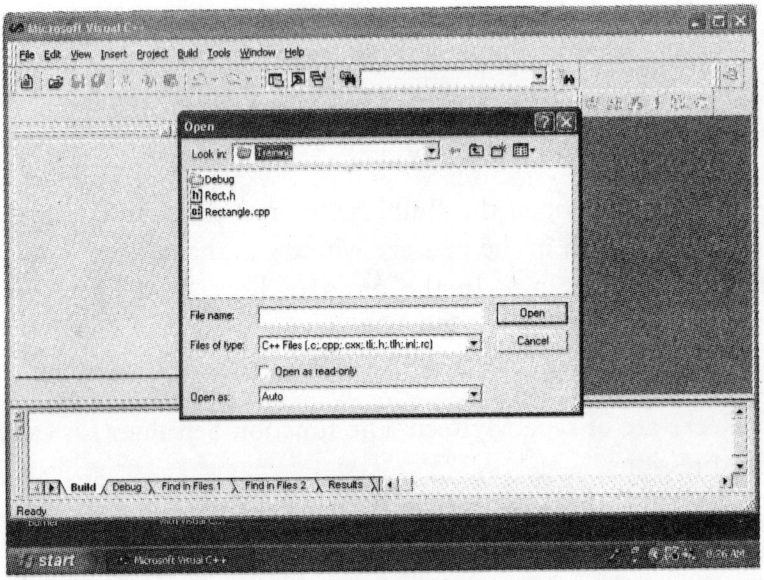

Fig. 12

ooo

Subject Index

A

D

E

G

H

I

T